Machiavelli's Children

Machiavelli's Children

Leaders and Their Legacies in Italy and Japan

RICHARD J. SAMUELS

CORNELL UNIVERSITY PRESS

Ithaca and London

First published 2003 by Cornell University Press
First printing, Cornell paperbacks, 2005

Printed in the United States of America

Library of Congress Cataloging-in-Publication Data

Samuels, Richard J.
   Machiavelli's children : leaders and their legacies in Italy and Japan / Richard J. Samuels.
      p. cm.
Includes bibliographical references and index.
   ISBN 0-8014-3492-0 (cloth : alk. paper)
   ISBN 0-8014-8982-2 (pbk. : alk. paper)
   1.   Political leadership—Italy—History—19th century. 2.   Political leadership—Italy—History—20th century. 3.   Political leadership—Japan—History—19th century. 4.   Political leadership—Japan—History—20th century. I.   Title.
   JN5345 .S25 2003
   303.3'4'094509034—dc21
                                        2002015019

Cornell University Press strives to use environmentally responsible suppliers and materials to the fullest extent possible in the publishing of its books. Such materials include vegetable-based, low-VOC inks and acid-free papers that are recycled, totally chlorine-free, or partly composed of nonwood fibers. For further information, visit our website at www.cornellpress.cornell.edu.

Cloth printing 10 9 8 7 6 5 4 3 2 1
Paperback printing 10 9 8 7 6 5 4 3 2 1

For Lucian Pye and in memory of Myron Weiner:

mentors, *menschen* . . . leaders

Contents

CONTENTS

Preface:

LEADERS MATTER

> [It is] essential to recognize in the great man an outstanding individual who is at once a product and an agent of the historical process, at once the representative and the creator of social forces which change the shape of the world and the thoughts of men.
>
> E. H. Carr, *What Is History?*

This is a book about great leaders and historical choices. It starts with a puzzle: our common sense tells us that leaders and their decisions matter, but our social science theories tell us that constraints determine all major societal outcomes. My ambition here is to expose how much we have to gain by exploring leadership and the strategic, tactical, and moral choices that leaders make. History is not only a tale of great men, their will and their imagination, but it is partly that story. We need to include leaders in our understanding of the world and in our reckoning of what is possible and desirable in human societies.

The past is as restless as the present, and as elusive as the future. It never stands still in its retellings, and its retelling takes many forms. Versions of history that put great leaders at center stage became passé long ago. The impersonal, offstage forces that replaced them—ideology, social movements, class conflict, culture, state power—have dominated our discourse. More recently, these forces too have been discounted, as newer great forces—personality, cognition, representation, rationality, social networks—have taken their place. The retelling of history continues, and it depends on the shifting preferences of the viewer.

The range of our preferences and the speed with which they shift seem to doom us to live in a babel of parochial conversations about history and political change. Oddly, although we focus on change, the "great forces" we privilege are biased toward inertia. That is, each one privileges *constraints* that trump the capabilities of individuals.

Karl Marx was one of the earliest—and certainly the most famous—offender. He addressed political choice directly in his *Eighteenth Brumaire of Louis Bonaparte,* written immediately after a French coup d'état in December 1851. Arguing against other chroniclers who, he felt, made too much of Bonaparte's leadership, Marx proclaimed his well-known dictum about the limits to autonomous political action:

> Men make their own history, but they do not make it just as they please; they do not make it under circumstances chosen by themselves, but under circumstances directly encountered, given, and transmitted from the past. The tradition of all the dead generations weighs like a nightmare on the brain of the living. And just when they seem engaged in revolutionizing themselves and things, in creating something that has never yet existed, precisely in such periods of revolutionary crisis they anxiously conjure up the spirits of the past to their service and borrow from them names, battle cries, and costumes, in order to present the new scene of world history in this time-honoured disguise and this borrowed language.[1]

For Marx—and for most who have written since—leaders pick from the menus they are handed, and dine on cuisines not of their own choosing. They read scripts, but they do not often write them.

We know too much about constraints and not enough about choices. In this book, I pair leaders at (nearly) the same moment and place in history—in late developing Italy and Japan, two of the world's most constrained settings—to show how leaders routinely strain at and stretch the constraints they face. I focus on how they use Marx's "names, battle cries, and costumes" in remarkably creative ways, often tipping the balance of historical inertia in directions of their choosing and thereby transforming economic, social, and political institutions. We will see how different individuals can make different choices under similar constraints. Some act strategically, others do not. John Dunn responds to Marx well: "Humans may seldom know very well what they are doing and they certainly make their history under conditions unchosen by themselves. But there is no escaping the large measure of discretion which they enjoy in making their history."[2]

The contemporary Middle East offers particularly good examples. In the summer of 2000, U.S.-brokered peace talks between Israeli Prime Minister Ehud Barak and Palestinian President Yasser Arafat moved the two sides closer to an agreement than ever before, though not close enough to achieve peace. Renewed violence erupted in the Middle East after conservative Israeli politician Ariel Sharon visited a Muslim holy site in Jerusalem in the autumn of 2000. As a result, U.S.-brokered peace talks were not resumed until shortly before elections in Israel, which Sharon won, defeating Barak. One influential columnist, Thomas Friedman, wrote in the *New York Times:*

> Mr. Arafat had a dilemma: make some compromises, build on Mr. Barak's opening bid and try to get it closer to 100 percent—and regain moral high ground that way—or provoke the Israelis into brutalizing again, and regain the moral high ground that way. Mr. Arafat chose the latter . . . Imagine if when Mr. Sharon visited Temple Mount, Mr. Arafat had ordered his people to welcome him with open arms and say, "When this area is under Palestinian sovereignty, Jews will be welcome, even you, Mr. Sharon." Imagine the impact that would have had on Israelis.[3]

That such choices for peace were possible despite considerable constraints was made clear one week later by King Abdullah II of Jordan, who signed the first-ever free-trade agreement between the United States and an Arab country. It looked as though it would have been easier for him to concede to the pressure of his neighbors—and to the demands of his large Palestinian population—and maintain his political distance from Washington. He chose instead to innovate, to write a new script that could transform fundamentally the political economy of the region.

In this book I argue for the benefits of leaving room for an active voice in political analysis. Many commentators stress constraints and preach, in effect, that necessity is the mother of invention. I consider the reverse, that invention need not be born of necessity at all. Indeed, creative choice may have no particular parent: creativity can overcome existing constraints and create new ones. Of course I acknowledge that all choices are subject to powerful constraints. Still, it is clear that political actors—particularly leaders—routinely *stretch* these constraints. How much, in what direction, with what tools, and with what consequences—these are critical questions for political analysis. I address these questions in the rich and remarkably parallel histories of Italy and Japan.

Like Neil Simon's Oscar Madison and Felix Unger, Italy and Japan seem to make an odd couple.[4] In the popular imagination, Italy seems more the undisciplined, slightly antiauthoritarian and insouciant Oscar, Japan more the disciplined, neurotically fastidious Felix. One of Italy's most respected observers offers a catalog of Oscar-like stereotypes of the deficits in Italian political culture, and concludes: "Governing Italy is not difficult, it is useless."[5] The late psychiatrist Miyamoto Masao wrote that Japan was excessively conformist and that the system was "neurotic."[6] Japanese wonder why they do not cross the street against a red light, even if there is no car in sight, while the Italians wonder why it takes so long to get their traffic lights fixed when they are broken. Japan and Italy seem completely different.

But few nations have as many important common features; their political lives have proceeded in uncanny parallel for more than a century. Neither Italy nor Japan even existed as modern states when Great Britain and the United States embarked on their industrial revolutions. In both Italy and Japan rapid late industrialization was accompanied by a groping experimentation with parliamentary democracy before each succumbed to authoritarianism. And they paid the same price—devastation in the Second World War and subordinate roles in the new American world order.

Close comparison may be the most powerful tool in the social science tool kit. Similarities and dissimilarities illuminate important mechanisms of social change. Italian and Japanese leaders who sorted through similar options and made different choices offer up many compelling comparisons. But so do those who made similar choices when their options were different. Pairing Italy and Japan provides a rare chance to compare across wide terrain while illuminating the narrow band of factors that animate power, wealth, and identity.

Long ago, when I knew only that this book would be a comparative political and economic history of Japan and Italy, I was discussing the project with a Japanese government official. He was very uncomfortable with the comparison. He told me that his father, a veteran of the Pacific War, used to say "kondo itaria nashi de yaroo" (Next time, let's do it without Italy). I heard variants of that story on other occasions, and I concluded that (beyond a dissatisfaction with the outcome of the war) there must be a widely held view in Japan of an incompetent and backward Italy. The idea was reinforced when I interviewed a member of the Japanese House of Councilors who confided that it was one thing to be bested by Germany or by the United States, but "we don't want Italy to be ahead of us" (itaria ni wa maketakunai). Meanwhile—after they get over the shock that I could find anything in common between the two cases—Italians to whom I have spoken usually puff up with pride at the comparison to the Japanese, whom they admire but whose rules and rigidities they do not quite understand. Then, unfailingly, they would ask: "But how could you live in such a place?" "Do they ever have fun?"

Over the past two decades, my work has volleyed back and forth between structural and cultural explanations for the dynamics of Japanese politics. In a book on local politics and regional policy, I went out of my way to dismiss sociological explanations and argued that there were no cultural impediments to horizontal solidarity in Japan. In a book on energy markets, I struck the same general tone; the efficacy of Japanese industrial policy is due to the stable structure of business-government relations. But the next book—focused on the aerospace and defense industries—took a different tack; I suggested that institutions are informed by enduring ideas that constrain elite choices and shape institutional development. I do not believe that any of these accounts is wrong. Nor do I even believe they are contradictory. Structural and cultural explanations can and do coexist because they can and do explain different things. The problem has been that few authors (myself included) have been terribly clear about which and what and when and why. For me at least, such a sorting out is the next natural step in my intellectual journey. When I first characterized the journey in this way to one colleague who understood immediately how difficult this project would be, I was told (only half jokingly) that I ought to "quit while I'm ahead." This may have been the best advice I never took.

Along the way I sought and received plenty of advice—all of it generous and well intended, only some of it heeded. I have never had so many colleagues to thank and I have never done so with more heartfelt gratitude. In the United States, Gabriel Almond, Donald Blackmer, George Breslauer, Kanchan Chandra, Joshua Cohen, Gerald Curtis, Giuseppe Di Palma, John Dower, David Friedman, Sheldon Garon, Andrew Gordon, Chalmers Johnson, Peter Katzenstein, Ira Katznelson, David Kertzer, Herbert Kitschelt, Ellis Krauss, Ed Lincoln, Richard Locke, T.J. Pempel, Susan Pharr, Roland Sarti, Frank Schwartz, Sidney Tarrow, and David Titus each read and reacted to various pieces of this manuscript. I am particularly indebted to Suzanne Berger for wrestling vigorously with the entire manuscript and for helping me see clearly what it really meant. She has been a teacher and colleague of unbounded insight and generosity. I must also thank Professor Almond for gently pointing out that I had "reinvented Plutarch's wheel."

My colleagues in Italy were extraordinary in every way. Paul Ginsborg provided incalculably important support by bringing this project to Einaudi and by trying (without conspicuous success) to protect me from my disciplinary instincts. Paolo Pombeni deserves special mention for his unflagging enthusiasm and close reading of the manuscript. I am happy to acknowledge also the long conversations with Fulvio Cammaranno, Roberto Cartocci, Donatella della Porta, Giuseppe Di Federico, Ronald Dore, Giorgio Freddi, Mark Gilbert, Carlo Guarnieri, Giovanfrancesco Lanzara, Fernando Mezzetti, Gianfranco Pasquino, Patrizia Pederezoli, Marino Regini, Michele Salvati, and Carlo Tregilia, all of whom struggled to educate me on *le cose italiane*.

In Japan there are also a great many friends to thank, both old and new.[7] Aburaki Kiyoaki, Ariga Kenichi, Moreno Bertoldi, Herbert Bix, Verena Blechinger, Fujiwara Kiichi, Hara Yoshihisa, Hiwatari Nobuhiro, Honda Masaru, Andrew Horvatt, Llewelyn Hughes, Inoguchi Takashi,

Ishida Hiroshi, Kitaoka Shinichi, Tessa Morris-Suzuki, Christopher Redl, Suzuki Masabumi, Takahata Akio, Tanaka Akihiko, and Yamakage Susumu all needled, cajoled, and/or advised in very constructive ways.

I am particularly grateful to Shimizu Isao in Kawasaki and to Cinzia Bibolotti in Forte Dei Marmi for opening their cartoon archives to me. Ted Postol helped enormously with the digital camera and the images derived therefrom. Thanks too to Lucia Bonfreschi, Patrick Boyd, Brett Kubicek, Sara Jane McCaffrey, Sakaguchi Isao, Lisa Sansoucy, and Andrew Tagliabue—wonderfully able research assistants all. Finally—though he deserves better—I thank Roger Haydon, whose editorial judgments were, as always, as extraordinary as they were indispensable.

Institutional support was of enormous importance. I am delighted to acknowledge grants from the German Marshall Fund and the Abe Fellowship Program of the Japan Foundation's Center for Global Partnership (administered by the Social Science Research Council), which kept me afloat in Bologna and Tokyo. The Rockefeller Foundation's Bellagio Study and Conference Center is any scholar's paradise. Thanks to Gianna Celli and her staff for their pampering. Visiting appointments at the Dipartimento di Politica, Storia, Istituzioni at the University of Bologna and at the Shakai Kakgaku Kenkyūjo at the University of Tokyo were critical as well. They were made possible through the enthusiastic sponsorship of Professors Pasquino and Hiwatari, on both of whom I heaped a great many administrative burdens. In Bologna, Antonella Cuccoli did everything she could to help us get settled comfortably—and always with a smile. At MIT, Paula Kreutzer's indefatigable assistance afforded me complete peace of mind. Nothing was going to fall between the stools on her watch! Laurie Scheffler inherited me, and made finishing this book passably pain free. I am grateful as well to my enthusiastic Italian teachers at the ABC Center in Porto Azzurro and at Harvard University Extension School, where Professor Ubaldo DeBenedetto was a charismatic presence and a great teacher.

There was never any greater support than that from my wife, Debbie. She remains a woman of endless beauty and grace. Thirty years together is still not enough. It is simply not possible to thank her adequately or to acknowledge her properly.

RICHARD J. SAMUELS

Cambridge, Massachusetts

Machiavelli's Children

Introduction:

WHY LEADERS MATTER

> For my part, I detest these absolute systems, which represent all the events of history as depending upon first great causes linked by the chain of fatality, and which, as it were, suppress men from the history of the human race. They seem narrow, to my mind, under their pretense of broadness, and false beneath their air of mathematical exactness.
>
> Alexis de Tocqueville, *The Recollections of Alexis de Tocqueville*

It is obvious that leaders matter. What Bismarck did, what Churchill configured, and how Mandela calculated all clearly changed the world. Few will disagree that Mrs. Thatcher transformed Britain or that Mao and Gandhi inspired epochal change in China and India. Indeed, it is so obvious that it is puzzling that so many intellectuals routinely subordinate the choices made by individuals to large and impersonal forces. Few embrace the idea that there is no choice in history, and no one admits that leaders do only what the "great forces" dictate. Yet, in our collective retelling of the past, we routinely limit choices. Our histories privilege constraint over choice.

Not everything under the sun is possible, to be sure. A great deal always lies beyond the control of even the most able strategist. Moreover, we can be certain that far more opportunities are lost than are seized in history. But if determined individuals can make their political space more capacious—if they can "stretch their constraints"—then those analysts who privilege constraint risk missing how actors mobilize creativity, prejudice, spite, passion, history, and philosophy. In the real world, some leaders do little more than bob like corks on a restless sea. But others—many others—do much more. Some revolutionaries invent futures using wholly new materials. Others tinker with the materials at hand, first making a new past before constructing a future. And even those who are not revolutionaries, "normal" politicians, will routinely select among equally plausible alternatives. In short, constraints may be greater in the historian's narrative than they are in the real world, where social, political, and economic forces can be tipped into the balance to abet the leader's scheme.

In this book, I conceive of leaders as political actors who have a greater range of assets than others in the community for "stretching" the constraints of geography and natural resources, institutional legacies and international location. This book uses dozens of episodes from Italian and Japanese history to show what difference individuals can make. No societies have been so constrained as those that developed late and lost wars. Italy and Japan did both, and so they are particularly useful as laboratories. Here we can show how even under the same constraints, different leaders can choose—and choose differently. Some use history, or invent a usable history. Others create alliances where none ought to have existed or were even perceived as possible. Some find new, more effective ways to compel or deter rivals. We shall learn that choices can be constructed from a range of often-contradictory possibilities—each legitimate in its own context, but none predetermined. We shall see how individual agents use and even perturb the inertia of great forces. We shall examine how individuals often nudge political trajectories in new and unexpected directions. Some read from the scripts they are given, others write their own, and still others ad lib. In this book, in short, we will take choice and creativity seriously in our account of change. And, in so doing, we will revalidate notions of individual responsibility and culpability—a normative lesson of transcendent importance for the continued health of the body politic.

The Great Forces

Sidney Hook derided historians who presented leaders as little more than "colorful nodes and points on the curve of social evolution to which no tangents could be drawn."[1] But such historians have distinguished company. Each discipline tells its own version of history, and the broad repertoire of scholarly explanations has left very little room for human agency in general, or for leadership in particular. Each one partially explains historical change while simultaneously discounting the importance of leaders. Although a range of great forces is invoked, it is as if none of the blind men in the famous parable had found—or tried to describe—the elephant's brain.

Personality is the great force most closely linked to the brain. Psychological accounts of history were wracked for decades by debate about whether personality was fixed or variable. Cognition has now dislodged personality as the great force for psychological accounts, and the dominant metaphor

2

for the brain has become the computer. Either way, though, psychologists and psychobiographers have trouble explaining how the same individual could act so variously. Harry Truman, the meek haberdasher and failed Kansas City machine politician, wrestled General Douglas MacArthur to defeat and committed the United States to a Cold War against communism. Ulysses S. Grant, a Civil War general of great self-assurance, honesty, and unquestioned authority, proved a bewildered president who associated with known scoundrels and failed to control the widespread corruption that marred his administration. Psychology does a better job explaining how leaders might fail to use information than explaining how they might transform a political landscape. And it has largely abandoned charisma, that particular personal quality of some great leaders.[2]

Culture is an alternative that works at the group level. It explains choice by means of norms and values that are derived from shared historical experience and reproduced through education, family, and civic participation. These norms and shared experiences powerfully limit options. What is possible in one culture is impossible—even inconceivable—in another. But culture is simultaneously too ambitious and underspecified.[3] Who was acting more "Chinese": Mao Zedong, the Marxist revolutionary, or Chiang Kai-shek, the reactionary generalissimo? And which was more characteristically "American": Alexander Hamilton's preference for manufacturing or Thomas Jefferson's preference for agriculture? Culture—at least in this reified application—is a "great force" that fails to provide for the possibility of different brains. A good example is found in twentieth-century Canada. Pierre Trudeau and Rene Levesque, both leading Francophone politicians, were born after World War I, just three years apart. The former held a vision of a strong, federal Canada, whereas the latter dedicated himself to leading a strong, independent Quebec. Although the choices of both had great consequences, it is hard to argue that culture animated their fundamental differences.[4]

Then there is *structure*—those elements of a social system that produce regularized patterns of behavior that we call social roles and functions. When these roles and functions become routine, structures can empower a strong, *causal* argument about historical development.[5] On this account, individuals are highly constrained by processes such as secularization, market rationalization, and scientific revolution. Structures powerfully shape choice, often setting in train particular courses of action that may prove to be difficult if not impossible to reverse. Accounts of revolution may omit the revolutionaries.[6] Political actors are "embedded agents operating within relational structural fields that distinguish the possible from the impossible and the likely from the less likely."[7] Scholars thus bet against the likelihood that individuals will select against the logic prescribed by their social role. This sort of "probabilistic wagering" can lead to big surprises. When Mikhail Gorbachev selected glasnost and perestroika and against Soviet communism in the 1980s, when Pol Pot selected against Cambodian modernization in the 1980s, and when Helmut Kohl voluntarily surrendered German autonomy to a stronger Europe in the 1990s, each was selecting against their prescribed role.

The border between society and politics is highly permeable. The great forces of structure and *power* are often twinned. Like any other structure, power relations—as embedded in received institutions and norms—constrain, resist, or transform individual preferences. As a result, politics is biased toward inertia and power is slow to change.[8] But since power relations *do* change—sometimes violently and unexpectedly—"contingency" becomes the scholar's wild card. Contingency is an important but ambiguous concept with two equally relevant meanings. The first refers to something accidental—an unforeseen and unexplained occurrence that happens by chance. The other refers to the dependence of one event on a prior one. Both meanings suggest that once something happens, new trajectories of change are created. These trajectories, informed by the past, become in their turn difficult to reverse.[9]

Indeed, much power is contingent—both on accident and on what the past bequeaths. Still, we do not always understand what is internal to the system. Contingency cannot adequately explain why Czechoslovakia, a pastiche of Czech, Romanian, Polish, and Germanic peoples, split peacefully after the end of the Cold War, whereas Yugoslavia dissolved into civil war and genocide. The contingency here may have been leadership itself, and so we may be overlooking a regular element in historical change. Leaders such as Gandhi and Lenin may have become colossal figures not only because they seized opportunities presented by shifting global forces but also because they constructed the most consequential "contingencies" of their age. Power sometimes is bequeathed, but at other times it is built—and building requires builders.[10]

Often, we think of such building as a process animated by the rational, cost-benefit calculation of individuals. *Utility* becomes the greatest "great force" of all. Although self-interest works at the individual level, it has joined these other great forces in focusing scholars on the constraints that channel action.[11] Individual rationality is presumed in order to test models; it is not an object of testing itself. But there are many ways to calculate utility, and when a model predicts many outcomes, there is no way to tell which will be chosen.[12] Even Douglass North, one of its most distinguished theorists, rejects the "instrumental rationality" of rational choice in favor of incorporating ideology and other "subjective models."[13] He and others acknowledge that even with full information about the preferences of particular leaders, it was not possible to have known a priori when—or even if—Richard Nixon would unilaterally dismantle the Bretton Woods system of world trade and international finance; when/if Charles de Gaulle would remove France from the joint military command of the North Atlantic Treaty Organization; or if Winston Churchill would yield to Hitler in the dark months prior to U.S. entry into the Second World War.[14]

To be sure, scholars have begun to entertain a more ecumenical, agency-based view of how to think about historical change. Political psychologists appreciate how individuals fix new bounds to rationality; political anthropologists have provided for the possibility that culture can be constructed and wielded by determined leaders; historical sociologists have reassessed the impact of contingent events on structural change; political economists now accept that ideology plays its part in the construction of self-interest; political sociologists have begun to mix contingency with structure in creative ways; economic historians have infused their narratives with game theory; and economic sociologists have identified how leaders matter in institutional transformation.[15] Still, a range of constraints continues to dominate our analytic lenses. We must address two questions: Are real leaders as constrained as most scholars assume? What alternatives do we have to the privileging of constraints and the discounting of choice?

STRETCHING CONSTRAINTS

Let us begin by imagining political leadership as the "stretching of constraints."[16] By "constraints," I refer to the great forces that seem to limit the choices of political actors. By "stretching," I refer to the ways in which these actors bring resources in, take resources out, or mobilize existing resources in new ways. These resources may be institutional, ideological, or material. Complicating matters, the constraints that leaders confront may reinforce each other more tightly at some times than at others, making the job of stretching them all the more difficult. But, unless they manage to stretch these constraints, leaders are unlikely to mobilize the resources that give them power or that transform their systems. Able leaders may regularly figure out how to circumvent the constraints that bind other, less effective ones. More important for our purposes in this book, the solutions devised by "transformational" leaders may leave legacies: changes that constrain or enable their successors (hence demonstrating that invention may be the mother of necessity).

Change need not be accidental or compelled by great forces. Even if it

5

occurs at unexpected times and in unexpected ways, it can be nudged by the choices of individuals. But how often, and under what conditions? Can we do better than dismiss change as the product of some under-theorized "contingency"? Can we understand change as the product of more than accident, luck, or serendipity? One way is to combine choice and context systematically. Leadership is where they intersect, and it has been under our noses all along. In short, leadership may be a "normal" contingency.[17]

John Kingdon builds a compelling argument about the relationship of ideas, opportunities, and leaders (whom he calls "policy entrepreneurs").[18] Building from cases of "normal politics" in the United States, he shows how luck, constraint, and skill always work in parallel. Leaders may lie in wait for the opening of a "policy window." For Kingdon, opportunities come and opportunities go, and leaders must be alert and prepared to seize them. Structure and choice are joined by the efforts of an individual.

I also believe that leadership is that constrained place where imagination, resources, and opportunity converge. The imaginings need not be original to the leader, but he is the one who can control their use for his ends. The resources need not be entirely of her making, but she must be able to commandeer them for her own use. Opportunities will flow past individual entrepreneurs from time to time, and the successful leader will seize them. Most important of all, the constraints need not be determinant and the change need not be serendipitous. Determined individuals will demonstrate a range of creative ways to combine resources and ideas, and to seize opportunity. This book is about ideas applied, resources assembled, and opportunities seized . . . or lost. It is *Hamlet with* the prince—often a Machiavellian prince actively engaged in building support for new ways of getting politics to work.

There are many ways to think of leaders. The simplest, perhaps, is as the individual who exercises power. He not only can assert some control over the social relations in which he is embedded, but he can get others to do what he wants done.[19] At this level, leaders are granted (or seize) the authority to act as agents on behalf of the political collectivity. More interesting—and analytically far more difficult—is the leader who, having exercised power and having made choices, leaves a *legacy* that changes the world for his successors. We are interested in the leader who not only gets things done but affects future generations. Leaders who create new constraints and new opportunities are "transformational." They not only overcome the constraints that have stymied others, but they also influence—for better or worse—the ability of their political unit to survive and thrive.[20] As we shall see, many do not even survive in power long enough to consolidate their gains, much less see the transformations they imagined.

TRANSFORMATIONAL STRATEGIES

We can imagine two basic transformational strategies: *bricolage* and *revolution*. They are distinguished principally by the leaders' relationship to and use of the past. The revolutionary leader rejects a discredited past and focuses on building the future. The *bricoleur* is no less intent on change, but searches for a useable past. The revolutionary focuses more on exploring new forms, while the bricoleur is busy exploiting old ones.

History has romanticized the revolutionary, but it has been far more accommodating to the bricoleur. Even the most "revolutionary" leaders have sought some synthesis of the old and the new as a way to legitimate their grandiose transformations. Ho Chi Minh appealed for radical change, but he did so while invoking the French Declaration of the Rights of Man and Vietnamese history in equal measure. Revolutionaries and bricoleurs are not entirely different, though bricolage is a more nuanced representation of the mechanisms through which leaders bring change to their countries.

We owe this notion of the bricoleur to Claude Lévi-Strauss. Lévi-Strauss's bricoleur is a tinkerer, a practical problem-solver who uses only the materials and tools he has at hand. He operates with and redeploys heterogeneous "fragments" from the past. What earlier were ends now are means—his block of oak, once a doorstop, is now a pedestal. The bricoleur's challenge is to transform residual matériel into practical resources that will support change. In this sense, "institution building often occurs not *on the ruins* but *with the ruins* of the old regime."[21]

Too much reliance on the past is a problem because history limits the ways materials and components can be reassembled. The doorstop can become a pedestal but cannot become a wagon unless someone invents the wheel. Indeed, Lévi-Strauss acknowledges that bricoleurs can assemble new worlds from fragments of the old, but his bricoleur tends to be "imprisoned in the events and experiences [which he] never tires of ordering and reordering."[22] He stresses the "pre-constraints" in the bricoleur's leftover "oddments."[23]

But bricolage works differently in the world of politics. In the political world, where transformational leaders stretch constraints, those fragments of the old can be extremely valuable as repositories of the acceptable. They contain *legitimacy* as well as constraints, and are tools of creative

7

reinvention and change. Political bricoleurs reassemble and deploy fragments of legitimate action as they search for a useable past. Indeed, because legitimacy is so precious and elusive, the deeper and more ably the
political bricoleur reaches back to secure a serviceable history, the surer
may be his grip on the future.

Lévi-Strauss gave us the name and deep insight into this process, but
others had already appreciated the political function of bricolage. Machiavelli, for example, had warned against the sudden rejection of the past in
the construction of the future. His solution was to invoke the past to legitimate change:

> He who desires or proposes to change the form of government in a state and
> wishes it to be acceptable and to be able to maintain it to everyone's satisfac-
> tion, must retain at least the shadow of its ancient customs, so that institutions
> may not appear to its people to have been changed, though in point of fact
> the new institutions may be radically different from the old ones. This he
> must do because men in general are as much affected by what a thing appears
> to be as by what it is.[24]

Contemporary scholars have begun to catch on. Some now think of
symbols as an "irresistible strategic resource."[25] Leaders can both reassure
and manipulate followers, even while skimming the bulk of the material
rewards for themselves.[26] In this way, we can appreciate how collective action depends on persuasion and how individual action interacts with
norms and values. Culture becomes a tool—an *instrument* available for
leaders to use and manipulate. The revolutionary is usually a bricoleur,
and the bricoleur may be a persistent revolutionary.

MOBILIZING MECHANISMS

Beneath these grand strategies to stretch constraints lie three mobilizing mechanisms that transformational leaders use to build and maintain
power. Leaders may appeal to affect, by *inspiring*. They may appeal to material interests, by *buying*. And, by *bullying*, they may appeal to fear.[27]

The bricoleur's use of culture, often through the selective reconstruction of history, is designed to appeal strongly to affect. The bricoleur is a
master of symbolic politics and of inspiration. His power can derive from
the ability to name things—even (or especially) familiar things that are
experienced in a new way. The leader who controls the way the collectivity
is represented to itself—often through the words and rituals of historical
narrative and even "foundational fictions"—can control the future. As

Kertzer reminds us, naming comes from a battle among elites to define the past, to inspire, and to control affect. Leaders succeed or fail "depend[ing] on their ability to discredit the renaming efforts of their rivals and to substitute themselves as authors of any re-representation."[28] Thinkers as different as Machiavelli and Marx knew well that mantles must be grabbed and appropriated.[29]

This important insight about culture and history as instruments of the powerful has insinuated itself into political studies from several directions. Historians Eric Hobsbawm and Terence Ranger show how tradition is "invented." Leaders make largely fictitious references to history to legitimate their own power. Sociologist Ann Swidler offers an image of culture as a "'tool kit' of symbols, stories, rituals, and world views" that leaders selectively employ to sustain their power. And political scientist David Laitin demonstrates how culture is "Janus-faced": individuals are informed by the symbols of their culture but are also able to use these symbols instrumentally.[30] These insights remind us that legitimacy may be the most ubiquitous tool of power, perhaps because it is usually cheaper than bullying or buying.

Still, of course, leaders do bully and buy with abandon. Bullies are straightforward. They have insufficient legitimacy and act with the conviction that power wears out those who do not possess and deploy it. If they think their adversaries are weak, they surround and squeeze them, using every variety of material and ideational resources. They may court popularity and crave legitimacy, but being feared will usually suffice. They may invent threats to conjure support or, like Joshua, they may blow trumpets to knock down adversaries' already frail walls.[31]

Buyers come in many forms as well. Where bullies purge and consolidate, buyers may juggle and cajole: bullies dominate, buyers accommodate. Some trade. Some share. Others broker, balance, or co-opt. Rather than besiege opponents, they purchase support. Their choices can transform their world. Recall that the "creative destruction" posited by Joseph Schumpeter was driven not by faceless markets but by determined entrepreneurs—"buyers" who perceived new combinations and whose greatest power was obtained when they were monopolists.[32] So it is in the uncertain world of politics, where minimum winning coalitions may not be good enough. If buyers have sufficient resources, they are likely to over-insure their power. If, on the other hand, they are particularly conservative, they are as attentive to the reaction to change as to change itself. Some buyers center themselves between enemies and allies—always ready to make one into the other. Such centering cannot simply be a matter of finding the midpoint of a straight line, and it is more complicated than balancing weights on a scale or walking a tightrope. Centering is about balance—but a balance that is neither mechanical nor hydraulic. It requires agency. Like the juggler, the centerer manages a heterogeneous collection of shapes and weights and adjusts to the wind, to the noise, and to the excitement of the crowd. Successful centerers are the buyers who impose order so fully that the order they create becomes one of the forces that shape and is nudged by the creative stratagems of their successors.

Bullies, buyers, and inspirers can each be strategic actors—manipulators who busy themselves by creating and controlling the political agenda.[33] They focus on the structural conditions that make it easier for them to achieve and maintain power. They may bureaucratize politics, or politicize the bureaucracy. They understand that all else being equal, different agendas will result in different outcomes. They therefore enhance their chances of success by shaping their world so they can win. Creativity and opportunism are central.

As we have seen, there are a number of ways in which transformational leaders can stretch the constraints that operate on them. At the end of the day, creativity, flexibility, and opportunism—all combined with resources—may be their most distinguishing characteristics. Machiavelli understood this clearly. For Machiavelli, the wise prince knows there are many roads to Rome. He knows that some are safer and others more dangerous at different seasons, and so he knows which one to select at which time: "I have often thought that the reason why men are sometimes unfortunate, sometimes fortunate, depends upon whether their behavior is in conformity with the time."[34] Here, then, in the contingency of leadership, is where we are apt to find a connection between agency and structure. It is likely to reside where leaders shift their tactics, to adapt to new conditions and thereby perhaps change the conditions themselves. Thus, to take just three examples, the bully may reinvent himself as a buyer, as the onetime apparatchik Boris Yeltsin did after the fall of the Berlin Wall. The inspirer may resort to ruthless bullying, as Mao did after the Chinese Revolution succeeded. Or the buyer may choose to bully, as Fidel Castro did once he no longer needed alliances with the liberal opponents to Fulgencio Batista in Cuba. Having done well in one role hardly ensures success when times and challenges change. Flexibility joins invention and creativity as the sine qua non of the transformational leader.[35]

THE ODD COUPLE

I undertake to analyze leaders through a close comparison of Italian and Japanese history. The standard explanation for things Italian is jarring to observers of Japan who have heard the same characterization many times over:

> The most important thing for the foreigner to realize about Italy is that it is a poor country . . . One-third of Italy is mountains, another third is hills . . . Her total land area is only a little more than half that of France . . . [and] on this meager allotment of productive territory she must support a population larger than [France's]. Italy almost totally lacks mineral resources. She must import nearly all her coal and her iron ore . . . Italians have managed by ingenuity and hard work to make their country an important industrial power . . . A mere glance at Italy's situation on a map will show why the Italians have traditionally been famous as seafarers and traders. Italy is technically a peninsula, but it is at the same time practically an island.[36]

This characterization is identical to the mantra invoked by generations of Japan interpreters—Japanese as well as foreign. This mantra, the *shima-guni-ron,* is the ubiquitous claim that "Japan is a unique small island trading nation precariously dependent upon imported raw materials cut adrift in a hostile world." Former U.S. Ambassador Edwin O. Reischauer was its best-known purveyor:

> Because of Japan's narrow and poorly endowed geographic base, [its] industrialization has brought with it a heavy dependence on foreign sources of energy and raw materials and therefore an equal dependence on foreign markets for industrial exports to pay for necessary imports . . . Japan's dependence on global trade for its very survival is the single most important fact about its economic geography and the chief determinant of its relationship with the rest of the world.[37]

Even general statements that attempt to capture the nature of Italian democracy sound more than vaguely Japanese:

> Italy is in name a democratic republic—yet . . . it has never experienced the sort of classic, epoch-making revolution on which nations like France have founded their democratic tradition. Its modern, fluid, industrial society is a recent accretion superimposed on a hierarchical, unchanging, quasi-feudal society . . . How could a Western-type democracy evolve out of a society that remained basically conservative, stratified, and profoundly rooted in the manners of the pre-industrial age?[38]

While this sort of parallel language is fascinating, such general characterizations are not terribly useful. (Nor are they necessarily correct.) We need to unbundle accounts of Italy and Japan to explain their respective paths to the present. Today, Italy and Japan are democratic states, with high rates of electoral participation in free and fair elections, basic civil liberties, formal checks on central authority, civilian control over the military, the rule of law in social and economic relations, and robust civil societies. Yet, both countries also exhibit pathologies that contradict the more progressive requisites of "ideal" democracy: frequent changes of government, a problematic balance between deference to authority and individualism, some stubbornly authoritarian social relations, extensive corruption, limits to effective participation in decision making, problems of accountability, and increasing cynicism toward politicians and bureaucrats. Given these problems, one of the more important contemporary parallels between Italy and Japan is the synchronized effort to repair their respective democracies. Each is struggling to redefine its constitutional order in the wake of the Cold War.

Efforts to repair the status quo are a fixture of Japanese and Italian political life. Since the 1860s, from the very moment the two states were formed, both Italy and Japan have pursued parity with the rest of the world. Japanese leaders strove to eliminate the "unequal treaties" that were forced on them, and were openly determined to "catch up and surpass" (*oitsuku, oikosu*) the West and become a "first-class nation" (*ittō koku*). Italian leaders, for their part, were determined that Italy would become "the last of the great powers" (*l'ultima delle grande potenze*) and occupy a seat in the councils of Europe (*entrare nel concerto europeo*). Both had to overcome the repeated, humiliating slights of diplomats who treated them as "adolescents" in the grip of "inferiority complexes"; each was preoccupied by its national reputation in foreign eyes.[39] Each felt the sting of foreign condescension and scorn.[40] Today both are immensely prosperous, and each sits comfortably among the G-8—the most exclusive group of great powers in the world.

Judging from the persistent discourse about national shortcomings, however, neither is fully convinced that it has achieved parity with the world's leaders. Their "great chases" have never ended. What had been a pursuit of modernity is now a pursuit of "normality." Italians debate what it will take to become "*un paese normale*," while Japanese debate what it will take to become "*futsū no kuni*."[41] While the nominal terms are identical, the substance of these debates is different. Japanese wonder when they will become normal in foreign affairs, while the Italians wonder when their domestic politics will become "normally" stable. Each is still hotly in pursuit of parity.

The roads to contemporary Rome and Tokyo were built and traveled by "latecomers" who saw a world ahead of them. They were perpetually trying to catch up. Italy and Japan have different histories but long have felt

Italians in the 1890s spoke of their young state as "the last of the great powers" (*l'ultima delle grande potenze*). Reproduced courtesy of the Museo Civico del Risorgimento, Bologna.

Even as the Japanese celebrated their military victory over Russia in 1905, they saw themselves as childlike. They struggled to be a "first-class nation" (*ittō koku*). Reproduced courtesy of the Saitama Municipal Cartoon Art Museum (artist Rakuten Kitazawa, in *Tokyo Puck* 3, no. 8 [1907]).

a common need to come to grips with (and preferably to conquer) modernity. This was true in the 1860s, when creation of a nation-state and autonomous national *power* was the project; it was true in the economies of the nineteenth and early twentieth centuries, when each had to industrialize rapidly to create national *wealth;* and it was true in the manufacture of a national *identity* to bind state and economy to a common purpose. This book will examine each of these three constructions—power, wealth, and identity—and will show how this chase is still relevant today. The road builders were ever—and are still—vulnerable. They had to overcome common external shocks: war, depression, and, now, globalization. Theirs have always been stories of "becoming" something else, something different, something more advanced. Something "normal."

These roads seem to have taken Italians and Japanese to the same place—liberal democracy—with roughly the same detours along the way: socially dislocating industrial development, radical nationalism, authoritarian interludes, hegemonic party systems, and structural corruption. This seems a powerful argument for convergence. Since for most of this period the Italian economy was relatively more liberal and open, while Japan was relatively more insular, it even casts doubt on the relevance of ideology. Above all, it casts doubt on the relevance of agency and political leadership. If, after all, these countries came out in the same place and got there along similar routes, then the choices of leaders could not have mattered very much.

In this book I show why this interpretation is wrong. Through paired case studies of political leaders over the past 150 years, I demonstrate why few of these outcomes were inevitable—or, at a minimum, that few of the most consequential ones were as overdetermined as much social science would have it. To be sure, great political, social, and economic forces were unleashed by modernization and late development. Likewise, international politics operated on domestic choice at all times. But constraints on leaders, as significant as they were, masked enormous room for maneuver—room that the most able among them exploited.

In some cases, as we shall see, individuals led. In other cases they merely acted. But however we model their agency, as grand architecture or as creative bricolage, their stories suggest that neither social nor economic imperatives such as trade-induced convergence nor the "requirements" of democracy make nations so fully alike that choices are irrelevant. Choices *are* made and *do* have institutional legacy. The accounts in this book call into question the great categories many believe sufficiently capture "the end of history." We shall see that modernization and democracy have many faces, none of which ever emerged from dispassionate forces alone.

Plutarch's Wheel on Machiavelli's Cart

This book takes seriously the idea that leaders can stretch constraints and that this process requires determination and skill as well as opportunity. Toward that end, it takes a close look at specific cases from Italian and Japanese history, paired when possible to facilitate appreciation of intentional and consequential choice. The pairing of leaders is hardly my invention. Plutarch first did it two thousand years ago.[42] But Plutarch's was a moral evaluation. He selected pairs of leaders—one Greek, the other Roman—because one or the other provided a good example to emulate. They were virtuous, honorable, generous, or caring. For Plutarch, "there is no perfecter endowment in man than political virtue," and he added that "To seek power by servility to the people is a disgrace, but to maintain it by terror, violence, and oppression is not a disgrace only, but an injustice."[43]

Machiavelli is famous for a different idea. His reputation notwithstanding, however, Machiavelli was not unconcerned with the higher good. Even his classical formulation of the ends justifying the means was warranted on moral grounds: "It is a sound maxim that reprehensible actions may be justified by their effects, and that when the effect is good . . . it always justifies the action. For it is the man who uses violence to spoil things, not the man who uses it to mend them, that is blameworthy."[44] His distinction between *fortuna* (luck, accident, circumstance, constraint) and *virtú* (skill, ability, fortitude, audacity) continues to inform our understanding.[45] The leaders Machiavelli most admired—and those he deemed most powerful—became princes more by their own abilities than by dumb luck, though he understood clearly the difficulties they encountered:

> I believe that it is probably true that fortune is the arbiter of half the things we do, leaving the other half or so to be controlled by ourselves. I compare fortune to one of those violent rivers which, when they are enraged, flood the plains, tear down trees and buildings, wash soil to deposit it from one place to another. Everyone flees before them, everybody yields to their impetus, there is no possibility of resistance. Yet although such is their nature, it does not follow that when they are flowing quietly one cannot take precautions, constructing dykes and embankments . . . So it is with fortune. She shows her potency when there is no regulated power to resist her, and her impetus is felt when she knows there are no embankments and dykes to restrain her.[46]

Machiavelli's concern with *virtú* was about *virtuosity* as well as virtue. It was about skill as well as goodness and justice. And, while we will not ignore the ethical questions that leadership engenders, skill is also a central concern of this study.

Reinventing Plutarch's wheel and mounting it on Machiavelli's cart provides a tool for examining the "what ifs" of counterfactual history.[47] One possibility is to examine closely the alternatives considered by the same leader and imagine the consequences of a different choice made at the same juncture. As Max Weber noted, the question of "what might have happened if . . . Bismarck had not decided to make war is important if history is to be raised above the level of a mere chronicle of notable events and personalities."[48] The other possibility is Plutarch's: paired comparisons of choices by different leaders under similar constraints.

In this book I do both, for each provides its own kind of analytical leverage. In a series of paired comparisons of Japanese and Italian leaders across four historical periods, I am able to hold structural differences relatively constant and focus on how each leader sorted through and developed choices. I scrutinize both the choices *and* the context in which they are made and attempt to reconstruct their scripts and stratagems.[49]

In selecting cases for comparison, I looked for leaders who were either catalysts of political change despite "great forces" that might easily have dictated otherwise or who resisted change effectively. Either way, they will have made choices that mattered for (and possibly even constrained) subsequent leaders. I have also sought pairs of leaders who, despite shared structural constraints across different political landscapes, had very different conversations with history. Finally, I have sought (though not always successfully) to identify choices that were not clearly overdetermined. To be sure, anyone looking for creative leadership is apt to find it and is apt to undervalue the great forces shaping outcomes. Selection bias is clearly a problem.[50] That acknowledged, there remain good reasons for proceeding.

First, by looking simultaneously at cases from similar historical settings in which Japanese and Italian leaders made *different* choices, the risk of privileging structural explanations is reduced. Second, by starting with striking similarities, the bias shifts *toward* structure, a framework against which this analysis is arguing. Third, by using paired biographies from different sectors of economic and political life, one can hedge against *both* individual and structural bias. Fourth, if leaders make choices among multiple—or, better yet, equally plausible alternatives, then assumptions about single correct choices and the limitations of great constraints are rendered less compelling. Leaders may not be all that matters in politics, but they are surely more than mere vessels for irresistible and inevitable change.[51] In the end, I hope to emerge with a fuller, more nuanced understanding of the interactions among creativity, choice, constraint, and their consequences.

IMPROVING ON CONTINGENCY

There is room for many kinds of leadership in the evaluation of political change. Choice is what leaders do, and the consequences of their choices are worth studying: leadership can have an independent legacy. I have suggested that leaders can bully, buy, or inspire without stretching constraints, but they cannot stretch constraints without bullying, buying, or inspiring. Leaders design and build with given resources and tools, but these tools and resources depend on leaders' skills and imagination as well as on external forces. Mine is not a story of choice over constraint, but a story of choice within constraint. The job in the rest of this book is to determine when leaders are connected to outcomes, how often outcomes are connected to intentions, and if these outcomes constitute legacies in any systematic way. This book does not develop and propose any particular theory of agency. Instead, it induces from Japanese and Italian history just how limited and unsatisfactory our ability is to understand the world without an operative sense of how agency matters. In this sense, it makes a positive, but not specific claim: It does not exhort scholars to "do agency" in any special way, but rather to "do agency" to make our explanations more robust.

Here, then, we return to the dismissal of historical theory with which this chapter opened. Its fuller context reveals that Tocqueville was arguing not just against the pretentiousness of social science or for the efficacy of strategic leadership, but also in favor of the incorporation of serendipity: "Antecedent facts, the nature of institutions, the cast of minds and the state of morals are the materials of which are composed those impromptus which astonish and alarm us. The Revolution of February, in common with all other great events of this class, sprang from general causes, impregnated, if I am permitted the expression, by accidents."[52]

My purpose here is to see whether we can do better than that. This book travels through Italian and Japanese history in order to theorize from what has heretofore been routinely dismissed as "contingency." I hope to demonstrate that contingency is itself routine, and thereby to show that in political analysis it is critical to connect context to agency and to marry leadership to the great forces that constrain it.

PART I

CREATION STORIES:
THE NINETEENTH CENTURY

CHAPTER ONE

Chasing Prestige and Security

If one impartially compares our country with European countries, we are . . .
abreast of Italy.

Editorial, *Kokumin no Tomo*, 1891

There is no doubt that England was our teacher. But it is not unusual for students to overtake their teachers. And we can truly say that Italy has now overtaken its tutor in many respects.

Gaetano Arangio Ruiz, 1911

Determined, audacious oligarchs built modern states in Japan and Italy at precisely the same moment in history. And, in so doing, they left institutional legacies that neither subsequent political engineering nor great external shocks could erase. The Italian and Japanese state-builders had a great deal in common. They were drawn from the educated classes; they were alienated from what they perceived as a decaying aristocratic order; they feared populism, yet they were able to channel popular support to legitimate their own power. Above all, both the Japanese and Italian state-builders were profoundly conscious of their own backwardness and of developments abroad; each was animated by the fear (and very real prospect) of foreign domination. These "conservative revolutionaries" raced to create states that could withstand the tremors of great power conflict while going to great lengths to deny that anything like a revolution was occurring.

Italy was born of liberal aspirations for the nation, Japan of nationalist ones for the state. From the beginning, liberalism was a tool of autocrats in Italy, and altogether a chimera in Japan. Liberty, the great rallying cry among Risorgimento intellectuals, held at least two separate promises. The first was freedom from foreign rule and the second was freedom from absolutist or papal domination. Unification of the Italian state—the modernizing project—was a tool to accomplish both. Italy would be accepted into the system of European states, or be devoured by foreign tyrants. It would sit beside Britain, Hungary, France, and Germany, or be dominated by them like Spain and the Netherlands.[1] Japan would meet the rapacious Western powers on their own terms by developing a "rich nation and strong army" (*fukoku kyōhei*) or, like China, it would become their vassal.

Whereas nineteenth-century Italy had been the "footfall" of foreign dynasties and their armies, nineteenth-century Japan had never been invaded; its "Pax Tokugawa," more than two and a half centuries (1600–1868) of peaceful isolation, is unequaled in modern history.[2] Threatened repeatedly by European powers and, in 1853, very convincingly by the "black ships" of Commodore Matthew Perry, Japan had long since established a central government under the military control of a hereditary shogun. Thus, the Italian Risorgimento was a movement to unify Italy and dislodge foreign and clerical powers, but the Meiji Restoration was aimed at fortifying an already unified Japan. Japanese state-builders could appeal to symbols of the primordial Japanese nation. Their Piedmontese counterparts could appeal only wanly to Roman glory and equally feebly to a "sacred" monarch.[3]

Yet, the monarchies were useful tools as state-builders grabbed for power. Neither the House of Savoy (which was more French than Italian), nor the Japanese imperial household (which was largely unknown to the masses) appears at first glance a propitious institution on which to build fundamental political change. In Japan, thousands of years of an unbroken imperial line and two and a half centuries of what scholars have termed "centralized feudalism" were incalculably valuable resources, and those who controlled the prerogatives of the emperor learned they could control the empire itself. But they had to be cautious. Rather than rush headlong to embrace Western values and institutions, the Japanese chose and adapted Western forms that could be legitimated by their divine emperor. In Italy, where liberalism was a serious idea, the task was different.[4] State-builders first had to establish the principle of liberty and set limits on aristocracy. They had to locate sovereignty within the Italian state. Only after Cavour had sold the House of Savoy on the framework of a liberal constitution (Lo Statuto) could King Victor Emmanuel II of Sardinia be transformed into King Victor Emmanuel II of Italy. Only then could that old and generally alien dynasty legitimate a new state.[5]

Despite the Risorgimento and the Meiji Restoration, the ruling classes retained their power, avoided agrarian reform, and blocked major social change. If the Risorgimento was "a civil war between the old and new ruling classes," the Japanese Restoration was a civil war *within* the old ruling class.[6] As Barrington Moore noted a generation ago, neither the Italian nor the Japanese ruling class was confronted by the sort of politicized bourgeoisie that became politically active in France and England.[7] Italian

22

dissenters sought greater egalitarianism than the liberals would provide. Japanese dissenters sought more liberalism.

There was no social revolution in either case, but there certainly was protracted civil war, which in the Italian case never healed completely. After Italian unification, the defeated parties—Republicans, Garibaldians, and Catholics, inter alia—"all nursed various degrees of indignation."[8] They sapped the strength of the new state, which consequently had great difficulty establishing its authority evenly throughout the peninsula. Persistent unrest was called brigandage by the young liberal state as a way to understate the problem, but it was nothing less than civil war. More soldiers fought and died in the aftershocks of unification than in the Risorgimento itself. Italy remained weak, and it was years before it could install the king in Rome or reclaim its *terra irredenta*—much less establish an empire of its own.[9]

The young Meiji state repressed a smaller number of more limited challenges to its claim to power, but civil conflict did not end until nearly a decade after the Restoration. There were a half-dozen samurai rebellions between 1874 and 1877, a "predictably violent reaction of a traditional elite displaced by a modern revolution."[10] The largest, the so-called Satsuma Rebellion, was led in 1877 by Saigo Takamori, one of the original oligarchs; imperial forces suppressed the rebellion after a six-month campaign. As in Italy, the link between civil unrest and the goal of establishing international power was abundantly clear. Saigo had left the government to protest its unwillingness to invade Korea. Japanese oligarchs were straining to establish their international power and prestige, and even the Emperor Meiji was pressed into service, writing to U.S. President Ulysses Grant: "It is our purpose to select from the various institutions prevailing among enlightened nations such as are best suited to our present condition and adopt them . . . so as to be upon equality with them."[11]

Both Italy and Japan were "catch-up imperialists."[12] For the Italians, finally privileged to participate in this entente and that alliance, it was important to feast on colonial victuals. The problem, as one politician observed at the turn of the century, was that "Italy had an enormous appetite, but rotten teeth."[13] Italian colonial wars in North Africa, like Japanese adventures against China and Russia, stimulated great national pride and dramatic defense buildups. But the gains on the battlefield were often annulled at the conference tables. Neither country got the respect that its mobilized populace was led to believe it deserved. When Japanese negotiators returned from Portsmouth, New Hampshire, in 1905, they were met with mass protests that Japan had not won due respect. Meanwhile, Bismarck had proclaimed that Italy "does not count" and later, in 1919 at Versailles, where both Italy and Japan joined the other victorious Allies at last, a senior British diplomat referred to the Italians as "the beggars of Europe."[14]

Italy and Japan were each a hodgepodge of imported laws and administration. Cavour's Lo Statuto and Itō's Meiji Constitution each combined Prussian legal doctrine with a British-style parliament and French-inspired system of centralized domestic governance supervised by a powerful interior ministry. In Japan, foreign law was grafted onto a bureaucracy of long reach and firm grasp. The state assumed jurisdiction in every aspect of social life, and few groups escaped supervision.[15] By contrast, Italian public administration was adopted de novo and the sudden introduction of more than one hundred thousand laws and directives all but paralyzed a nascent civil service. The Italian state was centralized, but remained inefficient.[16]

Inefficiencies aside, the sources of legitimacy bear closer examination. Neither state was built by extolling the new and abhorring the old.[17] Still, there was a crucial difference. The royal title assumed by Victor Emmanuel was "king by the grace of God and by the will of the nation,"[18] while the Meiji emperor was a divine ruler of his subjects. Sectarian groups and institutions have long competed for citizens' primary loyalty in Italy with no analogue in modern Japan.[19] The oldest and most enduring competitor for power in Italy has been the Roman Catholic Church.

THE CHURCH

For seven hundred years—from the fifth to the twelfth centuries—the Church was the only indigenous power governing the public realm on the Italian peninsula. Machiavelli, no admirer of the papacy, anticipated that the Church would become a powerful reactionary force and an impediment to the unification of Italy.

> It is the Church that has kept, and keeps, Italy divided . . . For though the Church has its headquarters in Italy and has temporal power, neither its power nor its virtue has been sufficiently great for it to be able to usurp power in Italy and become its leader; nor yet, on the other hand, has it been so weak that it could not, when afraid of losing its dominion over things temporal, call upon one of the powers to defend it against the Italian state that had become too powerful.[20]

The pope's ability to mobilize foreign support finally evaporated in September 1870, when the king's troops breached the Porta Pia in Rome, sending the defenders into flight. No surprise, then, that the Church was the young Italian state's greatest enemy. In the years after the Risorgimento the churches were abandoned; priests were excluded from civil life and often jeered in public. Pope Pius IX responded with intransigence and "unrelenting opposition to national unification."[21] He refused to recognize the Italian state, excommunicated its founders—both democrats and monarchists alike—and sought assistance from every possible enemy of Italy. The state-builders prevailed, of course, and stripped the Vatican of territorial sovereignty. Their March 1871 "Law of Guarantees" authorized the pope's use of the Vatican, the Lateran Palace, and a villa. He could keep an independent guard and diplomatic immunities, and the new Italian state promised to abstain from interference in Church affairs. Pope Pius IX continued to claim his sovereignty. His successor, Leo XIII, regarded himself as a prisoner and, in his encyclical *Non Expedit*, forbade Italian Catholics from voting or running for office (*né eletti, né elettori*).[22]

But when intransigence failed, the Church shifted to subversion in pursuit of a "Catholic Italy." The church determined to undermine the liberal state by building a dense set of capillary networks that mirrored—and sapped the strength from—secular institutions. A state would be built within the state.[23] Local governments were targeted in order to preserve the (now optional) religious instruction in public schools. In 1891, Pope Leo XIII issued the encyclical *Rerum Novarum,* which addressed the conditions of the working classes, reintroduced corporatist notions of solidarity, condemned liberal capitalism, and reoriented the Church toward social action.[24] The Federation of Catholic Organizations (Opera dei Congressi) and Catholic Action (Azione Cattolica) were used to coordinate good deeds as well as opposition to liberal doctrine.[25] Rural cooperative associations and banks rapidly formed as alternatives to the state's own institutions.[26]

Once having established a highly articulated social and economic base, the Church shifted more overtly toward politics. After 1904, Pius X partially lifted the *Non Expedit* and allowed Catholics to participate in politics "at the discretion of their bishop." It was a slow start. Catholic deputies received less than 1 percent of the vote in 1904, a figure that grew to 6 percent in 1913. But, the first Catholic political party, Partito Popolare (PP)—formed in 1919—won more than one-fifth of the popular vote in the 1920 election.[27] By having stranded its faithful on the margins of Italian political life for decades, the Church had dealt a profound blow to the liberal state, one which it helped make fatal by supporting fascist designs on power in the early 1920s. As the Liberal Prime Minister Giovanni Giolitti struggled between the Church and the Socialists, the Church flirted with him, and then moved right. Later, in 1924, it made peace with the Fascists, sealing it with the Lateran Pacts in 1929. Now the Catholic Church was recognized as the official religion of the Italian state, religious education was compulsory in public schools, and the state treasury would pay the salaries of parish priests.[28]

THE SOCIALIST LEFT

The Roman Catholic Church was not concerned exclusively with the liberal state. As industrialization progressed, the Church—like the state—grew increasingly concerned about the rise of the socialist Left. And for good reason. Unlike the elitist liberals who had never established a popular base, the socialists were direct competitors for the hearts and minds of the general public. They were also building an alternative to the Italian state, and Italy was becoming a nation of competing subcultures; Italians were being forced to choose between what would become *il mondo comunista* and *il mondo cattolico.*[29]

Like Catholic piety, socialist fervor was a genuinely popular phenomenon.[30] It was, of course, a much more recent, nineteenth-century phenomenon, which some date from Mazzini's agitation for an "associational" Italy in the 1840s.[31] By 1862 there were already one hundred and fifty mutual assistance societies for workers and artisans and nearly five hundred cooperatives, predominantly in the large industrial centers of the North.[32] These groups were not primarily political, but economic, social, and educational. Liberals who promoted these groups were wary of the socialist influence, but shared the Left's desire to wean the poor and working classes away from the influence of the clergy. Throughout the peninsula "Houses of the People" (Case del Popolo) provided a physical base for producer and consumer cooperatives, employment offices, child care, social and sports clubs, libraries, medical clinics, and other collective needs.[33] Ultimately, the Left—and the Communist Party in particular—would establish itself as the center of the social infrastructure for much of Italy's working class.[34]

By the turn of the century, Italy had witnessed the territorial consolidation of these rival subcultures.[35] A "Red Belt" of diffuse associational networks could be clearly identified in the industrial districts where modern factories and male workers—as well as self-employed artisans—dominated, as in Emilia-Romagna and Piedmont. The Church had greater success in "White" areas like the Veneto and Lombardy, where artisans were connected to the land and where women workers dominated. Each encompassed the social and economic lives of their faithful in a vigorous network of cooperatives. The Socialists and the Church each strove to eliminate what they considered the artificial distinctions between social, economic, and political life.

26

Some Socialist politicians became less intransigent, and by 1918 the Italian Socialist Party (PSI) got its first taste of power. During the so-called Biennio Rosso (1918–1920), the Left had greater electoral success than the Church. In the 1919 elections, the PSI outpolled the PP in both the big cities and the countryside. By 1920, more than one-quarter of Italy's municipalities was governed by leftist mayors.[36] But the tensions among the Church, the state, and the Left were hardly ameliorated by electoral success. If anything, they were exacerbated. Factory sit-ins and land squatting invited violent reactions from the Right that the Italian state could (or would) not suppress.

The Italian ruling elite alternated between force and conciliation as it tried to contain the Catholic and socialist mass movements. In the late 1870s and again between 1894 and 1900, liberals lashed out at worker and peasant organizations, but from 1900 to 1914, under Giolitti's leadership, they tried a policy of accommodation. From 1914 to 1920, "both strategies were applied inconsistently and incoherently."[37] For its part, the Japanese state ratcheted up suppression while consolidating its institutions, but the power of the Italian state was not consolidated until fascism was invented. Fascism in Japan was a natural development. In Italy it benefited enormously from perceived incoherence.

Two Faces of Fascism

After the First World War, both Italy and Japan were "semi-authoritarian states with pluralist trappings [that] gyrated into full authoritarianism."[38] Liberalism had defeated itself in Italy and had never gotten much traction in Japan. The crises of representative government that gripped Italy and Japan had many of the same features. In both cases liberalism and socialism had lost their luster; the claims of each had been discredited. The glorification of war, the magnification of national virtues, the transcendence of the individual, and the rejection of class conflict had enormous appeal to these late-developing states with shallow bourgeois traditions.[39] There was a shared disillusionment with politicians and their deal making; among the propertied classes, there was a common fear of communism. Most Italians and Japanese could be convinced that the loss of political freedom was a small price to pay for liberty from foreign tyrants, for a high standing in the world, and for stability at home.[40] There came to be broad popular consent to authoritarianism in both countries.

But, there were important differences in the paths that took each to fascism. Italian fascism was built from the outside, without the support of a coherent bureaucracy and even in the absence of a strong military. Japa-

27

nese authoritarianism was built from the inside out—by a strong military with powerful bureaucratic allies.[41] In Japan it was *parliamentary politics* rather than *fascism* that was an historical "parenthesis."[42] Maruyama's analysis remains the most insightful:

> The distinctive characteristic in the development of Japanese fascism was . . . that it never took the form of a fascist revolution with a mass organization occupying the state apparatus from outside the administration. The process was rather the gradual maturing of a fascist structure within the state effected by the established political forces of the military, the bureaucracy, and the political parties.[43]

There was no successful coup in Japan, and certainly no "March on Tokyo"; no mass party, no mobilization against the state, and no Duce.[44] Whereas the Italian fascists eradicated the opposition, the Japanese state absorbed it. Whereas the Italian bureaucracy had to be infiltrated by ideologues, the Japanese bureaucrats were already in place. Whereas the Italian military was insulated from political life, the Japanese military dominated it. It was the Japanese *state* that led the transition to authoritarianism. Italian fascism—itself a shifting ideological melange—paid lip service to agrarian interests, while in Japan these interests were the regime's main base of support.[45] Italian leadership was discontinuous, Japanese leadership was continuous:

> The Japanese government operated as before under the control of the same elites chosen from among Tokyo Imperial University graduates and, in the military, from among regular staff officers, who had gradually become dominant early in the twentieth century . . . [Japanese authoritarianism was] an impressive demonstration of the fundamental continuity of Japanese political life in modern times.[46]

These differences would be consequential. The violent, extrastatal origins of Italian fascism legitimated a wartime Resistance and a postwar democracy. In Japan, where there was no Resistance, postwar democracy could be legitimated only by a foreign power. We will explore the consequences of this fundamental difference in later chapters. First, however, we turn to the building and consolidation of national wealth.

BUILDING WEALTH

"Late development" was the animating force of economic transformation in nineteenth-century Japan and Italy. Economic policy choices were

28

forged in a crucible of aspirations to achieve parity with the great powers. From the beginning, and for nearly half a century, the Japanese strained at the trade restrictions imposed by the Western imperialists. Revision of degrading "unequal treaties" was as central to plans for Japanese development as were the study missions they sent abroad or the foreign teachers they imported to make Japan self-sufficient. Japan insisted on becoming a "rich nation" with a "strong army" in order to end humiliation at the hand of rapacious foreigners.[47] For its part, Italy hoped to once again be the font of global knowledge and scientific progress.[48] Each was disgraced by its technological backwardness and determined to find its proper place in the world's pecking order. Nor did the sense of backwardness disappear with industrialization. Finance Minister Takahashi Korekiyo's farewell address to the students of one of Tokyo's elite universities captures this well: "Gentlemen, it is your duty to advance the status of Japan, bring her to a position of equality with the civilized powers, and then carry on to build a foundation from which we shall surpass them all."[49] But "late development" is more than an animating force. It is also a concept we can use to explain many of the common elements of early Italian and Japanese industrial transformation—particularly their parallel emphases on strategic industry, state ownership, and banking-industrial complexes with intimate ties to the state.[50]

After Italian credit collapsed in 1866, the finance ministry turned to the disposal of state property. In 1868 the state sold the canals, railways, and the tobacco monopoly to private firms. It also sold the land expropriated from the Church and the old states. These were precisely the contours of the Matsukata Reforms in the 1880s—the greatest uncoerced privatization in economic history—which abetted the rise of the Japanese *zaibatsu*. The largest of these integrated financial and manufacturing combines—for example, Mitsui and Mitsubishi—were fortified decisively by the purchase of state-owned firms in mining and manufacturing. And, dependent on political connections to the oligarchy, they seemed almost to follow an Italian script. The political fortunes of Italy's industrial leader, Ansaldo, were ensured when its Banca Nazionale became chief financier of Cavour's activities, and after unification, it "ventured into many areas where the interests of the state and of private investors intermingled."[51] Likewise, Mitsui cashed in on having been banker to the Restoration forces. Ansaldo also used its political connections to get contracts for navy vessels and military equipment in a manner wholly reminiscent of Mitsubishi. These Italian industry-government ties have been labeled "political capitalism," the identical term (*seisho*) used to characterize Japanese zaibatsu houses.[52]

The most striking difference in late development was Italy's extended embrace of free trade. Early Italian industrial development proceeded with foreign owners and entrepreneurs, and laissez-faire liberals had a longer and more consequential moment in Italy than in Japan.[53] Unlike the Japanese oligarchs, many Risorgimento elites had limited hopes for and indeed feared industrialization. Those who encouraged it did so in the hope that foreigners would provide the financing. Cavour was a confirmed believer in the virtues of liberal free trade—a set of beliefs that won Italy extended credits from London and Continental bankers.[54] He concluded free trade agreements with Britain and Belgium and presided over a doubling of Piedmontese foreign trade before the unification. As a result, laissez-faire liberalism had a privileged place in Italian debates. The simple fact of late development cannot explain both the sustained openness of Italy and the persistent insularity of Japan. Italian railway builders, for instance, used Rothschild and Pereire funds and foreign control was onerous. In contrast, Japan's first railroad was financed through a bond issue in London, but the Japanese refused to become dependent on foreign capital. There were no powerful advocates for free trade during the Meiji industrialization and, with the exception of two finance ministers in the 1920s (who were assassinated for embracing liberalism), none appeared until nearly a century later. Japan's economic program would always be more mercantilist than liberal.

Italy became dependent on some very powerful neighbors for technology and finance. Webster notes that "after 1866 the Italian government was dependent on the Paris money market for credit and was therefore in no position to do anything to alienate French lenders."[55] Its financial dependence was exacerbated by the way it handled its technological dependence. In 1894, Austrian and German financiers created the Banca Commerciale, which became the leading provider of industrial credit during Italy's industrialization. The bank dominated Italian electrification, steering contracts toward German machinery and technology (nearly 90% of all equipment came from Germany). German equipment was accompanied by German technicians and by German financiers who frequently served as directors of Italian banks and manufacturing firms.[56] The senior managers were all "acclimatized foreigners," and the bank was always caught in the squeeze between satisfying its foreign creditors, who demanded liquidity and diversification, and the needs of the Italian economy, which required patient and dedicated capital.[57]

The Japanese case was quite different. Although always eager to acquire foreign technology, the Meiji government made heroic efforts to avoid financial or technological dependence. Toward that end they created a set of quasi-official financial institutions, such as the Yokohama Specie Bank (1880), the Hypothec Bank (1896), and the Industrial Bank of Japan

(1900) to undertake industrial finance.[58] Although foreign borrowing was not rejected entirely, it was deliberately limited and channeled strategically into portfolio borrowing to avoid excessive vulnerability. As Lockwood notes, "Japan was drawing heavily on the West, but for knowledge and purchased equipment, not financial loans."[59] That the Japanese resisted foreign penetration so well, and Italy so poorly, would have enormous historical significance.

To be sure, the Japanese economy was never fully insulated. When its economy collapsed after 1918, Japan responded with a remarkably "Italian" debate over the appropriate extent of state control. This debate resulted ultimately in a corporatist solution. As in Italy, where the major private business interest group, Confindustria, supported legislation authorizing the fascist state to form compulsory cartels in 1932, the Japanese solution maintained private ownership.[60] Indeed, there are striking parallels. In both cases "the system was designed to bind labor and give capital an upper hand, if not a free one."[61] The interwar Japanese debate between "state control" (*kokka tōsei*) and "self-control" (*jishu tōsei*) was ultimately resolved in much the same way as the Italian debate over "collective self-regulation" (*autodisciplina delle categorie*). In Japan, cartels were established in each industrial sector and these cartels were formally supervised by state bureaucrats. The largest zaibatsu firms were responsible for their management, and were "encouraged" to participate in "public policy companies" by the state's guarantee of dividends to their shareholders.[62] As in Japan, Italian corporatism privileged the large producers and subordinated the smaller ones, even while the official ideology extolled the virtues of small and medium-sized industry.[63]

In the Italian context, state control has often seemed oxymoronic, while in the Japanese context, state control—or at least state participation in markets—has long been taken as a fundamental feature of governance. This is due in no small measure to one important institutional difference: the Italian Istituto per la Ricostruzione Industriale (IRI) created in 1933 to rescue banks and manufacturers on the verge of collapse because of excessive exposure to industrial finance. Unlike Japanese public policy companies, IRI was not the result of careful negotiation and planning. It was a quick response to an unprecedented crisis—the collapse of Italian capitalism. The difference matters: Japanese capitalists never had to recover from the excesses of state intervention *all'Italiana,* because they never surrendered control of their markets to Japanese bureaucrats.

Sarti observes that "every society that experienced the economic depression witnessed an increase in public regulation of business . . . but it was *only in Italy that public and private initiative became intimately and permanently linked by means of institutional innovations.*"[64] This is not exactly right.

The history of industrial policy in Japan consistently tells a story of bureaucrats thwarted by business interests from reestablishing state enterprise, instead diverting them to public-private joint ventures in which the state guarantees private returns.[65] As we shall see, the Italian state became a large stakeholder in the Italian economy and the Japanese state was virtually nowhere a commercial presence. Japan emerged from the Depression without the crushing burden of state ownership, while the Italian state found itself encumbered with one of the industrial world's most inefficient industrial organizations. In chapter 9 we will examine how this was subsequently exploited as a tool for political corruption. First, however, we turn to the third major resource built and deployed by leaders in their pursuit of parity with the developed countries—national identity.

ITALIANITÀ VS. NIHONJINRON

We are taught that the Japanese are a homogeneous people, constituents of the most natural nation-state in the world, while the Italians are a naturally divided, heterogeneous collection that find themselves living uneasily together—a pastiche of peoples and communities with too little in common. We are taught that Japan is the archetypal nation-state while, from the beginning, Italy has been a state without a nation. The first (and most common) phrase we encounter is the famous aphorism uttered by Massimo D'Azeglio after the unification of the peninsula: "Italy has been made; now we need to make the Italians" (L'italia è fatta, ora bisogna fare gli italiani).[66] The contrast could not be more stark: Japan, we are told, had subjects before it had citizens, but Italy had only inhabitants. As a result, it was "natural" for Japanese to feel solidarity, while the Italians groped—largely without success—to develop a common sense of themselves.

As with most generalizations, the truth misleads by burying the complexity. There has never been much that was natural about either the Italian or the Japanese national identity. Italianità and Nihonjinron were each constructed of available materials by political elites in the mid-nineteenth century, and each has been continuously contested and remade ever since. Like the Italians, the Japanese *also* had to be made; like the Japanese, the Italians *also* found deep reservoirs of common past and future purpose. Competition for control of national affect has shaped very different, domestic—and foreign—politics. In celebrating its homogeneous and unique national identity, Japan has (not inadvertently) built barriers to acceptance by the rest of the world. Italy, which celebrates its parentage of fifteen centuries of Latinate civilization, has been eager to dismantle remaining barriers to European integration and to consolidate national unity. A rather xenophobic Japan is united at home but remains uncomfortable in the world, while a more cosmopolitan Italy, less insecure than ever about its place in the world's councils, seems rather more divided at home.

Italy's identity and national mission began with an insistence on her former greatness. As Chabod points out, "Rome was a driving idea . . . an indispensable support for the affirmation of the national identity of the Italians as they faced other peoples long since constituted as nation-states."[67] A long line of intellectuals, from the eighteenth century forward, undertook the effort to identify the *essential* "Italian-ness" and the special place that Italy occupies in Western civilization.[68] A literary elite made the bricks, a revolutionary elite fired them, but it was an aristocratic elite that set them with mortar. It was a confused and highly contested process that, along the way, was captured by the nationalist Right. The literati taught that Italy had moral and intellectual primacy because it was the cradle of European civilization—of Roman law, of Christian thought, of the Renaissance. "Primacy" was Italy's great founding myth—the idea capable of animating and agitating, mobilizing, directing popular conscience, and sustaining action.[69] Italy could be the spiritual empire that transforms and unites Western civilization. In 1843 Vincenzo Gioberti exhorted Italians to sweep the church clean of corrupt and hypocritical clerics, free the peninsula of foreign princes, and restore the pope to full temporal authority. Even Mazzini, the republican with whom he had earlier split, imagined *italianità* embedded in *cristianità*. When the Kingdom of Italy was formed, "Italian" ceased being merely a referent to a cultural tradition or all that a diverse peninsula contained. For the first time, "Italian" had a political personality and legal substance; it referred to citizenship and to international diplomatic standing. But still there was no nation.

Despite centuries of ideas revolving around an Italian mission, and despite its civilizing, humanitarian, and occasionally imperial ambitions, the Italians have always harbored doubts about where they belong in the world. It did not help that the European princes, such as Metternich, thought of Italy as a mere "geographic expression," or that the Italy of European textbooks was the Italy of a collapsed empire long detached from living memory. Italians always wanted to be European, but feared that they would forever be merely Mediterranean. They obsessed over whether they could become "the last of the great powers." A flush of idealism for a "Third Italy" to again lead the way for human development was transformed by contact with European realpolitik: "Soon words like 'progress' and 'civilization' merged into words like 'power' and 'international prestige,' neither of which Italy had in long supply."[70]

Meanwhile, the Japanese were busy constructing their own national myths. Two hundred and fifty years of internal peace and millennia of racial fusion had provided a plausible basis for myths of homogeneity.[71] But Japanese state-builders were *also* confronted with powerful centrifugal forces. They *too* had to "make the Japanese." Until the 1880s, "the great majority of the common people did not recognize the emperor as the central Japanese national symbol, and the great masses of the Japanese people did not have a sense of national identity."[72] Indeed, the Meiji intellectual Fukuzawa Yukichi echoed Massimo D'Azeglio perfectly when he declared in 1875 that "Japan has never been a single country . . . In Japan there is a government but no nation."[73] The challenge before the Japanese oligarchs was not as great as that facing the Italians, but shogunal loyalties were local, not national, and the Restoration forces were led by southern enemies of the shogun. As Oguma explains, "consciousness of being Japanese [*nihonjin to iu ishiki*] is a post-Meiji phenomenon."[74] The great task before the Meiji oligarchs—one they embraced fervently—was to instill what Gluck has called "a national view of things in regional minds."[75]

As in the Italian case, much of this challenge was animated by Japan's pursuit of parity with the Western powers. Like the Italians, the Japanese were humiliated repeatedly. Fukuzawa warned in 1875 that "The civilization of Japan is less advanced than that of the West. When some countries are more advanced than others it is natural for the advanced to control the less advanced . . . Armed with this knowledge, our prime concern cannot help but be our country's independence."[76] By the late 1800s, therefore, "nation-mindedness" was bursting forth from every intellectual and institutional crevice.[77] Asia, once Japan's source of "civilization and enlightenment" (*bunmei kaika*), was now a backward continent that had to be "left behind" (*Datsu A*). Civilization and enlightenment could come only from the West. As a matter of national prestige, the rest of the world needed to understand that Japan was different from China and Korea, and its other neighbors: "If we keep bad company," Fukuzawa warned, "we cannot avoid a bad name. In my heart I favor breaking off with the bad company of east Asia."[78]

Japanese nation-builders had a number of tools at their disposal to build a "national essence" (*kokusui*)—the symbolic order that would unite the archipelago and enable Japan to achieve parity with the West. They did not have to abandon Japanese culture, and indeed they defended it vigorously as they transformed social relations. But there was no single canonical source of Meiji ideology. The oligarchs experimented in their

34

project to create "one dominant memory" from a "polychromatic" mix that included the sensibilities of the Heian court, the Spartan ethos of the samurai, the "boisterous arts" of the Edo townsmen, and the "austere puritanism" of Tokugawan Confucianism. Each found its use in what would be a trial and error process: agrarian values would be arrayed with warrior values; Shinto ideals with Confucian ethics; Chinese learning with German practice.[79]

No tool was more powerful than the imperial institution and the Meiji state wasted no time. It dispatched agents—state missionaries (*senkyōshi*) and national priests (*kyōdōshoku*)—in a well-orchestrated campaign to inform the masses about the emperor and how his divine rule would be their salvation.[80] In April 1868, within months of the "Restoration" of the emperor, the new governors reconstituted the Department of Shinto Affairs. The government issued uniform national guidelines for the practice of Japan's only native religion, endowing all Shinto ritual with imperial significance for the first time. Shinto was a particularly powerful tool because it predated Japan's pollution by foreign influences, and because it provided the insecure state with a mechanism for social control and a claim on legitimacy. National identity and national morality could be based upon native doctrines. By 1906 priests became subordinate to state bureaucrats who reduced the number of shrines and increased state subsidies to the remainder. Now shrines would be coordinated with the schools, the cooperative movements, the factories, and the local governments as part of a centrally directed effort to manufacture loyalty.[81] Basil Hall Chamberlain, the first to observe how much of "traditional" Japan was a Meiji reinvention, wrote in 1912 that Shinto, "which had fallen into discredit," had been "taken off the cupboard and dusted."[82] Italy, where the incompatibility of church and state could not be overcome, witnessed nothing quite like this. Also writing in 1912, Nitobe Inazō draws our attention to the way Japanese essentialism was constructed: "Shinto may be called a compact bundle of the primitive instincts of our race. All religion is conservative; but in the case of Shinto, this loyalty to the past has more truly than in the religious life of ancient Rome . . . developed from the status of an accidental attribute into that of an essential quality."[83]

The Meiji state deployed the figure of the emperor to impress upon the people that they were part of a great extended family that descended from a common imperial origin.[84] It established national holidays to honor the birthdays of Emperor Meiji and the first emperor, Jimmu. Even the most archaic-seeming imperial rituals were Meiji inventions—made up on the spot by leaders who grasped at whatever they could to justify their rule. The bond of emperor to subjects was embodied in the *kokutai,* a densely constructed, fundamentally cohesive national essence guided by the imperial presence. This model of a great extended family blended Confucian morality with nativist myth into a distinctive "civil religion."[85] For now this family would be biologically Japanese—a single, very old race that was both pure and homogeneous. References to its Korean or Chinese origins were conveniently buried.

In both Italy and Japan, war helped the nationalist Right win a protracted battle for control of national identity. In Italy, the ideas of the nationalist hero of the modernizing Left, Giuseppe Mazzini, were snuffed out by those of Gabriele D'Annunzio—and by Mussolini, who fired them in the crucible of his own power. Only after millions of peasants were outfitted in the same uniforms and stood shoulder to shoulder with comrades from distant regions and only after 600,000 of them died in the service of the nation during World War I, could they feel Italian at last. Using D'Annunzio's tools, Mussolini capitalized on the possibilities for national pride and identity. His nationalist Right defined who the Italians were. It was *they* who made the Italians from the crucible of self-vilification after the great European war. After two decades of squeezing contemporary pride from ancient Roman glory Mussolini authorized the folk identification that "we are a people of poets, of artists, of heroes, of saints, of scientists, of explorers, and of emigrants."[86]

In Japan, liberal ideals were snuffed out, stillborn, by fervid nationalism. The shift, already under way, was abetted by victories over China in 1895 and Russia in 1905. Images of inferiority were replaced by celebrations of the special advantages of the Japanese. Aggressive "patriotic societies" purveyed images of domestic racial purity and unique national gifts—but in the context of an expanding, multiethnic empire.[87] In 1907, Haga Yaichi enumerated the ten characteristics of the people. His Japanese were loyal and patriotic, reverent of ancestors, worldly and practical, lovers of nature, unburdened by trifles, simple and guileless, able to find beauty in small unadorned spaces, pure of body and spirit, courteous and mannered, and tolerant and forgiving.[88] A naïve, optimistic Japan was replaced by a self-esteeming exclusive one—in part as a consequence of putative Western awe at its achievements.[89] If Italy was a nation of poets and artists, Japan was a nation of warriors with a divine calling. Now every Japanese was a once and future samurai. Byas explains that by the 1920s, "the public had forgotten the insolence of the old samurai. Writers threw a halo of romance around them. The stage played dramas of chivalry from year-end to year-end. A name—Bushidō, the Way of the Warrior—was invented for a code of chivalry discovered after the thing itself had passed into limbo unregretted."[90] Samurai—now little more than gentlemen in kimonos—had an aesthetic sense, of course. Ethnographers wrote of "a sensitive appreciation of the beauties of poetry" as "the most important characteristic of Japaneseness."[91] But there were other distinguishing characteristics. The liberal Nitobe Inazō used Bushidō to explain Japan's "essential principles" and "moral atmosphere."[92] Its sources were Zen Buddhism, which taught calm trust in faith and submission to the inevitable, and Shinto and Confucianism, which taught loyalty, filial piety, and patriotism. In his construction, the Japanese had inherited and assimilated from their past a distinctive set of virtues: rectitude and a sense of justice, courage, benevolence, politeness, veracity and sincerity, honor, loyalty, and self-control. These virtues were further reified for children's consumption. As one wartime textbook explained:

> The Japanese land shines with a golden light, and for that reason the country is the most excellent in the world and its people are the most excellent people. The Japanese are golden people . . . neither white people nor brown people nor black people, but are a special race who live only in East Asia. However, the Golden People are not all the same . . . The Japanese are the true Golden People and the Chinese are the Quasi-Golden People. Why are the Japanese the true Golden People? It is because they are people who live directly under the shining golden light of the Imperial Way.[93]

Perhaps the Italians were too busy being poets, artists, heroes, saints, scientists, explorers, and emigrants to have the single "essence" of the Japanese. The Japanese taught themselves they had a consistent bundle of virtues—the Japanese Spirit (*Yamato damashi*). To soldiers, this spirit suggested sacrifice; to farmers, it reinforced family and community; to workers, it inculcated obedience. In World War II Japan, solidarity was "the hundred million hearts beating as one" (*ichioku isshin*); in wartime Italy, Mussolini lamented that "a people who for sixteen centuries have been an anvil cannot become a hammer within a few years."[94]

Eventually, the oligarchs succeeded in "making the Japanese." That emperors had rarely exercised any power in Japanese history, that these "divinities" had been deposed, manipulated, exiled, and even murdered, and that the imperial family actually originated in Korea, only underscores an obvious point. Facts matter less than what leaders can make of them.[95]

REGIONS AND NATION

Italian national identity grew out of the failures of the liberal state, whereas Japanese national identity grew out of the imagination of leaders determined to catch up with and surpass the West. A comparison of the persistent tug of regionalism in Italy with the unification of national identity in Japan is testimony to this difference. There were many utopias bundled into *italianità*—hopes that Italy, which had been the crossroads of so many great civilizations, would bridge East and West. After all, Italy owes its national identity in large measure to geographic position.[96] Greek, Byzantine, Islamic, and Christian influences washed up on Italian shores; perhaps Italy was where contradictions could be reconciled. But, of course, as Romano points out, "Italian cultural history cannot be more unified than the society of which it is an expression."[97] And that society has long been as deeply divided as any in Europe.

Italy bears the open wounds of its incomplete, recent, and unequal national unification. Italian feudalism had been administered by local notables who paid tribute to varying foreign monarchs, but never forged a national polity. In 1861, less than 3 percent of the population spoke Italian fluently. Mack Smith reports that "the new government of Italy countered these deep-rooted regional sentiments by an administrative centralization which perhaps exceeded in the urgency of the moment what was justified or wise . . . [It created] novel territorial units devoid of traditional sentiment."[98] Whereas regional disparities were allowed to widen in Italy, they were aggressively ameliorated in Japan. After the suppression of the Satsuma Rebellion, the Meiji state moved to Japanize its northern and southern frontiers (Hokkaido and Okinawa). In time—*no* time at all by Italian standards—regional identity slipped from the realm of the political to the realm of folklore. There would be no parallel in Japan to Italian irredentism.[99]

Internal colonialism in Hokkaido and Okinawa was merely a prelude for external colonialism in Taiwan and Korea.[100] The programs there were essentially the same: primitive natives were in need of the civilizing guidance Japan could provide.[101] Although Japan's colonial policy included forcing Koreans and Chinese to take Japanese names and speak Japanese, there was never any official pretense that ancient territory would be redeemed. Japan neither played on nor tried to create affect among those it conquered. The rhetoric of racial purity clearly had limits, especially as Japan became a full-fledged imperial power. It became counterproductive to project ideas of a unique, superior, and racially pure Japanese race. Nation-builders now turned toward construction of a Yamato people who themselves had come from mixed parentage. By the interwar period, they were underplaying descent from a divine ancestor and began constructing a Japanese race that originated in a mongrel people who millennia later had lost track of their ancestry.

So, while the Japanese contrived an identity of a great and special family, the "golden people" of Yamato damashi, the Italians were never entirely sure how best to proceed. They had asked themselves for centuries: "What unites us?" The priests? The Roman emperors? Dante? The popes?

The invaders? The catastrophes? The heroes? That Italian leaders failed to seize upon or to invent a legitimating symbol has had enormous costs.

Yet, we must not trust the easy conclusion that Italy was fragmented and Japan unified because of historical necessity. After all, regionalism was once the most politically relevant identity in Japan as well. Domination by regional allies of the shogun for nearly three centuries was replaced by domination by the Satsuma/Chōshū clique for two generations after the Restoration. The puzzle is why these divisions never became as politicized as in Italy, where domination by the Savoys of Piedmont was, in a sense, little different. To understand why regional identities have had no political relevance in Japan for more than one hundred years, yet remain significant political forces needling democracy in Italy, one must look closely at the ways in which leaders maintained and extended their power.

Japanese leaders never had to compete for citizens' loyalty. With the exception of Oda's suppression of Buddhist clerics in 1571, the only times in Japanese history when religion, loosely defined, mattered, the "church" was legitimated by the state, and not vice versa. It happened three times in Japanese history. The first time, in the early seventh century, Prince Regent Shōtoku Taishi used his influence to promote Buddhism, in part to strengthen his political position. A millennium later, the Tokugawa shogunate used Confucianism as state ideology to consolidate its power. Confucianism was ideally suited to a regime that sought to establish loyalty to its authority. It emphasized the proper relationship between father and son, husband and wife, ruler and ruled. This had a developmental dividend for, by valuing public service, education, and literacy, Confucianism also stimulated the emergence of a body of trained scholars within the samurai class who contributed to the making of a highly rational bureaucracy. Centuries later, these bureaucrats seized upon Shinto—the only indigenous Japanese religion—to mobilize a population threatened by rapacious foreign powers. Shinto was used to instill an intense and xenophobic nationalism through schools and workplaces in Japan until the end of the Pacific War.

The Roman Catholic Church acted as a check on the Italian state, while organized religion in Japan was used to consolidate state power. Thus, state Shinto and Christian Democracy were never analogous. Effective use of state Shinto was key to elite management of the Japanese polity during industrialization and wartime, but there was never an independent church—the population never had to choose. In Japan religion buttressed the legitimacy of the secular, while in Italy, conflict with the Church deprived the state of the "sacred" symbols of legitimacy. The state-church split in Italy created two separate affective spheres—the legitimate state on the one hand, and the spiritual church on the other. For Italians

39

this created the possibility of conflict between conscience and political authority, a possibility foreclosed for Japanese, for whom resistance and rebellion meant the violation of both spiritual *and* secular authority.[102]

As we have seen, Japanese leaders focused on making a nation in a way that the Italian leaders did not. They were determined not just to cut deals to remain in power but to consolidate power through the hegemonic construction of power, wealth, and identity. The most consequential differences between Italy and Japan may lie in the differential success of these projects, and it is to the nature of their leadership that this book next turns.

CHAPTER TWO

How to Build a State:

COUNT CAVOUR, ITŌ HIROBUMI, AND YAMAGATA ARITOMO

Rite makes might.
> David Titus, *Palace and Politics in Prewar Japan*

Modern Italy was born of liberal aspirations for the nation, modern Japan of nationalist aspirations for the state. In this chapter, we look closely at how these aspirations were realized through the designs of three political architects: Count Camillo Benso di Cavour, Itō Hirobumi, and Yamagata Aritomo. These men were by no means the only influential architects— nor, as we shall see, were their choices made in a vacuum. Cavour depended on allies at home and abroad, and the Japanese oligarchy was a collective effort. Yamagata and Itō gained power only after the shogunal forces had been defeated and much of the Restoration's architecture established. But to a remarkable extent, it is the choices of these three men that inform the institutions of modern Italy and Japan. Cavour engineered a liberal Italy free of foreign domination and, in the bargain, won unification as well. Itō produced a constitutional order that protected imperial prerogative and limited popular influence. Yamagata built authoritarianism into the modern Japanese state. We begin with the opportunities they perceived, and then explore their choices and legacies.

OPPORTUNITIES

There was no greater opportunity for dramatic historical change than the one presented by Commodore Matthew Perry when he sailed his "black ships" into Tokyo Bay in July 1853. The shogun—the fifteenth descendent of the founder, Tokugawa Ieyasu—was stuck. His legitimacy was based upon effective defense against foreigners, but he lacked the military capability to repel such advanced and determined barbarians. The shogunate's days—after two and a half centuries of isolation—were numbered. The end came shortly after the shogunate chose capitulation in the form of the "unequal treaties" of 1858, which granted foreign traders extraterritorial rights. In 1868 mid-level samurai—aristocrats all—from a small number of western domains led a coup d'etat in the name of the emperor.[1] The rebels wed loyalism to xenophobia in the slogan "Revere the Emperor, Expel the Barbarians!" (*sonnō jōi*), and fought a short, successful civil war.[2] Unlike in the Italian case, foreign powers stayed out.[3] More than two hundred and sixty feudal and semiautonomous domains (*han*) were replaced by a centralized state.

For years after the revolutionaries conquered the Edo Castle in 1868, however, they lacked the military and financial power to govern the nation. The nominally unified han could fly apart at any time. But the precocious rebels were not without a powerful—albeit latent—resource: the Chrysanthemum Throne. They seized upon the legitimacy of the emperor, even though no emperor had appeared on the political stage for almost three hundred years.[4] This was, as we shall see, a delicate game. The Meiji oligarchs did not wish the emperor or his courtiers to wield power, but merely to legitimate their rule.[5] The leaders of the rebellion seized their opportunity by creating one of the great fictions of modern history. They proclaimed "restoration" of the rule of Emperor Meiji—a boy emperor, whom few had ever seen, in an imperial line that had rarely ruled.

A similar set of resources and opportunities was available to Count Camillo Benso di Cavour. He, too, was confronted with regional divisions. And he, too, emerged at a moment when history was being punctuated by great military, moral, and intellectual forces. Cavour was an aristocrat who entered politics in 1848, at the age of thirty-seven, after having dabbled in agriculture and the family business, and—much like his Japanese counterparts—after foreign study. He had never traveled in Italy outside his native Piedmont and never spoke Italian very well, but he spent seven years (1834–1841) abroad: in Great Britain he studied law and parliamentary politics, in France philosophy, and in Switzerland business. He returned to Turin, capital of the Kingdom of Piedmont and Sardinia, and established himself in political debate by publishing, with Cesare Balbo, the journal *Il Risorgimento* in order to "raise the Italian question into the sunlight."[6] Within five years, the king would name this moderate, cautious, persuasive, and determined man head of the government.

To be sure, the parallels with Japan are imperfect. The strong anti-absolutist and antipapal undercurrents of Italian intellectual life were missing in Japan. The intellectual and moral elements that came to define the Risorgimento were evident even before the French Revolution, and it is clear that that great event—and the Napoleonic armies that followed hard upon it—stimulated a new co-identification of "Italians." Intellectuals, who otherwise spoke different languages and served different rulers, came to recognize a common patrimony born of Rome, and of Dante, Boccaccio, Petrarch, and Machiavelli.[7] The Risorgimento was deeply bound up with two great Continental ideas: liberty and nationality. The former was only wanly in play in post-Restoration Japan, whereas the latter was central to the oligarchs' program. Thus, the opportunities for national unification and for freedom from foreign domination were as attractive to Japanese as to Italian modernizers.

Indeed, these opportunities would be seized in both cases with the help of a monarchy. Like the Japanese oligarchs who built an absolutism they could control, Cavour was no republican. He served two kings. The first was Carl Albert who, tutored by Cavour in the dangers of revolution from below, granted Cavour his cherished constitution: Lo Statuto. The second was his son, Victor Emmanuel, who assumed the throne after the Savoyards' humiliating defeat at the hands of the Austrians in 1849. The count viewed the Savoy monarchy with barely veiled contempt for its parochialism and reaction. But, like his Japanese counterparts, Cavour perceived a way to use the monarchy both as a shield and as an anvil. On the one hand, he used it to provide political cover against threats of foreign intervention that would stimulate nationalist revolution. On the other, he used it as an anvil against which to bend domestic support for his ambitious transitions toward liberal government. Although Carl Albert gave the count his constitution in February 1848, Cavour knew that the monarchy's commitment to liberalism was extremely shallow. It remained for Cavour to "habituate" his kings to the practice of constitutional liberalism.[8] Both monarchs were always prepared to fall back on martial law, and Victor Emmanuel openly resented how much his father had conceded to Cavour.[9]

Like the Japanese oligarchs, Cavour used the monarchy, but he used it for different ends. Unlike Itō or Yamagata, he was comfortable with the idea of shifting majorities and was determined to establish a parliament. Perhaps he felt that he was dealing with a more independent monarchy— he understood that the king, in whose name he established a united Italy, was hopelessly self-serving.[10] Cavour would use the king to build a national identity and to defend his power from competitors, but he also had to seize other opportunities in his effort to establish a unified kingdom of Italy.

International politics provided another opportunity. Cavour was above all a skilled diplomat, one for whom the Japanese oligarchs had no counterpart. Demands for Italian independence in the 1830s and 1840s centered on eliminating direct Hapsburg rule in the north as well as Austrian influence elsewhere on the peninsula. Following the peninsula's short-lived freedom from Austrian influence in 1848–49, Austria returned to dominate in the early 1850s. Cavour's Kingdom of Piedmont and Sardinia was the only independent Italian state. In the north, Lombardy and Venice were part of the Austrian Empire, and important ones at that, for Lombardy alone provided one-third of the empire's revenue, despite having just one-sixth of its total population.[11] Other states—from the duchies of Tuscany, Parma, and Modena; the Papal States; and the Bourbon Kingdom of Two Sicilies—were dependent on Austria for protection and domestic tranquility.

Cavour wanted Austria ousted, but knew from the failed revolutions that he would need help. Making a calculation unthinkable to the more xenophobic and less diplomatically experienced Japanese, he sought the direct support of the French and the acquiescence of other great powers. It was no easy task, not least because he had little to offer. Italy was more attractive to the great powers as a weak congeries of client states than as a unified, competing power. French interests, in particular, lay in displacing Austria from northern Italy, not in assisting Piedmont to become powerful.

In July 1858, Cavour and Louis Napoleon conspired at Plombières to provoke a war with Austria. At this point, Cavour's goal was to expand Piedmont but not necessarily to unify the peninsula.[12] Without consulting his parliament (or his king), he agreed that upon Austria's defeat, Piedmont would cede Nice and Savoy to France. He expected that a victory would leave the political map fragmented, but with Piedmont the most powerful single state. Cavour and Louis Napoleon needed a casus belli, in the form of an Austrian attack, and they conspired to have the Savoy monarch publicly yearn for freedom. The French emperor personally penned the words for the king, who would declare himself unable to "remain insensitive to the cry of pain from so many parts of Italy."[13]

It worked, but not entirely as planned. Cavour's bloodied French allies nearly sued Austria for a separate peace, and the pope, who would have presided over a confederated parliament, remained hostile. But the war unleashed renewed revolutionary activity throughout the peninsula, and evoked strong diplomatic support in Britain. In the event, the French could not object to Cavour's new plan to annex central Italy, which was engineered through a remarkably ill-defined plebiscite. Garibaldi's subsequent military victories over the Bourbons in the South dealt the final blow for unification. Cavour arranged for two more plebiscites, but this time the question was put: "Italy under Victor Emmanuel?" After an overwhelming yes vote, Garibaldi rode into Naples with the king of a nearly united Italy—an outcome that Cavour had not intended, and one featuring two men whom Cavour frequently had tried to subvert. The opportunity Cavour had seized delivered far more than he ever imagined.

Cavour now could commandeer the initiative of the revolutionaries, led by the hapless intellectual Mazzini and the remarkable soldier Garibaldi. Many in the emerging middle classes warmly embraced their profoundly democratic and nationalist ideas—most centrally, that foreign absolutism must be abolished and that a united Italy could lead human civilization. The danger was that these ideals might mobilize the peasantry to overrun the country with mass democracy. Cavour judged the threat of revolution to be palpable. There were wealthy tenant farmers in Lombardy, sharecroppers in Tuscany, and peasant proprietors elsewhere in the North, but nearly half the Italian peasantry was comprised of landless laborers. The most wretched were in the South—where absentee owners controlled local power and were pillars of Bourbon rule—and by the 1850s they were embracing Garibaldi with unprecedented enthusiasm. Cavour co-opted them, abandoning the idea of an enlarged Piedmont and instead moving decisively toward an Italian kingdom. He had recognized a danger and harnessed the "moral energy" of others for his own ends.[14]

CHOICES

Cavour's Liberal Choice

By the mid-1850s, the democrats and republicans on Cavour's left were ever more impatient, the reactionaries on his right ever more defensive. Notwithstanding Mazzini's accusation that Cavour was a traitorous representative of the "old, greedy, timorous" House of Savoy[15] and notwithstanding his intensely antirevolutionary convictions, the count was committed to change. Revolution and romanticism represented for Cavour the height of irrationality; he sought a gradual progression toward a liberal political order.

The Continental liberalism of Cavour's day was bound up with modernity and progress. It competed vigorously with autocratic ideas deeply entrenched in the monarchies and with democratic ideas brewing in the wake of the French Revolution. Cavour's liberalism, like his diplomacy and politics, was pragmatic. In Cavour's very orthodox view, only liberty could release the energies vital to economic and social change. Liberty was necessary for progress. He was sure that autocracies were doomed, but believed that monarchy could be put to modernizing ends.[16] He was frightened not only by the enemy he knew—Austrian domination—but

Count Cavour is the spider conspiring with Louis Napoleon in this 1860 cartoon to entrap the Austrians, the Vatican, and the Masons while protecting the city-states that would combine to form modern Italy. Reproduced courtesy of the Museo Civico del Risorgimento, Bologna.

also by mass democracy.[17] He relentlessly attacked those to his left, like Garibaldi and Mazzini, who would have him move too fast, and those to his right, like the aristocracy or the pope, who would have him move too slowly or not at all.

By the time Italy was made, Cavour had already consolidated his other great contribution to the institutions of Italian politics—a liberal parliament. Cavour was just one of many Europeans of his day chafing at the excesses of absolutism and struggling to find a form of governance that would protect property and provide rudimentary political liberties—without surrendering to egalitarianism. Indeed, while his was the only liberal constitution to survive, it was, in fact, just one of many granted and retracted across the peninsula.[18]

The parliamentary form of contemporary Italy was embedded in a proto-constitution that Cavour, pointing to popular unrest in Genoa, convinced a reluctant King Carl Albert to accept in March 1848. Little more than a set of borrowed (and undebated) rules, Lo Statuto was adopted virtually unchanged as the first constitution of the Kingdom of Italy in 1861.

The Piedmont Constitution, like others of its day, guaranteed civil rights to a limited part of the male population. (The income- and literacy-qualified franchise extended to a mere 2 percent of the population.) It established an elected lower house, an appointed upper house, and an interior ministry to supervise local administration through appointed mayors and prefects. But with the Piedmont Constitution, Cavour *created* the traditions of parliamentary and cabinet rule.[19] Although Lo Statuto placed executive power in the hands of the king, Cavour effectively snatched that power for the prime minister and kept it away from his ministers. Apparently, executive power was too important to be left to a monarch or to be fully delegated to bureaucrats. What was nominally a government of the king would in fact be a government of the politician.

Confident in his abilities to manipulate these complicated matters, Cavour extolled parliament. In April 1858 he defended parliamentary government against an attack from the Right: "The people, the true people, have no other legal politics. I believe that the only representation of the people is found in this house . . . In fact, our system is one of the most liberal in Europe, and I believe it would be an enormous error to say that the opinions of the nation are not truly represented here."[20]

The maneuver that would establish parliamentary power and prefigure the dynamics of most subsequent Italian politics was Cavour's famous "Marriage" (Il Connubio) to the Center-Left in 1851—a sudden and successful coup that could just as aptly have been known as "The Divorce." Cavour sought to consolidate his power in order to resist republican pressures. To do so, he betrayed longtime political allies, including Massimo D'Azeglio with whom he had engineered the king's original acceptance of Lo Statuto. Cavour secretly arranged for Urbano Rattazzi to become president of the House, and Rattazzi, the leader of the Center-Left, agreed to renounce all republican aspirations and embrace Lo Statuto without reservation. Cavour's sudden announcement that he would now govern without the Right was met with howls of protest, but it also generated the stable majority he was seeking. Cavour now governed with deputies who owed their station to him directly. In one fell and very sudden swoop, Cavour had redefined the political Center. He had isolated both the extreme Right and Left, thereby diminishing the prospects for clerical or republican governance. Having consolidated his center, Cavour embarked on a series of state-building domestic reforms, including limitations on clerical privilege.[21] He used this stable base to undertake the diplomacy with France that would lead to unification and independence.[22] He also used it with confidence that he now could ignore parliament with impunity, and make his secret deals with foreign powers.

Cavour referred to his Il Connubio as his "political masterpiece."[23] And it was second only to the unification of Italy as a consequential act of state-craft. Cavour had defined the Center he insisted was a requisite element of liberal politics; it lay between anarchy on the Left and despotism on the Right. The "marriage" bought him protection from both revolutionary change and dissolute conservatism. Now he had a parliamentary center from which he could lean left or lean right without losing control.

The period between the incorporation of Lo Statuto in 1848 and the promulgation of the Italian Constitution in 1861 gave Cavour the chance to make a permanent imprint on Italian political life. Without changing the letter of the law, Cavour commandeered the king's prerogatives and elevated the parliament to a central place in Italian governance. Italy would have neither a government of the king nor a powerful bureaucratic state. In Japan different choices were made.

The Oligarchs' Anti-Liberal Choices

Cavour's Japanese counterparts had similar resources but different ideas about how to govern. The new government needed the symbolic power of the emperor, but it also needed to maintain independence from imperial interventions. In one of the greatest examples of conservative revolution the world has ever seen, the Meiji leaders chose to build a *double* governing system—one that would harness the legitimacy of the emperor while simultaneously monopolizing the power to wield the emperor's prerogatives.[24] To this extent, the oligarchs' choices resembled Cavour's. But the Japanese chose to face modernization by consolidating a bureaucratic state. Their parliament was on the margins, not at the center, of engineered change.

The new government issued its first proclamations of purpose in March 1868. One reassured the people that the emperor would console them and protect them from foreign aggressors. Another promised the government would seek peaceful relations with foreign countries. A third set out the regime's moral principles, prohibiting (among other things) the murder of foreigners.[25] One month later, a council of state system (Dajokan-sei) was established, placing the emperor atop a deliberative system that separated administration, legislation, and the courts. Suddenly the emperor was—at least nominally—the governor of Japan.[26] In February 1869, the government printed and distributed nationwide a declaration of Kyoto officials who were the first to try to explain the emperor's legitimacy: "Some would think that they have not ever received even a one *sen* coin from the Emperor and have not been helped by him. But everything of this country belongs to him because this is the country created by him. We all receive benefits from him from our birth until our death."[27] In the late 1860s the emperor and the imperial throne meant very little to the average Japanese. The Meiji government made the emperor visible for the first time, with short ceremonial visits (*junko*) to places like military academies and long pageants (*gyōkō*) that could last up to two months. The first of these pageants occurred soon after his "restoration," between September and December 1868, when the young Emperor Meiji left Kyoto for Tokyo with more than three thousand retainers.[28] Such shows of imperial splendor continued until the 1880s. Their number—and their size—increased at times of popular unrest and political opposition.[29]

The use of ritual was related to Japan's quest for acceptance in world councils. Over time, public pageantry became more cosmopolitan and less "oriental." Itō Hirobumi, now rising within the oligarchy, created ceremonial occasions at which the Meiji emperor would change his clothes as if to sustain the metaphorical "advance toward civilization." He would perform unseen rites inside the palace sanctuaries wearing priestly robes, while in public he rode in Western carriages wearing Western military garb. The mystery and divinity of the emperor was preserved, while his uniform and medals simultaneously suggested his direct involvement in public life and the extent to which Japan was ready to take the world stage.[30]

Yet, even as Ito cloaked the new government in the legitimacy of the imperial symbol, he was careful also to limit the power of the emperor and his courtiers. The system of policy deliberation sought to make sure that the government, not the emperor, would monopolize political initiative.[31]

As in Italy, the legitimation of the modern state was not uncontested.[32] Revolts and civil war continued. Popular support for the new government—and especially for the emperor—was still shallow. The revolutionaries may have taken the Edo Castle in April 1868 without shedding a drop of blood, but much instability remained ahead. A large number of the new rulers came from a small number of domains, and they were lower-level samurai. To counter suspicion and distrust across the rest of the archipelago, the new oligarchs urgently needed to establish their legitimacy.[33]

Indeed, there was limited public explanation for the change of government, and even less public support. Revolts, assassinations, and farmers' resistance (*nōmin ikki*) spread across the country.[34] Several domains fielded troops to confront the new government, while guerilla activity erupted in Edo itself.[35] Assassinations, failed coups d'état, and assaults continued through 1871, when the Meiji government finally established its authority in Tokyo and pacified the countryside. Even then its authority was still not completely consolidated.

The Restoration may have been "little more than a shift of power within the old ruling class," but the subsequent decades witnessed fundamental institutional changes.[36] Some of these changes were reactionary. In 1871, for example, Buddhist ceremonies were discontinued in the imperial court and Shinto was adopted as the state religion. More than eighteen thousand Buddhist temples were closed in the early Meiji period, and images were smashed.[37] Other changes were progressive. In August 1871 outcast classes were abolished.[38] The oligarchs then proceeded to sweep away the privileges of the old warrior aristocracy. In 1871, they had the emperor proclaim the end of daimyo rule. They took away the exclusive right of the samurai to bear arms and to hold office in 1873, when they introduced universal conscription. That same year, they established a home ministry that centralized many of the functions of the feudal domains: tax assessment, mail, health services, police, public works. Now the Meiji government would appoint all governors. In 1876, the government eliminated all hereditary titles and required that all hereditary stipends be surrendered for government bonds. In 1884 a meritocratic system was introduced that required all civil servants to pass examinations in law, economics, and political science.

Itō Hirobumi, the brilliant young oligarch who, by his own institutional design, would become first among equals, referred to the elimination of heredity as a determinant of government service as "one of the splendid results of the Restoration." He averred that the shogunate had distorted the relationship between the imperial ancestors and their subjects.[39] Yet, after the great leveling was completed, Itō had the emperor proclaim his desire to honor "high-born descendents of our illustrious ancestors" as well as those who had distinguished themselves in the Restoration struggle.[40] By creating a peerage, he was protecting the state from counterrevolution. Itō knew that a nobility would be "contrary to the spirit of the times," but he was every bit as cautious as Cavour. In 1881 he was very blunt about the benefits of peerage: "[It] is an absolutely indispensable instrument for fortifying the position of the Imperial House . . . [and to counter] the recent tendency of both the government and the people to slip into the spirit of republicanism."[41]

Historians assign responsibility for the manipulation of tradition and for the engineered modernization of Japan to a shifting group of oligarchs. Itō Hirobumi was always near the top of the list. But none was more directly responsible for consolidating power than Yamagata Aritomo, also from Chōshū. Yamagata returned in 1870 from study of the military organizations of continental Europe. He convinced feudal commanders to place their troops under imperial control and ended the special military privileges of the samurai. He was convinced that only a national military could secure domestic control against rebellious fiefs and defend Japan against avaricious foreign powers. Conscription—all twenty-year-old males would serve for seven years (three on active duty, four in the reserves)—engendered the most violent rural protests of the period. After four years of popular resistance and open defiance, Yamagata finally prevailed through repression and imperial sanction.

The loss of samurai status in 1876 was accompanied by the reduction and then commutation of hereditary stipends. The reduced charge was a enormous relief to the government budget, but predictably, the samurai rebelled.[42] The first deep split in the oligarchy reinforced their grievance. By the mid-1870s, Saigo Takamori and his allies were seeking external expansion in Korea, while Kido Kōin was focusing on the consolidation of domestic power. Saigo had maneuvered to get imperial permission to punish Korea for refusing to open to commerce with Japan. Believing that Japan was still too weak for an external war that would invite Russian or Chinese intervention, others in the oligarchy then convinced the emperor to rescind permission to attack Korea. Saigo left the government in 1873 with six others, five of whom went on to lead antigovernment rebellions. There were a half-dozen samurai rebellions between 1874 and 1877. The largest, led by Saigo in 1877, was fed by the several other samurai discontents. After a six month campaign, imperial forces suppressed the Satsuma Rebellion and eliminated the last prospect of armed counterrevolution.

But the oligarchs faced other threats, especially from liberals. Here their choice and Cavour's are most sharply contrasted. It was the liberals who unified Italy, but in Japan the liberals were one of several dissident groups that split—or were purged—from the oligarchy that unified the country. Never liberal, even in Cavour's limited sense, the Meiji oligarchs believed that public opinion encouraged political dissent, which was seditious and weakened the state.[43] Itō captured this view by referring to "the onslaught of extremely democratic ideas" that had to be resisted.[44] Itō would incorporate the people to achieve national unity, but not as a matter of any innate right to self-government. He chose to avoid popular control by appealing to "a higher transcendent moral order . . . that would deny any notion of private interest"—the emperor.[45] Itō ensured that the liberal road to Tokyo would remain unpaved. Cavour chose liberalism dressed in the regalia of the Savoy monarchy. Itō chose authoritarianism dressed in the morning coat of parliamentary procedure.

One group of liberals emerged quite early in the post-Restoration political firmament. After all, one motive for the Restoration had been to emulate the West as a way to strengthen Japan. Positivism, materialism, and utilitarianism were each introduced in short order. J. S. Mill's *On Liberty* was translated in 1871. Many of these "Enlightenment writers" (*meirokusha*), such as Fukuzawa Yukichi, had been abroad even before the

Restoration, and judged Japan's backwardness harshly: "In Japan's present condition there is nothing in which we may take pride vis-à-vis the West. All that Japan has to be proud of is its scenery."[46] There was politics in this. They attacked the oligarchs who were reconstituting a shogunate-like regime. They demanded greater popular control. In 1875, nearly a decade after the Restoration, Fukuzawa observed that "one government has been replaced by another, but the political trend of Japan as a whole has never changed. Power has always remained one-sided, and a great chasm divides the rulers and the ruled."[47]

The first liberal challenge came from within the oligarchy. No sooner had Saigo lost approval for a punitive expedition to Korea and left government than two of his allies, Itagaki Taisuke and Gotō Shōjirō, demanded an elected assembly. Itagaki returned to his native Kochi, where he gave lectures on the thought of Locke, Bentham, and Mill and established a self-help society for former samurai. By January 1874 both men were issuing public calls for a popularly elected national assembly and had formed a Public Party of Patriots (Aikokokōtō). Although historians question their liberal credentials, the effort attracted "enlightenment" intellectuals, as well as city dwellers, wealthy farmers, and radicals. Importantly—for it would be the liberals' undoing—they argued that there was full harmony between imperial and popular will, a harmony that was being distorted by despots and oligarchs in power.[48] When they were promised "gradual progress" toward representative government, Itagaki and Gotō reentered government. Within months, convinced that the oligarchs had no intention of making good on vague promises, Itagaki left again. By now the movement had a broader base and was known as the Popular Rights Movement (Jiyū Minken Undō).

By the late 1870s, the democratic movement had spread, assisted by government corruption scandals and resentment of the centralizing control of oligarchs.[49] As the voices of the Popular Rights Movement became louder, Yamagata wrote to Itō in July 1879 that "Every day we wait the evil poison will spread more and more over the provinces, penetrate the minds of the young, and inevitably produce unfathomable evils."[50]

Yamagata was perceptive, and Itō took heed. The initiative for popular participation in government diffused to hundreds of local political societies.[51] The tipping point came in the mid-1870s when—with the support of the press—the liberals began to call for new institutions of government, including a Western constitution. In 1875, and again in 1880, press regulation and libel laws were strengthened. Police were granted the authority to regulate the activities of political groups. All associations were required to submit membership lists and charters for official review. Permits had to be obtained before all public meetings, and uniformed police were empowered to monitor meetings and to intervene if, in their judgment, the discussion became seditious. Soldiers, teachers, police, and students were all banned from public assemblies. The repression notwithstanding, by the end of 1880 sixty petitions with more than a quarter million signatures supported representative government. Itagaki and Gotō had formed the Liberal Party and Ōkuma Shigenobu—still an oligarch—established the Progressive Party.

Itō's government countered brilliantly. In 1881, he engineered Ōkuma's expulsion from the oligarchy. Yet, as he was silencing the lone remaining progressive voice, he announced that before the end of the decade the emperor would "graciously grant" a constitution that would include a national assembly.[52] Since the advocates of representative government had argued for the harmony of democracy and imperial will, the clear and authoritative voice of the emperor—now controlled by committed enemies of liberalism—could easily stifle their activities. Vlastos puts it succinctly: "The liberals 'won' a constitution while losing the war against oligarchic rule."[53] Soon after this promise to establish a parliament, Itō began systematically to suppress the liberal parties. He dispatched a governor to Fukushima Prefecture, the stronghold of the Liberal Party, to eradicate it. His delegate arrested nearly three thousand, including the party chairman, sending fifty to Tokyo on charges of planning rebellion.[54] In 1883, the police arrested about twenty Liberal Party members in the northeast region on trumped-up charges.[55] Whatever prospects may have existed for liberal democracy were now seriously damaged.

Their demands co-opted and their position undercut, the Popular Rights Movement splintered. Movement leaders—many of whom were landlords and businessmen—realized that liberalism no longer suited their commercial interests and they traded "enlightenment" for "conservative realism." They were becoming the objects of protest, and now they welcomed a strong state to protect them. In short, liberalism was abandoned by a leadership that might never, in any event, have been fully committed to its ideals. What Pyle has called "Meiji Conservatism"—a politics that was bureaucratic and authoritarian, meritocratic and modern—was finally consolidated. After two decades of institutional reform, enlightenment ideas were abandoned by a conservative regime *and* by liberals who found common cause in a strong state and a stable social order.

Itō's Constitutional Choice

If Yamagata made the critical choices that protected the oligarchy from counterrevolution, Itō made the critical choices protecting it from the liberals. He did so by enshrining a strong state and stability in a Western-inspired constitution of his own design.[56] There was never public debate over the constitution, but there was considerable debate among the oligarchs—a debate that Itō never failed to control even if at times he was merely primus inter pares. The first call for a constitution came from Kido Kōin in 1873, but the idea—which included guarantees of freedoms of speech and assembly (but would have eliminated all religions except Buddhism)—was rejected by the other oligarchs as premature. Some advocated French democracy, others English parliamentarianism. Ōkubo Toshimichi offered up a more autocratic draft in 1878, including a division of powers between the imperial household and the legislature and Diet control of the imperial purse. Itō was quick to reject it as too foreign. A revised version was submitted to the emperor in December 1880, but disappeared altogether, discarded through Itō's intervention.[57]

The debates over the proper constitution for Japan clearly were surrogates for bare-knuckled contests about political power. Itō was threatened both by conservatives, who were seeking personal rule by the emperor, and by democrats, who were demanding immediate, direct election of a national assembly. At this point, as Silberman notes, "the transcendent position of the emperor was by no means assured."[58] Like Cavour, Itō centered brilliantly. He found a middle way between representative government and monarchical absolutism. For him, "the object was to disarm critics, not to cede real power."[59] To counter the conservatives, he abolished the Office of Palace Advisors in 1879, but reconfigured access to the emperor so that he would have greater control of the imperial will. To counter the democrats, he had Ōkuma purged in 1881. In March 1881 the government created an independent, unsupervised Bureau for the Investigation of Constitutional Systems "to shield the work of drafting the constitution from any contact with public opinion . . . [and to] create the illusion that the drafting was being done under the personal supervision of the Emperor."[60] Itō had himself made chairman of this bureau on the very same day that he was appointed minister of the Imperial Household Department, thus controlling access both to the emperor and to the architecture of the forthcoming constitution. He had constructed an institutional shield to protect both flanks.

In March 1882, his political control of the constitutional process now assured, Itō set off for Europe for more than a year of study and preparation. He was, of course, well aware of the wide range of possibilities that the term "Western constitution" concealed. Itō wrote to Iwakura from Germany that "the tendency of our country today is to erroneously believe in the works of the British, French, and American liberals," and he proudly declared that he had "found principles and means of combating this trend."[61] He found a congenial model in Germany, where bureaucratic power was not beholden to an elected legislature, and he returned to Japan in 1883 with German advisors in tow. Itō was determined to make the emperor even stronger than his German advisors proposed—and went beyond historical precedent to endow the emperor with formal authority.[62] Social harmony could be preserved if Itō and his colleagues could control imperial prerogative.

Itō found the legitimating institution he had been seeking in the imperial household. He rejected Shinto as too dangerously reactionary and Buddhism as too dissolute. In an oft-quoted explanation that reveals the political importance of this formulation—as well as his remarkable prescience—Itō spoke of the role that imperial myth would play in holding the new system together: "What is the cornerstone of our country? This is the problem we have to solve. If there is no cornerstone, politics will fall into the hands of the uncontrollable masses; and then the government will become powerless . . . In our country the one institution which can become the cornerstone of our constitution is the Imperial house."[63] Itō wished that "the affairs of the court should remain a mystery to ensure greater transcendence for the imperial institution."[64] And to ensure his authorship of this mystery, Itō served as imperial household minister from 1884 to 1887, while he penned the text of the new constitution in secret. It was politically salutary for Itō to reason that "if the Constitution is known to the people as having been drafted by a given individual, not only will this give rise to much public comment and criticism, but also the constitution will lose the people's respect."[65] Ever cognizant of the attraction of material incentive, Itō established fiscal autonomy for the imperial household. All imperial property was made available for the ministry's exclusive use. The ministry directed imperial investments in a range of firms and real estate—investments that returned handsome dividends.[66]

The political use of the emperor was changing. At the time of the Restoration he was used to promote national unity, and now he was used to legitimate a "constitutional future" against a premature democratic politics.[67] State-building—or at least the maintenance of oligarchic power—required better control of the emperor and of his courtiers, who were beginning to interfere more deeply in the affairs of state.[68] Itō initiated a government restructuring to separate civil from imperial activities. He abolished offices that Ōkubo Toshimichi had established in 1877, and he introduced the cabinet system in 1885. The emperor and his associates tried to block these administrative changes, and only the defection of a group of imperial advisors enabled the change. Itō now served as both imperial minister and, after 1885, prime minister.

Now only the cabinet was authorized to assist the emperor, and the prime minister controlled other ministers. The next year, Itō succeeded in further clarifying the relationship between the imperial household and the cabinet—largely on his terms. The emperor would not participate in ·cabinet meetings unless petitioned to do so; ministers and vice-ministers could advise the emperor; when necessary, the emperor would travel outside Tokyo to be visible to the public; he would accept dinner invitations if petitioned to do so by a minister; he would meet ministers who petitioned to see him.

Itō had earlier been concerned that the imperial household would become too powerful. Now that he controlled it, the household could not be powerful enough. Predictably, and correctly, his enemies charged him with "using the emperor." At first his shields worked as designed: he was defended both by his cabinet and by the imperial court. In the event, however, his argument that only he could ensure successful constitutional government convinced few of his colleagues, and he resigned as minister of the imperial household in September 1887.[69] Never again did a prime minister—or even a former prime minister—also hold the post of imperial household minister.

But for Itō this was a remarkably small setback—if indeed it was a setback at all. By resigning, Itō actually managed to *enhance* his own power. He had already succeeded in replacing the hodgepodge of councilors and ministers with a cabinet he ran, with responsibility for appointment of ministers. Years ahead of the constitution that would enshrine many of these arrangements, Itō was already effectively responsible only to the emperor. Ever resourceful, he devised yet another institutional means of access to the imperial prerogative. In April 1888, at exactly the time that his draft constitution was completed, the oligarchs agreed to establish the Privy Council (Sūmitsuin)—a committee to advise the emperor on matters of policy. All legislation prepared by the government, and all treaties, now had to pass through the Privy Council before presentation to Diet. Itō was appointed first president of the Privy Council, and three of his closest associates were appointed secretaries.

The first task of the Privy Council was to "deliberate" on the constitution that Itō had drafted and for which he had already secured imperial approval. Ramseyer and Rosenbluth correctly argue that the Privy Council was the oligarchs' last "remaining grip" on power, and that "it rested almost entirely on the personal stature of the oligarchs who were its first members."[70] The oligarchs' power (particularly Itō's) was still considerable, despite his falsely modest claim that "The Emperor . . . has established the Privy Council so that in His wisdom He may have at command its assistance, and that the information He obtains may be thorough and impartial . . . The Privy Council is the palladium of the Constitution and of the law."[71]

In fact, Itō had very clear ideas about how to maintain and use power through the Privy Council. He made sure that none of its deliberations, and none of the "advice" it proffered to the emperor, would be made public. He kept the Privy Council outside the formal structure of government. It was to become a "watchdog" (*bannin*) to protect oligarchic power from popular encroachment, and de facto the most powerful organ of the Japanese state until the end of the Pacific War. The "gatekeepers of the Imperial Will" were, like Itō, all politically astute leaders who understood the need to keep the emperor's preferences hidden from public view. No attacks on the monarch could be allowed to undermine the legitimacy of the system, and they would not be tolerated.[72]

A decade after a constitution was first promised—and only after Itō, Yamagata, and their close allies had solidified their grip on the imperial prerogative—the system was enshrined in the Meiji Constitution. For all his public insistence on the transcendental superiority of the emperor, Itō did not hesitate to argue for limits on monarchical power. During deliberations about his draft constitution, Itō explained that "constitutional politics means the *restriction* of the monarchical right."[73] Just as he refused to cede too much to the emperor, Itō also refused to allow the constitution to be ratified by an open constitutional convention. Only in the closed environment of the Privy Council, which Itō effectively controlled, were the constitution and all foundational laws debated, in forty-one conferences between May 1888 and January 1889.[74]

Finally, in February 1889—on the invented anniversary of the assumption by Emperor Jimmu to the imperial throne two and a half millennia earlier—a formal ratification ceremony took place in Tokyo. The emperor "bestowed" the Constitution on his subjects. In a room filled with foreign dignitaries upon whom the oligarchs wished to impress Japan's modernity and its worthiness "of the autonomy denied it by the unequal treaties," the document was passed by Itō to the emperor, who then handed it to the prime minister—all the while only Itō and his closest associates knew the contents.[75]

The contents of Japan's modern constitution were entirely Itō's, despite his hollow insistence that the emperor was its "sole author."[76] Its highest purpose was the protection of imperial sovereignty. The parliament (Diet) established by the Constitution was a far cry from the British model that so attracted Count Cavour. It was at best a "safety valve for political and social unrest."[77] Itō intended the power of representatives to be severely circumscribed, and he achieved this by establishing in the first chapter the "sacred and inviolable position of the Emperor."[78] It was a loophole they would ultimately learn to exploit, but formally Diet representatives could do little more than deny the government new taxing and spending powers. The Diet was a mere appendage of imperial power. Itō declared forthrightly that "without the sanction of the Emperor, no project can become law, even if it has received the consent of Diet."[79]

Clearly, the Constitution was not "popular," and "liberty" was not a constitutional principle. It was instead an elaborate and carefully constructed legal justification for an authoritarian government. The oligarchs had a bare minimum of responsibility to the people. The preamble was straightforward:

> Having, by virtue of the glories of our ancestors, ascended the Throne of a lineal succession unbroken for ages eternal; desiring to promote the welfare of, and give development to the moral and intellectual faculties of Our beloved subjects, the very same that have been favored with the benevolent care and affectionate vigilance of Our ancestors; and hoping to maintain the prosperity of the State, in concert with Our people and with their support, We hereby promulgate . . . a fundamental law of State, to exhibit the principles by which We are to be guided in Our conduct, and to point out to what Our descendents and Our subjects and their descendents are forever to conform.[80]

Rights were bestowed on "subjects" with one hand, and taken away with the other. While the Constitution guaranteed equal access to public service and the right to property, it clearly circumscribed other rights. Privacy was guaranteed "except for cases provided for in law"; freedom of petition was granted "by observing proper forms of respect"; freedoms of speech, press, movement and trial were available "within the limits of the law."[81]

In the event, the emperor was to be "a prop," a matter of "pragmatic necessity."[82] Those who controlled access to the emperor controlled Japanese governance. But, it is a measure of Itō's political genius that even as he was establishing himself as both head of government and conduit between government and emperor, he was simultaneously stripping the emperor of personal responsibility in order to maintain the important fiction that the emperor was inviolable. That is, the emperor served the oligarchs best by serving as a medium, through rites, between his subjects and his ancestors. Itō legitimated his power through an unassailable mechanism that only he and a select few could control.[83] At the same time, he was demonstrating to the rest of the world that Japan had come of age and was worthy of the respect due a great power. While Japanese self-confidence and self-respect had never been higher, possibilities for popular control of government were all but eliminated.

Yamagata's Military Choice

Itō's constitution was the first of two choices for Japanese authoritarianism. The second was Yamagata's creation of an independent military. Like Itō, Yamagata was suspicious of party politics, and worked diligently to thwart liberal democrats. Itō's instrument was a constitution free from both imperial and political control, Yamagata's was a *military* system with the same attributes.[84] If Itō succeeded by playing his cards close to his vest, Yamagata succeeded by building a highly articulated network within every important political and bureaucratic organization—including the Imperial Household Agency. If the consequences of the Constitution were fatal for democracy at home, the consequences of the independent military were fatal for people throughout Asia.

The reconstruction of the military on the Prussian model was Yamagata's first big step.[85] The oligarchs had collectively decided military issues, and the ministers of the Imperial Army and Navy depended on the oligarchs.[86] Borrowing a page from Itō's playbook, Yamagata created a new institution under his own control. In 1878, he established the General Staff Office (*sanbō honbu*) directly under the emperor and, resigning as army minister, he made himself its first commander in chief. He thereby became one of only four "direct advisors" to the emperor and the only one who, with the emperor's "permission," could give orders to the armed forces.[87] The army minister was responsible to the prime minister on matters of administration, but on matters of military command, only to the commander of the general staff, and he only to the emperor. Yamagata's control of the military lasted nearly until his death in 1922.[88]

There was great irony in Yamagata's efforts to separate the military from politics. After he had had fifty soldiers executed for an abortive mutiny at Takebashi in August 1878, he wrote an admonition to the military warning against political activity of any kind. He reinforced this stand after the political crisis of 1881. Yamagata drafted and had the emperor promulgate the "Rescript to Soldiers and Sailors" in January 1882, to impress upon them the importance of loyalty and the dangers of politics.[89] Yet, when Itō went off to Europe, Yamagata took up some of Itō's political duties, monitoring the development of political parties and increasing state repression along the way. Just before Itō returned, Yamagata had become home minister, and now had full control of the civilian bureaucracy, which he reorganized and filled with his protégés. By December 1889, when Yamagata began service as first prime minister under the new Constitution, he had thoroughly transformed Japan's civil and military bureaucracies. Yamagata's innovations made subsequent military and bureaucratic intervention in politics not only possible but virtually certain of success.

Yamagata, already established as Japan's chief military strategist, became president of the Privy Council in 1893. Now he turned his attention to Japanese expansion and to thwarting Russian expansion. His war planning and his control of the military and the emperor paid off in a massively popular victory in China two years later, in the consequent consolidation of popular Japanese nationalism, and in the West's recognition of Japan's industrial and military prowess after the Russo-Japanese War a decade later.

After Japan's victory over China, and before its stunning defeat of Russia, the Yamagata government took another giant step toward protecting the oligarchy. Concerned that some army ministers were cooperating with political parties that opposed his plans for military expansion, Yamagata asked for and received an imperial order in 1900 that all army and navy ministers be active duty general officers. In a cabinet system in which the prime minister was merely primus inter pares, this order effectively made the military (and Yamagata) an independent—indeed paramount—force in government. It gave the military (Yamagata) the power to dissolve the cabinet, for if the military refused to recommend a new minister of the army or the navy, a cabinet could not be formed.[90]

Still, Yamagata soon learned that he had not gone quite far enough. His erstwhile ally, Itō Hirobumi, opposed his foreign policy. Itō was concerned that Japan not provoke the intervention of the great powers. Declaring that "Manchuria is in no respect Japanese territory" and that "the responsibility for administering Manchuria rests with the Chinese government," Itō blocked the ambitions of Army Chief of Staff Kodama Gentarō to extend Japanese control in 1905–6.[91] Yamagata moved quickly. In 1907 he had the emperor proclaim a new order of command (*gunrei ni kansuru ken*), eliminating the prime minister and peers' roles in the deliberation of military policy. Even the emperor could act in military affairs only with the advice of the ministers of the army and navy.[92] Those ministers could now issue imperial orders without the consent of the prime minister.

Itō had made a terrible mistake by transferring the prerogatives of the prime minister to the emperor after 1885. Thinking that he had wrapped

Yamagata Aritomo protects the military's perquisites in 1906 as Itō Hirobumi tries to gain control. Prime Minister Saionji, a civilian, sits helplessly to the side. Reproduced courtesy of Shimizu Isao.

up control of the imperial voice, he had discounted the possibility that the emperor would have his own opinions. Nor had he bargained for the possibility that other oligarchs could gain access to the emperor. Yamagata had skillfully used the institutions Itō had created to enhance his own control. In 1907, reversing course, Itō attempted to keep the military from becoming independent by specifying the powers for each minister of state and by elevating the status of the prime minister. He failed. The emperor took Yamagata's counsel instead.

The military did not hesitate to use its power to destroy cabinets—even very popular ones. In 1898, when Ōkuma and Itagaki formed a party cabinet after winning an overwhelming electoral victory (244 of 300 seats), the two military ministers paralyzed the government. In 1908 and again in 1912, they brought down cabinets when they felt the political leadership was insufficiently attentive to the military budget.[93] They blocked the formation of another cabinet in 1914. After Yamagata's death, they intervened regularly to bring down cabinets—as in 1927, when they judged Prime Minister Wakatsuki Reijirō too soft on China. At least as consequential as these public displays were the unseen deterrent effects of an independent military in shaping the course of early twentieth-century Japanese governance.[94] In 1914 the system was overturned temporarily when Prime Minister (and Admiral) Yamamoto Gonnohyōei introduced legislation over army protests that permitted reserve and retired officers not subject to military control to serve as ministers of army and navy.[95] None did, however, and in May 1936 these ministerial positions were again restricted to active duty officers. The army rarely hesitated, even in the face of opposition from the emperor, to bring down cabinets it opposed, including that of Admiral Yonai Mitsumasa in July 1940. We cannot know how much policy went unintroduced by elected politicians for fear of arousing the opposition of the powerful armed services.

Yamagata served in the Privy Council for seventeen years and continuously as president from 1909 (when Itō was assassinated in Korea) until 1922, when he died.[96] He was even more successful than Itō in insinuating his bureaucratic allies into the Privy Council. He placed his protégés strategically within each of the institutions he sought to control: the civilian bureaucracy, the military, the House of Peers, the colonial administrations, the Privy Council.[97] He was never reluctant to use and reward his supporters or, conversely, to punish his opponents by intervening in elections, by excluding them from important posts, or by dissolving political groups altogether.[98] Among Yamagata's protégés in the Ministry of Army, three would become prime minister. Another, Kodama Genichirō, became governor-general of Taiwan.[99] He tried to control the House of Peers to assure support for military expansion and favorable budgets.[100] But he constructed his most influential network around the emperor, both in the Privy Council and in the imperial household.[101] By the time he was done, Yamagata had outlived his competitors, and had completed institutional arrangements to preclude the rise of others. He was "*genrō* of the *genrō*," oligarch of the oligarchs.[102]

Liberalism, already severely constrained by the new Constitution, was forced further away, and even when parliamentary politics returned in the early twentieth century, it would not be healthy. Until the divinity of the emperor was finally rejected—and it took the disaster of the Pacific War for this to come about—Japan had no legal basis for freedom of belief or expression. The *kokutai*, the national body politic under the "sacred and inviolable" throne, was the locus of moral values.[103] The oligarchs controlled the kokutai as long as they survived, but they failed to establish rules for succession. Since none but the radical Left was ever willing to reject the kokutai, succession involved an extended political battle within the Right from which Japanese politics never really recovered. We turn, now, to examine the institutional legacies of these choices against liberalism in Japan and for liberalism in Italy.

LEGACIES

A unified Italy was the greatest legacy of Cavour's relentless political leadership. A peninsula that had been the "footfall" of foreign armies for centuries would soon be poised to become "the last of the great powers." Cavour must be credited for transcending, indeed for bending, the interests of the great powers to achieve in 1861 a unification that no one thought possible a year earlier. He was not above fomenting war, betraying his allies, manipulating his king, and ignoring his parliament. As Seton-Watson suggests: "Cavour's diplomatic achievement will always rank beside Bismarck's as a masterpiece of the nineteenth century."[104] It is no small irony that Louis Napoleon's dynasty ended soon after the war, whereas Victor Emmanuel's survived for nearly a century.

But the Risorgimento was hardly "Cavour's soliloquy."[105] *La bell'italia* owes its unified existence to a great many protagonists. Cavour conspired with Louis Bonaparte, King Victor Emmanuel, Mazzini, and Garibaldi, but each played an individual part in the pulling and tugging that created a unified state. And it must be said that Cavour also enjoyed a large share of *fortuna*. He was lucky that the Bourbon king was weak, that the pope's grip on temporal authority was slack, that the revolutionaries' ideas could be co-opted, and that he could play the English and the French, the Republicans and the Austrians, the monarchy and the parliament against each other. Add it all up, however, and one cannot but acknowledge that only the most skilled politician could have managed so many conflicting demands, relationships, and opportunities. Cavour repeatedly manufactured resources, commandeered others', and identified opportunities in which to use them. More important, Cavour's choices transformed Italian politics forever.

As great a legacy as national unification was, however, it was an opportunity seized, not a plan implemented. Cavour's most consequential strategic choice was the establishment of a liberal constitutional order. But as the contrast with Itō's machinations makes plain, Cavour's contribution went beyond the formal institution of parliament. He shaped a distinctive *form* of parliamentary politics, ensuring that parties would dominate the state and that skilled politicians could dominate the parties. What Cavour crafted, including the seesaw oscillation of alliances and shifting purposes, entered the tool kit of subsequent generations of Italian politicians. Cavour's centering was more than a onetime, pragmatic exercise in coalition building. It became the prototype for democratic politics in Italy, and its significance can hardly be overstated. Cavour pioneered *trasformismo*—those opportunistic shifts that governments make when they abandon programs in order to remain in power and that oppositions make when they seek to accommodate to power.[106] Centering ultimately became the backbone of Italy's democratic politics. But there was no direct route to democracy. When the nation failed to find skilled politicians, Italy was left to drift with the great forces of the late nineteenth century and then succumb to the authoritarianism of Benito Mussolini. Cavour's legacy was limited.

Yet, as we shall see, once Mussolini was gone, Italian statesmen reached to their shelf of parliamentary experience and, blowing away two decades of dust, returned to the only representative politics they knew—the Cavourian politics of the *juste milieu*. When the new parliament convened in 1948, it adopted the Parliamentary Code (Regolamento) of pre-Fascist Italy with only minor revisions. Lanzara suggests that this decision "was highly symbolic, marking at the same time a discontinuity with respect to the Fascist period and a continuity and a link with the former political order."[107]

Cavour's norms have continued to resist change into the twenty-first century. Frustrated politicians have often sought to make the Italian parliament more efficient and less inconsistent; less proportional and more majoritarian. They have struggled against procedures; but they have never started afresh. Cavour's model of parliamentary politics has been inviolate. Few politicians ever achieve such a legacy.

Clearly, Cavour was an exceptional politician—perhaps the most exceptional Italy has ever produced. Starting from a modest base as prime minister of a regional kingdom, he married the ideas of liberalism and nation to an unexpected chance to establish a unified Italy. That these were not his ideas (or even his nation) was less important than his ability to make both come to life—and to provide them an institutional form that continues to sustain the Italian Republic today. If there was no architect of modern Italy, Cavour was, at a minimum, foreman on the construction site. It is unlikely that a recognizable Italy would exist today had Cavour not perceived and seized his opportunity, wielding others' powerful ideas to his opportunistic ends. The achievement of a unified Italy belongs to many, but its specific institutions are Cavour's legacy.[108] The count lived just long enough to convene the first parliament of the Kingdom of Italy in February 1861. He died weeks later, at age fifty.

Itō Hirobumi and Yamagata Aritomo, whose choices for authoritarianism were just as consequential as were Cavour's for liberalism, lived much longer. Indeed, Itō lived long enough to reinvent himself as a party politician, Yamagata long enough to constrain the choices of Hara Kei, Japan's first politician-prime minister. We have seen that Itō reaped what he had sown. He had worked relentlessly to insulate the bureaucracy and the emperor from all outside political influence. Until the eve of World War I, in fact, the oligarchs controlled both the palace and the government. They succeeded by achieving control of the imperial prerogative. But, in so doing, they created the possibility that competitors for power might gain the ability to define the imperial will.[109] Yamagata's victory over Itō, establishing a military beyond civilian *or* imperial control, is an example that continues to haunt Japan today. It enabled Japanese expansionism, was the reason for Japan's postwar "pacifism," and is the essence of Japan's continuing search for "normality" in the twenty-first century.

It was a remarkably short distance from the Meiji Constitution of 1890 to the Japanese garrison state of the 1930s. That brutal road was paved by choices made not only by Itō but by Japan's "first soldier." Yamagata's "frank distrust" of politicians was reflected in his ceaseless and, alas, successful efforts to build a Japanese state immune from popular control.[110] In sum, Yamagata's impact had two faces. First, he contrived to separate the military from other political bodies. By placing the military directly under the authority of an emperor he felt he could instruct, he prevented other officials or politicians from intervening in military issues. Second, by limiting the posts of army and navy ministers to active duty general officers whom he controlled, Yamagata gave the military effective veto power over all cabinet decisions.

At times the politicians asserted themselves. The government eliminated four army divisions in the 1920s and blocked the army's expansion in Manchuria in 1928. It even capitulated at the 1930 London Naval Conference. But the military always used its control of the imperial prerogative to counterattack.[111] Wrapping itself in the emperor's old clothes, it transformed Japan into a garrison state. By the 1930s, even the commander of the Kwantung Army had a direct line to the emperor—whereas the ambassador to Manchukuo had to report to the prime minister.[112]

On his death, some politicians reviled Yamagata as an "enemy of mankind and suppressor of democratic institutions."[113] The military was now responsible only to a pliable emperor. The only challenge to army prerogatives came from the navy, and to ensure that politicians would not reassert civilian control, the army and navy forged an agreement that Ramseyer and Rosenbluth sum up neatly as an exchange of army autonomy in continental Asia for navy control of all points south.[114] Before 1946, sixteen prime ministers were retired military officers. He had already been dead for more than two decades, but Yamagata is widely held culpable for the Pacific War. He built the road to Japan's ruin.[115]

No single individual achieved the stature or amassed the raw power to dominate the Meiji system. Scholars document two distinct generations of oligarchs. The first defeated the shogunate: among them, Iwakura Tomomi, Saigo Takamori, Ōkubo Toshimichi, and Kido Kōin. We have examined their handiwork as a collective product. The second, including Itō Hirobumi and Yamagata Aritomo, took Japanese government into the twentieth century. Most commentators take the view that the oligarchs acted strategically and in the national interest as they defined it: "What is particularly impressive about the statecraft of the Japanese leaders is the clarity with which they understood the historical process through which they were leading the nation."[116] In this account, the oligarchs consciously aroused passions to extract resources without stimulating expectations or seeming to license excessive demands. They wisely balanced empowerment and repression to avoid the revolutionary violence they observed in Europe.

Others posit a very different picture, in which the selfish competition for power among oligarchs was far more consequential than any devotion to the nation: "Because none alone was strong enough, the leaders of the Meiji Restoration had to band their forces together to overthrow the Tokugawa shogunate. But once collectively in power, each individually had an incentive to wrest more power from the others for himself."[117] Neither interpretation presents leaders as mere receptacles of the great forces of history. Were their interventions selfish or selfless, competitive or collaborative? In the longer term it does not matter. A set of larger, highly malleable institutions emerged from their interventions to shape subsequent Japanese history. Ever searching for a useable past, the oligarchs relentlessly scanned the horizon of Japanese traditions. When the horizon was empty and "tradition" did not oblige, they invented one. Their search would turn up instruments of great contemporary value, such as contrivances about the Japanese "family" and other notions of collective harmony, but their first and most valuable discovery was the emperor himself.

Itō Hirobumi designed the Meiji Constitution and Yamagata Aritomo was father of the imperial military. Both sought to harness the imperial prerogative, and each found ways to use the emperor to enhance his own political program. Their legacies extend to the present: debates over bureaucratic dominance and about civilian control of the military are as central to contemporary Japanese discourse about becoming a "normal nation" as they were central to the process by which Meiji leaders built the modern Japanese state and the new Japanese nation.

Cavour's legacy seems more limited. His fear of popular control invited fascism, and his liberalism was insufficiently robust to preclude it. His Japanese counterparts established institutions that constrained their successors, while Cavour's broke down. Japanese leaders programmed fascism into their new state, but for the Italians, fascism had to be forced on them from outside. Japanese fascism was evidence of the success of the system, whereas in Italy it derived from the system's failures.

Cavour's legacy was more enduring in other respects. A unified peninsula might have been dragged toward a Soviet model (Mazzini's victory gone wrong), toward a Greek model (Garibaldi's victory gone wrong), or toward a Balkan model (the foreign powers' victory gone wrong). None of these possibilities was ever liberal in the sense that Cavour established. This particular leader mattered not just for the changes he wrought but for the institutions he created.

Where Cavour built a parliament to counteract the powers of the monarchy, Itō and Yamagata built a bureaucracy to serve a monarchy that would not challenge state power. Where Cavour created *citizens* of an Italian state who actually voted for their king in the 1860 plebiscite, Itō created *subjects* of a Japanese emperor. No two monarchs could have been put to more different political use. Cavour used the monarch and Itō and Yamagata used the monarchy.

Nor could two states develop more different institutional resources. Cavour's Italy was centered on parliamentary politics; Italians were governed for better or worse by politicians of varying skills. The first generation of Italian politicians were also able bureaucrats but were unwilling to cede institutional power to a state bureaucracy. Itō's Japan was a bureaucratic state, governed by dedicated and able technicians who cared little for popular support. Liberal politicians had to wrest political power from bureaucrats in Japan, whereas in Italy politicians monopolized political power, and the state never quite evolved a balancing executive—until it overcompensated with fascism. Cavour built a parliamentary state, Itō and Yamagata built a bureaucratic one. Each had an excess of what the other lacked. Both were incomplete.

Italian and Japanese state-builders both sensed that the world of the mid-nineteenth century was not one in which the weak or the divided could survive. Cavour closely monitored nationalist movements in Poland, Greece, and Germany, just as Itō monitored events in continental Asia. Both invoked ideas of nationality. But while Cavour sought foreign support for his efforts, Itō fortified Japan by sustaining its insularity. For Cavour, liberty from religious and secular autocracy was as important as liberty from foreign domination; foreign states could be harnessed to help Italy. For Itō, Yamagata, and the other oligarchs, liberty at home was a nonstarter.

There remains one inescapable difference we have yet to explore—the ways in which leaders chose to organize their economy. The difference distinguishes mercantilist oligarchs who had a very clear idea of how to achieve prosperity and liberal leaders who were inconsistent and often confused. Italian liberals became mercantilists when they decided that liberalism was exhausted, but by then it was too late. Japanese mercantilism worked more fully. In the next chapter we will show how each was the product of a real choice and each had a price. Mistakes made by leaders in Italy made that price even dearer.

CHAPTER THREE

How to Build Wealth:

ALESSANDRO ROSSI, ŌKUBO TOSHIMICHI, AND

SHIBUSAWA EICHI

> It is possible for a nation to possess too many philosophers, philologers, and literati, and too few skilled artisans, merchants, and seamen. This is the consequence of highly advanced and learned culture which is not supported by a highly advanced manufacturing power and by an extensive internal and external trade, it is as if in a pin manufactory far more pin heads were manufactured than pin points.
>
> George Friedrich List, *National System of Political Economy*

This chapter explores nineteenth and early twentieth century choices about how to build wealth—perhaps the most fundamental difference between Italy and Japan as they chased parity with the great powers. In both cases, state-builders and early entrepreneurs appreciated the backwardness of their economies. In both cases, talented individuals occupied high offices and established major industrial firms without particular regard for distinctions between public and private sectors. In both cases, "political merchants" commandeered state resources for private gain. Finally, in both cases, material and ideational resources were diverse and abundant. Often the terms of debate were identical. We will focus on three debates in particular: a) free trade vs. protectionism; b) national economic policy and state intervention; and c) relations between entrepreneurs and the state. Resources and opportunities may have been similar, but the choices—and, perforce, their legacies—were profoundly different.

LEGACIES FROM THE START

In May 1861, just before his death, Count Cavour addressed Parliament to outline a strategy for economic development based on free trade.

69

Cavour believed that Italian economic backwardness was the natural result of its fragmented markets. Now, he argued, Italy could integrate itself into the larger European economy by exporting primary goods and developing light manufacturing. Cavour was aware of the risks and exhorted his colleagues to stimulate industrial development—although he ruled out heavy industry for such a weak and agricultural economy. Toward that end, he focused especially on helping manufacturers by reducing duties on imported machinery. He also called for a broadly based program of technical education.[1]

Cavour's views were not concocted in the first flush of unification. A decade earlier, while serving as minister of economic affairs to the Savoy monarchy, he had opposed assisting producers at the expense of consumers. Singling out the textile industry as a paragon of aggressive modernization without protection—and without regard for the fact that it was dominated by foreign entrepreneurs—he had sought to steer a course away from state intervention, which, in his view, could lead only to socialism and reduced wealth for all.[2] Toward that end, he concluded tariff-reducing commercial treaties with major trading partners, including France, Great Britain, and Switzerland.

Before the unification, of course, every state had its own trade tariffs and customs. Piedmont was oriented toward free trade, and France was its leading trade partner. Its general customs tariff of July 1859—averaging about 10 percent—was one of the lowest in Europe.[3] Unification extended this rate to annexed provinces and to the Kingdom of Two Sicilies, whose producers suddenly lost up to 80 percent of the protection they had enjoyed under the Bourbon regime.[4] And, of course, all internal customs were abolished within a new country of twenty-seven million people.

Cavour supported free trade for two reasons: First, he thought it a quicker route to sustained economic growth. And second, he viewed trade as an instrument of statecraft. He wanted diplomatic support from Great Britain and France, two free-trading states, for the annexation of Venice and Rome, which remained just beyond the kingdom's grasp.[5]

His liberalism notwithstanding, Cavour understood the dangers of free trade applied wholesale to a young industrial economy. Unfortunately for the young Kingdom of Italy, his successors had a less subtle understanding of economic issues.[6] While Cavour's successors acted on his exhortations concerning free trade, they ignored his admonitions about its dangers. They recklessly eliminated most tariffs; and by late 1861, just six months after Cavour's death, Italian duties were merely 15 percent of French levels.[7] In the event, debates about economic principles, like debates about political alliances, would be captured more by cynical bargains than by lofty ideals.

The Japanese oligarchs also were constrained by prior choices, for the shogunate had begun to lose control of the economy well before the Restoration. Despite the low nominal status of the merchant class, a national commercial economy—with thriving urban centers—had been consolidated by the early nineteenth century. The shogunate had no power to enforce trade regulations across domains, and foreign trade, long proscribed, expanded rapidly once it was available. From the opening of trade in 1859 until the Restoration in 1868, Japanese exports, led by raw silk, generated a trade surplus.[8]

Limited economic success notwithstanding, the shogunate grew weak. It was unable to protect Japan from foreign coercion. For example, Commodore Perry ignored with impunity 1852 legislation requiring that wholesale merchants belong to state-sanctioned trade associations. When the government tried to impose a separate tax and a fee on transactions in Yokohama between foreign and Japanese traders, the resident foreign powers forced rescission of the order.[9] Most humiliating of all were British demands that the shogunate reduce and recalculate tariffs.[10] The unequal treaties forced upon Japan in 1859 committed her in perpetuity to a fixed, across-the-board tariff of only 5 percent.

The shogunate was unable to protect itself from protests sparked by foreign coercion and by economic change. It could not prevent—or effectively ameliorate—the unrest that emerged in the countryside, where commercial agriculture had led to often-violent resentment from wealthy farmers (*gōnō*).[11] Worse, from the shogunate's perspective, was the crisis in domestic relations precipitated by the opening to trade. Edo sought to impose controls that the han—with foreign support—successfully resisted. The Satsuma han, for example, was far ahead of the shogunate in dealing with foreign threats. Worried about the seizure by British and French forces of his Ryūkyū holdings, Nariakira, the Satsuma lord, moved vigorously to build naval defenses. With his talented deputy, Ōkubo Toshimichi, he built a modern shipyard, an iron foundry, and an arsenal.[12] Ōkubo would use these arms against Edo before long and would invoke this program of autonomous technology development on a national scale within two decades.

Clearly, ideas now associated with the Meiji leadership, such as *wakon yōsai* ("Japanese spirit and Western technology") and *fukoku kyōhei* ("rich nation, strong army"), were not unknown before the Restoration. Late Tokugawa thinkers had been developing coherent ideas for Japanese technonationalism well before Perry's "black ships" appeared in Edo Bay. Intellectuals recognized that Western knowledge was both a source of enormous power and a threat; "controlling the barbarians with their own methods" was seen as the only solution.[13] The shogunate negotiated with

71

the French to acquire shipbuilding and military expertise, and dispatched six separate missions to the West in the 1860s to study advanced technology and administration. It knew that Japan would have to be opened, and it took steps to do so. But its modernization program was too little, too late.

UNCERTAIN GAINS FROM TRADE

There were different ways to "open" an economy in the nineteenth century, and in both countries the debate was joined between free trade and protectionism. In Japan, the liberal alternative, though weak, did have its advocates. Indeed, for a time the only choice that made sense to outward-looking Japanese intellectuals was the liberalism of Great Britain, the dominant global power. Laissez-faire and its application to international trade was the most important topic of economic debate in the leading journals.[14] Liberals were fighting a losing battle, however. Morris-Suzuki sums up the balance of intellectual forces at the time: "The liberal theories of the British classical economists . . . had relatively little appeal to the self-interest of Meiji businessmen, and, from the government's point of view, had the additional disadvantage of being associated with the suspect political ideology of parliamentary democracy."[15]

European treatises on protectionism came to Japan after the Restoration but before the formal adoption of mercantilist economic policy. In 1870, Wakayama Norikazu, a finance ministry official who earlier had supported liberal economics, invoked foreign protectionist thinkers to the effect that weak states cannot afford to open markets too soon. Open markets would invite imports of luxury goods that would sap the national reserves of precious metals.[16] By the mid-1870s the mercantilist argument had become more nuanced; now it recognized the difference between protection of infant industries and the importance of dismantling protection for internationally competitive sectors.[17] Not until the late 1880s, when Friedrich List's influential *National System of Political Economy* first became available in Japanese translation, were the missing pieces—the ideas that economic laws were not universal, that comparative advantage could be constructed, that the state could play an important role in economic life—in place. But Meiji economic planners—especially Ōkubo Toshimichi and Ōkuma Shigenobu—were already well ahead of the intellectuals in denying the relevance of Smith's "invisible hand." They were not of a single mind, but neither did they entertain the extended debate endured by their Italian contemporaries.[18]

Despite constraints imposed by the unequal treaties, Japanese policy-makers made important choices about how the nation might become rich and strong—choices available to but ignored by contemporary Italian leaders. Their early choice for economic intervention and technonationalism was made *despite* an international trade regime and a still uncertain national consolidation that appeared to make free trade and openness the more compelling option. Like the Italian economy of the time, moreover, the Japanese economy was short on capital and long on labor. But unlike Italian leaders, the Japanese elected to pursue capital-intensive economic growth without inviting foreign investment.

In January 1863 Italy signed its first trade treaties—a twelve-year pact with France (its largest trading partner) and a navigation accord with Britain (its second largest).[19] A treaty with Switzerland followed in 1867, and one with Austria the next year. None generated much opposition. Industrialists seemed unaware of the consequences and, in any event, were scarcely organized. There were no trade associations to produce analyses or coordinate political activity on behalf of their members. That Italy's first treaties, unlike Japan's, were entered into freely and equitably makes their consequences all the more painful to evaluate.

Confidence in Italy's future was widespread. It was thought that Italy needed only to exploit its comparative advantage in agriculture, where 70 percent of the workforce was engaged and 60 percent of the GNP generated, and use its geopolitical advantages as a Mediterranean trader. The southern agricultural economy, so badly mismanaged by the Bourbon monarchy, would thrive under liberal government and commercial freedom—most agreed that the South's renaissance was at hand.[20] Intellectuals organized the Adam Smith Society to promote free trade and liberal values. They had few opponents, and boundary duties were not a political issue until 1870.[21]

In the dominant view, duties would be used only to recoup the state's cost of supervising trade and rarely needed to be greater than 5–6 percent of the value of goods traded. Some Milanese journalists even campaigned to abolish all duties.[22] Despite Cavour's admonitions, precious few understood that Italian industry could not sustain competition without protection.[23] For a time, optimism seemed justified, and throughout the 1860s and 1870s trade grew. Indeed, there was 33 percent average growth in tonnage through Italian ports between 1871 and 1880. Genoa, which had five commercial harbors in 1868, had nineteen—all at full capacity—five years later.[24] Agricultural exports boomed. Yet trade and budget deficits grew faster. Italy was importing nearly all of its cast iron, railway equipment, and industrial machinery.[25]

The treaty with France not only required Italy to reduce its tariffs considerably but, through a "most favored nation" clause, to apply similar reductions to other trading partners. The young kingdom, now spending with abandon to build a modern army and navy, soon felt the loss of revenue. Limits on the convertibility of the lira helped protect domestic manufacturers but stunted imports and choked off needed revenues. With the government struggling to make ends meet, Italian credit collapsed in 1866.[26] Mark Twain, who visited Italy the next year, offered an astute account: "Italy has achieved the dearest wish of her heart and become an independent state—and in so doing she has drawn an elephant in the political lottery. She has nothing to feed it on. Inexperienced in government, she plunged into all manner of expenditure and swamped her treasury almost in a day."[27] The new state, nearly bankrupt, could no longer borrow abroad and found it necessary to deflate the economy and dispose of state property. In 1868, the finance ministry sold the canals and railways as well as the tobacco monopoly. It also sold land expropriated from the Church and the old states. Many of the bargain hunters were foreigners. Seton-Watson puts Italy's dilemma in striking terms that Japanese oligarchs anticipated mutatis mutandis: "The new state had to prove that it could hold its own in a competitive industrial world. If it failed, the fate of Egypt or Tunis awaited it, and effective sovereignty would pass into the hands of foreign bankers and investors."[28] Here was Italy's first, painful lesson in free trade. The textbook might have been more explicit—or Italian elites might have read between its lines more carefully—for the recurring blasts of foreign competition that swept across the peninsula were not always salutary.

To be sure, the pain was not shared equally. In the North, the silk industry earned nearly half of Italy's foreign exchange in the 1860s, and, after the introduction of mechanical looms in 1869, northern Italy boasted an active and growing industry. As in Japan, a patrician oligarchy was learning, albeit slowly and tentatively, to engage in the real economy. But these northern successes further distanced the northern and southern economies.[29] These differences were further exacerbated when the national railway system opened, exposing Italian manufacturers to vigorous foreign competition. English textile manufacturers dumped their products; free trade was leaving Italy vulnerable, and some feared she was doomed to an agrarian future.

A decade and a half of free trade and a severe fiscal crisis resulted in sustained trade deficits and stunted growth. Foreign domination no longer seemed temporary; it seemed unending. Illusions about the benefits of laissez-faire were shattered, and northern industrialists began to organize themselves politically for the first time.[30] Southern elites were unhappy with northern taxes.[31] The heirs of Mazzini—the so-called Extreme Left—had their first chance in 1876 when the king invited Agostino Depretis to form a government.[32] They bungled it. They governed for twenty years, but Depretis and his successor, Francesco Crispi, could not sustain a coherent program. In the end, abandoning hope for coherence, they were left to practice and refine Cavour's *juste milieu*. Depretis reprised the Cavourian *connubio* by pulling in the Right and transforming his program, and Crispi would further practice this fine art. But this was not Cavour's balancing act. Empty of strategic purpose, Depretis and Crispi pandered to interests and blurred their differences to maintain power.[33]

There were plenty of interests to which they and their opposition could pander. Italian industry was anything but unified, and the consensus on free trade was coming undone. Candy and biscuit makers opposed the duties sought by sugar processors. Furniture makers opposed the duties sought by wood and timber interests. Machinery makers fought against protection for iron and steel makers. And so it went on, upstream and down, in every sector.

In 1869 northern industrialists succeeded with their demands for Italy's first official trade agency: the Council of Industry and Trade. The next year, the council launched an official inquiry into Italian competitiveness. Among the commissioners was a woolen textile factory owner named Alessandro Rossi (1819–1898) who had been instrumental in pressing for the council and who would shortly emerge to lead Italy toward protectionism.[34] Finally, a leader was stepping into the breach.

In the end Rossi would not be up to the task, but that could not have been known at the time. Politicians had good reason to listen to him. His Venetian factory, Rossi Wool, was Italy's largest and most advanced, employing two thousand looms and five thousand workers in 1876.[35] Rossi was elected to Parliament as a confirmed free trader in 1866, but four years later—as he was coming around to his "brutal realism"—he was named senator.[36] By 1876 Rossi was the leading spokesman for industrial protectionism, for the elimination of foreign dependence, and for corporate paternalism. His model of a national political economy was very close to that of Friedrich List—and the one Japan's economic leadership would embrace. Like List, Rossi believed that "economic autonomy gave a nation strength."[37] Rossi advocated a national state *institutionally* predisposed to intervention in economic affairs. He would privilege manufacturers but included agrarian allies as needed. Rossi's state would not compete with producers, nor legislate social policy, but would finance and protect national industries.[38] Amid enormous controversy, the commission concluded in 1874 that manufacturers needed better protection. It prescribed tax relief and customs duties.[39] Revisions of Italy's treaties, at last high on the government's agenda, took several years. These new plans for trade protection were met by a commensurate rise in demands for protection in France, where free traders were soundly defeated in the 1875 elections.

In Italy, the picture was mixed. Southern agriculture, which was still competitive abroad; silk manufacturers, who made enormous profits from foreign sales; and Tuscan banks, closely tied to foreign capital, fought Rossi and his allies. Rossi responded with new mechanisms to help the fight for protection. He created and led the Italian Cotton Association and helped stimulate creation of the Mechanical and Metallurgical Workers Assembly.[40] Brewers, leather workers, and silk and paper manufacturers joined them in Italy's first coherent national bloc of business interests. Rossi used his newspapers to win public support, but he was coming up short in the Parliament. Just fifteen of more than five hundred deputies represented business interests, and only three of them (Rossi included) were manufacturers.[41]

When Depretis formed his government in March 1876, he seemed determined to reduce tariffs and resist protectionism. But Depretis was presiding over a fragile government, had no support from the Church and precious little from the Republicans, was exasperated by negotiations with the French, and was clearly cowed by the prospects of social movements that Rossi predicted would get out of hand if jobs were lost to free trade. Rossi used his media and intellectuals to hound the government. Depretis promised help for industry.[42] He did help, but not as much as Rossi had hoped; and, in the event, it was more help than was good for the Italian economy.

Rossi had helped position Italy for a trade war with France. A new treaty with France was signed in July 1877, at a time when the French were absorbing 30 percent of Italy's exports and the Italian government and industry depended on the Paris money market for credit. The Italian Parliament passed the treaty easily in early 1878, but not with all the protection that Rossi and his northern industrial allies had sought.[43] In fact, the treaty was only slightly less liberal than the previous one. Industry was still fragmented and largely beholden to foreign interests, and many were convinced that Italy could not survive a trade war with France—not least because French financiers owned an enormous piece of Italian debt.

Even if the treaty was not all that the protectionists sought, it turned out to be more than they bargained for. In June, the French Parliament refused to ratify the treaty. Rossi and his allies were emboldened by Paris's hostility and forged ahead.[44] Some manufacturers benefited, especially the textile industry, and most notably Rossi. Within a year of the tariff of 1878 production in his mills was back to pre-crisis levels, and his firm's share prices had stabilized.[45] Rossi crowed: "The reality of economic development was one of struggle among interests and countries. The stronger countries hide behind liberal principles: Every illusion of competitive equilibrium hides the pitiless hegemony of those nations who had first started the industrial revolution."[46] Predictably, however, economic and political relations with France deteriorated. Rossi's personal gains notwithstanding, Italy proved vulnerable. French manufactures and banks continued to dominate the Italian economy, while Italian exports to France of cattle and milk products fell off. Silk and wine producers reeled from the loss of their largest market, and grain producers now had to compete with American and Russian producers. By 1881, France was no longer Italy's top trading partner.

Geopolitics were important, of course, and Italo-French competition in the Mediterranean complicated matters considerably. In 1881 France proclaimed sovereignty over Tunisia, and anti-French demonstrations across the peninsula provoked anti-Italian counterdemonstrations in Marseilles. Depretis lost support on the Left, and he turned back to the Right. When he tried to negotiate with the French, France responded with higher tariffs against Italian imports. Italy, which had hoped to balance German and French power, found itself tipping decisively in favor of Germany. (France responded by supporting the papacy and irredentists.)

Depretis may have been at a loss, but Rossi was undeterred—possibly because his own woolen mills had prospered or possibly because he simply did not understand the consequences of the game he was playing. By the late 1880s, he perceived an opportunity to build a new, broader protectionist initiative. This northern industrial senator reinvented himself as the most committed defender of southern agricultural interests in Parliament.[47] He began to aggressively promote protection for agriculture against the "invasion of Russian and American grain."[48] As a Catholic, Rossi could argue that stable agricultural production was essential for social order. It bolstered "traditional values" while also serving as an important source of capital accumulation for industrial investment. Everything came together in what in retrospect looks remarkably like proto-corporatism: the "social question"—essentially public order—would be resolved through cross-sectoral cooperation and a dose of protection. Rossi was aided by a resurgence of nationalism in Italy and a surge of protectionism across the Continent, both of which he had had a part in stimulating. Now he redirected indiscriminate demands for protection into a coherent economic argument—one that included support from the working class. Rossi vigorously supported higher duties on grain and rice. He was engineering an "iron-and-rye coalition" *alla italiana,* and brought government policy along with him.[49]

Industrial development had to reinforce and maintain traditional social balances in the national interest. Rossi, arguing the Catholic line, averred that protection would strengthen bonds between workers and employers and between peasants and landlords. Then, invoking nationalism, he insisted that protection would enhance national prestige. Rossi saw the opportunity to fuse social reform, nationalism, public works, cross-class solidarity, and military spending more clearly than any other leader.[50] And he got what he sought. After the partial tariff of 1878 became a punitive one a decade later, however, Rossi watched this package destroy large parts of the Italian economy and stimulate economic nationalism.

Rossi expected that a new general tariff would be a panacea at home and cause only limited reaction abroad. In October 1887, despite a decade of evidence to the contrary, Rossi wrote in *Il Sole* that Italy did not need French manufactures as much as France needed Italian exports. Italy would be safe from reprisals.[51] Although his assessment was dangerously wrong, Rossi had broad support. In mid-1887, Parliament passed a new protectionist general tariff that would apply only to trade with countries that had no commercial treaty with Italy. In 1888, with the expiration of the earlier treaty, this tariff became effective in trade with France, and a rupture of commercial relations loomed. Duties on iron and steel and many manufactured goods reached as high as 200–300 percent, and trade with France was cut in half before the end of the century. Italy had joined continental Europe's protectionist mainstream, and this new tariff would be the basis of Italian commercial policy until the First World War. Senator Rossi and his ally Ernesto Breda, whose firm built railways, celebrated only for a short time, for relations with France deteriorated into a full-scale trade war. Hardest hit were finance and agriculture—precisely those sectors that had held out in favor of free trade. The Italian silk industry tumbled into disorder, and 200,000 workers lost their jobs. The largest foreign market for Italian wines was eliminated, and the largest banks in Rome, Tuscany, and Naples failed when French financiers took their money home. German financiers, with the blessing of the liberal Italian state, replaced them. Protectionism *alla italiana* was a late, unnecessary, and devastatingly wrong choice for the Italian economy.

A NATIONAL ECONOMIC POLICY?

The prominence of foreign investors and entrepreneurs in late nineteenth-century Italy stands in stark contrast with the Japanese experience. The Japanese sought no foreign capital and welcomed no foreign investment. By contrast, French bankers held Italian debt, Swiss dominated the textile industry, and British dominated in metallurgy. The Italian treasury subsidized foreign investors in railroads and even guaranteed a minimum return per kilometer of line in operation. Not only was the capital imported and profits repatriated but management and equipment were likewise brought in from other countries. Hence, as Webster notes, "rail construction was not the stimulus to industrial development in Italy that it had been elsewhere."[52]

Italy's dependence on foreign capital and technology was a defining structural feature of the early economy. So was a dearth of local entrepreneurial talent. As in Japan, investment and risk taking did not come naturally to aristocrats who had clipped coupons for generations. The private sector failed to create collective goods, and the state responded to their fragmented pleas with inconsistent policies. Historians have long decried the lack of vision and the self-serving leadership of late nineteenth-century Italy. Playing off D'Azeglio's aphorism, some have observed that "they made Italy to devour her."[53] Until the 1880s, when Alessandro Rossi stepped forward to champion protectionism, no leader articulated a comprehensive national interest, and, as we shall see, Rossi's vision was not nearly comprehensive enough. He and others badly misjudged the Italian economy, and their failures would whipsaw generations of Italian economic planners and industrialists.

Like Italy and other late industrializing economies, Japan had a choice between two different paths toward national economic development. The first option was the liberal free trade advocated by British economists and by local intellectuals impressed with ideas of civilization and enlightenment. As we have seen, this way was rejected in Japan and accepted (at least nominally) in Italy. The second was to find a way to nurture domestic industries without the protection of tariffs. The Japanese leadership, in a desperate effort to retain political autonomy, chose industrial nurturance (*shokusan kōgyō*). This program, designed by the powerful oligarch Ōkubo Toshimichi and his associates, protected Japan against foreign military threats and reduced trade deficits through import substitution.[54] Shokusan kōgyō was an effective substitute for trade protection and proved to be a central instrument in Japan's national development.

Ōkubo's domination of the young Meiji state between 1873 and his assassination in 1878 is sometimes called the "Ōkubo dictatorship." He was the first Restoration activist to advocate a "rich nation and strong army" (*fukoku kyōhei*).[55] One source of his convictions was the success of his Satsuma han in industrial development before the Restoration. By 1848, Satsuma had built its own arsenals, iron mills, and shipyards, and the han treasury enjoyed a substantial surplus. But industrial development was only half of the story. The other half was about protection. In September 1865, while still a bureaucrat in Satsuma, Ōkubo had witnessed the shelling of Kagoshima by British ships. He wrote to colleagues in England

79

that he had had his eyes opened. Expelling the barbarians (*jōi*) was not an option. The foreigners were far too strong and the shogunate hopelessly weak. He made a strategic choice to join forces with other han and selectively to open to the West in order to raise Japan's military capabilities. "Consequently," he averred, "there is no alternative than to aim for the fundamental policy of protecting the Court and establishing Imperial prestige abroad by resorting to the energetic execution of *fukoku kyō-hei.*"[56]

Ōkubo was a creative, relentlessly opportunistic, and single-minded leader. He spoke of "protecting the Court" but ignored imperial orders that were inconvenient. Without understating his unwavering grip on power, historians concur that he was concerned above all with keeping the West at (a strong) arm's length. Craig argues that "Ōkubo was burdened with a sense of mission. Power was his means . . ."[57] Once Ōkubo made his critical choice for Japan rather than for Satsuma, he insisted on doing whatever it would take to enrich the nation and strengthen the army. By one account, Ōkubo "almost single-handedly" held the young Meiji government together during its delicate early years between 1868 and 1871.[58] He coaxed (and alternately threatened) the han into "devoting themselves to the national ideal," and replaced them with prefectures. He was an expert in no field of public administration, but dominated virtually all by empowering protégés such as Itō and Yamagata, who would, in turn, dominate Japanese politics for decades after his demise. And, as we shall see, Ōkubo also nurtured private capitalists, such as Shibusawa Eichi and Iwasaki Yatarō, who would use the relationship to create some of the world's greatest corporate empires.[59]

A national economic policy was difficult to implement. At first, the young Meiji state fared no better than the shogunate in asserting authority over the feudal domains. Six months after the Restoration, when the oligarchs took up the failed plan for national economic control, including government licensing and supervision of commercial and financial activities, foreign interests again intervened to block central control of trade.[60] There were also serious fiscal constraints. For one thing, the new leaders had only limited access to revenues from duties on trade. For another, fearing a further loss of sovereignty more than delays in their economic program, the government ruled out foreign borrowing. Third, while they wished to tax commerce and industry lightly to speed capital formation, they were also concerned about alienating the peasantry. As a consequence, they devised a remarkably equitable tax program, which, while it did not eliminate peasant unrest, was better accepted than its Tokugawan predecessor.[61]

Despite these considerable constraints, and perhaps because Japan was beyond the easy reach of foreign powers, plans for industrial development fared rather well. The Meiji government inherited modern factories established by the han before the Restoration, including Japan's first modern ironworks, shipyards, and arsenals.[62] While the oligarchs held no particular brief for state ownership, they acknowledged that domestic capital was limited and stepped into the breach with public investment as a way to break bottlenecks in basic industries, mining, communications, and transportation.[63] Their insistence on security drove these investments, and they immediately seized on technology as the key to successful industrial development. The Japanese leaders would not make the Chinese mistake of thinking of the foreigners as nothing more than "barbarians who were no different from birds and beasts."[64] They were ready to learn foreign technology in order to make Japan rich and strong. Indeed, the fifth of the five clauses of the April 1868 Charter Oath of the Meiji emperor proclaimed that "intellect and learning should be sought for throughout the world in order to establish the foundations of the empire."

The first industrial policy of the Meiji government was designed by Ōkuma Shigenobu. Ōkuma argued for the establishment of a ministry of industry in 1870 to coordinate the importation of foreign transport and communication technologies. He explicitly rejected the British model of private leadership, arguing that only a powerful public agency could direct industrial development.[65] Ōkubo, first minister of finance, initially opposed him, wanting to focus exclusively on the military industries, but Ōkuma prevailed. Meanwhile, Ōkubo and his deputy, Inoue Kaoru, grew concerned that traditional Japanese industries were being heavily damaged by imports and argued that the government should protect them as well.[66]

In November 1871, Ōkubo joined the Iwakura mission to the United States and Europe to study industrial development and attempt to restore Japan's tariff powers. Itō Hirobumi, another of the remarkable group that made the voyage, wrote to his colleagues in Tokyo from Washington, D.C. early in the trip, seconding Ōkubo's call for the use of tariffs to protect Japan's infant industries.[67] In Sacramento, Itō explained that he and his colleagues had come West "to study your strength, that, by adopting wisely your better ways, we may hereafter be stronger ourselves."[68] Although President Grant expressed a willingness to renegotiate the treaties, the Europeans would not, and the mission abandoned that part of the effort. Instead, it focused on administrative and economic reform. While Ōkubo was impressed with the British and German economies, he appreciated Germany's centralized bureaucracy, and saw in the Germans a mirror of the Japanese, a "thrifty, hardworking, and unpretentious" people.[69] Bismarck personally tutored the mission on the German experience of industrial development. He explained that Germany proceeded without the assistance of England or France, two powers that, in any event, could not be trusted. Bismarck warned them of the territorial ambitions of these great powers and exhorted Ōkubo and his colleagues to pursue industrial autonomy.[70]

Ōkubo had heard what he came to hear, and he listened carefully. Upon the mission's return in 1873, he identified his priorities: "Because of the critical times through which the nation is traversing, it behooves every government official to concentrate upon the encouragement of manufacturing industries and the increase of production generally in view of establishing the basis for wealth and power."[71] Ōkubo wasted no time implementing plans for the rapid modernization of Japanese industry. In the process, he experimented with the entire panoply of industrial policy ideas—import substitution, limited state ownership, technological borrowing, national champions—that would guide Japan for the next century and a half. He was now convinced that state-run enterprise would be essential for Japan "even if it goes against the laws of political economy." Ōkubo argued Japan was "different" and therefore needed "different laws" to catch up with and surpass the West.[72] He immediately arranged for the establishment of a home ministry—with himself as minister—through which every variety of industrial policy (save the impossible protective tariff) could be implemented. He left the Ministry of Finance to Ōkuma and gave the Ministry of Industry to Itō.

It was Ōkubo's new home ministry, and especially its Industrial Promotion Bureau, that implemented the widest range of economic development programs. Its first act was to cancel orders for imported military uniforms and to subsidize Japanese sheep husbandry to build a domestic industry. Looking further downstream, Ōkubo authorized importation of spinning factories to enable the export of processed, as well as raw, silk. He urged Japanese commercial firms to bypass Western traders when exporting their products, leading to the establishment of Japan's first "general trading companies."[73] Rossi's scheme may have been proto-corporatist, but there is little in Japanese or Italian economic history that has had a longer, deeper, or more pervasive legacy than Ōkubo's technonationalism.

Interestingly, Ōkubo's formal plan for industrial nurturance (*shokusan kōgyō ni kansuru kengi*), although German-inspired, also acknowledged a British precedent—albeit not the one that the British were urging on Japan. Ōkubo distinguished between the contemporary free-trading Britain and the mercantilist Britain that had nurtured its domestic industries before opening them to foreign competition: "Britain prevented the inflow of foreign goods and promoted the development of local industries. It was not until local industries developed and until their production capacity exceeded local consumption that Britain abolished its protectionist trade policy and allowed liberal free trade. This is why Britain emerged as a great power today."[74]

By 1873, Ōkubo's policy priorities were firmly established. His opposition to an assault on Korea in 1873 was decisive for the first major crisis of the Meiji state. He based his opposition on seven factors, each of which speaks to the care with which he had considered the relationship of national wealth and national strength. He reckoned that intervention would lead to disturbances at home, cost more than the treasury could bear, require the abandonment of the industrial nurturing program, deplete gold reserves, invite Russian adventure in Sakhalin, invite British intervention in Japanese domestic affairs, and divert attention from the more pressing issue of treaty revision.[75] It was a bad idea, in short, because Japan needed time to develop the industrial capabilities it would need to establish its place as a secure world power. Ōkubo was so convinced of the correctness of his position that he was willing to risk civil war.

Two elements of Ōkubo's general strategy—what I have elsewhere described as a "three-note chord of Japanese technonationalism"—bear closer scrutiny for their legacy.[76] First, he insisted that Japanese firms should displace foreign ones whenever possible. In 1875, Ōkubo moved to eliminate the dominance of foreign shipping firms in northeast Asia, and in particular among Japan's treaty ports. He authorized state funds for the training of merchant seamen and for the transfer of thirty-one ships free of charge—with fifteen years of state subsidy—to Iwasaki Yatarō's Mitsubishi Company. Iwasaki had started Mitsubishi two years earlier by taking ownership of the ships of his Tosa han on its dissolution. Building shipping routes between Tokyo and Osaka, he added military transports (again at the state's expense) for use in the Taiwan expedition of 1874. With Mitsubishi thus favored, virtually all foreign competitors disappeared—including the American Pacific Mail Steamship Company, which sold its ships and warehouses to Iwasaki on its way out of the market. As a result, Mitsubishi came to dominate Pacific shipping and to monopolize coastal trade. It would become one of Japan's national champions—and one of the largest global corporations of the twentieth century.[77]

Second, he excluded foreign direct investment and avoided the dependence of Japanese industry on foreign capital. He might not have had full control of tariff policy, but Ōkubo was resourceful enough to find other ways to reduce foreign control of the fragile Japanese economy. Foreigners were allowed neither to buy real estate in Japan nor to live outside carefully monitored foreign settlements.[78] The Ōkubo government began building transportation and communication infrastructure "partly to forestall foreign investors who had shown a keen interest in direct investment in this area."[79] In contrast to the Italian leadership of the same period, the Meiji government saw dependence upon Western financiers and governments as perilous to national security and would have as little of it as possible. What little existed was undone through a program of "exclusion of foreign capital" (*gaishi haijo*) in the late 1870s.[80] Former Prime Minister Yoshida Shigeru described Ōkubo's approach with characteristic bluntness: "Japan's leaders in the Meiji era were above all realists. Thus, fearing that the importation of foreign capital would permit alien interests to obtain control of the nation's economy, they prohibited the introduction of such funds. But at the same time, they saw no danger in employing foreigners for the purpose of acquiring foreign knowledge, and this was encouraged."[81]

The government did take a foreign loan to build the first railway between Tokyo and Yokohama, but domestic capital paid for the largest part of Japan's infrastructure investments. Moreover, the decision to proceed with this railway loan—taken by Ōkuma and Itō (who negotiated directly with the British)—was vigorously criticized by Ōkubo and was not repeated, even after his death. In 1880, with Ōkubo gone and the yen highly depreciated, Ōkuma tried again to open Japan to foreign investment. He argued that such a measure would restore international confidence in the yen, and sought approval for a fifty-million-yen bond issue in London. Itō refused to support him, and Iwakura expressed what surely would have been Ōkubo's own sentiment: "Rather than raise a foreign loan . . . we would do better to sell Kyushu and Shikoku to a foreign country."[82] In the event, the emperor was asked to "intervene" and Ōkuma's plans were scuttled. Instead, the government would begin to sell its state-owned firms to get its fiscal house in order. The contrast to Italy's response to the same opportunities was stark.

DIFFERENT CHOICES FOR STATE INTERVENTION

By the early 1880s, the *shokusan kōgyō* program was bearing less fruit than costs. The government had spent nearly two years worth of tax receipts on infrastructure, but government factories were being run in a profligate and haphazard manner. Inflation was hampering development. Japanese foreign reserves had fallen to dangerously low levels. Rice prices had soared, and the Satsuma Rebellion had drained the treasury.

In November 1880, the government announced that it would increase taxes, dispose of government factories, and discontinue some of the most direct industrial promotion programs. This reform measure may have been a pragmatic response to pressing economic exigencies, but it was brilliantly prosecuted by Matsukata Masayoshi, the oligarch who typically gets credit for the largest uncoerced privatization in economic history.[83]

Matsukata, who succeeded Ōkuma as minister of finance after Ōkuma's ouster in 1881, sounded more like Adam Smith than Friedrich List when he declared that the state would never be able to rival "in shrewdness, foresight, and enterprise men who are actuated by immediate motives of self-interest."[84] The fact, however, was that transfer of ownership from the state had nothing to do with liberal principles. Matsukata was aligned with those who opposed Ōkuma's plans to raise foreign capital. Rather than risk inviting foreign control of the Japanese economy, he chose to drastically cut government spending, reduce the money supply, create a single central bank, and raise taxes. By 1886 both inflation and government spending were under control, and the fortunes of Japan's largest private firms were assured by cheap acquisition of government factories and mines.

Indeed, of the eight major zaibatsu, five (Mitsubishi and Mitsui the largest) were built through the favored acquisitions. The government selected its buyers carefully. It refused to transfer assets to foreign interests, even though there were few domestic buyers and the government needed the cash. The initial guidelines established in 1880 for the sale of government factories excluded armories, post and telegraphs, railways, and mines, while including industrial plants. When the buyers wanted more, the government placed the mines for sale; Mitsubishi and Mitsui each acquired mines that would become the cash cows of their burgeoning empires.[85] All transactions carefully observed the preferences of private investors. Transferees were allowed to lease facilities for one to two years to determine whether they were worth purchasing—all at concessionary rates.[86]

The liberal Italian state was struggling too, and its policy began at this point to resemble Japan's—at least superficially. Rossi railed at laissez-faire policies that would leave Italy at the mercy of the German-led steel cartels. Foreign steel makers had considerably greater access to raw materials and could deliver to Italy at half the price that domestic manufacturers had to charge. Never mind that the users of steel did not see it his way. Rossi saw a profound threat to the prospects for a modern and competitive Italian industry, and he had success in invoking arguments for military security.[87] As late as 1878, the Italian government had continued to favor textile producers and light manufacturers. Now, however, the decision was taken to construct a powerful Mediterranean fleet, and the navy and army budgets were sharply increased. Strategic military calculations prevailed, and little thought was given to the commercial potential

CREATION STORIES

of the industry. Suddenly, the steel industry was a model for state-led industrialization and for protection from cheaper foreign competition (a precedent to which other sectors would later appeal).[88] No government official could be too concerned for the performance and cost of this equipment. In 1883 the minister of navy, Ferdinando Acton, was forced to resign because of what his political enemies insisted was an insufficiently deep commitment to national industry.

Admiral Benedetto Brin replaced Acton. Brin used his control of the shipyards to protect Italy's machinery and shipbuilding industries. The dominant protectionist coalition in Italy resembled the German iron-and-rye coalition, but with a twist. Rather than a straight combination of industry and agriculture, the Italian protectionists comprised I Dazi e Commesse—those sectors, such as military industries and agriculture, that were most dependent on state procurement would receive the highest protective tariffs. By Japanese standards, of course, this was not sound logic. Brin would make sure that Italy was self-sufficient in steel plate, but he would fit his warships with British artillery. Indeed, he encouraged Britain's arms manufacturer Armstrong to establish a manufacturing presence in Naples as a way around Italian tariffs. He used government funds to build seawalls for the British plant and guaranteed it supplies of fresh water.[89]

Thus, the picture is mixed. On the one hand, Italian heavy industrialization was dominated by a "naval-industrial complex."[90] The pivot of this delicate system was the steel plant of Terni, whose construction had been started in 1884 after the navy called for domestic steel. Terni made poor steel at high cost. Wearing its product as political armor, Terni would liberate Italian industry from dependence on British, French, and German suppliers—even though Germans would control its lead bank.[91] The Italian navy soon became the second largest in the world, and Italy had a viable shipbuilding industry along with it. The state's desire to enhance its military power, and the thirst of some industrialists for expansion, led the Italian state to support it without considering costs. It also had the perverse effect of drawing in the financial sector; capital for these enterprises was being guaranteed by the reckless Italian state. Hostility between financial and industrial interests was eliminated, and agriculture was now on board. Rossi had helped engineer a winning protectionist coalition. Italy's economic growth would be led by a small number of highly protected, cartelized, and often state-owned firms that cared little about international trade so long as their home market continued to absorb their high-priced products.

Confirmed liberals had become an ineffectual minority, but there never developed as coherent a technonational ideology in Italy as in

Japan. Despite the claim that "state support for heavy industry was based on a solid political and ideological consensus,"[92] technonationalism was a contested and only partially acquired taste in Italy. Italian economic development and industrial policy left considerable room for foreign participation. By the turn of the century, Italy's underdeveloped capital markets in general—and the Terni military-industrial complex in particular—were dominated by German "mixed banks," particularly the Banca Commerciale.[93]

NURTURING POLITICAL MERCHANTS

These stories of late-developers' industrial growth have been well understood since Gerschenkron's pioneering work on the subject. They are particularly familiar to students of Japan, where precisely the same considerations at precisely the same historical moment led to the nationalization of steel and the nurturing of a formidable shipbuilding industry. However, the Italian commitment was haphazard, patched together by occasional initiatives of clearly self-serving individuals like Rossi, who benefited more from Italy's protectionism than Italy did, and by politicians like Depretis and even Crispi, who as often lost their way as they found a new one. Champions of Italian state intervention were comfortable demanding autonomy in the military industries, while their railways—arguably of equal strategic significance—were owned by foreign firms.[94] It was as if Italy had read only random paragraphs of List.

By the time the Japanese economy recovered from the Matsukata deflation in 1882, the zaibatsu were in place. They would dominate the burgeoning economy—and complicate Japan's political life considerably.[95] Even if the great privatization was largely an opportunistic solution to a fiscal crisis rather than a farsighted strategic action, the zaibatsu were created in collaboration with the Japanese state. This collaboration had important implications. Virtually all their founders—like virtually all of the leaders of Japan's business associations for generations to follow—began their careers as economic bureaucrats. From the beginning, these firms balanced national and shareholder interests. Shibusawa Eichi, one of Japan's earliest and most active entrepreneurs, said it best: "I believe that engaging in true commerce is not a matter of private interest and public desires, but of the public interest and the public good . . . Discussing commerce by distinguishing private interest and public good is a complete mistake."[96]

Clouding the distinction between public and private sectors came naturally to Shibusawa. He began his career working for the shogunate and after the Restoration was persuaded to join the Meiji finance ministry by Ōkuma personally.[97] He worked in the ministry for four years, reporting directly to Ōkuma, but left the ministry to create the Daiichi Bank in 1872. By "stepping down" into the despised world of business, Shibusawa paved the way for the development of a business elite that—the result in no small measure of his efforts—ultimately achieved parity with the state.[98] This elite, however, would always maintain its national characteristics even when in deep conflict with the state.

Shibusawa's contributions to modern Japanese capitalism were manifold. The most obvious was as an entrepreneur. Shibusawa pioneered the joint stock company and created more than five hundred of Japan's largest industrial and financial enterprises, including what today are Toshiba, Tokyo Gas, Tokyo Electric, the Tokyo Stock Exchange, and the Mizuho Financial Group. He also was Japan's first successful cotton textile industrialist. His Osaka Spinning Company, established in 1882, combined Western technology with cheap local labor and stimulated a rush of private investment. His second contribution was as an organizer of capitalists. With government subsidy, Shibusawa organized Japan's first modern business associations, including the Cotton Spinners Association and the Tokyo Chamber of Commerce. His third contribution was as a political activist. In 1899 he assumed the presidency of the League to Revise the House of Representatives Election Law, a group of businessmen who sought redistricting in favor of urban areas, and the league prevailed.[99]

Known widely as "the father of Japanese capitalism," Shibusawa never fully embraced liberal ideas—and never ceased serving the state or national ends. He understood his social responsibility was "to build modern enterprise with the abacus and the Analects of Confucius."[100] Like many another leader under review here, Shibusawa searched widely to find a useable past that would legitimate capitalism on Japanese terms. In 1912, he exhorted the Ryūmonsha, a group he had created for young business leaders, to propagate Japanese ideas about the spirit of capitalism: "The essence of Bushidō is a mixture of such virtues as righteousness, integrity, heroism, daring, and respectfulness . . . Now is the time to convert Bushidō [the way of the warrior] into Jitsugyōdō [the way of the businessman]."[101] Like other early Japanese capitalists, Shibusawa explicitly rejected Anglo-American ideas about the proper organization of the economy and denounced the liberal notion of economic individualism. Businessmen, he argued, should be patriots as well as profit maximizers. They were "modern samurai."[102] Shibusawa was an incorrigible promoter of *national* capitalism, a missionary who never ventured far from his con-

Entrepreneur Shibusawa Eichi is depicted in 1909 as the "Idol of the Business Temple." Reproduced courtesy of Shimizu Isao.

nections to the state. He became an entrepreneur in part because so few merchants were fit to meet the challenge of national industrial development. Ministries frequently called upon him to organize businesses or to design industrial relations programs—calls he never refused.[103]

Iwasaki Yatarō—much hated by Shibusawa for his dictatorial ways—was another classic case of what the Japanese call the "political merchant" (*seishō*).[104] Like Shibusawa, he began his career as a government official, a Tosa han bureaucrat in charge of its commercial office. When the han were abolished in 1871 he created a firm (eventually Mitsubishi) that assumed Tosa's liabilities and assets, including its ships. With Ōkubo's assistance, he built a shipping line that soon monopolized trade between Tokyo and Osaka; Ōkubo's government gave Mitsubishi an exclusive contract to transport imperial troops to the Satsuma battlefront in 1877—on ships the government imported and provided. These loaned ships soon became outright gifts. By 1881 the favorite of Ōkuma, Iwasaki had opened shipping routes to Hong Kong and Vladivostok. He used his profits to integrate vertically. Mitsubishi entered the maritime insurance business, built dockside warehouses, and built a shipyard in Yokohama with a foreign partner (whom Iwasaki soon discarded). In 1881, in one of the first of the Matsukata privatizations, Mitsubishi acquired the state's coal mines in Takashima.

In 1881, with Ōkubo dead and Ōkuma expelled, Iwasaki's fortunes turned. Ōkuma's political foes made an issue of Iwasaki's subsidized gouging as he built the Mitsubishi empire. They protested that he had channeled state subsidies into unrelated businesses and pilloried him for being a "self-centered capitalist entrepreneur."[105] In 1882 Mitsubishi was ordered to engage in no business other than shipping, and, to break the monopoly it had helped create, the government created a public-sector competitor. Iwasaki had the last laugh, however. The state firm went bankrupt two years later, after a protracted price war, and the government was forced to broker a merger that gave Mitsubishi even greater control of shipping (with a fifteen-year guaranteed return of 8 percent to boot). The Mitsubishi fortunes improved further when the government leased its Nagasaki shipyards to Iwasaki in 1884, the year before he died. The guarantees that Iwasaki negotiated with the state became standard practice for all "public policy companies" (*kokusaku gaisha*) for the next seventy years. If the state wanted to do business without foreign investors, it would have to guarantee returns to Japanese capitalists.[106]

Although the Japanese economy clearly was never liberal, neither was it a command economy. The negotiations between Iwasaki and the state—like those between the state and Shibusawa—became a template for negotiated participation in state programs. These negotiations have been remarkably consistent in following the contours first shaped by Shibusawa and by Iwasaki. The Japanese state would enjoy jurisdiction in the market in exchange for ceding control to business in what I have elsewhere characterized as "reciprocal consent."[107]

Italian state intervention needed allies, and its success was accomplished with the active collaboration of "political merchants."[108] If Mitsubishi founder Iwasaki is an icon for the collaborating military industrialist in Japan, in Italy it is Carlo Bombrini (and his successors, the Perrone brothers), through the firm, Ansaldo, which he founded in 1846.[109] The Triple Alliance required Italy to build bigger warships and more munitions, and Italian industrialists were happy to oblige. None could have been more pleased than Ansaldo and few benefited more extensively. In a remarkable echo of the Japanese pattern, Ansaldo's early fortunes were made in banking, and its political fortunes were ensured when its Banca Nazionale became chief financier of Cavour's activities. This relationship continued after unification. Bombrini used his political connections to get contracts for navy vessels and military equipment. His aim was to create a vertically integrated combine powered by the Italian treasury.[110] The price Ansaldo paid was subordination to the state. This "arsenal of

Garibaldi's Thousand" seems profoundly Mitsubishi-like to observers of Japan: "Ansaldo represents a striking case of a private industrial company whose fortunes were shaped by state intervention to promote economic development . . . State economic policies and Ansaldo's management strategy were strongly conditioned by an economic nationalism which sought to make Italy both a great industrial and a strong military power."[111]

Yet it is the *differences* between Mitsubishi and Ansaldo that reveal larger truths. Bombrini's initiatives may have been a response to Cavour's efforts to stimulate the military economy, but he established Ansaldo with a *British* partner. Ansaldo's fortunes were as closely tied to foreign capital as they were to state procurement. In Italy, Ansaldo and other firms—even those built by the state—accepted foreign technology *and* foreign capital, and so at certain key points, Ansaldo was at the forefront of the struggle *against* protectionism. In the mid-1880s, Ansaldo vigorously protested higher prices for steel. Early in Italian industrialization, Italy had Rossi pushing one way and Bombrini pulling in another. Not surprisingly, Ansaldo's fortunes, like those of the economy as a whole, were whipped about wildly by the whims of the Italian state, which between the 1880s and 1920s shifted often from direct support of industry to fiscal retrenchment.

Rossi's expectation, the emergence of a collective national industrial interest, had been dashed. And, much worse, the tariffs he had done so much to promote stimulated precisely the social unrest he had warned would result from free trade. Meanwhile, Italian exporters lost their most important markets, and industrial jobs were threatened by the high costs of imported iron and steel.[112] Railroad and shipping firms imported their carriages and vessels because they were cheaper than those available through local procurement. Even Ansaldo had to pay as much in duties on materials to build a locomotive as it would have cost merely to import one whole. Only state procurement saved the firm in the late 1880s. Indeed, Ansaldo was the paradigmatic victim of Italy's rather porous protectionism.

By the late 1880s, the Left began organizing the nation's first industrial strikes. Northern industrialists and southern landlords were locked in common cause—both codependents of the state. Social unrest increased, and Crispi's government—despite promising social harmony in the spirit of Mazzini—responded to calls from landlords and industrialists to repress protest. Peasants joined *fasci* to force concessions from landowners. The government faced secessionist movements and possible civil war. It was not at all what Rossi had expected and a lot more than he had bargained for. The Italian economy had grown, but very unevenly and with far more difficulty than any of its architects had imagined. Per capita income before the turn of the century was barely half that of France, with which it had tried to do battle.[113] Italy enjoyed a trade surplus only once between 1861 and 1890. Fiscal crises had come and gone . . . and come again. Social unrest threatened other gains.

In 1892 Italy got its first taste of Giovanni Giolitti, who would be the last leader of liberal Italy. Giolitti's solution was to reconfigure the nation's economy. His first move was to open agricultural markets in a unilateral effort to seek a new, freer trade regime. Proclaiming his intention "above all to facilitate the exportation of agrarian products," he negotiated commercial treaties in 1892 first with Switzerland, then with Germany and Austria.[114] With state firms and cartels taking care of heavy industry, he sought to reduce tariffs on manufactured goods while favoring agriculture and producers of semifinished manufactured goods.

Giolitti acknowledged that he was as flexible in economics as he was in politics. During a debate on trade in May 1890, he spoke from the floor of the Senate, presumably with Alessandro Rossi in attendance. His declaration nicely (and critically) summarized the distance Italy had traveled in the previous half century, and anticipated how far it would travel by the time his own work was done:

> I declare frankly that in economic matters I do not recognize dogmas. I remember when I was a youth it was considered impossible that protectionist ideas could still be adhered to. I heard people speak of protectionism as a thing of the past and anyone who would have spoken of it as a serious thing would have been considered a person foreign to the modern world. Now, instead, we are in a period in which the free traders, in turn, are considered somewhat backwards. I do not know what the current of ideas will be in ten or fifteen years, but for my part I do not believe that a government can profess dogmas either in one sense or the other.[115]

Giolitti accelerated Italy's geopolitical tilt toward its northern neighbors and encouraged the substitution of German for French dominance in domestic financial markets. Under his program the German-controlled Banca Commerciale replaced French banks as the lead industrial creditor in Italy's modernization.[116] The needs of the Italian economy were routinely sacrificed to foreign payment schedules. Northern machinery makers and chemical manufacturers bore the brunt of these changes, but agriculture prospered. Giolitti rejected Rossi's demands for wholesale protection and "national industry," but was willing to intervene selectively. He explained to Rossi that protectionism at home invited retaliation abroad and that a "stable and prosperous protectionism" was as oxymoronic as a "stable and prosperous free trade." That said, he erected moderate barriers and reoriented Italy's industrial structure.[117]

But Giolitti could satisfy no one and was roundly distrusted by all. Some southerners complained that northern manufacturers still got too much from the arrangements. Northern industrialists refused to go along with protection of southern agriculture. Each side was convinced Giolitti was pandering to the other. Vilfredo Pareto insisted that Giolitti was pandering to *everyone* with equal vigor, even the working class. As we shall see in chapter 4, Giolitti was an outspoken proponent of social justice. Still, his efforts were dismissed as rank extortion and distributional excesses, designed to pay off workers and keep the social peace: "We are today living under a regime that is the worst of all possible. A regime in which a small band of sharks holds itself in power by throwing some mouthfuls to the future proletariat bandit . . . Social revolution is by far preferable to a continuation of this demagogic plutocracy which makes the proletarians the blackmailers of the nation and has rendered meaningless the power of the state."[118]

Amid all the criticism and mistrust, the old banking system collapsed in 1893 after French financiers withdrew much of their funds. The new banking system put German financiers in their place. Many created holding companies on the German model that controlled even Italian munitions firms. When Giolitti formed his second government in 1903, he reaffirmed his tariff policy of 1892 and moved closer than ever to the Banca Commerciale—the so-called German Bank (Banca Tedesca)—which he used for diplomatic interventions and for campaign finance. In the years leading up to World War I, Italian duties on manufactured products were among the lowest in Europe and North America. It all seemed to work. Italy enjoyed its first economic miracle, one that included rapid large-scale electrification and heavy industrial development.

Meanwhile, Ansaldo had entered into a joint venture with Armstrong, one of the world's largest arms makers. This pitted them against a Vickers-Terni alliance that formed in 1903. Unlike the strategic partnering that characterized Japanese joint ventures with foreign firms (whereby firms collaborated with the state to acquire needed technology that was then shared across the industry), Terni and Ansaldo were engaged in a bareknuckled war. For its part, the Italian state made no effort to reduce the predictably overheated, excessive competition that resulted.[119] It is hard to make the case for an economic nationalism that was anything like what had developed in Japan.

The tie between Ansaldo and Armstrong was broken in 1912, but the Ansaldo-Terni fratricide continued to take its toll. Ansaldo created its own bank, the Banca di Sconto, to rival the Banca Commerciale, and had just begun exploring export markets in Argentina and Turkey when war found the firm on the wrong side. For a short time, it did not matter. After all, the Banca Commerciale, with its German technology and resources, was in even greater danger in Italy. Ansaldo, waving the Italian flag, grew from six thousand to nearly one hundred thousand workers during the First World War, and its capital increased nearly tenfold.[120] Because "the Banca Commerciale was the financial heart of an industrial system which embraced virtually all of Ansaldo's rivals," the larger battle was Ansaldo's "crusade" against it.[121]

But Ansaldo had its own contradictions. It was now the beneficiary of French diplomacy aimed at weaning Italy from the Triple Alliance. Ansaldo, with French support, became the leading financier of nationalist politicians.[122] Together they attacked Giolitti and the Banca Commerciale relentlessly, calling the latter a Trojan horse through which Germany would dominate Italy. "Nationalist" Ansaldo also used French support to bankroll the leading nationalist newspaper, *L'Idea Nazionale,* as well as Mussolini's own *Il Popolo d'Italia.*[123] It is no small irony—and no irrelevant contrast to Japan—that the ultranationalists who sought to emancipate Italy from dependence on Germany would do so with French coins in their pockets.

Eventually, of course, these nationalists and industrialists succeeded in bringing Italy into the war. Among the many lasting economic lessons of the First World War were three that the Japanese learned as well. First, industry and government planners could collaborate to mutual advantage. Second, manufacturing and finance could draw closer together in giant combines. Third, this concentration could destabilize the larger economy.[124] Italy lost six hundred thousand men in the war—but even more were demobilized into unemployment when the Italian government discontinued war orders in November 1918. Ansaldo's domestic market collapsed. The Perrone brothers pleaded for government support and pressed for a state-run employment program that would prop up the economy. The government never responded.[125] In 1920, teetering on bankruptcy, this nominally nationalist firm appealed to the French government to intervene. The French wisely stayed out of it. Rather than stimulate the economy, Giolitti instituted an austerity program to reduce spending and balance the budget.

DIFFERENT IDEAS

This compact account of three critical choices made in the industrial development of Japan and Italy is punctuated by parallels and by surprises. Japan may be known as an archetypally dirigiste economy, but it was Japan that undertook the earliest and most extensive privatization in economic history. Meanwhile Italy, known as a chronically *weak* state, saw a massive reallocation of ownership once the state began its military mobilization. Similarly, we are forced to reconsider the standard sketch of Italian entrepreneurs, who are normally depicted as a lethargic, grasping bunch—individuals who could not sustain the energy required for growth.[126] Without suggesting that Italian entrepreneurs were visionary collectivists (they were not) or that Japanese business leaders were mere utility maximizers (they were not), we have seen how Italian entrepreneurs made critical (albeit late) choices for a mercantilist economy, and how Japanese entrepreneurs made sure to keep the state at arm's length. Political merchants in both countries benefited from and contributed to their state as much as they benefited from and contributed to their corporate empires. As we shall see, these relationships would endure.

We also examined the resources available to the architects of the modern Italian and Japanese economies. While the basic factor endowments of land, labor, and capital were not dramatically different, leaders in the two economies faced industrialization with material resources different in at least one important respect. In Italy, because the kingdoms were separate and mutually hostile, there was virtually no economic integration before the Risorgimento. Cavour had to eliminate internal tariffs before he could address foreign trade. By contrast, Japanese economic integration had proceeded throughout the Edo period. A national commercial economy was already in place by the time of the Restoration.

Ideational resources seem to have mattered even more. Leaders in both countries had liberal and mercantilist models before them—each could draw lessons from England or from Germany. Their specialists studied best practices across Europe and North America. Each had a fairly unrestricted view of the successes and errors of those who went before them. They had the same enhanced range of options available to all late developers, and each took care to understand the British, the German, and the American experiences. But, they made different choices about how to organize their economy.

Although Japanese government leaders were less prescient than some have posited—they had no coherent master plan—they *were* quicker than their Italian contemporaries to understand the risks and benefits of self-reliance. They made very different policy choices. The Japanese oligarchs—particularly Ōkubo Toshimichi—accelerated growth and technological learning while preserving national autonomy. Indeed, Ōkubo opted for protection even when it was the most difficult choice Japan could make. As the process unwound, Japanese private capital extracted considerable benefits from the state in exchange for cooperation. Despite a voracious appetite for foreign technology, Japanese leaders sought no foreign loans and welcomed no foreign investment. By contrast, Italian leaders tried to close the barn door after the horse had bolted. Italy's was at best a *porous* protectionism. Tariffs were high for traded goods, while foreign financiers were always welcomed. Japan insulated itself far more effectively. Japan's developmental ideology was coherent and consistently applied. Italian leaders embraced and abandoned ideas about economic management, and economic nationalism was often invoked for mere convenience.[127]

Industry would retain degrees of freedom, but the public would do less well. After all, it was fascism and not liberalism that would prevail. Liberals fought a losing battle in both countries, but they would lose this battle for different reasons. In the Japanese case, marginalized liberals fought with both arms tied behind their back, while in Italy, empowered liberals had two arms free, but dropped their weapons . . . and their guard. We turn next to the ways in which liberalism died. The outcome turns on the choices made by Prime Ministers Giovanni Giolitti and Hara Kei as they confronted massive social change in the early twentieth century.

PART II

LIBERAL EXHAUSTION:
THE EARLY TWENTIETH CENTURY

CHAPTER FOUR

The Death of Liberalism:

GIOVANNI GIOLITTI AND HARA KEI

> Let it be taken for granted that workman and employer should, as a rule, make free agreements, in particular should agree freely as to wages; nevertheless, there is a dictate of natural justice more imperious and ancient than any bargain between man and man, that remuneration should be sufficient to maintain the wage earner in reasonable and frugal comfort. If through necessity or fear of a worse evil the workman accepts harder conditions because an employer or contractor will afford him no better, he is made the victim of force and injustice.
>
> Pope Leo XIII, *Rerum Novarum*, 1891

Giovanni Giolitti (1842–1928) and Hara Takashi (Kei) (1856–1921) were the last important liberal politicians before the authoritarian curtains were lowered after World War I. Each stood above and apart from his peers in his ability to manipulate, co-opt, and coerce. Each governed effectively, stretching similar constraints imposed by industry, nationalists, left-wing parties, and rural landowners. They also shared the common challenge of expanding the electorate during a period when mass politics was becoming an insistent presence. Trade unions and working-class parties were exerting significant pressure, while capitalists divided their support among rival conservative parties and pressed for the repression of strikes and union bargaining.

Giolitti and Hara responded to the exigencies of mass politics in strikingly different ways. In the end, neither succeeded fully, but each left an institutional legacy for parliamentary politics—a blueprint for how to manage democratic participation that post-authoritarian leaders freely borrowed and used to better advantage. While both learned how to distribute state resources to win support, Giolitti showed how liberalism could accommodate social policy and social justice, a lesson not lost on those who designed the First Italian Republic after 1945. Hara took a different

99

route, constricting liberalism in favor of a statist social policy and a distributional politics that excluded labor. He pioneered a model of compensation and exchange built on single party dominance in concert with the bureaucracy that would become the backbone of conservative rule after competitive politics was reintroduced in 1946.

Both men cut their teeth as domestic policy bureaucrats in the first flush of national industrial development. Giolitti was the first of Italy's great politicians to come of age after the Risorgimento. But he was a bureaucrat first. For twenty years, Giolitti served virtually all the post-unification leaders, and helped write Italy's tax and civil codes and the regulations for local public administration. Hara was the son of a high-ranking northeastern samurai who had risen to defend the shogunate. His native Morioka was an enemy of the Restoration forces and, after a Western education, Hara began his career as a journalist who argued in favor of extending "liberty and popular rights."[1] His opposition to a constitutional monarchy notwithstanding, in 1882 he became an imperial bureaucrat, first in the Ministry of Foreign Affairs, and then in the Ministry of Agriculture and Commerce. Like Giolitti a world away, Hara had remarkably bold ideas about governance, and wasted little time working to politicize the bureaucracy. In 1890, he began pressing for ability as a criterion for promotion. He openly sought to weaken the oligarchs' hold over key posts, to replace them with his own allies, and to co-opt the remaining bureaucrats.

In 1900 Hara helped Itō Hirobumi and Saionji Kinmochi form the Seiyūkai, the first party to reconcile the oligarchs and bureaucrats with politicians. He was rewarded for his efforts with the portfolio of the powerful home ministry three times in the decade 1905–1915. Given his rank, he might easily have received an appointment to the House of Peers. Instead, Hara chose to stand for a lower house seat.[2] From his post as home minister, he appointed the nation's governors and police chiefs, and placed loyal associates in important positions in communications, civil engineering, economic development, and elections. Like Giolitti, Hara appointed governors and police chiefs friendly to the Seiyūkai who could be counted on to harass political opponents. Also like Giolitti, he appointed election officials who would stuff ballot boxes if the need arose.[3] Hara's use of fiscal policy to win political support was also widespread. Working with his minister of finance, Takahashi Koreikyo, Hara adopted a vigorous program of public works to expand local support for the party, including plans to build nearly two hundred new rail lines. Hara learned early that "it was more important to win friends than to win arguments."[4] And as Hara himself put it: "If you don't give men official position or money, they won't be moved."[5] Long before becoming prime minister in 1918, he had turned the Seiyūkai into a formidable political machine.[6] By 1913 the party was formally his, as were—informally—a significant number of bureaucrats.

Giovanni Giolitti's path was remarkably similar. In 1892, a decade after his first election to Parliament, Giolitti formed his first of five governments. By the time his career was finished, he had established himself as "the dominant political figure of the first decade of the twentieth century in Italy."[7] That is not to suggest that Giolitti was popular or admired. To the contrary, he was widely reviled. To his many detractors, he was "Minister of the Underworld," a corrupt master of spoils and a betrayer of democratic ideals. Contemporaries labeled his governments the "Giolittian Dictatorship."[8] Historians, however, have been more generous. He so dominated politics from 1890 to 1921 that they routinely label it "The Giolittian Age."[9] Giovanni Giolitti was a leader who might have stepped from the pages of a Machiavellian thesaurus: manipulative, unscrupulous, shrewd, opportunistic, cunning. Without even a hint of irony, his successor, Benito Mussolini—one of the most amoral politicians in world history—says that Giolitti "never gave any evidence of believing in the deep idealistic springs and streams of Italian life."[10] Don Sturzo, the founder of Italy's first Catholic political party, and a highly principled enemy of both Mussolini and Giolitti, wrote that Giolitti was "as devoid of scruple as of idealism."[11] Antonio Gramsci, who inspired generations of Italian communists, was never impressed with the support Giolitti extended to labor, which he derided as mere tactical shifts—famously remarking that Giolitti was merely "shifting his rifle from one shoulder to the other."[12] As we shall see, Mussolini, Sturzo, and Gramsci were not entirely right.

It was not their *methods* that distinguished Hara and Giolitti, but their *choices*. And these choices—Giolitti for the incorporation of the Left, Hara for its exclusion—were made in remarkably similar political contexts and with remarkably similar resources.

THEIR CONTEXTS

Giolitti

Italian liberalism was in disarray when Giolitti arrived on the scene. The party that had been the expression of Italian unification now stood for everything in general and nothing in particular. Liberals had both called for the extension of suffrage and repressed workers' rights. They had championed political freedoms—but had broken opposition coalitions apart and crushed local autonomy. Some called for mass participation, while others sought a royal dictatorship. Liberalism in Italy—as in Japan—was pre-democratic.[13] It preceded and (Giolitti excepted) failed to anticipate mass politics. Uninterrupted liberal rule, whether of the so-called Left or so-called Right, was a period of unrelenting tumult. Rather than mirror the stable alternation of mutually correcting parties that characterized the England that Cavour so admired, Italian liberals dissolved into temporary cliques of self-interested politicians. "[Then they would] . . . change again when opportunity or vanity or interest provided a motive or pretext. Thus, ideas and programs, interests and personal power merged continually one into the other, democrats acted as reactionaries, pacifists were imperialists, moderates became anti-clericals."[14] This was a drifting, amoebic party of conservative elites, one accustomed to hand-to-hand combat. As Salomone says, Italian liberalism "seemed to have lost the heroic efficiency which a generation of statesmen, economists, and myth-makers had given it . . . The only remnant of liberalism appeared to be a skill in the art of government which succeeded in tempering its oligarchical tendencies . . . (T)he heritage of the *Risorgimento* and of Cavourian liberalism . . . [was] *giolittismo*."[15]

The Italy that Giolitti would govern was not the new Rome that Mazzini had envisioned but a degenerating state rife with social unrest. Although Giolitti would accomplish much of what the Risorgimento had failed to achieve, his efforts to adapt liberalism to mass democracy would fail. He would be attacked from every direction, and ultimately—in large part because he failed to understand how to organize mass publics—the result would be a lost generation. The Italian state would be captured and transformed by Mussolini.

Hara

The social unrest in the Japan that Hara inherited was complicated by Japanese foreign affairs. In July 1894, Japan's leaders felt ready for a test of her international strength. Under terms of an earlier treaty, Japan sent troops to Korea to meet forces sent by China at the request of the Korean government. The Japanese defeated the Chinese, and advanced northward into Manchuria. Her navy dominated Chinese coastal waters as well. At the March 1895 treaty of Shimonoseki, China ceded Formosa, the Pescadores, and the Liaotung Peninsula to Japan, as well as opening new ports for preferential trade and paying a large indemnity.

The response at home was euphoric—and universally characterized in terms of Japan's chase of parity with the great powers. The *Mainichi Shimbun* editorialized after early victories that "hitherto Europe was blind to

Japan's true greatness and apt to slight her . . . This . . . is the beginning of a new era of Japanese greatness."[16] Japan's first modern military victory was a matter of pride for liberal intellectuals for the same reason. The liberal Fukuzawa Yukichi was among those who celebrated Japan's coming of age as an imperial power:

> One can scarcely enumerate all of our civilized undertakings since the Restoration—the abolition of feudalism, the lowering of class barriers, revision of our laws, promotion of education, railroads, electricity, postal service, printing and on and on. Yet among these enterprises, the one thing none of us Western scholars ever expected, thirty or forty years ago, was the establishment of Japan's imperial prestige in a great war . . . When I think of our marvelous fortune, I feel as though in a dream and can only weep tears of joy."[17]

The euphoria was short-lived, however. It turned to widespread indignation and civil discontent when, a week after the peace treaty was signed, Russia organized a "Triple Intervention" with France and Germany, forcing Japan to relinquish all claims on the Liaotung Peninsula. The United States and Britain stood aside. Japan's leadership, humiliated at home, was determined to maintain in peace what it would next win in war.

In February 1902, as a measure of just how far she had come, Japan entered her first modern alliance—with Great Britain, the world's greatest power. Japan and Britain found common cause in blocking Russian expansion after Russia took the Liaotung Peninsula in 1898. The treaty recognized British rights in China and Japanese rights in China and Korea. If either signatory became engaged in hostilities in the region, the other was required to remain neutral. It was the first time Japan had been treated as an equal.

A test soon came. In 1904, when Russia refused to withdraw from Manchuria after protracted negotiations, Japan initiated hostilities. After a prolonged and deadly land war through which the Japanese pushed the Russian army back toward Mukden, the Imperial Navy annihilated the Russian fleet in the Straits of Tsushima. U.S. mediation in Portsmouth, New Hampshire, led to Japanese rights in Manchuria—where Japan could enjoy the mixed blessing of broad colonial autonomy without a formally established colony. Japan also received the naval base at Port Arthur and the South Manchurian Railway system, as well as a twenty-five-year lease on Kwantung and effective carte blanche on the Korean Peninsula, where Itō Hirobumi made himself resident-general.[18]

Unlike the war with China, a crumbling and already semicolonial state, victory over Russia was a victory over a European power. Now Japan could demonstrate the righteousness of its claims for equality and for a "proper" place in the world. Its state-building and industrial development were vindicated. The success further opened the door to revision of the unequal treaties, and heartened many with its racial message: a European people can be defeated in war by non-Europeans. In August 1905, Japanese ambitions were rewarded with an extension of the alliance with Great Britain to include protection of British interests in India. After two military victories, Japan's great power aspirations—fully in keeping with those of the Europeans and Americans—were ever more transparent.

The Japanese negotiators who went to Portsmouth as victors returned with less than they sought and less than most Japanese thought they deserved. There was no indemnification from Russia, although Japan's treasury had been drained by the war. Once again, pride in military victory was transformed by diplomatic defeat. Newspapers demanded that the treaty not be ratified; some even obliquely advocated physical violence against government officials. The government declared martial law, but not before a week of riots in Tokyo, the destruction of churches, and efforts to burn the homes of cabinet ministers.[19] The success of Japan's chase for parity had fueled a demand for even fuller international recognition—a demand that was politically manifest at home.

At the turn of the century a new group of leaders was settling into power. The original Meiji oligarchs would soon pass from the scene without having prepared for their succession.[20] Those who followed represented a broader swatch of institutions and regions than their predecessors. Some were politicians, others were bureaucrats in the powerful home ministry and the military. Despite the best efforts of Yamagata and Itō, the social mobilization unleashed by Japan's rapid economic development had helped transform politics. This politics was still what Titus has called a "competition to declare the imperial will," but what had been control by fewer than a dozen men was now a battle between the home ministry and the army for control of the police, between the army and the navy for control of the military, between politicians and bureaucrats for control of the economy, and between the army and the foreign ministry for control of foreign policy.[21]

The rise of the politicians was perhaps the greatest frustration for Yamagata and Itō, who had worked so diligently to keep the Diet weak. It began with the first parliamentary elections in 1890, when three parties led by former oligarchs captured the majority of seats. Yamagata and Itō were quick to recognize what was happening, but only Itō was willing to make an early peace with party politicians. When Itō reached out to co-opt one of them, Yamagata blocked him. Indeed, within a month, Yamagata revised the regulations for Public Meetings and Political Associations to forbid parties from combining or even communicating with one another.[22] The February 1892 elections, which produced an anti-Yamagata majority in the House of Representatives, were notorious for police interference and for the deaths of twenty-five people in election-related violence.[23]

It was an inauspicious start; the lines were being drawn not only between the oligarchs and the politicians, but also between Yamagata and Itō. By 1900, even Itō resorted to forming a political party in order to control increasingly fractious relations between the parties and the state.[24] Itō's Seiyūkai drew heavily upon his bureaucratic allies. He also added support from the urban business class. Itō was not above playing the imperial card, however—a trump card largely of his own design. During a particularly heated confrontation with political opponents who demanded his resignation in 1901, Itō declared, "You seem to be determined to force the resignation of my government . . . But in so much as I still have the confidence of the Emperor, I could not possibly relinquish my post on account of a mere resolution."[25] He and Yamagata now parted ways. Japanese government shifted back and forth between the Yamagata forces of order and the Itō forces of limited representation for the next decade, as each jockeyed to control the voice of the emperor.

Between 1905 and 1918, Yamagata enhanced state powers at every turn, yet had to accommodate the fact that each cabinet had the support of a majority. Not only did the number of politicians who held cabinet positions steadily increase, but by the 1910s, in what is surely a measure of the changing balance of power, bureaucrats and even some soldiers were beginning to resign in large numbers to run for political office.[26] One stood out for his skills and for his potential to transform the institutions of Japanese politics: Hara Kei. His failure to confront Yamagata and enhance parliamentary governance, at what likely was the last moment that chance was available, was made all the more tragic by the fact that, like Giovanni Giolitti in Italy, he was fully aware that such a moment existed.

Their Resources and Choices

Giolitti

One observer has concluded that "Giolitti's genius was to comprehend what must be done."[27] Giolitti believed that liberalism could accommodate workers—and that this was in the nation's best interests. In the incorporation of the masses, he saw the possibility of marginalizing the *real* threats to liberal values: the church, the socialists, and the nationalists.

His was a new Italian liberalism, one infused with the social conscience so conspicuously absent in the old version. Even Benedetto Croce admired this idea as a "widening of the spiritual horizon" in Italy.[28] For Giolitti, social peace and material progress both depended on the way in which workers would be brought into the system. His reactionary forebears (and contemporary opponents on the right) considered all trade unions dangerous. For Giolitti, however, "The amelioration of the condition of the workers was in my opinion the dominating problem of the moment . . . The future of our civilization and the prosperity and greatness of our country depended directly, I believed, on the gradual and pacific improvement of the moral and material conditions of the masses."[29] He was convinced that the alternative—"put[ting] obstacles in the way of this movement"—"would have no other effect than to render the working classes enemies of the state."[30]

The Left was the object of Giolitti's most energetic blandishments.[31] Filippo Turati gathered more than two hundred delegates in Genoa to create the Italian Socialist Party (PSI) in 1892, the same year that Giolitti formed his first government. The PSI was an admixture of diverse and schismatic working-class movements, some violent and revolutionary, others moderate and reformist—all of which had been repressed in the 1880s. It immediately split in two when a group of anarchists refused to accept reformist norms. Still, within five years the PSI had more that twenty-five thousand members and in 1900 it won thirty-two seats in Parliament. By 1902 it had established seventy-six "Chambers of Labor" (Camere del lavoro) throughout central and northern Italy to coordinate workers' demands and protect employment. Italy was developing a large, albeit as yet incoherent, socialist subculture that could challenge both church and state.

The failures of repeated authoritarian experiments by earlier liberals convinced Giolitti that Italy's rapid economic development was creating a new politics. Novel politically relevant groups—such as organized labor—would join, rather than displace, existing actors in the panoply of Italian political forces. He was developing strategies to "center" his ideas and actions when opportunities presented themselves. At different times and in different measures, he found ways to tease business, trade unions, left-wing parties, the Church, regional interests, and nationalists on the far Right into one or another temporary coalition.

As a liberal, Giolitti had something of a natural claim on the support of industry and the landed elite. As we have seen, he governed during Italy's first economic miracle, and was able to take some credit for the immense expansion in the North, which had become one of Europe's leading industrial regions by the turn of the century. The number of industrial workers nearly doubled between 1903 and 1921. By 1913, industry was for the first time a larger share of the economy than agriculture. Despite rapid growth in military industries, textile manufactures—led by silk and cotton—still had the largest workforce of any industry in Italy. Now Italian industrialists would organize. In 1900 the League of Industrialists of Biella was established to confront organized labor in the textile industry. In 1906, representatives of seventy-five sectors established the Industrial League of Turin for the same purpose. This Piedmont group was followed by one in Lombardy, and in 1910 they reorganized as the Italian Confederation of Industry, the progenitor of Confindustria, Italy's peak business group, which was finally established in April 1919.[32] In short, industry— excluding small and medium-sized enterprises—secured a powerful place in Italian politics long before the rise of fascism. In Italy, as in Japan, large financial and industrial interests divided their support among conservative cliques.

The most powerful regional interests were the southern landlords on whose support Giolitti depended. The South was far behind the North on every social and economic indicator. Giolitti rejected the "myth of the South" (*il mito del mezzogiorno*)—that it was the garden of Italy that would forever support the nation by exporting cash crops. To the contrary, he believed that the South was a special problem that required state intervention. Rural landowners claimed to be insulted by what they termed Giolitti's "charity" but accepted it without flinching. He launched rural development programs, from Naples on south, to build canals, electrification, irrigation, and to provide potable water. Crispi's repression of the Sicilian *fasci* in the mid-1890s was just the sort of polarizing inheritance that animated Giolitti's new liberalism.

Like early twentieth-century capitalists everywhere, Italian industrialists were selectively liberal, railing against state intervention except in the cases of tariffs and suppression of worker organization. They expected Giolitti's government to support them in confrontations with workers. But Giolitti considered labor conflict merely another form of free economic competition, one in which the state had only limited jurisdiction. He sarcastically compared conservative attacks on him for "encouraging" labor struggle as akin to "blaming an astronomer for having 'encouraged the moon to pass before the sun' because he foresaw an eclipse."[33]

Initially, Giolitti directed the state toward mediation between employers and workers; he held that it was the "social apostolate" of state officials to step in. If their liberalism (like Hara's) was selective, his was comprehensive. Giolitti adopted the pragmatic position that workers were free to strike, but that nonstrikers were equally free to work. Thus, his prefects ended up defending both the strikers and the scabs—something more than both the Socialists and the industrialists had bargained for. In 1901, as part of his seduction of the Left, Giolitti instructed his prefects to remain neutral in labor disputes. The predictable consequence was an immediate, rapid increase in strikes. None were violent.

Within a year, Giolitti was allowing his prefects to use force selectively against strikers. In 1903, to end a railway workers' strike he saw as a threat to the national interest, Giolitti militarized the workers, subjecting them to military discipline and ending the strike by government fiat.[34] But labor unrest was never fully ameliorated, and in 1904 the maximalist Socialists, following the lead of southern rioters, organized the world's first successful general strike. Reform Socialists, unable to moderate their more radical brethren and unwilling to bolt the party, capitulated. Enraging liberals and conservatives alike, Giolitti refused to force the workers back.

Characteristically, Giolitti hedged his bet on the Left by attempting to co-opt the Church. In 1904, after the general strike, Pope Pius X modified the ban on Catholic participation in politics (*Non expedit*). Preoccupied by the threat from freemasons and radicals, the Church now allowed Catholics to "do as their conscience dictates"—to vote and to serve as elected representatives. Although the Vatican was not yet ready for a mass-based political party, it became more openly engaged in politics—and policy. Amid fears of "theocratic tyranny" from one side and "Masonic conspiracy" from the other, Giolitti recused himself from a controversial divorce bill, compensated the Vatican for seized property, entertained the idea of compulsory religious education, and even placed Catholics in the Ottoman Empire under the protection of the Italian state. He proclaimed that the Center was the proper place for the state: "The Italian people," he declared, "did not intend to permit certain limits to be exceeded by any side."[35] With Church support, Giolitti was able to achieve reasonably stable majorities across the next several elections.

But he never stopped trying to placate the Left. Early in his second government, he reversed his position on universal male suffrage. To the "general wonderment" of his opponents, who believed that a broader suffrage would break his southern electoral grip, he judged his social policies had helped create conditions that made an electoral machine necessary.[36] Believing that he could control the electorate just as he had controlled the Parliament, he moved to co-opt the socialist position on voting rights by endorsing the extension of suffrage.[37] Meanwhile, he persuaded his Parliament that the entry of the masses into politics could be negotiated on favorable terms. Workers were, he argued, now well enough educated to participate responsibly in politics, as collaborators with the existing powers rather than as exasperated revolutionaries.[38]

In March 1911, his Parliament agreed to a limited extension of suffrage.[39] Giolitti convinced himself and his allies that he was buying an-

Avoiding strikes, social revolution, and foreign intervention, Giovanni Giolitti steers the Italian "ship of state" toward the rising sun of Filippo Turati's Socialist Party in 1902. Reproduced courtesy of the Biblioteca Comunale dell'Archiginnasio, Bologna.

other generation of domestic tranquility rather than opening Pandora's box. It seemed a brilliant stroke, for the number of socialists would be limited, and Catholics would be compelled to make deals directly with Giolitti in order to maximize their representation. No liberal politician before him had had to worry quite as much about masses of voters. Giolitti attended to his southern clientele and his northern industrial partners ever more carefully. When his opponents demanded a wider extension, Giolitti responded by advocating universal suffrage for the first time. Meanwhile, he moved to pacify the Left by introducing a national insurance scheme and by financing other social welfare programs in an effort to keep control of social policy away from the Church.[40]

Like Cavour before him, Giolitti hoped for a Church that would accept the formula of "a free church in a free state" (*libera chiesa in libero stato*). He wished that church and state would forever remain parallel forces— and never meet. His ministries would not challenge the Church, if the Church would not challenge his ministries. He might have known this could not be. It was, after all, already several decades since the pope had issued his encyclical *Rerum Novarum* in May 1891, the first formal effort to articulate a social program compatible with democratic ideals. Opposed both to the materialism of the Left and to the conservatism of the Right, the Church was moving in fits and starts toward establishing a place for itself that was dangerously close to Giolitti's. For the Church, of course, an alliance with workers could galvanize the poor against the liberal state.

Although Pope Leo XIII had formally endorsed "Christian democracy" in 1901, just two years before Giolitti's second government, the Church's fundamentalist wing, fearing democracy and modernism, succeeded in having Christian democracy condemned just one year later. Giolitti had some breathing room, and moved vigorously to expand suffrage. It was not until 1919, after a decade in which a reactionary Vatican actively purged those who would make peace with secular politicians, that Don Sturzo would form the Popular Party (PP) with Vatican support. The Church finally had grown comfortable with Christian democratic promotion of civil liberties, political freedom, universal suffrage, local autonomy, and pacifism. Or at least it finally had come to terms with these ideas. Limits on Catholic participation in politics were rescinded, giving Giolitti a dangerous new competitor for power.

Meanwhile, Giolitti's political enemies on the right claimed Cavour's mantle for themselves.[41] Between his first and second governments, Sidney Sonnino and Antonio Salandra argued for a return to the more aristocratic letter of Lo Statuto. They sought an elite rule based on liberal principles, among which individual freedom, opposition to the Church, and the wise and patriotic exercise of power by an elite would suffice. They, and the reactionary General Pelloux, pushed Giolitti aside for a time in the 1890s, as Italy turned to repression again. Freedoms of speech, press, and assembly were suspended. Giolitti called their invocation of Cavour "one of the most audacious falsifications of history."[42] He stood before the Chamber in 1898 and asked: "And should we, after fifty years of free life, restrict our liberties on account of tumults which had their origin in an exceptional misery?"[43] He later described these right-wing liberals as "conservatives coated with a thin varnish of liberalism."[44] Both in and out of power, Giolitti stood against them, arguing that reaction and liberalism could not coexist. But, his attractive rhetorical flourishes notwithstanding, he was always prepared to accommodate an ally.

These aristocratic reactionaries knew little of—and cared little for—the general public. Following hard upon them were populist reactionaries, who would capture nationalism, dress it in Mazzini's clothing, and carry it (and Giolitti) to disastrous foreign adventures. Part of the problem was that unlike Cavour, who deeply understood the diplomacy he used for domestic ends, Giolitti had paid little attention to the world outside Italy, except in economic affairs. Giolitti valued Germany as an ally in part because he did not want to be burdened with foreign policy. This was not enough. Nationalism, still a weak reed at the turn of the century, was, by

World War I, Italy's most virulent political force and Giolitti's most implacable political problem. It began in literary circles, as a "revivalist movement" that stressed past failures and the promise of a greater future.[45] Its main competitor was socialism, but Giolitti was in the way. There would be many casualties, and no prisoners taken.

The nationalist Right and the Church had never been more threatening to Giolitti. Miscalculating badly, he chose to appease them by undertaking a foreign war that fundamentally changed the balance of domestic forces. Diplomats and the military wanted to control the eastern Mediterranean coast of Africa. Nationalists wanted Italy's humiliating 1896 loss to Ethiopian troops avenged. Industry wanted war orders. Republicans saw an opportunity to break away from German influence. Southern peasants preferred emigration to an Italian colony over emigration to a foreign Western Hemisphere. And the Vatican urged Italy to push the Turks further from Italian shores.[46]

In September 1911, Giolitti declared war on the Ottoman Empire. He expected that the European powers would support Italian claims, but the Turks elicited German help, and European diplomacy leaned away from the Italian cause. The Socialist reaction to the war split the party. A young Benito Mussolini, then the most energetic of antiwar maximalists, railed against those who cooperated, and had them expelled from the party. Others, like Turati, who did not actively support the war, could never again collaborate with Giolitti. For his efforts, Mussolini was rewarded with the editorship of *Avanti!*, a perch from which he garnered national attention. Worst of all, war, which Giolitti had hoped would placate the nationalists, just made them more voracious.

Historians disagree on Giolitti's calculus. The dominant interpretation holds that war in Libya was the compensation Giolitti reluctantly paid for the Right's acquiescence to social reforms. On this view, Giolitti was throwing them a bone that got caught in his own throat. He wanted to gain points with the Right, the military, and the Crown, and speculated that a successful colonial policy would keep them in his camp. On the other side are those who see a Cavour-like maneuver that Giolitti could not control. They argue that he moved left expecting to benefit from reduced opposition to a war he intended to prosecute.[47] Giolitti himself denied he would "encourage a diplomatic incident abroad in order to extinguish domestic political conflicts." And he claimed that the Libyan war was "a simple consequence, a thing very different from a design." (He does not, however, indicate if it was a consequence of designs.)

Italy now had Libya, but Giolitti had neither the nationalists nor the Left on his side. In the first election after the Libyan War (the first election after suffrage had been extended), in October 1913, the Socialists abandoned Giolitti and ran a separate slate. Giolitti had few options, and no organized political base, so he moved to embrace the Church. More than two hundred Liberal deputies were elected with Catholic support. The price was state guarantees of the rights of the Church—more promises that would be costly to keep.[48]

Giolitti's accommodation of the Church was followed by a national debate about entry into the Great War in Europe and by one final, fatally miscalculated accommodation: his dance with fascism. The two were closely connected. Throughout the summer of 1914, Mussolini used his editorship of *Avanti!* to relentlessly propagandize for Italian neutrality: War, he declared, was the "maximum exploitation of the proletarian class." Further, he argued that "to declare war against nations with whom Italy was allied for over thirty years and until yesterday . . . would be repugnant to the Italian conscience [and would constitute a] stab in the back."[49] Then, without warning, Mussolini took out his own dagger. In October he disavowed his antimilitarism and demanded intervention against Germany and Austria. The same Mussolini who had reasoned that "war and socialism are profound and irreconcilable opposites," and who had purged party executives two years earlier for supporting the war in Libya, now proclaimed that this war was different. The man who had engineered purges of reformists in 1912 and of freemasons in 1914 now found himself expelled from the ever schismatic Socialist Party.[50] No matter. With money from the French government, which stood to gain from Italian help against Germany, Mussolini established a new newspaper, *Il Popolo d'Italia.* Reinventing himself as a nationalist, he also attracted support from the domestic military industry, so that after the French no longer needed Italian blood and withdrew support, he could turn to Ansaldo for money.[51]

In August 1914, Italy was in an enviable position. With no treaty obligations to uphold, Italy was free to enter negotiations with both the Entente and the Central Powers. While nationalists (now including Mussolini) and most Liberals saw the opportunity to regain lost territory from a crumbling Austro-Hungarian Empire and to gain territory from a crumbling Ottoman Empire, neither the remaining Socialists nor the Church wanted Italy to enter the war. And neither did Giolitti.

Giolitti had already stepped away from the prime ministership in March. Contrary to his expectations (and to his prior experience), the king did not call him back to lead the nation. Antonio Salandra, the man Giolitti had urged the king to appoint in his stead, had outmaneuvered him. In April 1915, Sidney Sonnino signed the Treaty of London, pledging to intervene against the Central Powers. (Just eight months earlier, he had pledged Italy's neutrality, but now much better terms were offered.)

In exchange for its participation, Italy would receive Trentino, Trieste, South Tyrol, a free hand in Albania, a large slice of Dalmatia, and colonial compensation in the Near East and Africa. In May 1915, nine months after the war had started, the king declared war on the Central Powers. Giolitti kept quiet for nearly the duration, but he opposed the war. He spoke out only in August 1917 in favor of self-determination, and against both his king and Salandra for their duplicity. He would not return to power until the guns were silent and the peace treaty signed.

Italy picked the winning side but lost the 1918 peace. Despite the 1915 treaty, the victors denied most of Italy's territorial claims. Woodrow Wilson, who had not been in London in 1915, now led the victors: Italy could "redeem" Trieste and Trentino, but the "overriding principles" of self-determination nullified any additional concessions promised by the British and French. Not only would Italy not gain territory, but it would also be confronted by a new Yugoslav state on its eastern border. Italy, which had sought to exploit the alliance, was betrayed and exploited instead.

Some believed that Italy did well enough and did not need most of the territories whose loss it was mourning, but the dominant reaction was fervently nationalist. Most blamed the result on diplomatic ineptitude. The socialist Gaetano Salvemini—enemy of both Giolitti and the fascists—would later compare postwar Italy to Molière's *malade imaginaire,* a country "unhappy about ailments it did not have. She needed no more than wisdom and a rest cure. She had little wisdom and instead of the rest cure she got Mussolini."[52]

First, however, she got Gabriele D'Annunzio, the audacious poet who forced the national issue in September 1919 when he and a group of regular troops and *arditi*, clad in uniforms of their own design, marched past cooperating Italian military units into Fiume to "redeem" it for the motherland. Within days, having stimulated a nationalist fervor and with a force of 15,000 troops, D'Annunzio founded his Regency of Carnaro. Even if, as Mack Smith says, the occupation of Fiume was a "petty and ridiculous affair in itself," the nationalists had their first flush of success; and they had the measure of the liberals who cowered before them.[53]

They were not finished. The Fiume experience was a prototype Mussolini would develop into a fuller working model three years later. Giolitti formed his fifth and final government at seventy-seven years of age in 1920. Abandoned by the Left and by the Catholics, he betrayed his liberal ideals, using fascists to intimidate voters. But he had to get D'Annunzio out of Fiume if he were to have any chance of electoral success. In November he signed a treaty with Yugoslavia in Rapallo, fixing their borders and making Fiume a free state. The next month he ordered the military to remove D'Annunzio; they did so, with the loss of fifty-three lives. In January 1921 the Socialists split as he expected, but the split left the reformists unexpectedly weak—and with a new Communist Party on their left. Giolitti, now formally allied with the fascists, called an election. He abandoned his Catholic allies, calling them "white Bolsheviks," and sought to govern on the right. Amid all this juggling he got the worst possible result: the Socialists, the Communists, and the Catholics all gained, and he could not control the bloc of thirty-five fascist deputies he brought into the Chamber. Giolitti's last government fell in June 1921, unable to survive even six months. His Liberal colleagues rushed to cultivate Mussolini, with industrialists cheering in the background. Within a year, and after considerable extraparliamentary intimidation of the body politic, Italy had a fascist prime minister. The former intransigent socialist Benito Mussolini, now wrapped in D'Annunzio's nationalist mantle, would rule fascist Italy for two decades.

Giolitti is often blamed for delivering Italy to Mussolini.[54] And he did. After using fascist thugs to wring votes for his government—and after failing to convince Don Sturzo and the Catholic Popolari to join the government—Giolitti brought Mussolini into his coalition. He confidently assumed he could tame Mussolini and temper the fascist arditi by binding them with the reins of power. "Absorbing troublemakers" was, after all, an old Italian practice, and no one had practiced it as often or as well as Giolitti.[55] He confidently predicted at the time that "the fascist candidates will be like fireworks. They will make a lot of noise, but leave nothing behind except smoke."[56] The actual result was more like smoldering ruins.

Hara

Hara was dealt a much stronger hand, in part because his predecessors had repressed and/or co-opted the labor movement. With regard to nationalism, he helped himself by winning support from the aging Yamagata Aritomo. This took no small measure of conjuring. Yamagata's politics and Hara's were at odds from the beginning, and as we have seen, Yamagata did not trust politicians. Hara, as the most skilled, was surely one of the least trusted. In 1908, Yamagata bypassed Home Minister Hara and went directly to the emperor to seek additional repressive powers for the state. He understood that a Hara government would be a party government, the natural enemy of his carefully constructed bureaucratic state. Still, Hara had worked diligently to win over the aging oligarch. Like Yamagata, Hara worried about the rise of socialism and the dangers of subversive movements. After all, in 1907 he ordered the suppression of Ashio copper mine strikers, the first time imperial soldiers had been ordered to intervene in a labor disturbance at a specific firm.[57] He made sure that his social policies were conservative, and that his educational program was designed to instill patriotism. He proved to Yamagata that he, too, was comfortable resorting to repression as the occasion demanded. Yamagata ultimately came to accept Hara as a "temporary expedient," and even nominated him for prime minister.[58]

Hara became prime minister in 1918 at a most delicate moment. The end of the wartime economic boom would be sudden and dislocating. Rice riots, farm tenancy disputes, and labor unrest grew out of legitimate grievances and were received by the government as the harbinger of an irresistible "mass awakening."[59] While the state perceived a serious threat to social order, liberal politicians argued that the government should relax its authoritarianism; otherwise, the people would turn sharply leftward and Japan would face revolution. Thus began a great debate on the "Social Problem" and the "Livelihood Problem" not at all unlike the one that had gripped Italy. There is abundant evidence that, like Giolitti, Hara understood and fully appreciated the choices. Indeed, it was Hara who, in 1919, prevailed upon Yamagata to accept electoral reform—particularly in the countryside—as a way to preclude revolution.

Hara also echoed Giolitti by referring often to "knowing the trends of the time (*jisei*) . . . To be in a position of power and not know which way the tide is running is very dangerous."[60] He argued consistently that change could be encouraged, but not forced. Neither could it be resisted if the historical conditions were propitious. As if reading from a Giolittian script, Hara held that leaders had to read the trends and act accordingly: "If changes are not carried out when the conditions require them, high and low will be torn asunder and it will be impossible to maintain the political structure . . . If changes are carried out when conditions are not ready for them, then chaos will result."[61] But to political opponents who wanted a more active response to the "trends of the time," Hara appeared to be merely an opportunist. Some conclude that Hara did not respond to the challenge of social change because he thought that he would not be able to accomplish much. He preferred, according to Duus, to "let sleeping dogs lie."[62] But, in fact, the dogs were not sleeping—and neither was Hara. He understood exactly what was going on but reckoned that popular pressure, if strategically managed, would not overwhelm state capacity. Indeed he compared the Japanese situation to that in Europe: "[Some people] are inclined to assert that there has occurred a great spiritual and material change in our country. Naturally we recognize this. It is a fact that there has been some degree of change. However . . . it is not change such as there has been in the various countries of Europe."[63] Hara was more than an opportunist. He was a strategist who calculated that responding to social demands with selective repression was the safer alternative.

His cabinet turned far more vigorously to electoral than to social reform. Electoral reform had two important components. One involved redistricting. Sensing electoral advantage, Hara moved to strengthen the hand of party government over the regional cliques by replacing the very large, multimember district system (of Yamagata's design) with a primarily single-member district system.[64] The second component was expansion of the franchise. Unlike Giolitti, Hara tended to "discount the importance of the 'mass awakening' [and] was skeptical of the country's having undergone any significant changes since the war."[65] He agreed to enlarge the franchise to eight million male voters, but he steadfastly refused the universal male suffrage demanded by the opposition parties and the trade unions. Ignoring massive protests in Tokyo, Hara insisted that universal suffrage was "premature."[66] Like Giolitti, he recognized that the franchise was a salient issue in politics, but he calculated that it was not so pressing that his government needed to acquiesce to opposition demands. He might plausibly have championed universal suffrage (or some more limited expansion of the electorate) as part of the electoral reform laws. That he decided not to do so reflected his reading of the Seiyūkai's electoral advantage.

In the event, Hara got what he wanted and more. The Seiyūkai electoral reform bill that passed in 1919 expanded the electorate slightly, but boosted Seiyūkai strength in the countryside at the expense of the urban areas, relieving pressure for universal suffrage. Meanwhile, mass demonstrations in favor of universal suffrage provided the pretext Hara needed to dissolve the Diet and hold a new election under the new electoral laws. Universal male suffrage would have to wait until 1925—when it would be paired with a draconian Peace Preservation Law. Hara was operating quite effectively in an environment hostile to democratic reform. He had hard-line oligarchs like Yamagata on his right, and disenfranchised masses threatening instability on his left. Moreover, politicians who believed in truly open competition were in short supply. Democrats outnumbered liberals by far, and autocrats continued to trump both under the rules drawn up by Itō Hirobumi in the Meiji Constitution.[67]

This well-entrenched hostility to competitive politics notwithstanding, the constraints operating on Hara can be overstated. Yamagata had empowered him, but was growing weak. Party forces were gaining strength. And, after all, over the course of more than two decades Hara had often confronted Yamagata and other conservatives with impunity and, indeed, with some measure of success. As home minister in the first Saionji cabinet, for example, Hara had allowed the formation of the Japan Socialist Party in 1906, which Yamagata had blocked in 1901. Hara's early criticism of the suppression of labor never disadvantaged him politically. Moreover, Hara had been to the United States and Europe, and often acknowledged that industrialization was unleashing popular forces.[68] Hara was, after a statist fashion, an aggressive social reformer. He ordered his home minister, Tokonami Takejirō, to address social issues through state intervention and he was the first prime minister to grasp the possibilities for political modernization opened up by the absence of a performing monarch.[69] He even anticipated the threat arising from the military's arbitrary intervention in politics and tried to do something about it. Hara was moving to secure control of the imperial house when he was assassinated in November 1921 amid demands for an end to the political corruption that his government had abetted.

In short, Hara understood his situation well. He had choices, and he made them only after careful calculation. Unlike Giolitti, he moved to control the monarchy rather than to expand the electorate, leaving unexplored the possibilities for parliamentary coalitions and structural if not democratic reform.[70] Whereas Giolitti would use the state to appease society, Hara would use it to control society. In the end, Hara was a machine politician, not a populist; Giolitti was neither. Hara reached for the monarchy, Giolitti for the masses. Despite his rhetoric and democratic credentials, Hara was, according to Najita, "not a political leader with great vision . . . [but] a strategist with conviction . . . Thoughts of structural reform and social legislation were, at best, secondary and tertiary considerations."[71]

It is here that the liberal politics of Giovanni Giolitti and Hara Kei diverge most clearly. Hara showed only limited sympathy for working class demands. He chose a minimalist course in dealing with labor unrest, neither supporting all the activist designs of his home minister nor accepting the view that workers needed protection from employers. He adopted what we might call a liberalism of convenience, a laissez-faire approach to labor issues that benefited his industrialist supporters by defending the status quo. His approach to labor issues was democratizing, but minimalist. Reversing prior repressive policies, he accepted the basic right of workers to organize but did nothing to define workers' rights. Intervention—usually violent intervention—and the arrest of workers in labor disputes became routine. The government repeatedly invoked Article 17 of the Police Regulations to break strikes, encouraged managers to fire striking workers, and supported their refusal to rehire them. The doctrine of laissez-faire liberalism gave Hara an excuse to remain aloof when he wished to be. By the time Hara was assassinated, his government had moved deci-

Hara Kei presides over the transportation ministry in 1906 as it flattens the general population with rate increases. Reproduced courtesy of the Saitama Municipal Cartoon Art Museum (artist Rakuten Kitazawa, in *Tokyo Puck* 2, no. 16).

sively to the right. He intended to control the emperor, and to keep that control out of the hands of the military—something Yamagata, the last active oligarch and defender of the military prerogative, had dedicated his life to achieving.

MODALITIES AS LEGACIES

There have been few political outcomes more overdetermined than the failures of liberalism in Italy and Japan—failures that clearly were abetted by choices made by both Giovanni Giolitti and Hara Kei. Each country took its own route away from democratic mass politics, and so the roads back would also be different. Giolitti and Hara used similar modalities, but deployed them to different ends. They elaborated two instruments of governance that became indelibly identified with national politics. The first was bureaucratic. Giolitti and Hara each politicized the executive. For his part, Giolitti nominated each prefect and all of the senior executives of the judiciary, military, and administrative hierarchy. When he was uncertain of the loyalties or capabilities of his subordinates, Giolitti kept the portfolio for himself. His governments prodigiously increased public spending on infrastructure and on the military as well. Although the imperial bureaucracy was more difficult to infiltrate, Hara played a similar game. Hara's allies in the Seiyūkai were placed strategically in administrative posts—from governors and police chiefs to election supervisors. But Hara pressed less hard upon (and surrendered more to) the prerogatives of the Japanese bureaucracy. The second modality was electoral. Each moved decisively to control parliament and to manipulate the electorate. But whereas Giolitti struck multiple, shifting alliances, Hara reaffirmed existing ones. Let us explore each in turn, for each created lasting institutional features of Italian and Japanese governance.

The Italian case is more clear-cut. Giolitti bound the landed classes to his programs through a generous distribution of spoils. They would have their tariffs and their irrigation projects, if he could have their parliamentary support. He openly intervened to manipulate southern elections and was known to use police to intimidate voters and even to enroll convicts to vote for government candidates or to threaten the opposition. By "selling prefects to buy deputies," Giolitti developed a prototype for an Italian political machine.[72] He constructed a remarkably effective system of state largesse comprising unequal measures of fraud, intimidation, and reward.

But he eschewed the development of a disciplined mass party. He preferred "conjuring" majorities of parliamentarians to building a permanent electoral base.[73] He opposed proportional representation, believing it would contribute to instability.[74] Instead, he sought to control small parties through enticements and rewards outside the electoral system. He believed that cooperation could be continuously bought without a party program or party discipline, and that the considerable instruments of the state could be more effective and less costly than maintaining a disciplined party of his own. He was wrong.

On the evidence examined here, Giolitti might have known better. He acknowledged that peaceful incorporation of a mass electorate was the only alternative to violence in an industrial state: "Only the nations in whose progress the masses took an active part—nations such as England, Germany, France and the United States—were economically powerful . . . The social security and the economic wealth of the country had always appeared to me to be closely connected with the well-being and the material and moral elevation of the lower classes."[75] It was also a way to prevent the masses from being won over by the Church or by the Socialists.

Consistent with this understanding, Giolitti engineered Italy's first "opening to the Left." Betting that he could obtain support from the Center-Right when necessary, Giolitti chose to center around a base of left Liberals and moderate Socialists. Giolitti was determined to promote industrial expansion *and* allow for the satisfaction of mass demands simultaneously.[76] In a bold stroke of co-optation, he reached out to the moderate Socialists in 1901 to create a "Lib-Lab Coalition." Giolitti embraced issues dear to the Left. He openly stood for freedoms of speech and assembly. He stood against the Right's preference to "return to the Constitution." Sensing he might be able to divide the Socialists and create a strong Center, he tried unsuccessfully to entice PSI leader Filippo Turati to serve in his government.

Even if the Socialists would not accept his portfolios, they (like the southern elites) would gladly accept his largesse. In an audacious move, Giolitti assigned control of Italy's fledgling cooperatives to the Socialists, which had championed them, providing state subsidy in the bargain. These Socialists proved adept at establishing themselves as local bosses. When they exceeded their formal authority, Giolitti even restrained his prefects from intervening, in the interest of maintaining their parliamentary and electoral support.[77] He called openly for redistribution of land, and introduced a range of programs, including night education, workmen's compensation, maternity insurance, and industrial safety regulations. He adopted the greater part of the moderate socialist program, and his second government hardly lagged behind other European states in the extension of social programs. What he wrought in his effort to split the Socialists was revolutionary.[78] Still, he dismissed the strategic importance of a mass base, believing that it would ensnare him and limit his creative freedom. Giolitti deliberately never built a liberal democratic party of his own.[79] He would pay for this choice in ignominy and failure.

His failure would later turn to success, and his ignominy to a grudging admiration. Two generations later, Giolitti would be credited as a pioneer of conciliation in a divided polity. His early "opening to the Left" would be rediscovered twice—first in the Constituent Assembly in the mid-1940s and again by the Christian Democrats in the late 1950s. By trying to peacefully incorporate the working class, he demonstrated that a Center-Left was possible in this stubbornly divided polity. It is hard to escape the conclusion that Giolitti's democratic liberalism and early concessions to the Socialists left the working class relatively strong and protected in Italy.[80]

Giolitti was also the first to recognize that the resources and institutions of the state could be put to partisan ends. He realized, as Christian Democrats would later rediscover, that knowledge of the machinery of the state was a surer route to power than ideas alone. He prefigured Christian Democratic rule by institutionalizing the distribution of spoils. It was part and parcel of his dualism. While pursuing a progressive program of social welfare in the North, Giolitti practiced a corrupt clientelistic politics in the South. Subsequent Italian governments did not embrace his social program for half a century, but they copied Giolittian clientelism almost from the very beginning of the new republic in 1947. The Giolittian legacy was less *what* he delivered than the mechanisms he pioneered for their delivery.

Finally, Giolitti understood better than any Italian politician—except perhaps Cavour himself—how to center among competing elites. Unlike Crispi, Giolitti never succumbed to his personal antipathies; unlike Zanardelli, he never succumbed to the blandishments of populist ideology; unlike Depretis, he never succumbed to the temptation to temporize under pressure. Giolitti opened to the Left by introducing universal male suffrage and by recognizing the legitimacy of unions, and reopened to the Right by declaring war. He supported workers in order to co-opt them and prevent Socialist gains. He supported industry with tariffs and state investment to create prosperity. When the Socialists wanted cooperatives, he gave them state subsidies and management authority. When the Republicans wanted universal suffrage, he supplied it. When the Church wanted pressure on freemasonry, he obliged. While massaging old political forces, he was also attempting (sometimes subtly, sometimes not) to harness new ones. Many of the standard views of Giolitti are overstated. Given his clear and sustained commitment to the liberal democratic project, he was neither the unprincipled mediator between plutocrats and proletarians that Pareto averred, nor was he the detached, pedestrian "breeder and teacher of neutrality" against whom Mussolini blustered.[81]

In the end, Giolitti remained in the Center. But the Center proved to be a vice, and his project—situated in the middle of the road and without armor—was crushed. A postwar coalition of socialists and liberal democrats, who recognized how much they had lost, would resuscitate it.

Hara Kei wrought less and more than Giovanni Giolitti. Hara was less engaged in "stretching" constraints than in maximizing the political benefits he could derive from them. If Giolitti pioneered Italy's characteristic "openings to the Left," Hara pioneered Japan's equally characteristic politics of compensation and accommodation. Giolitti experimented with new systems; Hara fine-tuned existing systems to his advantage. He was a party politician who chose to limit his popular base and bolster it with state support. Contra Giolitti, Hara opted to exclude labor and to empower the bureaucracy with responsibility for a paternalistic social policy. He experimented far less with shifting alliances than did Giolitti—but he showed how politicians could cut deals with local elites without surrendering power to local publics. His great dream was single-party dominance, a hegemony cemented by close ties between politicians and bureaucrats.[82] He built the prototype for political machines that would govern Japan for generations to come.

Hara's legacy is more indirect than Giolitti's, but just as clear. Japanese fascism intervened before the postwar Liberal Democrats could actualize Hara's dream. Importantly, it intervened differently than Italian fascism. Japanese fascism was animated by the institutional constructions of authoritarian oligarchs as well as by the intimidation of liberal elites and by the failure of party politicians. Hara was not responsible for Japanese fascism, but he was at least as culpable as any other political leader. By pressing bureaucratic power, he diminished the chance for party control and failed to seize the chance to give teeth to Taishō democracy. In his reluctance to expand the electorate or to incorporate the Left, and in his determination to aggrandize the bureaucracy, Hara ensured that Taishō democracy would remain merely a "parliamentary parenthesis." For all his prodigious tinkering with a spoils system, Hara left the larger system much as he found it—one designed by oligarchs to remain beyond the reach of ordinary party politicians and the general public. An extraordinary politician had his chance to institute democratic politics, but he chose to forego it for what he believed was surer power. He was wrong. His ideas and hopes for parliamentary politics died with him.

The death of Italian and Japanese liberalism was due in part to the failure of Hara and Giolitti to reach the masses with compelling ideas about a shared national project. Neither of these two consummate logrollers inspired citizens; buying voters seemed enough. And, in the event, buying gave way to bullying in both countries. Hara Kei and Giovanni Giolitti were insufficiently creative. They did not appreciate how to use the past to secure power. Each was displaced by remarkably creative *bricoleurs*—Mussolini in Italy and ultranationalists in Japan—who would make different mistakes.

As we shall see in the next chapter, Japan's fascism came not from a break with the past but from a *refusal* to break with it. It was prosecuted by zealous bureaucrats and senior military officers—Japan's best and brightest—who were, after the emperor, Japan's only legitimate governors. Party politicians stood by, collecting political rents, and allowed it to happen. From the beginning, fascism was legitimate in Japan in a way not true in Italy. It was widely accepted by the general population, abetted by the existing order, and largely unresisted. No Duce was required.

Hara was not alone in failing to block Japanese fascism. Indeed, he was taking steps against the military when he was murdered. But he did fail to seize opportunities to legitimate parliamentary politics. These opportunities might not have generated immediate alternatives, but, as was clearly the case in Italy, they would have provided guidance for political leaders who emerged after the war to pick up the pieces. Giovanni Giolitti's legacy was a Left strong enough to resist fascism and claim a place at the table when the postwar order was being determined. Hara Kei's legacy was realized first in Japanese fascism and later in the hegemony of the Liberal Democratic Party and its bureaucratic partners.

CHAPTER FIVE

The Birth of Corporatism:

MUTŌ SANJI, ALESSANDRO ROSSI, KISHI NOBUSUKE,

GIOVANNI AGNELLI, AND AYUKAWA GISUKE

> Political sentiment is the subjective, and the political constitution the objective substance of the state. The logical development from the family and civil society to the state is thus pure appearance . . ."
>
> Karl Marx, *Critique of Hegel's Philosophy of Right*

The inability of Italian liberals to prevent—or at least to ameliorate—the destabilizing effects of class-based politics was perhaps the greatest lost opportunity in the first century of Italian modernization. In contrast, as we have seen, Japanese leaders found ways to contain similarly massive forces. In both cases, what was perceived as the threat of mass politics invited authoritarian solutions. But however much these solutions resembled each other, they were made of different stuff. And these differences had profoundly different consequences for political legitimacy in each country—and for their institutions.

This chapter explores interwar corporatism in Italy and Japan. First, I focus on contrasting choices made by private entrepreneurs as they confronted mass politics. Japan is famous for having reinvented the institutions of capitalism, in particular for deploying the distinctive institutions and ideology of "firm as family" corporate paternalism.[1] It is less well known that Italy missed its own chance to do the same. Indeed, the protectionist senator and entrepreneur Alessandro Rossi clearly understood these forces and brilliantly articulated a mechanism to ameliorate them. The similarities between Rossi's ideas and those of his Japanese counterparts help us appreciate how many possibilities were never realized. By focusing on leadership, we can understand better why. We explore each experience separately before turning to the negotiated arrangements between capitalists and their state as both hurtled toward authoritarianism and war.

Corporate Paternalism *alla italiana*

Alessandro Rossi's advocacy of a national economy was, as we have seen, decisive in Italy's delayed turn toward protectionism in the late nineteenth century. But like many nineteenth-century captains of industry, Rossi had other irons in the developmental fire. In particular, he was renowned for his deep and passionate sense of responsibility for his workers. As Vilfredo Pareto acknowledged, Rossi was one of the very few protectionists animated by ideas as outsized as his material interests.[2] Rossi was a religious Catholic, a "clerical moderate" who had spent five years in Britain in the 1840s where he developed fervent beliefs that jobs were necessary for individuals, and that providing them was the responsibility of the entrepreneur. That responsibility included provision of housing and educational facilities to enhance the capabilities of the workers. He practiced what he preached. Rossi started and sustained a network of philanthropic initiatives for his workers in Schio, the home of his woolen mills.[3]

Rossi believed that the tariff would prevent social dislocation and the growth of socialism—but only if its benefits were shared widely. Rossi's moral crusade seemed as important as his political one—although all was not what it seemed. He saw a properly functioning industrial economy as one that did not need (and that would not spawn) the class-based politics he had observed in England. For Rossi, society would be better off if class-based politics could be avoided. Look, he demanded, at "England, that very country whose qualities we are used to admiring and whose vices they are used to hiding . . . What were Roman slave~ in comparison with mine workers of Newcastle? . . . Industrialists opposed trade unions to the point where [they had to meet each other with] forces of violence . . . But in those battles all moral sense disappeared [and] socialism was nourished."[4] Italy still had time to avoid these politics. Rossi proposed to trump socialism by avoiding the laissez-faire capitalism that spawned it. He preferred a paternal Christian order based on workers, and he even advocated profit sharing with employees.[5] A national and paternal order would resolve class conflict within the system.[6]

Rossi encountered two significant problems. First, his Modello Veneto attracted adherents in the northeast, but he failed to convince entrepreneurs elsewhere—especially in the South—to adopt it.[7] Engaged though he was in politics, Rossi always held politicians in contempt. He never joined a political party and, without a national association of manufacturers to embrace his scheme, he never saw it widely adopted. Second, Rossi fought social legislation at every turn.[8] He opposed legislation in 1907 to abolish night work by women and children. He opposed the mandatory day off, suggesting that it would lead to idleness and alcoholism. This most nationalistic of industrialists, who built paternalism on his own shop floor, retreated from advocating his formula as national policy.

Rossi insisted that Italian industrialists could be trusted to do the right thing for their workers—they need not be required to do so. He expected they would see that supporting workers was in their self-interest. Left to their own devices, however, Italian industrialists demurred. It seems a clear judgment of history that the Modello Veneto never became a Modello Nazionale because its protagonist fumbled every opportunity to promote it. Rossi ran headlong into a classic public goods problem: others would not make voluntary contributions to national solidarity from which all could profit.[9] For all his sincere dedication to a "philosophy of industrialization"—a philosophy entirely consistent with the ideas that would succeed and transform Japan—Rossi squandered a remarkable opportunity that he had helped to create. With his failure, Italian politics took a giant step deeper into class and regional pathologies.

MAKING CORPORATE PATERNALISM WORK IN JAPAN

These were pathologies the Japanese—armed with remarkably similar ideas—were determined to avoid. Like Rossi, Japanese business leaders reflected upon the class-based turn taken in European industrial relations, and they resorted to the bricolage earlier pursued with such success by state-builders Itō Hirobumi and Yamagata Aritomo. They scanned the past for Japanese values that they could use to keep change under control—*their* control. Their discovery—acknowledged today as in equal part their invention—resulted from yet another extended search for a useable past.[10] The formula they developed was based on the claim that Japanese factories were like traditional Japanese families and villages—which were called "exceptional sites of warmhearted social relations." This vision would inform Japanese industrial relations for the next several generations.[11] In its (highly evolved) contemporary form, this "traditional" model includes permanent employment, seniority-based advancement, and company-based unions that emphasize corporate rather than class loyalty. It is the base of the social contract that globalization seemed poised to rupture at the turn of the twenty-first century.

In Japan, as in Italy, corporate paternalism is sometimes indistinguishable from corporate despotism. Not everyone who advocated warmheartedness had the workers' interests in mind. Indeed, the model was useful for individuals with varied motives. There were those who wanted only to prevent change, those who invoked it as evidence that Japan had found a new way to organize a modern economy, even those who rejected it as the corrupt foundation of a feudal order. Still, the effort was remarkably successful. Japan was hardly immune to the "great forces" associated with proletarianization and social change, but leaders found a way to cope with these forces and avoid some of their most dislocating consequences.[12]

This invention was not the work of any single individual, although the person credited with early efforts to find the model was also the one most clearly associated with its national diffusion—the textile industrialist, politician, and polemicist Mutō Sanji (1867–1934). By the late Meiji period, skilled workers were in short supply, and factory managers like Mutō found themselves competing for workers. They also found that they were driving up wages and facilitating labor mobility. And, even before they began to face challenges from trade unions, they faced government pressure to improve working conditions. In the mid-1890s, for instance, the Ministry of Agriculture and Commerce issued draft legislation to regulate hours and establish minimum health and safety standards for women and children.[13] Mutō picked up elements of "familism" and warmheartedness from studying the practices of Krupp in Germany and NCR in the United States, but he insisted that he was infusing them with traditional Japanese values.[14] As senior manager at the Kanegafuchi Spinning Company, he coined the term "large familism" (*dai kazoku shugi*) and stressed the differences between what he observed in Europe and what he would introduce to Japan.[15] Mutō seized upon the idea that corporate paternalism could be used to combat both unionization and state intervention: "To develop Japanese manufacturing industry, corporate leaders must moderate the labor movement. To prevent active labor unions, corporate paternalism must focus on both employees' satisfaction and public benefit. Solving misunderstanding between the employer and employees is as important as preventing public outcry."[16] Like Rossi, Mutō saw no inherent contradiction between warmheartedness and profit-seeking. Indeed, the former could contribute to the latter: "The owner of a shop or company must think of clerks and employees as if they were children in his care, and must look after them with tenderness as if they were his own family members. If he does this, a kind of affection will naturally develop between employers and employees; the quality of their work will improve and the expenses on their welfare will be repaid."[17]

Again like Rossi, Mutō practiced what he preached. In 1896 he introduced Japan's first works committees and even established mechanisms whereby workers could elect representatives to handle discipline problems in the plant.[18] In addition to paying higher wages and establishing a special welfare and pension fund for longtime workers, Kanegafuchi ran a hospital for employees, provided sewing lessons, subsidized consumer cooperatives, provided funeral benefits, published magazines, and introduced profit sharing. By the time Mutō was finished, he had introduced more than three dozen welfare and educational programs, all designed to engender affection for the firm.[19]

At first, these innovations were not well received by competing textile firms whose workers left to join Kanegafuchi. The Spinners Industry Association tried to isolate Kanegafuchi, but Mutō appealed to his lead bank, Mitsui, to break their blockade. He also convinced other spinners to adopt some of his paternalistic practices.[20] Initially dubious, the government picked up the idea as well. In 1911 legislation was introduced that incorporated the "beautiful custom" of paternalism as the basis for a stable social order. A tradition invented by businessmen would prevent social disorder when underscored by state power.[21] As Dore points out, "slowly these innovations spread—from the textile firms to other branches of industry. So, too, did the ideology."[22] Thanks in large part to Mutō's persistence, the textile sector was where "familism" was born and bred as Japan's dominant model of industrial relations.

His persistence was remarkable. Mutō formed a national association, the Greater Japan Business Association (Dainippon Jitsugyō Rengōkai), to propagate paternalistic programs and to teach "the true meaning of paternalism."[23] Numerous firms signed on to his five basic principles: respect workers' skills, promote lifetime employment, enable worker concentration, reduce illness and injury, and promote dual-income families.[24] Even the Chambers of Commerce that represented numerous smaller firms now insisted that Japan's familial social organization of production enveloped workers in "a mist of affectionate feelings."[25] With Mutō pushing his colleagues—and with workers pressing managers for concessions—the model began to take hold. Mutō's brand of paternalism was adopted by the National Railways in 1906, and in 1910 by the Ōji Paper Company and by the Nikko Electric Copper Refinery. Later it was extended to other heavy industrial firms.[26]

But this was not a smooth process, for corporate paternalism was not an uncontested idea. It was invoked by labor as well as by management, by reformers as well as by reactionaries. On the eve of World War I, some workers found the model useful for their demands for higher wages and better working conditions. The newspaper of Japan's most important labor organization editorialized in 1914 that "we workers are powerless souls born and raised under pitiful circumstances. We crave powerful protectors with warm human feelings. We beg you to show hearts of parents. If you do, we will show you hearts of children, by working hard for you."[27] But it was also vigorously endorsed by industrialists who opposed factory legislation that the state had been trying to implement for nearly three decades. Such social policy, they argued, would empower workers, undermine discipline, create social classes, and upset the harmonious social order that was held together by their warmheartedness.[28] In a transparent excuse for doing nothing, a senior manager at the Mitsubishi Shipyards protested, "We cannot agree to something that will destroy the beautiful custom of master-servant relations and wreak havoc on our industrial peace."[29]

But doing nothing was not an option. Yamagata used the Public Order Law of 1900 to shut down the first Socialist Party just hours after it proclaimed its existence, and to outlaw collective bargaining and strikes, but he could not eliminate class-based politics completely.[30] Corporate paternalism and beautiful Japanese customs notwithstanding, some 10 percent of the industrial workforce were children under the age of fourteen, and working conditions were "scandalously inadequate."[31] A three-day riot by workers at the Ashio copper mines in 1907 sparked the worst fears of many industrialists.

Labor unrest escalated. Between 1915 and 1917 the annual number of labor disputes rose sixfold. The Yūaikai, a moderate labor group associated with the Unitarian Church, emerged from a decade of repression in 1912. Some prominent business leaders accepted the Yūaikai because it rejected class struggle; but it did not reject strikes.[32] By 1917—amid the wartime economic boom—the Yūaikai had been involved in some seventy labor disputes. The boom fueled inflation, driving up rice prices for a growing mass of urban industrial workers. Riots over commodity prices, particularly rice, were accompanied by strikes by printers, postal workers, teachers, and longshoremen. By 1919, Japan had nearly two hundred unions engaged in nearly five hundred disputes. At this point, the Hara government, under pressure to conform to international labor standards and sensitive to the harm noncompliance would have for integration in the world economy, called upon both Mutō Sanji and an old ally, Shibusawa Eichi, for assistance. Mutō went off in 1919 to represent Japan at the International Labor Conference in Washington, D.C.[33] Ignoring his personal observations in the United States and Germany, Mutō argued that Japanese warmheartedness was unique, and Japan should therefore be exempt from evolving international standards. Anticipating the arguments of subsequent generations of Japanese trade negotiators, Mutō rejected universal rights for their corrosive effects on traditional Japanese ties of sentiment. Since conditions in Japan were different, he argued, its industrial relations should be different as well. A rights-based approach amounted to "senseless attacks on the principle of familial affection."[34]

Shibusawa, now a baron, was asked by Home Minister Tokonami Takejirō to convince the business community to create and fund a Harmonization Society (Kyōchōkai) to promote labor-management cooperation and to develop enterprise unionism—the institutional form of corporate paternalism.[35] The home ministry proposed to selectively enforce the police laws against class-based trade unions. The plan was rejected by the Yūaikai, which noticed that Tokonami was simultaneously creating an auxiliary police force of foremen and thugs to suppress unruly workers. But the state insisted that cooperation with labor could not be based on individual rights. It had to be organic—a matter of "living and prospering together" (kyōson kyōei).[36]

Shibusawa was on record supporting corporate paternalism and supporting the Yūaikai. In July 1909 he had written:

> In the West they embrace an extreme individualism . . . On the contrary, we earnestly embrace the family system, and so the person who is at the head of a family not only supports those in his family . . . but . . . is also rich in a benevolence that goes out to his neighbors, and warmheartedness is communicated between the capitalist and the worker, so that relations between the two proceed smoothly, and the employer loves the employee, the employee respects the employer, and everything is able to proceed harmoniously.[37]

The Harmonization Society was formed, but resolved few disputes.[38]

The failure of the Harmonization Society did not bode well for Japanese industrial relations. After the Russian Revolution, the moderate Yūaikai was transformed by new leaders into the more militant Sōdōmei. Predictably, the Japanese state responded in two ways. It used the National Essence Society and the police to repress independent unions, and it continued to discriminate in favor of what the police called "patriotic" unions like the Seamen's Union, which were allowed to engage in collective bargaining.[39] By the early 1930s business leaders and bureaucrats designed their "Japanese-style" alternative to unemployment insurance, and labor unrest came to an end in 1937 with the establishment of a national labor federation, the Industrial Patriotic Service Movement (Sanpō). This was Japan's version of the corporatist experiments of Fascist Italy and Nazi Germany. It involved the same pyramidal network of national, regional, and workplace councils and featured the same racialist rhetoric and anti-Marxist class-leveling.

In constructing this system, Japan's bureaucrat-intellectuals built directly upon Mutō's original model—morphed to suit their purposes. Adopting his rhetoric, if not his warm heart, the state announced there would now be paternal unions in each plant, formally recognized and subsidized by the home ministry. Each enterprise was now formally recognized in law as a "family" (*jigyō ikka*). Each Sanpō unit was configured as a "comprehensive community concerned with all aspects of work and life."[40]

The institutional connections to postwar labor organization are well documented.[41] Japanese industrial relations would after all remain unique. But as Sako points out, feudalism did not naturally "slip into the domain of modern corporations."[42] There was nothing "natural" or "organic" about the connection between preindustrial Japanese social norms and Japan's "uniquely" paternalistic system of industrial relations. The system evolved by embracing practices that worked and that were actively promoted by leaders such as Mutō Sanji. That said, it is far from clear that the fascist model was the "traditional" approach Mutō had in mind for Japan. The state had to proceed without Mutō's assistance because, ironically, unemployed workers assassinated him in March 1934.

CORPORATIST SOLUTIONS

By the time the industrial workforce came of political age after 1945, it was clear in both countries that the state had broad jurisdiction in the economy. War, which generated enormous demand for heavy industrial products and for the technology used to build them, was one entry point for the state.[43] Another, as we have seen, was concern about the destabilizing effects of class-based politics.

The Japanese recognized this first. They intervened to create as well as to manage business interest groups. And they introduced cooperatives in part to rationalize the economy for rural producers and in part to consolidate a national identity. The contrast to the Italian experience is profound. Italian entrepreneurs had much more difficulty organizing themselves. And, whereas Italian cooperatives were built by outsiders to consolidate *alternatives* to the state, Japanese cooperatives were introduced by state planners to consolidate a *national* identity and to forestall the social divisions inherent in economic development.[44] The home ministry exhortation, "Cooperative Groups for the State" (*kokka no tame no kyōdōtai*), could not have been more different from those of contemporaneous Catholics and Socialists in Italy.[45]

In 1900, the same year as the Public Order Law, the modern cooperative movement started in Japan. The Japanese home ministry introduced, nearly verbatim, German legislation to combine small producers for the purposes of providing capital and credit, facilitating savings, joint marketing, joint purchasing, and other collective action.[46] The German legislation was the result of a popular movement. But the Japanese bureaucrats did not wait for rural groups to organize and make potentially destabilizing demands. Instead, they let the rural poor "share in the blessings of civilization along with the great capitalists." Society and order would prevail.[47]

The borrowers were selective. They left out the German paragraphs on "self-governing workshops" which, they feared, might provide legal justification for trade union organization or, worse, socialism. The legislation was accompanied by systematic state proselytizing, village by village, for the creation of cooperatives. In 1908 the home minister drafted an imperial rescript exhorting people to save and to cooperate with one another so that Japan could become a great power.[48] The effort was so successful that within a decade Japan had more cooperatives than villages. By 1918 one in four families was participating in a producer or consumer cooperative. Whereas Giolitti had used cooperatives to co-opt Socialists and Catholics, the Japanese home ministry used them to preclude competitors to the state.

The Japanese took these measures because they wished to avoid fragmentation of authority. Their efforts were repaid in the years before and during World War I. But, after the war, the economy soured. Labor conflict became a major problem for the first time, and the economy was punctuated by recurring panics in the 1920s—some of which generated mass violence. Throughout these difficulties and despite inflation, large firms continued to expand until stock and commodity markets crashed. The four largest zaibatsu had resisted much of the speculative frenzy, and picked up the pieces after successive bank failures in 1922 and 1927.

At the turn of the twentieth century, all firms in Japan with capital exceeding half a million yen, with only one exception, were zaibatsu affiliates. Japan was already a dual economy. Zaibatsu firms produced mainly for the large, now protected home market, and small enterprises concentrated on production for export (with exceptions such as synthetic fibers and textiles). The smaller firms—where more than half the manufacturing labor force was employed—were responsible for two-thirds of Japan's exports and 30 percent of GDP by the mid-1920s. But they were losing money, in part because the zaibatsu firms supplied their raw materials and controlled their trade.

The conflict between large and small producers was mirrored by clashes between industry and agriculture. The New York Stock Exchange crashed in October 1929, just three months after Japan's ill-timed return to the gold standard. Exports went into free fall, as did rural commodity prices. Raw silk prices plummeted by more than 50 percent, as did rice prices.

Rural distress was exacerbated when female workers went home to their villages and young men joined the now highly politicized military. The Japanese population had nearly doubled since the Restoration, and widespread rural poverty now combined with urban unemployment and landlord-tenant disputes.

A great battle was joined between those advocating fuller state control and those who were sympathetic to the zaibatsu. The government was running out of short-term fixes. Finance Minister Takahashi Koreikiyo struggled to bring Japan out of recession by inventing what would later be known as Keynesianism. In 1932 he used massive fiscal stimulus—mostly in the form of agricultural relief and military spending—which had a salutary, if temporary, effect. With the approval of his prime minister, Inukai Tsuyoshi, Takahashi had taken Japan off the gold standard the year before. Their move—effectively a last, futile lurch toward liberalism—devalued the yen and stimulated exports, but it also enriched speculators and enraged the general public. Liberal solutions, never widely accepted in any event, were now perceived as a large part of the problem. As Marshall astutely points out:

In the 1930s Japanese business leaders found themselves faced with a foe over whom they no longer held an advantage, as they had with their liberal and Marxist opponents in preceding decades. Whereas in the 1920s businessmen had been able to say they were defending traditional Japanese social doctrines against the "foreign radicalism" of socialism and labor unionism, now the tables were turned, and it was the right wing that had assumed the role of champion of the traditional virtues.[49]

And the right wing, which mobilized to assassinate Inukai, Takahashi, and a number of zaibatsu leaders, already had powerful allies within the Japanese state.

This was not the case in Italy, where the right wing had to come in from the outside. Giolitti's liberal economic and trade program stayed in place until 1921, just before he delivered Italian governance to Benito Mussolini. That was also the year that Ansaldo—shorn of liquidity and without a friend in government—collapsed. But Ansaldo and the other industrial firms that opposed Giolitti's liberalism and felt threatened by the socialist labor movement would not be without a friend for long. This friend— Benito Mussolini—came from an odd corner of the Italian polity.

Until his March on Rome in October 1922, it was not at all clear whether Mussolini was a friend or foe of industry. After all, Mussolini had cut his teeth on socialist activism, he had taken the proletarian weapon from the socialist arsenal, and he had brought large groups of workers along with him to a fascist movement undertaken largely in their name.[50] Ultimately, industrialists came to presume that he was "just another candidate for the job of Prime Minister . . . It was simply a business transaction."[51] Like Giolitti, they felt that they could do business with him.

Political and social unrest spread across Italy in the early 1920s. Anarcho-syndicalists challenged state authority at every turn in the North; peasants seized land in the South; and violence, especially fascist violence, went unchallenged by a weak liberal state. Industry wanted a strong government to confront these threats to its privilege.[52] Mussolini seemed to provide what they wanted. Confindustria, the Italian employers association, announced its support for Mussolini as soon as his government was formed. Business had nowhere else to turn: the liberal solution was bankrupt and the socialist solution was directly and unambiguously hostile to industry.[53] They hoped, and half-expected, that fascism might be divided and conquered. They believed that the fascists were likely to "dissolve into the mainstream of traditional liberal politics."[54] They were right that they could do business with him, but wrong about their ability to put the brakes on the fascist movement. Mussolini would conjure up some of the most revolutionary transformations in modern political economy. His state corporatism was widely copied, not least by Japan, and its legacy persists to this day across the nominally "neoliberal" industrial world.[55]

After 1918, new ideas began to emerge under the banner of "productionism" or "syndicalism"—an attempt to find common ground between capital and labor. Class interests would be abandoned in favor of national interests. Unions should abandon their insistence on class warfare, and employers should abandon exploitation in the interest of higher production.[56] In Italy, the players were bound together ideologically by nationalism and operationally by the fascists, who had captured the nationalist high ground. Fascist ideologues like Alfredo Rocco believed that unfettered competition would lead to waste, class conflict, and degeneracy. They argued for discipline and cartels. But they also insisted on private ownership, because only private property would generate the capital needed for national strength. Their instrument was corporatism, a state-supervised system of dispute resolution in which labor and capital would both sacrifice for common goals. Only through the authoritative coordination of sectoral groups and interests could a stable and productive society be maintained. The corporations would represent a "third way" between capitalism and socialism. It was the state's role to harmonize these interests—by coercion if need be.

A system of coercion, of course, was a system that played to Mussolini's strength. He had risen to power through intimidation: extreme nationalism justified extreme violence against the Left. Fascist attacks against newspapers, socialist clubs, and peasant leagues endeared him to industrialists and to the middle classes that sought (and expected) a prosperous status quo ante. Instead, Mussolini delivered his revolutionary third way of economic governance. Even before he consolidated full dictatorial powers, his minions began to insinuate themselves into the Italian government.

In April 1926, fascist Italy enacted the corporate state. At the base of a national pyramid of governance were one hundred and sixty national federations of employers, workers, and professional associations. Atop them were twenty-two sectoral corporations. A National Council of Corporations that reported to the state's Ministry of Corporations supervised decisions on the regulation of production and employment, on social welfare, and on labor relations. The units at each level were nominally equal, and syndicalist language extolled the solidarity of workers and employers. In practice, the dictatorial state atop the structure left little room for ambiguity about the locus of power. Exile Gaetano Salvemini, one of fascism's most distinguished victims, captured this eloquently: "Labor has in the fascist corporative state no more active part than have the animals in a society for the protection of animals."[57]

This was not true for business, however. In very short order, liberalism would dissolve into something less than a tribal memory. Italian industry nestled itself comfortably inside the corporatist framework. Under this system, Confindustria became a powerful quasi-state institution. The Fascist Confederation of Industry was granted formal monopoly to represent all industrial employers vis-à-vis trade unions and the state. It was Confindustria that generated all the industrial data that the state needed for economic and industrial policy decisions. Several Confindustria presidents were made fascist ministers of state. Under corporatism, all businesses were more equal than labor organizations, but some businesses were more equal than others. Those responsible for licensing new industrial capacity often licensed themselves in violation of limits on duplicate investment, and then paid fines as insurance against competitors.[58] As in Japan, industrialists manipulated state control through corporatist channels. Industrialists went along with corporatism for its guarantees of labor peace and general stability, and to maximize their share of state procurement.

By the mid-1930s Mussolini grew frustrated with industry's preference for stability, with its timidity, and with its self-dealing. He sought political control of the economy through the use of an entirely unexpected instrument: public enterprise. Earlier he had dismantled the state insurance and telephone monopolies, and used the proceeds to pay back Ansaldo, an early ally.[59] Now, however, he needed something new.

The Istituto per la Ricostruzione Industriale (IRI) was quite new. It was created in 1933 to rescue banks and manufacturers on the verge of collapse. It was not the result of careful planning, but a response to an unprecedented crisis—a collapse of Italian capitalism. The 1929 stock market crash hit Italy at a moment of extreme economic concentration. The creation of IRI was "the most sweeping reallocation of ownership in the history of Italy."[60] The architect of the rescue, Alberto Beneduce, perhaps the most influential economist in fascist Italy, was no fascist. Beneduce had been instrumental in Giolitti's nationalization of life insurance. After the war, he had directed massive public works programs and pushed successfully for the state to assume the industrial assets of failed banks. Through his IRI, the Italian state came to own a greater share of the national economy than any other industrial state with the exception of the Soviet Union. But the closer model was Weimar Germany, which owned the three leading banks as well as the steel, shipbuilding, and engineering firms.[61] Ansaldo, once the greatest manufacturer in Italy, was liquidated and absorbed into IRI in 1936.

Mussolini mobilized IRI firms in his program of economic autarky, but this did not work as planned. The per capita income of Italy declined relative to that of France and Germany.[62] Still, the results were less than disastrous for some parts of Italian industry. As autarky became a more explicit goal, the regime seemed to lose degrees of freedom in dealing with the manufacturers who would achieve it for them. Some industry leaders bargained with the fascists from a position of relative strength:

> The industrial leadership of Italy dealt with fascism as the hedgehog deals with a fox ... The industrialists concentrated on retaining maximum independence in the management of their enterprises and trade associations ... Their vast network of trade associations ... gave them political leverage to counterbalance the influence of self-styled social revolutionaries within the Fascist Party.[63]

The cagiest hedgehog of all may have been Giovanni Agnelli, the founder of Fiat, Italy's largest employer. His relationship to the fascists offers insight into the workings of the corporatist Italian state. It also provides a splendid contrast to the relationship of Nissan founder Ayukawa Yoshisuke to the wartime Japanese state.

AGNELLI'S GAMES

Giovanni Agnelli was the first Italian industrialist to see the possibilities for mass consumption. By 1906 he had become the largest shareholder in

Fabbrica Italiana Automobili Torino (FIAT), a company he had founded with some two dozen other automobile enthusiasts in 1899.[64] The firm prospered. Italy's liberal politicians were drawn from the class of people that Agnelli knew well, and he was close to many of them. He opposed protectionism, and favored a larger European federation. Many employers disliked Giolitti's inclusive, conciliatory approach to industrial relations, but Agnelli was not among them. He rejected government intervention even to assist employers vis-à-vis striking workers.[65] Yet he was also deeply involved in the formation of the Lega Industriale, the association of employers formed in 1906 that eventually became Confindustria.

When Mussolini assumed power, the pragmatic Agnelli adjusted quite easily. He was as pro-government under fascism as he had been under liberalism—and as distant from state power as he could reasonably remain. So long as the government did not tread too heavily on Agnelli's business interests, Mussolini could have his support; but Agnelli would not openly countenance the extremism of some of the fascists.[66]

It was not difficult to go along with fascist economic policy. Mussolini's first minister of finance (1922–25), Alberto De Stefani, was a strong defender of free trade, and the early fascist program included reduction of business regulation and a modicum of interventionist measures that large firms welcomed, including a tariff that favored exporters. When speculation against the lire adversely affected Fiat's foreign trade in 1925, Confindustria sought a replacement for De Stefani. Their choice, Count Giuseppe Volpi di Misurata, a Confindustria leader, stabilized the lire and returned Italy to the gold standard. This move hurt export industries like Fiat, and so the government increased protective tariffs and provided various forms of financial assistance, including large procurement orders, favorable contracts, and tax breaks. Under the 1925 Palazzo Vidoni Pact, Confindustria and the fascist unions won exclusive recognition as the corporatist representatives of employers and workers. Confindustria's president and secretary became ex-officio members of the Fascist Grand Council. Business support for the regime—including Agnelli's—was considerable.[67]

It was important for Mussolini to establish good relations with Agnelli. Industrialists remained a latent threat to the young fascist state and Fiat, Italy's largest employer and most advanced firm, had not supported agitation by the Black Shirts during the economic crisis of 1920–21. The fascist state had to deal with Fiat and its politicized workforce explicitly. They danced a careful, if elaborate, tarantella that began with Mussolini's appointment of Agnelli as senator for life in 1923. Agnelli's appointment was seen as an "opening" to the capitalists of the North and an expression of Mussolini's tolerance toward those known not to agree with him.[68] Agnelli chose to work with the fascists and accepted their political control. He downplayed the consequences of corporatist offices and he welcomed the protection they afforded him from Ford, his most threatening market competitor.[69] It was a relationship of mutual convenience. With the support of the fascist syndicates and corporations, Agnelli upgraded Fiat's industrial output and effectively brought about wage reductions. Productivity soared. The state was supportive on fiscal issues as well. From 1924 until the end of fascism, Fiat operated without any increase in capital, evidence of Agnelli's adaptation to the fascist system of risk-free finance.

But it was not always easy. Fiat spent several years retooling in order to profit from military procurement after being caught flat-footed by Italy's foreign adventures. Indeed it was Ford, rather than Fiat, that supplied the trucks that carried Italian soldiers to the Ethiopian front.[70] Eventually, though, Fiat and Italy's other large firms profited from Mussolini's ambitions. Fiat ramped up production of military vehicles in time to peddle them in other hot spots. With government guarantees, it sold armored vehicles to Franco's forces in the Spanish Civil War and aircraft to China. Fiat's sales nearly tripled between 1935 and 1937, and its workforce more than doubled.[71]

On the other hand, the sanctions imposed by the League of Nations hindered Italian exports. Although temporary and limited, they changed Italy's commercial landscape, for the sanctions prompted Italy's turn toward autarky in 1936. The autarky plan was the apex of fascist industrial policy. It included fiscal austerity, currency controls, import substitution, and state control of imports of raw materials. Agnelli was only mildly critical. He admitted that Fiat benefited from state support, but added disingenuously that this was only to ease the "passage from the current exceptional period of war production to normal production without disruptive jolts."[72] It is unclear whether Agnelli did not understand the portent of the events in Ethiopia, Spain, and Manchuria; found them inconvenient to confront; or welcomed them more than he let on.

Even after Mussolini and Hitler signed their Pact of Steel, Agnelli and other Piedmont industrialists continued to advocate a comparatively open economy and good economic relations with the United States. Agnelli's first reaction to military tensions in Europe was annoyance. Germany's invasion of Czechoslovakia in March 1939 deeply clouded Fiat's eastern European strategy, especially in Poland, where it sold armored vehicles, aviation products, and railroad carriages, as well as automobiles.[73] Agnelli was scornful of Germany and its leader.[74] Fiat's preferences were shaped by the need to preserve foreign markets. Good relations with Britain were also important, because preferential treaty arrangements gave Fiat access to markets in the British Empire that otherwise would be closed. Agnelli

Giovanni Agnelli's Fiat was just one of many Italian firms that embraced fascist iconography during the 1930s. In *La Stampa italiana: sotto il fascismo, 1919–1943* (The Italian press: Under fascism, 1919–1943), edited by Oreste Del Buono (Milan: Feltrinelli, 1971).

praised the Anglo-Italian accords of April 1938. Still, he played every angle. Three months later, an Italo-Japanese commercial accord set aside for Fiat a small share of the motor vehicle market in Japan and Manchuria, one that Agnelli hoped to expand. American sanctions against Japan further aided Fiat by reducing competition from Ford in Asia.

Fiat faced the European political situation in 1939 and 1940 with growing apprehension. The company knew how ill-prepared it—and Italy—was to produce the military armament necessary for an all-out war. Civilian production was still strong and important for the maintenance of the firm.[75] Agnelli sent his deputy to Rome in September 1939 to meet Mussolini and inform him that conversion to military production would take six months. He was stalling. Agnelli continued to believe—and was clearly betting—that Italy would not enter a war for which Italy was unprepared. He had no concerns beyond commerce, and sought to avoid war because of the disruption it would cause to his business. He feared German dominance, hoped for peace, and preferred to maintain healthy commerce with France, England, and the United States.[76] Right up until the spring of 1940, Agnelli continued to expand operations in the Allied states. Thereafter, of course, he aggressively ramped up military production for the Axis powers.

His worst fears were confirmed. In November 1942, Fiat's industrial complex in Turin was bombed by the Allies. That winter—and especially after Mussolini was forced out of Rome and chased to his Republic of Salò—Agnelli began playing an even more delicate game. With defeat certain but with Germany still Mussolini's nominal partner, Fiat secretly provided supplies to the Resistance and covert information to the Allies.[77] But this latest turn was too late. Giovanni Agnelli was tainted by his long dance with Mussolini. His final months were full of bitterness as he was stripped of his position as senator and tarred for his ties to the fascist regime. Agnelli died in 1945 at age seventy-nine. His narrow business vision was overwhelmed by a combination of unbridled opportunism and limited conviction. Agnelli responded to the great forces of history by embracing them; he never stretched them hard enough to change their shape or direction. Meanwhile, in Japan, there were entrepreneurs who were far more audacious.

KISHI'S BRAND OF STATE CONTROL

"Reformist" bureaucrats (*kakushin kanryō*) replaced what was left of liberal economic policy with state control. They were determined to end electoral corruption, political influence in the ministries, and the empowerment of corrupt zaibatsu. Working hand in mailed fist with the military, they would try to "return to a social harmony and national unity thought to have been shattered by class conflict and political partisanship in the 1920s."[78] A "Shōwa Restoration" would renovate flagging national solidarity in the name of the new emperor.[79] It promised freedom from foreign domination, the elimination of Marxism as a political force, and increased national strength through centralized planning.[80] The reformers borrowed heavily from the Italian experiment—via Germany—pressing for industrial rationalization by forming "public policy companies" (*kokusaku gaisha*) in each strategic industrial sector and by forming sectoral cartels. In what amounted to a natural extension of the institutional handiwork of Ōkubo, Itō, and Yamagata, these bureaucrats cemented a statist pact. Military power, of course, had grown in tandem with bureaucratic power since the Restoration. Anti-party and anti-zaibatsu sentiment was strong in the bureaucracy and the military, and both believed that their combination—in alliance with the peasantry—would enable Japan to realize its mission at home and in Asia. Japan would lead a new regional economic order built on privileged access to the resources of north China and Southeast Asia. They would build an empire—a yen bloc with guns.

The control bureaucrat who pioneered the alliance between the military and civilian planners even in defiance of his supervisors was a young official in the Ministry of Commerce and Industry (MCI), Kishi Nobusuke. He was the linchpin of a "factional alignment that would shape the national economy for generations to come."[81] Even a great novelist would have difficulty imagining the twists and turns in the career of this extraordinary man. Kishi would not only become the architect of the corporatist Japanese state and "transwar" economic system, but would return after the war from the political graveyard—he was a Class A war criminal at Sugamo Prison—reinvented as a democrat to design and lead the "1955 System" of conservative consolidation and Liberal Democratic Party hegemony. His was a long road from bona fide fascism to nominal democracy, from signatory of a resolution for war against the United States in 1941 to the most determined protector of the U.S.-Japan alliance. No single individual had a greater impact on Japan in the twentieth century.

At Tokyo Imperial University in the years just after Versailles, Kishi found himself buffeted by debates over the status of the Meiji Constitution and roiled by passions over two great ideologies of the day—socialism and nationalism. Politicians led by Hara Kei were experimenting with parliamentary politics, but Kishi had little in common with Hara. Kishi was an ardent nationalist who was keenly aware of his Chōshū forebears, Ōkubo Toshimichi and Itō Hirobumi, who had developed the economic and political institutions that Kishi would extend.[82] Kishi was pulled rightward by three doctrines. Two were developed by his professors at Todai—the "Greater Asianism" of Ōkawa Shūmei, which included plans for colonizing India, and the "Confucian Nationalism" of Uesugi Shinkichi.

It was Kita Ikki, the radical national socialist, whose *General Outline Plan for the Reconstruction of Japan* most inspired Kishi. Kita called for a coup against the emperor, the elimination of the Meiji Constitution, the dissolution of the Diet, and the redistribution of wealth and public ownership. Kishi—who met Kita only once—hand copied Kita's clandestine pamphlet and, by his own account, was "overwhelmed by [Kita's] revolutionary spirit and his commanding appearance."[83] Kishi could comfortably accommodate to the emperor system, and was less inclined to assault private property, but it was abundantly clear that Kishi saw little in democracy that would serve the state. Declining Uesugi's invitation to teach at the university, the precocious Kishi passed his civil service examination after only his second year of college, and joined the Ministry of Agriculture and Commerce (MAC) in 1920.[84]

At MAC Kishi worked for Yoshino Shinji, eight years his senior, whom he credits as the intellectual father of the "control economy."[85] Yoshino first gathered academics and bureaucrats to design sector policies, and he lobbied successfully for the creation of a separate Ministry of Commerce and Industry (MCI). Still, Kishi also acknowledges that Yoshino delegated most of the substantive policy planning to him: "He trusted me, and left it all for me to do . . . I did my best to respond to his expectations and it was all a very beneficial learning experience for me."[86]

It was surely more than that. In Kishi's hands, these plans became a distinctive form of capitalism. Kishi would soon head a group of elite bureaucrats, including future LDP kingmaker Shiina Etsusaburō, who would build common cause with the military, cut their policy teeth in Manchuria, and bring their experience home. As Johnson suggests, "if the Yoshino-Kishi line prevailed in the Ministry during the first half of the 1930s, the Kishi-Shiina line dominated it during the 1940s, 1950s, and well into the 1960s."[87] Indeed, Kishi handpicked reform bureaucrats to fulfill the army's requests, a remarkable number of whom became senior officials in the Ministry of International Trade and Industry (MITI) after the war's end. Together, these bureaucrats believed that the primary purpose of private companies was not to seek profit but to increase productivity to meet the nation's purpose. Their goal was to separate management from ownership, so the state could control industry without obligating the government's budget.[88]

In 1926, like so many other Japanese planners before him, Kishi left for a study tour of the United States and Western Europe. The United States was celebrating its 150th birthday, and Kishi was overwhelmed by the scale of U.S. production and consumption. But also like his predecessors, he was far more impressed with the relevance of the German model. Kishi observed how a state control program rescued Germany from the crushing burden of high unemployment and inflation. He was impressed with the level of technical sophistication and, above all, with Germany's program of industrial rationalization (*sangyō gōrika*). He was especially taken by the use of cartels to address problems associated with "excessive competition" (*katō kyōsō*)—a lesson that would be enshrined in every subsequent document of Japanese industrial policy.[89]

Even before he could digest the results of this trip, Kishi and his colleagues were stunned by the Soviet Union's first five-year plan announced in 1928. Kishi reports that he was "shocked and impressed" by Soviet boldness. Indeed, he recalls feeling threatened by what successful planning could give Japan's neighbor.[90] He and Yoshino used the Soviet plans both as a model and as an incentive. Their efforts to promote rationalization were opposed by the zaibatsu but abetted by an imperial military that showed a particular interest in planning. The following year, the MCI created its Rationalization Bureau, and Kishi was assigned to return to Germany for blueprints to develop the program. The results were codified in the Important Industries Control Law (Jūyō Sangyō Tōsei Hō) of April 1931. Kishi's fingerprints were all over the document.

Indeed, Kishi's fingerprints are found on many innovations in industrial policy. The Important Industries Control Law compelled large firms to establish cartels, known as "control associations" (*tōseikai*).[91] Sector-specific industry laws followed in short order, first in petroleum in 1934, then in automobile manufacturing, machine tools, aircraft, aluminum, light metals, and organic chemicals. If two-thirds of the firms in a sector agreed, a cartel could be created with membership compelled for the rest. As a result, twenty-six control associations were created. The provisions were consistent: firms had to respond to the public interest and the government could intervene to direct investment and production levels. Cartels needed approval for annual plans. In exchange, losses would be covered and the firms would enjoy trade protection and tax benefits. There was less state control than met the eye: in every case, the zaibatsu firms that dominated the sector dominated the cartel as well.[92]

Kishi was equally deeply involved in the establishment of so-called public policy companies (*kokusaku gaisha*) in most strategic sectors. The formula was invariably the same: half the capital was provided by the state and half was raised from large firms, which were guaranteed dividends, given a policy role, and granted significant tax holidays. Some companies, such as Nippon Steel and Nippon Coal, came to dominate economic activity in their sectors. Once again, private capitalists maintained their autonomy and resisted the most onerous interventions of the state. As we shall see, these two measures were liberally applied to postwar Japan.[93]

The third innovation was an institutional umbrella beneath which cartels and public policy companies were shielded from political control. After the Manchurian Incident in September 1931, Kishi and allied bureaucrats formed what Berger calls "superagencies." These networks cut across existing ministries, linking bureaucrats and soldiers in order to marginalize politicians and to facilitate planning.[94] The most important were the Cabinet Research Bureau (Naikaku Chōsa Kyoku), created in 1935, and the Manchurian Affairs Bureau, established in 1934. Kishi became the MCI section chief responsible for the industrial development of Manchuria in 1934, and was elevated to Industrial Affairs Bureau chief in 1935, working directly with the military general staff on the expansion of the defense industry and military procurement.

In these capacities, Kishi was building fascist economic policy from within. He was responsible for the strategic industrial policy laws described above, from petroleum to automobiles, and from electric power to fertilizers. Kishi recalls being very blunt about the need for industrial policy. If domestic manufacturers could not make a strategic product, or if foreign competition threatened to knock them out of the business, it was a matter of national security for the state to protect them.[95] For example, he and his subordinates developed plans to bring corvée labor from China and Korea to work in Japan's coal mines.[96]

Kishi claims that he never fully embraced the idea of "separating management and capital," a central tenet of Japanese industrial-policy planning in the 1930s.[97] In fact, the Japanese state never ran roughshod over Japanese industry. Still, the accession of military officials to senior political posts made the Yoshino-Kishi "team" (*konbi*) seem particularly dangerous to party politicians and their zaibatsu supporters.[98] MCI Minister Ogawa Gōtarō, a Minseitō politician, decided to send Yoshino—then the MCI vice minister—to run the Tohoku Development Company, a public policy company modeled after the Tennessee Valley Authority. He sent Kishi to Manchuria, where the occupying army—including the future wartime Prime Minister Tōjō Hideki and senior military planner Ishiwara Kanji—were all too eager to welcome him. Their collaboration on plans for the industrial development of Manchuria was but a part of their Greater East Asia Co-Prosperity Sphere.

Kishi's first post was as the vice-minister for industrial development of Manchukuo. As the second-highest-ranking civilian official in the territory, Kishi enjoyed free rein on all matters related to the economy.[99] After having struggled for years against entrenched interests in Japan, Kishi considered Manchukuo—which was under the strict control of the Japanese Kwantung Army—"a bureaucrat's paradise."[100] His only instruction was to implement the five-year plan that he had been developing in Tokyo, a plan designed to extract raw materials, develop agriculture, and produce industrial equipment that would feed the war economy. It is difficult to overstate the ambition of this plan. Japan would depart from standard imperialist practice and actually *build* a foreign industrial base.

From the beginning, however, he faced two problems. First, the government provided no funding for the plan, and the financial resources of the South Manchurian Railway (Mantetsu) were insufficient. The military had already failed to break up Mantetsu and transfer its assets to an army holding company. Business leaders in Tokyo had rejected this plan for an economic general headquarters.[101] Second, the military had expanded territorial control without considering the costs. Nor had the military made any arrangements for private capital. Their distrust of the zaibatsu had hardly abated, but now they had to reconsider.

The original industrial policy for Manchukuo was clearly failing by the mid-1930s. That policy was based on "one industry, one firm" (*ichigyō issha*). Military economic planners created specially licensed policy firms in each strategic sector, and excluded all direct investment from Japan. The slogans "denounce capitalism" and "keep out the zaibatsu" were official policy. Mantetsu, so useful to the Army before 1931, was by now an albatross around its neck:

> By the mid thirties, danger signs began to appear in the Manchurian controlled economy . . . Most worrisome was the failing health of Mantetsu, still the anchor of Manchurian development. Under army direction, Mantetsu resources had been diverted into such unprofitable military-related activities as the construction of strategic railroads and the development of special companies like the Dowa Automobile Manufacturing Company and the Manchurian Chemical Industry Company. Bankers complained that Mantetsu's recent activities had badly overextended it, turning a healthy company into one whose prospects were "unpromising.[102]

The solution—for which Kishi must share credit with Ishiwara Kanji, the Kwantung Army officer responsible for the military's five-year plan (and apparently for the Manchurian Incident of 1931)—has been called "legendary."[103] They decided to abandon "one industry, one firm" in favor of "all industries, one firm." Now the challenge was to find the one right firm.[104]

AYUKAWA ON STAGE RIGHT

Like Mussolini, who cultivated Agnelli's support, Kishi and Ishiwara knew what they were looking for. They wanted "new zaibatsu"—conglomerates that would be independent of existing Japanese capital, and eager to exploit the potential wealth of northern China. Eight leading industrial figures—some with zaibatsu ties—were invited to tour Manchuria during the autumn of 1936 as guests of the army. Ayukawa Yoshisuke, the president of Nippon Sangyō (Nissan for short), was one of these invitees.[105] Kishi recalls disingenuously that he was still willing to work with the zaibatsu: "I believed that the military and the bureaucracy could not develop Manchuria alone. We needed first rate private industrialists to come there. I did not want their capital, I wanted their talent. Mitsui and Mitsubishi had assembled managers whom I wanted in Manchuria."[106]

But the military was not similarly disposed, and Kishi shifted plans to build his five-year plan around one huge firm. Ayukawa's Nissan was an excellent candidate. It was not Japan's only "new zaibatsu"—but it was the one best integrated across industrial sectors. It comprised firms in mining, transport, chemicals, fishery, and civil engineering, including Hitachi Manufacturing, Nippon Mining, Nihon Kagaku Kōgyō, and nearly one hundred and thirty other firms. By June 1937, just months before Ayukawa consummated a deal with Kishi and the military, Nissan was, after Mitsubishi and Mitsui, the third largest conglomerate in Japan.[107] The deal was extraordinary in every respect. Because of opposition from the finance ministry and zaibatsu, the army and MCI were authorized to negotiate with Ayukawa only on a limited basis. Ayukawa did not respond positively to this limited overture. He insisted on moving Nissan in its entirety to Manchuria, per the original, far grander plan.[108] He even insisted that he be permitted to raise non-Japanese capital to develop any new firm they might approve for Manchukuo. The military reluctantly approved.[109] Now he ran into opposition from some within the Kwantung Army who hesitated to antagonize Mantetsu officials by taking industrial activities away from them.

Kishi intervened on behalf of the Manchukuo government. He and Ayukawa developed a provisional plan that met with the approval of Army Minister Sugiyama Gen and was approved by the cabinet in July 1937. Sugiyama prevailed upon Matsuoka Yōsuke, the president of Mantetsu (and Kishi's uncle), and upon the Kwantung Army planners. A final plan was approved by the Japanese cabinet and by the Manchukuo state council in October 1937.

The final plan created a new firm, Manchurian Heavy Industries Company (Manshū Jūkōgyō Kaisha—Mangyō for short). The Nissan zaibatsu

Ayukawa Gisuke runs from his original firm, Kuhara Industries, and dashes past his "new zaibatsu" Nissan, to sit atop his new Manchurian operation in 1938. Reproduced courtesy of Chikako Okuyama.

would move its headquarters to Hsinking and form the core of Mangyō, which would be owned half by Nissan and half by the government of Manchukuo. Ayukawa won guarantees of 6 percent annual returns for ten years, funding from the Industrial Bank of Japan, allowances for the raising of foreign direct investment, and protection from fluctuations in his firms' share prices.[110] Mangyō was given monopoly control over many industrial sectors, including steel, light metals, heavy industry (automotive and aircraft), and coal mining. Most state-owned enterprises, previously subsidiaries of Mantetsu, were turned over to Mangyō, which became a giant holding company for most Manchurian heavy industry. Mantetsu operations were confined mainly to ports and railroads.

This was an extraordinary—indeed, unprecedented—move for a private firm. But Ayukawa had a number of good reasons to find the transplantation to Manchuria attractive. First was the opportunity to create— and to manage free from zaibatsu control—an immensely powerful industrial group that dominated an economy that could rival Japan's in size and scope. Second, Kishi and the military made it possible to transform Nissan at relatively little cost. The safety of Ayukawa's own investment in Mangyō was protected by specific guarantees from the Manchukuo government. Third, Ayukawa envisioned difficulties for Nissan if it remained in Japan. The 1937 Japanese tax reform affected Nissan's fiscal solvency—dividends paid from one company to another became subject to income tax, hitting holding companies like Nissan with heavy double taxation.[111]

Ayukawa's Mangyō got under way in December 1937. Its integration with the former Mantetsu firms never worked smoothly, and Ayukawa never secured foreign capital because of international sanctions imposed on Japan as a result of the war with China. The business community in Japan resented Manchuria as a drain on domestic resources. After the Pacific War got under way, "private capital was no longer willing to allow the government to run the Manchurian economy single-handedly."[112] Despite a 1941 reorganization of the company, continuing poor performance forced Ayukawa to resign from active management of Mangyō in December 1942. Ayukawa had failed to attract American capital and had, in any event, miscalculated the enormous costs of resource development.[113] Worse, he effectively lost control of his firm when, like Mantetsu before it, Mangyō fell prey to the army's whims.[114] Unlike the zaibatsu elite, who weathered this period successfully, Ayukawa's empire collapsed under the weight of international politics and military discipline.

KISHI'S TRANSWAR LEGACIES

Kishi, for his part, created no less modest—but much more durable—economic institutions. He was brought back to Tokyo in 1939 to serve as vice minister of MCI, where he could take credit for a Manchurian economy that was still running far more smoothly and profitably than when he had arrived three years earlier.[115] He returned at the request of Prime Minister Konoe, who promised him a free hand in implementing at home what he had learned about building an industrial economy in Manchuria. Kishi looked forward to instituting, in the name of the "security state" (*kokubō kokka*), the same planning and programs of state control. He explained that because of war mobilization, "it would be unavoidable to have to reduce the freedoms of people's daily lives somewhat."[116] But he had not banked on resistance from private capitalists. Indeed, his problems started with Konoe's minister, Kobayashi Ichizō, a zaibatsu-related politician. Kobayashi labeled the control bureaucrats "communists." Kishi resigned in protest in January 1941, and Kobayashi, realizing the Konoe government was laden with reformist bureaucrats, resigned soon thereafter.[117]

Prime Minister Tōjō Hideki brought Kishi back into government in October 1941 as his minister of commerce and industry. Kishi, just forty-four years old, was Japan's leading control bureaucrat. He now would have responsibility for the entire economy. He immediately replaced pro-zaibatsu senior ministry officials with his former Manchukuo deputies, such as Shiina Etsusaburō. Within two months he had affixed his signature on a resolution for war with the United States and Great Britain. Firmly ensconced as Japan's industrial czar, Kishi found himself in a "whirlpool of conflicting interests."[118] Private firms refused to invest in such businesses as rare metals mining, judging their prospects after the war as negligible, and the military services refused Kishi's request that they create a common pool of raw materials.[119] Trapped between two intransigent groups—and with war mobilization going badly—in late 1943 Kishi and Tōjō combined the Ministry of Commerce and Industry, the Economic Planning Board, and three other agencies to further centralize state control in a new, consolidated Ministry of Munitions (Gunjūshō). To protect the ministry from two implacable constituents, the military and business, Prime Minister Tōjō agreed to serve concurrently as munitions minister. Kishi would serve as vice minister and hold a portfolio as minister of state.

Here was the highest expression of state control that Japanese capital would ever abide. The government now held nominal power to determine production and transport schedules, storage, and investment decisions for all "munitions" firms. The zaibatsu kept their heads down. The next incarnation of the munitions ministry would be as the Ministry of International Trade and Industry after the war. MITI would be endowed with many of the same policy instruments pioneered during the war mobilization—including an "economic general staff," the ability to invoke "priority production," and a range of sector-specific industrial laws that enshrined close cooperation between ministry and industry.[120] Indeed, the continuities between MCI and MITI were biographical as well as institutional. Although Kishi was purged by the Occupation authorities, most of his disciples were not. Virtually every MITI vice minister from the inception of the ministry until the early 1960s had, earlier in his career, been a reformist bureaucrat under Kishi Nobusuke, either in Tokyo or in Manchuria.[121]

In the meantime, of course, the war did not go well for Japan. Even after the United States took control of Saipan in June 1944, placing their bombers within range of the home islands, Tōjō did not budge from his refusal to negotiate for a peaceful settlement. Kishi began to undermine the government. Publicly he organized to oppose the Yokosan Seijikai, and privately he joined a group led by Marquis Kido Kōichi, the lord privy seal, that conspired to bring Tōjō down. His critics called him "Double Kishi" (*ryō Kishi*) for his rank opportunism. In the eyes of one scholar, Kishi was merely "buying futures" to prepay his way out of jail at war's end.[122] In the event, neither he nor Kido bought enough. Both were imprisoned—with Tōjō—soon after the Occupation began. Kishi Nobusuke spent three years and three months in Sugamo Prison. There he consolidated his ties to powerful right-wingers—many of whom his Manchurian development projects had enriched. Upon his release, the architect of the "transwar" system of economic planning would turn to more singularly political pursuits.

What Johnson has aptly labeled "the institutions of Japan's high speed growth" and Noguchi called "the 1940 System" of postwar economic organization clearly originated in wartime economic mobilization.[123] Survivals in the areas of finance and industry are legion.[124] They include the establishment of an "economic general staff" to undertake industrial planning by "picking winners" and easing the economy away from losers on a sectoral basis through "industry laws" (*jigyō hō*); competition policy; controls on foreign currency exchange; and administrative guidance that allowed bureaucrats and businessmen to conspire on a sectoral and, often, company basis.[125] They also involve Japan's innovative system of indirect finance (*kansetu kinyū*), by which the government ordered banks to provide corporate finance. Supervised and protected by the Ministry of Finance and the Bank of Japan, this system persisted long into the postwar era.[126]

Given the anticapitalist bias of Kishi Nobusuke and other "control bureaucrats," the period of military hegemony was remarkably favorable to private business. Industrial output rose from 6 billion yen in 1930 to 30 billion yen in 1941. Light and heavy industries reversed positions in the economy—heavy industry accounted for a little more than one-third of total production in 1930, nearly three-quarters in 1941. The four great zaibatsu houses, Mitsui, Mitsubishi, Sumitomo, and Yasuda, ended the war with three billion yen in assets, about 20 percent of the total assets in the Japanese economy. They had learned how to work with an interventionist state and to turn many of its interventions to their own advantage. Meanwhile, state planners like Kishi Nobusuke had been learning the limits of their own power. They institutionalized, indeed ritualized, the process of reciprocal consent pioneered a generation earlier. Negotiation for control and jurisdiction in the market would continue to shape business-government relations far into the postwar period.

Legacies

A wide range of leaders served as midwife to the birth of corporatism. In Japan Mutō Sanji and his industrial allies were busy reinventing a "warmhearted" past, while Kishi Nobusuke was always justifying his actions by looking forward to a new, pan-Asian empire. Likewise in Italy, there were those who, like Giovanni Agnelli, cared only for what worked—usually in the present and with whatever ally was at hand—as well as those who, like Alessandro Rossi, chased solutions halfheartedly and so ensured their failure. Indeed, the path to corporatism in Italy was paved with failure, while in Japan it had a measure of strategic success.

The conventional view of Italian entrepreneurs holds that they were unable to adjust to modernity: "Employers projected the values of a pre-industrial, family-oriented society into industrial labor relations."[127] But there is another plausible interpretation. Perhaps the problem was not a preindustrial model, but that Italian business leaders simply failed to inject new meaning into old forms. Those, like Rossi, who had shucked the old-fashioned paternalism, failed to develop their preferred alternatives. The comparison to Japan makes them look especially inept. After all, the Italians had a more credible tradition to draw from than did Japanese entrepreneurs. As we have seen, Mutō and the others first had to invent a tradition of corporate paternalism before they could spread it through the economy. The consequence was a substantially different kind of labor politics and industrial relations in the two countries.

There were related differences in the organization of the economy more generally. Japanese leaders largely chose to organize the economy from the top down or from the inside out. Unlike their Italian counterparts, Japanese leaders—whether bureaucrats, politicians, or businessmen—left little to chance. Many were engaged in a competitive struggle to find and control a useable past. Others were obsessed with designing the future from scratch. The only question was, whose choice would prevail?

The legacies of Italy's economic leadership would be no less consequential but rather less salutary. IRI, the most important institutional legacy of this period, would be revived after World War II. After a strong but short-lived contribution to Italy's first postwar economic miracle, the Christian Democrats would undermine IRI for political ends. Ironically, it was at the turn of the twenty-first century, just as IRI finally disappeared, that the Japanese model of technonationalism finally seemed to run out of steam. Choices have long and often very sticky consequences. But here we are getting ahead of our story. First, we must look at some hugely consequential choices, for repression and for war.

CHAPTER SIX

The Total Leader:

BENITO MUSSOLINI

> I felt the pride of the victor . . . I had solved . . . such a problem as sometimes withdraws itself beyond the will and influence of any political man, and becomes subjected to the tyranny and mechanism of mere material relations under the influence of various and infinite factors.
>
> Benito Mussolini, *My Rise and Fall*

Japan's "parliamentary parenthesis" ended within a decade of Hara's assassination, and Giolitti failed to occupy the middle ground in Italy. Thereafter politics in both countries was largely about elite accommodation to naked force and public support for full-throated nationalism. Successful leaders were able to mobilize an antipathy for liberalism and use violence (their own or others') to capture the national imagination. The liberal window was effectively nailed shut after the March on Rome in 1922 and with the Manchurian Incident in 1931. Benito Mussolini stepped in from outside the state, armed and very dangerous, whereas Japanese authoritarianism was the handiwork of the state itself, abetted covertly by ultranationalists. Kita Ikki was one of several such ideologues who helped inspire a government by assassination, eliminating the slim and rapidly diminishing chances for liberal democracy in Japan in the 1920s and 1930s.[1] This chapter examines the ideas and intimidation used by a total leader in Italy and by a collective leadership in Japan to win domestic support for national expansion and fascism.

CLOSING THE PARLIAMENTARY PARENTHESIS IN JAPAN

After the assassination of Hara Kei in 1921 a full decade of parliamentary politics would pass before the bureaucracy and military gyrated into full fascist authoritarianism. During this extended, incandescent moment, possibilities for democracy seemed enhanced. Prime ministers represented parties that alternated in power; those parties debated policy alternatives and supplied cabinet ministers who led governments.

But Taishō democracy was less than it seemed, for these politicians feared to stretch the Meiji Constitution. They never challenged the fundamental institutions of a system designed to omit a formal role for the cabinet and the prime minister. As Itō had intended, power was wielded only in the name of the emperor, and each minister was left to fend for himself. Hara had taught that deals could be cut across elite groups. So parliamentarians—often purchased by businessmen—brought bureaucrats and army officers into the parties and collaborated with those inside the state.[2] This elite game was becoming ever more fractious. The conservative parties differed in the extent to which each would accommodate social forces, but neither trusted the masses, and neither dared affirm the principle of popular sovereignty.[3] The 1920s was replete with party competition, but democracy had precious little to do with governance.

Indeed, the parties responded to mass politics with schizophrenia. The more "liberal" Minseitō had long argued for universal male suffrage as a safety valve for popular unrest and endorsed workers' rights. When it finally got the chance to govern in 1925, Minseitō expanded the franchise but also enhanced police powers to stifle dissent through the Peace Preservation Law. Making matters worse, these party politicians badly mismanaged the economy. By the late 1920s, Japan was in desperate straits. Primary product prices were stagnant, export markets had collapsed, and incomes had fallen precipitously, especially in rural Japan. The government compounded the pain by returning Japan to the gold standard in 1929. By then, violence fed by resentment of politicians and businessmen was becoming commonplace.

It was easy for the nationalist Right to assign blame. Party politicians were transparently corrupt, and scandal wracked nearly every cabinet. Nationalists depicted the politicians as immoral imitators of indecent Western ideas and the growth of industry as an undermining of Japanese values. According to one, "electricity is discovered and the world is darkened."[4] Politicians routinely were portrayed as "intruders who sundered a sacred and mystical bond between the emperor and his subjects."[5] Despite considerable precedent, Taishō era leaders utterly failed to use (or to invent) the past to their advantage. As Pyle notes with penetrating insight, "their ultimate failure to justify or legitimize themselves within the realm of Japanese values" doomed them.[6] They met a prevailing ideology of social harmony with an ill-suited politics of partisan advantage.

Ultranationalists were much better at marrying symbols to power. As in Italy, many came from outside the state, and others, like the young army officers, were inside but disaffected. Young officers—sensitive to the distress of hardscrabble rural communities from which they and most of their conscripts came—felt keenly the disparities between their spartan existence and capitalist opulence. They were also distressed by the betrayal of "traditional" values by corrupt party politicians.[7]

The most influential of the ultranationalist ideologues of the 1920s was Kita Ikki (1883–1937). Kita was never easy to categorize. His first book, published in 1906, denied the emperor's authority as a god and was banned immediately. His participation in Chinese revolutionary movements in the early 1910s suggested to some that he was a socialist, but his *Outline Plan for the Reconstruction of Japan* (*Nippon Kaizō Hōan Taikō*), published in 1919, established him as the "father of Japanese fascism."[8] Kita was animated by the same race with the West that had motivated so many Meiji elites. But rather than seek parity, Kita sought Japanese domination of Asia. Kita's Japan would expel Western powers and would build an empire from Australia to Siberia so that "Japan could at last march to its destined place on the scale of historical evolution." His *Outline Plan* ended with the rousing reminder that "peace without war is not the way of heaven."[9]

Kita cooked up a stew using ingredients from a large number of doctrines. He called for temporary martial law to remove the corrupt politicians and plutocrats. Meiji institutions that no longer responded to the people's welfare had to be reformed—Kita argued for removing all barriers that separated the emperor from his subjects, including the Constitution, the House of Peers, and the Privy Council. He was a radical populist as well. He would expropriate private property—of the zaibatsu and of the imperial household—and redistribute Japan's wealth with widespread social programs. Japan, he taught, needed to be "purified" if it was to achieve its great destiny. His ideas were promulgated through the ultranationalist "Society of Those Who Still Remain" (Yūzonsha).

Kita was more than just another radical nationalist. His plan prefigured much of the wartime program, with a prototype for the Greater East Asia Co-Prosperity Sphere and an outline for a national defense state, state control of major industries, and, above all, a military seizure of power. This prefiguring, of course, was no coincidence. Kita inspired military and economic planners such as Kishi Nobusuke by squaring the circle of communism and capitalism with his Japanese-style national socialism.

Disciples, such as Ōkawa Shūmei, who planned for "Eight Corners of the Universe under a Single Roof" (Hakko Ichiu) and "The Imperial Way" (Kōdō), inspired restless officers. These idealistic men, resentful of elite privileges, willingly took up arms against the state in defense of a transcendent emperor. Groups of officers determined to destroy the "wicked men around the throne" (*kunsoku no kan*) so that Japan could realize its great ambitions and the emperor could rule beneficently through his own "great heart" (*ōmikokoro*). The first concrete plans toward a Shōwa Restoration were undertaken by the Cherry Blossom Society (Sakurakai). Their intended coup d'etat, undertaken with Ōkawa in March 1931, was aborted when senior military leaders balked. The planners went unpunished.

The situation changed dramatically in September 1931, however, when the government and even the general staff lost control of junior officers in Manchuria. The Kwantung Army staff bombed the South Manchurian Railway and blamed it on the Chinese. The bombing was used as an excuse to mobilize troops and assume control of Manchuria, against the known wishes of the cabinet. In October the Sakurakai attempted another coup, to eliminate leading cabinet members and imperial advisors and install General Araki Sadao as military governor, per Kita's *Outline Plan.* However, Araki turned on the plotters and as a reward was named minister of war. Once again, sympathy for the miscreants prevented the government from punishing them, and the Wakatsuki Cabinet resigned instead. Party politicians were slipping into cowed irrelevance. Far worse was yet to come.

The violence accelerated. In February 1932, the "Blood League" (Ketsumeidan), with connections to the Imperial Navy, murdered Minseitō Party leader—and former finance minister—Inoue Junnosuke for his alleged betrayal of Japan through financial policies that enriched capitalists and impoverished farmers. The zaibatsu responded as best they knew—by spending money. After its chairman, Dan Takuma, was assassinated in March 1932, Mitsui created a "Kindness Repayment Association" (Mitsui Hōonkai), which undertook social projects to improve its image. Mitsui also began to pay ultranationalists for "protection" of their senior executives.[10] This "conversion" (*zaibatsu tenkō*) was far too little and much too late. "Government by assassination" was already well under way.

On 15 May 1932 the Sakurakai attempted yet another coup d'etat in the name of the emperor. This time they murdered Prime Minister Inukai, attacked officials of the imperial household, and tried to provoke demands for the long-awaited Shōwa Restoration. Once again, senior military officers stood aside. And, once again, the perpetrators were treated with sympathy. Astonishingly, War Minister Araki, the nation's senior military official, declared that the assassins of the nation's prime minister were not traitors because they acted with high moral purpose: "We cannot restrain our tears when we consider the mentality expressed in these pure and naïve young men. They were not actions for fame, or for personal gain,

155

nor are they traitorous. They were performed in the sincere belief that they were for the benefit of Imperial Japan."[11]

In the decade since Hara's assassination, many more politicians and businessmen suffered the same fate. Party cabinets were now finished for good, and most prime ministers until 1945 would be drawn from the military. But still the violence was not over. There was one last convulsive display of national purification to come.

This time, an attempted coup would reveal deep divisions within the military itself. An Imperial Way faction, which had been supporting political agitation, now was confronted by a "Control" faction, which preferred political stability while biding time to seize power itself. On 26 February 1936, a group of fourteen hundred soldiers marched from their barracks and occupied central Tokyo. Demanding "restoration of the emperor" and "destruction of the wicked," they surrounded the Parliament building, the prime minister's residence, the Metropolitan Police headquarters, and other government agencies.[12] They murdered the emperor's most senior advisor, the Lord Keeper of the Privy Seal, as well as the finance minister and the inspector general of military education. They also attacked the prime minister and other senior leaders. But the officers overplayed their hand. The incident ended when the Imperial Navy sailed into Tokyo Bay and the emperor "personally" intervened to declare that the rebels had "breached authority."[13]

The officers arrested in the May 15 Incident had a public trial and were treated leniently, but the leaders of the 2/26 Incident were court-martialed in camera. Thirteen officers were executed, as were four civilians— including Kita Ikki, who had not even participated in the insurrection. As the Chinese proverb says: "When the cunning hares have been killed, the hunting dogs go into the cooking pot." The Imperial Way faction had killed the hares of party politicians, but were now consumed by their erstwhile military colleagues.[14]

By July 1937, however, the army had more freedom to prosecute war with China. There would be no more politicians compromising Japanese strength at international conferences, as at the Washington Naval Conference in 1921–22 and again at the London Naval Conference in 1930. As we saw in the previous chapter, the government had shifted to national mobilization (*kokka sōdōin taisei*) through which state control policies guided the economy, the press, and social relations in general. And, there was no one to stop them.

Corporatism had arrived in Japan. Laissez-faire capitalism was rejected for stimulating selfishness and unbridled competition, socialism for impeding the national purpose. No mass movement would capture the state, and no total leader would capture the masses. Militarists and bureaucrats would share full control. They deputized civic groups, such as the Boy Scouts, the Red Cross, women's groups, and religious organizations, to watch for banned views that would "impair fundamental national policies."[15] In 1940 they folded all civic associations in Japan, including political parties, trade unions, and civic groups, into a corporatist Imperial Rule Assistance Association (Taisei Yokusankai) established to "mobilize the Japanese spirit." The home ministry required all Shintō shrines be rededicated to Amaterasu Ōmikami, the sun goddess (the emperor was a direct descendent). Zen Buddhist leaders fell into line, proudly celebrating the connection between Bushidō and the militarists now in power. The absolute Japanese state would serve as the great protector of the Buddha-Dharma, for "the Imperial wind and the Buddha's sun are," they declared, "non-dual."[16] The "Emperor System" was now under the control of the military and its bureaucratic allies, its "ideological orthodoxy" now "rigidified."[17] Japanese leadership, the Japanese body politic, the Japanese nation—in short, the kokutai—was now united and purified. And bent on destroying itself.

IL DUCE

Benito Mussolini (1883–1945) has no counterpart in Japanese history and few in the annals of Western civilization. He would surely have been the first to insist that he stood alone, sui generis, as he made history—and he would not have been incorrect. Much of what he wrought has already been documented in these pages. Here we focus less on the institutions he built (and destroyed) than on the way he built (and destroyed) them. For here was a leader—indeed, as he would have it, *the* leader (Il Duce)—who invited but always defied easy characterization.[18] Mussolini may have been singular, but he did what great leaders do. He was easy to caricature; at once a clown and a poseur, timorous and courageous. He was ruthless and opportunistic, and simultaneously productive and destructive. He could inspire and conspire, and he could manipulate yet bend. His rhetoric was always voluble, but he kept it controlled: he could make it vertiginous or subtle. In short, the way he deployed power gains us an opportunity to understand some of the essential mechanisms of leadership.

The one constant was change: few have reinvented themselves as relentlessly as Mussolini. Until 1919 he was a socialist; then he proclaimed himself an anarchist. Having turned on his socialist fraternity before 1914, he turned on his democratic fraternity afterwards. In 1925, he said he was a free-trade liberal, who subsequently adopted the posture of a monopoly capitalist—always black-shirted, to play to adoring crowds. One distinguished observer argues that "one transient phase succeeded another . . . [in] violent oscillations [of] fundamental unseriousness."[19] But Mussolini was always deadly serious. He shifted easily from intransigent socialism to ardent nationalism once the opportunity presented itself. He was as comfortable sleeping with republicans as with monarchists, with Catholics as with liberals, with J. P. Morgan as with Adolf Hitler. All these liaisons (save the last) were temporary, each merely a "one night stand" on his way to total power.[20] Mussolini's profound amorality was consistent. His was an eclectic "church of all the heresies," one that absconded with slogans indiscriminately, without regard for their origins, so long as he could put them to use.[21] Ideas were justified only by their success.

Mussolini's most distinguished political enemies, the socialist Gaetano Salvemini and the prelate Don Luigi Sturzo, captured Mussolini's absolute moral indifference in caustic tones, which they tinted only slightly with grudging admiration. Both underestimated Mussolini's skills, and each would spend decades in exile. In 1926, Sturzo argued, "Of mediocre culture and meagre political experience, Mussolini has the brilliant qualities of the extemporizer and none of the scruples of those who, convinced of an idea, fear to be false to it."[22] Salvemini, speaking of the time in 1929 when Mussolini was simultaneously Duce of the Fascist Party, Commander in Chief of the Fascist Militia, Head of the Government, Home Secretary, Foreign Minister, Minister of War, Minister of the Army, Minister of the Navy, Minister of the Air Force, and Minister of Corporations, declared sardonically that "he broke the record of Pooh-Bah in the *Mikado* . . . always representing himself as responsible for all that was happening . . . [while] the only department to which he devoted himself wholeheartedly and with boundless success was advertising and public relations . . . He knew as few have known that a lie goes round the world in the time truth takes to tie its shoes."[23]

Mussolini himself could not have agreed more. Indeed, he *celebrated* his amorality: "We do not believe in dogmatic programs . . . We will permit ourselves the luxury of being aristocrats and democrats, conservatives and progressives, reactionaries and revolutionaries, legalists and illegalists, according to time, place, and circumstances."[24] Morality was for fools, and Mussolini was no fool. He knew what he was up to: "Every revolution," he told a German reporter in 1932, "creates new forms, new myths, and new rites."[25] His dictum, "Everything in the State, nothing outside the State, nothing against the State," was, characteristically, mere rhetoric. Mussolini made sure that neither would the state absorb the party nor the party the state.[26] All roads may have led to Rome, but more to the point, they all led to *his* Rome, to the historic, long-awaited "Third Rome" that he alone could build.

Le maschere e il volto

Mussolini seen in 1925 with frustratingly many personae. Reproduced courtesy of Dino Aloi. Cartoon by Camerini, "Il travaso," 1925—in *L'altra storia d'Italia* (The other history of Italy), edited by Dino Aloi. Published by Il Pennino, 1996, in collaboration with Regione Piemonte, Italy.

If Mussolini had to empty the state by besieging those within it, he would. If, after bombast and violence failed, he had to accommodate to a rival's superior position, he would. There was always a larger project to attend to—the project to make Il Duce and his work eternal. There were two mechanisms in this project: Mussolini's meticulous use of history and his besieging of opponents. Each was linked directly to his ultimate, fatally miscalculated decision for war.

POLICING HISTORY TO BUILD THE "THIRD ROME"

We have already seen how many Italians responded to Mazzini's promise of a "Third Italy." The liberal state never delivered, but Mussolini would. His "Third Italy" would not last long, but its evanescence would be brilliantly lit by the past. Mussolini tenaciously policed the aesthetics and rhetoric of historical representation.[27] His fascist state was always linked back to Rome through the Risorgimento—and always viewed through lenses he personally would grind. Among all else he was and did, Il Duce was a publicist—a master of the past as well as of the present. He promoted a renascent Rome that would again impart its civilization to the world. Rome was Mussolini's most fecund inspiration and his most powerful tool. He used it more effectively than any Italian leader before or since to inspire, to mobilize, and to stir national passion. Rome was the foundation of Western civilization, and fascism would recapture for Italy the same respect Rome had once enjoyed.[28] He selectively borrowed its symbols: the Roman salute, the eagle, he even put Romulus and Remus to work for the Fascist boy scouts. Roman forms of address were taught in schools, as were (and here he trod carefully) Roman religious traditions.[29] Although rebel Sicilian peasants had already used the *fascio*—the bundle of rods enclosing an axe that symbolized the authority and discipline of the Roman lectors—during the land revolts of the late nineteenth century, Mussolini deployed it to define his regime. There was no higher totem than the fascio; it adorned every variety of artistic and architectural undertaking and, lending its name to a fully developed ideology, it blurred the distinction between state and civil society.[30]

Rome was neither his sole inspiration nor his only tool. Mussolini eagerly grabbed and used anything glorious in Italy's past. Virtually everything was a possible "predecessor and prefigurer of fascism," even Dante.[31] The fascist anthem combines his vision with the full range of national themes: youth, heroism, immortality, rebirth, war, discovery, beauty, even liberty:

Salve, o popolo d'Eroi,
Salve, o patria immortale,
Son rinati i figli tuoi
Con la fe'nell'ideale.

Il valor de' tuoi guerrieri,
La virtù dei tuoi pionieri,
La vision de l'Alighieri,
Oggi brilla in tutti i cuor.

Giovinezza, Giovinezza,
Primavera di bellezza
Nel fascismo è la salvezza
Della nostra libertà.[32]

Greetings, people of heroes,
Greetings, immortal nation,
Your children are reborn
With the faith of ideals.

The valor of your soldiers,
The skills of your pioneers,
The vision of [Dante] Alighieri
Shine today in every heart.

Youth, Youth
Spring of beauty
In fascism is the salvation
Of our liberty.

Just as in Roman times, time would restart at the foundation of empire.[33]

Mussolini would dress up as Caesar but invoke Napoleon and Garibaldi. Indeed, the Risorgimento also provided a rich vein of instrumentally reconstructed history—as an incomplete spiritual rebirth of Italy whose promises now would be fulfilled by fascism. He celebrated the anniversary of Cavour's Lo Statuto, but skipped back past liberalism to inject fascism directly into the veins of Mazzinian Republicanism and Garibaldian revolution. Mazzini and Garibaldi surely would have brushed him off, but Mussolini stood on the shoulders of both. Mazzini's garb of national mourning inspired the black shirts of Mussolini's thugs. Mazzini's anti-Marxian and antiliberal ideas, not just the "Third Italy" but also his later call for an Italian mission in the Mediterranean and North Africa, legitimated Mussolini's ambitions.[34] Mazzini, denounced during his lifetime by Bakunin for being too available to the Right (because he rejected materialism and embraced religion), made it easy for others to abscond with his formulations.[35]

Garibaldi was nearly as powerful an icon. The fiftieth anniversary of Garibaldi's death (1932) coincided with the tenth year of the fascist state, a confluence that Mussolini could not let pass. Mussolini personally took control of the fascist reconstruction of Garibaldi. The government financed a Garibaldian Exhibition, pilgrimage to his tomb, publication of the first national edition of his writings, commemorative stamps, even a lottery in Garibaldi's honor. National holidays were declared, replete with speeches by fascist *gerarchi* (officials) in the major squares. And, of greatest significance, Mussolini ordered the building of a monument to Garibaldi's first wife, Anita, an event laden with symbolic attacks on the Church and on liberalism.[36] Rome, the Risorgimento, and fascism all came together in one brilliant symbolic moment in October 1928, when Mussolini ordered a public celebration on the anniversary of the March on Rome in which World War I debt certificates were burned on an ancient Roman altar taken from a museum and placed atop the steps of the Victor Emmanuel monument in central Rome.[37]

The man who choreographed all this—the man who invented Mussolini's "national liturgy" and many of the rituals of Romanità—was the voluptuary poet Gabriele D'Annunzio.[38] Roman history had long been a feature of popular education, but it was D'Annunzio who turned "patriotism and the cult of Rome into a rhetorical, passional mourning for the past."[39] He did this through direct political action as well as through the written word. As reported in chapter 4, D'Annunzio had led a regiment of regular army troops and *arditi* into Fiume in September 1919 in the first instance of international violence in Europe since the Armistice. D'Annunzio's open defiance of the temporizing Italian state—the first by an "organized" military force—was abetted by a general staff that let him pass unchallenged through Istria, and met with an outpouring of popular support. This was, he argued, Italy's destiny, and the people agreed. He had taken this step in the name of Roman glory:

[Italy] shall be greater by conquest, purchasing territory not in shame, but at the price of blood and glory . . . After long years of national humiliation, God has been pleased to grant us proof of our privileged blood . . . No, we are not and do not want to be just a museum, a hotel, a vacation resort, a Prussian-blue horizon where foreigners come for their honeymoons . . . Our genius demands that we should put our stamp on the molten metal of the new world . . . If it is a crime to incite people to violence, I boast now of committing that crime . . . This war, though it may seem destructive, will be the most fruitful means of creating beauty and virtue that has appeared on the earth.[40]

D'Annunzio was everything Giolitti and the Liberals were not. He was lustful and passionate, while they claimed to seek reason and solved problems through material exchange. He sought glory, while they sought economic development and personal enrichment. There was no question which was more closely attuned to "the collective appetites of his generation" or to the individual appetites of the future dictator.[41] Mussolini visited D'Annunzio in Fiume and saw firsthand "how dead elements of the Roman culture had come to life under the breath of D'Annunzio's creative spirit."[42] By now Mussolini was firmly in the thrall of reaction. None put his transformation better than Salvemini: "The more he watered his revolutionary wine, the more alcohol he added to his nationalist cocktail."[43] Mussolini's own band of men (*fascio*) was joined by those who had been with D'Annunzio in Fiume. More importantly, D'Annunzio provided Mussolini a road map replete with intimidation, glorification of violence, operatic costumes, visions of modernity, government by guild, foreign funding, and, above all, an object lesson in what could be accomplished in openly confronting the weak, liberal state. Kita Ikki played this role in Japan, but no single leader ever dared exhibit Mussolini's audacity.

Lest we forget, Mussolini's standoff against this state, like his use of symbols and "rituals of consensus," met considerable support from the masses and underwhelming opposition from elites. He succeeded in building a sense of solidarity where others had failed. Mussolini's project was at the height of its popular appeal when, in May 1936, he proclaimed the Italian Empire from the balcony of the Palazzo Venezia in Rome.[44] He had by then long since squeezed the life from the Italian center—in his words, he had "broken the bones of the democrats."[45] How he did this, beyond the brilliantly manipulative and instrumental use of history and symbolic politics, bears closer scrutiny.

EVERY WHICH WAY AGAINST THE MIDDLE

Measured against Italy's glorious past and Mussolini's ambitions for its future, the present was simply humiliating. Victories on the battlefield had been stolen at the peace table. Splendor had been reduced to insignificance. If D'Annunzio was correct that Italy was little more than a holiday destination, it was the fault of a cowardly, flaccid, inconsequential, egotistical Liberal state, a state characterized by "moral senility."[46] The

Right promised virile action. Nationalists conquered the *piazze*, taking the public squares from the Left with impunity.[47]

Mussolini founded his Fasci di Combattimento in Milan in March 1919 and, after months of intimidation and thuggery, the fascists were widely known to the public. In the May 1921 election his Partito Nazionale Fascista won more than a fifth of the popular vote—more than Don Sturzo's Catholic Popolari and only slightly less than the Socialists (26%). Despite internal divisions, his party had something for everyone: eight-hour days for workers, land for peasants, confiscation of Church property for the Republicans, industrial peace for the industrialists, national prestige for the military. Mussolini could be the enemy of the socialists and the friend of the workers at the same time. His party's violence became profoundly useful. Giolitti had found it convenient to bring in Mussolini to intimidate voters, industrialists employed the *fascisti* to bully unionists, and shopkeepers found them useful to coerce managers of competing cooperatives.

Mussolini's fascists had something for everyone—but each time the party took the stage it stole power from its patron. D'Annunzio initially had invented the idea of a coup d'etat to be effected through a "March on Rome," but he abandoned it after being paid off in November 1921.[48] When Fascist squads took over many of Italy's smaller northern cities in the summer of 1922—having already seized power in Trieste, Bologna, Florence, and elsewhere—Liberals continued to delude themselves that they were still in control. They talked themselves into believing they had domesticated Mussolini. Senator Luigi Albertini, influential editor of *Il Corriere della Sera*, confided to his associates that "once he is in Rome, he will be much more subject to influence."[49] Even when Mussolini's newspaper, *Il Popolo d'Italia*, published military regulations for an illegal Fascist militia in early October, the government did nothing. It issued no challenge until the March on Rome began, by which time it was too late. Unlike Emperor Hirohito, who suppressed the 2/26 mutineers, the king refused to decree a state of siege. No monarch had ever withdrawn support from an Italian government in crisis, but this was no ordinary crisis. It was the beginning of the end of the Kingdom of Italy, and it was most certainly the end of the liberal Italian state.

Benito Mussolini became Italy's youngest prime minister ever at thirty-nine years old, and his first cabinet seemed normal enough. He was invited to form a coalition government that included two Catholic Popolari, four Liberals, a nationalist, and only four Fascists. Legitimating this unholy mix were the philosopher Giovanni Gentile and two war heroes. The government was confirmed in regular constitutional form, 306 in favor, 116 opposed, and he assumed power as the economy recovered from postwar recession. After 1923, Italy would enjoy rapid economic growth, the expansion of exports, and balanced budgets. But little would be normal, as Mussolini actively suppressed the opposition, increased the level of terror, and created a Grand Council of Fascism that would displace the Chamber of Deputies as the locus of legislative and executive authority.[50] The small group that marched on Rome in October 1922 grew to fifteen million strong by 1937. Everyone loves a winner—except for vanquished enemies.

And enemies would not go unpunished. In a sustained, carefully managed attack, Mussolini emptied the center of Italian politics. The defining moment of his strategy came very soon. In May 1924, a Socialist deputy, Giacomo Matteotti, openly denounced the Fascists.[51] Soon thereafter a fascist death squad assassinated him, generating a firestorm of protests, including formation of Italy's first and most sustained antifascist alliance and the flowering of an antifascist press. A group of opposition deputies left the Chamber in protest—an act known as the Aventine Secession—and stayed away for sixteen months.

In the event, Mussolini owed his survival to ruthlessness and the unwillingness of Italy's most respected institutions—Vatican, press, monarchy—to intervene. From outside the Parliament, the Aventine group could do nothing to stop reforms that further consolidated Mussolini's power. For example, one of Mussolini's deputies, Giacomo Acerbo, authored an electoral reform that tilted the existing system of proportional representation dramatically in the Fascists' favor.[52] Mussolini arrested editors, threatened politicians, and tried to intimidate everyone else. Giovanni Giolitti appealed to Fiat's powerful chairman Giovanni Agnelli, who had a minority interest in the newspaper *La Stampa*, to use it to oppose Mussolini, but Agnelli demurred. Instead, Alfredo Frassati, the majority shareholder, was forced out, and Agnelli assumed control with Mussolini's tacit blessing. In October 1924, the Communist Party appealed to the other secessionists to declare themselves a legal parliament, but they declined, fearing civil war. Instead, the secessionists, in disarray, tried to return to the Chamber. Mussolini, declaring that their electoral mandate had lapsed while they were away, blocked their entry. It was the end of antifascist politics in Italy—at least during Mussolini's time in Rome. According to one historian, "The only value of the Aventine protest was that it forced Fascism to reveal itself as totalitarian."[53]

Mussolini was free to play the routine game of *trasformismo* from a position of great strength.[54] It took time, but by the late 1930s he had changed a normal constitutional government into a thoroughly Fascist state that maximized his own personal tyranny. His party was now another ministry in a machine of state that would indoctrinate, co-opt, intimidate, and empty the center. His deals with the monarchy, business, and the Church were visible. From early on, fascism had been republican; Mussolini had promised to "liquidate" the monarchy. In the end, though, he maintained the monarchy—after stripping it of power. King Victor Emmanuel—whom Mussolini called a "dolt"—never gave Mussolini any trouble. Until 1943, when fascism was chased north to Salò, the crown stayed out of Mussolini's way.[55]

Business was, as we have seen, nearly as easy to digest. It is possible to overestimate the degree of support fascism received from the business community, and business did remain fragmented during the corporatist period. Still, Mussolini reneged on his promises to end statism, he established IRI as preeminent in the Italian economy, and he tamed Confindustria. Like the monarchy, organized business was no threat to the fascist state.

His crowning conciliation was with the Vatican. Mussolini in his socialist youth had authored a steamy novel, *The Cardinal's Mistress*, and he was no friend of the Church. Fascism was based on antireligious principles, yet to many Catholics, the fascists had looked like natural allies. They shared fundamental antipathies toward the anticlerical Liberals and the Communists, and each controlled something the other coveted. Mussolini wanted to eliminate political competition from the Partito Popolare, and the Church wanted enhanced defense against socialism.[56] The Church was quite willing to sacrifice its political party, and Mussolini agreed to rescue the Vatican's Bank of Rome from bankruptcy. In February 1929, after six years of secret meetings, Mussolini and the Church signed the historic Lateran Pacts. The Roman Catholic Church, squeezed into a postage stamp-sized territory and marginalized by the liberal state, now would enjoy public support. Catholicism would be the "sole religion of the state," religious marriages would have the force of law, divorce would not be recognized, and there would be compulsory religious education in state schools. The Lateran Pacts reversed sixty years of church-state separation. The Church's complicity with fascism was substantial, although protest by traditional clergy and Popolari who went underground ensured that the door would be open for reconciliation between the Church and the postwar republic. In the meantime, Church and Fascist state would remain uneasy partners.[57]

By most conventional measures of national power, of wealth, and of national identity, Fascism was a success. All those who believed they could domesticate Mussolini—the Liberals, the Church, business, the monarchy—had fatally miscalculated. Each underestimated his capacity for brutality, his vigor, and above all his public support. But, in the event, their miscalculation was not the only one. Amid the best economic performance in Italian history, Mussolini made his own fatal misstep—his decision for war on the side of Nazi Germany.

Mussolini was depicted as a student of Machiavelli in 1924. In *Come ridevano gli italiani* (How the Italians laugh), edited by Adolfo Chiesa. Rome: Newton Compton, 1984.

THE OTHER FATAL MISCALCULATION

To casual students of twentieth-century European history, fascism means war. Indeed, because Mussolini's Italy and Hitler's Germany were "natural" allies, fascism means war *in alliance with* nazism. After all, each was built on a base of aggressive nationalism.[58] But the historical record suggests otherwise, at least from the Italian perspective. Mussolini entertained a number of foreign policy options, only one of which was the so-called Pact of Steel with Hitler. His policy inconsistencies should make ideological affinity a thin reed upon which to build political analysis, and anyway he had other plausible choices.[59] For at least a decade after 1924, for example, the British and the French, allies during the Great War, courted Italy. Mussolini might have maintained that alliance and balanced against Germany. Alternatively, he could have consolidated the Fascist state and destroyed his socialist enemies at home by confronting the Soviet Union. In the event, Mussolini elected to march with Nazi revisionism, "perform[ing] the feat of making his country the instrument of its traditional enemy for injury against its traditional friend."[60]

There were geopolitical limits to any "natural" relationship between Nazi Germany and Fascist Italy. Mussolini was more concerned about preserving Italian sovereignty in Alto Adige than about the rise of a group of Bavarian "clowns" (*buffoni*) who modeled their National Socialism on his original. Long before he was terrorized by Hitler, Mussolini expressed his contempt (or at least what he called "majestic pity") for him. Until Hitler became chancellor, Mussolini refused his repeated requests for a meeting, and even declined to send him an autographed portrait. Nazis were ever the barbarians of Tacitus, "descendents of people who were illiterate in the days when Rome boasted a Caesar, a Virgil, and an Augustus."[61] Only after assurances that the Nazis would respect Italian claims in Southern Tyrol should they gain power did Mussolini provide financial support.[62]

With the British he shared common (albeit limited) geopolitical interests in the Middle East, particularly shared opposition to pan-Arabism. Of course, this too was a delicate game. In 1922, before the March on Rome, Mussolini declared that Italy must break from its "subjugation" to Great Britain. He proclaimed that he would drive Britain out of the Mediterranean and turn it into an "Italian lake"—a position to which he would return in the late 1930s.[63] For a decade, however, he and the British explored their common interests in a European and Mediterranean status quo. Churchill was particularly effusive. Like most British conservatives, he welcomed fascism as a counterweight to "the bestial appetites of Leninism."[64] Churchill declared Mussolini a "Roman genius" and described him as the "greatest law giver among modern men."[65] And, after Austen Chamberlain secured Mussolini's support in 1925 for British claims against Turkey, he proclaimed that Mussolini was "the simplest and sincerest of all men when he is not posing as a dictator . . . I am confident he is a patriot and a sincere man, I trust his word when given, and I think we might easily go far before finding an Italian with whom it would be as easy for the British government to work."[66] Mussolini began securing what he believed was British support for an African empire. And indeed, until the imperialist adventure in Ethiopia in 1935, British diplomats worked closely with Mussolini. Even after the Ethiopian misunderstanding, the British struggled to keep Mussolini and Hitler apart. They nearly succeeded. When they failed, it was Mussolini's choice, not theirs.[67]

With the British eager after 1925 for further cooperation, Mussolini turned to France. Here another Franco-German conflict promised two possibilities. Either he would extract rewards for helping France against Germany, or he would extract concessions from Germany for doing the opposite. Salvemini argues that Mussolini preferred the former but could easily have gone either way.[68] In February 1927 he told a French newspaper that "the German peril should draw Italy and France ever nearer together," and he strongly objected to German-Austrian unification.[69]

In short, by the mid-1930s, Mussolini had created a world of multiple possibilities for Italian foreign policy. The future Pact of Steel was by no means a foregone conclusion. In fact, it seemed unlikely. Mussolini met Hitler in Venice in June 1934, and came away certain of his own superiority and convinced that the German chancellor was a "dangerous fool."[70] Mussolini confided "there is no way of reaching an agreement with that man."[71] One month later, in July 1934, he was proved correct. Despite Hitler's promise not to meddle in Austrian affairs, local Nazis assassinated the Italian-supported chancellor, Engelbert Dollfuss, and tried to seize power in Vienna. Mussolini declared that "It would be the end of European civilization if that country of murderers were to overrun Europe . . . [National Socialism is] a revolution of the old German tribes of the primeval forest against the Latin civilization of Rome . . . Perhaps the Great Powers will recognize the German danger."[72] Mussolini made an ostentatious show of hosting Dolfuss's widow and family at his home near Rimini.

During the failed putsch Mussolini mobilized four mountain divisions and dispatched them to the Brenner Pass at the Austrian border. He proclaimed "Hands off Austria" (*L'Austria non si tocca*), let the Italian press vilify Hitler, and provided the new chancellor, Kurt von Schuschnigg, with

When Mussolini chose war in 1940, he had a real choice of allies. Reproduced courtesy of the *Richmond Times-Dispatch*.

funds to counter Nazi propaganda. The French saw a natural ally: "Italy's cause is ours. We are mounting guard for her on the Rhine. She is mounting guard for us at the Brenner."[73]

The next step was an effort to parlay European relief into support for imperial ambition. Mussolini invited the British and French foreign ministers to the northern Italian town of Stresa in April 1935 to discuss an anti-German front. Their official communiqué denounced German "undermin[ing of] public confidence in the security of a peaceful order" and concluded with an agreement to oppose by all "practicable [means] any unilateral repudiation of treaties which might endanger the peace of Europe."[74] The communiqué never mentioned what Mussolini believed he had really achieved—a carte blanche from Britain and France for an Italian empire in Africa.[75] Still, Mussolini had every reason for confidence. After all, he had assurances—tacit and otherwise—from the French and the British. He had seen the world stand idly by as the Japanese advanced into Manchuria in 1931.[76] And, to underscore the important point that Italy and Germany were not natural allies, as late as 1935 Germany was training Austrian "volunteers" to fight in Ethiopia *against* Italy and was preparing troops for resistance against Italy in Southern Tyrol, should Mussolini have decided against the German alliance.

Mussolini moved against Haile Selassie in October, and immediately met with opposition from France and Great Britain and the League of Nations. The League had failed on Manchuria, and world leaders knew it would collapse if it failed again. Even if the British and the French had intended to appease Mussolini, they were constrained by an unexpected public outcry at the invasion. Britain redeployed forces in the Mediterranean even as conservatives, who did not want to alienate Mussolini, made known their preference for neutrality. France and Britain approved only mild sanctions. In December 1935 they also devised the so-called Hoare-Laval Plan: to preserve the European balance of power, Britain and France were prepared to veto the League's sanctions and deliver half of Ethiopia to Italy. Incredibly, Mussolini rejected the plan. Hoare was forced to resign, and Laval was left to mumble that Mussolini was mad.[77] Mussolini had sabotaged the best chance for a balance of power that would contain Germany.

The judgment of historians diverges at this point. Was Mussolini pushed into Hitler's open arms by a Britain unwilling to cede sufficient space in the Mediterranean and Africa? Or was Mussolini simply continuing to lurch inconsistently toward a future he continued to misperceive? There is evidence on both sides. On the one hand, Italian and British interests in the Mediterranean were increasingly in conflict, and Mussolini was unmoved by persistent British efforts to appease him. Moreover, Hitler's arms were becoming wider, stronger, and more irresistible. On the other hand, Mussolini's foreign policy did appear to take on "a terrifying wobble" in the late 1930s.[78] Mussolini overestimated the desire of British public opinion to keep out of a European war as well as the willingness of British conservatives to continue appeasing Hitler. For whatever reason, Italy and Germany came together in late 1936 with Mussolini's proclamation of empire and a joint determination to support Francisco Franco in Spain. Now, however, Germany was far more powerful. When Hitler intensified his Nazification of Austria, there was little Mussolini could do. In March 1938, Hitler attacked Austria before it could hold a plebiscite on independence. Italy stood by and observed the *anschlüss* in what Cassel has called "the beginning of the end of fascist Italy."[79]

Mussolini enjoyed one last chance to bask in Western praise. In September 1938, after months of Hitler's railing against his Czech neighbors, Mussolini called for a conference to broker the peaceful dismemberment of Czechoslovakia. The Munich Pact, perhaps history's most often invoked example of appeasement, won great public acclaim at the time. Mussolini prevailed upon Hitler to settle for annexation of the Sudetenland, home of a German-speaking minority (and of fortifications and industry). He was admired for his role as peacemaker at home and abroad. Relations with Britain improved, and there was a surprisingly deep (or surprisingly naive) sense that war could be kept at bay. Mussolini seemed educable again to the ways of European stability.[80]

But chances for an Italian volte-face slipped away forever in May 1939, when Hitler and Mussolini signed their famous Pact of Steel one month after Hitler had burned the Munich accord and (without informing Mussolini) invaded the rest of Czechoslovakia. Mussolini now seemed to have cast his lot. He believed that if Italy were left out of European war, it would be left out of history. Credit for keeping the peace was not the same to him as getting credit for winning the war. Hitler and Mussolini agreed that war need not be provoked before 1943, but German forces struck Poland in September 1939 and the Allies responded with declarations of war.

Italy was not ready for war. Mussolini's air force had less than two months of fuel stockpiled, and Italian steel production was one-twentieth of Germany's and one-fifth of Britain's. Mussolini had neglected the military industries in the 1920s and had bankrupted the treasury in the 1930s. Although his "instincts led him toward war, prudence drew him back. Eventually he settled for delay."[81] He convinced Hitler to release Italy from its treaty obligations because it was not ready with men and matériel. Hitler declared that the Italians were behaving "exactly as they did in 1914," a reference to Italian temporizing until the Treaty of London promised them maximum prizes from participation.[82] This time, though, the chance to play both ends against the middle had been frittered away. Instead, invoking a term unknown to international law, Mussolini declared that Italy would be a "nonbelligerent."

Hitler let Mussolini off the hook. To his chagrin, if not humiliation, Mussolini was immensely popular at home for "dismounting"—for keeping Italy out of the war.[83] Italy won strategic and diplomatic benefits from the Allies as well. The British acquiesced to Italian nonbelligerency and withheld their planned attack on the peninsula. Mussolini did in fact temporize. Now concerned about Soviet-German friendship, for the Non-Aggression Pact had been signed in August, Mussolini informed the Benelux countries of impending German invasion in late 1939. Hitler cancelled earlier pledges to respect Italy's Balkan and Mediterranean interests, as well as its Austrian frontier. Count Ciano, Mussolini's foreign minister and son-in-law, was prepared to break with Germany at this point. He wrote in his diary that he had urged Mussolini to tear up the pact with Hitler and become the continent's "natural leader of the anti-German crusade."[84] Mussolini revealed that he would denounce the Pact of Steel if Hitler "committed other irreparable errors," but in the end he responded with little more than "anti-German fulminations."[85]

The Allied powers did not make enough of all this. Sumner Welles, President Roosevelt's envoy, met with Mussolini several times to explore the possibility of a separate, negotiated peace. Although Churchill was pessimistic that he could keep Italy out of the war, Britain and France promised Mussolini considerable concessions in the Mediterranean.[86] The British war cabinet even approved a plan to provide Italy 70 percent of its coal requirements in 1940 in return for armaments and agricultural products, if Italy would reduce trade with Germany. Mussolini rejected the offer, and ultimately he determined that Italy could not "remain with hands folded while others write history."[87] In what the Allies disingenuously labeled the "stab in the back," Mussolini entered the war alongside Hitler in June 1940, after France had been defeated.

"Fascist Italy's fatal error"—Mussolini's decision, taken against the advice of his foreign minister and other councilors—marked the beginning of a quick end.[88] It seemed a straightforward calculation: Hitler would win with or without Italy, and Italy stood to gain more from an alliance with the victor. Mussolini's ambitions in the Mediterranean depended on the displacement of British and French power, something only an alliance with Germany could accomplish. He judged, moreover, that a weak or nonbelligerent Italy would attract only German domination. Mussolini preferred to sit at the peace table beside Hitler than to sit, trussed up, on the dinner table in front of him. A Germany that could devour France could devour Italy as well.

Churchill, whose admiration for Mussolini had known no bounds, now abandoned flattery. He called Mussolini's choice "the tragedy of Italian history." Mussolini, he declared, has "arranged the trustees and inheritors of ancient Rome upon the side of the ferocious pagan barbarians."[89] Years later, Churchill reflected further on Mussolini's "fatal mistake":

Had he not [allied with Hitler] he might have well maintained Italy in a balancing position, courted and rewarded by both sides and deriving an unusual wealth and prosperity from the struggle of other countries. Even when the issue of war became certain, Mussolini would have been welcomed by the Allies. He had much to give to shorten its course. He could have timed his moment to declare war on Hitler with art and care. Instead he took the wrong turning . . . Thus he marched to ruin.[90]

And thus, despite plausible alternatives, he set in stone what we mean by "wartime" and "postwar" Italy.

PERSONIFYING FASCISM

In 1912, still a Socialist, Mussolini evoked Machiavelli: "It is faith that moves mountains because it gives the illusion that the mountains move. Illusion is, perhaps, the only reality in life."[91] But Mussolini's power, his popularity, and his legacies were no illusions. They were more substantial than those of any Italian before or since. Mussolini was a master bricoleur. He took pieces, often broken pieces, of the past and arranged them to provide himself unparalleled legitimacy. He coined and proudly invoked the term "totalitarian" to describe his handiwork. He would oppose class struggle because through his Fascist state he could represent *all* of society.

In Japan, the emperor represented all of society. His authority was unassailable, but his prerogatives were controlled. Ultranationalists provided the language, bureaucrats the tools, and soldiers the muscle to sustain Japanese fascism. When Japanese liberals squandered the rare opportunities they had to challenge them, the institutions of the authoritarian state prevailed. Fascism may not have been inevitable in Japan, but neither was it imposed upon the state from the outside. Alternatives were never seriously tested.

In contrast, fascism was already an alternative on the peninsula before Mussolini was converted. Certainly fascism—or something like it—might have erupted under the leadership of others, as it did in Japan under no leader in particular. But Mussolini transformed it into something personal. His success made it a seductive model for other regimes. Perhaps Herman Finer made the most prescient analysis of its prospects during its heyday. In 1935 he addressed the "inevitability" and "natural development" of fascism, arguing: "It looks as though it were the product of an unbroken deterministic chain: economic contradictions, political confusion, parliamentary weakness . . . Yet Fascism seems to me to have been avoidable if Mussolini had not functioned as he did . . . His will to power, and the ruthlessness in its realization, alone made Fascism inevitable, even as it now continues to make it possible."[92] In Italy, at least, social conditions alone may not have nurtured fascism to maturity. It needed a creative leader who could capitalize on opportunities. And no leader in history was more creative, especially in policing the past and besieging his opponents, than Benito Mussolini. Like fascists Francisco Franco in Spain and António de Oliveira Salazar in Portugal, he might have survived for decades more had his political judgment about war and peace been more discriminating.

PART III

IN THE AMERICAN IMPERIUM:
THE COLD WAR

CHAPTER SEVEN

Chasing Democracy

> The true measure of nations is what they can do when they are tired.
> Winston Churchill, 1919 speech at the English-Speaking Union

We have seen how in the anarchic world of the late nineteenth and early twentieth centuries Italian and Japanese leaders deployed a formidable range of resources in their pursuit of prestige. Leaders used what was at hand, sometimes in novel ways, to win acceptance in the world's councils. It seemed for a time that acceptance was in the offing, but ultimately, of course, Italian and Japanese leaders failed terribly. With the end of the Second World War, new leaders, and some more experienced politicians appropriately reinvented, would have to rebuild national power and reconfigure national identity in exhausted nations. There was still no "natural" course leading inexorably to status as a great power. Complicating matters was subordination to the United States, which expected them to establish democracy under its global—anticommunist—leadership. It was a tall order, especially since few of those chasing democracy had ever been democrats. This chapter explores in general terms the ways in which leaders in both countries reconsolidated identity, power, and wealth after the war.

Leaders, as we have seen repeatedly, are not granted the luxury of starting with a blank slate. Nor, since the past can be useful, do many wish to do so. This is true even when there appears to be sharp historical discontinuity. Organization theorists understand that "when an old regime collapses and a new one needs to be established, institution building is constrained by the existing repertoires of competencies and resources... What can realistically be accomplished in a transitional, 'building' phase is thus dependent on the skills and competencies of the people which were most closely aligned with the old institutions."[1] This compelling irony captures the "transwar" histories of Italy and Japan. The interaction among existing institutions, the experience of the war, and the shifting interests of the victor became dominant facts in the regeneration of Japan and Italy. The first dismantling of some institutions pointed toward a democratic future, but the preservation of others and the growing indifference of the victors gestured at an authoritarian past.

Importantly, the chase after parity with the other great powers was never diminished. Prime Minister Yoshida's goal after the war was to "return Japan to its place in international society."[2] He reflected on "setbacks and miscalculations in the recent past" and pledged his determination that "Japan would become the acknowledged financial and economic equal of the industrially advanced West" thanks to the "inherent qualities of the Yamato race."[3] To do so, he would have to search for, elaborate on, and sometimes even invent democratic elements of Japanese political culture. Italian leaders made similar calculations. Communist Party (PCI) leader Palmiro Togliatti was quick to reach for what was left of Italy's democratic mantle. He proclaimed the PCI a "*partito nuovo*" but also insisted it was the "inheritor of the Liberal tradition."[4] Alcide De Gasperi, leader of the Christian Democrats (DC), also used the old to accommodate to the new. He sought to reinvent Christian democracy as a broad movement led by a mass-based "national party." He would combine what was once Mussolini's with what was once Giolitti's, binding these two failures with democratic norms, anticommunism, and Catholic morality. The Italians, however, as weary of war and authoritarianism as the Japanese, were less sure just what they were now pursuing. They were not even sure whether they had lost or won the war. The debate about the war was central to the rebuilding of national identity in both countries.

Rebuilding Identity

By the end of World War II, Italians were more than ready to shed the baggage of imperial Rome. They were eager to be part of Europe rather than to help dominate it. The idea of an Italian nation was widely rejected as so much patriotic swill. In postwar Japan, likewise, a gentler, pacifist self-image had to be crafted. Bushidō had to be transferred from military to commercial associations. Again, Japanese history and traditions were pressed into service and were flexible enough to support a new national story. There was no "stubborn reality" of Japanese identity, only determined reinterpretations—many of which were made under the close supervision of Americans who intended to "redefine the Japanese nation away from ethnic and toward civic models."[5]

Italy, the nation that had had a lust for historical glorification, now harbored a palpable disgust for what that lust had wrought. The very core of Italy's majesty was also her greatest disappointment. Gaetano Salvemini called it "the Roman-Imperial cancer," filled with "dreams of impossible primacies," and it was for him a history that had crushed Italy.[6] After the war, many shared Salvemini's self-abasing, masochistic national image. Italians were fit to do great things but became convinced they would not. Their hopes were denied by great forces from the outside (Italy ever the victim of cunning, malicious foreign powers) and by inadequacies from within (localism, familism, egoism, incompetence).[7] Both the Japanese and the Italians felt vulnerable and victimized. But the Japanese saw in themselves special competencies the Italians did not. The Renaissance had happened in Italy, but Italy did not become a nation-state. Machiavelli taught princes how to rule, but Italian princes were too incompetent to do it well or too stupid to learn. Italy produced great bankers and traders, and political analysts, but could not gain advantages over other nations. It was a nation of heroes, of stars: it produced great generals but poor armies; great scholars but poor universities; great jurists but poor administrations. Japan, by contrast, told itself that its leaders were weak or wrongheaded but that its institutions were strong and worth preserving. Individuals could be subsumed in groups, and creativity could be collective. The stars might be small, but the constellations could be stunning.

In both countries national identity had been invented and affirmed through mobilization, sacrifice, and foreign wars. The Japanese had contrived an identity as a great and special family, the "golden people" of *Yamato damashi*, and reinvoked it after the war for commercial rather than military conquest. The Italians seemed less sure how to proceed. They proclaimed themselves poets, saints, and scientists, but for centuries they had asked what united them.[8] They embraced a pastiche and they resorted to self-vilification. An established *Italian* national image remained elusive. That their leaders failed to seize upon a legitimating symbol would have costs.

While patriotism became suspect in both countries after the war, the Italians held one advantage over the Japanese as each tried to reconstruct itself as a peaceful and democratic people. The Italians could point to growing popular disaffection with fascism, even before Mussolini's decision to enter the war, and they could remind themselves of armed resistance even before his demise. Then, too, they could speak of valiant Italians who fought side by side with the Allies against the Germans. Never mind that there were fewer than four thousand men under arms before Mussolini's fall; never mind that many of those who joined them subsequently, swelling their ranks to some sixty-five thousand, were opportunists or turncoats. The central point of the comparison to Japan is that

in Italy "every citizen was faced with crucial moral and political choices."
Many (especially in the reconstruction) made the right one.[9]

The Japanese had generated no mass movement to oppose their militarists. There had been no early defiance of the regime, as there had been in the June 1924 Aventine Secession, no community of exiles to needle the regime and await their postwar turn at power.[10] Indeed, beyond a few doubts expressed by intellectuals who were quickly silenced and forced to recant and by conspirators who found themselves cornered late in the game, there had been virtually no elite opposition to the regime.[11] The Japanese had no obvious heroes to invoke as they rebuilt their polity. They were perforce freed of some of the postwar violence that wracked Italy, but were burdened with finding other ways to legitimate a democratic politics. Given how dispirited the people were, leaders had to be particularly inventive in reasserting the superiority of the Japanese spirit. It was not easy to recover their confidence, but they did. They discovered or created "traditional" elements to justify the wholesale shift from the Meiji to the U.S.-imposed constitution, claiming continuity from the welfare policies of the home ministry to the progressive programs of General MacArthur's Occupation, from Taishō liberalism to U.S.-style democracy and state-led economic growth. They even found a history of Japanese pacifism, with the emperor merely a symbol of the state, to justify the view that nothing was changing.[12]

So the two nations proceeded to reconstruct their postwar identities in different ways. Italians across the political spectrum gathered openly to design a new political order. Their 1947 Constituente continued the broad collaboration of the Resistance. The process was hardly uncontentious, but compromise dominated the proceedings.[13] The Left and the Church would soon return to their posture as the most implacable foes in Italian politics, but for a crucial moment the Communists approved reaffirmation of the Lateran Pacts, recognizing Catholicism as the official religion of the Italian state and accepting religious education in the public schools.[14] For its part, the Church was convinced to confront modernity and accept democracy. Church and party would agree on important issues of local autonomy, land reform, and the fundamental values of the new Italian state. When they could not settle matters by logrolling, they put the issue to the people. The most important referendum, in June 1946, concerned "the institutional question": a republic or a monarchy? Italians had seen Victor Emmanuel III lift Mussolini to power in 1922 and fourteen years later they heard him proclaim the Kingdom of Italy as the "fascist fatherland." They also saw him abandon Rome to the Germans, fleeing the country in 1943. The republican idea prevailed, constitutional monarchy was rejected, and the royal family was expelled. The central cleavage in Italian politics thereupon shifted, from Republicanism versus Catholicism to Christianity versus Communism.

Japan, where the Showa emperor had been a tool of, and possibly even an active participant in, militarist decision making, saw no eruption of republican sentiment. Although there was considerable debate, the Japanese people ultimately accepted a version of war responsibility that placed blame on the military rather than on the emperor, whom they continued to embrace even while "embracing defeat."[15] Where Croce famously viewed fascism as a "parenthesis," the Japanese public accepted a view of the recent past as a "dark valley" (*kurai tanima*).[16] Postwar Japan would be like Meiji Japan before it, "restored" rather than "new." Elites that had used the emperor now gambled that the imperial presence was too deep a part of the national identity to be abandoned. Concerned that the U.S. Occupation would impose an end to the imperial house—or, worse, that it would try the emperor as a war criminal—they pressed vigorously and successfully for at least a constitutional monarchy. None of this was put to an open test of popular will. A constitution written by U.S. officials was imposed upon the Japanese people with little more than pro forma review and approval. To be sure, Japanese identity was being transformed, but even so a mortal emperor would remain a touchstone for the nation.

In these ways, an official morality repudiating militarism and embracing democracy was carefully constructed in both countries. In Japan the new "democratic" self-image remained largely untested, and delicately balanced against an inheritance of conservatism if not authoritarianism. It was as if the Japanese did not trust themselves with democracy. (Certainly their U.S. overlords did not.) When the new image was tested, it was tested by the Right, which vowed to revise the Constitution. There was never an open test of popular support for the document. Instead, the Left used the military alliance with the United States as a surrogate. After massive, generation-defining protests, the Japanese Left lost its effort to prevent a strengthening of the U.S.-Japan Mutual Security Treaty (Nichibei Anzen Honshō Jōyaku, or Ampō). The Liberal Democratic Party emerged from the 1960 demonstrations shaken but in better control of national identity and power than ever. The Italian dynamics were uncannily similar. A parallel antifascism dominated postwar Italy's national formula; any open effort to return to authoritarianism met with immediate protest. The crucial moment was also in mid-1960. The Italian Left attacked the government for having accepted neofascist support in Parliament and, after street battles broke out, forced the postponement of the neofascists' Missini Congress in Genoa. Neofascists in Italy, who over time fashioned a less nostalgic position, would continue to enjoy significant electoral support and representation in Parliament, whereas the Japanese Right would be incorporated as an anti-mainstream minority inside the LDP itself. Neither would disappear, but it is important to note that antiauthoritarian official moralities held in both countries.[17]

Rebuilding Power

It is as easy to overstate how much had changed in Italy as it is to understate how much had changed in Japan. At first, the United States was extremely aggressive about "democratizing" its former adversaries. In Japan, a U.S. military government assumed unambiguous, albeit formally indirect, political control for seven years (1945–1952). The Occupation (known as SCAP, or Supreme Command for the Allied Powers) wasted no time. Its lawyers, determined to replace the authoritarian order with a popular one, overshadowed its soldiers. In October 1945, just months after arriving in Tokyo, General MacArthur announced a five-point program based on: 1) equality of the sexes, 2) rights for organized labor, 3) liberal education, 4) abolition of autocracy, and 5) reorganization of the economy through dissolution of the zaibatsu. The home ministry would be abolished, the people would become sovereign, and left-wing parties would be legalized. In Italy, meanwhile, the U.S. forces cheered as progressive parties came in from the fascist cold. They supported former exile Carlo Sforza's High Commission for Sanctions against Fascism and the Italians' determination to cleanse their own house.

In fact, neither Italy nor Japan was reinvented from scratch after 1945. Despite constitutional changes, the bureaucracy, the entrepreneurial class, and many institutions survived virtually unscathed.[18] Although hundreds of thousands of officials were investigated, most of the judges, civil servants, and businessmen who had served the authoritarian states also served their democratic successors.[19] There would be no wholesale purge of the fascists in Italy or in Japan. Aggressive housecleaning in Italy, where membership in the Fascist Party had been "obligatory" for all public officials, would have shut down the government altogether. In Japan, the home ministry was hit harder than other agencies, but only 12 percent of Japan's upper-level civil servants were purged by SCAP. The Tokyo War Crime Trials netted several big fish, but other "Class A" war criminals went unindicted and were soon freed to pursue careers as powerful political fixers. Politicians who had served in the wartime parliaments reappeared under the banner of democratic parties. In Japan, the old Minseitō became the new Progressive Party; the old Seiyūkai became the new Liberal Party. Neither waited for its leaders to be de-purged. Within three years, one of these men would be prime minister and within five, another—an

unindicted "Class A" war criminal who had spent three years in prison—
would succeed him. Despite institutional reforms, in October 1952, just
six months after the peace treaty went into effect and the U.S. occupation
ended, nearly half of the representatives in the Diet were former
purgees.[20] Italian and Japanese newspaper editors and business leaders
who had collaborated were investigated, but rarely punished. Nor were
university professors who had signed Italy's racial manifesto in 1938.

The U.S. New Dealers were beaten back at home and distracted abroad,
and there was a "reverse course" in both Italy and Japan. Many of the most
progressive constitutional reforms were undone. In Italy, progressive ar-
ticles of the 1946 Constitution were quickly vitiated; local taxing powers
were circumscribed and proved "woefully inadequate for their purposes"[21]; prefects retained considerable control. In Japan, the decentralization of the police and education, as well as many of the new regulatory
agencies, were undone systematically. Liberal democracy in postwar Japan
would have a centralized cast, just like its counterpart in Italy.[22]

Overall, the Japanese and Italian experiences were quite similar. In
both cases, contra the hopes of Croce, "fascism turned out not to be a 'historical parenthesis' that would cease to have any effect on the country's
political life as soon as democratic principles and institutions were introduced. Although they were painted over with democratic colors, some of
the features of the fascist era continued to be operative after 1945."[23] This
outcome can be attributed in no small measure to the fact that by 1948,
the United States, once avid about democratization, now preferred stability in its confrontation with communism.

Indeed, there are few political facts more consequential than the way
Japan and Italy shared the Cold War.[24] The tribute exacted by the United
States was their junior partnership. Faithful support for U.S. foreign policy earned Italy the sobriquet "the Bulgaria of NATO," while Japan served
as the U.S. workshop, its East Germany.[25] Critics saw both as America's lap-
dogs, the more polite version holding that Japan pursued a "Pulled Along
by America Diplomacy" (*taibei tsuijū gaikō*). Conservative elites stretched
these alliances to allow for some degree of independent foreign policy,
but the wisdom of tying national security to the American hegemon defined each nation's political debate. In both cases the Right insisted this
was the only way to preserve freedom, whereas the Left feared being
drawn into unwanted and unwarranted conflicts abroad. In both cases,
Italy and Japan would play much lesser roles in world affairs than their
economies or ambitions might otherwise have supported.

These junior partnerships entailed a second tribute to the American
hegemon. Japanese and Italian leaders effectively ceded to the United
States the ability if not quite the right to intervene in their domestic poli-

tics for as long as the Cold War lasted. In the first blush of democratization, both countries had elected short-lived governments with leftist participants; in Japan the socialists formed a government. These governments soon gave way—with unambiguous U.S. encouragement—to expanding coalitions of anticommunist politicians who would hold power for decades. U.S. bullying was commonplace. The United States was not shy about insisting on the elimination of Soviet influence, nor was it reluctant to extend its own. In 1955, for example, U.S. Ambassador Clare Booth Luce announced that no more U.S. defense contracts would be forthcoming for Italian factories where leftist unions had more than half the support—pressure echoed as late as the 1970s by President Jimmy Carter. In Japan, a large U.S.-constructed slush fund may have been placed at the disposal of anticommunist politicians throughout the Cold War.[26]

A number of America's other Cold War allies remained authoritarian two and three decades into the Cold War, so one must take care not to attribute too much of domestic politics to U.S. power. That said, it is surely no coincidence that the Liberal Democrats and the Christian Democrats forged dominant and remarkably similar party systems. Each system was built on patronage, rural voters, and business support, enabling a pragmatic but splintered political class to govern at the center without flying apart.

The Italian DC and the Japanese LDP governed for decades without alternation of power in what have been characterized as "one and a half party systems."[27] Fashioning itself as the only mass-based alternative to the PCI, the DC reached from the Center to the socialist Left. It dominated government but after 1953 never governed alone. Behind a façade of instability, Italy was perhaps the most stable of western European democracies, for the DC was in power from 1946 until well after the end of the Cold War. Meanwhile, the LDP, which depended upon a stable coalition of business and agriculture, reached from the Center to the Right. It, too, would not leave power until well after the Cold War had ended. Alliance politics dominated the political strategies of party leaders. For the LDP these alliances were internal and for the DC they were external.

Both parties were first, and above all else, anticommunist. Each "governed from the center, disarmed the communist opposition, and became an essential lynchpin in political exchange."[28] Each "digested" its opponents with consummate political skill, generously distributing material benefits, enticing the extremes to abandon anti-system views, and establishing for themselves a popular image as indispensably sturdy democrats and friend of the American protector.[29] In short, both were conservative forces capable of extraordinary innovation and creativity.[30] The price of this flexibility was ideological diversity. Three currents co-existed uneasily within Christian democracy: the Christian Left, which believed in governing in the interests of the poor but which had been allied with fascist corporatists; the Center, which sought to govern in the interests of the nation but was suspected of having a class bias in favor of industrialists; and the Right, which hoped to govern in the interests of the Church. The LDP was similar, though narrower, comprising a nationalist Right that hoped for a quick return to prewar statist principles and a pragmatic Center that preached fiscal constraint but succumbed regularly to the political exigencies of the pork barrel. It could be said of each that there was less ideological coherence than met the eye: the LDP was routinely described as neither liberal, nor democratic, nor even a party, and the DC was often characterized as neither democratic nor Christian.[31]

These internal differences were not unimportant, but neither did they determine how the LDP and the DC dominated. In both cases, clientelistic factions built on material exchange were far more important than ideological ones built on ideas about governance. In both countries, an expanding conservative Center reached out to deliver to both Left and Right, giving and taking with increasing proficiency.[32] In both countries, the term "structural corruption" was widely used to characterize governance. The key "structure" was the electoral system. In Japan, factionalism was born of multimember districting, a system that pitted members of the same party against one another, and therefore raised their costs of doing business. In Italy, proportional representation was the functional equivalent. Both countries saw more vigorous and better-organized political competition *inside* the governing parties. In Japan this could be handled within the LDP. Italy's Cold War *pentapartito* delivered the goodies to five political parties.

Credible and dramatic challenges to these "creative conservatives," to use T.J. Pempel's term, came well before the scandals of the late 1980s. They came first at the local level in the 1960s and early 1970s as leftist-led coalitions achieved power in the rapidly industrializing urban centers. In all, the Left controlled six of twenty regions and most of Italy's major cities north of Naples after the 1975 and 1980 local elections. Japan had great expectations for a locally generated challenge to conservative dominance.[33] By the mid-1970s, half the Japanese population lived in localities governed by the Left, which demonstrated that innovative social policy was possible even inside a "conservative's paradise." These leftist administrations were the first to introduce welfare programs, health care, environmental restrictions, and social infrastructure projects overlooked during the postwar emphasis on economic growth.[34]

Partisan change at the center was delayed until the Soviet Union disappeared. As if on cue, and as if freed of U.S. restrictions, both the Italians and the Japanese simultaneously rejected their party systems and some of their more corrupt politicians. Nearly simultaneous electoral reforms in 1994 created hybrid systems of proportional representation and first-past-the-post balloting. Until then, one had heard a great deal of "partyocracy" in Italy and of the "plunder" of the state by the DC.[35] The competition for spoils was no less central to LDP dominance, whereas in Italy, the spoils sustained personalized factions. Italian cabinets were the largest in any Western democracy and Japanese cabinets were the fastest to be recycled because each fief had to be fattened.[36]

Of course, this is not just about politicians. It is also about their relationship to bureaucrats. Cold War Italy was conventionally portrayed as a party-dominated system with a weak executive, whereas Cold War Japan was a case of bureaucratic dominance of a weak governing party. The Japanese bureaucrat emerged from an intensely meritocratic and (purportedly) politically neutral system; the Italian bureaucrat was distinguished more by his connections than by his administrative skill.[37] Consequently, the Italian system was "patently inefficient" and corrupt, the Japanese system the paragon of the developmental state in which "bureaucrats rule, while the politicians reign."[38] But in fact the administrative consequence of party dominance was the same. In both cases, ministries constituted a sort of "sealed compartment, a power unto itself" in which there were discrete, functional ties between particular politicians and their bureaucratic allies.[39] In Japan, this was called "tribal politics" (*zoku seiji*), and particular faction leaders (many of whom were former bureaucrats) were renowned for their ability to control particular ministries. In Italy, civil servants were instruments of the parties before they were instruments of the state. Without alternation of parties, the Italian and Japanese bureaucracies grew increasingly vulnerable to political pressure. In Italy the bureaucracy became very southern, and in Japan the "regional" focus of the mandarin bureaucracy remained the Hongo campus of the Tokyo University law faculty.[40]

Italian governance evolved through a set of loosely connected centers of power that Ginsborg calls the "collateral organizations" of an "archipelago state."[41] Special agencies (*ente pubblici*) proliferated in a baroque congeries of poorly integrated institutions. This "archipelago" model also applies to Japanese public administration, but the Japanese use a different metaphor: the "evil of vertical administration" (*tatewari gyōsei no heigai*). As in Italy, Japanese bureaucrats rely heavily on "third sector companies"—separate administrative units designed to deflect or reflect political control.[42] The key difference is state ownership. It dominated the Cold War

Italian economy but was never a factor in the Japanese case. Economic bureaucrats had to resort to different instruments to rebuild national wealth.

Finally, governance was abetted in both cases by organized crime—Japanese *yakuza* and the Italian Mafia, whose fortunes were built on gambling, drug trafficking, prostitution, immigrant smuggling, extortion, and murder. These criminal syndicates served public functions avoided by the state, and were welcomed as "in-laws" as often as they were reviled as "outlaws." The modern yakuza received huge infusions of manpower from disaffected youths and demobilized soldiers following defeat in World War II.[43] Nationalistic and right-wing gangs were mobilized first by the U.S. Occupation and later by the LDP right to help suppress left-wing groups. Over time, the yakuza—concentrated in Kobe and Tokyo—came to enjoy a remarkable degree of social acceptance. Many gangs have their own business cards and occupy clearly marked neighborhood headquarters, and the yakuza operated largely in the open for much of the postwar era.[44] Japanese citizens often rely on gangsters to mediate disputes and extract compensation. The business community also has a history of association with the yakuza, particularly in real estate and construction.

From the beginning of the Cold War, the DC was just as willing to use criminal muscle as the LDP—likely with the same connivance of the United States. In Sicily's regional elections of 1947, the Left had unexpectedly triumphed over the Christian Democrats, posing a threat to the interests of southern landholders, the Catholic Church, and international anticommunist forces (the United States). Traditional southern elites used the Mafia in response. Just weeks after the election, Mafiosi opened fire at a May Day rally, killing eleven and wounding fifty-five. Attacks on Communist Party offices continued throughout the early years of the Cold War, and union leaders were common targets.[45] The DC used the Mafia to mobilize its own voters as well, especially in areas of the South.[46] In exchange for electoral support and muscle, the Mafia received regulatory favors such as the granting of permits, kickbacks from public works projects, and protection from law enforcement. The electoral benefits of collaboration with organized crime were not lost on national politicians. Factional competition within the DC led ambitious northern politicians with national aspirations to enlist the support of southern parliamentarians. In return, southern politicians pushed for regional industrial development from which they could extract rents. In these ways, organized crime played a public function avoided by the state and demanded by civil society. In both cases, as we shall see, these functions entailed enormous and often tragic costs.

REBUILDING WEALTH

Japan and Italy began the postwar era with nearly identical levels of economic output and quite similar sectoral distributions. Both had gross domestic products in the $20 billion range, both had nearly as many agricultural workers as blue-collar workers, and both had manufacturing industries made up largely of small firms. Both faced the same obstacles to reconstruction—most immediately, shortages of raw materials and foreign exchange. Black markets for essential commodities drained a great many resources from the "official" system. Both embarked on active programs to import foreign technology and accelerate economic reconstruction. Export-led "economic miracles" stimulated migrations from the countryside, leaving each nation richer than virtually any other industrial democracy. In the first decades after the war, per capita income rose faster in Italy and Japan than anywhere else in the developed world. Even after the first oil shock in 1973, GDP growth rates were the highest in the OECD.[47] Italy was the sixth largest manufacturing economy in the world by 1975 and surpassed Great Britain as number five in the early 1980s. Japan was by then the second largest economy in the world and challenging the dominance of the United States.[48]

Japanese and Italian reconstruction benefited from a very favorable world trading system. The largest market, the United States, was wide open, and both countries catered to voracious American consumers. That, combined with low defense burdens, cheap imported energy, and acceptance of government intervention, facilitated unprecedented prosperity. While both countries benefited from a liberal world trading system, Italy grew as a more fully open economy, Japan as a more protected one. Japan is touted as the exemplar of the industrial trading nation, but in fact Italy's dependence upon trade and exports has long been significantly higher. The Italian government removed all foreign exchange controls in 1946 and all quantitative controls of industrial exports in 1951, whereas the Japanese were still defending a range of formidable non-tariff barriers to trade as late as the 1980s.[49] Productivity growth and savings were higher in Italy than in Japan for significant periods, but the Japanese economic miracle was more equitably distributed and better sustained. It was also better protected from foreign competition. The Meiji consensus on the dangers of foreign direct investment was never challenged.

There were other striking continuities after the war. Corporatism was formally dismantled, but the same officials managed industrial firms inside IRI and within the zaibatsu. By one account, the corporatists "bleach[ed] their black shirts" and simply carried on.[50] Hughes frames the Italian continuity in a way that evokes the Japanese experience: "It was not too hard a task to eliminate the formal structure of corporatism. But it was something else to change the habits of nearly twenty years. Corporative procedures and the corporative mentality remained . . . [The employers] were roughly the same people who ran the economic activity of the country under Fascism, and they continued to operate in similar fashion."[51] In Japan, as we have seen, the ideas that had animated economic policy in Manchuria were redeployed at home—largely by the very same bureaucrats.

These continuities were also enabled by limits on institutional reform. The Occupation New Dealers began with a steadfast determination to remake Japan, but the Cold War changed all that. Within two years, SCAP would subordinate its interest in transforming the Japanese economy to an interest in strengthening it to help contain communism. It made every variety of concessions to the old guard. One of the planners reflected on the new imperatives:

> The most highly industrialized country in the Far East must remain outside the Soviet orbit if there is to be a free Asia, and to this end U.S. policy should be directed, by whatsoever means are necessary, military or economic, to assist in the establishment of political tranquillity and economic betterment in all of free Asia . . . Until it is clear that Japan can stand firmly on its own feet, the United States must of necessity lend support, even to the extent of providing an unrestricted market for such Japanese goods as American consumers find attractive.[52]

Thus ended U.S. efforts to recast the Japanese economy. Zaibatsu dissolution was abandoned. Japan would rebuild its economy in its own way and on its own terms. Japanese economic planners devised a program of "priority production" that emphasized four industries: 1) iron and steel, 2) coal mining, 3) electricity, and 4) shipbuilding. Only one-fourth of all retained profits were in these four industries in 1950–1954, but they received 60–90 percent of all government subsidies and grants. Moreover, private banks were instructed to make capital available—in this sense small manufacturers funded the reconstruction of heavy industry. But they hardly suffered for it. The Special Procurement program of the U.S. military during the Korean War was a great stimulus. Within a year of its start in July 1950, Japanese manufacturing output had risen 50 percent and corporate revenues had trebled. By 1952 Japan had nearly regained its prewar level of industrial production, and by 1954 Japanese manufacturing stood at 174 percent of the prewar average. Between 1952 and 1960 Japanese exports tripled. By 1956 Japanese shipbuilding had surpassed British levels, and Japanese shipyards were the most productive in the world.

Two forms of industrial organization emerged from the effort to reconsolidate the Japanese economy. The zaibatsu morphed into *keiretsu* when SCAP forced them to abandon the family-owned holding company model. These well-established groups—accounting for some one-quarter of the paid-up capital in the economy—wasted no time in reconsolidating, especially after they succeeded in having the antimonopoly law revised. Interlocking directorates and cartels became the norm. "Horizontal" groups comprised a formal web of coordinated activities, usually spanning a full range of production and financial activities, and centered around a dominant banking and/or trading firm. Companies such as Mitsubishi Electric, Kirin Beer, and Nikon Optical were tied to each other not by contractual obligations but by interlocking stock holdings and a common dependence on the Mitsubishi Bank. This arrangement was replicated across six groups, each of which strove to have one firm in each sector. On the other hand, "vertical" groups, such as Toyota and Matsushita, were characterized by integrated operations, usually within a single industry or several related ones. These groups tended to be managed as though the various units were divisions of the same giant corporation, in contrast to the much looser mechanisms of consultation employed by the horizontal groups, and they lacked any central financial institution. Whether vertical or horizontal, these keiretsu were exceptionally resistant to foreign competition, and the Occupation did remarkably little to require otherwise.[53]

In Italy there was less consensus on economic nationalism. At the end of 1945, IRI, which controlled more than two hundred firms and had 135,000 employees, became the focus of an intense debate. Liberal economists argued for its dissolution, but the business community was split. Some, following a national rather than a liberal logic, feared that privatization would invite foreign investment and foreign control. For them, a state-owned IRI was a necessary evil because there was insufficient domestic capital to assure Italian control. Others preferred American capital over control of the state sector by the Left or the political strings involved in continued state ownership.[54]

The Communists insisted that nationalized firms were essential for national reconstruction, and the DC was divided between the old Popolari who wanted privatization and the social Christians who preferred public intervention. Great Britain and the United States were eager to see the end of high-cost autarkic production, but, as in Japan, they would not encourage foreign direct investment. After considerable debate, the state presence in the Italian economy—the so-called *ente pubblici*—was reinforced. A nationalized energy sector was consolidated in 1953. Over time, these legacies of fascism would become indispensable instruments of the political class. The maintenance of zaibatsu (albeit as keiretsu) in Japan and of IRI in Italy, and the continuity in attitudes toward foreign direct investment, were transwar legacies that continued to affect the shape, pace, and direction of the postwar economies.

There were other ideological legacies. Few Italian and far fewer Japanese economic planners worshipped at the liberal church. Both embraced the possibilities of industrial policy. While the Occupation reformers challenged the wartime system of policy supervision by the Ministry of Commerce and Industry (MCI), Japan's "strategic view of the economy" and, in particular, its developmental orientation survived.[55] MCI, the government ministry that had morphed into the Ministry of Munitions during the war, was again transformed into the Ministry of International Trade and Industry (MITI). Governed by the same men, it invoked many of the same rules. MITI routinely nurtured entire industrial sectors—steel and autos in the 1950s and 1960s, aerospace and semiconductors in the 1970s and 1980s. MITI's programs could include authorization of foreign currency, direct funding through its Japan Development Bank, licenses for the importation of technology, tax benefits, and the authorization of cartels that would regulate competition and coordinate investment with the state's blessing.

In Italy the state came to own nearly all the steel, shipbuilding, communications, aviation, energy, and engineering industries. But there was far more state ownership than coordinated state control. When the government created the Ministry of State Participation in 1956 as "the central organ of the mixed economy," there were two central government ministries with an institutional base in the economy.[56] State-owned firms attracted first-rate managers but were colonized by politicians, who put the state sector to partisan use.[57] Meanwhile, private entrepreneurs became increasingly marginalized. After 1956, when the government prohibited participation by state-owned firms in Confindustria, private capital was cut out of a large swath of economic policymaking. Some entrepreneurs, such as Fiat, Pirelli, and Olivetti, supported the DC's Center-Left strategy, in the hope that it would reduce labor unrest, but others who faced the prospect of nationalization fought the state at every turn. Confindustria's relations with the state and, in particular, with the DC became strained and, after the DC reached out to the Socialists to nationalize the electric utilities, public-private cooperation effectively ceased. Confindustria became the "custodian of the past."[58]

By contrast, Japanese business rebuffed every effort by MITI to create "national champions." Business leaders, organized in the Federation of Economic Organizations (Keidanren), were willing to accept state jurisdiction but drew the line at state control. Japan would face the liberalizing international economy with private oligopolies rather than with public monopolies. As Confindustria watched its membership base dissipate, Keidanren took special care to consolidate its power. Partly as a consequence, Japan's industrial policy was a matter of extensive coordination between bureaucrats and businessmen, largely without party intervention for the first decades of reconstruction. Italian politicians did not wait so long and, since they "owned" the firms, they did not have to.

The political management of land reform provides a second, equally important, contrast in the ways wealth was rebuilt in postwar Japan and Italy. The absence of aggressive land reform in Italy led to peasant revolts, land seizures, and farm labor strikes, after which the United States pressed the government—over British objections—to break up large estates. But the reform, passed by Parliament in May 1950, was eviscerated, and large estates remained untouched. As a result, peasants supported the Left, and the landowners moved further right. In October 1946, by contrast, SCAP directed the Japanese government to undertake the most comprehensive land reform in history. The share of owner-cultivators rose to 90 percent from less than 50 percent before the war, and tenant unrest was effectively removed from the political agenda. By 1950, Japanese agriculture had returned to prewar production levels and farmers—now independent businessmen—became the electoral backbone of LDP dominance.

In both countries peasants moved off the land in record numbers during the "miracle years" immediately after the war, though in Italy regional income disparities grew wider.[59] By 1970 Turin had more southern-born residents than any southern city save Palermo and Naples. At the same time, more than 80 percent of Tokyoites had been born in the provinces.[60] But De Gasperi did not have the same "advantage" enjoyed by his Japanese counterparts—a U.S. military force to repress unruly workers or compel redistribution of the land. He had to buy social peace with large "special indemnities" to workers and farmers. He did so at the cost of dividing his DC.

If the disproportionately large public sector was the major structural defect of the Italian system, small and medium-sized manufacturers were its greatest strength. Most analysts have focused on the keiretsu in Japan and on the state-owned firms in Italy, but in fact both economies were remarkably dependent on small and medium-sized enterprises (SMEs). Small-scale production was big business. In fact, the SME share of manufacturing employment in Italy and in Japan was well over 50 percent, higher than anywhere else in the industrial democracies. And unlike elsewhere, the SME share of value-added production grew after the war. So, too, did their level of technological sophistication.[61] On some accounts, their success engendered an entirely distinct economic sociology. Clearly some larger firms exploited their smaller suppliers in both countries, but the economic miracles in both countries were also enabled—if not actually led—by these smaller, more flexible, and highly cooperative firms.[62]

If cooperation among small firms was an evolving norm in Italy and—to a lesser extent—in Japan, workers and managers had a much tougher row to hoe in the large firms. From the beginning of the postwar period, industrial relations were in a state of war. Free to organize workers for the first time in decades, leftist parties actively politicized the workplace. In Japan, General MacArthur blocked a massive general strike and demonstrations in 1947, and workplace unrest in Italy's northern plants was both commonplace and disruptive through the 1950s and 1960s.[63] Employers' federations were created to resist the demands of organized labor. An important—and from their perspective, largely successful—part of their strategy was to divide the labor movement between Socialist- and Communist-affiliated unions. By the high-growth 1960s, strikes had taken on a quasi-ritualistic character. In Japan, accompanied by a largely ceremonial "Spring Struggle" (*shuntō*), the labor federations took turns negotiating contracts that became boilerplate for the rest of the industrial workforce. In Italy, the trade unions became particularly strong in the 1960s, when the Italian economy enjoyed full employment for the first time. By the end of the decade, they were following rather than leading the workers. Ad hoc workers' committees organized more than three hundred million man-hours of strikes during the "Hot Autumn" of 1969, inducing the Center-Left government to buy peace. The DC agreed to unprecedented measures to protect jobs, to index wages to inflation, and to raise wages by more than 12 percent annually for three years.[64] As a result, the large factories increased their subcontracting, inflation continued, and the trade unions began to experiment with concertation. Italian industrial relations finally took on a more cooperative cast when wage indexation (*scala mobile*) was dropped in the early 1990s.

In Japan, in the early 1980s, decades of wage gains were followed by intransigent political activity by the Socialists and their allied labor federation, Sōhyō. Business leaders and the LDP set out to destroy them both through administrative reform. There could be concertation only after taming the trade unions. Former Prime Minister Nakasone Yasuhiro recalls that he had been battling the railway workers since their strikes in the 1970s, when he was secretary-general of the LDP in the Miki Cabinet. He acknowledges that "It was my intention for years to crush Sōhyō. I had counseled breaking their strike in 1975, even though Prime Minister Miki and others wanted to compromise with them. Confronting labor was my strategy from even before Administrative Reform (*rinchō*) got under way. I was in my own World War II with Sōhyō."[65] Working closely with Keidanren Chairman Dokō Toshio, he won his war. They crushed Sōhyō, and in the process bought Japan another several decades of conservative dominance.

It was different in Italy. Italy ended the Cold War with only a piecemeal and fragmentary approach to industrial relations. Italian workers and employers never quite developed mutual trust, nor did the Italian state have the coercive tools that the Japanese state enjoyed. By the 1980s, Italy had tried and failed with economic planning, proto-concertation, and political bargains, whereas Japan proceeded to consolidate its economic miracle and to destroy the socialist Left.

These, then, were the ideological, political, and economic resources available to political entrepreneurs in Cold War Japan and Italy. These entrepreneurs—and their opponents—operated with a pervasive sense that U.S. power was never far away. In the following chapters we examine how they deployed the resources generated in this rebuilding of both countries—and how they continued to chase an elusive democratic "normality."

CHAPTER EIGHT

What Kind of Ally to Be:

ALCIDE DE GASPERI AND YOSHIDA SHIGERU

> Soviet domination of the potential power of Eurasia, whether achieved by armed aggression or by political and subversive means, would be strategically and politically unacceptable to the United States.
> *United States Objectives and Programs for National Security* (NSC-68), 1950

Alcide De Gasperi was known as the "solitary man" (*l'uomo solo*) and Yoshida Shigeru as "One Man Yoshida" (*wanman Yoshida*). They led Italy and Japan through political and social turmoil after World War II, and their legacy is still in place at the start of the twenty-first century.

Pressures from the United States and its allies exacerbated their domestic difficulties as the world edged into a half century of Cold War. They were significantly constrained by political opponents and by foreign powers. Still, each found ways to tailor a junior partnership with the United States. This partnership meant surrendering aspirations for great power status, something their electorates now welcomed after a generation of war and broken promises. In addition to providing national security at relatively low cost, it also gave their manufacturers access to the world's largest markets and sources of advanced technology.

De Gasperi had regional advantages that Yoshida could only envy. He could join a multilateral NATO and the European Coal and Steel Community. And he could initiate European unification directly, over beer (rather than wine) and in German, with his Catholic colleagues Robert Schuman and Konrad Adenauer. Yoshida remained aloof from (and distrusted by) his neighbors, tethered to a United States that would stick around to reassure the rest of Asia that Japan would not again preen with imperial ambition.

That said, both Italy and Japan used similarly favorable international circumstances to achieve unprecedented prosperity. The skilled statecraft of Yoshida and De Gasperi abroad was matched by determined politics at home: exclusion of the Left and tacit license to the United States to intervene. Each centered his program among hostile and contrary interests, making choices that others could not imagine, much less implement. They provide particularly clear examples of the ways in which resources, opportunities, and imagination can coalesce to reorient national identity, power, and wealth.

De Gasperi: The Singular Man

Alcide De Gasperi (1881–1954) grew up as a Catholic Italian in Austria.[1] The Christian Social Movement in which he participated was dedicated to helping the poor while eschewing revolutionary methods. He leaned early toward compromise. As a student in Austrian Trento active in Italian nationalist politics, he resisted the posturing of socialists and liberals, convinced that "to say 'all or nothing' means that we . . . will have the second part."[2] He used his editorship of *Il Trentino*, a Catholic newspaper, as a forum for his evolving politics of *possibilismo*—the art of conjuring conciliation across wide political divides. His ideas quickly attracted Socialist disapprobation. In a confrontation that would showcase two future Italian leaders in characteristic postures, De Gasperi was challenged to a debate by (an even younger) Benito Mussolini, then head of a local Socialist labor union. Mussolini argued that Christian democracy was a fraud, a recent invention of a "clever pope." De Gasperi urged Catholics and Socialists to join forces and improve workers' conditions. They were still decades away from national leadership, but each had already found a comfortable way of politics: Mussolini the bully, De Gasperi the buyer.

De Gasperi's first elective office was as the youngest of nineteen Italian deputies in the Austrian Reichsrat, in 1911. After the Great War, with the dismemberment of the empire, he demanded self-determination for the Italians in Southern Tyrol. When they joined the Kingdom of Italy, he became an Italian citizen. Soon his politics took him to the Chamber of Deputies in Rome, to unexpected leadership of the Partito Popolare (PP) and another important interaction with Mussolini. This time, after four months of heated debate about the wisdom of allying with the Fascists, De Gasperi prevailed and the PP approved participation by six deputies in Mussolini's first government.[3]

Collaboration with Mussolini ended in disaster. Like Giolitti before him, De Gasperi gambled on a tactical move to sate Mussolini's hunger for power. He had hoped to avoid a split in the Catholic party, or at least to avoid a civil war. He got a split when the so-called clerico-fascists bolted the PP to embrace Mussolini's *corporatismo*.[4] And he got worse than civil war when Mussolini consolidated power without a fight. De Gasperi wanly claimed to have gotten Mussolini to agree to respect proportional representation, but Mussolini would not cease his attacks on the Catholic social movement. The PP split in 1924. Don Sturzo fled to London, and the Church actively collaborated.

De Gasperi stayed to fight. He reclaimed his democratic credentials when he joined the Aventine Secession in 1924—the most important demonstration of antifascist solidarity during Mussolini's reign. With full dictatorship, De Gasperi began actively to criticize the government. For its part, the Church was already collaborating with Mussolini, and after De Gasperi had spent a year in jail, the Church intervened to both save and silence him.[5] In 1929, De Gasperi started fourteen years in "exile" within the walls of the Vatican, where he worked as a librarian.

By 1942 De Gasperi, trying to reconstruct Christian democracy, was working with other antifascists in the Committee for National Liberation (CLN)—the central committee of the Italian Resistance. After Mussolini was defeated, De Gasperi would serve as foreign minister in the short-lived Parri government.[6] He formed his first government in December 1945, and continued to govern with other antifascist forces while the Constituent Assembly was meeting to create Italy's republican constitution (1946–1947). Alcide De Gasperi served as head of government continuously from December 1945 until July 1953.

He was an inveterate conciliator. The period formally labeled Centrismo (1947–1953) was briefer than the practice itself. Like Cavour—and even more like Giolitti—De Gasperi was a genius at keeping coalitions intact. He believed in a moderate politics, and had to balance left and right, church and lay interests, monarchists and republicans, liberal and dirigiste economic interests, foreign and domestic pressures, and most of all, the diverse currents within his governing Christian Democratic Party.

Addressing the first dimension, De Gasperi wrote to Don Sturzo in early 1945 to express his profound concern for the future of Italian democracy. There are, he said, "two enormous specters on our political horizon. One is the threat of a totalitarian communist state, and the other is the fear haunting me of a *coup d'etat* a la Franco."[7] In a February 1949 letter to the pope he situated the second dimension with powerful clarity. He expressed his great fear that a dysfunctional bureaucracy would combine with republicans and some social democrats under "a common denominator of anti-clericalism" that would also appeal to industrialists and landlords.[8]

Holding this all together was no small accomplishment. But did it require strategic genius? De Gasperi has been credited with an "acute historical intuition," and there is little debate about his high moral purpose and incorruptibility, but many question his vision.[9] On most accounts, De Gasperi's politics were "ineffable." His centrism was Giolitti redux. He had no vision, no cultural identity, no articulated motives or obvious inspiration. His politics were pragmatic but embraced no ideals.[10] The consensus of historians is that De Gasperi could conjure but not inspire. As we shall see, this judgment is too harsh.

"ONE MAN" YOSHIDA

Until the late 1960s, Japanese historians were similarly harsh on Yoshida Shigeru. Like De Gasperi, Yoshida skillfully manipulated the forces that opposed him. He dealt with the Left by opposing communism but promising long-term disarmament; with the Right by opposing rearmament but delivering economic reconstruction and ending the Occupation; and with the Americans by supporting the alliance but keeping it (and its reformers) at arm's length. He accomplished all this as De Gasperi did—by centering. And, he suffered the same fate. After his preferences had been firmly institutionalized, he was replaced at the polls by more conservative opponents. And like De Gasperi, his name and ideas would become a yardstick against which all would measure their own successes and failures.

Although the son of a Tosa political activist, Yoshida Shigeru (1878–1967) identified closely with the oligarchs. He openly revered Itō Hirobumi and married the granddaughter of Ōkubo Toshimichi.[11] Yoshida began his career as a foreign service officer after graduation from Tokyo University in 1906. In his early years he advocated Japanese control of Manchuria, but by the time he had gained seniority in the ministry—including an ambassadorship to Italy in 1931 and to Great Britain five years later—his career had, in the eyes of many militarists, rendered him a weak-kneed liberal. In 1936, he tried to broker a deal on Manchuria, proposing that Japan would recognize British trading rights in Manchuria in exchange for British recognition of the puppet government of Manchukuo. Before any deal could be negotiated, however, the Japanese military precipitated war, and Yoshida resigned from the foreign service.

Yoshida sat out the war, but maintained close contacts with associates in the Japanese state. In February 1945, fearing that social unrest would follow Japan's certain defeat, he helped former Prime Minister Konoe Fumimaro draft a proposal to the emperor calling for surrender. Some in the military had begun to consider a Soviet alliance as a way out of the war. The system was convulsed by mutual recriminations between a military that had lost all perspective and a peerage that saw state control bureaucrats and the mass-based army as crypto-communists. Each group was

clutching for the remaining shreds of a dying empire.[12] Yoshida was arrested for his help with this "Konoe Memorial."

Yoshida's open contempt for the military, his opposition to the Axis
Pact, his resignation, his arrest, his anticommunism, and his ease in English all helped him win SCAP's confidence. Like De Gasperi, he served as
foreign minister during the transition to the new constitutional order,
and formed multiple governments during reconstruction. Yoshida
formed five governments between May 1946 and December 1954, and
served as prime minister for eighty-six months, the longest tenure of any
Japanese leader since Itō Hirobumi. Already sixty-seven years old when
Japan surrendered, if SCAP had not revived his career Yoshida Shigeru
would have been remembered—if at all—as a diplomat who tried to moderate the military's ambitions. "Instead," says Dower, "he left his name on
an era."[13] Yoshida and his protégés—such as Ikeda Hayato and Satō
Eisaku—would dominate governance for three and a half decades and become the mainstream of postwar conservative power. Yoshida Shigeru engineered the strong current against which all aspiring political opponents
would have to swim. Many more drowned than made it to shore. And he
did it by practicing a creative politics of centering that closely resembled
De Gasperi's.

CENTERING FROM THE CONSTITUTION

Yoshida backed into control of the Liberal Party on the eve of Japan's
first postwar election in April 1946 after its leader, Hatoyama Ichirō, was
suddenly (some say suspiciously) purged for wartime statements. It was a
chaotic time. Just seven months earlier, in October 1945, SCAP had eliminated all restrictions on speech, assembly, and religion. It lowered the
voting age, enfranchised women, released all political prisoners, and ordered the Japanese government to draft a new constitution. Political parties sprang up like bamboo shoots after spring rain.[14] Within those dramatic first two hundred days—when the Occupation was eager for reform
and the Japanese receptive to it—a tidal wave of institutional change
flooded the Japanese polity and society.[15] The government that Yoshida
formed in May had to surf these waves of change.

Yoshida had powerful opponents on the Left and the Right, but principally he had to deal with the formidable power of the United States. Arguably a liberal, but never even nominally a democrat, Yoshida bowed
pragmatically to the Americans. His support for SCAP's land reform was
particularly salutary, as most of the four million peasants who would own
land for the first time became strong supporters of his Liberals and, later,

of the LDP. But the greatest test was the new Constitution. He tried to put the best face on what was surely bitter medicine. As he later recalled: "I cannot entirely agree that [the] postwar constitution was forced upon us . . . There was nothing that could properly be termed coercive or over-bearing in the attitude of the Occupation authorities towards us."[16] Of course, the Occupation's reforms *were* coercive. SCAP forced a new demo-cratic politics on Japan, transforming it fundamentally. For the first time ever, Japanese sovereignty would reside in the people. The cabinet would be responsible to an elected Diet, not to an emperor. Human and civil rights would be guaranteed, as would the independence of the judiciary and local autonomy. And, most controversial of all, Article 9 of the Con-stitution would require Japan to renounce war and maintenance of a mili-tary forever.

On the other hand, Yoshida wanted all this change to remain within comfortable limits. He worked diligently to sell the Japanese people on the idea that the values of the "new" Japan were consistent with the values of "traditional" Japan. Like Itō before him, he turned to history to legiti-mate wholesale change. The greatest initial challenge was the disposition of the emperor. Some in the Occupation wanted to try the emperor as a war criminal, but Yoshida and others persuaded MacArthur that the em-peror was too beloved. MacArthur held that the Japanese would accept democracy if the emperor ordered them to do so, and would develop a de-structive resentment of the United States if their god were put on trial. Leaving the emperor merely a "symbol of the state" was not exactly what Yoshida had been angling for, but he accepted it, and argued (with feigned conviction) to the Japanese people that the emperor had *always* been little more than a symbol. And he sounded what would become the hegemonic idea of the postwar settlement: that the militarists were to blame for abusing the imperial prerogative.

The Meiji Constitution was one piece of Itō's handiwork that Yoshida could not salvage. Indeed, he initially miscalculated SCAP's determination to transform the Japanese polity and society. The first drafts of a new con-stitution his government submitted to the Occupation authorities were largely unchanged from the Meiji document and unceremoniously re-jected. MacArthur told Yoshida that there was no room for compromise: the only way to save the imperial throne was to accept a SCAP draft as the law of the land. In the event, it was the emperor himself who, fearing the alternative, signaled his acceptance.[17]

Yoshida argued in the Diet that he had believed the Meiji Constitution "an immutable set of laws to be accorded all the respect that was due through the ages." But, militarists had undermined its spirit. Hence, "in order to enable Japan *to preserve its traditional system of government* . . . we should frame the new constitution along the lines of democracy and pacifism." And, he further claimed, "*democracy . . . had always formed part of the traditions of our country*," and so its introduction to the political process would not be a novelty.[18] He quoted from the "august poems of the emperors through the ages" and insisted that the Meiji Constitution was "preeminently democratic, preeminently unmilitaristic . . . There is [not] a hair's breath of variance between this and the intent of the new constitution."[19] Much of Yoshida's political genius lay in his understanding that the absence of truth in these claims rendered them no less reassuring.

Later, Yoshida would reflect on the maturity of democracy in early postwar Japan and, no longer having to sell contrived connections, he would sound much more like Itō Hirobumi than like Alcide de Gasperi: "The so-called democratic form of government is still in its infancy in my country . . . So far we see little indication that its spirit has come to live amongst us . . . Years must pass before what is now new and strange to us in democratic politics becomes common-sense procedure."[20] Yoshida resembled Itō in another important respect. While others focused on "Japan's international role," Yoshida concentrated his policy choices entirely on Japan's national interests.[21] Like his role model, Yoshida Shigeru was a consummate realist, one whose skills were tested and affirmed in his dealings with the Americans over the terms of Japanese sovereignty.

Many on the Japanese right believe that Yoshida sold out to the United States. Nakasone Yasuhiro derides Yoshida as "MacArthur's entertainer," and argues that Yoshida failed to prepare the Japanese people for the idea that a nation must defend itself. Overall, Nakasone says, Yoshida's policy was "a loss for Japan" (*son o shita*).[22] But historians have come to a different conclusion. Dower points out that Yoshida never capitulated meekly to U.S. demands. He was determined to negotiate with the Americans at every turn. Dower argues that Yoshida "met America's needs, but never nestled complacently in its pocket."[23] This is Yoshida's own view: "When policies drafted by the Occupation authorities appeared to me to be mistaken through ignorance of the facts, or where they were not compatible with the actual situation in Japan at the time, I would clearly state my views. But if, in spite of my suggestions, the decision remained unaltered, I would abide by their wish and wait for the time when they might reverse the policy."[24]

Historians go further. They document how, rather than wait patiently for the United States to reverse its policies, he persistently nudged, cajoled, dissembled, and delayed in order to effect the changes he sought. What looked like passivity born of defeat is better understood as "an opportunistic adaptation to the conditions" within which Yoshida shrewdly pursued national security.[25] Pyle concludes that Yoshida was "the key figure in shaping the postwar conception of Japanese national purpose."[26] His strategic doctrine—which competes with the decision for war in 1941 as the most consequential decision ever made by a Japanese strategist— was a sharply etched maneuver of lasting political benefit to Japan.

CENTERING THE ALLIANCE

While navigating the dizzying maze of postwar domestic politics and responding to SCAP's demands for reform, Yoshida also spent a great deal of energy during the late 1940s sorting through Japan's foreign policy. His freedom was very limited. In October 1945, as foreign minister in the Shidehara government, Yoshida ordered a review of Japan's strategic options. In retrospect, it seems a foregone conclusion that Japan would become an ally of the United States, but there were always other possibilities. Moreover, even those who supported alliance held fundamentally different views of how to work with the United States.

Yoshida's staff reviewed unarmed neutrality, collective security, and security provided through great power (and later United Nations) guarantees.[27] Unarmed neutrality was a nonstarter for Yoshida—he had spent too many years watching great powers act like great powers. Collective security was also problematic. Although the United States repeatedly tried to pull Japan into a regional security regime, "Yoshida was too much of a nationalist to favor anything but economic ties with Asia."[28] Unlike De Gasperi or Adenauer, both of whom were eager for integration in a common European defense, Yoshida shied away from collective security, in part because he wished to maintain a separate Japanese cultural and national identity because, among other things, he feared being dragged into larger conflicts.[29] Too much the realist for neutrality and too much the nationalist for collective security, he turned toward great power guarantees. The UN would be untested until the 1950 Korean War, by which time the organization would be as divided as the world it was designed to police, and so Yoshida turned to a tried and true Japanese strategy. As it had with the Dutch in the seventeenth century, the British in the early twentieth century, and the Germans most recently, Japan would try to make the most of an alliance with the world's greatest power.

The advent of the Cold War changed Yoshida's security calculus. On the one hand, it complicated matters. By 1949, no issue was more divisive than national security. The Left rallied around the idea of "unarmed neutrality," the Right insisted on rearmament. On the other hand, the Cold War made Japan ever more valuable to the United States and, after the People's Republic of China was established in 1949, American policy in the Far East would become founded on Japan.[30] Now operating under guidelines set forth by strategist George Kennan, the United States had as its central purpose to contain communism. Yoshida recognized the chance to elevate Japan's status and regain sovereignty in the bargain. Japan could become an "ally in training" (*kenshūchū no dōmeikoku*) and prove its value to the United States.[31] He accepted U.S. bases and would leverage that decision into an early peace treaty and a return of Japanese sovereignty.

In the spring of 1950, Yoshida made a secret proposal to the United States through his finance minister, Ikeda Hayato, who was ostensibly on an economic mission to Washington.[32] Judging that the United States badly wanted to keep its bases in Asia—though possibly underestimating just how much the United States would be willing to pay—Yoshida argued that this could be Japan's contribution to the Cold War. Ikeda explained that if the stationing of U.S. troops in Japan was politically too difficult for Washington to propose, Japan would make a formal request.[33] Yoshida was confident that there would be no legal problem with such an arrangement. Political problems were another matter. Clearly, Yoshida was prepared to absorb enormous domestic pressure to gain the separate peace and an end to the Occupation. The idea for "post-treaty" basing of U.S. troops in Japan, which would become the central feature of U.S. strategic power in Cold War Asia, was the handiwork of Yoshida Shigeru.

John Foster Dulles came to Japan in June 1950 as a special adviser to Secretary of State Dean Acheson with a countersuggestion: Japan could do more than Yoshida proposed. To enjoy its place in the postwar free world, it should rearm. Dulles offered a conciliatory peace, one that would free Japan of the restrictions imposed on her by Article 9, but it would have cost Japan more than Yoshida was willing to pay.[34] Yoshida rejected the idea out of hand:

> I opposed [Dulles' suggestion] outright, because my country had not completed its economic recovery . . . To have invested vast sums of money in armaments would seriously have retarded hopes of completing our recovery and of creating a civilized standard of life for our people through peaceful trade . . . To equip the nation with an effective means of defense would have been tantamount to crippling Japan's convalescent economy.[35]

Yoshida's response centered him in Japanese domestic politics and enabled him to win a great many concessions from a position of weakness. Revision of Article 9 was out of the question because the Japanese people had no stomach for war and in any case it would alarm Japan's Asian neighbors. He hinted, moreover, that rearmament might provoke a constitutional crisis just when the United States most needed a stable ally. When news of U.S. pressure became known, he promised the Diet that if the Americans insisted, he would invoke Article 9 and simply refuse.[36] Yoshida ruled out rearmament variously as unconstitutional, or ineffective, or too expensive. Rearmament, he later recalled, was akin to "idiocy."[37]

He even had General MacArthur, who opposed Japanese rearmament for strategic reasons, weigh in on his behalf.[38] Dulles had not expected Yoshida to make demands on the occupying power, and he had no choice but to negotiate. Yoshida won the round, in a victory made easier by the outbreak of the Korean War two days before the end of Dulles's visit. The world—and the Far East in particular—had dramatically changed. In Yoshida's words, "history intervened."[39] The Americans, he realized, needed Japan more than ever, and recognized the *political* as well as strategic benefits of keeping Japan on board.[40]

Although MacArthur stood by Yoshida while Yoshida stood up to Dulles, the Korean War changed the dynamics. At the outbreak of the war, General MacArthur ordered Japan to establish a National Police Reserve (*keisatsu yobitai*, hereafter NPR) of 75,000 men. This was no ordinary police force. Although the recruiting posters featured doves to attract recruits who would serve a peaceful Japan, officers were recruited from those purged from the Imperial Army. The NPR was equipped with U.S. artillery, tanks, bazookas, and other distinctly non-police-like weapons. Appreciating that the Constitution forbade a Japanese military, the Americans urged the Japanese do some creative labeling. NPR officers should not be assigned military ranks; tanks were called "special vehicles."[41] Even though the U.S. government announced that the NPR was "the beginning of the [new] Japanese army," Yoshida denied that it was anything of the sort. He insisted that there was no rearmament afoot (few believed him), and, concerned about domestic unrest, Yoshida confessed privately that he was "grateful" he had been compelled to create this unit.[42]

Meanwhile, negotiations continued with the United States.[43] Dulles returned to Japan in January 1951. He came having consulted with the allies, each of whom (excluding the USSR) was prepared—after some U.S. strong-arming—to negotiate a peace treaty with Japan. Germany had just been enlisted in the integrated defense of Europe, and now it was Japan's turn to support the free world.[44] Dangling a treaty before Yoshida, Dulles again demanded large-scale rearmament, but Yoshida, however hungry, still would not bite—at least not hard enough. He perceived that Dulles was convinced that World War III was imminent, and was betting that the Americans would back down from their demands. If he was correct, Japan could focus its prodigious energies on economic reconstruction. Yoshida once again was able to use General MacArthur to good advantage. MacArthur, acting as what Yoshida would later refer to as a "lifeboat," explained to Dulles in Yoshida's presence that Japan could make a larger contribution to the free world as an economic power. Better be the workshop than the arsenal of the free world.[45]

Dulles kept pressing. He was armed with a congressional resolution requiring U.S. allies to make effective contributions to their own security, and told Yoshida that unless Japan took steps, he could not guarantee U.S. forces would remain in Japan. His bluff did not impress Yoshida. Convinced that Japan had become strategically crucial to the United States, Yoshida played every card in his surprisingly full hand. He warned about a nationalist revival and the return of militarists who had gone "underground." He warned about communist violence and leftists who would exploit any economic downturn caused by rearmament. He even encouraged the Socialists to take to the streets to protest rearmament.

In the event, Yoshida conceded that Japan "should be willing to make some contribution"—but clung tenaciously to the position that Japan needed its independence first.[46] That concession took the form of a secret agreement to gradual rearmament, with no specific timetable. Yoshida batted aside suggestions for a 300,000 man force and agreed only to a 50,000 man security force and a Ministry of National Security (soon abandoned) to supervise it.[47] Indeed, Yoshida quietly told his foreign ministry, conservative colleagues, and industrialists to be patient.[48] He was not going to rule out rearmament, but he was certainly not going to take giant steps in that direction. He would allow it "little by little" (*sukoshi zutsu*) as the Japanese economy and public opinion became ready to accept it.[49] Yoshida would refuse for years to acknowledge he had created a new military. He insisted that the NPR (and the Self-Defense Forces within which it was later absorbed) was "a means of national defense with forces not equipped to conduct wars."[50]

Yoshida had won a great deal. Remarkably, an occupied power had resisted and even transformed many of the demands of its military governors. As terms of the peace treaty were hammered out, Yoshida received formal understandings that Japan could undo any of the Occupation reforms, that war reparations could be paid in services rather than in foreign currency, that the list of war criminals would be closed, and that sentences already handed down could be reviewed.[51] Above all, it was agreed that there would be a separate U.S.-Japan Mutual Security Treaty (Ampō). Under the terms of this highly controversial treaty, the United States would station troops in Japan indefinitely "to maintain peace and security in the Far East." It could project force at will and without consultation with its hosts; it could intervene to quell domestic disturbances; and it

Yoshida Shigeru opens the jail of U.S. Occupation in 1951 only to imprison the Japanese people in an alliance with the United States. Reproduced courtesy of Kato Koji.

could veto any Japanese offer of bases to other states. Japan would be home base to the U.S. Pacific Fleet, and would maintain fourteen hundred U.S. military installations.

The Americans understood that (in General MacArthur's terms) the Occupation was a "wasting asset."[52] A nonpunitive peace was of enormous importance, because some allies, particularly the British, were pressing for treaty-based restrictions on Japanese trade. Others, such as the Soviet Union, the Philippines, Australia, and New Zealand, pressed for Japan's permanent demilitarization. Even the Pentagon was uncomfortable with the conciliatory terms favored by General MacArthur, Dulles, and Secretary of State Acheson.[53] Still, the diplomats and SCAP prevailed. Yoshida was relieved that the United States "had arrived at a better understanding of conditions in my country," and had become Japan's advocate in the councils of peace.[54] Of course, the United States was far more self-interested than this claim implies. There were those who sought a dual containment—keeping a lid on Japan was as useful as keeping a cordon around China and the Soviet Union. Acheson couches the Cold War calculus driving U.S. policy in characteristically diplomatic terms: "American purposes went beyond a settlement of the issues raised by Japan's challenge and defeat. They had to do as well with interests and desires brought forth in the intervening years."[55]

A second fundamental issue had to be resolved. With whom would Japan make peace? The Soviet ally was now behind an "iron curtain," the object of a U.S.-led policy of containment. The Chinese ally was now split in two; the United States was at war with Peking in Korea and refused to allow the Chinese Communists to sit at the peace table. The U.S. Senate, which would have to ratify any peace treaty, made it clear to Yoshida that recognition of Peking would render any negotiated treaty dead on arrival.[56] India, Burma, and Yugoslavia refused to participate; neither Peking nor Taipei was invited; and the Soviet Union, Poland, and Czechoslovakia refused to sign.

The United States and Japan did just what they wished. The peace treaty and the separate U.S.-Japan Mutual Security Treaty were signed on the same day—8 September 1951—in San Francisco. Japan came to terms with forty-eight countries, with assurances that terms would subsequently be worked out with the rest.[57] Matters may have been concluded to the satisfaction of the United States and Japan, but the long-awaited "settling of accounts" (*sōkessan*) was incomplete. The Soviet Union never signed a peace treaty with Japan and, because the United States bullied Japan so relentlessly, Peking and Tokyo did not come to terms until the late 1970s. The treaty was enormously popular in Japan, where Yoshida's approval rating soared to record levels.[58] Even better, the postwar settlement split the opposition Socialist Party: the right-wing Socialists opposed the security treaty but approved the peace treaty, while the left-wing Socialists opposed both.

Not all of the domestic political consequences were salutary for Yoshida, however. In 1952–53 he was tested directly by the arms industry, and its allies in Keidanren and MITI, who wanted to use defense production as the engine for postwar reconstruction.[59] For years Yoshida had argued that arms production would slow overall economic growth, but now with two years of "special procurement" by the U.S. military, Japanese industry knew better. The so-called divine wind (*kamikaze*) of the Korean War boom was over; industry was facing its first postwar recession and demanded investment in arms production. It was prepared to abandon Yoshida's Liberals to get what it wanted. The most ambitious remilitarization plans of the Right were defeated in the Diet, in large measure because the finance ministry and the banks balked at military Keynesianism, and the fall 1953 election was decided in favor of Yoshida's Liberals. The battle lines were clearly drawn, however, and his conservative opponents were gaining the upper hand. Yoshida had sown the seeds of his own political destruction.[60]

In the interim the man who had once insisted in the Diet that Article 9 unambiguously prohibited rearmament *even for self-defense*—a position with which even the Communists had difficulty—now had to reverse field.[61] Yoshida had clung tightly to the public fiction that Japan could not legally rearm, but the concession he had made to the Americans was now becoming a political liability. Yoshida testified in the Diet in 1952 that the Constitution did not, after all, preclude rearming for self-defense. He added that, for the sake of clarity, revision of Article 9—demanded by the conservative opposition led by Hatoyama Ichirō and Kishi Nobusuke—would be possible once the economy was strong and once Japan's neighbors were satisfied with Japan's peaceful intentions. The Americans now were packaging their food and development aid inside a Mutual Security Assistance Agreement that required recipient nations to have a military. In 1954 Yoshida again sent Ikeda to Washington to buy time and slow the pace of rearmament. Ikeda poor-mouthed the Japanese economy, insisting that its rapid postwar development remained very "shallow," and therefore could not sustain high levels of military expenditure.[62]

Yoshida was bending, however. Japan would have a military, even if it could not call it such. Rearmament became for Yoshida a matter of timing. Yoshida understood that if Japan were to continue its cheap ride on U.S. security guarantees, it would have to provide more of the collective goods the United States was seeking. It was time for a softer, more conciliatory line with the Americans. He approved creation of the Self-Defense

Forces, an act that entailed a vigorous bending of the past—and of both the spirit and the letter of the law. Dower compares Yoshida to a circus performer: "He was virtually a one man show: now the sword swallower, now the contortionist, now the Houdini who made elephants appear and disappear . . . Under his government, Article 9 was blown up like a balloon, twisted like a pretzel, kneaded like plasticene. In the end, however, it still remained unamended, and its survival was as significant as its mutilation."[63]

By the end of Yoshida's political reign, Japan had a military academy (Bōei Daigaku), military expenditures had become a routine part of the budget, air and maritime forces had been added to ground self-defense, and Japanese firms were again producing tanks, aircraft, and naval vessels. But none of this was at the level of America's other allies, nor would it be for decades. Yoshida had skillfully resisted American—and right-wing Japanese—importuning to become a major Asian military power. He had read public opinion as carefully as he had crafted it. Yoshida devised the widely accepted fiction that Japan had assumed a uniquely "pacifist" bearing. It had (and could have) no military, it would contribute to the free world by becoming rich, and it would become rich by supplying goods to nations around the world. Some of his allies may have been frustrated with the pace of Japan's rearmament, but he won their acceptance. Yoshida's tortured reinterpretation of Article 9 continued as government policy into the twenty-first century—by which time Japan had long since built one of the most formidable militaries in the world. He was, indeed, a magician.

CENTERING, ITALIAN STYLE

So was De Gasperi. It was no easier for De Gasperi to find a stable domestic center, and indeed Christian democracy had to be rebuilt from the bottom up. To make matters worse, and unlike in Japan, the Center-Right was tainted in the national imagination. The Communist Party had maintained a clandestine struggle against fascism, whereas the Church had cut its deal with Mussolini in 1929. Antifascism in general, and the Resistance in particular, were the legitimating touchstones for any credible leadership.

Leading Christian Democrats were actively engaged in the Resistance, especially after 1943, but the Communist Party deservedly got more credit. The DC was not formally established until July 1943. By then, Palmiro Togliatti—the man who would lead the PCI from 1926 until his death in 1964—had already proclaimed that the PCI had inherited the

Liberal mantle. Togliatti spent the war in Moscow, where he was closely tied to the international communist movement. Upon his return to Italy in 1944, he followed the guidance in the writings of Antonio Gramsci, co-founder of the PCI and his former Turin classmate, as well as the instructions of Stalin. Togliatti rejected the revolutionary path to power in favor of parliamentary democracy.

Togliatti and his *partito nuovo* benefited from their fight against fascism, but they suffered even more from their close ties to Moscow. Although the Italian Communist Party would become the largest nongoverning communist party in the world, and although its leaders made repeated efforts to demonstrate their commitment to democratic freedoms, they never convinced enough of the electorate—and certainly never convinced the United States or the Italian right. Togliatti was intent on building a mass (rather than vanguard) party. With the support of Stalin, who did not believe that the Americans or British would accept a communist Italy, he put the brakes on revolutionaries within the party. Togliatti reached out to the Italian center with his famous "handshake" (*mano tesa*); the PCI joined the government for four years and played a leading part in drafting a constitution for the first Italian Republic. The party announced its respect for religious freedom and opposed anticlericalism. It controlled the finance ministry portfolio for more than two years after December 1944 but postponed major structural change in land reform and state control of the economy. It agreed to a shared role in a unified national Confederation of Italian Labor (CGIL). It compromised on economic issues, studiously avoiding moves that might antagonize the middle class. Togliatti proclaimed an "Italian road to Socialism" (*la via italiana*) in an effort to construct a mass base, something Tarrow aptly calls "a rough analogue to DC centrism."[64]

The awkward embrace of Togliatti and De Gasperi—the great protagonists of the era—has been called the second Connubio by historians who draw parallels to Cavour's relationship to the Left. The marriage was extraordinary, durable, and utterly opportunistic on both sides.[65] Togliatti knew that revolution was impossible and he was unwilling to jeopardize nascent working class power for ideological reasons.[66] He cultivated the Catholic left and calculated that the Catholic social movement would rouse the populace to benefit the PCI. To pull progressive Christian Democrats away from the Church, Togliatti recognized individual and religious freedoms and endorsed the Vatican's agenda at the Constituent Assembly. De Gasperi used the arrangement in much the same way. He needed to show the lay public that it need not fear a Catholic party.[67]

Political expediency fueled their cooperation long enough to draft a new constitution and to ratify the peace treaty. The Center-Left governed as the new constitution dismantled the Savoy monarchy, assured women the right to vote, reaffirmed the Lateran Pacts, and revalidated the role of the Italian state in the economy. De Gasperi never gave Togliatti as much as he had sought. One of De Gasperi's first acts was to eliminate leftist control of local jurisdictions. Ginsborg sees this clearly: "It was part of De Gasperi's genius that he continued to inspire the respect and even the faith of the left, while consistently denying them their objectives."[68]

The Italian Communist Party had come a long way, but not far enough to achieve power. Too few believed that the working and middle classes could form a stable alliance under the Communist Party or, more fundamentally, that Togliatti could ever be free of Soviet influence. Moreover, the electorate had alternatives that seemed safer to the middle classes and that promised more rapid reconstruction. The leading alternative was Christian democracy. That this was also a choice for American influence was not entirely clear when the reconstruction of Christian democracy got under way.

De Gasperi began the project with a group of ex-Popolari while still underground in mid-1942. Just as Togliatti would shrewdly try to make the PCI a partito nuovo, De Gasperi sought to reinvent Christian democracy as a broad movement. He would exclude the communist Left and the far Right, but incorporate everyone in between—peasant proprietors and Catholic workers, shopkeepers, small businessmen, employers, and salaried workers.[69] He would take what was once Mussolini's and combine it with what was once Giolitti's, binding these two failures with democratic norms, anticommunism, and Catholic morality. In 1944, the young Aldo Moro wrote an article, "Dynamism of the Center," in which he articulated De Gasperi's program. He declared that the Center is "the natural position of Catholics, one truly consistent with our basic faith and Christian morals . . . It is this calling that leads us to the Center against entrenched conservatism that in the name of a presumed divine right would consecrate the existing order, and against the revolutionary movement of the left that appeals to Christians who cannot live with injustice."[70]

Finding this center, making it stable, was no small undertaking. De Gasperi was the first Catholic head of government in Italy who could speak to the pope on behalf of the large number of Italians who tempered their affection for the Church. But he also knew that reinvention of Christian democracy would distance Church and party. De Gasperi could no more afford for the DC to be perceived as the Roman party than Togliatti could afford for the PCI to be thought Moscow's tool.[71] De Gasperi needed the Church to support democracy.[72] Knowing that the Church's collaboration with fascism had helped destroy the PP, he sought a formula that would assure cooperation with non-Catholic forces without losing the support of the Church. He would remain "honor[ed] to be considered among [the pope's] devoted sons," but he also made sure the Church understood that it was only one of *two* legitimate powers on the peninsula—the other being the Italian Republic.[73]

Just before his death in 1954, De Gasperi reflected on his message to the electorate: "We [did] not say: You are Catholic, thus you are a Christian Democrat. We [said] that if you are a Christian Democrat, we have the right to think that you are a Catholic who feels the duty to exercise a public function."[74] Although the DC was not created by the Church nor under the Vatican's direct control, the Vatican went along. In 1944 the Church gave its tacit blessing. Clergy were encouraged to speak out in its favor, and parish churches were used as political headquarters during election campaigns. Church officials lobbied in public forums and in the media in support of DC programs. Without mentioning the party by name, in May 1946 Pope Pius XII announced that Catholics should vote only for candidates who "guarantee they respect the rights of God and religion."[75] De Gasperi was grateful to have the support of the Church, but he frequently needed to restrain its more authoritarian preferences.[76] In 1952 he blocked Church plans for an electoral coalition among non-leftist forces that would have included the neofascists. It is a measure of De Gasperi's success that historians would come to refer to the "fusion between the Christian Democratic Party and the republican state," and not to a fusion of DC and Vatican.[77]

Others within the DC needed to be "centered." The right of the party had been allied with the fascists and with monarchists, all of which De Gasperi declared out of bounds. The DC left was no easier to manage. The Catholic left shared his strong and uncompromising antifascism, but several factions were more concerned with social action, agrarian reform, state intervention in the economy, and redistributive justice than De Gasperi felt the party could afford. Unlike the DC right, which believed the DC should govern in the interest of the Church, and unlike the DC left, which argued the DC should follow the true mission of the Church and govern in the interest of the poor, De Gasperi steered the DC to govern in what he believed to be the interest of the nation.

This belief, as we have seen, required a heavy dose of conciliation outside the party as well. De Gasperi made common cause with Socialists and Communists for as long as it took to secure their commitments to religious freedom and to establish the bona fides of Christian Democracy as a responsible, nonauthoritarian force. As Ginsborg notes, "De Gasperi did not want the coalition to continue any longer than necessary, but he reserved the right to choose his moment to destroy it."[78] The moment he chose was when the Western bloc was being consolidated under U.S. control. If limited collaboration with the Communists was one of De Gasperi's great *tactical* choices, the creation of a mass-based DC was one of his two great *strategic* insights. The other was the alliance with the Western democracies.

CENTERING WEST

If foreign affairs was merely an "inescapable burden and necessity of government"[79] for Giovanni Giolitti, and for Benito Mussolini the chimerical opportunity for empire, for Alcide De Gasperi it was a singular opportunity for national reconstruction. Like Cavour, De Gasperi understood that the prosperity and security of Italy depended on a relationship he had to build with a foreign power. Also like Cavour (and like Yoshida), he looked realistically at the postwar configuration of international power and manipulated it from an acknowledged position of weakness. He understood that the Allies considered Italy, like Japan, unreliable at worst and a burden at best. But he concluded that neutrality would not suffice. Italy would need access to the resources the West could provide. Pride in Italianità would not protect Italy from being squeezed out like Egypt, Greece, or Portugal, detritus in the world power game.[80] According to his deputy, Amintore Fanfani, De Gasperi had three foreign policy goals: 1) return Italy to good standing in the family of nations, with full dignity and rights; 2) gain membership in the Western alliance of free nations; and 3) promote a united Europe.[81] None was a foregone conclusion.

At the end of the war, Italy remained subject to the terms of the 1943 Armistice and was supervised by the Allied Commission of Control. In late 1944 the Resistance received funds and arms but also agreed to Allied control and to dissolve immediately upon the cessation of hostilities. Control was never quite what Japan experienced, but neither would Italy get much credit for the contributions of its antifascists to the Allied cause. Cobelligerency counted for little, especially with Churchill, whose interventions were often heavy-handed. Churchill supported the monarchy and landowners, and personally vetoed the nomination of the antimonarchist Republican Carlo Sforza as prime minister and as foreign minister.[82] As in Japan, the Allies began by dismantling the Italian war machine. Italy was left with no ships and was forbidden to build or buy new ones. Rearmament, as in Japan, would come only with U.S. support after the start of the Cold War a half decade later.

Allied support was earned, in part, by the appointment of Alcide De Gasperi as foreign minister in December 1944.[83] His primary goal in these early years was to recover Italy's full standing as a member of the international community and, as far as possible, Italy's prefascist boundaries and colonies. When De Gasperi assumed his ministry, he was determined to craft a "cautious and balanced neutrality."[84] He needed Soviet support. In August 1945, he wrote to his Soviet counterpart, Foreign Minister Vyacheslav Molotov, pledging that Italy has no "prejudicial anticommunism" and did not intend to participate in any anti-Soviet bloc. He added "the fact that I write this as Minister of Foreign Affairs and as head of the Christian Democratic Party should give my words more weight."[85] Yet he was "certainly the quickest of the Christian Democrats to 'discover America,' "[86] and by the time he formed his first government in December 1945, he had abandoned any illusions about neutrality. The Western alliance was the best hope for Italian revival, and he retained the foreign minister's portfolio until February 1947 to steer Italy in that direction.

How could he continue to believe this given the Paris Peace Treaty of mid-1946? Italian representatives sought for Trieste and half of Istria to become Italian, to retain the boundary with Austria, and to restore Italian sovereignty to Libya, Eritrea, and Italian Somaliland.[87] These national aims had remarkably broad support, from the unpurged formerly fascist diplomats who drafted them to the Socialists and Communists.[88] But the Allies would not distinguish between the fascist Italians who provoked the European war and the democratic Italians who helped them end it. They went out of their way to humiliate De Gasperi at the conference.[89] In the final treaty, signed in February 1947, only the boundary with Austria was unadjusted—and this despite strong opposition from London and, earlier, Paris. None of Trieste (Italy's most visibly "unredeemed" land) was assigned to Italy. Instead, a Free Territory of Trieste was established, occupied by American and English troops. In addition, Italy had to pay reparations to Russia, Albania, Greece, Yugoslavia, and Ethiopia, and renounce its former colonies. Limits of 185,000 soldiers and 65,000 carabinieri were placed on the Italian military.

It was a punitive peace, but De Gasperi and Foreign Minister Sforza believed that Italy had received the best terms possible. Togliatti and the Left went along at Stalin's behest. Elder statesmen like Benedetto Croce, Don Luigi Sturzo, and Vittorio Emanuele Orlando claimed that Italy did not get the peace it deserved, and the treaty was attacked by the nationalist Right that had gotten Italy into this situation in the first place.[90] Some feared that foreign powers would seize the chance to reduce the Italian state to impotence, possibly even to its pre-Risorgimento divisions.[91] De Gasperi sensed he would lose the ratification vote and postponed it, giving him time to pacify domestic critics but raising suspicion abroad. The United States was losing patience. De Gasperi scheduled a vote only after the U.S. government informed him that it would suspend economic aid if

Italy did not move on the treaty. The Constituent Assembly grudgingly approved it in July. The best De Gasperi could do was put the Allies on notice that Italy would seek an early revision.[92]

Like Yoshida, De Gasperi would have far more leverage during the Cold War. By January 1947 De Gasperi, notionally in favor of "independent nations in a world unified above and beyond spheres of influence," was leaning hard toward the Western alliance.[93] Washington, whose support for De Gasperi had been oblique and tenuous, now would provide aid to assure the "stability and consolidation of democracy"—that is, to keep Italy out of the Soviet orbit.[94] By supporting Italy—and Turkey and Greece—the United States saw an opportunity simultaneously to contain Soviet communism and displace Britain in the Mediterranean.[95] In January, while still allied with the Communists and Socialists, De Gasperi visited Washington to obtain economic aid. He took the opportunity to convince American leaders that Italy could be a reliable partner in the emerging Cold War. Pushing exactly the right buttons, he told Secretary of State James F. Byrnes that the Italian communists were pressing hard "to bring Italy into Russia's orbit."[96]

De Gasperi came home with his pockets bulging, confident of U.S. support for reconstruction and an end to Italy's diplomatic isolation.[97] What looked to most Christian Democrats like De Gasperi's great success looked to most outside the party as the transformation of the DC into "*il partito americano.*"[98] In late January the Communist daily *L'Unità* published a scathing article by Togliatti accusing De Gasperi of "selling out to foreigners." De Gasperi's alliance was ever more uneasy: the Socialists split, the Communists were organizing demonstrations, and a group of nearly four dozen Christian Democrats supported by the Church pressed De Gasperi to create a new government by allying with the Right.[99] De Gasperi waited several months. In May 1947, after the announcement of the Truman Doctrine and on the eve of the Marshall Plan, he formed a government with no coalition partners. To this day, his was the only so-called *monocolore* cabinet in modern Italian history. The Italian left would not participate in government again for nearly fifteen years, and the PCI not for forty.

As the Cold War began to take shape, and domestic politics settled into a confrontation between Left and Right, Italian foreign policy faced a momentous choice. Did Italians want to be under the protection of the United States, or did they not? The forces for neutralism were not inconsiderable: the Socialists, the Communists, some Christian Democrats, the military, the Vatican, the nationalist Right. Even the Social-Democrats were split. That Alcide De Gasperi made Italy a full and integral part of the Atlantic alliance despite initial resistance from the British and indif-

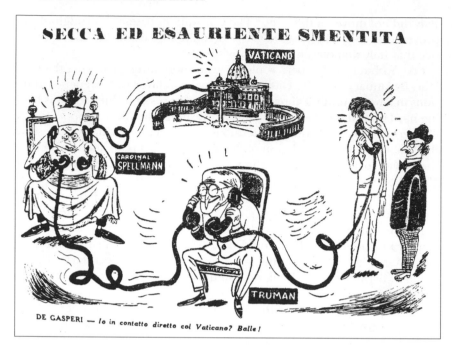

De Gasperi's "direct line" to the Vatican in the late 1940s went through President Truman and Cardinal Spellman, a power in the U.S. Catholic Church. In *Il Meglio del Don Basilico* (The best of Don Basilico), edited by Casa Editrice Roberto Napoleone, 1988.

ference from the Americans was a triumph of political leadership, and one with an immeasurably important legacy.

He did it by delivering the goods—and there were a lot of goods to deliver. In June 1947, Secretary of State George Marshall announced his program to reconstruct the European economies and to stabilize politics. Italy, which had already received more than $1 billion in U.S. relief, was invited to the inauguration of the Marshall Plan Secretariat in Paris in July 1947.[100] It was Italy's first opportunity to participate as an equal at an international conference. The American focus on Italy in the context of a European program, rather than a bilateral relationship, gave De Gasperi room to maneuver: now Liberals and Republicans could comfortably join Christian Democrats. They were encouraged also by the American invitation to Eastern European participation. The Soviet Union refused to allow its allies to participate, and created the Cominform in September. Italian participation came under mounting criticism from the Italian left.[101] The Cold War divide was becoming ever more sharply etched.

And now the stakes were getting higher. Even the British began to see the desirability of Italian participation in a united, anticommunist Western Europe. In January 1948, Foreign Minister Ernest Bevin appealed to "Western free nations" to join forces in a European military alliance.[102] Foreign Minister Sforza was positively inclined, but De Gasperi feared that Italian participation in a military alliance could undermine the domestic coalition he had constructed. Few Italian politicians wanted to follow popular participation in the Marshall Plan with a military alliance that war-weary voters might perceive as dangerous.

De Gasperi had good reason to be cautious. Elections were dominated by debate over the Marshall Plan and by the larger debate over foreign policy. The Americans lavished funds on Italy, but the Soviets also worked diligently. In February, for example, the Soviet Union announced support for Italian trusteeship over its former colonies. The United States countered with a promise of support for Italian acquisition of Trieste. Sensing they had bungled their diplomacy, De Gasperi and Sforza delayed a decision until after the election. Worse, they tried to play the French off against the British to extract a few additional concessions. Bevin was furious about Italian "blackmail" and refused to negotiate.[103] He and the other Europeans regarded Italian reluctance as characteristically perfidious—evidence that Italy could not be a reliable ally.[104] In the event, the Western European Union, a military pact of Britain, Belgium, Luxembourg, France, and the Netherlands—but excluding Italy—was realized in March 1948 after the communist takeover in Czechoslovakia. The treaty called for mutual military assistance but included economic, social, and cultural cooperation as well.

De Gasperi's calculation of domestic politics was more accurate than his calculation of foreign affairs. The profound opposition of the communist and socialist Left to an anti-Soviet foreign policy proved to be less a problem than widespread opposition from within his own Catholic world. Catholics were divided between those with an idealist faith in universal brotherhood, who preferred neutrality, and those with a realist fear of anticlerical communist power.[105] Many in the DC left, like Giuseppe Dossetti, imagined Christianity as the spiritual foundation for a bridge between East and West. A neutral, Catholic Italy would bring the two foolish giants to their senses. Dossetti, whose followers included the leaders of the next generation of left-wing Christian Democrats, was motivated by a curious combination of spirituality and realism. He wanted an autonomous foreign policy that would give Italy an active role in European affairs while avoiding the two "super-imperialisms" of East and West.[106] Giovanni Gronchi, a founding member of the PP, leader of the prefascist Catholic trade unions, and the second most powerful politician in the DC, also argued for neutrality. He argued for Catholic Italy to play the role of "third force," free from but guiding each of the two blocs. He touched on the sense that Italy deserved "moral and political parity" with the great powers, an unlikely prospect if it joined the Western camp.

Thus, the Catholic left preferred neutrality, and so did some on the Catholic right. The Vatican was slow to support the Western alliance.[107] Cardinal Montini, the Vatican's undersecretary for foreign affairs, later Pope Paul VI, advocated neutrality. Even the anticommunist Pope Pius XII was not immediately persuaded that the United States was Italy's best bet for peace and security; he feared the Church would have less influence in an Italy that looked like Franco's Spain. An inconsistent mixture of antimodern, antistate, and occasionally anti-European sentiment fed Catholic neutralism.[108] As the young Aldo Moro noted at the time, the division of the world into opposing blocs "posed grave problems for Christian life."[109]

De Gasperi prevailed, thanks in part to the poorly timed coup in Prague, in part to ethnic cleansing near Trieste, and in part to a great deal of heavy-handed help from his American friends. The Americans kept the development dollars flowing, and Secretary Marshall made it clear that a left-wing victory would lead the United States "to conclude that Italy had removed itself" from the list of beneficiaries of the European Recovery Program. Covert funding of the DC was also up and running based on a March 1947 recommendation of the National Security Council, and the Justice Department even went so far as to deny an entry visa to any Italian who voted for the PCI.[110] The United States openly studied the possibility of military intervention. For its part, the AFL-CIO provided funds to noncommunist trade unions.[111] Ginsborg concludes that during the run-up to the April 1948 elections "American intervention was breathtaking in its size, its ingenuity, and its flagrant contempt for any principle of non-interference in the internal affairs of another country."[112]

The Italian electorate got the message. On 18 April 1948, in what amounted to a national referendum on communism, the DC received its first (and last) absolute majority in Parliament. It won 305 of 574 seats, with 49 percent of the vote.[113] The Christian Democrats now fully controlled the Italian government—and would continue to do so alone and in coalition for the next four decades.

Having convinced the electorate of the material benefits of the Western side and defeated a broad-based neutralism, De Gasperi now needed to do two more things. First, he needed to integrate Italy into European diplomacy. The United States was prepared to accept Italy in the broader alliance, but the French and the British still needed to be convinced. In mid-September, the United States expressed the hope that Italy would join a new, larger Atlantic Alliance, and De Gasperi reassured U.S. officials that Italy would be a reliable ally. Second, he still had to win over the neutralists.

This second task was made more difficult by the PCI, which intensified its campaign for Italian neutrality. The PCI called for a general strike in July. Togliatti sought to drive a wedge between the neutralist and Atlanticist wings of the DC, hoping to win over leftist Catholics.[114] At first they seemed willing to listen, but the Communist agitation was counterproductive. Although the PCI showed that it retained significant popular support, the violence that it engendered turned away the Catholic left.[115] It also reconfirmed for many that Italy would need a strong and determined centrist leader if it was to survive as a democratic republic. Togliatti may have unintentionally united the DC.

In November 1948, two months after the American overture, PSI leader Pietro Nenni submitted a motion to Parliament that neutrality be Italy's declared foreign policy. In addition to support from Togliatti, Nenni expected allies within the Church and the left-wing of the DC who believed that "choosing neutrality was choosing peace."[116] De Gasperi convinced the DC neutralists that the Atlantic Alliance offered better opportunities for economic development and for Italian independence in foreign affairs. Nenni's motion was defeated, and the DC held together. De Gasperi immediately requested admission to the Council of Europe. Echoing the long struggle of Italian leaders to achieve parity with the great powers, he proclaimed "[Now] we go out from our humiliating situation after the war to again take our place among European nations."[117]

This outcome left one last convulsive debate.[118] In early 1949 the Italian Parliament began to consider joining what would soon become the North Atlantic Treaty Organization (NATO). De Gasperi took the offensive, appealing to every collective anxiety in the Italian nation. Equidistance and neutrality were illusions, he suggested, and Italy could not become the passive object of others' struggles. He reminded the deputies of the errors of fascist imperialism and Italy's need to inculcate trust among its neighbors. U.S. support would, he averred, be critical if Italy were "to maintain trust, openness, and loyalty." Then "a united Europe will have the chance to speak its mind to the two giants."[119] Italy, he promised, would not "be servile to foreign ideals or interests, but would bring to this peaceful alliance the bounty of our civilization."[120] It was a masterful performance, one aided by De Gasperi's promise of active support for social programs demanded by left-wing Catholics. In the end, only one DC deputy voted against the Atlantic Pact, and the DC was leading Italy. As we shall see, this claim—like the claim that Italy would be subservient to the United States—was exaggerated. Still, the Atlantic Pact was signed in Washington in April 1949 with Italy as a full participant. De Gasperi had moved mountains—both at home and abroad. Italian politics and public policy would never be the same.

THE FUTURE IS ALSO INVENTED

The terms of the postwar partnerships with the United States were not preordained. Each was the product of aggressive political manipulation by a creative political leader. Both Alcide De Gasperi and Yoshida Shigeru centered among domestic pressures and mobilized a remarkable set of political resources to achieve the outcome he sought. Each was criticized for a high-handed politics that marginalized his governing parties. While De Gasperi "centered" to the left, Yoshida "centered" to the right. Yoshida took care to protect the imperial institution and reinvented Japanese conservatism in democratic terms. Although he operated under the close supervision of an occupying army with its own strong ideas about democracy and national security, Yoshida struck a strategic bargain so that Japan would avoid a remilitarization that might derail its economic recovery. For his part, De Gasperi convinced reluctant allies to support Italian participation as a charter member in the European Community and the Atlantic Alliance.

There are two popular images of Alcide De Gasperi's "Western choice." One has it that there was no choice. On this account, he was forced into junior partnership by the United States. The other has him pushing on an open door of Western solidarity. Both are derived from a reading of the "great forces" that shaped the postwar world, and both are wrong. De Gasperi had to nudge these forces. He was not "pushed" into alliance with the West. He aggressively "pulled" Italy into it—over the doubts of the United States and Great Britain, and over the strong opposition of his domestic allies. He knew that Churchill had told Parliament in 1945 that "we have no need of Italy, just as we have no need of Spain," and he knew that the United States was then inclined to defer to Britain on matters related to the Mediterranean.[121] He also understood that, while the United States strongly preferred a noncommunist Italy, it did not have to be a democratic one. De Gasperi fought creatively and tenaciously to convince these allies that Italy ought not to go that way and played up Italian vulnerability to communism to win their support.[122]

De Gasperi sculpted a democratic political Center from what was at hand, using parts of Italy's many competing political forces. He saw an anti-system Left, but also a democratic one. He saw an anti-system Right, but also one committed to republican institutions. He understood all too well that these currents were also to be found within Christian Democracy.[123] He turned to the Left for support for social reform, and he turned to the Right for help with his foreign affairs and economic policy. He won grudging admiration from each. His Socialist adversary, Pietro Nenni, observed on De Gasperi's death that it was good for Italy that "he had his foot on the brake [while] I had mine on the accelerator."[124] And Giulio Andreotti, anchor of the Christian Democratic right, admired De Gasperi for having made it possible for the Socialists to "join the ranks of international democracy," and for "start[ing] the Italian Communist Party's long march."[125] Today, Alcide De Gasperi is the only postwar politician invoked by both Left and Right as a statesman and founding father of the Italian Republic. Ironically, years after his political opponents and his allies discarded him, all now want a piece of his mantle.[126]

Both De Gasperi and Yoshida signed on to the Pax Americana as the fast lane to prosperity and national security, but Yoshida had to accept more constraints. Yoshida spent more time untying the strings that came with the deal. But he did so, to Japan's enduring national advantage. The "Yoshida Doctrine" was his greatest legacy. Through it, he effectively set the terms of political debate for a half century.[127] It was the enduring result of a dazzling calculation, for it ran counter to the demands of several major principals. Yoshida's formulation split the political opposition. He prevailed by *inventing* a position for which there was no "natural" constituency. The Japanese left wanted complete disarmament, what it called "unarmed neutrality." It would accept neither U.S. bases nor rearmament, and was prepared to fight both on constitutional grounds. The Right wanted full rearmament and a return to national autonomy, and was eager to revise the Constitution to make it happen. The United States wanted both Japanese rearmament and basing rights in Japan, and was willing for Japan to ignore the Constitution that it had written for her.

Yoshida had a different idea. He used U.S. bases to buy Japanese independence, at a price far lower than the full cost of large-scale rearmament. He used Article 9 of the Constitution for domestic political protection. Japan could take a "cheap ride" on American defense spending, and free its resources for economic growth. Of course, it was debatable whether Japan could truly be independent in this position. After all, the success of this strategy rested in large part on Japan's ability to demonstrate that it could be a loyal ally. But, if he could survive attacks from Left and Right for toadying to the United States, the strategy would enable Japan to pursue the sort of security Yoshida most valued. Kosaka calls his preference "economics first-ism" (*keizai chūshin shugi*) and frames it with particular clarity: "Yoshida believed that the most important thing in international relations was whether a country was prosperous or not. He held this so-called mercantile view of international politics from before the Second World War. This is why using Article Nine as a negotiating tool was so natural for him."[128] Over time, the subordination of military power to economic power would become the institutionalized center of Japan's political consensus—"comprehensive security." It would also become identified with fundamental "Japanese values."[129]

When he became prime minister in 1982, Nakasone Yasuhiro reflected on Yoshida Shigeru's leadership:

> In hindsight one could argue that Prime Minister Yoshida's strategy represented, in its own way, a rational decision. By leaving Japan's defense to another country, he was able to reduce the defense burden, allowing the country to concentrate on rebuilding its devastated economy . . . Yet I cannot help but wonder, even now, about what might have happened had Japan made a different choice at that critical juncture.[130]

The "different choice" Nakasone had in mind, of course, was the one he, Kishi Nobusuke, and others on the Right had lobbied for: constitutional revision, rapid and full rearmament, sovereignty in matters of national security. The Right believed that Yoshida Shigeru had mortgaged Japan's pride and sense of national purpose.

Still, Yoshida's deliberate, step-by-step pursuit of national security, economic reconstruction, and acceptable peace terms achieved a great deal. Centering at home and negotiating relentlessly with his U.S. allies, he was able to preserve the imperial household, eviscerate the Left, and restore much of the prewar bureaucratic, economic (and even aristocratic) elite to leadership without giving the militarists a way back in and while empowering his supporters. He did nothing less than help reinvent Japan as what Benfell calls "the prosperous peace state"—one that in Yoshida's own conception had lost the war but won the diplomacy.[131] If his critics saw this as the result of kowtowing to U.S. demands, they were not listening to Yoshida: "Just as the United States was once the colony of Great Britain but now . . . is the stronger of the two, if Japan becomes a colony of the United States, it will eventually become the stronger."[132]

Yoshida Shigeru and Alcide De Gasperi were each exemplary bricoleurs. They identified possibilities no one else had perceived. Both used what was at hand to stretch, indeed to overcome, the daunting constraints of foreign occupation and domestic turbulence. Each recombined shards of the past into a novel, functional, and resilient present. More than any modern Japanese leader other than Itō Hirobumi, Yoshida shaped Japan's future. More than any modern Italian leader apart from Count Cavour, De Gasperi did the same for Italy. Rarely have political leaders made so much from so little that endured for so long.

CHAPTER NINE

Putting Corruption in Its Place:

KISHI NOBUSUKE AND AMINTORE FANFANI

> People have got to know whether or not their president is a crook. Well, I'm
> not a crook. I've earned everything I've got.
>
> Richard M. Nixon, November 1973

Important political choices remained to be made well after Alcide De
Gasperi and Yoshida Shigeru cast their lots with the United States. Democrats had to be found—or invented. Socialists had to be repressed or
placated. Conservatives had to be unified. And parties had to be
funded. The chief architects were two former fascists: Amintore Fanfani
and Kishi Nobusuke. Fanfani's flirtation with fascist corporatism pales
beside Kishi's extensive responsibility for wartime economic planning,
but each emerged from a pre-democratic past to mobilize resources for
a democratic present. Kishi's success suggests that even war crimes can
be forgiven under the right circumstances, whereas Fanfani's suggests
limits to the familiar claim that politicians needed a deep association
with the Resistance to establish postwar legitimacy. Their common
choices—for personal reinvention, for conservative consolidation, for
"structural corruption"—served as the institutional base of the postwar
political order.

JAPAN AND THE LDP

Single-party (LDP) dominance in Japanese politics—what has come to
be known as the "1955 System"—was virtually coterminous with the Cold
War. Yoshida Shigeru laid the foundation of this system, but his "mainstream" conservatism was just one of several rivers flowing into the reser-
voir of postwar Japanese power.[1] Yoshida's preeminence was challenged
by a very different conservative, Kishi Nobusuke, whom we have already

225

seen as an architect of the "transwar" system. Yoshida and his disciples represented the more decorous "mainstream" of LDP hegemony, and worked comfortably with the "orthodox" business community (*seitōha zaikai*). Kishi, by contrast, connected the non-zaibatsu business community and the discredited prewar world of ultranationalist politicians and control bureaucrats to conservative hegemony.

Political choices contributed directly to "structural corruption."[2] Yoshida's contribution was made before the consolidation of the conservative camp, Kishi's later, and the system was the result not of their collusion but of their vigorous competition. Yoshida never belonged to the Liberal Democratic Party, for the LDP was created by Kishi and his allies to take power *away* from Yoshida. Kishi wove together the disparate threads of conservatism in postwar Japan. He did not *displace* the Yoshida mainstream, he *widened* conservative hegemony, and Japanese politicians are still responding to the choices he made.[3] Although LDP dominance would not be consolidated until Kishi's revisionist platform was rejected and the LDP could move back toward the center, Kishi made the golden age of the LDP possible—for Tanaka Kakuei, who transformed his model of money politics, and for maverick successors like Nakasone Yasuhiro and Ozawa Ichirō, who took up his ideas for constitutional reform. Kishi Nobusuke did not dictate the final terms of the conservative project or of LDP dominance—but he contributed more than any other to its form and functions. Nakasone has identified Kishi Nobusuke as Japan's greatest postwar political leader.[4]

REINVENTION AND REDISCOVERY

Even in a Cold War world of cynical opportunism and rapidly shifting alliances, Kishi's resurrection was remarkable. Kishi had been General Tōjō's closest deputy for nearly a decade. Yet, in June 1957, in the same Senate chamber where the U.S. declaration of war against Japan had been approved a decade and a half earlier, Vice President Richard Nixon banged the gavel to introduce Prime Minister Kishi Nobusuke, one of the men who had been jailed for plotting that war. Nixon now proclaimed him an "honored guest" who was "not only a great leader of the free world, but also a loyal and great friend of the people of the United States."[5] Kishi responded grandiloquently, proclaiming his "belie[f] in the lofty principles of democracy—in the liberty and dignity of the individual."[6] His postwar ascent to power had been enabled by friends in high places and by his ability to reinvent himself. Upon his release from prison, for example, Kishi had driven directly to the prime minister's residence, where he met his brother, Satō Eisaku, the chief cabinet secretary. He literally exchanged his prison uniform for a business suit. More than the clothing felt odd: "Strange, isn't it?" he told his brother. "We're all democrats now."[7]

Kishi began building his political career long before the end of the war. There were rumors that Kishi had already enriched himself and his political allies while a bureaucrat in Manchuria. Connections to the opium trade, combined with his personal control of the movement of capital in and out of the puppet state, made Kishi singularly influential—and likely very rich.[8] Indeed, it was said that he could move as much money around as he wished "with a single telephone call," and that he did so both legally and illegally, and for both public and private purposes.[9] By the time Kishi returned to Tokyo in 1939, he was already the prototypical LDP political elder with an impressive network of allies inside and outside of government.[10] He first ran for elective office in 1942, while serving as minister of commerce and industry. The minimally competitive campaign gave him considerable insight into the darker side of campaign finance.[11]

In 1944, Kishi began mobilizing his network and lubricating it with cash. He created the "Kishi New Party" (Kishi Shintō) and recruited thirty-two Dietmen.[12] It was an eclectic mixture. Some, like his future foreign minister, Fujiyama Aichirō, were independent businessmen with whom he had collaborated in China.[13] Others were ultranationalists who had planned the ill-fated coups d'etat in 1931. Standing ready to help were senior executives of the "public policy companies" that Kishi had helped to create, independent (non-zaibatsu) businesses that Kishi had helped to nurture, and a large number of small and medium-sized businesses that had profited from his control program.

Corrupt politicians were no strangers to Japan. Hokkaido land scandals had rocked the Meiji oligarchy and the Yamamoto cabinet was forced to resign in 1914 after it was revealed that officials had accepted money from Siemens, the German arms maker. We have already seen how Taishō- and early Shōwa-era politicians were corrupted by their relations with businessmen. The early postwar period rediscovered some of the financial benefits of politics. The spring 1947 election campaign saw nearly three thousand violations of election law, resulting in seventy-one jail terms for open vote buying or selling.[14] A 1948 law required public reporting of campaign donations and set limits on the amounts that politicians could receive. Although the law was difficult to enforce, some powerful men fell.[15] The first major casualty was the deputy prime minister in the Ashida cabinet, Socialist Nishio Suehiro, who perjured himself about receiving unreported funds in 1948. The rest of the Ashida cabinet, which had come to power on the promise of cleaning up money politics, was felled later that year when it was learned that executives of Shōwa Denkō, a fertilizer manufacturer, had been bribing government officials to gain access to low-interest government loans. The dragnet pulled in such future LDP leaders as Fukuda Takeo (future scion of the Kishi faction), Ōno Bamboku, and even the prime minister, who was arrested after he resigned.[16] Soon thereafter coal mine owners bribed Diet members to block nationalization; Tanaka Kakuei, the most gifted among many corrupt politicians, was jailed.

Even if politics was corrupt and the laws were insufficient to deter it, people believed that at least an independent judiciary was immune to political pressure. Most believed that the new legal system gave prosecutors strong discretionary powers.[17] But there was one enormous loophole. Occupation reformers had decided that only public accountability would protect citizens' rights. Toward this laudable end, they inserted Article 14 into the Public Prosecutors Law, giving the publicly elected prime minister the authority to exercise "command and supervision" (*shikiken hatsudō*) over the prosecutors through his justice minister.

Until April 1954 the work of prosecutors had been considered inviolable. Then the prime minister invoked his authority to halt prosecution of senior political figures.[18] Prosecutors had learned that Japanese shipbuilding firms, seeking special legislation for government assistance to rebuild their shipyards, had bribed a large number of politicians, including the deputy prime minister, Ogata Taketora; the head of the Liberal Party's Policy Affairs Research Council, Ikeda Hayato; and the secretary-general of the party, Satō Eisaku. Thirty-four bureaucrats from the Ministry of Transportation and seventy-one businessmen were arrested as well. But Justice Minister Inukai Takeru refused permission to arrest Satō and Ogata (who as sitting Diet members were otherwise immune) under orders from Prime Minister Yoshida, and then resigned. For his part, Yoshida hung on for another eight months in the face of withering public attacks. He left office for good in December 1954.

The damage was done. A former director of the Tokyo Special Investigation Division lamented that most senior prosecutors now "tend to cave in to political pressure."[19] In the next three and a half decades nearly half of Japan's postwar prime ministers and a strikingly large number of cabinet ministers would be arrested or investigated on serious charges of corruption at one time or another. Among them, only one major political figure—Tanaka Kakuei—was ever prosecuted for political finance violations.[20]

SORTING OUT THE PARTIES

The first postwar decade was a period of intense upheaval for political parties. The Japan Socialist Party (JSP) had led a coalition government under Prime Minister Katayama for ten months from April 1947 to February 1948. The bulk of the JSP remained together until October 1951, when the party split over ratification of the Peace and Security Treaties. The Communist Party, which had done so well in the 1949 elections, veered off into a strategy of violent revolution, which cost it popular support. The conservative parties were even more divided. In 1945, there were three major conservative parties: the Liberals (Nihon Jiyūtō), the Progressives (Nihon Shinpotō), and the Cooperative Party (Nihon Kyō-dōtō). Their ranks were decimated by the purge of those with wartime ties. Their greatest loss was Liberal Party leader Hatoyama Ichirō, purged in 1946. In his place, Yoshida Shigeru became party leader and prime minister. By the early 1950s the conservatives had settled into the mainstream Liberal Party and the Japan Reform Party (Nihon Kaishintō), but the conservative political landscape was still far from settled. Prewar associations, enmities, and personal debts were all in play, and no unified conservative solution seemed possible.

It was not only personal. Much of the dispute was substantive—and, indeed, began with the Constitution itself. No politician was more outspoken on the importance of revising the Constitution than Kishi Nobusuke. He worked relentlessly for revision so that Japan could rearm, become an equal security partner of the United States, and enjoy an autonomous foreign policy.[21] He captured the concern of most of Japan's postwar Right when he wrote: "If Japan is alone in renouncing war . . . she will not be able to prevent others from invading her land. If, on the other hand, Japan could defend herself, there would be no further need of keeping United States garrison forces in Japan . . . Japan should be strong enough to defend herself."[22]

Kishi was determined to lead the Right to power. Kishi had a well-developed vision of a stable Japanese polity ruled by a dominant party. On his release from prison, Kishi revived the model of his wartime Kishi New Party and his prewar Association for Defense of the Fatherland (Gokoku Dōshikai) in the form of a Japan Reconstruction Federation (Nippon Saiken Renmei). He built the party around former Minseitō politicians and control bureaucrats, and placed Shigemitsu Mamoru, the former foreign minister, at its helm. The party would pursue an independent anti-communism, promote small and medium-sized businesses, deepen U.S.-Japan economic relations, and revise the Constitution.[23] Yet despite having raised hundreds of millions of yen from industrialists—many in the defense industry—Kishi's federation failed in its first (and only) electoral test. When Yoshida Shigeru called for elections in the autumn of 1952, his young party was crushed at the polls. Kishi had to consider other options.[24]

He even flirted with joining the Socialist Party but, at the urging of his brother Satō Eisaku, he turned reluctantly to Yoshida's Liberal Party so that he might transform it from within.[25] At first, Yoshida—whose first battles with Kishi dated from the wartime mobilization—wanted no part of Kishi.[26] He had, in fact, intervened with the Occupation authorities to remove Kishi from the list of politicians to be de-purged. But this was a time of fluid ideological borders and political desperation. Moreover, Kishi had money and (not unrelatedly) a battalion of politicians, both of which made partnership palatable, if not appealing, to Yoshida.[27] In the event, Yoshida took him in and Kishi won his first postwar Diet seat in 1953.

Kishi lost no time in denouncing the party's defects from within. He painted a picture of his own party leader as a collaborator unable to defend Japanese interests. Kishi argued vigorously for his signature issues, Japanese rearmament and economic planning, based on a "democratic" anticommunism. The constitutional issue was tougher. Yoshida tried to co-opt Kishi, appointing him chairman of a Diet committee to study constitutional reform. Kishi used the committee as a bully pulpit and pulled away several of Yoshida's most senior colleagues as well as the Japan Federation of Employers (Nikkeiren).[28] "We Liberals," Kishi argued with extraordinary chutzpah, "must be prepared to make concessions to our fellow conservatives. We must not insist that Yoshida be returned as Prime Minister if this issue is a stumbling block to unity. We must be realistic."[29]

Kishi Nobusuke was surely the equal of any realist politician in history. There was no stratagem too cynical, no ally too close to betray, in his pursuit of power. He joined Ishibashi Tanzan and Ashida Hitoshi in April 1954 to create a New Party Formation Promotion Council (Shintō Kessei Sokushin Kyōgikai). Flashing "show money" (*misegane*) as evidence of his close ties to deep corporate pockets, Kishi and his colleagues convinced two hundred politicians to join their call for a new conservative alternative to Yoshida's Liberal Party.[30] Not surprisingly, Kishi's open revolt earned him expulsion.

In November, Kishi took his faction with him and joined with Hatoyama, the sometime Seiyūkai politician, to form the Democratic Party. Hatoyama became the party head. In Japanese parlance, he was atop the *omikoshi*, the portable shrine carried (and steered) by Kishi Nobusuke, who was party secretary-general. The Democrats gained the support of the Left-Wing and Right-Wing Socialist Parties for a no-confidence vote that ended the political career of Yoshida Shigeru.[31] In the subsequent election, the Democrats took 185 of 467 seats, and the Liberals lost nearly half their Diet strength. Kishi, now widely recognized as the kingmaker, immediately reached out to the rump Liberal Party to complete the conservative consolidation.[32]

Just one day after the Hatoyama government was installed, Kishi began negotiations with Ishii Mitsujirō, the secretary-general of the Liberal Party, and other powerful conservatives. Hatoyama was hardly enthused, for once again the indefatigably ambitious Kishi was subverting his party leader.[33] This time he got more than he sought. What had begun as a campaign to create a stable two-party system, to prevent the Left from gaining power, became a "one and a half party system" in which the conservatives, under the expansive Liberal Democratic Party, would govern Japan for more than four decades.[34]

It is now recognized that Kishi was the father of LDP dominance, the central figure in building the 1955 System.[35] Still, the formation of the Liberal Democratic Party in November 1955 must be one of the most overdetermined events in Japanese political history. Kishi had been maneuvering for it for half a decade; the business community and U.S. Secretary of State John Foster Dulles each openly demanded it. The proximate cause was reunification of the Japan Socialist Party one month earlier, in October 1955.[36]

Mutually mistrustful conservative Japanese politicians were feeling pressure from all sides, and it was Kishi Nobusuke who moved to take them all in hand. He had his work cut out for him. There were deep—nearly irreconcilable—factional divisions in the conservative camp.[37] Kishi convened at least ten meetings, and the discussions frequently stalled over fundamentals: Were they aiming merely for cooperation, or for full consolidation— and on whose terms? Would the Liberals be forced to join the Democratic Party, or would a new party be created? Kishi pressed for yet another incarnation of his long-sought "New Party." After a summer of protracted negotiations, the Socialists inadvertently helped break the logjam. Their consolidation in October led to formation of the Liberal Democratic Party one month later.

Kishi felt he could maximize his own chances at a future premiership by refusing a cabinet post and by becoming party secretary-general (*kanji-chō*). He already had the knowledge, experience, and financial resources that a cabinet post would bestow, and as secretary-general he would be responsible for all decisions about party endorsements and campaign funding. Distrusted by many former Liberals, he saw in this post the chance to build their dependence on him.[38] In his first test, the LDP won an absolute majority of seats in the Diet.

Given this irresistible confluence of factors, it is impossible to argue that Kishi Nobusuke created the LDP single-handedly. But it is clear that Kishi's strategic choices shaped the new party. It was he who devised the mechanisms for stable collaboration that had eluded so many other ambitious politicians. It was he who pursued policies and devised stratagems that would become identified with LDP dominance. The most important among the former was his relentless pressure to undo Occupation reforms and to revise the Japanese alliance with the United States. The most important among the latter was his enduring influence on political finance.

THE REVERSE COURSE

The start of Japan's strategic and highly contested move away from Occupation reforms can be pegged to the announcement in 1947 of the Truman Doctrine, when the United States indicated it cared more about anticommunism than it did about democratization. It continued after the Occupation ended, with Yoshida's support. But Kishi would take it even further. Once the LDP was returned to power in the June 1958 election, his government moved vigorously to amend laws related to national defense—resulting in a 10,000 man increase in the number of Japanese uniformed soldiers.[39] Concerned that the teachers were too sympathetic to communism, the Kishi government also introduced legislation to oblige public schools to provide moral education and to evaluate the teachers.[40]

Kishi's efforts to revise the Police Law and to amend the Constitution were his most conspicuous failures. Widely seen as returning the police to prewar levels of power, the new legislation would have enabled the police to conduct searches and seizures without warrants.[41] Kishi's proposals had to be abandoned in face of protests by *both* the Left (general strikes by Sōhyō) and within the LDP (three cabinet members resigned in protest). His effort to revise the Constitution dragged on interminably, and was finally abandoned in the tumult over the Security Treaty revision in 1960.

The political consequences of the battle to revise the U.S.-Japan Security Treaty (Ampō) are widely understood as Kishi's greatest legacy. For his supporters the revision stands as his "monument."[42] For his detractors, it stands as evidence of his unreconstructed authoritarianism. However viewed, it was a turning point in conservative hegemony. To proud nationalists, Ampō was yet another unequal treaty. U.S. troops were allowed to quell domestic disturbances even after the Occupation had ended, and could prevent the use of Japanese bases by any other power.

Revision of the treaty became the main item on Kishi's agenda.[43] The Americans were relatively easy to deal with. The United States was more than willing to change the terms of the treaty, and through secret side agreements protected those privileges—such as the introduction of nuclear weapons—that it most cared about.[44] Kishi battled forces within his own party, squared off against a popular Left, and had to contend with the largest mass demonstrations in modern Japanese history. In June 1960, hundreds of thousands of demonstrators surrounded the national Diet building in central Tokyo. They forced Prime Minister Kishi to cancel a scheduled visit by President Dwight Eisenhower, for what was supposed to be his crowning achievement as an international statesman. A week later, after forcing the treaty bill through the Diet without debate and without the opposition present, Kishi abruptly announced his resignation. Now the LDP could reject Kishi's leadership, turn away from the reverse course, and lock arms with the business community to champion high-speed growth.

THE PUBLIC FACE OF POLITICAL FINANCE

Business disillusionment with Kishi's leadership was already widespread. Business leaders were calling for his resignation as a way to restore political stability. Kishi claimed that "the business community was not divided" in its support for him, but Keidanren Chairman Uemura abandoned him in favor of the less controversial Ikeda Hayato. Of the major business interest groups, only the Nikkeiren stood by him throughout the crisis.[45]

Keidanren's political influence was threatened. By 1960 Uemura's "Economic Reconstruction Group" accounted for some 60 percent of all reported political contributions.[46] Although the group gave funds to all parties (excluding the Communists), more than 90 percent went to the LDP.[47] This was only a *part* of the total funds flowing from business to the LDP, and the bigger problem for Uemura was that it was a *declining* part. Kishi was contributing to the problem by unleashing factional competition for funds and seeking to broaden LDP sources.

Two tracks had developed for business support of conservative Japanese politicians. On the one hand was the formal track, Uemura's single channel. Uemura and the Keidanren wished to fund only the party, and insisted that contributions be earmarked for election campaigns. These funds were fully legal and reported.[48] (This single channel also provided firms an excuse to decline direct requests from the party and politicians.)

On the other hand, *internal* campaigns among faction leaders were becoming even more critical. Factional considerations came to dominate, and the factions needed money.[49] Kishi turned to the non-Keidanren business class. In principle, Keidanren became the source of "clean" funds and other sources were identified for factional support.

Kishi knew how to suck money from both pipes. He was undeterred by Keidanren complaints about the escalating demands of LDP politicians. One of Kishi's political secretaries says: "Individual politicians and individual faction leaders were all going to the same businessmen for money. The competition got so intense that some of them made direct promises to the businessmen. It wasn't 'dirty' money (*kitanai*) exactly, but the business leaders did want to avoid giving 'inconvenient' (*guai ga warui*) and 'strange' (*henna*) money."[50] Under Kishi's leadership, LDP factions became the leading object of political fund-raising. Kishi resorted to the frequent reshuffling of his cabinet as a way to balance factions and to rotate needy politicians through the high-rent district of ministerial real estate. Rather than replace individual ministers, as Yoshida had done, Kishi changed entire cabinets to spread the wealth. His successors took the idea further and routinely rotated cabinets on an annual basis. As a result, politicians continuously sought "the money from which sprouts the wings that let us fly."[51]

There was little Uemura and the Keidanren could do, as Uemura explained:

> It takes money to run a party—staff, meetings, study. But parties do not have their own source of funds. Someone has to give it to them. The same is true at election time. There are fees for filing for candidacy, costs for speech meetings, publications, and so forth . . . Instead of giving separately to each faction member, we think it better to give to the party headquarters. Then again, there are still a number of businessmen who give funds directly to individual politicians; we cannot control this.[52]

But Uemura certainly tried to. In fact, after Kishi's chaotic departure, Keidanren tried to moderate what it perceived as Kishi's excesses.[53] Under pressure from other business interest groups, Uemura abolished the Economic Reconstruction Group and replaced it with a more noble-sounding Citizens' Association (Kokumin Kyōkai) in March 1961. His purpose was to broaden the sources of conservative party support.[54]

Kishi was not invited to speak at the inauguration of this group; his successors and rivals displayed the LDP's "kinder, gentler" face to the Japanese public. Ikeda Hayato, the new prime minister, delivered a speech at the inauguration in which he barely veiled his disdain for Kishi's practices:

Ever since I became Prime Minister in the midst of the uproar surrounding
the Security Treaty crisis, I have not been able to keep the issue of 'correct political posture' out of my mind . . . Our LDP, on its own, has reflected about
political finance and factional problems, as well as about the way in which we
connect to the people. We have come up with a major new program—shedding our old practices in name and in fact, as a modern party.[55]

But skins are not shed so easily.

As one observer has aptly noted, "two distinct classes of leadership
evolved in the LDP in the 1950s and 1960s, the bagmen and the statesmen."[56] Kishi wanted to be recognized as the latter, but was far from averse
to being the former. Indeed, Kishi himself offered the bluntest assessment
of Japanese money politics. During the battle for control of the party in
1957, he had been attacked by Ishii Mitsujiro for raising dirty money. Ishii
remarked of Kishi that "no matter how tightly you seal a bucket of shit, you
still can't put it in the *tokonoma* [place of honor in a Japanese home]." Kishi
reflected on the charge and concluded years later that "there are plenty of
buckets of shit to go around."[57] Despite the best efforts of Keidanren to
perfume them, these buckets would only get larger.

Many political observers comment on the sharp increase in funds consumed by the LDP after Kishi became prime minister.[58] Kishi recalls (with
decided understatement) that he was not without resources during his
rise to power: "Among business leaders at that time, I was closest to Fujiyama Aichiro, the Chairman of the Japan Chambers of Commerce and
Industry, and to Uemura Kogoro at Keidanren. Because I was at the Ministry of Commerce and Industry for so long, I had connections with businessmen in Osaka, Nagoya, other local areas, and was relatively well
known all around."[59] Understandably, his account is not complete. Kishi's
power to collect political money resulted from his experience in MCI, especially in Manchuria. The staffs at Keidanren and at the Japan Chamber
of Commerce and Industry (Nissho) were filled with retired MCI officials.
They were called "Kishi's piggy banks" (*Kishi no chokinbako*).[60] Other associates had remained in industry, where they were also in a position to help
him. In particular, a great many "descended from heaven" (*amakudari*)
into the steel industry, and Yawata and Fuji Steel—both once under his supervision—donated much more political money to Kishi than any other
companies.[61] Only after Kishi formed his first cabinet did he begin to attract funds from the elite trading companies, such as Mitsubishi and Mitsui, and manufacturing firms, such as Sumitomo Chemicals.[62] Even then,
he depended on relationships to non-zaibatsu companies such as Nissan,
Marubeni, and Itochu, relationships cemented in Manchuria two decades
earlier.

These connections, nurtured so long and so diligently, had allowed Kishi to exploit alternative sources of funding. Throughout his time in office—and likely for much longer after that—Kishi moved aggressively to raise and conceal additional funds. His former Manchukuo ally, Ayukawa Gisuke, was made head of the leading association of small and medium-sized firms after his release from jail. It was Kishi who originated the most sophisticated money laundering operation (*roka sōchi*) in Japanese politics. Kishi built what one biographer has called an "exquisitely institutionalized" system of money politics (*seichi na kōzōka*).[63] His system took at least three forms. Each is close to impossible to document adequately, but each had important institutional ramifications. Each is associated with less-reputable aspects of LDP dominance that were as important as any positive reforms pioneered by Yoshida Shigeru. And some, of course, intersected with Yoshida's mainstream. Together they constituted what are still only dimly understood resources of the 1955 System.

PUTTING OTHER RESOURCES INTO THE SYSTEM

Using American Money

The first form was Kishi's exploitation of American paranoia about communism. Schaller reports that Ambassador Douglas MacArthur II, the general's nephew, convinced Secretary of State Dulles that the United States had to support Kishi or risk losing the alliance. Kishi returned triumphant from his June 1957 visit to Washington with promises that the Security Treaty would be revised and, possibly, with promises of secret funding from the Central Intelligence Agency.[64] Rumors have flowed for decades about a secret "M-Fund" that was built from the sale of surplus military materiél.[65] These stockpiles allegedly included rare metals and diamonds, the sale of which funded a sort of Japan-specific secret Marshall Plan run by General Marquat, chief of SCAP's Economic and Science Section. The fund was also purportedly used to underwrite the sudden (and unbudgeted) formation of the National Police Reserve at the start of the Korean War and to buy conservative political support for the U.S. alliance.

According to Kanō and Takano, there were two channels of M-funding, both managed jointly with U.S. officials.[66] One was to mainstream conservatives led by Yoshida Shigeru, the other to Kishi Nobusuke and the anti-mainstream group. Schlei alleges that Vice President Richard Nixon turned over exclusive control of the M-Fund to Kishi, presumably during their 1957 Washington meeting, and things changed:

Beginning with Prime Minister Kishi, the Fund has been treated as a private preserve of the individuals into whose control it has fallen. Those individuals have felt able to appropriate huge sums from the Fund for their own personal and political purposes . . . The litany of abuses begins with Kishi who, after obtaining control of the fund from [then Vice President Richard] Nixon, helped himself to a fortune of one trillion yen . . . Kakuei Tanaka, who dominated the Fund for longer than any other individual, took from it personally some ten trillion yen . . . Others who are said to have obtained personal fortunes from the Fund include Mrs. Eisaku Sato . . . and Masaharu Gotoda, a Nakasone ally and former chief cabinet secretary.[67]

All, or some, or none of this may be true, but we know for certain that Kishi and his brother Satō Eisaku frequently played the anticommunist card. According to Kishi's own account, he frequently used the good offices of his friend Harry Kern, a former *Newsweek* bureau chief, to make arrangements for him at the U.S. embassy in Tokyo.[68] Declassified records show Satō, then Kishi's finance minister, seeking U.S. funds "to combat extremist forces." In July 1958 Satō met secretly with S. S. Carpenter, first secretary of the U.S. Embassy. According to Carpenter's memorandum on the conversation, Satō told him that the LDP had established a "secret organization [of] top business and financial leaders," and that this group had "contributed heavily" to the recent electoral campaign. Satō explained that the party would shortly have to return to these business leaders for an expensive upper-house campaign, and felt that the LDP and the *zaikai* (business community) could not "combat communism" alone. If an M-Fund deal existed to cover these requests, Carpenter did not let on. He told Satō that the ambassador "had always tried to help Mr. Kishi and the Conservatives in every way possible," but he declined to authorize the funds Satō was seeking.[69] In short, it is plausible but not proven that Kishi Nobusuke played a central role in establishing a financial relationship between conservative Japanese politicians and the government of the United States.

Using Public Resources

Now that the archives of the Ministry of Foreign Affairs have been opened, we have a better understanding of how Kishi pioneered an intriguing alternative source of political funds.[70] He systematically employed government programs to generate business for political supporters that, in turn, may have generated substantial kickbacks. This public resources model opened a new and lucrative avenue for political finance. It was significantly expanded and deepened in the capable hands of Tanaka Kakuei.[71]

Kishi seized a splendid opportunity that Yoshida had dismissed out of hand: Southeast Asian demands for reparations (*baishō*) after the Pacific War.[72] Acting at first on behalf of the Hatoyama government, and then on his own account, Kishi negotiated reparations agreements with Burma, Thailand, the Philippines, Indonesia, and Cambodia. Yoshida had stalled all negotiations, and criticized foreign aid. In his view, "you have to trade with rich men; you can't trade with beggars."[73] The foreign ministry followed suit—it promised little and dragged out negotiations interminably. Kishi showed Japanese politicians that one could trade with beggars and enrich oneself at the same time. His innovation was deceptively simple. Kishi reinterpreted Japan's peace treaty pledge to provide reparations so that they would be paid predominantly in Japanese-manufactured capital goods and services—and he made sure that his business supporters would reap the windfall.[74] Once word of Kishi's program was known, industry lobbied the foreign ministry vigorously to qualify under the agreement.[75] Kishi even increased the amounts offered in reparations as a way to direct even more resources toward Japanese industry.[76] Kishi's lesson was not lost. His pioneering use of Indonesian and Korean aid seems to have inspired Tanaka Kakuei, who applied the technique to China, as well as Nakasone Yasuhiro, who expanded the practice elsewhere in the region.[77]

The most visible and controversial early use of reparations for political finance was a contract let to the Kinoshita Trading Company for the provision of ships to the Sukarno government in Indonesia in February 1958.[78] Kinoshita Trading was run by Kinoshita Shigeru, a metals broker in Manchuria before the war. When Kishi had returned to Japan in the late 1930s, so did Kinoshita; he was placed in the Iron and Steel Control Company, where he established close relationships with Nagano Shigeo of Fuji Iron and Steel and Inayama Yoshihiro of Yawata Steel, both of whom became enormously influential business leaders after the war. There was nothing subtle about these relationships. When Kishi was released from prison in December 1948, Kinoshita hired him as president of his trading company, a nominal post Kishi held until he could return to politics in 1952. Much to the chagrin of established firms, Kinoshita Trading won the first reparations-based contract for Indonesia even though it had never dealt in ships before. According to declassified records, in April 1958 Kishi told Indonesian Foreign Minister Soebandrio that he would appreciate the award of boat contracts to Kinoshita Trading.[79] The deal was roundly criticized in the Diet and in the press, but Kishi escaped unscathed.[80] In addition, Kinoshita won contracts for office buildings, machinery factories, and hotels. It was the largest recipient of reparations contractors among Japanese firms and by 1964, when it went bankrupt, Kinoshita Trading was Japan's seventh-largest trading firm.

The large and prestigious trading houses were shut out of the early reparations business in Southeast Asia. The winners were all non-zaibatsu, independent houses that had Manchurian ties to Kishi and other non-mainstream factions. No complete list of reparations contracts was ever published, but a 1968 MITI report showed that Kinoshita Trading had the largest share, followed by Nippon Kōei, run by a former Manchurian economic planner under Kishi and by Itōchū (C. Itoh & Co.), in which a former Kwantung Army officer, Sejima Ryūzō, was a rising star.[81] A fourth major winner was an unknown firm called Tōnichi Trading, whose board members included Kishi's factional rival, Kōno Ichirō, as well as their mutual ally, the Mob-connected Kodama Yoshio.

The system worked in much the same way as it did with domestic contractors for local projects, but involved many fewer competitors. Also, because it involved no open bidding, it required less collusion and fewer compensating payments. Kishi institutionalized the program by establishing an "Overseas Economic Cooperation Fund" in 1957 to distribute reparations and, later, foreign aid (Overseas Development Assistance or ODA). The system involved considerable collusion among LDP politicians, aid recipients, and conservative business interests in Japan. Nishihara reports that the reparations payments involved "large sums of money," much of which ended in the pockets of high-ranking Indonesian officials who "were given a cut from [inflated] profits."[82] The practice never disappeared.[83] As late as the mid-1980s, there was abundant criticism of ODA. According to one Diet member: "Aid money is like spy money. The Diet doesn't decide how much goes to which country, and the people are not told how it is being used. Moreover, it keeps growing and growing. As far as being the goose that lays the golden egg in financing political payoffs, it is super high grade."[84] The Diet never enacted a basic law to regulate either the reparations programs or the larger ODA program. Each time legislation was proposed, the bureaucracy and some in the LDP strongly opposed it.

Kishi's public resources model was a prototype for the even more aggressive Tanaka Kakuei who, as Chalmers Johnson suggests, "carried the system to its logical conclusion."[85] During Japan's phenomenal high-speed growth in the 1960s, Tanaka built a general hospital to take care of his constituents, faction members, and himself.[86] Resources were generated in a variety of ways. One was "land flipping," whereby officials would confiscate unclaimed property to sell to Tanaka's associates for a consideration, when he was minister of finance in the Ikeda cabinet. In another scam, a dummy corporation controlled by Tanaka or his family would buy underpriced stocks to be resold at market price. The firms bought and sold would incur large paper losses due to inflated expenses while they

239

were stripped of cash.[87] Other firms benefited from Tanaka's inside knowledge of (and control over) the location of new public works projects: chosen construction and real estate companies made vast fortunes from public spending on railroads, schools, and other infrastructure. Tanaka's famous "Plan for Remodeling the Japanese Archipelago" once he took office was essentially a blueprint for personal and factional enrichment.[88] Eventually, Masumi argues, the process of amassing a personal and factional fortune even emptied the LDP's safe.[89] This may help explain why Tanaka was the only senior postwar Japanese politician to be prosecuted without political intervention.

The man who could have intervened to block his prosecution, but chose not to, was Miki Takeo. Miki had been anointed prime minister by Kishi's former disciple and comrade, Shiina Etsusaburō. Some expected that Miki would invoke Article 14 of the Public Prosecutors Law to end Tanaka's prosecution, but the irascible Miki refused to accommodate them. Instead, he proposed to abolish all corporate contributions to politicians. LDP leaders eviscerated his proposals. The reform, which would have shifted contributions from "a few sources of large sums" (*shōsū tagaku hōshiki*) to "lots of sources of small sums" (*tasū shōgaku hōshiki*), had as many loopholes as it had teeth, and even legalized some formerly illegal conduits of funds. It was to be business as usual under the 1955 System.[90]

This, despite the best efforts of Keidanren. At his first press conference as Keidanren chairman in May 1974, Dokō Toshio made a startling announcement:

> The LDP should be based on its party members and supporters, and it is strange for it to be based on commercial firms. If firm managers wish to support the LDP, they should join a citizens' association on an individual basis. In general, there is something wrong with Keidanren's having the role of collecting political funds. In the course of time, I want to go about correcting this somehow.[91]

Dokō correctly anticipated what was ahead. In the July elections Keidanren provided Tanaka's LDP with a thirty billion yen war chest, but an LDP majority was barely returned. Dokō was so annoyed by Tanaka's profligacy that he demanded political reform. The electric and gas utilities refused further political donations as well. Dokō announced that Keidanren was ceasing immediately the work of collecting political funds for the Citizens' Association, and firmly supported political reform. Dokō declared that the LDP's faction system was the source of the problem. Henceforth firms would have to make contributions to political parties directly; Keidanren would exclude from its ranks any firm found to have contributed to a faction.

It sounded good, and it played well in the press and public opinion, but "the System" still had legs. Dokō ran into stiff opposition. Nagano Shigeo, head of the rival Japan Chamber of Commerce and Industry (and former close associate of Kishi Nobusuke) called him a "damn fool" (*ano baka yarō*), and refused to cooperate. Within the LDP, anger at Dokō was so great that no one from the Miki cabinet attended Keidanren's 1974 annual councilors' meeting—an unprecedented gesture.[92]

Dokō gamely pressed on. Keidanren formed a committee to study the "modernization" of political funding, but advocates of reform were worn down.[93] The best they could do was to return to a Kishi-era common pool of funds. A year after his remarkable press conferences, Dokō was out making the rounds of companies and collecting political contributions. Despite severe cost-saving measures adopted after the drop-off in contributions during 1974, the LDP had accumulated an operating debt of five billion yen. Keidanren managing director Hanamura Nihachirō quietly collected contributions from members and paid off the debt.

After a short interlude, Keidanren's support for the LDP was even stronger than before. Even the *reported* contributions tripled over the next decade, and the number of political organizations receiving donations increased from under two thousand to nearly five thousand. There was no increased mobilization of the electorate, just a new set of rules that allowed a politician to establish as many as fifty separate paper organizations to receive funds.[94] Dokō calmed the public and restored a modicum of propriety to big business, but his reform of political funding was slight.

One important consequence of his failures bears examination. Factional competition had grown ever more intense, and the competition for funds now was devolving to the level of individual politicians. By the late 1980s, every conservative politician with national aspirations was desperate to secure a corporate backer. Public resources alone were not sufficient. The use of public resources was compounded by a return to the use of inside information, and voracious parvenu businessmen embraced equally voracious politicians. Hanamura Nihachirō, who ought to know, estimated that it now took three times more money than Keidanren distributed to run a political campaign.[95] Japan was in the midst of its "bubble economy," and money was demanded by and flowing to politicians from every direction.

It all came to a head in the famous Recruit Scandal of 1989, in which more than forty politicians—including virtually every ranking LDP official—were named as having profited from "pre-floated" shares of stock in a new company, Recruit Cosmos.[96] The president of the upstart firm, Ezoe

Hiromasa, also provided shares to the chairman of the Democratic Social- ist Party, several Socialist Party members, the president of the Nihon Keizai Shimbun, the chairman of Nippon Telegraph and Telephone (NTT), and senior bureaucrats in the education and transport industries as well.[97] There were twelve indictments, but only two were politicians. Others fell from power but climbed back up in short order. Miyazawa be- came prime minister, Takeshita became kingmaker of the party's largest faction, and Nakasone resumed his role as respected party elder. Once again the political world was under pressure to reform, and once again, the institutions of the 1955 System would prove resistant to change. The scandal ended with a whimper.

Using Fixers

The previous innovations are poorly documented, but even *more* diffi- cult to document (and likely even *more* consequential) are Kishi's rela- tionships with ultranationalists and the underworld. He became con- nected to them through two of the most controversial figures in twentieth-century Japanese politics, the political "fixers" (*kuromaku*) Sasakawa Ryōichi and Kodama Yoshio.[98] These three men were cellmates for three years in Sugamo Prison, where it is alleged they concocted a plan for mutual assistance. These are, of course, large and contested claims.[99]

Kodama Yoshio (1911–1984) casts a ubiquitous shadow over many of the less pleasant aspects of Japanese politics. After jail time for plotting the assassination of business and party leaders, Kodama served the mili- tary in China as a procurer of strategic materials during the war. The ac- tivities of his Kodama Agency reportedly included drug trafficking, smug- gling, and black marketeering. War profiteering made Kodama a personal fortune he was quick to turn to political advantage.[100] He was released from prison after allegedly making a deal to work for U.S. intelligence agencies. Upon his release he served on the board of the National Coun- cil of Patriotic Societies, which was comprised of more than four hundred right-wing and underworld groups, some of which he mobilized to combat labor demonstrations. He is also credited with providing the funds used to create Hatoyama's Liberal and Democratic parties.[101] Kishi first called upon Kodama, whose "modus operandi was blackmail, intimidation, and violence," to provide protection for Indonesian President Sukarno during the latter's visit to Tokyo in early 1958 (the Tokyo Metropolitan Police re- fused on the grounds that it was a personal rather than official visit).[102] He again called upon Kodama to use his gangland connections in 1960 to battle student demonstrators and to help protect President Eisenhower during his abortive Ampō visit.[103] Kodama's connections with U.S. intelligence may have provided an entrée to the Lockheed Aircraft Corporation, which used him twice as a "representative"—once in the successful effort to get Prime Minister Kishi to select the Lockheed F-104 over the Grumman F-11 fighter favored by the air force, and again in the successful effort to convince Prime Minister Tanaka to intervene with All Nippon Airways on behalf of the Lockheed 1011.[104] The former bribery case was never proved, or even prosecuted. The latter brought down the Tanaka government.

Sasakawa Ryōichi (1899–1995) was a more complex figure. Sasakawa's name evokes the same range of reactions as Kishi's, from derision to admiration, for their political lives, aspirations, and enemies were parallel. Drafted into the Imperial Navy as a pilot in 1918, Sasakawa returned home after two years to expand the family fortune by speculating in rice futures. He later turned his energies to right-wing politics, possibly including membership in the violent Black Dragon Society.[105] In 1931, Sasakawa established the National Essence Mass Party (Kokusui Taishūtō); his 15,000 party members—among whom was Kodama Yoshio—wore black shirts modeled on the Italian fascists. Sasakawa was a maverick. He controlled a small air force of twenty-two airplanes, and took it upon himself to airlift supplies to Japanese troops after the 1931 Manchurian Incident. Later he was arrested for planning "patriotic violence," including plots against the prime minister, and spent two and a half years in jail (1935–1938).[106] On the eve of the Pacific War, Sasakawa introduced Kodama Yoshio to Imperial Navy officers and even claimed credit for creating the Kodama Agency.[107] During this period, he spent considerable time with Kodama in Shanghai, where they bought mines and sold minerals to the military.[108] They are alleged to have plundered millions of dollars worth of Chinese gold, diamonds, and other rare matériel. According to one account, Kodama shipped vast quantities of precious metals to Japan at war's end, storing a portion in warehouses rented by Sasakawa.[109]

Sasakawa formally entered politics with a successful run for Diet as an independent in the 1942 election. Although a vigorous critic of the Tōjō cabinet in which Kishi Nobusuke served, Sasakawa ardently supported Kishi in the wartime Diet, even joining the group of Diet members that organized to make Kishi prime minister.[110] After Japan's surrender, Sasakawa remained active in politics, entering into negotiations with leading politicians in an attempt to create a new "Japan Mass Party." When this effort failed, he threw his support behind Hatoyama's Liberal Party, attending its inaugural ceremony with a contingent of local yakuza.[111] Various accounts trace the seed money for this new conservative party to sale of a portion of the Kodama Agency loot.[112] Despite this auspicious beginning, however, Sasakawa was imprisoned as a war criminal.

After release from prison in 1948, Sasakawa began to promote motorboat racing as a form of legal gambling in Japan. Working with cellmates Kishi and Kodama to cultivate political support, Sasakawa won Diet approval of a Motorboat Racing Law in 1951 that granted him monopoly control of the sport.[113] Seventy-five percent of all gambling revenue would be returned to gamblers, 10 percent would go to local governments, 11.7 percent was earmarked for the Motorboat Racing Association, and 3.3 percent went to the Japan Shipbuilding Industry Foundation. By 1962, when Sasakawa gained permanent chairmanship of the foundation—once again with Kishi's help—he personally controlled both organizations. He made Kodama head of the Tokyo Motorboat Racing Association and used the revenues—more than $8 billion annually by the early 1980s—to build a financial and philanthropic empire that rivaled the greatest foundations in the world.[114] Legal philanthropy benefited organizations controlled by himself and his family, and he expanded his vast personal fortune by gaining control of virtually all businesses associated with the motorboat racing circuit.[115] In his later years, Sasakawa began to target foreign charities, many associated with the United Nations, in order to bolster his aggressive case for the Nobel Peace Prize. In 1990, the Japan Shipbuilding Industry Foundation was renamed the Sasakawa Foundation, and after his death in 1995, it became the Nippon Foundation. In 1978, Sasakawa was awarded the highest honor of the emperor, the "First Class Order of the Sacred Treasure."

Of course Sasakawa Ryōichi continued to pursue a political agenda, and much of it involved nurturing conservative politicians.[116] By the late 1980s, some fifty-five Diet representatives were asking the Sasakawa Foundation for "support for their districts," notably the once and future prime ministers Nakasone Yasuhiro and Hashimoto Ryūtarō and LDP faction head Katō Kōichi.[117] Sasakawa built "sports clubs" and other facilities in the districts of friendly politicians. He gave "gift vouchers" to transport ministry bureaucrats after golf outings, and it is widely assumed that his influence routinely shielded public officials and politicians from the law.[118] Sasakawa never again ran for public office himself, but he aggressively promoted the political careers of Sasakawa Takashi, his second son, and Itoyama Eitarō, his business associate and former secretary to Nakasone Yasuhiro. The junior Sasakawa originally ran unsuccessfully as an independent, but both Takashi and Itoyama served in the Diet as members of the LDP.[119] Equipped with several levers of political influence, Sasakawa publicly boasted of his role as a powerful political insider and was a key figure in the succession struggles that led to the governments of Kishi Nobusuke, Satō Eisaku, and Tanaka Kakuei.[120]

Sasakawa's anticommunism dovetailed neatly with his efforts in conservative politics. Working closely with Kishi Nobusuke, he cultivated relationships with anticommunists throughout Asia. This activity brought them into contact with the Reverend Sun Myung Moon, founder of the Unification Church, in the mid-1960s.[121] In 1967, Sasakawa invited the church to use his motorboat racing center in Yamanashi for its first rally in Japan. The following year, three months after the Reverend Moon established his "Federation for Victory over Communism" (Shōkyō Rengō) in Korea, Sasakawa became honorary chairman in Japan. Kishi was impressed: "If all younger people were like Shōkyō Rengō members, Japan would have a bright future."[122] Sasakawa and Kishi shielded what would become one of the most widely reviled groups in contemporary Japan.[123]

As loathed as the Unification Church was for alleged kidnappings and mind control of young Japanese, it proved (and may still prove) to be of incalculable benefit to many Japanese politicians. Its Japan headquarters was built on Tokyo land once owned by Kishi. By the early 1970s, church members—so-called Moonies—were serving some LDP politicians without compensation as industrious and highly valued campaign workers. For many years the church enjoyed protection from prosecution for often fraudulent and aggressive sales and conversion tactics.[124] By the 1980s, Japan reportedly provided some four-fifths of Unification Church revenues worldwide.[125]

The Kishi-Sasakawa link to Moon was broadened through the Kishi and allied factions. Fukuda Takeo, direct inheritor of the Kishi faction, praised Reverend Moon as "one of Asia's great leaders" in 1974, and Nakasone Yasuhiro, the youngest member of the Kishi cabinet and scion of the allied Kōno faction, similarly honored Moon.[126] Abe Shintarō, Kishi's son-in-law, also depended on Moonies in his election campaigns.[127] A list prepared by the Japanese Communist Party of 126 LDP and DSP politicians who used church "volunteers" to staff their campaign included Ozawa Ichirō, Hashimoto Ryūtarō, and other senior party leaders.[128] In the 1990 general election, more than one hundred Diet members apparently received support from the Federation for Victory over Communism.[129] Moon's influence is shown by the special permission he received in 1992 to enter the country. Japanese law forbids entry to a foreign national who has served more than one year in jail. Moon had served eighteen months in a U.S. prison for tax evasion, but in March 1992, Kanemaru Shin, vice president of the LDP and head of the largest faction within the party, intervened on Moon's behalf with the minister of justice.[130]

Sasakawa also had a purely pecuniary motivation in his political activity: to defend his state-granted gambling monopoly. The management of all other legal gambling in Japan had been entrusted to public organizations, and Sasakawa had to defend his gambling concession against reformers and opportunists. First, as we have noted, he cultivated strong personal and financial ties with LDP politicians. Second, to deaden bureaucratic assertiveness, his Shipbuilding Industry Foundation provided trillions of yen to research institutes, training centers, community associations, sports clubs, and other nonprofit organizations associated with Japanese government ministries. Recipient organizations also served as retirement havens (*amakudarisaki*) for more than one hundred former bureaucrats from the Ministry of Transport, the government organ with jurisdiction over motorboat racing.[131] Finally, Sasakawa defeated political challenges to his control with ruthless efficiency.[132]

The most striking example was his rebuff of an attempt by then-Prime Minister Tanaka Kakuei to control the Shipbuilding Industry Foundation. After he rejected the prime minister's request to install a Tanaka ally among the foundation's leadership, Sasakawa became the subject of a police investigation widely believed to have been encouraged by Tanaka.[133] Although the investigation ended with the arrest of his brother, Sasakawa emerged unscathed. Now a vocal critic of Tanaka, Sasakawa contributed mightily to the storm that followed revelations of Tanaka's own questionable financial practices and led to his resignation as prime minister in late 1974.[134] The culmination of Sasakawa's counterattack, however, is his alleged role as a key information broker in the development of the Lockheed bribery scandal that resulted in Tanaka's arrest and conviction.[135] Although most of these allegations remain unconfirmed, Sasakawa's media campaign against Tanaka is a matter of public record. Following Tanaka's arrest, Sasakawa made public statements that both suggested an intimate knowledge of the details and pointed specifically to the culpability of Tanaka and his cohorts.[136] Although Sasakawa was also investigated by the Lockheed prosecutors (at the time he was chairman of the association that combined the three aircraft industry groups), he was never indicted.[137]

He seemed made of Teflon, like Kishi. Between 1955, when Kishi helped create the LDP, and 1960, when he resigned as prime minister, there were fourteen separate corruption cases that involved politicians and/or bureaucrats.[138] Kishi's name never appeared on the formal docket of the prosecutors, but it was ubiquitously associated with them in the popular imagination. Many of these scandals are associated, moreover, with the three alternative routes that Kishi took toward money politics: the acceptance of U.S. support, the use of public resources, and reliance on political fixers.

Before leaving his post in Manchuria in 1939, Kishi Nobusuke reportedly told his colleagues: "Political funds should be accepted only after they have passed through a 'filter' and been 'cleansed.' If a problem arises, the 'filter' itself will then become the center of the affair, while the politician, who has consumed the 'clean water,' will not be implicated. Political funds become the basis of corruption scandals only when they have not been sufficiently 'filtered.' "[139] More than fifty years later, virtually the entire leadership of the LDP would be tainted by the Recruit Scandal; Kanemaru Shin, Tanaka Kakuei's disciple and Ozawa Ichirō's mentor, was prosecuted for accepting funds that had not been properly 'filtered' (in this case, $4 million from a gang-related trucking company); and Prime Minister Takeshita Noboru was toppled for his ties to yakuza. Kishi's advice was still valuable. Kishi first connected the discredited world of prewar politics to postwar conservative hegemony, and it was Kishi who welcomed organized crime and the nationalist right-wing into the LDP mainstream. By the 1990s, however, Kodama was dead, Sasakawa was dying, and newly founded religious organizations had become active—indeed indispensable—supporters of the LDP.[140] Structural corruption was no longer Kishi's invention; it was taken for granted. It was just the way things worked.

KISHI'S LEGACIES

There are limits to the claims one can make for Kishi Nobusuke. He was by no means Japan's first (or even most) corrupt politician. Nor was he singularly responsible for the creation of the Liberal Democratic Party. It was not Kishi who created factions—they were the logical result of an electoral system that obliged members of the same party to compete with one another. Structural corruption was overdetermined: had Kishi not taken the lead, others would have built many of the same institutions. Moreover, there was little of the bricoleur in Kishi Nobusuke. Although he was intensely patriotic, he rarely invoked or invented the past to justify his political decisions. Unlike virtually every other leader examined in this book, Kishi was always reinventing himself by *ignoring* the past, especially his own: he was active only in the present. There was nothing fancy about his leadership except his footwork; his secretive and unrelenting machinations for power were always in the present tense.

Still, Kishi's legacies are colossal. Structural corruption—a central institutional feature of the 1955 System—developed along lines he pioneered and continues to shape contemporary Japanese politics. He may not have invented structural corruption, but it was a first-order consequence of the system he helped build. After Kishi's demise, his practices diffused across the LDP's ruling class. Kishi walked away unscathed, but the corruption deepened. Between 1955 and 1993, Japan had an average of one major

LDP architect Kishi is depicted by the Japan Communist Party newspaper in 1959 as "traitorous" on the one hand and "corrupt" on the other. Reproduced courtesy of Shin Nihon Shuppansha (artist Matsuyama Fumio, from the book *Manga de miru sengoshi* [Postwar history as seen through cartoons]).

corruption scandal per year, and by the mid-1990s these were as apt to involve upper-level civil servants as politicians.[141] As late as the mid-1990s, after the curtain had come down on the 1955 System, reformers were *still* demanding fuller transparency and tighter restrictions in matters of political finance. Even those tarred by the brush of structural corruption acknowledge its origins in the 1955 System.[142]

At a minimum, Kishi Nobusuke personified Japan's transwar continuities. The industrial policy instruments he pioneered in the 1930s in Japan and in Manchukuo served as boilerplate for Japan's postwar economic miracle. In matters of politics he connects backwards to ultranationalists and power brokers, such as his cellmates Kodama Yoshio and Sasakawa Ryōichi, and he connects forward to the highly refined instruments of what we now call structural corruption. Indeed, Kishi represents these changes even more vividly than Yoshida Shigeru. Yoshida met the Occupation forces in the morning coat of a former diplomat who had opposed the war, and Kishi met them in handcuffs. Schaller is correct, the resurrection of Kishi Nobusuke (who he calls "America's favorite war criminal"), "symbolized the transformation of Japanese-American relations during the 1950s. In a literal sense, Kishi's life mirrored Japan's evolution from enemy to ally, the emergence of the Cold War in Asia, and the role played by the United States in forging Japan's postwar political and economic structure."[143]

But Kishi was no mere personification or symbol. Like Yoshida Shigeru, Kishi Nobusuke intervened in Japanese history, almost always at critical times. Indeed, these interventions earned him the unflattering sobriquet "The Monster of Shōwa."[144] Like the Shōwa era, Kishi was a large and constant institutional presence before and after the war. And like the Shōwa emperor, his public persona changed dramatically along the way. He put together disparate elements of power and fused them into institutions that served his short-term political goals as well as his long-range vision. Most persisted long after he had passed from the scene, and many became accepted elements of Japanese conservative hegemony. His doppelgänger in Italy was Amintore Fanfani.

ITALY AND CHRISTIAN DEMOCRACY

Fanfani and Fascism

Amintore Fanfani died in November 1999 and was celebrated in the press as a founding father of the Italian Republic. But he had to grow into the role of left Christian Democrat. Fanfani began his career closer to clerico-fascism than to Christian democracy. He was a "reformer" who "pursued a simple project of grave consequence: to shift the balance of the country by subordinating the economy to politics."[145] His most lasting contribution to Italian politics—the diversion of state enterprises to partisan ends—corroded the Italian Republic. Few political architects built structures at once so transformative, so robust, and so defective. And few so effectively reinvented a political persona.[146]

At the end of World War II, Fanfani faced much the same challenge as Kishi: he had to reinvent himself as a democrat. Fanfani did not have to change as much as Kishi, nor did he have to serve time in prison. But a close reading of his political philosophy shows remarkable continuity across a career of university teaching, active intellectual support for the fascist regime, and political leadership of the center-left of Christian democracy. This continuity suggests a strong, unyielding ideological core in Italian political life that is often overlooked, and it deserves a closer look.

249

Fanfani's ideas derived from his education at the Università Cattólica del Sacro Cuore, where he embraced the most conservative, antimodern models of the Church's social doctrine.[147] Catholic theorists, struggling to confront both democracy and fascism in the 1930s, invented the oxymoron "reactionary modernism" to specify a Christian way to embrace change.[148] They posited "good" and "bad" modernities. Radio was good because it enabled the pope to reach a wider audience, liberalism was bad because it celebrated selfishness. "Medieval values" of social solidarity could be joined with the best achievements of modern science to rebuild a Christian society. Fanfani came of age amid this ideological struggle to redimension modernity. His central concern was to reconstruct a traditional Catholic civilization discarded by the modern world. The Christian doctrine of "voluntarism" was his connection to fascism.[149] On this view, the economy is subordinate to politics, and politics is subordinate to Christian morality.[150] He was one of many Catholic intellectuals who found in fascism a shared aversion to both laissez-faire liberal doctrines and Marxist materialism.[151] Corporatism was a fundamentally reactionary "third way" between capitalism and communism that suited Catholics and fascists alike.[152]

Although he never became a party activist, like most intellectuals employed in state universities, Fanfani joined the Fascist Party in 1933. As editor of the *Rivista Internazionale di Scienze Sociali*, he elaborated the Christian character of corporatism, in particular collaboration between classes as a way to reconstruct the moral basis of the nation.[153] Although his central concern was social justice, he was not beyond nationalist sentiment. Fanfani celebrated Italian imperialism in Ethiopia, for bringing "Roman virtue combined with Christian consecration" to Ethiopia.[154] He praised Mussolini, whom he called "the conqueror of all in the struggle for civilization," for inculcating a new patriotism among youth and for raising Italy's stature abroad.[155] He had no education in or affect for liberal or democratic values. In 1937 he wrote that he did not consider fascism a form of tyranny because it limited "only the noxious and dysfunctional liberties."[156] Totalitarianism, he argued, was acceptable because it organized the inequalities among citizens for desirable collective ends and subordinated rights to duties.

Fanfani's views were no more incompatible with democracy than were the Church's, of course. It was not until the fall of Mussolini that the pope recognized democracy as consistent with the principles of the natural law.[157] Until that time Fanfani's education and guidance came from a church that officially accepted fascist corporatism. Once the Lateran Pacts were signed in 1929, as Robert Bellah notes:

"No [fascist] party initiative . . . ever lacked the cooperation of the clergy . . . After 1929 . . . one would have been hard put to find a bishop's pastoral or sermon, an inaugural speech at a diocesan conference, that did not contain the word, the invocation, the blessing, the epithet appropriate to the *Duce*. And the epithets chosen became progressively more sonorous, and the person invoked tended more and more to assume the likeness not of a Head of Government, but of the pioneer of a civilization.[158]

Early successes helped make fascism look correct. Fanfani continued to write of its virtues as late as 1942, arguing that it had succeeded traditional corporatism with its powerful ideas for "organic reconstruction of society and cross-class cooperation."[159] At this point Fanfani was convinced that fascist corporatism echoed the moral teachings of the Catholic Church, a "coincidence [that] should not serve to diminish the originality and merit of fascist corporatism, but [that] should demonstrate the profound sense of justice that animates the new [fascist] doctrine."[160]

Like many Italians, Fanfani became disenchanted when the regime's fortunes turned. He broke with the regime in 1943, as Mussolini scrambled north to found the Republic of Salò. Fanfani escaped to Switzerland, where he resumed his writing and taught Italians in exile. He became engaged with a group of Catholic intellectuals in a reassessment of the relationship between church doctrine and the fascist state. Unlike Giuseppe Dossetti, who remained active in the Resistance, or Alcide De Gasperi, exiled to the basement of the Vatican library after a time in Mussolini's jails, Fanfani took no active part in confronting the Fascist state. Refuge in Switzerland would provide him only a partial, shadowy legitimacy.[161]

Reinvention

After the war Fanfani returned to help build the new Italy. Although he never disavowed his previous doctrines, he edged toward democratic ideas—ideas built on social control rather than on individual rights. He saw public policy in corporatist terms and never abandoned his preference for political control of the economy. Individual economic activities had a social function; democratic control of public intervention in the economy was the best way yet developed to attain social harmony. What he had earlier harmonized with fascism he could now harmonize with democracy. In a report he prepared for the Constituent Assembly, he claimed: "Social control of the economy, organized in a country in which every citizen can openly and without danger influence the Government and take part in correcting public mistakes and abuses, is the only means found until now to prevent the state becoming prey to rapacious oligarchies, clever tyrants . . . or dominated by shrewd politicians."[162]

In 1945 he published his first reflections on the problems of democratic control. The mission of each individual is to realize the powers God gave him. The task of society is to distribute goods in a self-regulating and stable manner, and toward this end, public opinion should determine government activity.[163] Nonetheless, his work for the Constituent Assembly stressed neo-voluntarism. One report, "Social Control of Economic Activity," was entirely in accord with the doctrine elaborated under fascism, whose general corporatist principles of rationality and elite control were reasserted.[164]

Fanfani's views were evolving in parallel with the Church's. Fanfani had been attracted to fascism in part because fascist corporatism was consistent with Catholic social doctrine and in part because fascism was politically dominant.[165] He reinvented himself as a center-left Christian Democrat at a time when democracy had become the only means to realize his social doctrine or to achieve political power. Fanfani was a man of the thirties, and the thirties had passed. Times change, and his public persona, if not his ideological center of gravity, could too. Fanfani carried successfully the irreconcilable contradictions of his past, of his party, and of his country.[166]

Indeed, perhaps because so many of the new top cadres in the DC had been recruited from the fascist left (and had been far more active within fascism than he was), Fanfani's "fascist moment" was the object of only limited embarrassment.[167] In November 1951, he was not named by the party to a weeklong "Democracy Initiative" designed by Christian Democrats, although his two deputies were. Three years later, when Fanfani was presented to Parliament for his first term as president of the council, PCI leader Palmiro Togliatti protested that Italy could not be governed by a man "who had worn the [fascist] beret with the eagle." (Fanfani snapped back indignantly that Togliatti had no authority in the matter, for he had worn the hat of a Cossack.)[168]

For all his intellectual baggage—and for all that a fascist past was presumed to be a liability—Fanfani inherited the leadership of the Catholic Action wing of the DC when Dossetti left political life in 1951. By that time, Fanfani had demonstrated his formidable skills as a political operative. He had served as De Gasperi's minister of labor and produced projects to improve the daily lives of workers, reform agriculture, and reduce social tensions. Like Kishi, who chafed first under Yoshida and then under Hatoyama, Fanfani began moving away from De Gasperi, taking advantage of De Gasperi's narrow but crushing defeat in 1953 to assume control of the DC. He began immediately to revamp the organization. Fanfani sought to construct a DC that would "collaborate with the forces of the center, proceed with reforms, promote development in the depressed areas, defend liberty, provide peace and security through NATO, and pursue a united Europe."[169] It all sounded consistent with the De Gasperi program, but was different in one very important respect: De Gasperi never freed himself from the burdens of parliamentary politics whereas Fanfani believed that the DC had within itself the potential to govern and to redistribute wealth and power in Italy.[170] To realize this potential, Fanfani reached back to his fundamental views about the subordination of the economy and the government to political leadership. He would use the party to control both.

The House that Fanfani Built

This was not an easy project, of course. As we have seen, the DC was riddled with factions and burdened by obligations to clients in business, the United States, the Church, and the countryside. Aldo Moro and others on the DC left were concerned that Fanfani would try to make good on his aspirations to become an Italian de Gaulle. While defending a role for the Church in Italian social life, Fanfani had to deny persistent claims that the DC was seeking to "clericalize" the Italian state. Now fully reinvented, the former clerico-fascist could write in 1958 that "The DC has not forgotten that it is an Italian party, created and operated in the bosom of the Italian state, a state consolidated in liberty and democracy, based on the autonomy given it by the people."[171] By his own account, Fanfani clearly relished his ability to embrace and frustrate forces across the Italian political spectrum. In December 1957 alone the Communists and the Socialists accused Fanfani of embracing the Right and big business, and the Liberals accused the DC of threatening the nation through too much social policy. Meanwhile, the business press in Milan accused him of being unable to resist Socialist and Communist pressures.[172]

Fanfani so profoundly frustrated his opponents that many had little choice but to combine with him when he was ready for their help. He was abetted by Enrico Mattei, who emerged from the Resistance to establish the state holding company Ente Nazionale di Idrocarburi (ENI) in 1953.[173] Mattei shared Fanfani's idea that state firms could be political tools. Mattei was a brilliant operative, a latter-day Renaissance condottiere who linked himself to each faction within the DC to create a broad set of intimacies.[174] Together he and Fanfani sought to stabilize party power and provide the independence that would allow them to subordinate Italian political and social life to their goals. Fanfani wanted the DC to penetrate

Fanfani depicted as a liar in 1974. In *Referendum*, edited by Pino Zac. Rome: Partito Socialista Italiano, 1975.

the economy and society, Mattei wanted autonomy from foreign oil companies and private capital at home. They began by peeling away small firms from Confindustria, "violat[ing] the stable rules of the game . . . [and using] economic power to pursue the ends of the party."[175] Slowly and inexorably Fanfani and Mattei stabilized control of the DC through state firms such as ENI and IRI, through agrarian reform agencies, and through the Cassa del Mezzogiorno, which was created to develop the South. Inside each they built cadres of technocrats linked directly to the DC.

This idea was not novel. Discussions in Parliament to place political controls on state enterprises had begun in 1949. In 1951, and again two years later, the Republican Ugo LaMalfa proposed a ministry to supervise public firms.[176] Finally, with Socialist support, the DC government formally established the Ministry of State Holdings (Ministro della Partecipazione Statale) in 1956. The formal justification was to impede the development of private sector monopolies and to promote equitable industrial progress. The unstated purpose was to pull state firms out of the orbit of Confindustria and to begin political control of the largest part of the economy.[177] The Mattei/Fanfani alliance was succeeding.

To establish political control they had to replace some of the most dedicated and politically independent managers Italy has ever had.[178] As we have seen, in the early years of the postwar recovery, the decision was taken to maintain—and even enhance—the role of state firms. Liberal and Catholic economists accepted the necessary role of state enterprise—firms such as IRI that had originated in fascist times. What these *tecnici* did not bargain for was Fanfani's insinuation of the party into the operation of these firms, and the ways in which these firms would thereby subordinate economic judgments to political ones. Politics weighed heavily in all investment and location decisions. Preferences for the South, already privileged in DC plans through the Cassa, were elevated.[179] The DC was prepared to sacrifice marginal independence to gain political control over the free world's largest public sector. And, it should be added, Fanfani did not appreciate the extent to which these political operations would corrode the very moral basis of Italian life that he had aspired to aggrandize: "It would not be an exaggeration to attribute the long crisis of the Italian economy in the 1960s, among other factors, to a finally successful effort on the part of the political class to wrest power over the public agencies and enterprises away from the technocrats and to replace them with their own, often frankly inferior, but politically loyal, appointees."[180] The "fatal consequence" was the formation of a muscular public sector directed by an elite whose first concerns were not with the marketplace and whose first loyalties were to the party.[181]

Fanfani was building a spoils system, Italian-style. Senior managers were selected on the basis of their political affiliation with the DC. Preference went to candidates educated at the Catholic universities who shared the same career experiences as senior DC leaders and party staff.[182] Fanfani, who supervised these appointments as general secretary of the party, denied any preferential treatment. The charges, he insisted, were "false, one of the legends of this decade, a wrong we have been left with." He noted how many positions in government and state firms were occupied by non-DC managers, adding rhetorically how few from the DC occupied posts in the universities or the cultural centers of Italy.[183]

Fanfani may have been protesting too much. After all, he had enabled the expansion of the *ente pubblici* from just 841 in 1947 to more than three thousand by 1973. The selective political placement of managers was soon expanded from state firms to the central government bureaucracy—particularly in the post office and social service agencies.[184] Fanfani also was the first to understand the implications of political control of the state television network. In addition, funds were diverted from the state enterprises to finance DC-related organizations as well as the political campaigns of individual politicians.[185]

These innovations seemed promising. A May 1958 electoral victory emboldened Fanfani to deepen "partisan extraction."[186] Working with Social

Democrats, he established a Center-Left government that emphasized state intervention and social safety nets while accelerating the extension of economic power to the political class.[187] The move was premature, and Fanfani was cut down by a Vatican-supported insurrection from the right-wing of the DC with monarchist and neofascist support. The Right lost control when it used armed force to break up antifascist protests in 1960, and Fanfani responded with perhaps his boldest move of all. He won a large electoral victory and formed his third cabinet dedicated to an opening to the [noncommunist] Left. He saw the Italian left as too strong to be ignored but not too strong to be split apart. The best way to divide it was to create new channels for the distribution of state resources. After his "opening to the left" in March 1962, the DC's coalition partners were included in the distribution. Italian *trasformismo* had been rediscovered.

The cost to the DC was a bruising battle over nationalization of the electric power industry.[188] The party also agreed to enact the constitutional provisions for regional autonomy, which the Left had long sought. The cost to the Socialists was the loss (again) of their left wing, which refused to cooperate with the DC. The Socialists also had to accept Italian membership in NATO and the European Community. PSI chief Pietro Nenni had to abandon collaboration with the PCI—something Fanfani was clearly banking upon. Finally convinced that the Socialists were distancing themselves from the Communists, Giulio Andreotti quipped that Nenni was "a free man, walking out of General Togliatti's barracks."[189] The cost to Fanfani, whose faction had split in 1959, was reliance on his party rivals, most notably Aldo Moro. It was Moro who became the head of the first truly collaborative cabinet in December 1963, when the DC finally delivered sensitive portfolios to Socialist ministers. While the DC would not relinquish its hold on the crown jewel—the Ministry of State Holdings—for nearly two decades, it and the PSI deepened and routinized their division of government operations and the spoils derived therefrom.

By the late 1970s, this would become too much to bear. Moro heeded the call of PCI leader Enrico Berlinguer to fashion a "historic compromise" (*compromesso storico*) and bring the Communist Party into the system.[190] Berlinguer had become PCI secretary in March 1972. Watching the United States support a coup against Salvador Allende in Chile and convinced that a PCI victory would invite a similar backlash, Berlinguer began calling publicly for a compromise between Marxists and Catholics. He rejected an alliance with the Socialists, believing that even if they could garner 51 percent of the votes (and they were close in the mid-1970s), the excluded 49 percent would be driven rightward. He argued for a grand alliance modeled on the one that governed Italy between 1943 and 1947.

Berlinguer had leverage. The PCI was now a serious electoral force, governing at the local level in much of the center and north of Italy, and polling one-third of the vote in parliamentary elections. By 1976, the DC, faced with terrorism from the far Left and the far Right, realized that it needed PCI cooperation to maintain power. In a sense, Berlinguer walked through an open door. He clinched the deal by dramatically ending "monolithic communism." He announced before the 1976 election that the PCI accepted Italian participation in NATO as a shield behind which to build socialism with freedom. Talks with the DC began after DC leaders anointed right-wing leader Giulio Andreotti to lead the government. Moro, for his part, was kidnapped and murdered by the Red Brigades in April 1978 while en route to Parliament to lead the vote that would cement the historic compromise. Ironically, the Red Brigades, who saw themselves as the last unsullied Marxist revolutionaries, strengthened power-sharing within the Italian Republic. A "government of national solidarity" including the PCI became indispensable, despite open U.S. hostility to the idea. The PCI remained relatively free of corruption, although its support for DC governments abetted the inexorable corrosion of the Italian party system.

The Italian case contrasts markedly with the Japanese in that the proceeds of corruption were so regularly divided between parties of government and opposition: "The share-out of resources generated from public works contracts was explicit and governed by clear rules. The PSI took the lion's share and distributed a few crumbs to the PSDI. The DC took a lesser cut and looked after the PRI [Radical Party]; both the DC and the PSI reserved a large part (as much as 25 percent) of any single *tangente* [kickbacks or bribes] for the nominal opposition, the PCI."[191] The fundamental problem was that in a multiparty system based on proportional representation, a generally benign and even functional spoils system degenerates into corruption. Old appointees are added onto, rather than substituted for, existing ones. In different areas, the parties' shares differed to reflect varying local strengths, but everywhere there were clear rules for distribution.[192] The single television station that Fanfani was so quick to dominate had become a set of networks divided among the parties.[193] In cases involving *enti pubblici*, payoffs would also vary according to party strength. Until the "historic compromise" the PCI was ordinarily compensated indirectly, through contracts awarded to communist cooperatives; as funding from the Soviet Union and Eastern Europe declined and as PCI cooperation became more important to maintain DC power, however, the PCI sought to be included.[194]

What had been designed as a means to redistribute wealth and power had become a highly refined system of *lottizzazione* by which coalition partners and factions divided up political appointments in proportion to their electoral strength. As the number of partners expanded, the system itself virtually displaced public service to become the purpose of Italian public life.[195] Fanfani's laudable goal of building social solidarity was reduced to a mechanism for resource extraction. By the 1980s, all parties had access to the trough, and the consequences for Italy's party system were fatal. Public managers no longer focused on economic gains but on electoral gains. By the 1970s and 1980s, parties routinely favored those decisions that were most productive in terms of *tangenti*. Better public policy, Fanfani's original goal, had long since been buried by cash transactions. The means had become the ends.

It worked well for a time. Italy had a relatively stable consociational arrangement among the parties. Each got its piece of the action. But the house that Fanfani built was rotting from the inside. With the "party-ocracy" (*partitocrazia*) fully institutionalized, parties, rather than the executive branch, tightly controlled the public sector—dividing it among themselves by creating multiple, often conflicting loyalties among the public servants.[196] Substantive power came to reside not with ministers but with party secretaries.[197] Too often the spoils that should have gone to the party went to the bank account of the politician instead.

Scandal followed hard upon scandal. Although commissions had been established to review the system as early as 1975, nothing would change for another fifteen years. A relatively benign power sharing and balancing (*consociativismo*) was transformed into something cancerous.[198] No longer was the business of the state being distorted by political goals; now political goals were being sacrificed to bosses who were interested in little but business. Italian politicians insisted for a long time that even if money had been taken, it had been taken for the party. By the mid-1990s, however, it became clear that the proceeds of corruption were not flowing to the party organizations.

The formal party system that evolved from Fanfani's strategic choices came to a crushing end in the early 1990s. In a paroxysm of anticorruption sentiment—the so-called Clean Hands (Mani Pulite) investigation of the 1990s—the entire party system was destroyed. The house that Fanfani built came crashing down. A Milan prosecutor, Gerardo D'Ambrosio, described what happened with exceptional clarity: "The two largest parties, the DC and the PSI, were financed through illegal mechanisms that were at base corrupt . . . The results are before everyone's eyes: our national economy and democracy have been defiled and placed in danger . . . There has been an era of corruption and the systematic occupation of the state."[199] He could have been describing structural corruption in Japan.

INSTITUTIONALIZING CONSERVATIVE HEGEMONY

Amintore Fanfani and Kishi Nobusuke made critical choices that institutionalized conservative hegemony in postwar Italy and Japan. They deployed different resources to similar ends. Originally orientated toward fascism, Fanfani found allies in the "legitimate" soil of the Resistance, while Kishi "legitimated" many of the same radical nationalists who had supported his wartime authoritarianism. However different their political resources, Fanfani and Kishi seized similar political opportunities. They made parallel choices for generating political cash—choices that involved above all the creative use of public resources. Kishi found ways to steer foreign aid to the domestic firms that would support the LDP. Fanfani pioneered a more direct route, colonizing public corporations. Both choices were institutionalized in a structural corruption that engaged the creative energy of politicians, businessmen, and public officials.

Fanfani sought to enable the DC to govern by using the considerable resources generated by the state firms. In this sense, he moved centering, as practiced by Cavour, Giolitti, and De Gasperi, out of the confines of the Parliament and into Italian society. It was the next logical step in an evolving Italian tradition. Unfortunately for Italy, Fanfani's successors confused his means for ends. His Center-Left program degenerated and came to a crashing end with the destruction of the parties it involved. There had not been so profound a challenge to the Italian political class since Mussolini loosed his Black Shirts on the system.

Kishi, on the other hand, never saw the promised land of sustained personal power. Only after he had resigned in the wake of the Ampō unrest would the 1955 System, which he engineered, begin to pay high dividends. His successors, mostly from the Yoshida mainstream, turned inward and refocused the nation on stable economic development. They abandoned his leadership, but not the tools he inherited from Hara Kei. Succeeding generations of LDP politicians purchased the affections of a broad swath of the Japanese electorate. Kishi's legacy—the factionally riven and corrupt, but effective, LDP—would prove as enduring as Yoshida's.

These choices and these legacies provide an important lesson for contemporary Italy and Japan. However "overdetermined" conservative dominance and structural corruption may now seem, creative leaders have always had a range of possibilities to consider. This was as true for the architects who built the system as for their successors on the path to "normality" in the wake of the Cold War.

PART IV

DEGREES OF FREEDOM:
AFTER THE COLD WAR

CHAPTER TEN

Chasing Normality

Normality in general [is] an ideal fiction.
     Sigmund Freud, *Analysis Terminable and Interminable*

Nothing seemed more singly determinant of late twentieth-century life than the Cold War. In Italy and Japan the central choices for voters—and for producers and consumers—were framed by the preferences of Washington and Moscow. What people bought, where they traveled and studied, and how their taxes were spent were powerfully shaped by the great powers. Domestic politics may not have been frozen in place, but the freedoms of leaders were clearly circumscribed.

The Left wanted to stand for progress and equality but came to represent authoritarianism. Washington and its local allies routinely reminded voters that alliance with the Soviet Union could rob them of their freedoms. The Right wanted to stand for freedom but came to represent hypocrisy and bullying. Moscow and *its* local allies routinely reminded voters that an American alliance could drag them into war. Italy and Japan were pawns in a global ideological war, and their citizens were pawns in ideological civil wars. Direct and indirect interventions were resented, but each great power was insinuated fully into domestic institutions. Their battles were reproduced everywhere, making it difficult to govern from the Center.

Both the United States and the Soviet Union made concessions to maintain their alliances. They paid their friends handsomely for the right to dominate, and in the process deeply corrupted both countries. These interventions were ubiquitous but not quotidian. It was enough for the great powers to be assured that their interests would be "considered" when the Italians and the Japanese made their "own" decisions. Skilled leaders like De Gasperi and Yoshida were able to stretch the constraints imposed by the great powers. But the great powers could be extremely heavy-handed, and the constraints were real.[1] Then, suddenly, the Cold War was gone.

Now nearly *everything* was up for grabs, and becoming "normal" took on new urgency.

One of the most interesting aspects of their parallel development after the Cold War was the extent to which Italy and Japan traded places. Suddenly, "stable" and "consensus-oriented" Japan was more unhinged than "unstable" and "contentious" Italy. Cooperation succeeded in Italy, but collapsed in Japan. The Italian economy grew, the Japanese economy slowed.[2] Suddenly Japan, the model of the strong state, was riddled with bureaucratic incompetence and corruption, while so-called technocrats (*tecnici*) were fixing much of what was broken in Italian governance and steering her comfortably into the European mainstream. If Italy was not yet a strong state, it was becoming a surprisingly competent one. Italy grew during the 1990s while reducing massive public debt; Japan went on a public spending spree in a failed effort to stimulate a slowing economy. Italian reforms went further, and Japan's international prestige declined.[3] We can observe these shifts in our three areas of central concern: identity, power, and wealth. First, though, we examine the renewed commitment to becoming "normal" after the Cold War ended.

Cleansing

Corrupt Politicians and "Clean Hands"

Italian and Japanese voters no longer had to tolerate criminality to assure U.S. support. Italian prosecutors, realizing that foreign patrons had lost interest, filled a domestic power vacuum and rebuilt the party system. In Japan, prosecutors sidled up to but ultimately backed away from a reconstruction of the political system, and a weakened LDP soldiered on. Some suggest that Italian prosecutors operated within (and pushed against) different constraints.[4] But as we shall see, both calculated the possibilities: the Japanese prosecutors *chose* to be compliant, the Italian *chose* to attack the political class. As a result, Fanfani's Christian Democracy disappeared as an organized political force, whereas Kishi's Liberal Democrats continued to govern into the twenty-first century.

That said, there are institutional differences. The Japanese legal code kept the door open to political intervention (via Article 14), whereas the Italian Constitution incorporated two mechanisms to insulate the judiciary from unwelcome partisan influence. First, Article 104 stipulated that recruitment and all career decisions, including salaries and promotions, would come from a Higher Judicial Council (Consiglio Superiore della Magistratura, hereafter HJC), mostly the judges and public prosecutors themselves. Even the minister of justice would be kept at arm's length. Second, Article 112 stipulated that prosecutors were *obliged* to prosecute. They could not select cases arbitrarily, and likewise could not arbitrarily be taken off cases. In these ways, the Italian system of justice provided broad guarantees of independence to the magistracy.[5] The HJC, established in 1959 after the DC had consolidated its power, has ever since jealously guarded the political independence of the *magistratura*.

Article 112 is very clear: prosecutors *must* prosecute whenever there is suspicion. But when they felt that a prosecution was not in order, the magistratura simply "opened a file" and dragged their heels, sometimes until the statute of limitations had expired. Together, the system of self-governance and the de facto ability of prosecutors to pick and choose targets allowed the magistratura considerable power. To its critics, the Italian judiciary had ample opportunity for abuse.[6] To its supporters, it merely exercised the authority granted by law to squeeze corruption out of the system.

Most important of all, there is no effective separation of powers in Italy. Magistrates operate openly, and often with monopoly power, in each of the branches of Italian government.[7] They can be elected to Parliament, where they routinely sit on judiciary committees; they monopolize the executive ranks of the Ministry of Justice; and they serve as both prosecutor and judge in the courts.[8] Very little can force their hand, not even public opinion. No case better illustrates their power than the "Clean Hands Case" of the early 1990s.

In February 1992, as part of a sting known as Mani Pulite or "Operation Clean Hands," Milanese prosecutors arrested Mario Chiesa, a minor Socialist-appointed administrator at a Milanese old-age home, for collecting kickbacks (*tangenti*) on laundry contracts amounting to less than $5,000. Chiesa had been appointed to create a small political machine to deliver seven thousand votes. Naturally, he explained to the investigators, this took money, and the nursing home produced it.[9] Chiesa's confessions led to wave after wave of arrests, waves that washed bigger and bigger political fish ashore. The prosecutors charged the most lowly to the most elevated—among them seven-time Prime Minister Giulio Andreotti and former Prime Minister Bettino Craxi—with extortion, conspiracy, receipt of stolen property, corruption, and association with organized crime. By May 1993 nearly one-third of the country's deputies and one-quarter of its senators were under investigation. By the end of the following year, seven thousand current or former public officials were defending themselves.[10] The scandal, known as Tangentopoli ("Bribesville"), caused the wholesale destruction of the national party system.

In Japan scandals were merely bumps in the road of LDP hegemony.

Italy, by contrast, came completely unraveled. Parties dissolved, as leaders abandoned colleagues in doomed efforts to save their own skins. In September 1992, Craxi's PSI was first to split. When DC politicians were indicted, however, the effect was shocking, because the charges revealed how closely the DC leadership had conspired with organized crime in southern Italy. Tangenti paid in the South had to be arranged with the Mafia. The effect was to ratchet up the degree of public outrage.

Efforts by the political establishment to move beyond the scandals were frustrated by public opinion and by prosecutors who smelled blood in the water. In March 1993, the Amato government suggested that tangenti were merely a fund-raising excess, not a matter of personal corruption.[11] It introduced retroactive legislation to decriminalize the use of illegal funds to finance political parties. The public and the prosecutors would have none of it. Prosecutor Gerardo D'Ambrosio put it succinctly: "The political class that is responsible for a system of bribes has decided to absolve itself."[12] Street demonstrations and public denunciations by magistrates convinced President Oscar Luigi Scalfaro not to sign the legislation.

Repeated government attempts to end the investigations were to no avail. Every step to contain the revelations seemed only to exacerbate public disillusionment. Justice ministers were powerless to influence a determined judiciary or to stop the spread of investigations from Milan to more than thirty other cities. The judiciary was protected by the rule of obligatory prosecution, and politicians could not argue that prosecutors should be restrained in some larger interest.[13]

The prosecutors relied on three tools during Clean Hands. The primary one was leaks to the press of information generated by the second tool, the formal notification of inquiry (*avviso di garanzia*). Notification is required by law and is intended to protect the rights of the accused. It does not signal guilt, but the public widely perceives that it does. Prosecutors have wide discretion over timing. By notifying early, and letting the media know the details of the charges, they can do significant damage to political targets. Even the president of the Republic protested the prejudicial and abusive consequences of public disclosure but the magistracy rebuffed him with impunity.[14]

The third tool was detention. In Italy more than three-fifths of all prisoners are detainees awaiting trial, and punitive detention can last up to ten years.[15] Doing time is as much a reflection of the charge as of a verdict. The Mani Pulite investigation presumed guilt rather than innocence. Detention was used to force the accused to name names and implicate their superiors. Those who pointed fingers, the so-called penitents (*pentiti*), typically received lighter sentences. The pressure to confess was overwhelming, and Clean Hands provoked more than two dozen suicides, including a parliamentary deputy and several prominent businessmen. The effort to root out political corruption created an imbalance between two fundamental values: prosecutorial independence and the democratic principle of accountability. Public opinion would eventually recognize that the abuse of power was the underside of prosecutorial independence.[16]

What was gained? More than one thousand individuals were formally indicted, but only two served prison terms after a finding of guilt in court.[17] It has become commonplace to speak of a Second Republic, but protracted efforts to draft a new constitution failed in 1998. The political lives of Bettino Craxi and Giulio Andreotti were destroyed, and their legacies transformed. But many other "old boys" were still thriving a half decade later.[18] There was no wholesale decapitation of the political class, but there was wholesale devastation of the political infrastructure.[19] Moreover, the reconstitution of Italy's political class was accompanied by a new correlation of institutional forces. An imbalanced system in which parties governed a weak executive became an imbalanced system in which strong judges came to govern weak parties and the larger bureaucracy. The politicians began to regroup.

Explaining Protagonismo

Aggressive Milan prosecutors forced this dramatic change. But what explains their remarkable *protagonismo* (agency)? There are four possibilities: 1) The system of obligatory prosecution required them to act; 2) The public demanded it; 3) They were motivated by partisan political concerns; or 4) They wanted to protect their considerable prerogatives—and could.

Obligatory prosecution is the weakest of the four. As we have seen, judges and prosecutors can merely open files to meet the letter of this requirement. Indeed, until the mid-1960s, few believed that the judiciary would ever become politically active. Of course, the prosecutors could claim that they had no choice, but until the early 1990s they had been willing and able to ignore political corruption.

Public opinion was not insignificant. The chief prosecutor of the Milan pool, Francesco Saverio Borelli, set the investigation in the context of strong popular disaffection with the "house that Fanfani built": "Our investigation had gone forward . . . above all due to the nausea felt throughout the public from the systematic and predatory occupation of some public sectors."[20] Small and medium-sized businesses seemed especially enthusiastic. Small-business owners resented the nagging and costly inefficiencies of the corrupted state sector. The Italian public roared with satisfaction as every one of the ruling parties of the First Republic either died or reinvented itself.[21] In April 1993, in the midst of Mani Pulite, the electorate overwhelmingly supported (80%) a national referendum to change the Italian electoral system to first-past-the-post. They approved other measures to strike at structural corruption, including abolition of public financing of parties, eliminating party control over nominations of directors of savings banks, and abolition of the Ministry of State Participation that Fanfani and Mattei had crafted nearly forty years earlier. The Italian electorate was apparently convinced that political life could not be fixed by their elected representatives.[22]

Were the Milan prosecutors "waging politics" on behalf of or in collusion with the former Communist Party (the Democratic Party of the Left, or "PDS")? The magistrates needed political support to succeed, and the PCI had always supported a stronger judiciary. In a celebrated dismissal, one prosecutor, Tiziana Parenti, claimed that her supervisors "made me understand that no *avviso di garanzia* should be sent to PDS members."[23] Francesco Cossiga, a leading DC politician and president of the Republic when the investigation got underway, claimed the prosecution was taking the country down the "judicial road to socialism."[24]

Other observers suggest that industrialists, tired of the parties' escalating demands for money, used their newspapers to generate public support for Mani Pulite.[25] The charge is supportable—it does seem, for example, that the prosecutors went easier on some of the larger industrial interests than on the upstart Silvio Berlusconi, for example. Umberto Agnelli, chairman of the Fiat Group and scion of the founding family, never denied paying tangenti; he welcomed the investigations as a way to be rid of demands for money. Carlo DeBenedetti, the head of Olivetti, went further. He took full responsibility for payments of tangenti, explaining that firms were paying not to buy policies but to avoid "lethal damage" from state managers. He served a short sentence. The treatment of Fiat and Olivetti was significantly less aggressive than it might have been, lending credibility to the charge that large industrialists benefited from supporting the prosecutors.

Were industrialists and former Communists colluding to bring down the political class? Prosecutors had other reasons to be soft on the PDS. Former Communists, having been out of power, may have been less involved in corrupt practices.[26] Second, the Communists were more disciplined and hence had fewer *pentiti* to implicate their comrades. Finally, Antonio DiPietro, who initiated the investigation and stole most of the media spotlight, openly claimed that he was "not a man of the Left." He explained that he would have stood for office with the Center-Right, had it not been led by Berlusconi, the man he was presently prosecuting.[27]

268

Other prosecutors were leftist, but their very diversity gave them legitimacy and lent force to the investigations.[28]

The fourth explanation for prosecutorial vigor presents it as a straightforward matter of bureaucratic politics. As Borelli acknowledged, "Politicians are threatening the independence of the judiciary because they are trying to occupy all the interstices available and are grabbing what is not theirs."[29] In May 1992, just three months after the beginning of the investigation, Borelli acknowledged that he perceived an opportunity to advance the institutional interests of the judiciary against politicians. He already knew that he could bring the system down.[30]

Each of these explanations is plausible, but we should also recognize that the Italian judicial system, especially criminal prosecution, provides express lanes for individual prosecutors to rise to fame and fortune. The Milan prosecutors became celebrities. Francesco Saverio Borelli was the political strategist of the group. Gherardo Colombo, one of his assistant prosecutors, and Gerardo D'Ambrosio, the number-two man in the office, were the judicial strategists. But no one captured the public imagination more than Antonio DiPietro, the assistant prosecutor who started it all. The least polished and most popular member, DiPietro touched a raw nerve of public resentment and found deep public support for his relentless attacks on politicians.[31]

Borelli acknowledged that DiPietro was more cop than lawyer and that his lack of judicial reserve had hampered his career.[32] It certainly did not hamper his public appeal. By the mid-1990s he was arguably the most popular public figure in Italy.[33] He was celebrated on T-shirts, in graffiti, and in every form of popular media—even wines were named after him.[34] DiPietro left the magistracy to create his own "Party of Values," which he merged into Romano Prodi's Democrats and center-left Olive Coalition. Even revelations of illegal gifts received while he was a public servant failed to cut into the public adoration. DiPietro understood that in contemporary Italy, political success required him to be "nominally left."[35] He ran for Senate with the support of PDS leader Massimo D'Alema, and Prodi appointed him minister for public works—head of the very ministry that Fanfani and Mattei had created and that DiPietro had prosecuted.

Mani Pulite is not a standard story of political leadership. None of the prosecutors, least of all DiPietro, started out to destroy the party system. None deserves individual credit for transforming Italian politics. A rank and file prosecutor began it, Colombo and D'Ambrosio plotted it, and Borelli guided it to a political conclusion. Nor is there evidence of any grand strategy. But Mani Pulite *is* a story of agency. A group of determined prosecutors acted decisively after recognizing that Italy's politicians had lost the ability to defend themselves. DC strategists like Moro and Fanfani had left the scene, and their party nemesis Andreotti was on trial for murder. There was, Colajanni argues, "No De Gaulle for us."[36] But there was a magistracy. They felt their way, learning how to use alliances with other parts of the political class. Operating behind a shield of prosecutorial independence, these unlikely protagonists destroyed the "house that Fanfani built." There was no compelling reason for them to act when they did. Their career paths—among the most prestigious and remunerative in Italian society—were already assured, and the politicians could not threaten their perquisites. But, they understood that the corrupt party system was vulnerable. By the time they were done, politics would never be quite the same again.

Organized Crime

Organized crime was also subject to cleansing in post-Cold War Italy and Japan. In Italy, Giulio Andreotti was indicted in 1993—shortly after two anti-Mob prosecutors were assassinated in Palermo—for alleged ties to the Sicilian Mafia.[37] He was acquitted in September 1999, but the Mafia had been put on notice that the rules had changed. In Japan, influential politicians were revealed to have particularly close relationships with Mob leaders. Prime Minister Takeshita was the first senior LDP leader whose ties to the underworld would become a liability. Here too the rules seem to have changed.

Or had they? Japanese crime syndicates remain "among the world's largest and most powerful criminal confederations."[38] A 1989 survey conducted by the National Police Agency (NPA) estimated that annual revenues of yakuza-connected operations exceeded 1.3 trillion yen ($13 billion).[39] Ten years later, the NPA estimated that there were over three thousand yakuza gangs with a total of about eighty thousand members—some five times the size of the Italian Mafia.[40]

The strength of the yakuza was demonstrated by the speed and efficiency with which criminal groups provided aid to victims of the Great Hanshin Earthquake in 1995, an effort that compared favorably to the lethargic response of the government.[41]

The Japanese police did step up their operations against organized crime in the 1990s. An anticrime law, passed in 1992 and updated in 1997, granted them authority to designate groups as gangs based on the criminal records of members. Once designated, these groups could be blocked from deriving profits from otherwise legal activities.[42] Armed with these new powers, police nationwide arrested more than thirty thousand gang members annually, disbanded hundreds of small gangs, and helped over four thousand former gang members return to civilian life. Between 1990 and 1998, gang-related shootings and murders fell by nearly one-half.[43]

Still, estimates of overall yakuza membership remained stable. Organized crime became increasingly concentrated, and mobsters shifted their emphasis from traditional sources of income—drugs and prostitution—to legitimate business. The police cracked down on corporate blackmail (*sōkaiya*) in the late 1990s, but the major syndicates remain healthy, in part because Japanese banks extended credit to them. The slowed Japanese economy of the 1990s provided new business opportunities in debt collection, bankruptcy management, and consumer finance. Soon, the Japanese financial crisis was being referred to as "the yakuza recession" because gangsters held significant portions of the city banks' nonperforming loans.[44] According to one 1998 estimate, the combined annual revenue of organized crime may have risen as high as 5–6 trillion yen ($50–60 billion).[45] According to another, the yakuza had invested that much in the U.S. economy alone.[46]

Moreover, it is alleged, the yakuza still raise funds for right-wing candidates and "get the vote out" on Election Day. The *Far Eastern Economic Review* asserts that the Yamaguchi-gumi (Japan's largest gang) conducted campaign activities for "scores of politicians" in the June 2000 lower house election. It quotes one unnamed political source as stating "there isn't a single Japanese politician who doesn't know his local yakuza boss."[47] It is further alleged that many Japanese police are equally indebted to the gangsters who hire them when they retire.[48] Although the exact nature of these relationships is unclear, it is not difficult to doubt the government's resolve.

The Italian Mafia never achieved the same public acceptance, but it continues to play a prominent role in civil society.[49] Otherwise legitimate firms appreciate the Mafia's ability to reduce risk, clear bureaucratic hurdles, and guarantee a market share. Italian prosecutors pursued organized crime and its allies in the DC after the Cold War. By 1995, more than six thousand Italian bureaucrats, corporate executives, and politicians were under investigation.[50] Italians who had 'held their nose' and voted DC finally got tired of the stench. Della Porta and Vannucci make a compelling case that the complex interdependence of corruption, clientelism, and maladministration collapsed of its own weight.[51]

Not that this was easy for prosecutors. Between 1978 and 1992 nearly every public official in Sicily who interfered with the business of Cosa Nostra—including the chief of detectives, the deputy chief of police in Palermo, three chief prosecutors, the local head of the carabinieri, the local DC party chief, two former Palermo mayors, and the regional president—was murdered.[52] By 2000, the anti-Mafia movement showed signs of fatigue.[53] The Andreotti trial came up empty, and prosecutors were still appealing to business owners to refuse extortion demands. As in Japan, it was in many respects business as usual.

REALIGNMENT

Much else did change. The new international balance of power removed many of the external pressures that had shaped postwar Italy and Japan. Suddenly it was less important to be anticommunist and—at least in Italy—suddenly it was less important to *be* Communist. No longer did any group or party *have* to be included or excluded from power. When the Soviet Union disappeared, the Communists in Italy reinvented themselves, and the Christian Democrats disappeared in ignominy, falling from power and then dissolving in 1992. It turned out that *both* parties had depended upon the Soviet Union for their identity and purpose, and the PCI leaders proved to be more inventive. Centrist politicians in both countries could now imagine coalition possibilities precluded under the old system—and many, like Romano Prodi in Italy and Hatoyama Yukio in Japan, embraced old enemies. Italian *trasformismo* and Japanese *mochitsu motaretsu seiji* (two metaphorical variations on the theme of "political exchange") could be revived with new vigor. Politics was more unpredictable than it had been for decades; political parties stood for less and less; voting rates declined sharply in both countries. The number of independent ("floating") voters multiplied. Politicians could no longer rely on their machines or their ideological label.[54]

The most striking institutional change was the simultaneous and identical transformation of electoral systems. Both had suffered from extreme proportionality. In Italy, a 1993 referendum dictated that three-quarters of the 475 seats in the Chamber of Deputies would be determined in first-past-the-post competitions, one-quarter by proportional party lists.[55] Months later, in January 1994, Japanese politicians engineered what Curtis has called "the most far-reaching political reform in Japan since the U.S. Occupation."[56] Their reform created a hybrid system modeled upon Italy's: in a 500-seat Diet, 300 representatives would be elected from small, single-seat constituencies, and 200 would be elected from regionwide party lists. In both countries, each voter gets two ballots, one for the small district and one for the party list.

Dramatic as the reform was, in neither country did it diminish party fragmentation. Debate over electoral reform goes on.[57] So does the game of musical chairs played by politicians who have difficulty finding a party to call home. By late 1999, nearly one-quarter (109) of Italy's deputies had changed parties at least once; twenty had changed parties twice, and ten had changed three times.[58] In Japan, after the June 2000 lower-house election, 35 percent (170 of 480) of lower house members had changed parties at least once in the previous six years.[59]

This instability is a stunning change from the days of single-party dominance. The LDP split and recombined several times—starting with the dramatic vote of no confidence in the Miyazawa cabinet in June 1993.[60] A rapid succession of weak, unsteady coalition governments followed. Between 1989 and 2000, Japan had ten prime ministers, nearly as many as it had during the entire Cold War. In the twelve months between mid-1993 and mid-1994, every single party except the JCP participated in a governing coalition. No one could say with certainty just what was "normal," for "the dynamics and logic of the political system had changed."[61]

Defectors from the most powerful and corrupt LDP faction led the Japanese realignment; former Communists and social Catholics from the DC, untouched by scandal, led the Italian one.[62] Their "Olive Coalition" brought relative stability. Romano Prodi became the longest-lasting Italian prime minister since Alcide De Gasperi. But he had to contend with persistent party fragmentation—and an even greater degree of polarization. The Cold War, it seems, had constrained the Right *and* the Left. Apparently, as many voters with neofascist as with centrist preferences had been holding their noses and voting for the DC because they judged it better able to prevent leftist government.[63] Now, many were attracted to the territorial politics of the Lega Nord (Northern League) and to the once-fascist politics of the Alleanza Nazionale. With the end of the Cold War, as Berselli notes, "The barriers fell that had kept right-wing voters in a center party."[64] In 1994, Italy became the first Western democracy to enlist the far Right in its ruling coalition.[65]

Even things that seem not to have changed have in fact changed profoundly. Italy saw the emergence of new political forces, but more than a decade after the demolition of the Berlin Wall, the LDP still governed Japan. The LDP that returned to govern after 1994, however, was not the same LDP. For the first time since its formation in 1955, the party was dependent on former adversaries, such as the Kōmeitō and (for a time) even the Socialists. The DC disappeared in Italy, but the Church remained an important—if diminished—political force. Both countries remain allies of the United States. Each debates how (and if) to revise its constitution, and each continues to seek an elusive "normality." Some things never change.

"NORMALITY"

"Normality" became the Holy Grail for Italy and Japan in the early twenty-first century. Italy has felt abnormal for several reasons. First, despite decades of effort, Italy has failed to rectify regional economic imbalances—its efforts betrayed by the sticky fingers of politicians and their patrons. Second, the political use of the public sector was markedly more corrosive of democratic institutions than elsewhere. In part as a result, Italy's public services—postal, civil engineering, educational, and so on—have been inefficient. Finally, the Italian Center has always had to contend with both a Right and a Left more sizeable than in the rest of Europe.

For its part, Japan has felt abnormal in at least three fundamental ways. First, Japan has never had a "normal" military. Until 1945, Japan's military was beyond civilian control, and after 1945, its legitimacy was limited by its history. Second, Japan has never had a "normal" economy. Its consumers have served its producers, rather than vice versa. Third, Japanese *politics* has been abnormal. There has been no alternation in power as in the two-party systems of Great Britain and the United States.

Two politicians have defined "normality" in the Italian and Japanese contexts. Ozawa Ichirō and Massimo D'Alema are both reinvented politicians—the conservative Ozawa having foresworn ties to the LDP and the progressive D'Alema having done likewise vis-à-vis communism. Each has written about "normality" in ways that have challenged conventional practice and refocused national debate.[66]

Ozawa elaborated his "normal nation theory" (*futsu no kuni ron*) in the early 1990s after he bolted from the LDP. For him, "normality" is above all a matter of standing in the community of nations. No nation can be "normal" until and unless it shoulders those responsibilities "regarded as natural in the international community," something he argues Japan has not done: "Japan has reaped the harvest of peace and free world markets more than any other nation [but has borne] hardly any of the costs of maintaining peace and freedom."[67] It is abnormal that Japan "continue[s] to receive and not to give."[68] A "normal" nation meets its responsibilities willingly—it does not avoid them out of concern for domestic opposition nor does it accept them only under foreign pressure.

Ozawa speaks bluntly of Japan's "national interest." He stresses that free trade and international security are "normally" created for the sake of one's *own* prosperity and safety. Specifically, Japan must abrogate or amend Article 9 of the Constitution, expand the roles and missions of its Self-Defense Forces within UN peacekeeping and the U.S. alliance, and shoulder a greater share of international responsibility.[69] Like many conservative politicians, he blames Yoshida Shigeru for distorting Japanese security policy and Yoshida's successors for failing to heed Yoshida's recognition that his "doctrine" had outlived its usefulness.[70] Ozawa calls for a new "Restoration" (*isshin*) and compares Japan to Venice. Both, he says, are great trading states that enjoyed enormous prosperity, but Venice provided for its own security and in its day was "normal."[71]

Massimo D'Alema published his treatise on normality (*Un paese normale*) in 1995, and it involves many of the same strivings. Where Ozawa stresses Japan's international contribution and her national interest, however, D'Alema focuses on the need to be "accountable" and to look more like other European states. Like Ozawa, D'Alema became convinced that there was something pathological and backward about his nation's institutions. But where Ozawa blames the bureaucrats and wants to strengthen political control, D'Alema blames the politicians and wants to introduce bureaucratic accountability. He blames Italy's "peculiar condition" on a frozen ruling class.[72] Italy is unique in lacking a responsible Center-Right that "is able and willing to promote conservative values without ransacking the state."[73] D'Alema argues that the majority and the opposition must come to agreement about the rules and norms of democratic practice. Only after they agree on "limits," he argues, will "the majority govern without pretending to command, and will the opposition chase the majority without impeding governance."[74] The opposition must be prepared to govern, but must refrain from destroying the majority's work. In a normal nation, each will have its turn.[75]

For D'Alema, Europe is "the yardstick of our normality,"[76] and he declares that Italy "is not European enough."[77] He seeks an Italian commitment to a larger democratic Europe, one with a single currency, full economic integration, and a shared set of values. While both Ozawa and D'Alema speak of making more generous contributions to world and regional order, Ozawa pursues "normality" by enhancing national independence whereas D'Alema does so by subordinating it to larger, more cosmopolitan goals. D'Alema is chasing European standards to achieve normality, Ozawa is chasing global standards.

"Normality," the ideological heir to "modernization" and "catch-up," enjoys broad legitimacy across the political spectrum. Yoshida Shigeru anticipated this in 1967 when he wrote that "what we need today, one hundred years [after the Meiji Restoration], is a far-reaching vision and the ability to assume our rightful role in the ever-widening arena of international relations."[78] In Italy, "normality" was coined on the Left, but is also embraced by the Right. Silvio Berlusconi routinely refers to "the challenge of Europe" (*la grande sfida europea*) and the importance of making Italy a nation of the first rank; like D'Alema, he insists that Italy meet European standards: "We are just 'minor league' Europeans [*Europei di serie*

B]. Our citizens have fewer rights, fewer guarantees, and less freedom than their brethren in England, France, or Germany. Italy is not truly the 'normal nation' that some would like to have us to believe it is."[79] Italian and Japanese leaders continue to pursue the great powers in the twenty-first century. The development of "normal" economic and political modalities is complicated by post-Cold War realignments of identity, power, and wealth.

IDENTITY

The consolidation of national identity remains far more an Italian problem than a Japanese one. The crisis of the Italian state after the Cold War was also a crisis for the Italian nation. The end of longstanding political arrangements transformed the Communist and Catholic subcultures. Regional identities assumed new political relevance, and Italians began to associate with one another in different ways. In Japan, none of this happened. Even regional identities with political potential, such as in Okinawa, are objects of nostalgia, not of politics. Today Japan celebrates its homogeneity.

Italy has more minorities, and far greater regional economic disparities, than any other European state. Although nearly 90 percent of the population can speak Italian, less than one-third does so all the time.[80] Italians celebrate their localism as *campanilismo,* "the idea that one's basic territorial, ethnic, social, cultural, and political identities center on the bell tower" of the local church.[81] Identity resides in piazzas, cathedrals, towers. There is a glorious municipal tradition and, it is often claimed, only a latent national one.[82] But localism does not overpower national identity.

Three-quarters of the Italians surveyed in 1994 expressed pride in being Italian—somewhat more than the levels of pride expressed in being from a particular city (51%) or region (62%).[83] At the same time, however, Italians are deeply ashamed of their state. In Italy, trust in the political system has been significantly lower than the European average for decades.[84] Indeed, Italy is the only established democracy to rank in the lower half worldwide on the issue of trust in government, alongside the Philippines and the former Soviet bloc countries.[85] Italians place more hope in European institutions than in Italian ones and feel a higher level of attachment to Europe than do citizens of most other EU members. They trust the European Parliament and the European Central Bank more than do citizens of any other EU state.[86] Two-thirds of Italians are proud of being European.[87]

The Japanese have a much weaker attachment to Asia. Although more than 90 percent of the Japanese respondents typically express affection for their region or locality, less than two-thirds report affection for Asia. Moreover, the Japanese express pride in *both* their nation and their state institutions. More than four-fifths of the Japanese say that Japan is a better country than any other, and nearly 90 percent say they would rather be Japanese than any other nationality. Their attitudes about the superiority of Japan have changed over time, in directions consistent with Japan's economic performance (see table 10.1). In an international survey of national identity, Japan ranks far higher than average on indicators of pride—including pride in achievements in the economy, sports, world leadership, art, and literature. Italy ranks well below average.[88] Italians are far less proud of their government, political influence, and economy than the Japanese are of theirs.

Both by stereotype and by self-identification, Italians are less willing than others to sacrifice for their nation, whereas the Japanese are immensely patriotic and more willing to sacrifice their personal preferences for collective ones. Those who are selfish are still considered "unusual for a Japanese."[89] Japanese are as proud of their economic achievements as Americans are of theirs—at twice the level of pride exhibited by Italians.[90] And, while three of four Japanese agree strongly with the statement that "I would rather be a citizen of my country than of any other country in the world" (a higher rate than any other nation in the survey), only one in four Italians agree—the lowest of any country except Spain or Holland. Yet Japanese and Italian identifications overlap in some respects. Like the Italians, the Japanese exhibit low trust in politicians, both are significantly less proud of their democratic institutions than are Americans, and both the Italians and the Japanese are far more inclined to identify their family rather than themselves or their nation as "important."[91]

Of greatest interest are the parallels and differences in their respective self-identifications. The Italians celebrate many characteristics—pragma-

Table 10.1 Compared with Westerners, the Japanese Are (in Percent of Total):

	1953 (immediate postwar)	1968 (during high growth)	1983 (during economic bubble)	1998 (after bubble burst)
Superior	20	47	53	33
Inferior	28	11	8	11
Same	14	12	12	32
Cannot Say	21	21	21	19

Source: Tōkei Sūri Kenkyūjo, 1999, 140.
Note: Because of rounding, numbers in rows do not total 100%.

tism, individualism, and creativity—that few Japanese report recognizing in themselves.[92] The majority of Italians identify themselves as "center-left" and an even larger majority of Japanese identify themselves as "center-right," but both the Japanese and the Italians today are deeply committed to liberal democratic values.[93] Italians have less interest in politics than they had earlier but are a far cry from the "amoral familism" that was identified as central to their civic culture in the 1950s.[94] The Japanese react with indignation when their political leaders invoke prewar authoritarian norms.

In Italy, local, regional, and national identities coexist, and there remains the potential for fragmentation.[95] Perhaps Italians are Italians *because* they are Sicilian or Genovese or Abruzzese. One is Florentine, and *therefore* Tuscan, and *therefore* Italian. Italians have no difficulty feeling Italian in this way, but may have trouble when ordered to behave collectively because national institutions have been corrupt or inept for centuries. The problem is how much to localize one's fundamental identity. In this regard, a revealing exchange took place in Bergamo between the "Padanian" separatist Umberto Bossi and a local supporter of his Northern League in 1996. After he exhorted her to "remember, we are Padanians first, and then Italians," she corrected him: "I think that I am a Bergaman first, and then a Padanian."[96]

There is, of course, politics in identity. Bossi's Lega Nord first captured a place in Italy's ruling coalition in 1994.[97] In 1996 he won the most popular votes he ever got and proclaimed his intention to establish an independent state of Padania north of the River Po. The Lega is linked directly to Italy's most intractable regional problem, the inequality between a wealthy North and an impoverished South. In Japan industrialization narrowed regional inequalities; in Italy it deepened them. Numerous remedial efforts have failed. Disparities widened and northern resentment calcified.

There is still room in Japan for this kind of regional politics. Japan's largest minority groups are the Okinawans and the children and grandchildren of Korean and Chinese corvée—Japanese-born resident aliens who are denied citizenship. In a 1995 survey only one-eighth of Okinawans identified themselves as primarily "Japanese." Okinawa is Japan's poorest prefecture and has an unhappy history of occupation, first by the Chinese, then by the Japanese, and now by the U.S. military, whose bases cover one-fifth of its territory. Yet Okinawa's incomplete integration seems to have little political potential in a Japan that has convinced itself of its homogeneity.[98] While Umberto Bossi has proclaimed an independent "Republic of Padania," no one in Okinawa is demanding independence. Italians have become "accustomed to the idea that [they are] not a true nation," and the Japanese have become accustomed to the idea that they are.[99]

Still, ambitious Italian politicians have only rarely put regional identities to strategic use. And when they have, as in the case of the Northern League, they have failed. Meanwhile, Japanese battles for control of the state have taken a different form.

POWER

No instrument is more central to national power in a democratic state than the constitution. In contemporary Italy and Japan, none has been more contested. In Japan, a decades-long elite debate over constitutional revision has only recently engaged the general public. In Italy, the political class sandwiched efforts to revise the Constitution between public referenda. Debate in Japan has centered on Article 9 of the Constitution, which prohibits the use of force to settle international disputes. In Italy it has addressed the role of the presidency of the Republic. Italian reformers want to strengthen the presidency. Japanese reformers believe that the statute of limitations on the "peace clause" has expired.

Japanese Constitutional Reform

The constitution designed by the U.S. Occupation to democratize Japan soon became a political meridian. Despite its opposition to the U.S.-Japan alliance, the Left embraced the Constitution for its guarantees of freedom and civilian control of the military. The Right accepted it, but pressed relentlessly for revisions (*kaiken*) on three main points. First, the U.S. Occupation had imposed an "un-Japanese" constitution and it was the nation's duty to write a new one. Second, the emperor's constitutional status should change from "symbol of the state" (*shochō*) to "chief of state" (*genshu*). Finally, Article 9, the hotly disputed "no war" clause, should be revised or deleted. Revisionists led by Kishi Nobusuke, Hatoyama Ichirō, and their supporters in the Democratic Party claimed that Japan has the right to self-defense and the right to participate in collective security arrangements.[100]

Anti-revisionists (*gokensha*) opposed any formal amendment. Their ranks included centrists such as Prime Minister Yoshida Shigeru and his "mainstream" allies in the Liberal Party, leftist political parties, major labor unions, academics, and a wide range of citizen and student groups. Yoshida believed that Japan should become an economic power first and that Article 9 provided a convenient constraint on premature rearmament.[101] Peace and disarmament groups feared revision of Article 9 would lead to a return to militarism. Leftist parties viewed the existing Constitution as a check on "reactionary" conservatism. Labor unions feared that revision would limit the constitutional rights of organized labor. Academics argued that formal amendment might damage the legitimacy of the document. The anti-revisionists prevailed. Despite vigorous efforts to force changes, the Constitution has never been revised.[102]

The world changed, however, and with it public opinion. Iraq's 1990 invasion of Kuwait triggered a new constitutional debate in Japan.[103] Faced with U.S. requests for contributions, in October 1990 the Japanese government submitted a United Nations Peace Cooperation bill to the Diet. The bill, whose chief advocate was Ozawa Ichirō, then secretary-general of the ruling LDP, called for a "Cooperation Corps" to be dispatched to the Gulf. Previous LDP governments had interpreted Article 9 as forbidding involvement in collective self-defense. Prime Minister Kaifu now emphasized the "nonmilitary" aspect of the proposed deployment by arguing before the Diet that Japanese personnel would not be sent to "dangerous areas."[104] The government and LDP leaders advanced a new and controversial interpretation of Article 9—that overseas force was permissible in a United Nations operation.

Opposition to the bill hardened. Both the Democratic Socialist Party (DSP) and the Kōmeitō moved away from initially receptive positions.[105] The Japan Socialist Party (JSP) and the Japan Communist Party (JCP) strongly opposed the bill. Finally, an official in the Cabinet Legislation Bureau admitted during the Diet debate that there remained "some room for doubt about the constitutionality of SDF [Self-Defense Force] participation in a United Nations force."[106] The bill never came to a vote. Instead, the Diet approved a $9 billion financial contribution to the allied force, earmarked for transportation, food, and other logistical expenses. It denied it was "assisting the war" and thus in violation of Article 9.[107] The move may have placated domestic opposition, but Japan's contribution was belittled as mere "checkbook diplomacy" abroad.[108]

The debate had, however, nudged public opinion toward constitutional reform. Advocates focused in particular on Japan's "international contributions" (kokusai kōken). One senior politician, Murakami Masakuni, asked rhetorically: "Can we be proud of our constitution as [the product of] an independent nation? Unless the Japanese people quickly build [our own] constitution, we will not get respect from the world's nations."[109] As the United Nations became more active, demand for Japanese participation increased. Stung by domestic and international criticism, the LDP submitted a new Law on Cooperation for United Nations Peacekeeping Operations and Related Activities (the PKO bill) in the fall of 1991. Once again it met strong opposition, but after alteration of some controversial elements, it passed the Diet the following June. Japan could now dispatch soldiers overseas for the first time since the Pacific War. It did so, to Cambodia, in October 1992.[110]

Still, the Constitution went unrevised. Conservative politicians began to question whether Japan's "one state pacifism" could be sustained.[111] Ozawa Ichirō launched an LDP study group that in February 1992 called for reinterpretation or revision of the Constitution to ensure Japan could participate in international peacekeeping. Following passage of the PKO bill, other senior LDP leaders proposed a nonpartisan panel to consider constitutional revision.[112] Japan's largest circulation daily newspaper, the *Yomiuri Shimbun,* joined the debate by establishing a think tank to study constitutional revision. By 1993, constitutional reform, particularly with regard to security matters, had once again become a politically salient issue.

Proponents of constitutional reform, exasperated by attempts to equate reform with reactionary militarism, expressed their support for the general principles of the Constitution—democracy, liberalism, and pacifism—while advocating amendments to meet current challenges.[113] On Article 9, for instance, they called for changes to clarify Japan's right to self-defense and allow participation in collective security arrangements but also trumpeted their support for Article 9's pacifism.[114] Ozawa has even claimed that the nation's right to self-defense is the surest way to *prevent* a return to militarism.[115] Revisionists also emphasized their commitment to liberalism by considering new basic rights. Nakasone, for example, has contemplated the addition of environmental rights and "right to know" provisions relating to the disclosure of official information.[116] Revisionist positions on less divisive issues, such as direct election of the prime minister and rationalization of the relationship between the two houses of the Diet, similarly refer both to established constitutional principles and current national challenges.

The revisionist position incorporates a strongly conservative strain. In advocating special government powers for emergencies, for example, Ozawa has called for amendments specifying that the needs of public welfare can trump the rights of private individuals. Nakasone has suggested that there are only two fundamental approaches to the Constitution, the "national" position (*kokuminteki tachiba*), which places national interest above civil rights, and the reverse, "civic" position (*shiminteki tachiba*). While those who take the latter position—predominantly left-wing parties—will prevail in the short run, Nakasone believes that "those who regard national identity as most important, who respect national history and tradition, and who uphold the national position will prevail. This change," he adds, "will be the force that sustains the nation."[117]

Opponents of revision emphasize the Constitution's contribution to Japan's prosperity. On the Left, Socialists and Communists dismiss the liberal elements of the new revisionist agenda, such as the call for environmental rights, as disingenuous attempts to garner support.[118] They adamantly oppose any change in Article 9. SDP leader Doi Takako, for example, openly voiced suspicions regarding the revisionists' intentions.[119] On the Center-Right, LDP elder and former Prime Minister Miyazawa Kiichi has argued that formal amendment is unnecessary: judicial interpretation and administrative usage should remain the means of constitutional change. Regarding Article 9, he and other LDP members have expressed concern over the potentially negative reaction of the international community, particularly in Asia, and want international agreement before proceeding with revision.[120]

The debate would encompass far more than Article 9. In late 1994, the conservative *Yomiuri Shimbun* published its own draft constitution, a document that became a lightning rod for public debate. It included provisions to clarify the sovereignty of the people, the constitutionality of the SDF, and the division of power between upper and lower houses of the Diet, and to establish a constitutional court.[121] This move was unprecedented: it marked the debut of "advocacy journalism" (*teigen hōdō*).[122] Public support for constitutional debate—as well as for revision—rose. Those advocating revision reached a postwar high of 52 percent in 1998.[123]

There was no resisting the debate. In May 1997, a supra-partisan group was established by nearly two hundred Diet members from the newly formed Democratic Party (Minshutō) and conservative elements of both the New Frontier Party (Shinshintō) and the LDP. It sought a standing Diet committee to study the Constitution "on a broad national basis transcending party lines."[124] The group eventually achieved a Constitutional Review Committee in each house of the Diet. These standing committees, officially established in January 2000 for five years, included members from all parties. Indeed, there were active revisionists and anti-revisionists within every party except the JCP.[125] Former Prime Minister Nakasone, the most senior advocate for revision, explained in May 2000 that within the LDP "nearly everyone has come to support constitutional revision— except Miyazawa and Katō, and they are weak."[126] By mid-2000, opinion polls showed broad and deep public support for constitutional revision.[127] The convergence was striking: conservatives now embraced popular sovereignty and espoused limits on military development, whereas progressives accepted the legitimacy of the Japanese armed forces. This sea change had been anticipated by Yoshida Shigeru who, reflecting in his memoirs forty years earlier, had opined:

There is no reason why revision should not come in the long run . . . But the actual work of revision should only be undertaken when public opinion as a whole has finally come to demand it, and then only after listening to all that the people have to say on the issue. It should be a matter of long years of patient experiment and the product of much disinterested thought—factors which lie outside the scope of a single cabinet of a single political party.[128]

The experiment was nearly over, and Yoshida's conditions had been met.

Italian Constitutional Reform

Those seeking Italian "normality" after the Cold War pressed to replace extreme proportionality.[129] As in Japan, electoral reform proved exceedingly difficult. After all, electoral reform requires politicians, who know how to win under the existing system, to change the rules of the game. Voters in both countries were force-fed scandal-a-day news in the 1990s, but Italians would demand a radical restructuring of the system.

The instrument for reforms was the national referendum, an instrument not available to the Japanese.[130] In 1991, a mixed bag of reformers—including disaffected Christian Democrats, leftists, leaders of the Radical Party, and grassroots groups like Catholic Action—collected the half million signatures needed to submit electoral reform to referendum. Nearly two-thirds of the electorate went to the polls in June, and a whopping 95.5 percent voted for change. One leader of the Lega Nord described the vote as a swift "kick in the pants of the political class."[131]

The kick was softer than many had wished, and the political class soldiered on under new party banners. When Parliament deadlocked on electoral reform, a disgruntled Christian Democrat, Mario Segni, instigated a second referendum campaign. His measure to limit proportional representation to one-quarter of the seats in the Senate passed overwhelmingly in April 1993.[132] This vote (plus a drubbing of ruling parties in regional elections in June) would not be ignored. But Segni blinked at the chance to ride his popularity into the Italian premiership through an alliance with the PDS. No strong advocate of electoral reform was left, and the reform movement began to backslide.[133]

In 1996 Romano Prodi's center-left "Olive Coalition" (Ulivo) won power on a reform platform emphasizing institutional change and fiscal restraint. In August, Parliament authorized a special Bicameral Commission on Constitutional Reforms (Bicamerale) made up of thirty-five members from each house, selected according to party strength. Its existence enabled a division of labor in the coalition: Prodi, the centrist prime minister, would run the government and prepare for Italy's entry into the European Monetary Union (EMU), while Massimo D'Alema, head of the PDS, would oversee institutional reform.

The Bicamerale was charged with transforming Italy into a decentralized, federal state with a semi-presidential executive on the French model.[134] The growing strength of the large parties created a favorable environment for reform, and Italian politicians drafted an entirely new second half of the Constitution between February and July 1997. D'Alema hoped leadership of the Bicamerale would signal that former Communists could be trusted to lead a democratic Italy. He was not alone in using reform as an instrument for political legitimation. Gianfranco Fini, leader of the once-fascist Movimento Sociale Italiano (MSI), hoped that participation would underscore his new, more liberal image and gain respect for his new Alleanza Nazionale (AN). The Bicamerale adopted a relatively narrow agenda with three main goals: to increase federalism, to sharpen the definition of the executive branch, and to introduce French-style two-round elections. A fourth objective, reform of the judicial branch, was added at the insistence of former Prime Minister Silvio Berlusconi, who was under investigation for corruption by what he derided as "red-robed judges." Electoral reforms were addressed only at the very end—and when they were introduced, the entire package collapsed.[135]

The public explanation for failure centered on differences concerning the role of the executive. Parties on the Right wanted a strong, directly elected president, who could dissolve Parliament and directly oversee defense and foreign policy. The Center-Left preferred a directly elected prime minister and a weakened presidency. D'Alema reportedly accepted a directly elected president with limited powers, and reached agreement with Fini. Berlusconi did not get support for immunity from prosecution, however, and he rejected the compromise on the presidency. Eighteen months of focused energy dissolved in acrimony and finger-pointing. There would be no electoral or judicial reforms, no federalism, and the powers of the president of the Republic would be unchanged.

Now the public was exhausted. In April 1999, nine out of ten voters who went to the polls chose to adopt a first-past-the-post electoral system, but too few voted for their preference to be binding. The measure missed by less than one-half of 1 percent of the electorate.[136] In May 2000, the referendum on majoritarian elections was put to a vote, and this time, with Berlusconi instructing his supporters to stay home, only 30 percent went to the polls—not even close to a quorum. The electorate was fast demobilizing. Gianfranco Pasquino frames the failure of the Bicamerale as a failure of leadership:

Unfortunately there are few cases in which a single individual has been able to end a political-institutional transition and at the same time consolidate a democratic regime . . . The Italian system . . . seems condemned to navigate the transition without any institutional guidance other than that of the efficient but limited electoral referendum instrument. Although better than other instruments, the abrogative referendum is still insufficient to make Italy a European democracy.[137]

Italy's chase of normality had been frustrated yet again. The defeat of the May 2000 referendum slammed shut a window of opportunity for reform pried open by scandals in the early 1990s.

Bureaucratic Power

If that were the full story of Italy after the Cold War, it would be a tragedy. But despite these failures Italian leaders *did* achieve at least one notable success during the 1990s. In a demonstration that the Italian state still had considerable coherence, its political managers anchored Italy to the EMU. They did so while ameliorating the worst excesses of Italy's "partitocratic" spoils system. The Italian political world was not suddenly cleansed of corruption, but in an odd turn of events, trust in the Italian state would improve just as trust in the Japanese state went into free fall.[138]

Corrupt politicians were par for the Cold War course in both countries. The following passages, the first describing Italy and the second Japan, are both accurate and interchangeable:

Even though politicians are able to steer the bidding for contracts by introducing restrictive clauses in the notices calling for tenders, keeping the competitions semi-secret and distributing insider information, events . . . confirm that one of the key mechanisms used by entrepreneurs—with equally tainted effects—was collusion among the various enterprises attached to the same sector. Business cartels that coalesced on their own could, therefore, control the assignment of contracts, cut out underbidding and inflate prices.[139]

A collusive system of exploiting the public by massive corruption evolved . . . The system works like this: the [government agency] allocates contracts to firms that belong to officially recognized cartels . . . The prices, initially inflated, allow generous profit margins, even after the creaming off of a levy, usually between 1 and 3 percent, which goes to maintain the political system at local and national levels . . . Politics in the conventional sense is irrelevant. It is the business of the politician to serve as broker, articulating the interests of various social groups . . . Collusion, price fixing, and bribery have long characterized this industry.[140]

By the 1990s, such practices were pervasive. Both countries had their share of political corruption scandals during the Cold War. By one count, the Japanese media named eighty-two corruption scandals between 1947 and 1994.[141] In Italy, corruption was the norm from 1948 to 1974; regulations introduced in 1974 drove corruption to new heights by the 1980s.[142] With this precedent, the corruption scandals of the 1990s elicited a puzzlingly large degree of public scorn. But for the Japanese corruption in the *bureaucracy* was something quite new. Structural corruption had a new locus.

The Japanese civil service had long been the paragon of efficiency and honesty. It recruited Japan's best and brightest and provided a perch from which prosperity was enhanced, order maintained, and power flowed. No institution enjoyed higher levels of public trust.[143] It started coming apart in 1995. In January, an earthquake in Kobe killed more than six thousand people, Japan's worst natural disaster in nearly three-quarters of a century. The absence of centralized mechanisms to respond, inadequate preparation, and a refusal to accept international assistance were all roundly criticized. In some neighborhoods, yakuza played a more active role than the Self-Defense Forces or the police. Subsequently, it was learned that collusion between bureaucrats and the construction industry had led to lax inspections that surely multiplied the damage.[144] Then, in March, members of a religious cult, Aum Shinrikyō, used Sarin nerve gas to attack Tokyo subway trains during rush hour. The gas attack killed twelve and sickened over five thousand. It was soon learned that a similar attack had taken place in the town of Matsumoto the previous July, and the U.S. Department of Defense had warned of a larger attack. Finally, in November, officials in the Ministry of Health and Welfare were discovered colluding with commercial firms to introduce HIV-contaminated blood into Japan's blood supply. To avoid the cost of destroying tainted blood, the ministry and suppliers ignored safer blood-screening tests. After a patient undergoing liver surgery died from tainted blood, the practice was stopped—but only after the bureaucracy's prestige was dealt a blow.[145] For the first time ever, a senior MHW bureaucrat was arrested for professional negligence, and a former vice minister was charged with receiving bribes.

Now the sluice gates were opened. The once "infallible" and "incorruptible" Japanese bureaucracy was revealed to be thoroughly fallible and structurally corrupt—and they had no politicians to defend them. There were revelations of personal enrichment and abuse of bureaucratic prerogative. Senior officials were arrested, and others committed suicide to avoid arrest. In 1995, the deputy chief of the Budget Bureau—perhaps the most prestigious bureau in the most prestigious ministry—was arrested for accepting gifts from the president of a credit firm liquidated by court order. He and another official were forced to resign.[146] The chief of the Defense Agency's Central Procurement Office and his deputy were discovered to have granted special favors in exchange for well-paying jobs for retired defense officials.[147] The two senior officials were arrested, high-ranking bureaucrats were demoted, and the defense minister resigned.[148]

The LDP had always presented corruption as a matter of individual failures, and the media had always focused on politicians. Now all had changed. Bureaucrat bashing became a mainstream sport. Politicians who had suffered from charges of corruption now fired back at the bureaucrats who, they argued, had always been corrupt but had been protected from punishment.[149] For their part, the bureaucrats complained that they were scapegoats and that the charges were arbitrary. They were being punished for practices that had been routine.[150]

In October 1999, the former head of the Defense Agency's Procurement Division was sentenced to three years in prison for overcharging the government in favor of corporate suppliers.[151] At about the same time, nine former high-ranking Kanagawa prefectural police officials were charged with destroying evidence to cover up a former officer's drug use.[152] In February 2000, a national police inspector enjoyed a night on the town at a hot spring resort with the prefectural police chief he was supposed to be inspecting. Busy gambling, they failed to respond to reports that a nine-year long kidnapping victim had been found.[153] In January 2001, the Ministry of Foreign Affairs fired an official who had embezzled at least fifty-four million yen from a secret fund. He had apparently used the money to support three ex-wives, buy luxury housing, and acquire thoroughbred racehorses. The Japanese public divided its outrage evenly between the fact that these public funds were embezzled and that they were originally earmarked for the entertainment of diplomats and politicians traveling abroad.[154]

The Japanese state was revealed to be not only dishonest but incompetent as well. This charge seemed most clear in the case of the vaunted finance ministry. In the autumn of 1995 the ministry underestimated the volume of bad debts borne by large banks and tightened fiscal policy, a misjudgment that exacerbated the economic crisis. It also underestimated the impact of a depressed real estate market. Within two years, mismanagement of the economy and the subsequent recession undermined the authority of banking regulators. When it was discovered that regulators had been entertained by the banks they were regulating, the ministry was split apart by politicians who created a separate Financial Supervisory Agency.[155]

These incidents are part of a much longer litany, one that is hardly unique to Japan. But the sea change in public perceptions is difficult to overestimate. Perhaps the most discomfiting problem—where incompetence meets public safety head on—was the bureaucracy's inability to confront the threat from nuclear power plants. The first problems presented themselves in November 1995 when nearly three tons of highly combustible liquid sodium leaked from Japan's prototype fast-breeder reactor.[156] In March 1997, an accident at the Tōkai Mura reprocessing plant in Ibaraki Prefecture exposed thirty-seven workers to radiation.[157] The following month, a tritium leak at Japan's Advanced Thermal Reactor exposed eleven additional workers to low-level radiation. The plant's managers then admitted that they had failed to report eleven prior leaks over the previous three years.[158] Several months later, it was revealed that two thousand drums of stored nuclear waste at the Tōkai Mura Reprocessing Plant had been leaking over a thirty-year period.[159] After more than fifty tons of primary coolant water leaked from a reactor in Fukui Prefecture in July 1999, the troubled Tōkai Mura complex suffered the worst nuclear disaster in the nation's history in the autumn of 1999. Operators of one of the units in this complex failed to follow guidelines, and the result was a nuclear reaction and large-scale radiation leak. At least fifty-nine workers were exposed, and one died. More than one hundred local residents were exposed, and once again the government was criticized for its slow response. During the crucial first twelve hours, for example, communication between the Science and Technology Agency and the prime minister's office broke down. The minister for Home Affairs attended a party, the minister for Health and Welfare campaigned for a colleague in Niigata, and Prime Minister Obuchi continued to make telephone calls to complete a cabinet reshuffle.[160]

Perhaps because so much was expected of the Japanese bureaucracy and so little of the Italian, the "strong" Japanese state became perilously weak and the "weak" Italian state grew unprecedentedly coherent, if not exactly "strong." It was in Italy, where the state was reputedly infiltrated by politicians, that prosecutors rose to crush the political class. It was in Japan, where the state was reputedly insulated from political influence, where the bureaucracy was discredited. Implausible as it might sound, in the 1990s the Italian government established an unprecedented level of accountability. Politicians failed to reform the Italian state, but nonpoliticians—technocrats (*tecnici*) and politicians with a particularly high level of policy expertise, the so-called policy wonks—worked closely with "social partners" (employers, unions, and parties) to guide Italy. They brought a healthy Italian economy into the European Monetary Union, on schedule and under cost. They positioned Italy to build unprecedented wealth at precisely the same moment that Japanese economic bureaucrats were fumbling their nation's future.

WEALTH

Italian Concertation

Despite the failures of the Bicamerale and the referenda, Italy achieved fundamental economic reform during the 1990s. Its governors reduced inflation, restored fiscal solvency, and realized striking changes in industrial relations and social policy. Against all odds, the Italian state demonstrated the capacity to change. When the European Council met in May 1998 to determine the first wave of states to join the European Monetary Union (EMU), Italy had already met all the required "convergence criteria"—including targets for inflation rates, interest rate differentials, public debt, fiscal deficits, and currency stability. It had earned a place at the table with the other European powers. Success was won in part through a currency depreciation that boosted exports and in larger part through political bargains. Italian authorities exhibited, as Croci and Picci describe it, a "kind of political virtuosity that [they had] so often lacked in the past."[161]

Concertation is a means by which democratic states work with capital and labor to achieve otherwise impossible "social pacts."[162] It requires extensive coordination and clear articulation of preferences. Actors must each maintain control of their membership, come to trust the others, and bind themselves to difficult concessions. Italy's social pacts have always been responses to one or another emergency: the inflationary oil shocks of the 1970s, the public debt crisis of the 1980s, the pressure to enter the EMU in the 1990s. Most deals broke down before the ink had dried.[163] The state could not deliver on obligations it had incurred in making bargains because it activated a vicious cycle: the government used public funds to buy the cooperation of its social partners, but this engorged public debt made subsequent offers of compensation difficult and less generous. As offers became less attractive, the social partners grew less willing to make sacrifices, and the deal collapsed. Concertation was replaced by adversarial politics.

By the 1990s, however, the mix of constraints and resources had changed. The former seemed greater, the latter more limited. Italy could not have succeeded without the creative leadership of the technocrats at the Bank of Italy and other elite institutions, such as Lamberto Dini and Carlo Azeglio Ciampi, and policy wonk politicians such as Giuliano Amato and Romano Prodi. These tecnici worked with the social partners to hammer out reforms that enabled Italy to meet the Maastricht criteria. The new constraints came from Europe, and the domestic political landscape had been transformed. The PCI and the DC now were gone, and with them went many of their alliances. The system was realigning amid a widespread recognition that public debt had gotten out of hand, and that Italy had to change. In Italy, where the term *crisis* is a permanent fixture in the political discourse, a sense of true national emergency now emerged. Political bargaining between the unions and the state resumed with vigor.

The technocrats invented new modalities for the bargain between capital and labor. In July 1992, a tripartite agreement was reached on incomes policy in which the partners for the first time did not *get* goodies but *gave them up*. The government negotiated abolition of the *scala mobile* (the indexing of wages to inflation), long the most sensitive issue in Italian industrial relations. Company-level wage bargaining was suspended for a year as well. The partners agreed to bring public-sector industrial relations into line with private practice, and new agreements were signed on incomes policy, collective bargaining, and pensions. In the face of EU demands to contain public spending, it was now clear that the public enterprise sector would have to change as well. In September 1992 the Amato government announced a "Reorganization Plan" for public enterprise. By 1994, IRI had begun selling its assets, and ENI soon followed suit. There was no longer a DC to colonize management or to siphon off funds.[164]

The next agreement concerned pensions, and the Berlusconi government tried to break the evolving rules of the game. Its 1994 budget proposal abandoned shared burdens and tried to impose sacrifices on labor alone. Its plan to scrap seniority pensions and abrogate some earlier agreements provoked wildcat strikes and widespread protests; Berlusconi's government collapsed just seven months after it was formed.[165] A nonpartisan, "technocratic" government led by Lamberto Dini took its place. Dini governed effectively by avoiding Parliament altogether. His government set pension reform as a major objective, and he led negotiations between unions and the state using a union proposal as the starting point. The resulting agreement won a workplace ballot, and the government converted the agreement into legislation. The technocrats succeeded in "lowering the temperature" of Italian politics.[166] Dini's May 1995 agreement with the unions has been called "one of the most radical reforms in the history of the Italian welfare state."[167] The Bank of Italy could now devalue the lira by 50 percent vis-à-vis the deutsche mark without inflation or social unrest. Italian manufacturers improved their competitiveness faster than any others in Europe, thanks to wage moderation and productivity improvements.

This was just the beginning. In December 1998 the Italian state and thirty-two social partners signed an even broader agreement. Their Social Pact for Development and Jobs (colloquially referred to as "the Christmas Pact") was a comprehensive agreement to reduce unemployment, labor costs and taxes, to encourage investment, and to develop the South. No major player stayed out. All three labor federations and Confindustria, as well as the small and medium-sized firms and local and regional governments, signed on. To give the deal additional legitimacy, Prime Minister D'Alema subjected it to debate and put it to a vote by Parliament. Italy had won broad support for an institutionalized system of concertation just as other European states were giving up on the idea.[168]

Italian public administration experienced effective reform and enormous structural change. While Italian leaders displayed considerable "virtuosity," their choices were enabled by (welcome) pressure from Brussels. Now that capital could move easily across borders, and currency devaluation was no longer a policy option, many of the traditional instruments of economic policy making had been voided. Active industrial policy was also newly problematic, leaving little other than neoliberal cost control and productivity increases. Local governments as well as firms now saw the benefit of ceding power. The unions agreed to limit wage demands to the level of productivity increases, and even the Bank of Italy agreed to tie its own hands. The central bank, no longer subservient to Italian fiscal authorities, no longer had to finance their debt. With moral hazard thus eliminated, fiscal deficits were dramatically reduced and public debt was cut from nearly 9 percent of GDP to under 3 percent. Regini and Regalia hit upon a critical point: "Contrary to received wisdom, concertation involving a devolution of policymaking functions to interest organizations aimed at solving urgent and shared problems is more likely to succeed when such organizations cannot hope for selective benefits in exchange."[169]

Now all groups were making sacrifices for the first time. Enforcing this critical change was first a technocratic and then a Center-Left government. Each came to the table with the confidence of labor, and each worked to win the confidence of business. The elimination of the DC and the PCI made it less likely that any single group could seek or receive unilateral concessions. Berlusconi's Right could not inspire the necessary sacrifice in 1994, for it never had the trust of all parties. Only a Center-Left government could motivate labor to tighten its belt, because only the Center-Left could convince labor that every group would make concessions.

Notwithstanding Berlusconi's misstep, the Italian state made enormous economic progress. Still, there remained one point of fundamental continuity. To convince the Italian people to accept sacrifices, the government appealed to their longing for international prestige. The authorities explained that changes were necessary so as "not to miss the European train," to meet Italy's "appointment with Europe," "to prove Italian maturity."[170] As far as Italy had come—and it had come a very great distance—it was *still* chasing parity, it was *still* seeking prestige and acceptance, it was *still* intent upon becoming normal.

Japanese Reversal of Fortune

Japan had its own "reversal of fortune" during the 1990s—widely referred to as Japan's "lost decade."[171] The Ministry of Finance grossly miscalculated how best to let the air out of the speculative bubble it had allowed to inflate. The Japanese economy grew by less than half the rate of the previous decade. Slower growth, of course, could have indicated merely that the Japanese economy was "maturing" and "converging" with the performance of other rich economies. But dramatically slower growth was joined by a collapse in asset values. It seemed a temporary setback, but the decline never ended. Over the course of the 1990s the Nikkei index fell from close to 40,000 points to just over 13,000, and land prices fell by more than 50 percent. The remarkably under-regulated—and now transparently corrupt—banking system proved insolvent, and by the fourth quarter of 1999 retail sales had fallen for thirty-four consecutive months.[172]

Each time there were signs of recovery, Japan's leadership intervened with tax increases that drove the economy back into recession. They whipsawed the economy with fiscal policies of stimulus and restraint and experiments with eased monetary policy.[173] By 2000, Japanese public debt was at least 130 percent of GDP, the highest ever recorded by a developed economy.[174] Still, "extraordinarily inept" political managers of the Japanese economy pursued failed stimulus after failed stimulus.[175] They injected more than one trillion yen into the reeling economy—ten times more than the entire Marshall Plan, even adjusting for inflation—mostly for construction projects of little economic benefit.[176] Each new package provoked a temporary boost followed by negative growth. Repeated claims of incipient recovery were belied by lackluster economic performance, and often by recession. Meanwhile, the private sector was inundated by unrecoverable loans, and a mountain of bad debt devastated the credit ratings of leading firms. Now the characteristics invoked as sources of Japan's extraordinary strength and resiliency during the high-growth era—keiretsu, cartels, developmental bureaucrats, high levels of investment and savings, lifetime employment, industrial policy—were reinterpreted (if not revealed) as liabilities. The sources of Japan's economic miracle now seemed sources of excessive rigidity and "inner rot."[177]

To some it was the best thing that could have happened.[178] The old economy, with its barriers to foreign direct investment and to manufactured imports, its insulated capital markets subject to high levels of control, its exclusionary finance-centered conglomerates (keiretsu), and its captive domestic labor market, was coming undone.[179] Here, at last, was real and long overdue change pushed by the forces of globalization. Nor was it just a matter of foreign pressure alone. Irresistible demographic change and the escalating costs and risks of indigenous technological development were about to destroy Japan's celebrated exceptionalism. An insular economic system so well suited to the needs of late industrialization would have to yield to liberalization, deregulation, and transparent competition.[180]

Or would it? On the one hand, there is evidence that in the 1990s the Japanese economy finally responded to "universal" economic imperatives. It *was* changing from a manufacturing-centered, export-oriented growth generator to a more mature service-oriented wealth generator. More than one million manufacturing jobs were lost between 1991 and 1996 alone. By 1995, Japanese-owned firms were manufacturing more overseas than they were exporting from Japan.[181] This structural shift affected the political economy as well as the social contract itself. Lifetime employment began to disintegrate, and unemployment rose to levels unprecedented in postwar Japan.

The most dramatic change was in the financial sector. Seeking to make the Tokyo market competitive with those of New York and London, Prime Minister Hashimoto Ryūtarō announced plans in 1996 for a British-style deregulation of Japan's financial industry. His much-ballyhooed "Big Bang" opened a range of once-protected financial markets, including the large and lucrative business of pension-fund management. By 2001 foreigners owned nearly one-fifth of the equities traded on the Tokyo Stock Exchange.[182] Insolvency of the banking system also led to experimentation with venture capital and other equity instruments. The old firewalls that had separated various types of financial institutions were dismantled, and consolidations cut across keiretsu lines. Six city banks were suddenly reduced to four. Sony and Toyota entered the financial sector and began making significant profits. Foreign firms such as Merrill-Lynch and GE Capital penetrated the Japanese financial sector through mergers and acquisitions, and soon made inroads into the insular Japanese capital markets.

There was ample evidence of change elsewhere. Long-suffering (some might say long-complacent) Japanese consumers now seemed fiercely price sensitive. "Mom and pop" retailers succumbed as foreign megastores such as Toys-R-Us, Costco, and Wal-Mart came to Japan. Legal requirements were tightened to prevent companies from hiding losses or manipulating pension funds. In the late 1990s a Brazilian was hired as chief operating officer to run Nissan for Renault; a German assumed control of Mitsubishi Motors after Daimler-Chrysler took over; and an American became CEO of Mazda, now controlled by Ford. Market leaders in strategic sectors such as oil refining and shipbuilding saw an unprecedented number of mergers. Markets began to respond to supply and demand as well as to manipulation. For the first time, winners and losers were easy to identify, because share prices of competitors no longer moved in lockstep. A decade of economic hard times had perhaps unleashed forces of creative destruction. Change had come at last—and, for some analysts, not a moment too soon.

Still, a great many remained skeptical.[183] For them, change had come not at last, but only "at the very least." The "Big Bang" was actually a "Big Whimper." They note that despite lip service to deregulation and liberalization, economic bureaucrats have never really abandoned their deeply rooted proclivity to meddle. Competition was successfully introduced into the financial sector, into airlines, and into the electric power industry. But METI (formerly MITI) continued to pursue industrial policy and deregulation stalled.[184] Even the consolidations in the financial industry are seen as evidence of weakness, not of effective reform. It may be a story of *re*-regulation, rather than *de*-regulation.[185] The government, moreover, continued to intervene in the economy through industrial policy or by manipulating stock prices, thereby frustrating true reform.[186] Few institutions were abandoned, and many mercantile practices remained unchanged.

Hostility to inward foreign direct investment provides the best example. Foreigners held less than one-half of 1 percent of total assets, barely one-twentieth of the U.S. level. Moreover, although foreign direct investment had doubled between 1997 and 1998, and more than doubled again the next year, virtually all foreign acquisitions were of distressed assets. Healthy Japanese firms were still off-limits. Foreign holdings were overwhelmingly in fund portfolios—ownership that provided no direct managerial control. The stock of foreign direct investment remained markedly lower in Japan than any other advanced industrial country.[187]

Was keiretsu exclusivism truly dead? Although the "big six" keiretsu consolidated into four groups by 2000, more than 90 percent of all Japanese firms continued to rely on a "main bank" for their financing. Much change remains before the Japanese economy is comparable to that of Canada, the United States, or most European countries. Although Japan is not immune to global economic forces, it does continue to filter them in ways that render Japan unlike other markets. None of this is new, of course. Japan has often had to choose between embracing and resisting change, and more often than not it chose to resist. Japan surfed the tur-

Table 10.2 Q: How Would You Characterize Japan's Economic Power?

	1978	1988	1998
Very good	23%	42%	4%
Pretty good	43%	40%	28%
Pretty bad	19%	10%	42%
Very bad	5%	2%	23%

Source: Tōkei Sūri Kenkyūjo, 1999, 143. See Tōkei Sūri Kenkyūjo (1995, 712) for Italian and Japanese attitudes toward capitalism and socialism.
Note: Because of rounding, numbers in rows do not total 100%.

bulent waves of "liberalization" in the 1960s, when it was "compelled" to reduce tariffs as the cost of entering the Organization for Economic Cooperation and Development (OECD); it did so again in the 1970s, when it was compelled to dismantle nominal barriers to direct foreign investment. In neither case was there much de facto liberalization. Japan turned to similar "reforms" in the 1980s to "deregulate" domestic markets. If economic "normality" required the openness of North America and Europe, the Japanese social contract might be worth protecting to the bitter end.

Historians of the twentieth century may see the period of Japan's high-speed growth as merely a triumphal parenthesis separating more than a century of insecurity from continued decades of widespread anxiety. The Japanese were hardly satisfied with their situation at century's end (see table 10.2). Dissatisfied citizens remained very receptive to compensatory politics, however. Italy weaned itself from the fiscal teat, and public works spending in Italy declined to just 2 percent of GDP in 1997; in Japan it remained at more than three times that level.[188] The continuation of this compensation-as-usual politics helps explain why Japanese voters were so reluctant to rise up. Short-run cyclical recovery was always force-fed "just in time" for a new election, and the cumulative effects were never quite enough to precipitate true reform.

EXPLAINING THE REVERSAL OF FORTUNES

Immediately after the collapse of the Soviet Union, the oft-repeated quip that "the Cold War is over, and Japan won" seemed exactly right.[189] In 1989 Japan was rich, secure, and upwardly mobile. Its bankers and its engineers seemed poised to dominate world markets, and its U.S. ally seemed endlessly willing to protect them while they did so. Something even better than "normality" was within their grasp. Japan was attracting awe, admiration, and dread in equal measure, without fiddling even minimally with its domestic institutions or its social contract.

Meanwhile, Italy, a charter member of both NATO and the G-7, did not appear to have won much of anything. Germany and France were dictating the terms of the new European order. The Italian economy was gripped by massive inefficiency, its politics by transparent corruption, and its administration by frustrating sclerosis. Italy would be lucky to get as far as "normality," and many expected that it would have to settle for much less.

After a tumultuous decade, it all looked very different. Italians had mobilized to make sacrifices and change. They pruned their budget drastically, curtailed inflation, privatized state enterprises, and joined the common currency. The Italian economy became a model of structural reform. The two major Cold War political parties—the Christian Democrats and the Communists—disappeared. To be sure, Italy failed to complete its transition to the Second Republic. But even if the Italian bureaucracy remained sclerotic, even if the political class blinked at the chance to make wholesale administrative reforms, Italians were living richer, more dynamic lives than before the Wall came down. As a "normal" part of Europe, Italy could expect help to finish the job of reforming its public bureaucracy. It would not be relegated to Europe's "minor league" after all.

The Japanese harbored equally high hopes for political change, but they blinked sooner and kept their eyes closed longer. The economy drifted away from prosperity. Indeed, it began to sink, its rigidities pulling it under a tsunami of adverse changes in asset values, unemployment, and bankruptcies. Japanese consumers felt betrayed by their managers, and Japanese citizens felt betrayed by their bureaucrats and politicians. They had not felt so much economic insecurity since the famous Oil Shock in 1973 or so much political insecurity since the Vietnam War. Japan responded by hunkering down. The LDP was returned to power to govern in its time-honored way—deferring costs through extensive compensation. In May 2002, the authoritative Moody's service raised the rating of Italian government bonds, thereby relegating Japanese bonds to the lowest level of any in the G-7—and equal to those of Botswana.[190] Japan resisted change whereas Italy embraced it.

Why did Italy and Japan respond so differently? On one account, Japanese are naturally more quiescent than Italians. They demand (and expect) less from their leaders and are seldom disappointed. The Japanese identify themselves as tenacious and diligent, but also as irrational and uncreative. Freedom is not high on the list of values they claim to embrace. Yet Japanese citizens have taken to the streets to demand change in the past. Japanese environmental regulation and renewed investment in the social infrastructure was a direct result of citizens' movements.[191] Similarly, protests in the 1960s had yanked the LDP back to the center after it had strayed too far to the right.

Another interpretation holds that external pressures "forced" Italy's hand. Italy "had" to succumb to European demands for convergence. Pressures on Italy for reform were salutary and propitious it is true, but Japan was facing similar pressures. Few "outside pressures" (*gaiatsu*) could have been more irresistible that those of the U.S. trade negotiators. Few could have been as salutary or propitious as the growing acceptance of its products in global markets, its increasing productivity and persistent technological upgrading, or its expanding global investment reach. The forces acting upon Italy and Japan were not fundamentally different; both economies depended disproportionately on small and medium-sized, export-oriented firms.[192] Resources and opportunities for change were more abundant in both countries in the wake of the Cold War.

There is nothing inexorable about the changes we have observed on the Italian and Japanese paths toward "normality." There is instead considerable room for political choice as an explanation for change. Conventional characterizations of "weak" and "strong" states are inadequate. Public officials in an Italian state reputedly among the weakest in the industrial democracies transformed the party system, whereas Japanese bureaucrats—reputedly among the strongest in the industrial world—submitted to domination by politicians who resisted similar efforts to clean up corrupt practices. In Italy, as the Clean Hands investigation unfolded, decades of docile acceptance of corruption were discarded. Italian prosecutors tested the law that gave them "independence," and they succeeded. Their Japanese counterparts, presented with a similar opportunity in the Recruit Scandal, dared not test the constraints of Article 14 of the Public Prosecutors Law. Yet Japanese prosecutors had earlier succeeded in bringing down a prime minister without repercussions, suggesting that they may have been no more constrained than their Italian counterparts.

Japanese and Italian leaders—like Japanese and Italian citizens—might have accepted very different outcomes. We should not expect a single definition of "normality." The two countries will continue to differ in fundamental and irreconcilable ways. Yet both have been traveling much the same road, striving to catch up to the rest of the advanced nations in a century-long search for what once was called "prestige" and later "modernity." Their parallel roads have taken them past, around, and through some remarkably similar challenges.

Why do they remain so different? The easy answer is that they remain different because they were differently endowed from the beginning, with different resource mixes, different social forces in play, and different constraints on their leaders. But as we have seen, they were not so differently endowed. There were basic differences, but there were also remarkable similarities. We now turn to a closer analysis of how recent Japanese and Italian leaders have intervened as they pursue their visions of "normality." We begin with choices on the Left.

CHAPTER ELEVEN

Choices on the Left:

ACHILLE OCCHETTO AND FUWA TETSUZŌ

A wall had fallen, only a wall . . . Nothing remained as it was in the East and
in the West.

               Achille Occhetto, *Il sentimento e la ragione*

The most consequential choices made by Italian or Japanese political
leaders after the Cold War were made not by prime ministers or by government officials but by opposition politicians. The collapse of Soviet
communism posed a major strategic choice to the Communist Party of
Italy (PCI) and the Japan Communist Party (JCP). Although the JCP
never achieved the same degree of national power as the PCI, their political circumstances were remarkably similar. Both had seen their electoral fortunes wane during the 1980s, both had seen their most likely
coalition partners embrace the dominant conservative parties, and each
was engaged in a generational leadership transition. Their central committees immediately recognized the moment of opportunity, and debates flared over how best to respond to the collapse of Soviet communism. Party leaders, however, took the JCP and the PCI in markedly
different directions. Achille Occhetto chose to reinvent the PCI as a social democratic party, and the JCP's Fuwa Tetsuzō chose *not* to do likewise. Both proclaimed their continued commitment to democratic politics, but the PCI declared its own death and rebirth whereas the JCP
declared its determination not to change. The PCI would be revitalized,
the JCP reburied.

    Although the PCI was a mass party and the JCP was less broadly ac-
cepted, the two communist parties had a great deal in common. They
were both major opposition parties in pluralist democracies. They had
much the same history to draw on: a tradition of hard-won independence
from Soviet domination; the antipathy of (and toward) the American
hegemon; difficulties winning undivided support from organized labor;

299

broad support from cultural and intellectual elites; a pantheon of leaders who had pursued peaceful, parliamentary paths to power despite pressures from the far Left and foreign benefactors; a reputation for rectitude in a corrupt party system; and successful local governance in coalition with other parties. But the leaders drew on these parallel resources differently. Achille Occhetto reached back into party history to justify dramatic change; Miyamoto Kenji and his successor Fuwa Tetsuzō read their history as a justification to continue on the same path. The former used history to abandon communism, the latter to reaffirm it.

COMMON PATHS TO THE PRESENT

Marxism came slowly to Italy and Japan.[1] In both countries there were splits between revolutionaries and reformists from the very beginning, well before middle-class activists formally established communist parties after the Russian Revolution. The PCI was formed in 1921 under pressure from Moscow, when Antonio Gramsci and Amadeo Bordiga led a group out of the Socialist Party. The same drama was played out in Japan in July 1922, when a small group led by Yamakawa Hitoshi declared the need to move toward revolution from a mass base. The time seemed ripe for vast social change in Italy and Japan: industrial development had created a large working class and massive disparities in wealth in both countries. Both the PCI and the JCP submitted to the discipline of the Third Communist International (Comintern) operating out of Moscow.

Not surprisingly, each faced unrelenting hostility. Indeed, the JCP was dissolved and reestablished several times in the face of internal division and state repression. By 1928, after Japan had outlawed outdoor assemblies, virtually all Japanese Communists were in prison or had fled into exile. The party organization effectively was smashed.[2] In the 1930s, some Japanese Communists continued their struggle from prison, but a great many declared their "conversion" (tenkō).[3] In Italy the Communists fared little better—Gramsci began writing his influential *Prison Notebooks* in 1929. Both countries exhibit parallel stories of unequal struggle with an authoritarian state, including cyclical mass arrests, repression, and new instructions from Moscow to start over.[4]

From the beginning, the clandestine JCP and the PCI faced four great decisions. The first concerned when and how much to cooperate with other progressive forces. While each had been created out of the failure of others to support revolution, there still were tactical alliances to be debated. The second proved more difficult: how much and to what extent to nationalize Karl Marx. Each party was pulled between nationalist and internationalist values: some saw universal truth in Marx's diagnoses, others argued that different national conditions required different revolutionary approaches. This is connected to the third—and most constrained—decision: how much distance to keep between the national party and the Soviet Union. Indeed, in the Japanese case, where the Comintern regularly selected (or purged) its leadership, JCP leaders were always squeezed between Stalin and the imperial police. In Italy, Palmiro Togliatti resisted Stalinist purges in the 1920s and confronted the Comintern regularly— until he became a target himself of the Comintern at the end of the decade. At that point he submitted to Soviet authority.[5] Fourth, the Italian prewar and wartime communist parties had to decide how they would relate to popular nationalism. Unlike the JCP, the PCI had—and indeed seized—the opportunity to establish itself as a nationalist force against the fascist state. Without the mantle of resistance, the JCP never was able to overcome the popular perception that it followed foreign direction.

After 1945 the choices available to Italian and Japanese communist leaders were further limited. These leaders had survived both state repression and Stalinist purges. With support from the Soviet Union, each pursued conciliatory "popular front" programs. Togliatti, the most prominent of the Italian communists, had spent most of the war in Moscow. In Japan, three men assumed JCP leadership: Tokuda Kyūichi, who had been in Moscow; Nosaka Sanzō, who had returned from Moscow via Yenan, where he had worked with Chinese communists to propagandize Japanese soldiers; and Miyamoto Kenji, imprisoned for twelve years until SCAP opened the prisons in October 1945. At first, both leaderships eschewed the model of a vanguard party. The JCP strategy was to create what Nosaka called a "loveable party," attractive to a broad public. Togliatti, for his part, returned to lead a *partito nuovo*, one open to Catholics and former fascists as well as the doctrinally orthodox.[6]

Togliatti was the more successful. The "Italian professor" (as he was known to Stalin) returned in March 1944 and immediately began constructing a reformist and democratic PCI.[7] Convinced that there was no short run alternative to parliamentary democracy, Togliatti began to distance himself from the militant liturgy of the prewar period. He used Gramsci's mantle to give the PCI "national" characteristics, speaking of "unity in diversity" to characterize relations with others. He participated actively with Catholic, Liberal, Republican, and Socialist veterans of the Resistance in the construction of the new Italian constitution. Unlike the Socialists, he even threw PCI support behind renewal of the Lateran Pacts. Without ever completely breaking from Moscow, though he came perilously close at times, Togliatti was building a different kind of communist party. Even after the outbreak of the Korean War in 1950, when the Soviet

Union pressured communist parties to be more revolutionary, Togliatti pursued a parliamentary path.[8] Treading carefully between Stalinist controls and right-wing attacks as a pawn of Moscow, Togliatti built the most successful parliamentary communist party in the world by embracing an Italian national identity.

Nosaka's "loveable" JCP, reestablished in December 1945 after the jails were emptied of political prisoners, had less success. U.S. anticommunism, furthermore, was a substantial obstacle for both parties; but an American occupying army made it a greater problem for the JCP. At first, however, the JCP had extraordinary success. Like Togliatti, Tokuda and Nosaka returned from exile to stress moderation and develop a mass party within the context of parliamentary competition. They would pursue the same sort of united front—nominally independent of Moscow—that Togliatti was pursuing in Italy. Six Communists were elected in the first postwar election, in April 1946. The party had changed its position, after 1945 believing that the Japanese people needed the emperor a while longer. Indeed, the JCP saw itself aligned *with* the U.S. military: both would seek to democratize and demilitarize Japan. At first, party ideologues saw SCAP as little more than a "part of the progressive bourgeoisie" whose historic function was to expedite the revolution. Some U.S. officials welcomed Nosaka's program.[9]

This changed, of course, as U.S. policy shifted away from New Deal liberalism. In January 1947 SCAP blocked a general strike called by the JCP, but the party was doing well in establishing control of key unions. Party membership was under one thousand cadres in 1945, but as in Italy the JCP attracted most of the nation's progressive forces. By the spring of 1949, the JCP controlled the labor movement and registered 100,000 members. In elections that year, nearly three million voters sent thirty-five JCP representatives to the Diet. The party may have seemed "loveable" to the Japanese voting public, but SCAP was not impressed. With the outbreak of the Korean War, SCAP purged the central committee and suspended publication of *Akahata* (*Red Flag*), the party's daily newspaper.[10]

Unfortunately for the JCP, the American military was only part of its problem—perhaps the smaller part. No sooner had the JCP achieved electoral success than the Cominform—Stalin's postwar mechanism for controlling the communist parties abroad—issued a January 1950 editorial excoriating it for moderation. The JCP was *too* loveable and was "drifting into the arms of the social democrats."[11] The creative and remarkably successful Nosaka was singled out and vigorously denounced for his strategy of peaceful revolution.[12] His first reaction was disbelief. He blamed provocateurs seeking to disrupt party unity. When he realized that the only provocateur was Stalin himself, however, he quickly fell in line. Despite the success of the JCP, Nosaka confessed to past errors in a vigorous "self-criticism" (*jiko hihansho*) of his "rightist opportunistic tendencies."[13]

At Stalin's instruction and with Chinese support, the JCP adopted a radical program of violent struggle. The official party history understates this relapse into "ultraleft adventurism" when it claims that "unjustifiable interference by foreign parties of the big socialist powers" created "confusion" within the JCP.[14] What Langer more aptly calls "a virtual death plunge into violent action" created more than mere confusion.[15] It stimulated energetic repression by SCAP and the Japanese government, and it alienated Japanese voters. The next general election (1952) sent a single JCP representative to the Diet. The party was once again underground, pursuing a "national liberation democratic movement" strategy—that is, guerrilla war. With Stalin broadcasting messages about the Japanese "courageous fight for independence," the party staged large-scale demonstrations and occasional violence that led only to further repression.

This line was counterproductive, and party leaders knew it. By July 1955, with public support dissipated and Stalin and Tokuda both dead, the party was ready to start over again. At its Sixth Party Congress, the JCP selected a "new" leadership. Nosaka, who had been in hiding, returned to a tumultuous greeting to become first secretary and Miyamoto Kenji became chair of the party's Standing Committee.[16] The revolutionary line was formally abandoned. After a short apprenticeship, Miyamoto became secretary-general and Nosaka was elevated to the largely honorary post of chairman in 1958. Although the party would continue to make mistakes by tying itself too closely to foreign powers—as in 1963 when it embraced Chinese opposition to the partial nuclear test ban treaty in disregard of Japanese public sentiment—Miyamoto would lead the JCP to a relatively independent and relatively successful electoral path. Meanwhile, Nosaka betrayed the party by continuing to accept secret funding from Moscow, thereby ensuring difficulties for at least another decade.[17] That notwithstanding, under Miyamoto the JCP evolved from "an almost grudging acceptance of parliamentary tactics to an appreciation of the transformation of . . . Japan into an advanced industrial . . . democratic society, in which neither the Soviet nor the Chinese—only the Eurocommunist model—has any relevance."[18]

Meanwhile, Togliatti had his hands full trying to establish an image of independence. The PCI was never pressed by Moscow to plan violent revolution, and Togliatti was persuaded that "the domestic and international balance of forces" would not support an insurrection in any event.[19] But, he faced constant pressure from his left wing to do more than play a parliamentary game.[20] On his right, Togliatti faced reformists who wanted greater distance from Moscow. Togliatti, however, would never stray far from the Soviet Union. He struggled to balance the party's desire for autonomy with its commitment to the international communist movement. Togliatti steered the PCI along his winding and bumpy "*via italiana*" with one hand on the wheel, never attempting to force Stalin's foot off the brake. Indeed, he did not even use the term "via italiana" until three years after Stalin's death. Meanwhile, other communist parties—China, Yugoslavia, Albania—were building their own roads.

In the spring of 1956, at the Twentieth Party Congress of the Communist Party of the Soviet Union (CPSU), Nikita Khrushchev shocked the communist world with a speech denouncing Stalin's errors and excesses. Stalin was a hero of many in the Italian working class. Now he was dead, and his guiding myths were to be buried.[21] Characteristically, Togliatti adjusted. Now he would repudiate Stalin using tools provided by Khrushchev, who proclaimed that there could be different roads to socialism—albeit under Soviet leadership. Togliatti seized on this new line and began to speak of a "polycentric" international communist system.[22]

The new road in Moscow was important, but the new ones in Eastern Europe were treacherous. After the 1956 CPSU Congress, Togliatti declared the Soviet model should not be obligatory. He celebrated "the full autonomy of the individual movements and Communist parties."[23] But within months, rebellions in Eastern Europe confronted him with an epochal test of this doctrine. He failed. Togliatti retreated, in June 1956 denouncing workers in Poznan, Poland whose workplace grievances had taken them into the streets. He reaffirmed his loyalty to Moscow and supported Soviet repression, blaming the nascent revolt on capitalist meddling. In the autumn, he applauded the Soviet invasion of Hungary, labeling the revolt a reactionary uprising that could lead to a renascent fascism. As late as 1960 he was insisting that the Socialist Party's position of "neutralist autonomy" was retrograde. Since capitalism was organized globally, so must socialism be, and under Soviet leadership.[24] The Socialists, who openly condemned the Soviet Union, benefited; PCI membership dropped by more than one-third, and senior leaders bolted.[25] The PCI, which retreated from "polycentrism" because it grated on Soviet ears, was still a long way from Eurocommunism.

The same could be said of the JCP. Worse, the JCP had two potential foreign masters—the Chinese and the Soviets. Although it has been claimed that the JCP was "probably the least nationalist and assertive in its relations with the outside Communist world," by 1960 the JCP was openly insisting that the CPSU was no longer a vanguard of the world communist movement.[26] Miyamoto rejected Soviet efforts to reassert itself, declaring in Moscow that "all Marxist-Leninist parties are independent and have equal rights . . . The communist party of each country should decide the outlook and tasks of the revolution according to the specific historical and social conditions of its own country."[27] Rejecting Moscow did not mean full autonomy, however. It meant switching allegiances—at least temporarily. The JCP was wooed by China.[28] Although the Soviets never spoke of their ham-handed intervention in the ill-fated revolutionary period, Mao Tsetung personally apologized to Miyamoto in 1959 for China's role.[29] The communist world was dividing. The first big test was the Albanian tilt toward Peking in 1961. While the Italians and the French went along with the Soviets, the JCP refused to denounce Albania. Instead, the JCP raised the volume on its denunciation of Soviet efforts "to undermine" its position in Japan. Miyamoto referred to the JCP's "independence" (*jishu dokuritsu*) from Moscow for the first time in September 1963, but "independence" from Moscow was accompanied by what appeared to most observers as "out and out" (*chūkyō ippentō*) dependence on Peking.[30]

The Chinese were not much better at keeping their hands off the JCP. By 1966, the Chinese were renewing their insistence that the JCP pursue armed revolution, and the Chinese Communist Party (CCP) openly condemned the JCP for pursuing a parliamentary route and for its "betrayal of Lenin."[31] Believing the JCP to be on better terms with the Soviets than it in fact was, the CCP suddenly declared the JCP its "fourth enemy"— listed just behind U.S. imperialists, Soviet revisionists, and LDP reactionaries.[32] In a single remarkable stroke, Chou En-lai banned both Satō Eisaku and Kishi Nobusuke on the right, and Nosaka Sanzō and Miyamoto Kenji on the left, from travel to China. The CCP even began supplying funds to a Maoist group that had split from the JCP.

By the late 1960s, there were no more fraternal relations to be had. The only path that made sense was the one that Nosaka had started building in 1945. After a decade of frustrating fraternal denunciations—and after sustained successes at the polls—Miyamoto began to criticize the one-party model of governance. He declared in July 1969, when the JCP was winning 7 percent of the popular vote in the general elections, that if the JCP were to come to power, it would permit free functioning of opposition parties. By the early 1970s Miyamoto rejected the idea of socialist revolution in favor of a neutral, democratic Japan, and rejected all interference in the JCP's domestic affairs.[33] The JCP did not support unarmed neutrality and assumed nationalist positions vis-à-vis Japanese claims against the Soviets regarding the Northern Territories and vis-à-vis the Chinese regarding the Senkaku Islands. It disavowed any connection to student violence and acted as a responsible, non-corrupt, and principled competitor under established parliamentary rules. This all paid off at the polls. The JCP was governing widely in coalition at the local level, and was openly studying Eurocommunism—particularly the experience of the PCI.

The PCI had earned the status of role model. After the 1962 birth of the Center-Left in Italy the PCI shifted strategy, beginning with support for the European Economic Community.[34] Slower than China or Yugoslavia (or even the JCP) to declare independence from Moscow, Togliatti now stood his ground against a Soviet plan to coordinate the parties, and began to take on the role of loyal opposition. While the PCI would not be an open challenger, Togliatti did defend China against Soviet efforts to "excommunicate" the CCP from the international communist movement. By 1964 Togliatti had finally put some substance in his formula of "unity in diversity" by focusing on "bilateral parity" (*bilateralità*) with the CPSU.[35]

Togliatti made a real break just before his death (in August 1964), but it had an impact only posthumously. He had prepared a report to the CPSU outlining his views of the current state of international communism. Against General Secretary Brezhnev's wishes, the PCI published it as "Togliatti's Testament." The party used his blunt assessment—it was intended as an internal document—to justify the next fundamental transformation of the PCI. Enrico Belinguer had been in the party leadership since 1948, when he was a twenty-five-year-old representative of the Communist Youth. Togliatti had long used him to buffer Soviet demands, and Berlinguer moved vigorously to further distance the party from Moscow.[36]

Ironically, it was *American* rather than Soviet heavy-handedness that persuaded Berlinguer to take the final plunge. The U.S.-supported coup that toppled Salvador Allende in Chile in September 1973 convinced Berlinguer that the PCI could never govern Italy on its own. From that time forward, he ceased speaking of the "leftist alternative" and added reference to a "democratic alternative" and close cooperation with popular forces.[37] With the PCI doing well at the polls, Berlinguer reassured voters that the party stood for the great-power status quo—a PCI government would never take Italy out of NATO. He continued to insist (disingenuously) on the PCI's independence: "We have never had the least concern that the Soviet Union would tell us what we should or should not do."[38] He added with some justification that the *DC* had the greater problem, for the PCI's independence from the Soviet Union was surely greater than the DC's independence from the United States.[39]

By 1976, the PCI's decoupling from the Soviets was nearly complete. Berlinguer reaped enormous electoral benefits by criticizing the Portuguese Communist Party, which seemed poised to seize power with military support, and by fully endorsing European integration. The finishing touch was his speech to the Twenty-fifth Party Congress of the CPSU, where for the first time he dared to use the term "pluralism" and proclaimed the age of "Eurocommunism" in which personal freedom and cultural diversity would be guaranteed.[40] Despite the fact that he "punctiliously defended and wanted to preserve the Italian Communist identity," he was fundamentally repositioning the party.[41] Berlinguer had become by far the most popular politician in Italy, and the Italian center was listening carefully. In April 1978, despite initial U.S. and NATO reservations, the Communists and the Christian Democrats made their "Historic Compromise." The PCI supported a "national solidarity" cabinet, from the outside, and was rewarded with a variety of goodies, including control of one of the public television stations. For a time, the ease with which public policy was formulated—as well as its quality—improved markedly.

The PCI and the JCP, each having enjoyed considerable electoral success, were well positioned to seize the opportunities created by U.S.-Soviet détente. In the spring of 1976, as Berlinguer's PCI was winning an unprecedented level of confidence from the Italian electorate, Fuwa Tetsuzō, at forty-six the youngest member of the central committee of the JCP, published an essay praising the institutions of the democratic state. Four months later, the party formally embraced the ideals of the U.S. Declaration of Independence and the French Declaration of the Rights of Man.[42] Fuwa was Miyamoto's protégé, mirroring the relationship between Berlinguer and Togliatti. He had joined the party in 1947 while still a physics student at the University of Tokyo. Also like Berlinguer, he was of the first postwar generation, without personal experience of wartime repression.[43] The two men signaled possibilities for a new era of pragmatic communist party politics. In Italy these possibilities have been realized, while in Japan they have not.

CHOOSING TO CHANGE

In moving the party away from Moscow, Enrico Berlinguer had actively positioned the party for fundamental change before his untimely death in 1984.[44] Massimo D'Alema, editor of *L'Unità* under Berlinguer—and prime minister in 1997—says that Berlinguer "stopped at the border."[45] Achille Occhetto, who took the PCI "across the border" to become a social democratic party, credits Berlinguer with openly establishing the PCI as a critic of totalitarian politics.[46] But it was no smooth process, nor an easy choice.

The party was in deep crisis after Berlinguer's death.[47] It had gone along with Berlinguer's Historic Compromise but came away without palpable gains. Its great electoral surge was a decade old, and its deal with the DC and the Socialists was starting to come undone. The left and right wings, young and old cadres, were polarized. A resounding electoral defeat in 1987 left the PCI with fewer seats in Parliament than it had twenty years earlier. Both electoral support and the PCI organization were crumbling. Amid open criticism, the leadership cleaned house. Berlinguer's successor, Alessandro Natta, appointed the fifty-one-year-old Achille Occhetto as party vice-secretary. Natta used him to assuage the frustrations of the younger cadres, to float trial balloons calling for a return to a policy-based political strategy. Occhetto responded as an active and aggressive—if inconsistent—voice for change. When Natta fell ill in June 1988, he became general secretary of the party.

From the beginning, Occhetto undertook what some resented as desecration. Early on he criticized the extent to which Togliatti had allowed great power politics to undermine the "great political and moral victory of the Resistance [and] the ideals of our patrimony."[48] His pointed denunciations of Soviet communism were in open contrast with his admiration for Willy Brandt, the German Socialist who had led his party to abandon Marxism in 1958.[49] Yet, as late as June 1988, Occhetto was speaking to the central committee of "reconstruction." He was not exhorting his comrades to create a fundamentally new identity.[50] Indeed, although he introduced the idea of a "new course" at the March 1989 Communist Party Congress in Rome, Occhetto promised the PCI would never change its name: "Our name," he declared, "has been and is glorious and deserves respect."[51]

But that suddenly changed. Just days after the collapse of the Berlin Wall, on 12 November 1989, at a rally in Bolognina—an annual PCI event to reaffirm the party's ties to a heroic partisan battle—Occhetto announced a historic change (*svolta*).[52] In a stroke, he eliminated the deepest, most intractable fault line in Italian politics. He told the assembled Resistance veterans that with the Cold War now over "we must move ahead with the same courage that was then demonstrated by the Resistance."[53] The extant debate between socialist unity and neo-communism had become stale, and the time had come for a new vision for society and its institutions—"a new political formation" (*nuova formazione*) and a new identity. He declared: "Everything can change."[54]

Although he insisted that this transformation was not an impulsive invention, nor even that it was solely his idea, Occhetto at first refused to reveal precisely what he had in mind. Yet he insisted "everything in the whole world has changed." "It is," Occhetto insisted, "the end of everything."[55] It was certainly the end of "class struggle" as the unifying idea, but finding a new identity for Communists would take time. He was in uncharted waters, for this was a full-blown identity crisis. As Kertzer points out: "To immediately propose a new name risked provoking a trauma too great for party members to process. The new symbolism would have to be negotiated in a longer process . . . [for] what was most important *was* the name: the importance of not being Communist."[56] For a time, the new party identity was referred to simply as *la cosa* ("the thing"). Occhetto proclaimed: "First comes the thing and then the name."[57] He understood the challenge for the party faithful, many of whose very identities were "Communist" first and "Italian" second. Emotional bonds were deep. Occhetto—a member of the central committee for two decades—received support from the next generation of party elites who were convinced that the senior leadership (*capi storici*) was out of touch with political realities.[58] These younger men could lay no claim to the Resistance and wanted no association with Togliatti. They celebrated Berlinguer, but he had not gone far enough. They squared off against intransigent former Stalinists whose personal identification with the party, its symbols, and its icons— for example, the anthem (*bandiera rossa*), the hammer and sickle, and the venerated founding fathers such as Gramsci—rivaled (and likely superseded) the religious faith of Catholics and the patriotic fervor of nationalists. Catholics would have talked of excommunication, nationalists of exile.[59] The faithful mourned the passing of their party.

Occhetto understood that the battle for control of the future had first to be a battle for control of the past. Each step he took involved a legitimation of change through reference to a hallowed past. Battle lines were drawn between those who would reconstruct that past and those who would tenaciously defend the current version, between those who would control the naming of this "new thing" and those who would not countenance the very idea.[60] In the event, the reformers won a two-thirds majority at the 1990 Party Congress. Declaring that "the future has ancient roots," at the final PCI Party Congress in January 1991, they proclaimed the formation of the Democratic Party of the Left (Partito Democratico della Sinistra or PDS).[61]

The Italian communists had split irreconcilably. The PDS now faced off against the "Refounded Communists" and took their battle over the patrimony of the PCI—the legal right to use the symbols that stir the souls of the faithful—to the courts. The PDS, awarded the right to use the hammer and sickle of the PCI, thoughtfully deployed it at the roots of a solid oak tree with green leaves—representing its past and its future growth. A mixture of environmentalism, feminism, individualism, and even Catholic progressivism superseded the Marxist "class struggle."[62] The PDS stressed freedom and the rights of citizens. It sought to redistribute the tax burden, and favored the EU and NATO. It no longer embraced a coherent ideology, but neither would it attempt to be an all-encompassing subculture. It was now a thoroughly social-democratic political formation that sought to appeal as much to the middle classes as to workers.[63] And its

Party leader Achille Occhetto explains in 1990 that it is impossible to completely abandon the Communist heritage. Reproduced courtesy of Giorgio Forattini.

leader did not survive the transition. Achille Occhetto was shunted aside after he was defeated by Silvio Berlusconi. When Berlusconi stumbled within months, Occhetto's colleagues took power in a center-left "Olive Coalition" that governed for most of the next decade.[64]

CHOOSING NOT TO CHANGE

Just one month after the fall of the Berlin Wall—and barely weeks after Achille Occhetto announced the historical "*svolta*"—Miyamoto Kenji opened the Seventh Plenum of the Central Committee in December 1989 with an address entitled: "A Time of Historic Upheaval—Now Is the Time to Aspire to Realize Positive Goals." Expectations ran high that the JCP would follow the PCI, but he told delegates that it was imperative for Japanese communists to hold firmly to their belief in "scientific socialism." He insisted that the JCP *not* change. While others "yielded to the pressure of the Emperor system and collaborated in Japan's war of aggression, even dissolving their organizations to form the Imperial Rule Assistance Association and after the war emerged to form new parties," the JCP was still the JCP—and always would be.[65] Nothing had changed.

In 1972, one analyst had suggested that the JCP was already a "prisoner of the past . . . Only a minority group [those purged from the leadership] and the lower and younger Communist cadres show a tendency to reexamine Marxist premises in light of postwar Japanese reality."[66] Miyamoto's successor, Fuwa Tetsuzō, was one of that group. He long had been engaged in an effort to make Marxism-Leninism palatable to the electorate. He framed it in Eurocommunism in the 1970s, in perestroika in the 1980s, and in vitriolic critiques of Stalinism after the Soviet archives opened in the 1990s. But throughout, while emphasizing the JCP's independence, he insisted that the JCP was the "correct" inheritor of scientific socialism. Events in communist countries did not mean that the JCP should change, but rather showed that the JCP had been right all along. Despite his reputation for flexibility, Fuwa ordered party branches to concentrate on communist theory in order to rebuild the party. And he decried the idea of abandoning the communist label: "We have no intention of throwing away such a proud name. The JCP was the only Japanese political party that fought for democracy and against the war before the Second World War and we're proud of this."[67] He did not see the possibilities for the instrumental use of history that Occhetto seized so effectively.

Displaying a considerable understanding of the Italian situation, Fuwa denies that the Italian and Japanese communists have much in common.[68] The JCP was an "outlaw" from the start and never built the strong subculture that the PCI enjoyed. It never participated in an antifascist Resistance with other progressive forces. Says Fuwa: "We had no Resistance because we had no tradition of democracy in Japan . . . The young JCP faced state power naked and alone [*hadaka de butsukata*]."[69] Moreover, he argues that the Italian geopolitical situation was markedly different, and insists that the JCP was never as servile to the Soviets as the Italian communists had been.[70]

All this adds up for him to a different calculus. In 1997 Fuwa declared: "We will not change the party name to make it easier for voters to choose our party. Voters have become accustomed to the name we have. We hope that they realize from that name that we take responsibility for both our past and future behavior. More and more people understand this, and are telling us not to change our name."[71] Shii Kazuo, then director of the party secretariat and Fuwa's heir apparent, took umbrage at a radio interviewer's suggestion that Communism had failed:

You referred to 'the failure of communism.' But I do not think so. Soviet society, especially after Stalin, changed a great deal, both politically and eco-

Fuwa Tetsuzō as an inscrutable intellectual in 1990. Reproduced courtesy of Nishimura Koichi.

nomically. It is too early to conclude there has been a failure of communism just because such an oppressive regime collapsed . . . In our view, we will supersede capitalism over a long period of time and proceed to a more advanced society. We are a Party that takes responsibility for the past, the present and the future, and thus wish to use our name with care."[72]

There would be no svolta for the JCP. But there still was considerable room for fine-tuning the party's position. In the late 1990s Fuwa began criticizing Lenin for the first time.[73] In July 1998 the JCP announced that it would no longer demand abrogation of the Mutual Security Treaty with the United States as a condition for joining a ruling coalition.[74] That same month, in an election widely seen as a thorough repudiation of the LDP, the JCP increased its representation in the upper House of Councilors and won 13 percent of the vote (but it still had less than 10 percent of the seats). The Communists still had a long way to go before they could become an indispensable partner in a ruling coalition.

The JCP continued to work through incremental changes rather than through transformation. In early 2000, Fuwa declared the new decade to be an era of progressive possibilities. He reiterated that the JCP was prepared to help form a "democratic coalition government" if the ruling LDP coalition was defeated.[75] The problem was that he still had not opted for sufficient change. All the logical coalition partners in a "Japanese Olive Coalition"—most notably the largest opposition party, the Democratic Party (DP)—refused to consider an alliance until the JCP changed its name and thoroughly revised its platform. The Democrats insisted that all references to "revolution" be expunged. Fuwa refused. In the June 2000 election the DP made substantial gains while the JCP lost votes and seats. But with the opposition divided, the LDP continued in power.

The JCP was more marginal than ever. In 1999, the JCP had held twenty-six seats in the House of Representatives; in the July 2000 elections it lost six.[76] If the JCP was still "right," its message was lost on Japanese voters. In September 2000 the party responded by reorganizing its constitution, eliminating the preamble, and replacing the definition of the JCP as the "vanguard party of the working class" by the "party of the working class and the Japanese people." But it also reaffirmed its opposition to the alliance with the United States, to the imperial household, and to the Self-Defense Forces.[77] Despite repeated overtures from the Democrats—and even some from Ozawa's Liberals—the JCP was not going far enough to entice partners. A Japanese "Olive Coalition" was nowhere in prospect.

Even if we acknowledge the JCP's considerable pragmatism and its appeal as haven for protest voters, it is hard to argue with Peter Berton that "Fuwa, the physics graduate, seems to have a talent for commenting on Marxist-Leninist-Stalinist classics and engaging in sterile debates. He has yet to come up with a creative look at the present political, economic, and social reality in Japan . . . Prospects are not good for the JCP to overcome its history and ideology and present new, relevant, and attractive ideas."[78] Remarkably, it may still be as true in the early twenty-first century as it was in the middle of the Cold War that the JCP leadership is "more interested in being 'right' in terms of Marxist-Leninist orthodoxy than in having power as such."[79] Asked if any of the 187 members of the party's central committee has ever raised the issue of changing the party's identity, Fuwa explained: "It has never come up. We have no intention to change and will never toss aside our socialist identity . . . We intend to convince people to come around to our position, rather than the reverse."[80]

Change cannot be ruled out. At the Twenty-second Party Congress in November 2000, the JCP further softened its emphasis on revolutionary change and underwent a generational transition. Forty-seven-year-old Shii Kazuo succeeded Fuwa Tetsuzō as general secretary, and ten of the party's top twenty positions changed. Although they reaffirmed scientific socialism as the "theoretical basis" of the JCP, the younger JCP leadership conspicuously avoided terms such as "socialist revolution."[81] The choices that Fuwa declined to make are still available.

CONSTRAINTS AND CHOICES

From their very beginnings the communist parties of Italy and Japan have been subject to many of the same great forces. Internally, they were riven by disputes between reformers and revolutionaries and were repressed by similar forces of reaction. Externally, they faced an environment shaped by relations between the great powers, within which they seemed mere pawns. And for most of the Cold War, the PCI and the JCP stood on the losing side in most of their nation's crucial foreign policy choices. The PCI opposed Italian membership in NATO, in the European Coal and Steel Community, and in the Treaty of Rome that created the European Common Market. As late as 1978, the PCI opposed Italian membership in the European Monetary Union. The JCP opposed the separate peace treaty, the alliance with the United States, and the revision of the Mutual Security Treaty. It still seeks abrogation of the alliance with the United States and holds the Self-Defense Forces to be unconstitutional. It does not follow, however, as the Right would have it, that this was because the PCI and JCP were simply "servants of Moscow." Each had its own vision of national interests, one no more consistent with Moscow's preferences than were the positions of the DC or the LDP with Washington's.[82]

Nothing in the choices made by Occhetto or Fuwa after the Cold War was "natural" or predetermined. Nothing in Italian or Japanese history *required* the PCI and JCP to take particular tacks. Just as the mantles of Palmiro Togliatti and Enrico Berlinguer were available to Achille Occhetto, those of Nosaka Sanzō and Matsumoto Kenji were available to Fuwa Tetsuzō. Each elected to tailor his mantle in a different fashion. Plenty of history was available to each leader, however he might wish to deploy it. Indeed, as we have seen, each might have chosen the *opposite* of what he actually chose. Occhetto might have used Togliatti to continue a proud independence from other parties—in just the way that Fuwa used Matsumoto. Alternatively, Fuwa could have engineered the same abrupt shift that Nosaka had in 1945. He shed the mantle of Tokuda altogether, just as Occhetto shed the mantle of Gramsci, and chose to focus on Nosaka's perfidious betrayal of the party instead of his "loveable" strategy to achieve power.

Indeed, the PCI was a mass-based party, brimming with ritualized representations of a heroic past and swaddled in the legitimacy of the Resistance. It was surely *less* likely to break with the foundational elements of communist ideology than was the elite-led JCP, which had no popular past to build upon.[83] Even if the svolta was made easier by the fall of the Berlin Wall, the Italian communists were considerably more constrained than were the Japanese at the end of the Cold War. Occhetto and Fuwa give us a particularly clear window on why constraint is necessary but not sufficient in the analysis of change. It is easy to understate the ability of determined actors, as Lanzara reminds us:

> Identity—individual or collective—is a sunk cost: the higher the investment (cognitive, normative, ideological, emotional, existential) individuals or organizations make in a specific identity . . . the stronger the loyalty to that identity will be . . . Identities, similar to institutions, have inertial and resilient properties. Once they have clung to actors for a long time and have become deeply ingrained, they are hard to relinquish.[84]

The lesson we should learn is that the distance between "hard" and "impossible" is very great. That distance can be spanned by creative individuals who are determined to tease legitimacy for the new from affect for the old. Soon after he had set the svolta in motion, Occhetto insisted: "I did what I had to, nothing more and nothing less."[85] As we have seen, this was simply not the case. Occhetto did not *have* to do anything. What he *chose* to do, and the way he chose to do it, changed everything.

CHAPTER TWELVE

Options on the Right:

UMBERTO BOSSI, SILVIO BERLUSCONI, OZAWA ICHIRŌ, AND

ISHIHARA SHINTARŌ

> Nothing is more certain than that improvement in human affairs is wholly
> the work of the uncontented characters.
> J. S. Mill, *Considerations on Representative Government*

We have seen how Communists with limited and declining resources were
either choosing or using the past in the wake of the Cold War. While they
were sorting themselves out on the Left, ambitious politicians on the Right
were doing likewise. Mobilizing more abundant resources, conservatives in
both countries explored two distinct routes to power—one local and the
other national. If we consider resources alone, the local route ought to
have been more successful in Italy than in Japan. After all, by most accounts, regional identities remain more salient in Italy. But in fact the regional leader failed in Italy, whereas the one best poised to succeed in
Japan built a local, rather than national, base. In Italy, Umberto Bossi
"manufactured the North"—but Silvio Berlusconi trumped him by "consolidating the nation." In Japan, no one of comparable historical imagination appeared. Ozawa Ichirō spoke wanly of "restoration," but failed to sustain a coalition of elites at the center, while Ishihara Shintarō positioned
himself to succeed in national politics from his base as governor of Tokyo.
In short, it seems that neither large opportunity nor abundant resources is
more important than the imagination of the leaders who mobilize them.

BOSSI'S CONSTRUCTION PROJECT

Local political resources seem particularly abundant in Italy, and irre-
dentist claims have always hung over the modern Italian polity. In 1919,

316

Fiume was "occupied" by a faux army led by the poet Gabriele D'Annunzio. After the Great War, a half million Slovenes on the Istrian Peninsula lived as "compulsory Italians," and although most of the area was transferred to Yugoslavia after 1945, Slovenes in Italian Trieste are still a "majority minority" with special legal status.[1] French was the language of Val d'Aosta for three hundred years, and only the granting of local autonomy prevented a secessionist movement in 1945. In 1999, newly elected right-wing Austrian leader Joerg Haider suggested that the German speakers who dominate Southern Tyrol (Alto Adige) rejoin Austria.[2] Ethnic parties from these regions have been appealing to Rome and to Brussels for autonomy since the 1970s.

The northeast has been particularly fertile ground for political movements. All of Italy's new political movements of the past one hundred and twenty years—socialism, Christian democracy, and fascism among them—originated there.[3] In 1922, a full-scale taxpayers revolt coincided with the fascist assaults in northern Italy. Later, in the postwar confusion, other movements, such as the Uomo Qualunque (Any Man), emerged as a populist response to existing parties. None would have a major influence on Italian politics, but regionally based parties never disappeared. The Sudtiroler Volkspartei in Alto Adige, the Partito Sardo d'Azione in Sardinia, and the Union Valdôtaine in the Piedmont preceded the "new regional movements," the so-called *leghe* (leagues), that sought autonomy in the 1980s.[4] Indeed, it is surprising how few separatist movements have evolved into serious challenges to Italian unity.[5]

Past failures have not deterred present efforts. The latest and most ambitious attempt is the Lega Nord (Northern League), founded in December 1989 from the merger of local parties in Lombardy, Piedmont, Emilia-Romagna, Liguria, Tuscany, and Veneto. The leader is Umberto Bossi (b. 1942), a scruffy, unpolished man of immense charisma and unbounded ambition, who does nothing to discourage caricatures of the Lega as his own monocratic organization. The force of "King Bossi's" (Bossi Re) personality often deflects attention from questions about how much of the Lega's philosophy was original to Bossi, and how much the handiwork of his colleagues.[6] What clearly *was* his handiwork was the immediate assertion of his Lombard League. Bossi moved determinedly to eliminate other leaders, and he made sure that the symbols of the Lombard League dominated the Lega Nord. These symbols deserve attention, for their acceptance was the most difficult element of the Lega's mobilization and Umberto Bossi's most significant contribution to Italian politics.

Bossi did nothing less than manufacture the North.[7] He transformed a widespread resentment of central government into a regional identity that, in turn, redrew the electoral map of the entire peninsula. It is no

Umberto Bossi, champion of a decentralized Italy, is depicted in 1992 as a disjointed Lombard knight. Reproduced courtesy of Giorgio Forattini.

small irony that the North had never been much more than a mere geographic expression. The North had no political identity, no common history, no distinct set of collective values. Its "natural" divisions were among its cities, between city and countryside, and between Catholics and Communists. As Diamanti points out: "Not having a recognized fatherland, Bossi decided to invent one, and imposed its words and symbols on the political scene."[8] Because this was "a place without history"—a "virtual territory"—it was a place where history could be manufactured for political ends.[9] The Lega took this project upon itself. It declared in 1992 that "in order to do politics we need to produce culture."[10] Bossi correctly perceived that two targets would help him: widespread resentment of the South, and discontent with the central government. They came together in his pithy denunciation of the central government as the "Roman Thief" (Roma Ladrona). He spoke of how the South had picked the pockets of the North—too much northern wealth had been transferred to too many southern slackers. In his standard stump speech, Bossi quoted a shopkeeper from Bergamo who complained: "'For thirty years I paid for the Cassa del Mezzogiorno, having been told it is the right thing to do because the South is poor. I agree, in theory. But I do not understand how come now, having been given a sack of money, the South is still poor.' This woman has a point. If all the profuse resources of the North are not enough, isn't it a sign that the system is broken and needs to be changed?"[11] Although he conveniently ignored the fact that national unification entailed a net transfer of wealth from the South to the North, Bossi was correct that politicians had hijacked the development policies of the 1950s. The gap between the rich North and the poor South had widened.[12] Bossi called for taxpayers' strikes—"assaults" on an Italian fiscal system he denounced as "arrogant," "dishonorable," and "usurious."[13] He was playing to his supporters: tax revenue collected from their region ought to be spent in their region and politicians must not be allowed to steal from northerners to buy southern votes.

He was also playing to their prejudices. Surveys show that League members do not oppose marriage across regions, but they do show a lower toleration of Sicilians and Africans.[14] These prejudices have a distinguished pedigree. In October 1860, Luigi Carlo Farini wrote of the South to Count Cavour (who had never traveled on the peninsula outside of his native Piedmont): "What barbarians! This is not Italy! It is Africa. The Bedouins compare well to these louts. They are outside civil virtue."[15] For Bossi and the Lega, the North is European and the South is African. Bossi is blunt: "Mafia, thieves, delinquents, and vermin penetrated the North because we were distracted."[16] Not every supporter bought this racist package. In November 1995, Irene Pivetti, an early activist and one of its first deputies in Parliament, left the party, declaring: "I loved the League but . . . I did not join it to defend the white race."[17]

To be fair, Bossi was much busier with folkloric contrivances than he was with a strictly racist agenda. The first public ritual took place near Bergamo in 1990, when he took five hundred Lega faithful to the site where the Lombard knights had taken an oath of allegiance to fight Emperor Frederick Barbarossa in 1212. The five hundred became ten thousand by 1996, and the solemnity of an event designed to evoke an unfinished battle against oppressive foreign powers had become a boisterous, paramilitary gathering.[18]

They had a great deal to be boisterous about. Bossi's ardent manufacture of symbolic resources attracted the attention of the media, and the media got the attention of the public; his message got through to large numbers of voters.[19] The Lega won its first major victory at the polls in April 1992, when it took 9 percent of the popular vote and won fifty-five seats in the lower chamber and twenty-five in the upper chamber—all at the expense of traditional political forces. In June 1993, a *leghista* became mayor of Milan. The political map of Italy was being redrawn. The Lega was suddenly the second largest party in northern Italy and the third nationwide.[20] A short-lived ruling coalition with Fini and Berlusconi dissolved in mutual vituperation—Bossi referred to Fini as "Mussolini's grandchild" and to Berlusconi as "Berluskaiser."[21] Bossi also had little generosity for the Vatican. He argued that although the Church had the right to exist, it had no right to intervene in political affairs.[22] Flush with popular support, Bossi was going forward with his own project—making it up (and making enemies of all the major political forces) as he went along. His region might have been "virtual," but for a time at least his political clout was nearly as considerable as his bravado.

In July 1995, after years of groping for the right formula, Bossi declared the independence of his "Promised Land." Italy would have three separate republics, two named after proud civilizations (one fictional, the other real)—Padania in the North, Etruria in the Center—and the third, "Sud," in the South. There would be a Padanian parliament in Mantua and a capital in Venice.[23] The following year, in mid-September 1996, Bossi undertook a highly publicized and widely ridiculed journey starting at the Alpine source of the Po River, where he collected a cruet of "holy water, crystalline water, non-*mafia* water . . . Water that is within the fields, the trees, and the children of Padania." He poured this water into the Adriatic Sea.[24] Bossi was not only inventing an indigenous Padanian past. The preamble of the "Declaration of Independence and Sovereignty of Padania" has a familiar ring to American ears:

> We, the people of Padania, gathered on the great Po River of Emilia, of Friuli, of Liguria, of Lombardy, of Marche, of Piedmont, of Romagna, of Southern Tyrol/Alto Adige, of Tuscany, of Trentino, of Umbria, of the Aosta Valley, of Venice, and of Venezia-Giulia come together today, 15 September 1996, in a Constituent Assembly to affirm and declare that when in the course of human events it becomes necessary for the people to dissolve the political bonds which have connected them with another . . . [25]

The declaration goes on to claim that Padania forms "a natural cultural and social community, based on a shared patrimony of values, culture and common history," while "the history of the Italian state . . . is [one] of colonial oppression, economic exploitation, and moral violence." Amid the solemnity, Italian flags were lowered, Giuseppe Verdi's *Va Pensiero* was adopted as the Padanian national anthem, and international recognition was sought.

It was mostly downhill from there. Bossi was, after all, trying to build a nation on a segmented base. The proposition that there were two or three Italys foundered on the problem that there were an even greater number of "Norths."[26] As we have seen, Italians simultaneously take pride in their local, regional, national, and European identities. The number of Lega supporters who were proud to be Italian (61%) was nearly as high as the number of Lega supporters who were proud to be northerners (68%), and this was fatal to Bossi's plans.[27] It was also Umberto Bossi's bad luck that other, equally ambitious leaders could mobilize Italians on these other dimensions.

The Lega vote, greater than 10 percent in the 1996 legislative elections, slipped to less than 5 percent in the June 1999 European elections. It fell not only nationally but even in its own northeast and northwest bastions. Fully one-third of northern voters thought that independence was unattainable, and 10 percent thought it would be a "catastrophe for the country."[28] Even the majority of those who supported independence preferred federalism within an Italian state to secession.

Lega supporters were fed up with the status quo, but despite Bossi's most inventive efforts, they felt Italian. They were shopkeepers and small-firm owners—mostly middle-aged and middle-income postwar adults who had left the DC and the Socialists in equal numbers; the Lega never challenged the bastions of Communist or post-communist support.[29] In the event, the *leghisti* may have had little more in common than protest and an accident of geography. Bossi claimed that northerners were "different" and so should be treated differently, but they also differed among themselves. Their territorial identities could be activated and made politically salient, but were never uniform. They were mobilized at a time when the appeal of the existing political parties had been exhausted.[30] Bossi, however, had the bad fortune of colliding head-on with another political entrepreneur—Silvio Berlusconi—who had a different and *national* idea for mobilizing anti-system sentiment. In 2000 and 2001 Bossi would abandon his dream of an independent North and realign with Berlusconi. It was Berlusconi who would prevail, co-opting part of Bossi's program in the process.

FORZA ITALIA: BERLUSCONI'S NATIONAL ALTERNATIVE

The Milanese Silvio Berlusconi (b. 1937) is a self-made real estate and media mogul whose combined holdings form Italy's second-largest business empire. Like Bossi, Berlusconi is a relentless self-promoter with immense populist appeal, but his resources are much greater. Berlusconi owns three television networks as well as newspapers and one of Italy's best football clubs. Widely reported to be Italy's richest man (and officially its richest legislator), he has effectively bottomless pockets.[31] The comparison to Bossi is limited; a better comparison can be made to Ross Perot in the United States—with bits of Donald Trump, George Steinbrenner, and Michael Milkin mixed in.[32] The difference, of course, is that no American tycoon has succeeded to Berlusconi's extent.

Berlusconi had long been kept at a distance by polite society and, whether as cause or effect, he had disdain for Italy's mainstream business elite. Like other outsiders, Berlusconi benefited from relationships to politicians who eagerly accepted his funding, and who could ensure his further economic success.[33] With the loss of some of his political allies to Mani Pulite prosecution, Berlusconi perceived the need for a new political product. He understood that Socialist Bettino Craxi's day had passed, that the DC was lost in the post-Cold War wilderness, that the appeal of the Lega was too narrow.[34] Borrowing the slogan of the national football team, he declared the establishment of a new political party, Forza Italia (Go Italy!). Berlusconi made his formal appearance on the political stage in January 1994, just months before the first elections after the electoral reform.

Berlusconi insisted that the values of Forza Italia are those of all Western democracies: freedom, individual rights, and personal liberty. Like Bossi, Berlusconi appealed to those fed up with corruption, existing parties, public enterprise, immigrants, taxes, and other manifestations of an "unfair" and "unjust" state. He would lead Italy away from centralism, eliminate excessive bureaucracy, and stop abuse of the judicial system to damage political adversaries. Both politicians stressed the supremacy of the people over the state. Berlusconi's means transcended regional identities, however, and reached for an Italian pride long submerged beneath failed ambitions and corruption. His core appeal was *national.* Berlusconi positioned himself as the latest in a long line of Italian leaders: in an open letter to the Italian press he declared a "commitment to representing an Italy with international standing of the first rank."[35]

At Bossi's invitation, Berlusconi spoke before the Lega Nord in Milan in December 1993. He framed their fundamental difference, but with an outstretched hand, saying: "The name *leghista* is positive, and stands for improved federalism, above all in fiscal matters, [but] the unity of Italy is not under discussion."[36] Several months later, in his first appearance as the leader of Forza Italia, in Rome, he declared that his Italy would be "unified—diverse, and indissoluble." He included the South in his vision for Italian identity: "The Mezzogiorno needs trust, security, and hope. It is the true reserve for the development of all Italy if it is to win the challenge of Europe . . . Our work is itself to liberate the spontaneous forces of the South."[37] Nor had he omitted the Church. The Catholic Church had become openly hostile to the Lega, which it feared would undermine social solidarity and dismantle the social safety net.[38] Speaking in Palermo to a national Church conference, Berlusconi reaffirmed the importance of Catholic family values: "In this moment of difficult social, cultural, and political transition in which we are living, our nation needs more than ever the contribution and the testimony of the Catholic community."[39]

The popular "Clean Hands" investigation and the successful reconstruction of the communist Left should have led to a great victory for Achille Occhetto's PDS in the March 1994 election. But Occhetto, apparently spent by internal battles, failed to take Berlusconi seriously. The PDS managed only to paint "a gray horizon with vague outlines still recognizable as something dull and similar to the immediate past."[40] Berlusconi, by contrast, innovated brilliantly. He was the first leader since Mussolini to use Italian national identity as a palpable political resource. He transformed what once was "at best a loosely organized marketing vehicle for his candidacy" into a bona fide political party.[41] Bossi, who had once called Berlusconi a "detergent salesman [who] was born to remind us of the old regime," reluctantly joined Berlusconi's government in 1994.[42] Berlusconi's national appeal—no less manufactured than Bossi's regional one—proved successful. Berlusconi put the Left on notice that the Right was still a vigorous political force at the same time that he pulled the plug on Bossi's regional challenge.

Still, Berlusconi's early successes were punctuated by political miscalculation. He won power in 1994 with two separate electoral cartels—one in the North with Bossi and one in the Center-South with former fascists led

Silvio Berlusconi keeps Umberto Bossi on a short leash in 2001 and assures him that they are about to take power. Reproduced courtesy of *Corriere della Sera.*

by Gianfranco Fini.[43] His electoral strategy worked brilliantly and produced a comfortable majority. But Berlusconi had built a three-legged stool, and the legs were of unequal length. Fini and Bossi could not work together, and Berlusconi's alliances fell apart soon after the election. Bossi declared that Fini "comes from the darkest part of history," and called his party a group of "fascist hangmen."[44] He likewise dismissed Berlusconi as an egotistical dictator. Berlusconi's first government of "dubious allies" held office for only seven months.[45]

Berlusconi was soon under prosecution for the very corruption he had promised to eradicate. Although he was convicted of financial crimes in 1997 and 1998, he remained Italy's most popular politician, and his Forza Italia the most potent force on the Right. Berlusconi remained a critically important broker for—and ultimately against—reform. His convictions were overturned on appeal, and he continued to project a ubiquitous national presence through his control of Italy's private television networks and the nation's most powerful print empire.

Not surprisingly, Berlusconi's unrivaled control of the media generated charges of conflict of interest. These charges were not new. He had first had to respond to demands that he limit his media holdings in 1994. Berlusconi resigned from all managerial positions in his firms, but he turned management over to his closest associates and remained the majority shareholder. In February 2001, just months before the May election, the Italian Senate approved a conflict of interest bill designed to hamper

Berlusconi's election prospects.[46] The bill would make it illegal for any high-level public official to hold a stake worth more than $7 million in a business. It would also prevent a prime minister from holding any stake in a mass media company. When "conflict of interest" became a central issue in the spring campaign, Berlusconi struck an insouciant pose, claiming that he supported the bill.

The unlimited energy and funds he put into legitimating his politics and broadening his base were paying off. He even reached back to use Christian democracy. On 18 April 1998, the fiftieth anniversary of De Gasperi's greatest electoral victory, Berlusconi spoke in Milan of "our belief in the cultural values of our nation that are admired and loved throughout the world."[47] This admiration and love—couched in an open yearning for parity with the rest of Europe—were soon to be tested. Berlusconi threatened a lawsuit when *The Economist* pointed to "the known facts" and called him "not fit to lead the government of any country, least of all one of the world's richest democracies."[48] It was no small boost to Berlusconi's legitimacy when Gianni Agnelli, scion of the Fiat business empire, condemned foreign media for treating Italy as if it were some kind of "banana republic."[49] Berlusconi the outsider was now Berlusconi the centrist.

In May 2001, Berlusconi's "Freedom House Alliance" regained power in a hotly contested battle with the Center-Left, led by Rome Mayor Francesco Rutelli. Berlusconi won by reconstructing earlier alliances with Fini and Bossi, by cultivating the Center and the business community, and by appealing to the persistent sense that Italy deserved better than to be considered the "last of the great powers." In the wake of a neofascist resurgence in neighboring Austria, Berlusconi's alliances elicited open concern from some of Italy's EU partners. The French foreign minister warned that Berlusconi's government would be watched closely for signs of illiberality, and German Premier Gerhard Schroeder offered Berlusconi only lukewarm congratulations. Berlusconi needed the Right less this time, however, and the Center was securely his. Bossi's electoral appeal had tanked, and the Lega failed to garner even the threshold 4 percent needed to gain seats. Now Berlusconi could govern without worrying that Bossi would again defect and bring his government down.[50]

The election was a milestone in Italian political history. There were no cabinet reshuffles, no protracted deal making, no coalitions to achieve an arithmetical majority—and there were no coups. For the first time, an entire governing bloc was compelled by the electorate to deliver power to its opponents. Not only did the evolution of Italy's party system seem well under way but a historic generational transition was complete. Neither leader originated in Cold War Italy's major parties. Francesco Rutelli, originally a Radical Party activist, founded the Democrats after a short time with the Greens. There would be no Christian Democrats and few Communists in sight. Silvio Berlusconi would govern a newly national Italian polity that had a viable Center-Left and Center-Right. He demonstrated, moreover, that Italian localism is far less potent than most had imagined.[51] He understood better and sooner than anyone else that twenty-first century Italians were proudly Italian and looking toward Europe. For all its invention, Bossi's regionalism had failed. The "thousand Italys" that had been "united without a center" were one after all.[52]

This set of choices on the Right—one local, the other national—was mirrored by two of Japan's most vigorous and visible leaders: Ozawa Ichirō and Ishihara Shintarō. Unlike Bossi and Berlusconi, neither has much of the bricoleur in him; but each has reinvented himself several times in a determined effort to build a new system from the ashes of LDP hegemony. Ozawa was the "terminator" of the 1955 System, and Ishihara the "prophet" of the new order.

OZAWA ICHIRŌ KNOCKS OVER THE 1955 SYSTEM

Ozawa Ichirō (b. 1942) belongs atop the long list of conservative politicians who clambered out of the swamp of the "1955 System" to reinvent themselves as reformers. He also belongs atop the long list of politicians who bungled chances at key moments to control the reconstruction of the Japanese polity. Yet Ozawa's choices have had institutional consequences. He forced debate on Japan's participation in the Gulf War, which led to a new legitimacy for the Japanese military and, ultimately, to a constructive debate on the Constitution; he championed electoral reforms and forced the crucial split in the LDP. Had he succeeded in consolidating power for a new Center-Right he would have been praised as Japan's greatest leader since Yoshida Shigeru. Instead, he will be forever compared to Saigo Takamori, the Satsuma samurai who helped lead the Meiji rebellion, but who found no place on center stage in the new order.[53]

Like many contemporary Japanese politicians, Ozawa comes from a political family. His father, Ozawa Saeki, was a four-time cabinet minister and confidant of Kishi Nobusuke.[54] Ichirō inherited his father's Iwate constituency in 1968, with the active support of Tanaka Kakuei. In a short time, Ozawa became Tanaka's prized disciple, and was treated as his son.[55] Tanaka was not the only corrupt politician with whom Ozawa was close. Ozawa rose to power as an operative for Kanemaru Shin and Takeshita Noboru—the latest in a pedigree of "anti-mainstream" deal makers and money raisers. His "rite of passage" was in 1972, when he dispensed sufficient cash to make Tanaka prime minister. In the early 1980s, as LDP General Affairs Bureau chief, and after 1989, as LDP secretary-general, Ozawa masterminded LDP election strategy. By all accounts, his pièce de résistance was the collection of an unprecedented amount of money from business to support the LDP's 1990 campaign—in the teeth of the Recruit Scandal. Despite the scandal, the LDP increased its majority by thirty seats.[56] His connections and his fund-raising successes ensured Ozawa an "ear-popping rise" to power; he smashed through once strictly enforced rules of political seniority.[57] Some lambasted him for ham-handed, abrasive power plays, but others hailed him for attacking the LDP's inattention to policy, which was eroding trust in government.

Ozawa has had many political personae, from imperious and ruthless backroom operative to reforming, antiestablishment idealist. Indeed, as befits a reformer who rose to power on the back of the most corrupt faction in the LDP, he has been a man of infinite contradictions. He has been a backroom dealer who complains about the lack of transparency in government; he has been intensely stubborn but remarkably flexible; he wears both his principles and his pragmatism on his sleeve. He appeals to principle and to policy, but has achieved alliances with every one of Japan's political parties except the JCP. It is no surprise that he has inspired wide distrust. Immediately after the LDP split, how one viewed Ozawa became the litmus test of Japanese politics.[58] Through all this, the gruff, impatient Ozawa has also articulated a coherent vision for a Japan in which two-party democracy could be consolidated and Japan's national interests defended independently and without apology.[59]

Ozawa was LDP secretary-general during the Gulf War.[60] After Iraqi forces crossed the Kuwaiti border in August 1990, the Japanese government was openly uncertain about national policy. Four postwar decades of avoiding international conflict and stressing energy security left many officials inclined to accommodate Iraq. It took Prime Minister Kaifu three days to join the world's condemnation of Baghdad. The United States, busily constructing a global coalition against Iraq—a remarkable alliance that included the Soviet Union and the People's Republic of China—asked Japan to make a "direct contribution." When personnel and equipment were not forthcoming, the U.S. government shifted to demands for a large financial contribution.[61] Ozawa recalls: "America . . . expected Japan to stand with it against Saddam. Japan betrayed that expectation . . . Japan's response came too late; we were unable to cooperate when we were really needed."[62]

Japan's failure infuriated Ozawa. He was aghast that all Japan could muster was money, while the rest of the world was prepared to fight. Ozawa was determined to "force the Diet and the country to confront the issue [of Japan's contribution to global security] straight on."[63] He introduced legislation to create a United Nations Peace Cooperation Corps through which SDF forces could participate in UN peacekeeping, albeit in noncombat roles.[64] The LDP and the bureaucracy were divided. The foreign ministry generally supported an overseas role for the SDF, but MITI was firmly opposed.[65] Opposition also came from the Socialists and the Communists, and the Cabinet Legislation Bureau (CLB) was resolute in opposing any change in constitutional interpretation. CLB Deputy Director Kudo Atsuo insisted that overseas deployment of Japanese forces would be unconstitutional. After considerable debate, the LDP withdrew the bill without a vote.

After repeated U.S. requests, and only after the fighting was over, the Japanese government agreed to send minesweepers to the Gulf. Ozawa was embarrassed that debates over whether Japanese troops could legally carry side arms distracted the nation from the larger issues of world affairs: "Since the war, America's definition of 'ally' has become the twenty-eight countries that risked their people's lives on the battlefields of the Gulf War. Naturally, Japan is not counted as one among them."[66] From his perspective, Japan looked confused and irrelevant. The best Japan could do was sign a check for $13 billion—an enormous sum that virtually underwrote the entire enterprise but satisfied few at home or abroad.[67]

Ozawa was effectively stretching the constraints on Japanese foreign policy. He had forced the issue of international security into the open, making the LDP and the public at large confront the responsibilities of a great power. In February 1992, an LDP panel on Japan's security role took the position that SDF participation in UN peacekeeping activities was permissible under the Constitution. Its call for a shift from a passive to an active pacifism was accepted by politicians and, more importantly, by the general public.[68] Ultimately, an Ozawa-brokered agreement led to legislation permitting Japan to participate in UN peacekeeping operations. Within a decade, Japan had dispatched forces to Cambodia, Mozambique, and the Golan Heights, where they served with distinction and full public support.[69]

The monumental battle to redefine Japanese security policy was not the only one Ozawa fought during this period. The Gulf War debate was actually a detour around his plans for consolidation of a two-party electoral system. Well before the Gulf War, Ozawa had begun to press for replacing Japan's multimember system with a plurality system dominated by single-member districts.[70] He expected that this change would reduce the excesses of campaign finance and would force politicians to focus more on policy and less on personality. It would also force politicians to make compromises in order to achieve power, for there would be less room for narrowly constituted and obstreperous factions or parties. The consequence of this reform—as Ozawa envisioned it—would be a cleaner, more stable, alternating party system favoring a consolidated Center-Right that he could control.

Building on newly established ties with the Kōmeitō, Ozawa masterminded a vote-bartering agreement, which resulted in a defeat for the Socialists in the July 1992 upper house election.[71] The election results had a significant impact on Ozawa's views. First, he was convinced that the JSP could not reinvent itself as the core of a new Center-Left party.[72] Second, Ozawa learned that he was capable of working effectively with centrist politicians outside the LDP. A political realignment that pitted catchall centrist parties against each other was not only theoretically desirable but now seemed practically achievable. According to several accounts, in the weeks following the upper house election, Ozawa began to consider splitting the LDP and uniting centrist forces in a new party capable of challenging the LDP's decades-long stranglehold on power.[73]

However, Ozawa's vision was punctuated by scandals and crises. In August 1992, it was learned that a parcel delivery firm, Sagawa Kyūhin, had been providing cash illegally to prominent politicians, including LDP Vice President Kanemaru. After first denying the charges, Kanemaru admitted that he had accepted more than $4 million for distribution to his faction members. Ozawa, then deputy chairman of the same Takeshita faction, offered to resign, but Kanemaru refused the offer, leaving Ozawa as acting chairman of the most powerful faction in the LDP. But this faction was already on the cusp of dissolution. It contained seven ambitious men, three of whom would become prime minister and all of whom would occupy senior positions in party and government over the next decade.[74] There was certainly no consensus that Ozawa was entitled to be their leader.

By October 1992, the schism was widely acknowledged. Ozawa's rivals, miffed that he was running the faction, demanded his resignation.[75] They prevailed on Takeshita to overrule Kanemaru and anoint Obuchi Keizō instead. Meanwhile, Prime Minister Miyazawa, whose popularity was plummeting, tried to take advantage of the rift in a rival faction by initiating consultations about a cabinet reshuffle not with Ozawa but with Kajiyama Seiroku as the representative of the Takeshita faction.[76] In the reshuffle, Miyazawa not only offered three powerful cabinet posts to anti-Ozawa members of the faction, but he slighted Ozawa and his followers by offering them only two relatively minor positions.[77]

Miyazawa's plan to divide and conquer the party's largest faction backfired. In December, Ozawa took the first step toward what would be the LDP's defining split. He and Hata Tsutomu led forty-two other faction members in the creation of "Reform Forum 21," which they hoped would be the core of a new conservative party.[78] Now, Ozawa was running (in Hata's name) the fifth-largest faction in the LDP, but openly positioning himself as a reformer. Supported by Keidanren, Reform Forum 21 proclaimed itself a policy-centered (rather than deal-making) faction, with electoral reform its first priority.[79]

With battle lines drawn between Ozawa and Miyazawa, the correlation of forces did not favor Ozawa. Miyazawa was prime minister, and Kajiyama was LDP secretary-general, and they were determined to erode Ozawa's influence. Throughout the spring of 1993 they did little to discourage opposition demands for Diet investigations into the Sagawa scandal. Ozawa, forced to testify before the Diet, insisted that although he was at the 1987 meetings where Sagawa money and the use of thugs to silence rightists was discussed, he was too busy cleaning ashtrays and fetching drinks to know what was being discussed. He was ridiculed in the press, but no smoking gun was ever discovered.[80]

On the defensive within his own party, Ozawa began working across party lines. He mended fences with Yamagishi Akira, a moderate trade-union leader and powerful figure behind the JSP.[81] By May, Ozawa had helped orchestrate a compromise around a private reform proposal, which called for a combination of single-seat constituencies and proportional representation.[82] A reform bill that received the combined votes of the main opposition parties and Reform Forum 21 seemed guaranteed to pass. Ozawa appeared on the verge of achieving the first part of his plan to remodel Japanese politics.

While the LDP allowed open Diet debate over competing reform proposals, little headway was made toward a compromise. Finally, in the Diet session's waning days LDP Secretary-General Kajiyama abruptly announced the LDP would postpone electoral reform.[83] The anti-Ozawa members of the LDP leadership were unwilling to countenance any electoral reform that might be interpreted as a victory for Ozawa.[84] Outraged and unable to devise a counter, Ozawa and Hata threw the support of their faction behind an opposition no-confidence motion. The Miyazawa government fell on 18 June 1993.

Ozawa now faced a choice: he could leave the LDP and start a new party, or he could try to prevail over the LDP leadership. He had always imagined that electoral reform would precede political realignment.[85] His strategic calculus changed, however, with the departure of several pro-reform allies from the LDP.[86] Ozawa and Hata decided to roll the dice one more time, for even higher stakes. In less than a week, they drafted principles for a new Japan Renewal Party (Shinseitō) that started life with forty-four Diet members, and they selected candidates for the ensuing election. The LDP, bowed and bloodied by these defections, fell twenty-eight votes short of a majority in the July election. Worse, no party would join it to form a ruling coalition. Japan would have its first non-LDP government in thirty-eight years.

The Shinseitō became the most influential force in the short-lived, eight-party Hosokawa government, which included every party except the LDP and the JCP. By now Ozawa had become the nation's most prominent politician. His *Blueprint for a New Japan* was a best-seller that summer. It was the first time in living memory that a politician had articulated such an ambitious, idealistic national strategy for making Japan "normal": reform, decentralization, deregulation, international contributions. He was positioning himself to build a catchall party, the "large tent" that single-member districts would reward with a Diet majority and stable control of the government.

The bloom withered when investigative reporters learned that Ozawa owned a home in Tokyo valued at nearly one and a half billion yen. Ozawa was questioned vigorously about the land deals that made its construction possible.[87] After reports of funding from construction firms were made public, his Socialist coalition partners pressed for an investigation in the autumn of 1993—shaking an already fragile coalition. Ozawa insisted that the gifts were technically legal—they were divided into sums smaller than the legal limit—and unfazed, he seized the offensive, using the occasion as evidence of the need for political finance reform! The Socialists, under pressure from coalition partners, eventually limited their demands for hearings, but the coalition's days were numbered.

Between 1993, when he bolted the LDP to form the Japan Renewal Party, and January 1998, when he founded the Liberal Party (Jiyūtō), Ozawa experimented with the New Frontier Party (Shinshintō), to that point Japan's largest catchall party. Along the way, he built short-lived coalitions with the Socialists and the Kōmeitō. Even his alliance with Hata came undone. The reason was always the same—Ozawa typically made deals and promoted policy without consulting his allies. As a consequence, he watched his numerical strength—and his prospects for national leadership—shrink. By the summer of 1997, the New Frontier Party had declined to a 10 percent share of public support, while the apparently defunct but resilient LDP now garnered 40 percent. Ozawa had frittered away public support. Too focused on policy, he had suspended his usually astute political judgment and was trying to do too much. Ozawa had missed the chance to drive a stake through the heart of the LDP, and now members of his NFP began returning to the mother party. Just days after narrowly winning reelection as party president, Ozawa dissolved the NFP in December 1997. The following month he founded the Liberal Party out

Ozawa Ichirō remains enigmatic in 1993, even under a magnifying glass. Reproduced courtesy of Nishimura Koichi.

of the fifty-four seats that remained of his political base. Meanwhile, the LDP was back in the saddle. The Japanese political system returned to business as usual.

Now it was Ozawa who would return to the fold. In late 1998, just five years after he had bolted the LDP, Ozawa brought the LP into a governing coalition with the LDP. Still, Ozawa made the LDP agree that "decisions on security policies will be made by politicians" and insisted the LDP accept his views on the need to reinterpret the Constitution.[88] While the LP was part of the LDP government through most of 1999 and into 2000, Ozawa probed repeatedly for ways to establish a new conservative party. This effort went nowhere, and so did Ozawa. He threatened repeatedly to leave the coalition, and in April 2000 Prime Minister Obuchi called his bluff.

Ozawa's brinkmanship had backfired. Hours after the LP-LDP-Kōmeitō coalition was dissolved, Obuchi had a stroke and was replaced by party elders. A majority of the LP chose to remain in coalition with the LDP, and Ozawa was now left with the rump of the rump of the once-robust New Frontier Party—and was more isolated than ever before. In the June 2000 lower house elections, his LP increased its strength to a mere twenty-two, a far cry from the fifty Ozawa had targeted. With no leverage in the

Diet, he returned to Japan's "political wilderness," waiting for the LDP to collapse of its own weight. In the interim, the LDP found an improbable new life under the leadership of the immensely popular Koizumi Junichirō, the latest in Kishi Nobusuke's line of anti-mainstream conservatives reinvented as reformers. After 9 September 2001, it was Koizumi who led Japan to "show the flag" in an unprecedented demonstration of military support for the United States in its antiterrorist offensive in Afghanistan. Ozawa Ichirō, the once-muscular LDP leader who first dared insist that Japan act like a great power, found himself spent and isolated. Having missed his chance to eliminate the LDP as a political force, the best he could do was add his faint voice to the irrelevant chorus of Socialists and the Communists that protested the action.[89]

ISHIHARA SHINTARŌ PICKS UP THE PIECES

Ozawa Ichirō was instrumental in knocking over the 1955 System, but Ishihara Shintarō (b. 1932) was better positioned to pick up the pieces. This is ironic, for Ishihara removed himself from Diet politics in 1995 after having alienated Japan's leading politicians and business elites more thoroughly than even Ozawa had. Ishihara's is one of the most varied careers in Japanese political history. His long history of aggressive provocation catapulted him from 1950s cult litterateur to governor of Tokyo, and an exalted position in public opinion. Where Ozawa is admired and reviled for his backroom machinations, Ishihara gets marks—high as well as low—for his insouciance. For more than a decade in the 1990s and 2000s, Ishihara has consistently been one of the most popular choices for prime minister.[90] At a minimum, his successes and failures have demonstrated that there remains room in Japanese politics for the direct delivery of unvarnished ideas. While Ozawa suffers from aloofness and an inability to connect to voters, Ishihara offers the Japanese an additional, *populist* option on the Right—a Right that many had come to believe was calcified.

Ishihara first rose to prominence in Japan's early postwar youth movement. His first novel, *The Season of the Sun*, published while he was still a student at Hitotsubashi University, won the prestigious Akutagawa Prize in 1956.[91] Filled with the sexual energy of youth rejecting established morality, it sold more than a quarter million copies. Young men copied Ishihara's haircut and identified themselves as members of the "Sun Tribe" (Taiyō Zoku).[92] His younger brother, Yūjirō, who starred in the 1956 film version of *The Season of the Sun*, was also catapulted to fame as an actor and singer. Although his popular younger brother died of cancer in 1987, Ishihara still introduced himself as "Yūjirō's older brother" when he declared his candidacy for Tokyo governor in 1999.[93] Yet Shintarō was a superstar in his own right. By the late 1960s, having written more than thirty novels, plays, and films, he could claim to be the highest-paid author in Japan.[94]

In December 1966, Ishihara was sent by the *Yomiuri Shimbun* to cover the Christmas cease-fire in Vietnam. He returned to Japan a changed man, convinced that Vietnam would fall to communism. More important, he was alarmed by strong similarities he perceived between the apathy of the Vietnamese and what he encountered among the Japanese intelligentsia. Fearing a parallel collapse of order at home, Ishihara decided on a political career.[95] The following year, he surprised the public by running for a seat in the House of Councilors. Declaring himself a latter-day Gabriele D'Annunzio, an intellectual man of action, Ishihara rejected the idea of forming his own party, as well as joining one of the "progressive" parties, which he found unacceptably "conservative."[96] Ever the contrarian, Ishihara claimed that the best hope for Japan was an LDP reformed by big ideas from within.[97] In his first run for public office, Ishihara won with three million votes, the highest number ever recorded in a Diet race.[98]

Ishihara was always a man of open ambition and strong opinions, directly delivered. In 1970 he declared in the Diet that the U.S. nuclear umbrella was not reliable, and in 1974 he advocated Japan's acquisition of a nuclear bomb in order to gain international respect.[99] Echoing 1930s' patriotic exhortations, he bewailed Japan's empty materialism and lack of national purpose.[100] By then, Ishihara had moved to the more powerful lower house, ousting an eight-term LDP octogenarian, to the consternation of the party elders.[101] After he won as a nominal independent, they were compelled to welcome him back into the fold. Ishihara's campaign slogan, "Let's Get a Young Prime Minister from Tokyo," pulled no punches about his aspirations.[102]

His peculiar combination of ambition, independence, and volatility ensured that Ishihara would never be fully trusted by the mainstream LDP. In the lower house he was a founding member of the "Society of the New Japanese Generation" and the Seirankai, a high-profile group of young LDP members that pressed for higher defense spending, revision of the Constitution, and relations with Taiwan as well as the PRC.[103] One early mentor was Nakasone Yasuhiro. As early as 1959, long before Ishihara had entered politics, a Japanese weekly identified the young Ishihara and Nakasone as "kindred spirits" who sought reform and shared a hatred for Japan's pervasive postwar apathy.[104] Ishihara enjoyed the support of other nonmainstream LDP politicians, notably those, like Fukuda Takeo and Abe Shintarō, who were closely associated with Kishi Nobusuke.

Mainstream party elders suspended their mistrust in 1975, when they reluctantly supported Ishihara's bid to replace leftist Tokyo Governor Minobe Ryōkichi. The immensely popular Minobe, first elected in 1967 with the support of the Communist and Socialist parties, had long been a thorn in the side of the LDP. His aggressive environmental and welfare policies forced the LDP to repackage its "growth at all costs" program. Local governments across the nation followed his lead in what amounted to the first significant challenge to conservative dominance in postwar Japan.[105] Minobe reluctantly agreed to run for a third term in order to block Ishihara, whom he regarded as a fascist.[106] Getting LDP support was not easy for Ishihara. In the absence of other candidates, however, and with strong support from the local LDP branch, Ishihara stood as the LDP's candidate. He lost to Minobe in a hotly contested race.

In December 1976, as a reward, Ishihara was given his first cabinet post—the Environment Agency—by Prime Minister Fukuda. At forty-four, Ishihara was the youngest cabinet minister in postwar Japanese history. He was also one of the best known. Within a year, environmentalist groups were calling for Ishihara to resign because they felt he was insufficiently committed to environmental protection.[107] He hardly helped his case by picking a fight with public sector workers and the press corps, whom he accused of "moonlighting for the Communist Party," and by labeling efforts to revise the Environment Law in 1977 a "witch-hunt of industrialists."[108] His list of public brawls was growing remarkably long. He had tangled with the Japanese Sumo Association in 1963, accusing it of fixing bouts; he declared neckties "meaningless" in 1977, alienating LDP business support. More significant was his open denunciation of party colleagues, one of whom sued him for libel in the mid-1970s. When Ishihara declared several LDP ministers "meaningless," he was twice reprimanded by prime ministers—first by Satō Eisaku in 1970 and again by Fukuda Takeo in 1977.

After his faction boss, Nakagawa, committed suicide in January 1983, Ishihara took over the thirteen-member group and later made his only sustained, direct run for party president and prime minister. He went about his candidacy in a predictably unorthodox way. In October 1984, after his faction had dwindled to six members because he could not raise the necessary funds, Ishihara allowed its absorption into Fukuda's faction—soon to belong to Abe Shintarō, Kishi's son-in-law. Without the faction's support and without cash, Ishihara made a run at the LDP presidency in 1989. He gambled that in the midst of the Recruit Scandal, his bluff, populist message would be embraced. Clearly, he had underestimated Ozawa's resourcefulness and the party elders' determination to maintain order. When he lost, he was forced out of the Abe faction. He remained in the Diet but as a one-man band and nationalist ideologue. As one journal conjectured, Ishihara may have had only half the tool kit needed for political success: "The man is moved by ideas and the temptations of stage center. The cold calculation of political interest is not his province."[109]

He certainly deployed the half that he did possess with consummate skill. For a decade after his debacle, Ishihara kept in the limelight without pursuing higher office. He did this most famously in *The Japan that Can Say "No"*, his published conversation with Sony Chairman Morita Akio in which he spoke out against the "high-handed" arrogance of the United States and an accommodating Japanese government.[110] Ishihara fulminated that the U.S. economy and military depended on Japanese technology and yet Americans took Japan for granted. He exhorted the Japanese to stand up for themselves and stop being bullied, sell high technology to the Soviets and deny it to the United States.

Bashing the U.S. bully proved immensely popular. During trade negotiations in 1990, when the United States was demanding structural reform in Japan, he and a group of LDP colleagues issued a list of 109 items for reform of the *American* economy, including increased education spending, tougher penalties for sex offenders, reduced operating hours of ATM machines, and introduction of an industry-based trade union structure.[111] The Japanese government did not officially support these demands, but Ishihara won further public approbation for promulgating them. He also waded into the Gulf War debate—but not on Ozawa's side. Ishihara openly resented U.S. demands and called Japan's response "childish."[112] The next time, he argued, Japan should save its money, let the West get buried under Middle East race hatred, and use the funds to establish Japanese leadership of a new world order.[113] In 1991 he lambasted "degenerate" Americans, and in 1992 he proclaimed that American managers were inferior.[114] That same year he published another best-seller, *The Japan that Can Definitely Say "No"*, in which he claimed that Westerners are blinded by racial prejudice. In 1994 he co-authored a volume with Malaysian Prime Minister Mahathir Mohamad, *An Asia that Can Say "No"*, which continued his lambasting of Westerners as racist oppressors.[115]

Ishihara insisted that the United States had to stop blaming Japan for its own economic ills. When the reversal of fortunes became clear in the late 1990s, he started to blame the United States for *Japan's* ills. Now he attributed Japan's "empty materialism and lack of national purpose" to U.S. influence. By imposing an overvalued yen and pressing unfair and unilateral trade sanctions in violation of the GATT, the United States was seizing its chance to dominate. The United States was the global villain, and globalization was the villain's tool. In 1998 he called the Asian financial crisis part of this U.S. strategy, designed to leave Japan and its Asian neighbors "financial slaves." The United States had engineered the crisis as its next step after "singling out Saddam Hussein of Iraq as the fall guy to win control over the world's largest oil reserves."[116] The crisis was nothing less than a "takeover plot" by the Americans. And, he argued, the Japanese government has acquiesced. The Ministry of Finance was "the Japanese branch of the U.S. Treasury Department."[117] Japan should withdraw funds that prop up the American economy and bring down the new evil empire. The alternatively cosmopolitan and xenophobic Ishihara played the race card as well: "There is no hope for the U.S. Right now the modern civilization built by whites is coming close to its practical end."[118]

In April 1995, at a Diet ceremony honoring his twenty-five years in national politics, Ishihara abruptly resigned his lower house seat. In a terse speech, he declared his personal sense of shame at participating in a political system that allowed bureaucrats to control policy making.[119] As a consequence, Japan had become "unable to express its will as a nation, like a man who is unable to function as a man."[120] Taking responsibility for his part in this debacle, he apologized to his supporters. Following this sudden exit, Ishihara, then sixty-two, insisted he had no intention of running for political office again. However, the best-known Japanese politician at home or abroad did make it clear he would "not stop thinking about the nation and about politics."[121]

Despite his avowed lack of political aspirations, Ishihara was already considering the Tokyo governorship.[122] On 10 March 1999, just two weeks before the deadline, Ishihara became the last major candidate to enter the race.[123] He returned to his characteristically high-octane rhetoric. He would "reform Japan from Tokyo," he denounced the outgoing governor as "a good example of what not to do," and he promised to demand the return of the U.S. air base at Yokota to Japan, a move that infuriated the LDP government.[124] Ishihara had learned from his earlier experience of running against Minobe. This time, in addition to using the media, he spent considerable energy seeking endorsements and bloc votes from civic organizations, including religious groups.[125] His conservative opposition was splintered. The race ended in a landslide victory for Ishihara, while the LDP's candidate, a former United Nations undersecretary-general, finished a distant fourth. The sixty-six-year-old Ishihara now had a bully pulpit.

He wasted no time. Immediately after his election, Ishihara introduced a timetable for pollution controls on diesel-powered vehicles, antagonized metropolitan government workers, and insisted on improving "moral education," the euphemism for a nationalist educational agenda. He focused on local autonomy, on "saying 'no' to the central government."[126] He also put big business in his crosshairs. Exploiting a loophole in the Local Finance Law, he began taxing banks that do business within Tokyo at 3 percent of their gross profits. He sought to establish a junk bond market and announced his intention to privatize all public services. In addition, he called for the creation of a Tokyo Bay casino and a toll on cars that drive through the central city. In almost every instance (and remarkably like the leftist Minobe), Ishihara's aggressive creativity forced the LDP and the central bureaucracy to react. Although the LDP, supported by the Japanese Bankers Association, would not support his plan to tax banks, the cabinet admitted that it could not stop Ishihara without changing the Local Tax Law. More than a dozen governors announced that they planned to follow his lead.[127] In the best tradition of populism, Ishihara cut his salary and refused to move into the governor's mansion. Three months after taking office Ishihara enjoyed approval ratings of over 70 percent. Three years later, his poll ratings had risen to 78 percent.[128]

In his first official address, Ishihara proclaimed his ardent opposition to a long-standing plan to transfer the national seat of governance away from Tokyo. He reached out to neighboring local governments, some of which also housed national government facilities, to establish a coalition opposing the transfer. To defuse the strongest argument in favor of transferring the capital—that the national seat should be moved away from the earthquake-prone metropolitan area for safety reasons—Ishihara made Tokyo's disaster prevention capabilities a priority. In September 2000 he supervised the largest earthquake rescue drill in the city's history, a massive event that featured the mobilization of 7,100 Self-Defense Force troops and 18,000 rescue workers.[129] Although the exercise emphasized self-help, the unprecedented use of the SDF was also an attempt to promote the military and to show the resources available to the metropolitan government.[130] Ishihara again courted controversy by explaining that in the event of an earthquake, the SDF must protect Japan from rioting and looting by "third country nationals" (*sangokujin*), a derisive term used during the Occupation to refer to Koreans and Chinese.[131]

Ishihara's bully pulpit had considerable international reach. During the campaign he referred to China as "Shina," a pejorative holdover from the 1930s. At his inaugural press conference, in April 1999, he proclaimed that the PRC was violating the rights of Tibetans and that PRC threats to unify China by force were destabilizing the region. He described China as Japan's "biggest threat" and called for breaking it up into smaller states. The predictable result was an official protest from China and defensive measures from the Japanese foreign ministry.[132] In November 1999, in another clear provocation, Ishihara visited Taiwan, which he referred to as a "free state."[133] Adding fuel to the fire, he announced he would meet

Ishihara Shintarō, newly elected governor of Tokyo in 1999, is a train conductor with the general population securely on board. Reproduced courtesy of Nishimura Kōichi.

with the Dalai Lama in April 2000. Ishihara was livid when the Dalai Lama was forced to cancel his meeting by the foreign ministry.[134] He thereupon compared PRC President Jiang Zemin to Adolf Hitler.[135] Focusing on another favorite target, the United States, Ishihara met with U.S. Ambassador Thomas Foley only weeks after taking office and demanded the return to Japan of the U.S. air base in Yokota. When Foley diplomatically noted that the base's future was a national security issue, Ishihara responded, "Once I've built the public support, I'll see both the Japanese government and the White House move on this issue."[136]

Ishihara's steady stream of newspaper columns, television interviews, and Diet testimony have kept him in the public eye. In December 2000, in testimony to the lower house Constitutional Research Committee, Ishihara sharply criticized the "imposed" Constitution: "I want the Diet to reject the Constitution, which neither reflects the Japanese people's will nor has legitimacy from a historical point of view."[137] Predictably, this demand as well as Prime Minister Koizumi's subsequent sharp fall in popularity led to speculation that Ishihara was preparing to launch the "Ishihara New Party" (Ishihara Shintō), which might gain him a Diet seat and the chance to become prime minister. Ishihara has taken pains to distance himself from the pervasive corruption of the LDP, and expectations were high that he would attract defectors from the LDP as well as many unaffiliated voters.[138] One magazine reported that "all eyes are expected to remain on

Ishihara as the person holding the key to political realignment."[139] Indeed, in April 2001, the night before Koizumi Junichirō was formally anointed president of the LDP, he dined with Prime Minister Mori, Nakasone Yasuhiro, and the "independent" Ishihara Shintarō.[140]

In March 2001, a former Japan Defense Agency chief, Aichi Kazuo, told a Washington, D.C. audience that he saw only two politicians likely to emerge as national leaders in the near term: Ishihara Shintarō and Ozawa Ichirō. He thought that Ishihara, whose "style appeals to the Japanese who are beset by a sense of stagnation," would form a new party, run for a Diet seat, and be elected prime minister. He suggested that Ozawa "may have a chance" if he declares his ambitions openly.[141] Like Ozawa, Ishihara believes that the role of politicians is to discipline bureaucrats, a message now more popular than ever. But Ishihara has a far better nose for public opinion than Ozawa does. Ishihara has touched popular chords by confronting the banks, the Americans, and immigrants, and he is a proven magnet for disenchanted voters. Does he know how to use this, and will he seize the opportunities he can create? He has repeatedly dismissed suggestions that he create a new party. But in a newspaper interview, asked if citizens should be concerned that he is a nationalist or a hawk, his reply placed him in interesting company: "I am a nationalist . . . There is nothing wrong with being called a hawk. Japan's prominent postwar leaders—Shigeru Yoshida, Nobusuke Kishi, Eisaku Satō, and Yasuhiro Nakasone—have all been hawkish."[142]

Always provocative, ever self-absorbed, Ishihara has rarely been attentive to the organizational details required for party building. Yet he has proved more than able to attend to the organizational details required for municipal administration. As Tokyo governor, he has found creative solutions to enduring problems of finance and bureaucratism. He ran for office, he says, because he is "a man of ideas and courage."[143] After becoming governor in 1999, Ishihara expressed regret that he would not be able to finish the romantic novel he was working on, explaining: "I think my latest work could go down in literary history." Then he added that he wants to be remembered for his politics: "I hope to set off a revolution."[144]

RECASTING THE DEBATE

It may be too early to identify institutional legacies of the choices made by the four men examined in this chapter. Each remains active, and none has secured sustained power. Yet, each of these men took a turn at recasting the political debate. In his bold choice to abandon the mother party and to reinvent himself as a reformer, Ozawa Ichirō dealt the first significant blow to the hegemony of the LDP. In his choice to fight for "normality" during the Gulf War, he forced the Japanese public to accept new ideas about global roles and missions. His more populist counterpart, Ishihara Shintarō, made different choices. By confronting institutional totems on the Right—business, the LDP, and the United States—Ishihara injected new life into Japan's Gaullist options. The choices of Italian leaders have been even more sharply drawn. Contrary to most expectations, identity politics worked better at the national than at the regional level. As a result, Bossi's legacies may prove ephemeral, and Berlusconi's the more enduring.

In both Japan and Italy the Right remained unconsolidated more than a decade after the Cold War had ended. Voters in both countries watched a parade of would-be leaders come and go—and found none worthy of their sustained support. The use of history and identity was common to both countries but differently exploited. Ozawa and Berlusconi openly invoked great leaders of the past. Bossi simply invented leaders, while Ishihara largely ignored the past—except when he was distorting or denying it. The Italians proved the more active and able bricoleurs. Bossi and Berlusconi effectively recast history, refashioning old symbols in efforts to legitimate a new rule. Neither Ozawa nor Ishihara used the past effectively. For the most part, identity politics remained a latent weapon, sheathed and unwielded on the Japanese right.

Wealth was the surest instrument for Silvio Berlusconi. Unlike the other men examined in this chapter, Berlusconi could draw upon his vast personal fortune and apply it to generate attention. Ozawa had to rely on business contacts for material resources at a time when there were conflicting claims on their affection. Although he had once enjoyed unparalleled success in wringing contributions from the Japanese business community, Ozawa found the well was running dry. Populists Bossi and Ishihara each succeeded despite—or perhaps because—they alienated business support, but they had to find other ways to generate attention: such as regional bricolage for Bossi and the bully pulpit of local power for Ishihara.

There have been no consistently "Italian" or "Japanese" ways of doing politics on the post-Cold War right. As we have seen, Berlusconi, Bossi, and (albeit briefly and behind the scenes) Ozawa governed from the capital, while Ishihara governed even more effectively and durably from a locality. Localism was the key to Bossi's kingdom, while Ishihara and Berlusconi rediscovered nationalism. All played the reform card, but Ishihara and Bossi did so consistently, while Berlusconi and Ozawa had first to reinvent themselves many times over. And despite Cold War lessons about the breadth and stability of the Italian and Japanese centers, none effectively reached out to embrace the wavering voter. Battles over Italian regional identity were surrogates for battles to control the state. Battles over Japanese national purpose have been surrogates for battles to achieve autonomy from the United States.

All of these leaders have been self-conscious about leadership. Ozawa has argued that the absence of leadership is a "fundamental flaw" in Japan's political process.[145] In Japan, he argues, norms of consensus lead to indecision; the suppression of individual opinion has at times led to "lunatic decisions."[146] Yet, despite these cultural deficiencies, Japan has had effective homegrown leaders who "stand out for their ability to pursue bold nation-building efforts amid the dramatic historic change of their times."[147] He credits these "exceptional individuals" with having had "a firm grasp of the political system, built strong power bases, and . . . earned low marks from their contemporaries [for their] high-handed" politics.[148] Ishihara has expressed similar dissatisfaction with the quality of leadership in Japan, often using the same terms of reference: "The scary thing about this country," he avers, "is that our politicians don't have to say anything to succeed . . . In this country it's best to be mysterious; voters think that means there's something meaningful deeper down."[149]

Umberto Bossi and Silvio Berlusconi also have a great deal to say about leadership. In Bossi's view, Italian leaders have been too materially oriented. "Rule by party" has rewarded only "profiteers and professional careerists," an Italian political class he hopes to replace with "new politicians . . . pushed exclusively by a strong ideological motivation."[150] Italy's leadership, Bossi repeatedly intones, comprises scoundrels and criminals, men of *dis*-honor. His explanation is structural:

> Tangentopoli and the Mafia are not just a casual deviation by a few bad guys from correct practice followed by politicians at all levels. They are not the sudden disappearance, in the maze of illegality, of a tributary of the great river of politics, which for the rest of its course flows gently to the surface, easily seen by everyone. [They are] the poisoned fruit of a tree—the rule-by-party regime—which has five roots: centralism, the domination by powerful aristocratic families, political fragmentation, the lack of alternating government, and the collapse of ideology.[151]

Berlusconi, who immodestly declares himself "the best leader in the world," sees the central problem as a leadership deficit.[152] In 1994, he declared that "at the present time Italy needs an innovative, creative, and experienced leader with his head on his shoulders . . . if the state is to function," and offered himself as up to the challenge.[153]

The cultural explanations of Ozawa and Ishihara and the structural ones of Bossi and Berlusconi are old saws that echo across generations of analyses of Japanese and Italian leadership. But are they right? *Is* there a "Japanese" or an "Italian" way to lead? Are there peculiarly Japanese and Italian practices, norms, and institutions that preclude the emergence of effective leadership? We turn to these questions in chapter 13.

Conclusion:

HOW LEADERS HAVE MATTERED IN ITALY AND JAPAN

> The mutations of societies, then, from generation to generation, are in the main due directly or indirectly to the acts or the examples of individuals whose genius was so adapted to the receptivities of the moment, or whose accidental position of authority was so critical that they became ferments, initiators of movements, setters of precedent or fashion, centers of corruption, or destroyers of other persons, whose gifts, had they had free play, would have led society in another direction.
>
> William James, "Great Men, Great Thoughts, and the Environment"

Finding the right place for individuals is an old problem for political analysis. Do individuals make history, or does history make individuals who make history? Debates about the influence of leaders, and the great forces that compel their choices, have never been resolved. The theorist most closely associated with this delicate balance is Niccolò Machiavelli. His very name—in adjectival form—conjures the duplicity, manipulation, ruthlessness, and resolve that nourish and enable the archetypal political leader.

Machiavelli's was neither the first nor the last word on the subject. Plutarch and Livy had insisted that history was the study of personalities. They were later confronted by social scientists—Condorcet, Comte—who were confident that they could identify an underlying logic of historical change. When Thomas Carlyle famously argued that history is "the biography of great men," Herbert Spencer exhorted scholars to focus instead on the "antecedent modifications" that made leadership possible.[1] Biographers have never disappeared, but most historians have leaned hard into Spencer's wind. An "impersonal interpretation of historical change" prevailed.[2] E.H. Carr spoke sardonically for many historians: "The desire to postulate individual genius as the creative force in history is characteristic of the primitive stages of historical consciousness . . . We all learned this theory, so to speak, at our mother's knee; and today we should probably recognize that there is something childish, or at any rate childlike, about it."[3]

In this book, I have explored why we gain by reincorporating leadership into the analysis of politics. Although generations of scholars have embraced the idea that necessity is the mother of invention, I have shown that we can enhance analytical possibilities by rethinking the idea of necessity and the nature of invention. By definition, after all, leaders are inventors. As they challenge and stretch constraints, they do two things at once: they loosen the bonds of history that shackle them as they build a new set of constraints for their successors. In short, leadership and choice matter more—and more often—than many scholars acknowledge. Not every choice is strategic, but we gain analytical leverage when we understand the *transformational* consequences of political choice by powerful individuals. On this account, then, I reverse the maternity of causation: invention may be the mother of necessity. Contingency is no mere accident but an integral part of normal politics.

It is time now to take stock. Do invention and necessity really deserve equal attention? How can we begin to incorporate contingency systematically into the analysis of change?

We have to begin by acknowledging Machiavelli, who is invoked in almost every management text and primer on politics. Despite five hundreds years of theorizing about great forces, no one has devised a more effective, honest, or robust sense of human choice and motivation than he did. But there is another reason for returning to his teachings. Textbook writers and motivational speakers have narrowed our understanding of what Machiavelli has to offer. They have embraced his realism but discarded his moral maturity. Machiavelli gave us human beings and situated them within the limits of their skills (*virtú*) and their circumstance (*fortuna*). How many of the leaders we have reviewed were overwhelmed by the latter, and how many suffered from a deficit of the former? Either way, we have to be impressed with how many leaders fail.

Our comparative history is littered with failed leaders. Giuseppe Mazzini inspired many revolutionaries but fomented little successful revolution himself. Alessandro Rossi imagined clearly how to transform Catholic social values into cross-class solidarity, but he overestimated his program's attractiveness to other industrialists. Saigo Takamori dreamed of a continental base for the Japanese Empire but was crushed by more pragmatic oligarchs. Some leaders dropped mantles that on other more capable shoulders might have secured greater power. Palmiro Togliatti, for example, fabricated but mishandled the remarkable legacy of Antonio Gramsci by cleaving too tightly to Stalin's. The Italian Socialist Filippo Turati, at the turn of the twentieth century, like Eda Saburō and Giorgio Amendola fifty years later, planned for accommodation with democratic forces only to be overwhelmed by intransigents on the Left. Sometimes, as Machiavelli suggested, failures may be explained as a function of timing: Sidney Sonnino advocated the extension of suffrage twenty years before Giovanni Giolitti, but the *Left* feared that most new voters would simply vote as their priest or landlord instructed. By the time the Left had gained confidence in democratic politics, it was too late.

The miscalculations are manifold and striking—often in ways antici-pated by Machiavelli, who pointed out that "whoever is responsible for an-other's becoming powerful ruins himself."[4] In 1945 Socialist Pietro Nenni nominated Alcide De Gasperi for prime minister expecting that Christian Democracy would crash and burn. Instead, Nenni found himself excluded from power for eight long years while De Gasperi and his successors laid the foundations of a hegemonic party system. Otherwise successful leaders made some of the gravest miscalculations. We all understand the conse-quences of Giolitti's opening to Mussolini, of De Gasperi's cooperation with the fascists in 1922, of Mussolini's decision to ally with Hitler, and (in a more benign example) of Murayama Tomiichi's 1994 agreement to bring the Socialist Party into government with the Liberal Democrats. None of these choices brought benefits to the chooser.

GETTING THE MEASURE OF THE GREAT FORCES

Individuals often fail, but the great forces that have occupied historical and social scientific inquiry have also failed—and with considerable fre-quency. They often seem too general to explain change. Take *personality*, for example. Our data do not allow close psychobiographical analysis, but beyond the trite and obvious point that most leaders share a persistent, re-lentless thirst for power, they give us no direct links between personality and choices. To the contrary, we have observed remarkable variation. Some leaders pursued material gains, others normative ones. Some, like Fuwa Tetsuzō, allowed a vision to constrain agency and so compromised both. We have watched blustery self-promoters like D'Annunzio, Mus-solini, Umberto Bossi, and Ishihara Shintarō, as well as austere, quietly conniving bureaucrats like Cavour, Giolitti, Ōkubo Toshimichi, and Yoshida Shigeru. Some needed public adulation, like Ishihara and Mus-solini, and others, like Giuseppe Dossetti, Yamagata Aritomo, and Sasakawa Ryōichi, kept to the shadows. Some had charisma, but many had no need of it to be effective.

Most striking is the split between those who reinvented themselves and those who were consistent. The master of reinvention was Mussolini, who moved unapologetically from intransigent Left to intransigent Right, skipping over the democratic Center altogether. Others reinvented themselves no less broadly by drawing themselves into a parliamentary mainstream: Itō Hirobumi, designer of the authoritarian Meiji Constitution, founded the Seiyūkai as a hedge against the rise of party politics. Fascists Amintore Fanfani, Kishi Nobusuke, and Gianfranco Fini each became democrats. Communists Massimo D'Alema and Achille Occhetto became social democrats. Some, like Ozawa Ichirō, emerged from the most corrupt corner of party politics and reinvented themselves as reformers. Still, Yamagata Aritomo and Giulio Andreotti were no less effective even though they never manufactured new personas. In short, personality is not a consistent guide to choice.

Neither is *utility*, the other great force derived from individual preferences. To be sure, all our leaders were calculating. This is why so many reinvented themselves, and why some bullied while others bought or inspired. But by demonstrating that leaders *normally* have several equally plausible choices, we have seen repeated evidence of how difficult it is to calculate utility. Self-interest is rarely obvious, even to the self-interested. Two cases illustrate this ambiguity particularly well. The first is the way Achille Occhetto and Fuwa Tetsuzō each steered their communist parties after the Cold War. Both drew from much the same history. Each could point to hard-won independence from Soviet domination, consistent antipathy of (and toward) the American hegemon, broad support from cultural elites, tentative approaches from Center parties groping for a new alliance partner, and a pantheon of leaders who had pursued peaceful, parliamentary paths to power. The fall of the Berlin Wall was clearly a punctuating moment for both. But, despite parallel histories, similar resources, and a common structural break with the past, Occhetto and Fuwa made different calculations. Occhetto reached back into party history to justify dramatic change, whereas Fuwa read his history as reason to stay the course. *Both* choices dramatically shifted the trajectories of their parties, and both choices affected national politics profoundly. In Italy, power was consolidated by the Center-Left for the first time and, nearly half a decade later in 2001, it handed the government to the Center-Right in a transition unprecedented in Italian history. In Japan, nearly a decade and a half after the end of the Cold War, the Center and the Left remained unreconciled, thereby continuing to cede power to a resilient Center-Right.

The second case is Mussolini's decision to ally with Hitler in 1939 and enter the war in 1940, a choice that Machiavelli anticipated with chilling clarity:

It is always the case that one who is not your friend will request your neutrality, and that the one who is your friend will request your armed support. Princes who are irresolute usually follow the path of neutrality in order to escape immediate danger, and usually they come to grief. But when you boldly declare your support for one side, then if that side conquers, even though the victor is powerful and you are at his mercy, he is under an obligation to you and he has committed himself to friendly ties with you.[5]

An extraordinary fit between Machiavelli's imagination and Mussolini's dilemma? But there is a fundamental contradiction in how the prince ought to calculate his utility. Machiavelli also advised that a "prince should never join in an aggressive alliance with someone more powerful than himself, unless it is a matter of necessity . . . This is because if you are the victor, you emerge as his prisoner."[6] Both statements are plausible and each is rational, but they direct the prince in different directions. Only one choice is possible. Mussolini dithered, stockpiling tributes and assurances from the Allies and from Hitler. Finally, he chose, and history shifted perceptibly beneath his jackboots. Mussolini's options must have seemed clear to him, but even if analysts after the fact are sure of his calculation, to him the choice could not have been less obvious.

Most leaders seem preoccupied with material reward, a reward typically measured in *power*—another great, putatively irresistible force in determining choice. To be sure, we identified a great many cases in which power disparities seemed to make choice easy. For Yoshida and De Gasperi, the weak had to go along with the strong. The United States was determined that neither Italy nor Japan would ally with the Soviet Union. But this is mere tautology. We were also impressed by how often the weak conjured up an unexpected strength through extraordinary creativity. Both De Gasperi and Yoshida frustrated domestic competitors by inventing alliances that no other politician could imagine. Each found a way to maximize his nation's material well-being despite its weakness: De Gasperi maneuvered the Europeans into accepting Italy as a partner, Yoshida forced the United States to accept Japan as a cheap rider on its vision of global security. Both overcame the daunting constraints of foreign occupation, and both reconfigured the splinters of domestic power with dazzling, judo-like skill. Rarely have "weak" leaders made so much from so little that would endure for so long.

Power may be a great force, but like its competitors it is only a sometimes great force. The weak can become strong. Mussolini could not have started as a more marginal player in Italian politics. Many weak actors—Kita Ikki and Gabriele D'Annunzio, to take two—transformed the terms of politics even if they never achieved personal power. Among those who did, Enrico Mattei and Ozawa Ichirō are illustrative. Mattei inserted himself into an evolving party system by inventing a virtual bank for the dominant party. He defied the state and positioned himself to purchase the political establishment. Meanwhile, he constructed a state sector that would resist foreign intervention, particularly by U.S. oil companies, arguably the most powerful firms in indisputably the most powerful nation. Ozawa, passed over by LDP colleagues for party leadership, brought them down and pushed through electoral reforms that, though as yet unconsolidated, promise to make Japanese politics more "normal."

What endures are the *structures* of domestic and international power. Such structures and institutions—party systems, international alliances, balances of domestic power—have been an insistent force in our analysis. But so were the events that challenged and undid them. Put differently, our comparative history shows not only the remarkable extent to which contingencies are a normal part of historical change, but also the unexpected extent to which leaders introduce these contingencies in the course of normal events. In one sense, the leaders and the choices examined in this book are exceptional. There surely were many more choices that were not made, more constraints that were not stretched, in the histories of Italy and Japan. One might be unimpressed, therefore, with the power of leadership in the explanation of political change. Yet leaders' choices are part of normal political life. We have seen how often leaders transcend options that seem thoroughly limited, and how leadership itself becomes the contingency that shifts the trajectory of historical change.

This claim is worth reviewing briefly. Leaders often construct contingency in ways that defy nominal structural constraint. Consider the case of structural corruption, a central institutional feature of postwar Italy and Japan. Here one can tell a story of classical path dependence. As politicians came of age, they took up their roles as dutiful faction members and bided their time until, after considerable elbowing for advantage, they could assume leadership and cash in. The roles were set: senior faction leaders and dutiful rank and file members were bound together in a calcifying structure of clientage. The extortion, the distribution of spoils, and the immunity from popular control differed only trivially between Italy and Japan. Yet, structural corruption unraveled differently in the two countries. The magistracy transformed Italian politics by prosecuting politicians, whereas their Japanese counterparts cowered at the prospect of ministerial override. Structure can certainly account for this difference, for the Italians enjoyed more juridical independence.[7] But it cannot explain the timing. Why did they take so long to attack the Italian political class? Moreover, if Article 14 were such an impediment, how did Japanese prosecutors so aggressively and successfully dispatch Tanaka Kakuei in the

1970s? Even here, where structure seems so important, there is ample room to appreciate *protagonismo*—agency. Italian actors actively constructed a pathbreaking contingency; their Japanese counterparts, faced with the same possibility, blinked.

Roles are relevant to structure in another context. I designed this inquiry around pairs of individuals who played the same roles and operated under similar constraints. In both countries we identified state-builders and wealth-makers. We examined the choices of liberals under attack from mass politics and from grasping aristocrats. We looked at socialists who considered collaboration with conservatives after the Second World War and at communists who weighed the same choices after the Cold War. It was not difficult to find pairings. We could even pair the political enemies of our protagonists. All this is, of course, an argument for the defining power of structural forces. If there was no modernization, there would be no state-builders, and no one would have faced off in parliament over the great issues of industrial development and trade policy. Had there been no industrial development, there would have been no working class to incorporate or to repress. But this is precisely the point. The choice to incorporate or to repress was determined not by the role but by the agent. Alessandro Rossi accepted the recalcitrance of his business colleagues, while Mutō Sanji struggled to change the preferences of entrepreneurs. Giovanni Giolitti reached out to the masses; his role counterpart, Hara Kei, reached out to the police instead. Achille Occhetto proclaimed the death of communism, Fuwa Tetsuzō its continuing vitality.

When persons of different preferences act the same way under the same circumstances, we can speak of "actor dispensability."[8] But when they make different choices, we have to be impressed instead with the *in*-dispensability of actors. Their choices really *are* independent of their roles and their constraints. Structural explanations—especially those focused on increasing returns and fixed trajectories—emphasize reduction in the number of choices and their efficacy. In this book, where leadership intervenes between structure and outcome, we have seen something quite different. We have seen how choices and their efficacy can be multiplied.

The multiplication of choice is illuminated by focusing on the way *culture* works in history. This final "great force" has two different forms. The first, the reified and facile notion of identifiably "Japanese" and "Italian" styles of leadership, has limited utility. The second, a construction in which history and symbols are deployed for instrumental ends, is powerful across both cases.

The idea that there are national styles of leadership is widely embraced. It is generally accepted that Japanese and Italian leaders are very different—even though both prefer the English word *leadership* to anything in their own language.[9] Italy is a land of spiders, and Japan a land of webs. Italy has had great generals but poor armies, whereas Japan has had great armies but poor generals. Secular leaders appeared as angels or saints in Risorgimento iconography.[10] *L'uomo forte* (strong man), *l'uomo della Provi-denza* (man of Providence), or *il capo carismatico e plebiscitario* (charismatic populist) have always been welcomed in Italy. Bellah suggests that "Italian history has produced a continuous series of men larger than life."[11] Charismatic leaders such as Garibaldi and D'Annunzio, Mussolini and Bossi, who skillfully manipulate the "old and new languages of heroism," are pointedly missing from the Japanese historical landscape.[12] Yet, there may be less here than meets the eye. After all, the legacies of the less heroic Giolitti and De Gasperi, Fanfani and Occhetto, are no smaller than those of their charismatic compatriots.

Still, these are powerful stereotypes. Scholars depict Japan as a system with no center, a "leaderless nation incapable of decisive action."[13] Japa-nese leaders are effective managers, not because of any particular skills but because their patron bequeathed power to them a generation earlier. Protégés loom large in cultural accounts of Japanese leadership.[14] The stereotypical Japanese leader is not charismatic or creative. He is a bu-reaucrat, not a CEO.[15] His power comes from his ability to guide complex networks of interpersonal relationships. He avoids conflict and promotes consensus and cooperation. The most effective leader may spend his time behind the scenes, a fixer (*kuromaku*) rather than a public figure.[16] The consensus view holds that Japanese leaders are rarely inspiring, always conspiring, and transformational only in concert with others. They know how to navigate the Japanese "web."

But can there be a web without a spider? The Japanese web—in the form of bureaucratic organization—looms large in our history, but we also have identified a great number of Japanese "spiders." There may never have been a Japanese Duce, but Japanese history is filled with protago-nists: revolutionaries in the 1860s, *genrō* in the 1890s, businessmen in the 1910s, ultranationalists in the 1920s, and reinvented democrats during the Occupation. Whenever the nation's institutions were shaken, leaders were there to rebuild. And while the rebuilding was underway, they were always there to supervise. Today, however, most agree with Okuda Hiroshi, chair-man of a large business group, that there is a "leadership deficit" in Japan.[17] The Japanese press blames a system that retards leadership.[18]

How different are these stereotypes? The caricature of leadership in both countries includes the capacity to compromise and compensate. Trasformismo, celebrated or decried as a peculiarly Italian ability to ab-sorb or deflect political differences, looks very much like the way Japanese avoid conflict.[19] Even if Italian leaders are depicted as more passionate and outspoken, they are also said to understand the need to be tolerant behind the scenes; analyses of Italian leaders are just as likely to stress corruption, mutual suspicion, ideological rigidity, and rhetorical excess as they are to focus on charisma and gallantry. They can sound very Japanese.

To propose that there are no Japanese or Italian ways to lead is to suggest that there are no institutional or cultural differences between the two countries. Such a claim is surely wrong. Japanese leaders do seem to emerge from and work within existing organizations; Japanese leaders have taken great care to nurture their protégés in order to ensure their legacies. Yet as we saw both in Kishi's efforts to revise the Constitution and in De Gasperi's efforts to remake the electoral system, "nails that stick out" will be hammered down in both countries. Italy and Japan each have had a share of strong as well as weak, enlightened as well as parochial, creative as well as care taking, and consensual as well as risk-oriented leaders. In short, each country has its spiders and its webs. Caricatures of national leadership style that focus on only one or the other are, like most stereotypes, engaging but misleading.

Culture matters far more directly as a tool wielded by leaders. And here is the most striking commonality between Japan and Italy. As we have seen, leaders in both countries reacted to a fear of being left behind, a yearning to be powerful. Bending history and symbols, Italian and Japanese leaders nurtured a popular belief that they could consolidate national identity, wealth, and power. Leaders in *both* countries knew how to appeal to affect. They understood how to legitimate their power, and they recognized that popular yearnings could be nourished by symbols as well as by material gain. Culture mattered most not as a great force but as a social mechanism. It was the way culture inspired, rather than the way it constrained, that gave it the most force.

LEADERSHIP MECHANISMS

Italy and Japan, like new states everywhere, were imagined in multiple ways.[20] State-building and wealth-creating opportunities mattered only when they were seized and exploited by political actors. Likewise, identities had first to be selected and then sold. Leaders actively pursued particular versions of national and regional interests. And it was these same individuals who brokered the results of the conflicts their efforts stimulated. In short, social and political mechanisms had—indeed *had* to have—a human face. They were the instruments of agents who bullied, bought, and inspired.

Our narrative has been filled with examples of *buying*. Trasformismo—the co-optation of opposition and the conjuring of majorities—originated in Cavour's insistence on the ideal of a *juste milieu*, "the continuous rhyth-mical oscillation of group alliances" that stabilized politics and made change possible.[21] By the time the practice passed into the hands of his successors, Italy's Parliament had become a full-blown bazaar. Policy was subordinated to deals, and bargaining dominated purpose. Nimble lead-ers like Depretis turned first this way, then that. They distributed what they had and collected what they could—all without regard for principle. Giolitti, who flirted with every political force from socialists to fascists, did not invent this form of buying, but he may have been its most able practi-tioner. None of this was alien to Japanese practice, where compensation and logrolling became fine arts at about the same time. Long before Hara Kei, the oligarchs had established exchange as the most effective mecha-nism to retain power. Even Itō and Yamagata had to protect themselves against liberals on their left and direct imperial rule on their right. For his part, Itō bought off counterrevolution with peerages and the imperial household with a budget independent of political oversight. The differ-ence, it seemed, was that the Japanese oligarchs refined compensation as a political tool while also articulating a coherent vision of national trans-formation. In both cases, buying helped circumvent the problem of alter-nation between "ins" and "outs." As long as opponents could be manipu-lated toward a political center, leaders could muddle through.

The full institutional flower of buying came after the Second World War, when politicians struggled to identify and occupy the Center. Cen-terers like De Gasperi and Yoshida—and later, Fanfani and Kishi—faced choices much like those faced by Cavour (between despots and revolu-tionaries) and Itō (between liberals and aristocrats). Now, however, the public was in the game, and leaders had to be more inventive and nimble than ever. They had to find or build a Center in full view. Once the Cen-ter was in place, they had to consolidate and defend it, now with mass pol-itics playing a critical role. And the Center always had to be renewed. They may have received less attention than their romantic or heroic counter-parts on the Left and Right, but successful centerers were perforce bril-liant buyers (Kishi was a notable failure in this respect). Their tactics were diverse: they deftly divided and conquered; they expanded or shrank the Center to isolate opponents; they bought some opponents off and brought others in; they shifted the Center by inventing new opponents and reinvented the Center by co-opting others' issues. This "manipulative absorption" often involved clandestine bargaining and negotiation; it yielded shifting and heterogeneous coalitions, often of short duration. Centering through buying became enshrined as the standard operating procedure in both Italian and Japanese democratic practice. Its success depended on skilled leaders.[22]

Indeed, the failures of centering were the failures of leaders to understand who could be bought and at what price—and who could not be bought at any price. Di Palma argues that it was not centering that brought down liberal Italy, but its "wrong execution." Giolitti, who never took pains to build a mass party, "emptied the center and weakened its attraction" while making deals with extremists who would not play the game.[23] In Japan today, centerers who reach in from the Right continue to preempt those from the Left. The LDP co-opted most of the opposition's social programs in the 1970s, reconsolidated its leadership in the 1980s, and in the 1990s skillfully secured coalition partners from every party except the JCP. Unlike in Italy, where the Center has been occupied by the Left and the Right, no one on the Japanese left has learned how to center effectively.

Centering seems also to generate a perverse consequence. Each time a centerer tries to buy an ally, he generates a conflict for the prospective partner. Should it or should it not collaborate? Once again, Giolitti is illustrative. His deals with the Socialists alienated the syndicalists and maximalists, led by Mussolini at the time. His deals with the conservatives alienated the nationalist Right. His centering with the Church alienated the "modernists" who wanted greater reform. These disparate political forces—each rebelling against concessions made to Giolitti—found common cause against him. A similar coalition of intransigents would form in response to De Gasperi's effort to thicken the Center half a century later. After years of responding to the whims of minority parties, De Gasperi sought to free himself and eliminate the parliamentary uncertainties that frustrated his program. But each time he won a group over, he left behind purists whose opposition stiffened. By 1953, when his DC missed a majority by a mere 57,000 votes, De Gasperi was finished—a victim of his own centering. Giolitti and De Gasperi centered so ardently that they became the universal target of Left, Church, and Right intransigents who had little in common but their determination to end the Center's power. Yet within decades some of their most ardent opponents were openly and nostalgically admiring their skills and sensibilities.

There are other ways to eliminate the Center's power. The most direct is *bullying*. Again our narrative offers up many examples. First is the strong version, what we might call siege. Rather than tempt opponents with material incentives, the leader surrounds and destroys them. Mussolini was a repeat offender. He did not wait to become a fascist before sharpening his skills as a bully. While still a Socialist, he confronted the reformers at the 1912 party congress who were considering Giolitti's blandishments. Mussolini dismissed reform and parliamentary cooperation; he ridiculed universal suffrage as the grasping efforts of a dying regime. He split the party and demanded that collaborators be expelled. Mussolini made sure this would be the last united Socialist Party congress. The reformers departed, leaving the leadership posts—including the editorship of *Avanti!*—to Mussolini and his allies. Two years later, Mussolini turned his sights on freemasons within the party, whom he also succeeded in purging. He was a well-practiced bully long before he was himself expelled—at which point he took up his fascist cudgel and systematized his thuggery.

Itō Hirobumi may have been an even more accomplished—if far less vulgar—bully. Mussolini squeezed the life out of full-grown opponents, but Itō smothered his stillborn. Mussolini wielded a cudgel, Itō a scalpel. His ability to enforce his own vision of parliamentarianism ensured that many of the social coalitions that confronted Mussolini never even formed in Japan. Itō also purged opponents: he expelled Ōkuma before Ōkuma could generate support for a more liberal program. Like Mussolini, Itō was not even remotely a democrat. He was, however, consistently more skilled at anticipating how to limit the power of opponents. Inspiring, buying, and bullying as the situation suggested, he effectively controlled the political arena and patrolled it with his allies.

If siege is the strong version of bullying, the weak version is what might be called trumpet blowing. Here, like Joshua, leaders succeed by perceiving weakness and timing their assault. Francesco Saverio Borelli and his colleagues perceived a fatal weakness in the Italian party system when the political class did not react effectively to his investigations in early 1992. In May, Borelli told the press of an internal crisis in the Republic, and that he and his associates could bring it down. They did. Likewise, Achille Occhetto's dramatic reforms were abetted considerably by the internal weakening of the PCI that began when Enrico Berlinguer engineered the "Historic Compromise" with the DC in 1978.

But, for all this buying and bullying, the most striking mechanism of political leadership we have examined has been *inspiration*. Establishing legitimacy—by appealing to affect rather than to power—was consistently the most effective and inexpensive tool of Italian and Japanese leaders. We have observed it in many forms. In the weakest version, leaders cloak themselves in the mantles of national heroes, mentors, or fallen comrades. Manufacturing legitimacy in this way seemed to preoccupy the Italians, and every leader sought association with Cavour and Garibaldi. But it rarely sufficed. Few could monopolize the associations. In April 1948, even the leftist parties appropriated Garibaldi for their Popular Front. The Christian Democrats crushed them. Mussolini literally dressed as Caesar and positioned himself as the heir to Roman grandeur. His fate is well chronicled. The more austere De Gasperi held Don Sturzo's mantle, while Togliatti held Gramsci's. A generation later, Fanfani held Dossetti's mantle, while Berlinguer held Togliatti's. Most recently, in a particularly ironic turn, Berlusconi has reached for De Gasperi's, even after the demise of Christian Democracy.

Many Japanese took a more aggressive tack in the instrumental use of history and culture. They found historical figures less useful than mythical ones. Japanese leaders routinely recombined shards of the past into a novel and resilient present—and institutionalized a new future. Consider Itō and Yamagata's careful sacralization of the emperor. In one of history's great and most transformative fictions, a young oligarchy conjured its legitimacy from tatters. They invented a "natural" political community that was sustained across total war, total defeat, and unconditional surrender. The same was true of Mutō Sanji's construction of "Japanese values." Mutō aggressively scanned the past to find legitimating appeals that would stabilize industrial relations for generations. Yoshida Shigeru rummaged around in a drawer full of possibilities, and pulled out artifices that were immensely soothing to a war-weary but still proud populace. With an earnest voice and a straight face, Yoshida invented a story about the Meiji Constitution that convinced many Japanese that militarists had hijacked a pacifist nation that was poised on a democratic path.

Nor were all Italian leaders maladroit. Achille Occhetto was singularly attentive to Italy's communist subculture and for a time redeployed its symbols adeptly in a post-communist world. Silvio Berlusconi overwhelmed his opponents by commandeering a national football cheer for his own political slogan. As in all matters, Mussolini was the most aggressive. He did not merely invoke history—Roman or Risorgimento, fabricated or authentic, it did not matter—he *policed* it. Like the Japanese genrō, Mussolini worked diligently to control the aesthetics and the rhetoric of historical representation.[24] The most successful bricoleurs did more than "invent tradition." They defined and tried to monopolize its telling. The most successful among them—Itō, Mutō, Mussolini, Yoshida—owned the rights to their version of history and collected the rents. Some failed, of course. Sidney Sonnino tried to reconstruct Cavour's legitimating instruments, Lo Statuto and the monarchy, but was repudiated at the polls. A century later, Umberto Bossi manufactured a fanciful regional identity, only to discover that it had little appeal. Even Occhetto could not convert the new democratic Left into sustained personal power. We learn that bricolage is no more foolproof than any other leadership mechanism—and we can refer to a history of fools to prove it.

We know that the various mechanisms of buying, bullying, and inspiring can overlap—they can operate simultaneously or independently. It is not only that "leadership matters" but that different forms of leadership matter at different times—or at the same time but in different measure. We have seen bullies who buy and inspire, as when Mussolini concocted the

356

Lateran Pacts with the Vatican while simultaneously crushing his secular opponents. Itō bought protection from counterrevolution while repressing liberals at the same time. Cavour first bought support from the Right and then the Left, and finally, almost as an afterthought, he tried to inspire while bullying the revolutionaries into submission. Other bullies reinvent themselves as buyers, as when Kishi Nobusuke learned just how lucrative democratic politics could be. Some buyers, such as Crispi, resorted to bullying when they could not succeed at any price—and still failed. We are again reminded of Machiavelli's injunction that the wise prince is flexible and invokes strategies "in conformity with the time."[25]

LEADERSHIP AND LEGACIES IN NATIONAL CONSOLIDATION

In a striking historical template, this book has chronicled common moments of elite consolidation and institutional transformation in Italy and Japan.[26] Although the Italian ruling class shifted more palpably than the Japanese in each case, every transition was contested and each subsequent order was informed by choices made by earlier leaders—animated each time by the prospect of catching up to and being accepted by the great powers. Many of the same great forces were at work—nationalism, the rise of mass politics, industrialization. But the parallels we have observed were never simply a function of similar great forces; nor were the differences simply a function of differences in resources. Individuals refract these forces and mobilize these endowments. Their direct and indirect legacies were realized in each of three domains we have examined: national identity, national wealth, and national power.

Identity

Why, despite a recent experience with civil war, was *regional* nationalism so weak in late nineteenth-century Italy? McAdam, Tarrow, and Tilly wonder why "a weak and inefficient polity built from a dispersed and disconnected set of petty states avoided serious outbreaks of regional separatism" for most of the past 140 years.[27] Chalmers Johnson wonders "why . . . the Japanese were more nationalistic in 1930 than in 1830, since at both times they spoke the same language, held roughly the same religious views, and painted the same kind of pictures."[28]

Mutatis mutandis, these puzzles are the same, and so are their solutions. In the Italian case no policy entrepreneur emerged to seize the opportunity that regionalism offered. In Japan, elite leaders gave different political meaning to the common social features of 1830 and 1930. As no leaders successfully activated regional identities, the political meaning manufactured in Japan was *national.* In both countries, regional and national identities were potential political tools. They awaited activation by political leaders who would deploy them for their own strategic purposes.

That is what we see in the contemporary case of Umberto Bossi, but there is an important twist. Regionalism may have been a latent resource for him and his Northern League, but it was not going to activate itself. It needed to be manufactured, for identity is an outcome of politics, not a precondition. People need not "naturally" identify with one another to become convinced that such identification is desirable. Bossi missed his chance. He struggled in vain to construct a "northern" identity long after other leaders had made Italians and consolidated Italy.

Wealth

Between Cavour's death in 1861 and Giolitti's first government in 1892, Italy lacked decisive economic leadership and a consistent guiding ideology. In Japan at the same time, oligarchs established a cohesive ruling clique and clarified a uniform developmental ideology. In Italy no individual emerged who could challenge, tame, and redirect the "great forces" that shaped economic development and industrialization. Those who tried, like Alessandro Rossi, failed repeatedly. The Italians did not just make *wrong* choices; they made contradictory and incoherent ones. Japan faced many of the same challenges, but its leadership was never diverted from its chosen path toward national strength and techno-industrial autonomy. Determined leaders with firm control over the ideas that animated economic development created advantages for Japan that eluded Italy. In particular, Japanese leaders attended to many of the most likely sources of social and political unrest. Both nations became industrial powers, but beneath similar industrial façades, the differences had important consequences for what would follow. It mattered that Ōkubo and Kishi prevailed—and that Mutō and Shibusawa were creative—just as it mattered that Cavour's heirs misunderstood his "hardened liberalism," and that Rossi miscalculated his colleagues' willingness to collaborate.

Power

One cannot understand constitutional order, political discourse, or the possibilities for ruling coalitions in modern Italy or Japan without appreciating the choices of past leaders. The question of "normality" is a legacy of past choices. As we have seen, neither country ever felt fully part of the great power game. Each has flayed itself for perceived abnormalities. For its part, Japan has never had a "normal" military—at least as measured against the idea that in democracies, civilians should control soldiers. In what is surely one of the most durable political choices, Yamagata Aritomo preserved the military's prerogatives in a larger constitutional order that was designed by Itō Hirobumi to limit civil rights while appearing progressive. Itō and Yamagata ensured the unifying power of the imperial house and left a legacy of authoritarianism and statist intimidation that Japan has never fully shed. Their aggressively creative use of history stabilized a fragile young state. But that stability carried a price, and Japan is *still* struggling to balance bureaucratic prerogative, military legitimacy, and popular representation as it reaches toward "normality."[29]

Italy's defeat in the Second World War bequeathed it a similar constitutional ban on the deployment of its military, but Italian leaders had relatively little difficulty in legitimating a postwar military. They have had a different skin to shed: the scaly encumbrance of "transformist" inefficiency. Splintered parties in endlessly reconfigured alliances have caused persistent frustration. If Yamagata and Itō haunt Japanese political discourse today, the ghosts of Cavour and Giolitti haunt Italy. Cavour created a system imbalanced to favor not the state but the parliament, and Giolitti followed by institutionalizing mechanisms of exchange and reward. In so doing, Giolitti broadened the political landscape. His flirtation with the socialists was Italy's first, critically important, opening to the Left. The Left later consolidated its legitimacy during the Resistance, and no post-Giolittian Italian leader could avoid collaborating with some part of the Left. Italy may be frustrated by the fragmentation of its party system, but unlike Japan, it can celebrate a long history of wide-band political representation.

Some legacies have been direct and enduring—like those of the Japanese oligarchs—and others indirect and sporadic, like those of the Italian liberals. Some were injected directly into the new national bloodstream, like the legacy of the mercantilist planners and corporate paternalists in Japan. Others were set aside as part of an expanded repertoire of action available to future policy entrepreneurs, as in the case of Cavour's parliamentary code. Such legacies, like leaders, were not uniform, but they have been a ubiquitous part of the consolidation of both national systems.

CONJURING POSSIBILITIES FROM CONSTRAINTS

Most of our theories tell us that history *limits* possibilities. We have observed the opposite. We have seen real choices being made, across more than a century and a half in two surprisingly similar countries. These choices often stretched or transcended the constraints of culture and of institutions in sharply discontinuous ways. They followed no single institutional or technological logic.[30] At crucial moments, leaders select among plausible alternatives—Mussolini for war in 1940 and De Gasperi for Europe and Yoshida for "cheap riding" in 1950s. Some leaders fail to perceive alternatives that others understood in similar situations—Cavour unlike Itō in the 1860s, Rossi unlike Mutō in the 1890s, Fuwa unlike Occhetto in the 1990s. Perhaps our most important general finding is that history, rather than limiting or channeling choice, actually *enhances* choice and multiplies possibilities. Scholars all too often miss the creative possibilities for agency. They miss how history becomes a nearly bottomless well of resources in the hands of particularly able leaders. History is important, that is to say, not because it limits paths but because it creates so many.

We know the truth of this claim for two reasons. First, so many of the most creative choices we have examined were made under objectively limiting constraints. Second, we have *not* examined the choices of very many Italians and Japanese. After all, we have ignored the agency of groups and of classes. Women and others excluded from the elite ranks have been excluded here as well. Our top-down, elite-focused account of near-mythical historical figures has explored only a thin slice of Italian and Japanese history. By identifying common leadership mechanisms and by showing how normal is the contingency of choice, I can only begin to suggest the limits to our knowledge and the possibilities for the future.

Indeed, far more important than generating knowledge is an ethical claim about leadership. By focusing on leadership, we revive notions of individual responsibility and culpability at a time when each has been devalued. It is not only social science that has been looking past individuals. The same is true of civics education and international law. We need to monitor carefully how the past is deployed. A new generation of leaders—and not just in Italy or Japan—is always looking to fashion its preferred new order. Which past will be used, and for which future? We are waiting, but we should be watching as well.

Italy and Japan differ in fundamental and irreconcilable ways. Yet both have been traveling much the same road: striving to catch up and to join the advanced nations, to become "normal." Their journeys have taken them past, around, and through some remarkably similar challenges. The question that animates my research has been why they remain so different. The easy answer is that they remain different because they started different, with different resource mixes, different social forces, and different constraints.

In fact, they were not so differently endowed, and there were remarkable similarities. What we have seen is Japanese and Italian leaders, driving toward similar visions of modernity, but often intervening in different ways. This book reinserts choice between great social, economic, and political forces, on the one hand, and outcomes, on the other. It is a reminder that history has no shortcuts. Conventional interpretations of change suggest that each country responds to challenges in its own way. In the shortcut version, Japan responds with "traditional" centralization and authoritarianism, Italy with "traditional" fragmentation. I am impressed, by contrast, with the idea that while history matters, while contingency is ubiquitous and institutions have inertia, each country has many different histories and many different institutions. Many wait to be constructed, even to be imagined.

Specifically, there was always more than one "Italian," more than one "Japanese," way to respond to great forces. Human agency intervenes between the histories and the forces, to filter, to deflect, and to select responses. I have shown how human agents seized opportunities and actively sorted through or built newly "Italian" and "Japanese" alternatives.

We have learned that mid-nineteenth-century Italian leaders could have tried to develop their economy behind closed markets, but chose not to. Japanese leaders in the twentieth century could have opted for early liberalization, but chose not to. Italian leaders could have opted for authoritarianism rather than parliamentarianism, but chose not to. They might have engineered a divine monarchy, but they rejected the idea. They had the chance to develop corporate paternalism, but chose not to. They could have focused harder and more successfully on keeping nationalism away from the Right, but they failed to find a way to do so. Close comparative study allows us to see constraints in a new light. The study of leaders in these two countries, if we hold them up side by side, shows that similar constraints can be used differently, and that different constraints can be overcome creatively. The differences we observe in the two countries were not preordained by great forces any more than their disappearance is preordained by convergence at the "end of history." We live not in a world of predestination, but in a world of possibilities.

Notes

PREFACE: LEADERS MATTER

1. Marx 1972, 8.
2. Dunn 1985, 77.
3. Thomas Friedman, "Arafat's War," *New York Times*, 13 October 2000.
4. Tarrow (1994) is the first use of the "Odd Couple" analogy in the analysis of Italy and Japan. Boltho, et al., eds., (2001) demonstrates how much there is to learn from structured, theoretically informed comparison of these two countries.
5. Galli della Loggia 1998, 183. See especially his chap. 5, "The Missing History of the State."
6. Miyamoto 1995. See also Sengoku (1998, 108) for explanations of the norm-abiding behavior of Japanese.
7. Japanese names are presented in standard Japanese order, with family name first.

INTRODUCTION: WHY LEADERS MATTER

1. Hook 1943, 15. Hook celebrated prematurely: "That history is made by men and women is no longer denied except by some theologians and mystical metaphysicians" (xi).
2. Weber's original formulation of charisma is in Gerth and Mills 1958. In the mid-twentieth century, when great leaders seemed active everywhere, political scientists such as Rustow (1970) and Apter (1963) turned to Weberian "charisma" to explain the leadership capacities of Hitler, Churchill, Roosevelt, de Gaulle, Nkrumah, and Nehru. Like Weber, they concluded that charisma was a fragile base for legitimate rule. Others turned to "psychobiography"; Pye (1991) is a critique by a practitioner.
3. Geertz (1973, 312) calls this the "ethic of imprecision."
4. See Kubicek (forthcoming) for an elaboration of this example.
5. Barrington Moore's account of the transition from feudalism to contemporary society was particularly influential. His dictum "no bourgeoisie, no democracy" (1966, 418) was the touchstone for political scientists influenced by historical sociology.
6. Skocpol (1979) has been criticized for rejecting the "purposive image" of social change in her account of social revolutions. See critiques by Dunn (1985) and Laitin and Warner (1992).

363

7. Katznelson 1997, 83.

8. Hall 1992, 90.

9. See Pierson (2000) and Mahoney (2000) for analyses of "path dependence." Krasner (1984) and Sewell (1992) examine how stable institutions provide the rules for political choice until they are shaken by crises.

10. Most contemporary analyses of international politics exclude what Kenneth Waltz (1954) calls "first image" explanations, that is, those based on the choices made by individuals. See Byman and Pollack (2001) for an effort to reinsert leadership into realist international relations.

11. Tsebelis (1990, 40) makes this point clearly: "The rational choice approach focuses its attention on the constraints imposed on rational actors . . . The prevailing institutions (the rules of the game) determine the behavior of actors."

12. Ordeshook 1990. Some resist the idea that real people are not modeled well by rational choice/game theoretic analyses. See Levi 1997.

13. North 1990, 363. Cf. Levi (1997, 33) and Elster (1986, 24).

14. Betts (2000, 11) calls Churchill's choice to resist the Germans alone after the fall of France "among the epochal decisions of the past century."

15. For a creative combination of psychology with informational economics, see Kuran 1995. See also Nisbett and Ross (1980) and Khong (1992) for how "schema theory" attempts to capture group dynamics and individual calculations simultaneously. James Johnson (1997, 2000) is helpful on the instrumental use of culture and on symbolic action. See Kitschelt 1992, Immergut 1998, and Mahoney 2000 for particularly lucid insights into contingency and historical trajectories. Elster 1986, North 1990, and Levi 1997 are nuanced approaches to rationality and ideas. Bates et al. (1998) apply game theory to historical analysis. Kimeldorf (1988) and Granovetter and McGuire (1998) have situated networked individuals in the process of institutional change.

16. This is also the formulation of Ilchman and Uphoff (1969) and of Breslauer (2002).

17. This evokes the idea of "normal accidents" in Perrow 1985.

18. Kingdon 1995.

19. Sewell 1992, 20.

20. Burns (1978) makes this distinction. It is also used by Breslauer 2002.

21. Lanzara 1998, 28.

22. Lévi-Strauss 1966, 22.

23. Ibid., 19.

24. Machiavelli 1986, 175.

25. James Johnson 1997, 9. See also J. Johnson 2000.

26. See Brysk 1995.

27. Etzioni (1961) similarly distinguishes among coercive, material, and normative mechanisms of organizational control. Hedström and Swedberg (1998) is an important theoretical treatment of social mechanisms. McAdam, Tarrow, and Tilly (2001) is a comparative historical application of the concept.

28. Kertzer 1996, 66, 68. See also Bourdieu (1991) and Sommer (1991).

29. Machiavelli (1995, 17) wrote that "a prudent man must always follow in the footsteps of great men and imitate those who have been outstanding. If his own prowess fails to compare with theirs, at least it has an air of greatness about it." Marx agreed that some mantles might be too big for an aspiring leader. He ends the "18th Brumaire" with the expectation that Louis Bonaparte would not be up to the task of leading France, and that revolution would soon follow.

30. Hobsbawm and Ranger 1983, 1–2; Swidler 1986, 273; and Laitin 1986, 11–12. Vlastos (1998) is a fascinating application of this model to Japanese history.

31. In the language of "complexity theory" the piling up of actions and changes that weaken a structure and that render it weak enough to be destroyed by a trumpet blast is called "accumulated delay." The trumpeter ought not get too much credit for the victory. Indeed, this is how Marx (1972, 8) explained the success of Louis Bonaparte, whom he called a "grotesque mediocrity."

32. Schumpeter 1950.

33. William Riker (1986) described these actors as "heresthetes."
34. Machiavelli 1986, 430.
35. Kingdon (1995, 192) concurs. See also Ansell and Fish 1999.
36. Hughes 1965, 14. Kemp (1985, 150) offers a nearly identical geophysical explanation.
37. Reischauer 1988, 24–25. See Reed (1993) for a valuable critique.
38. Hughes 1965, 40–41.
39. These words of the British ambassador to Italy in 1911 (quoted by Bosworth 1979, 7) anticipate perfectly the characterizations of Japan by General Douglas MacArthur a half century later. See *Yomiuri Shimbun*, 24 July 2000, for MacArthur's condescension.
40. An 1893 editorial in *Kokumin no Tomo* addressed the issue of "Japan's National Dignity," with undisguised bitterness that "the most progressive, developed, civilized, intelligent and powerful nation in the Orient still cannot escape the scorn of white people." Quoted in Pyle 1969, 167.
41. Both terms are translated as "normal nation." The phrases were introduced in books written by conservative politician Ozawa Ichirō and leftist former Prime Minister Massimo D'Alema, both in 1995. See chap. 10.
42. Plutarch 1979.
43. Plutarch 1979, 433, 290–91.
44. Machiavelli 1986, 132.
45. Crick's introduction to Machiavelli (1986) and De Grazia (1989) offer excellent insight into Machiavelli's balancing of *fortuna* and *virtú*.
46. Machiavelli 1995, 77.
47. On counterfactual political analysis see Weber 1949, Fearon 1991, and Lebow 2000.
48. Weber 1949, 164.
49. Here I follow Luebbert (1991), who examined political coalitions in interwar Europe and "found little evidence that similarly situated leaders responded differently, or at least with different levels of success, to similar inherited inducements and constraints" (306–7). I wonder whether he looked carefully enough and in the right places.
50. See Lustick (1996) on the selection biases in the historical research by political scientists. Also see Fearon 1991, 179–80.
51. See Bates and Bianco (1990, 357) for a very similar assertion.
52. De Tocqueville 1949, 64.

Chapter 1: Chasing Prestige and Security

1. Chabod (1996), Bosworth (1979), and Cerasi (2002) are excellent accounts of Italy's drive to become "the last of the great powers." Cerasi (2002, 5) is the source of the epigram by Arangio Ruiz.
2. Albrecht-Carrié 1950, 4.
3. Mazzini embraced "a vision of Italy's past greatness, but this vision was never a central part of Risorgimento ideology." Indeed, it may have been particularly hard for him to make such an appeal, since the exiled Mazzini was "remarkably ignorant of Italy." Hales 1956, 16.
4. On Japanese liberalism, see Benfell 1997, chap. 3.
5. Cafagna (1999, 102) is helpful on this point.
6. Mack Smith 1959, 39. See also Kemp 1985, 152; LaPalombara 1987, 8; de Cecco and Giovannini 1989, 201. For more on the Japanese "revolution from above," see Trimberger 1972.
7. Moore 1966, 430–31. Lovett (1982) is a useful account of dissent in Liberal Italy. See also Kemp 1985, 151.
8. Mack Smith 1959, 68.
9. See Chabod (1996) and Bosworth (1979, 9) on this point.
10. Vlastos 1989, 382.
11. The imperial missive, undoubtedly written by the author of the Meiji Constitution, Itō Hirobumi, is quoted in Iwata (1964), 156.
12. I am grateful to Andrew Gordon for suggesting this term.

13. Quoted in Haycraft 1985, 4. See also Bosworth 1979, 5.

14. Bismarck and Sir Charles Hardinge are quoted in Bosworth 1979, 7.

15. Businessmen, doctors, lawyers, and youth groups were all first organized through the state. Academic historians are a particularly interesting case in point. The imperial rescript of 1869 declares that "historiography is forever immortal state ritual." See Mehl (1998) and Brownlee (1997) for more on how the Meiji state controlled the writing of history. Pyle (1973) and Garon (1987) address the ways in which state officials came to insinuate themselves into society.

16. Ginsborg 1990, 146. See also Dente 1989.

17. Salvemini (1973, 159) points out that the leaders of the Risorgimento "attacked the Vatican but did not touch the parishes." The Meiji oligarchs attacked the feudal lords and extracted surplus disproportionately from the peasants, but left the peasantry unchallenged in their dominion over the land.

18. Seton-Watson 1967, 13.

19. The closest analogue is the suppression of Buddhism by Oda Nobunaga in the late seventeenth century. Buddhism offered no competition to the modern Japanese state.

20. Machiavelli 1986, 145.

21. Seton-Watson 1967, 8; Kertzer 1980, 108.

22. Tullio-Altan 1997, 52–54. See also Formigoni 1998, chap. 2.

23. See Barzini 1964, 220. Note, too, that the Church was not monolithic: a strong Catholic left coexisted with a powerful reactionary right. See Tullio-Altan (1997) on this point.

24. Tullio-Altan (1997, 80) examines this opening to social action and explains how "fragments of the distant past mixed with particles of the future."

25. Trigilia 1986, 113–14.

26. In this way, the Church became a powerful instrument of social and economic policy, often more powerful than the state. See De Rosa and Malgeri 1995, 240. It was the Church that first integrated the Italian banking system by integrating workers and proprietors across class lines. By 1910, Catholic associations had enrolled nearly half a million people. Church banks accounted for more than 20 percent of all deposits nationwide. See also Trigilia (1986), 85, 114–20.

27. These data are from Trigilia 1986.

28. Pope Pius XI was sympathetic to the fascists as early as 1922. See Hughes 1965, 94. Members of the Partito Popolari served in Mussolini's first cabinet. See chap. 6 of this book.

29. Chubb and Vannicelli 1988, 131. See Kertzer (1980, 1988) for particular insight into these two worlds.

30. Bellah 1980, 14.

31. Ciuffoletti 1980; Earle 1986.

32. Manacorda (1966) is an excellent account. See also Earle 1986, 13–17.

33. See Degl'Innocenti 1980; Zangheri 1997; and Seidelman 1979.

34. While the Church denied it was possible to be both Catholic and communist, the Communist Party embraced Catholics who might join it. Swidler and Grace (1988, 51) report that the number of Italians who thought it possible to be both a good Catholic and a good communist grew from 21% in 1953 to 45% in 1977.

35. Trigilia 1986. Galli della Loggia (1998, 80) suggests that the PCI succeeded in the "Red Belt" because it could combine the strong communal and state traditions of the North. See also Ginsborg 1990, 195.

36. Trigilia 1986, 92; Hellman 1987, 334.

37. De Grand 1989, 4–5.

38. Tarrow 1994, 3.

39. Gordon (1991, 333–42) is an excellent review. Moore (1966) is the classic comparison.

40. Romano (1991, 24) makes this point about Italy. See also Bosworth (1998), who invokes Chabod (1963). Tullio-Altan (1997, 136) quotes Alfredo Rocco, who promised that fascism would rescue Italy from its "long medieval night" of anarchy and weakness.

41. Maruyama (1963, 27) prefers to label this "fascism from above."

42. Croce (1982) is the original formulation of fascism as a parenthesis.

43. Maruyama 1963, 65.

44. See Hori 1990; Wilson 1967–68.

45. Tullio-Altan (1997, 134) reminds us how incoherent and variable fascism was. Germino 1971, 105; Aquarone 1974, 103. Gramsci's notion of fascism as an armed dictatorship operating on behalf of the plutocracy and the landed elite seems not to capture its full palette. See Losito and Segre 1992, 66; see also Coppa (1971) and Seton-Watson (1967).

46. Wilson 1967–68, 406.

47. Marshall 1967; Pyle 1973 and 1989; and Duus 1988 are particularly useful accounts. See also Samuels 1994.

48. Bosworth 1979, 8; Chabod 1996.

49. Takahashi quoted in Crawcour 1988, 389. Takahashi was assassinated by rightists in 1936.

50. Gerschenkron 1966. For critiques of Gerschenkron's thesis in the Italian case, see Zamagni (1993) and Toniolo (1990).

51. Webster 1975, 77.

52. Webster 1975, 78. Yet, as in Italy, all was not left to powerful private interests. The Japanese government created the Yawata Works of Nippon Steel in 1901, in much the same way that the Italian government had built and financed a large steelworks in Terni in 1884—"to free the navy and railways from dependence on foreign supplics" (Seton-Watson 1967, 80–81). See the accounts in Zamagni (1993) and Toniolo (1990).

53. Kemp (1985, 158) calls the later Italian choice for protection "inevitable." If so, it was made far too late to consolidate its intended gains.

54. Sprigge 1969, 25–26. Kemp (1985, 152) calls Cavour a "doctrinaire free trader."

55. Webster 1975, 8.

56. Webster 1975, chap. 4; Seton-Watson 1967, 292; Zamagni 1993.

57. Webster 1975, 126.

58. Lockwood 1955, 249.

59. Ibid., 253–54.

60. Sarti 1971, 101.

61. Diggins 1972, 160.

62. See Johnson (1982) and Samuels (1987).

63. Sarti 1971, 107.

64. Ibid., 124 (emphasis added).

65. Samuels 1987.

66. Even earlier, in 1843, Vincenzo Gioberti identified the Italian people as "a desire, not a fact, a presupposition, not a reality, a name, and not a thing." Gioberti quoted in Bollati 1983, 44.

67. Chabod 1996, 170.

68. Galli della Loggia (1998), Formigoni (1998), and Chabod (1996) are particularly helpful sources.

69. Tullio-Altan (1997) and Romano (1991) are insightful here on Italian "primacy" (*primato morale e civile degli italiani*). See also Procacci 1968; Sprigge 1969.

70. Bosworth 1979, 8. Mazzini's "Third Italy" would be an era of association and fraternity that would follow eras of Roman liberty and Catholic equality.

71. Brown 1955, 7. Lie (2001) shows how the idea of the Japanese as monoethnic was first vigorously promoted only *after* World War II. Until then Japan described itself as a multiethnic empire. Weiner (1997, 7) reports that Prime Minister Itō solicited Herbert Spencer's view on the desirability of intermarrying Japan's lower classes with Westerners to enhance Japan's capacity for national development. The social Darwinist advised against the idea on the grounds that hybridizing the races would weaken both.

72. Fujitani 1993, 92.

73. Fukuzawa 1973, 144.

74. Oguma 1995, 6.

75. Gluck 1985, 37. For additional support of this view, see Fujitani (1993) and Oguma (1995).

76. Fukuzawa 1973, 171.

77. Gluck (1985, 23) is particularly eloquent on this point.

78. Fukuzawa quoted in Pyle 1969, 149.

79. Duus and Scheiner (1988, 654) speak of the absence of a single "great tradition" and the possibilities presented by a "polychromatic" mix. Gluck (1985) identifies the trial and error process and the lack of a "canonical source" for Meiji ideology. Fujitani (1993, 89) speaks of the "one dominant memory." See Greenfield (1992) on national identity as "created symbolic order." See also Doak 1997.

80. These agents were so alien that some were confused for Christian missionaries and attacked for antistate activities! See Fujitani 1993, 88. Weiner (1997) lucidly examines this project.

81. See Titus (1974), Gluck (1985), Hardacre (1989), and Pyle (1989) for excellent accounts of state Shinto.

82. Chamberlain quoted in Fujitani 1993, 78–79.

83. Nitobe 1912, 121. (Internal quote in the first sentence attributed to Jesse B. Carter.)

84. Weiner (1997) and Morris-Suzuki (1998) are excellent on this point.

85. Duus and Scheiner 1988, 655. Early in the summer 2000 general election campaign, Prime Minister Mori Yoshiro proclaimed that Japan was a "divine nation centered on the emperor," and three weeks before the election, used the word *kokutai* to describe the polity. His remarks raised a storm of protest in the media.

86. Mussolini had the phrase inscribed atop the Palazzo della Civiltà, the modernist coliseum he built for the 1942 Esposizione Universale di Roma.

87. The Black Dragon Society, established in 1901, dedicated itself to "the virtue and wisdom of the Japanese race." It counted both Itō Hirobumi and Kita Ikki in its membership. See chapters 2 and 6 of this book.

88. Haga 1968, 235–81. Minami (1994, 46–52) reports that Haga's 1907 essay, penned just after the Russo-Japanese War and the alliance with the British, made the Japanese feel they were part of a great nation for the first time.

89. Pyle 1969, 188; Minami 1994, 44.

90. Byas 1942, 130.

91. Torii Ryuzō quoted in Morris-Suzuki 1998, 16.

92. Nitobe 1936, 1, 20. In a speech to the United Nations in 1993, Prime Minister Hosokawa used this formulation to describe the Japanese. He advertised Nitobe's reissued book as holding the "key" to unlock Japan's "national mind." See Gluck 1998, 278–79.

93. These opening lines from *Basic Research into the Superiority of the Japanese People* are quoted in Morris-Suzuki 1998, 89–90. At the height of the Japanese Empire, when nearly one-third of the emperor's subjects were not Japanese, the notion of racial purity was reinterpreted. In some accounts, ethnicity and assimilation came to be valued over race and biology. See Oguma (1995, 4) and Morris-Suzuki 1998, 81–83, 91.

94. Mussolini quoted in Gibson 1973, 267.

95. Oguma (1995, 363) speaks of the Korean origins of the Yamato emperor. Chamberlain, in Fujitani (1993, 78–79), speaks of the emperors who had been hounded from office, and of one who had to escape from his pursuers by hiding under a load of dried fish. Gluck (1985, 3) might have had the Italy-Japan comparison in mind when she wrote that "although no society is innocent of collective notions about itself, some countries have made more of ideology than others."

96. Galli della Loggia 1998, chap. 1.

97. Romano 1991, 20.

98. Mack Smith 1959, 56.

99. See Novack (1970) for historical background on the various claims to the Julian/Istrian region. See Taira (1997), Morris-Suzuki (1998), and Weiner (1997) for analysis of how an expansive, but initially cautious, Meiji government made the indigenous Ainu in the north and Ryūkyūans in the south the objects of "redemptive projects." Even the liberal Nitobe Inazō considered the Ainu worthy of extinction. See Weiner 1997, 12. Morris-Suzuki (1998, 23–25) calls this program of assimilation "coloring in" and notes that the Japanese government invited Horace Capron, a former secretary of agriculture who had played a role in the suppression of Native Americans as the U.S. government expanded westward, to ad-

vise them. She reports that over time, as Japanese national identity was progressively reified, these people were transformed from "foreign" to "backward."

100. For more on this view, see Oguma (1995, 3) and Taira (1997, 144).

101. Weiner 1997, 10.

102. Thanks to Ellis Krauss for this interesting observation.

CHAPTER 2: HOW TO BUILD A STATE

1. Rebels from the domains of Satsuma and Chōshū dominated. Notehelfer (1990, 225) suggests more attention should be paid to local politics and mass movements.

2. See Iwata (1964), Jansen (1989), and Beasley (1989) for accounts of this period.

3. France had supported the shogunate's effort to suppress Chōshū in 1866, while Satsuma sought British help against the center.

4. Using the emperor as a shield against insurgency was not an idea original to the restorationists. Grasping for its own survival, the Tokugawa shogunate had itself "returned" governing rights to the emperor in October 1867. But it was too little, too late. Sasaki 1995, 117–19. Fujitani (1996) is the best account of this in English.

5. See Bix 2000.

6. Cafagna 1999, 152.

7. Cafagna 1999, 131–32.

8. Mack Smith 1985, 61.

9. When Cavour first became a minister, Victor Emmanuel told Massimo D'Azeglio, "You want me to nominate Cavour? I shall be pleased to, but be sure that before long he will take all your portfolios from you!" And he did. See Holt 1970, 181.

10. Cavour and D'Azeglio worked overtime to cultivate the image of the king as *galantuomo*—"a man who can be trusted"—when in fact Victor Emmanuel was, like his father before him, a rogue. He bragged to the nationalists that he would lead them to war against Austria, while simultaneously bragging to the Austrians that he would help them squash the nationalist movements. Cavour did not trust him.

11. Di Scala 1995, 76

12. Blumberg 1990.

13. Hearder 1994, 141–42.

14. Sprigge 1969, 71.

15. Ibid., 34.

16. Cafagna 1999, 99–100, and Hearder 1994, 48.

17. Mack Smith (1985, 137) reports that Cavour falsely accused Mazzinians of loving revolution more than they loved Italy, and they responded correctly by accusing him of fearing revolution more than loving a united Italy.

18. Manin's Venetian Republic and Mazzini's Roman Republic barely existed.

19. Mack Smith 1971, 56.

20. Pombeni 1994, 438. Also see Cammarrano 1997, 150.

21. Cavour was convinced that rule by priests was as damaging as rule by Austrians. His ultimate formula, "a free church in a free state," was designed to avoid the destruction of each.

22. Cafagna (1999) is a lovely account of these machinations.

23. Mack Smith 1971, 62.

24. See Beasley (1990, 79) for a good account. Akita (1967, 61) notes that as late as 1880 the emperor was still not the "unquestioned public symbol of reverence and awe" he would become. Bix (2000) questions the extent to which the emperor was the tool of the oligarchs.

25. Tanaka 1979, 67–69.

26. Sasaki 1995, 121.

27. This is from the *Kokuyu Taii*, quoted by Endo 1991, 91–94.

28. Sasaki 1995, 121–22. For fascinating details on the "Six Great Imperial Tours," see Fujitani 1996, chap. 2.

29. See Tanaka 1979, 224, 238–43. Also see Sasaki 1995, 132.

30. Fujitani 1996, 98–99.

31. Tanaka 1979, 67–69. Fujitani (1996, 162) notes that Itō and the other oligarchs feared that the emperor they had created could be used by their opponents.

32. Chap. 8 in McAdam, Tarrow, and Tilly (2001) is an excellent comparative account of post-Risorgimento unrest in Italy.

33. Silberman 1993, 175.

34. There were nearly three hundred documented revolts in 1868–69. See Tanaka (1979, 8) and White (1995).

35. Mōri 1969, 141–45; Tanaka 1979, 70–74.

36. Jansen 1989, 308.

37. Saigo Takamori, the most conservative of all the oligarchs, wanted to outlaw both Buddhism and Christianity. See Beasley 1990, 81; Hardacre (1989) is the most comprehensive account of the Meiji leaders' use of Shinto to sustain their rule. Also see Vlastos (1989, 386) and Titus 1974, 38.

38. Endo 1991, 110–11.

39. Itō 1906, 38–41.

40. Beasley 1989, 646.

41. Itō cited in Beckmann 1957, 74 ff. See also Titus (1974, 65) for more on Itō's calculation.

42. Vlastos 1989, 382.

43. This account is based on Pyle 1989, Vlastos 1989, and Notehelfer 1990.

44. Itō cited in Beasley 1990, 77.

45. Silberman (1993, 191) frames these choices clearly.

46. Fukuzawa quoted in Pyle 1989, 676.

47. Fukuzawa 1973, 142. See also Mitani 1988, 65.

48. They based their claims for representative government on the Meiji Charter Oath, the most authoritative statement of the Restoration's goals, which promised public debate and deliberative assemblies but which had been shelved by the oligarchs. Vlastos 1989, 404. See also Akita 1967, chap. 2.

49. Sakamoto 1989, 637–38.

50. Yamagata cited in Vlastos 1989, 411.

51. These are described by Vlastos 1989.

52. See Sakamoto (1989, 41–88, 684) and Lebra 1973, 52–53. Note too that Ōkuma was nominally expelled not for his advocacy of a British-style parliament but for his opposition to the government's corrupt dealings in Hokkaido.

53. Vlastos 1989, 413.

54. Sakamoto 1989, 590.

55. Ibid., 425.

56. Itō became convinced that Japan would have to learn from the West once he had visited Europe (illegally) in the mid-1860s. Hamada (1936) is a useful, if hagiographic, English language account of Itō's life.

57. See Akita 1967, 9–11. In 1843 the *daimyō* of Echizen had the Dutch constitution translated, and the shogunate established a constitutional study office. See Beckmann 1957, 26.

58. Silberman 1993, 193.

59. Beasley 1990, 73.

60. Beckmann 1957, 73.

61. Itō quoted in Beckmann 1957, 72 ff. See also Hamada (1936, 84) and Nish (1990).

62. Titus 1974, 37; Bix 2000.

63. Itō quoted in Pyle 1989, 700. See Titus (1974, 36) for a slightly different translation. Asukai (1995, 82–83) cites a similar passage.

64. Titus 1974, 43.

65. Itō quoted in Akita 1967, 61.

66. Sakamoto 1989, 115–43. In later years, these resources enabled the government to circumvent Diet spending caps—and, apparently, to bribe politicians when the need arose. See Gluck 1985, 78; Titus 1974, 127–28.

67. Gluck 1985, 76.

68. Sakamoto 1989, 11–14; Asukai 1995, 71–73, 77; Bix 2000.

69. Gluck 1985, 146; Titus 1974, 21, 24.

70. Ramseyer and Rosenbluth 1995, 34.

71. Itō, 1906, 108.

72. Titus (1974) is the best analysis. See p. 51 for "gatekeepers of the Imperial Will." Mitani (1988, 88) reports that between 1888 and 1924 all but one president of the Privy Council was a former prime minister.

73. Itō quoted in Asukai 1995, 83–84 (emphasis added). Ōkubo never identified himself as an imperial subject, and felt free to ignore imperial orders, claiming that "an Imperial order inconsistent with morality is not an Imperial order." Ōkubo quoted in Asukai, 54–55.

74. Beckmann 1957, 80–82.

75. Gluck 1985, 44.

76. Itō 1906, 154.

77. Pyle 1969, 144.

78. Itō 1906, 74.

79. Ibid., 12.

80. Ibid., 1.

81. Ibid., chap. 2.

82. Beasley 1989, 623. Bix (2000) argues that the emperor retained a considerably wider set of prerogatives.

83. Itō made it illegal for the emperor to be "made a topic of derogatory comment" or even "one of discussion." See Itō 1906, 7.

84. Fujimura 1961, 100–1.

85. Ibid., 47, 103–5; Hackett 1971, 50.

86. Fujimura, 1961, 65–66

87. Ibid., 94–95. Yamagata was just forty years old at this time. See also Hackett 1971, 83.

88. Fujimura, 1961, 15–17. See also Ramseyer and Rosenbluth 1995, 90.

89. Hackett 1971, 84–86.

90. Fujimura 1961, 197; Endo 1991, 280–81; Oka 1958, 123–25; Ramseyer and Rosenbluth 1995, 92–93.

91. Beasley 1990, 152–53. Yamagata never succeeded in gaining control of the Imperial Navy, which also maintained independent access to the emperor.

92. Fujimura 1961, 240.

93. See Mitani 1988, 68–69, 80.

94. In one of the most interesting uses of its veto, the Supreme Military Council agreed to a civilian cabinet in 1936 after the 2/26 Incident *only* on the condition that Yoshida Shigeru not be appointed foreign minister, thus blocking Japan's last chance for conciliatory diplomacy vis-à-vis the United States and Great Britain. See Byas 1942, 126.

95. This legal change is ignored in most accounts of the rise of military power in Japan, including Ramseyer and Rosenbluth 1995. See Heginbotham, forthcoming, for details.

96. Ramseyer and Rosenbluth (1995, 94) note that despite all the legal finagling that led to military independence, as long as Yamagata was alive "all this did not make an independent Army; instead it made a powerful Yamagata." Once Yamagata passed from the scene, the military was unfettered.

97. Hackett (1971, 213) compares Yamagata's "large circle of supporters both among the military and civil bureaucrats" with Itō's more narrowly constituted clique, and suggests this is why the latter turned to party politics in his later years.

98. He did this first in 1881 when his plan to reorganize the military on Prussian lines met internal opposition. See Fujimura 1961, 99–100, 146–48.

99. Fujimura 1961, 153–54; Oka 1958, 47, 55, 66–67, 72, 87, 99–100.

100. Kawada 1998, 196–97; Oka 1958, 47, 55, 66–67.

101. Sakamoto 1989, 370, 683–84; Fujimura 1961, 258; Oka 1958, 109.

102. Sakamoto 1989, 683–84; Fujimura 1961, 144–45, 268; Oka 1958, 109.

103. This argument is made elegantly by Maruyama 1963, 5.

104. Seton-Watson 1967, 6.

105. This is Piero Gobetti's metaphor. See Cafagna 1999, 12.

106. Di Palma (1978) makes this argument with particular clarity.

107. Lanzara 1999, 8.
108. This view is shared by observers as diverse as Sturzo (1926), Tivaroni (cited in Hearder 1994, 181), and Cafagna 1999.
109. See Ramseyer and Rosenbluth 1995, 39.
110. Hackett (1971, 344–45) suggests that "Yamagata's political power always rested squarely on his unquestioned position as the first soldier of the land." Ramseyer and Rosenbluth (1995, 91) exaggerate only slightly when they suggest that "the internal history of the Japanese army is a biography of Yamagata Aritomo." Hackett (1971, 2) also notes that Yamagata held "more power for a longer period than any other individual in modern Japanese history."
111. Kato 1998, 40–41.
112. Nish 1998, 183. See also Kato 1998, 41.
113. Diet speech quoted in Hackett 1971, 342.
114. Ramseyer and Rosenbluth 1995, 170.
115. Bix (2000) argues that the emperor was an autonomous political actor, more culpable even than Yamagata.
116. Pyle 1989, 697. Hackett (1971, 1) adds, "Of the many explanations for [the] rapid transition of Japan from an isolated, backward country to an advanced international power, the least contestable is the brilliant leadership provided by a group of able young men." Also see Akita 1967, Iwata 1964, Titus 1974, Jansen 1989, and Beasley 1989.
117. Ramseyer and Rosenbluth 1995, 17. See also Huffman (1983), who also stresses the oligarchs' self-seeking struggles for power, and Titus 1974, 20.

CHAPTER 3: HOW TO BUILD WEALTH

1. Cafagna (1999) has a vivid account of this speech. The full text is in Cavour 1942, 273–92. It contradicts accounts that represent him as excessively naïve, wedded to agriculture, or ambivalent about industrial development. See, for example, Webster 1975, 8; Adler 1995; and Davis 1996, 109.
2. See Mack Smith (1985) and Davis (1996).
3. Note the distinction between the *conventional* tariff, negotiated bilaterally by states, and the *general* tariff, which was applied to countries with which no treaty had been negotiated. See Del Vecchio (1979–80, vol. 1, 155, 166–67) and Izzo (1978, 70).
4. Pescosolido 1995, 280.
5. Coppa 1977, 221.
6. Del Vecchio, 1979–80, vol. 1, 155.
7. According to M. Block, as reported in Del Vecchio, 1979–80, vol. 1, 158. Bodio calculated the Italian average tariff at 3.50% in 1861. See Del Vecchio, 1979–80, vol. 1, 158.
8. Crawcour 1989, 602.
9. Shimomura 1962, 54–60.
10. Inō 1966, 37.
11. Vlastos 1986.
12. Iwata 1964, 33–34.
13. Sakuma Shōzan (1811–1864) quoted in Harootunian 1989, 241. See Harootunian (1989) and Pyle (1989) for more on the Tokugawa antecedents of Meiji mercantilism.
14. See Morris-Suzuki 1989, 53–55.
15. Morris-Suzuki 1989, 58.
16. Shimomura 1962, 125–26.
17. Morris-Suzuki 1989, 59.
18. Crawcour 1988, 448. Morris-Suzuki (1989, 60) calls the publication of List's book "a particularly important milestone in the development of Japanese protectionist thought." See Smith (1955, v) for an important clarification of the view that the oligarchs had only a single idea of best economic practice.
19. The previous treaty with France, signed in 1850, was revised by Cavour to reduce tariffs further. See Del Vecchio 1979–80, vol. 1, 236. France and Britain each enjoyed considerable trade surpluses with Italy in 1863.

20. Castronovo 1995, 37.
21. Francesco Ferrara, born in Palermo in 1810, was a leading figure in this movement. In 1867 he became minister of finance. See also Romanelli 1979.
22. *Il Sole* was founded for this purpose.
23. Vincenzo Rossi and Luigi Lasagno were early exceptions. Fedele Lampertico and Quintino Sella joined them later.
24. Romanelli 1979, 239.
25. Izzo 1978, 72; Coppa 1970b, 744.
26. Coppa 1977, 222.
27. Twain 1911, 263.
28. Seton-Watson 1967, 19. We explore below the parallel "Matsukata privatization," which delivered state property to Japanese entrepreneurs at a deep discount.
29. Webster 1975, 94; Toniolo 1990, 67; Seton-Watson 1967, 21. Italian silk held one-third of the world market until Japanese competition in the first decade of the twentieth century. See Zamagni 1993.
30. Baglioni 1974, 190.
31. We will return to this rich vein of irony in chap. 12.
32. *L'Estrema* comprised the Republican Party, orthodox Mazzinians who refused to cooperate with the Liberals and the Crown, and more moderate Radicals who were willing to accept the monarchy and work with both. Nearly all Radicals and Republicans—as well as many Liberals—were freemasons.
33. Salomone 1945, 14.
34. Prodi 1965, 614.
35. For more on Rossi, see Baglioni 1974, 297–98. See also Lanaro 1979; Romanelli 1979; Clark 1996; and Coppa 1970b.
36. Romanelli 1979, 238–39.
37. Seton-Watson 1967, 83. For more on other influential early protectionists such as Quintino Sella and Fedele Lampertico, see Coppa 1971, 51–52.
38. Lanaro 1967, 57.
39. Izzo 1978, 74. Del Vecchio, 1979–80, vol. 1, 75.
40. Prodi 1965, 623. Note how Italian industry associations were initiated by the firms themselves, Japanese associations by the state.
41. Coppa 1971, 55.
42. Prodi 1966, 42.
43. Ibid., 47; Coppa 1971, 59.
44. Webster 1975, 8.
45. Avagliano 1977, 343; Coppa 1970b, 745.
46. Rossi quoted in Romanelli 1979, 237–38.
47. Prodi 1966, 58.
48. Lanaro 1967, 70. Rossi sent his nephew to the United States in the early 1880s to collect data on American agriculture. See the accounts in Coppa (1971) and Romanelli (1979).
49. Romanelli 1979, 275–76.
50. Clark 1996, 94.
51. Prodi 1966, 76.
52. Webster 1975, 6.
53. Seton-Watson 1967, 91–92.
54. Did Ōkuma Shigenobu or Ōkubo Toshimichi dominate early Meiji industrial policy? See M. Kobayashi (1985, 56) for the former view; see Akita 1967, Craig 1970b, and Beasley 1990 for the latter. It is clear that both—with the assistance of others, including Itō Hirobumi and Inoue Kaoru—worked diligently to plan for Japan's industrial development. Samuels (1994) examines *shokusan kōgyō* in detail.
55. See Craig 1970b, 305–6. Ōkubo was murdered in Tokyo in May 1878 by six newly declassed samurai.
56. Ōkubo quoted in Iwata 1964, 88.
57. Craig 1970b, 291.
58. Iwata 1964, 116.

59. In his memoirs Shibusawa wrote that "Ōkubo—the supposed pillar of the nation and the most powerful man in the ministry—was not only deficient in financial expertise, but he seemed incapable of understanding the most rudimentary economic principles." Shibusawa 1994, 139.

60. Crawcour 1989, 605.

61. Vlastos 1989.

62. Samuels (1994) provides a detailed list of these plants.

63. See Smith 1955, chap. 4.

64. Harootunian 1989, 243.

65. M. Kobayashi 1985, 55.

66. Tamura 1977, 86–87; Shimomura 1962, 153.

67. See Inō 1976, 32.

68. Itō quoted in Hamada 1936, 66.

69. Brown 1962, 189–90.

70. Ōkubo quoted in Brown 1962, 189–90. Bismarck conversation from Iwata 1964, 159.

71. Ōkubo quoted in Iwata 1964, 237.

72. Craig 1970b, 296.

73. Kobayashi 1985, 57.

74. Ōkubo quoted in Tamura 1977, 113–14.

75. Iwata (1964, 168–69) reconstructs Ōkubo's priorities.

76. The three-note chord comprises import substitution, nurturance of domestic capabilities, and the diffusion of technology. See Samuels 1994.

77. For additional details, see Kobayashi 1985; Crawcour 1988; and Hirschmeier and Yui 1981.

78. Even traveling outside these settlements became a matter of great debate in the 1870s.

79. Crawcour 1989, 609.

80. Mason 1992, 18.

81. Yoshida 1967, 15–16.

82. Iwakura quoted in Smith 1955, 98. (Kyushu and Shikoku are two of Japan's four main islands.)

83. Marshall (1967, 21) calls Matsukata "Ōkubo's successor as the chief architect of government economic policy." Kobayashi (1985, 62–66) credits Ōkuma with the plan, while Smith (1955, 97–98) credits Inoue. For his part, Notehelfer (1990, 222) credits no one, arguing that it was merely "a pragmatic response to severe economic problems."

84. Matsukata quoted by Beasley 1990, 107. For the fuller quote, see Smith 1955, 95.

85. Samuels 1987.

86. Cement works, for example, were leased at 50% of net profits, with a 25-year payment schedule if the lessee was successful and wanted to make a purchase. Ironworks sold at just 10% of gross state investment. See Kobayashi 1985, 62–66.

87. Rossi's explanation for the success of his own mills included large military orders for uniforms. See Avagliano 1977, 345.

88. Prodi 1966, 54. Zamagni (1993, 161) reports that the Italian state's share of GDP during industrialization was greater than in any other country except, perhaps, Germany.

89. Row 1988, 43.

90. Clark 1996, 26–27.

91. The Banca Commerciale continued to serve as the lead bank for Terni—and for its competitors. See Clark 1996, 123.

92. Here Row (1988, 3) concurs with de Cecco and Giovannini (1989, 200), who claim "the Italian governing elite was . . . solidly interventionist and protectionist."

93. Mixed banks were a German innovation that used both credit and equity to support industrial firms. See Barca 1997.

94. Romanelli 1979, 265.

95. The "Matsukata deflation" led to the collapse of the rural economy.

96. Shibusawa quoted in Hazama 1992, 112.

97. Shibusawa 1994, 125–26.

98. Hirschmeier and Yui 1981, 127.

99. See Duus 1988, 46.
100. Shibusawa quoted in Crawcour 1988, 448.
101. Shibusawa quoted in Hazama 1992, 113.
102. Marshall (1967) is an excellent study of the ideas of early Japanese capitalists.
103. Shibusawa's simultaneous service to state agencies and to private firms became a model for generations of Japanese business leaders. See Allinson 1987, 388.
104. See Mitsubishi Jūkōgyō Kabushiki Gaisha Shashi Hensan Iinkai, ed., 1990. Also see Kobayashi (1985) and Hirschmeier and Yui (1981) for the fuller context of the privatization.
105. Crawcour 1988, 396–97.
106. Ibid., 394.
107. Samuels 1987.
108. Webster (1975, 78) speaks of an identical "political capitalism."
109. See Row (1988 and 1997) for a detailed account of Ansaldo.
110. Webster 1975, 76.
111. Row 1988, ii.
112. Sprigge 1969, 66. Total trade between Italy and France fell by two-thirds between 1887 and 1894. See Coppa 1977, 225.
113. Barca 1997, 6.
114. Coppa 1970a, 754.
115. Coppa 1971, 65.
116. Webster 1975, 126. Note, however, that French interests still held most of Italy's foreign debt.
117. This account is from Coppa 1971.
118. Mario Missiroli quoted in Coppa 1971, 46.
119. Row 1988, 56.
120. See de Cecco and Giovannini (1989, 199) and Bosworth (1996, 85).
121. Row 1988, 140–41.
122. Ibid., 135–36.
123. On the eve of World War II, Fiat also was a leading contributor to this newspaper. See Row 1988, 128.
124. See Sarti (1971) for more here.
125. Row 1988, 192.
126. See Kogan (1956) and Davis (1996).
127. Gerschenkron (1966) agrees that Italy lacked the "specific industrialization ideology" that guided Japanese economic development.

CHAPTER 4: THE DEATH OF LIBERALISM

1. Duus 1968, 71. See also Mitani (1995) and Kikuchi (1992).
2. Duus 1968, 78.
3. Berger 1977, 19.
4. Duus 1968, 80.
5. Hara quoted in Duus 1968, 137.
6. Beasley 1990, 135. See also Najita 1967, 221.
7. Coppa 1970a, 191. Mack Smith (1959, 287) calls Giolitti "one of the foremost statesmen of united Italy." In addition to the short-lived governments of 1892 and 1920, Giolitti served as prime minister between 1903–5, 1906–9, and 1911–14. He resigned frequently to demonstrate his own indispensability.
8. This from Gaetano Salvemini, one of Giolitti's many distinguished detractors. Gaetano Mosca passionately criticized the "moral cowardice" of liberal Italian politicians. See Salomone (1945) and Coppa (1971, chap. 1). With the passing of time, views softened. Salvemini retracted much of his criticism in his extraordinary introduction to Salomone 1945. See De Grand (2001, 270–71) and Sturzo (1926, 65).
9. See Coppa 1971; Salomone 1945.
10. Mussolini 1998, 108.

11. Sturzo 1926, 64.

12. Gramsci's quote reprinted in Ferrata and Gallo, 1964, 807–8. PCI head Palmiro Togliatti concluded years later that Gramsci had been too hard on Giolitti. See Togliatti (1973a, 1973b).

13. This point is made by Adler 1995, 1.

14. Sturzo 1926, 63.

15. Salomone 1945, 45.

16. *Mainichi Shimbun* editorial quoted in Brown 1955, 128.

17. Fukuzawa quoted in Pyle 1989, 696.

18. Itō tightened Japanese controls on the peninsula over the next four years. When he was assassinated by a Korean nationalist in October 1909, Japan annexed Korea as a formal colony.

19. See the accounts in Okamoto 1970, Nish 1998, Brown 1955, Beasley 1990, and Wilson 1969.

20. Ramseyer and Rosenbluth (1995) make a compelling case that the oligarchs were consumed by keeping power out of one another's hands.

21. Titus 1974, 324.

22. Akita 1967, 76.

23. Beasley 1990, 133.

24. For the Seiyūkai platform, see Hamada 1936, 122–26.

25. Itō quoted in Hamada 1936, 133. Itō did, in fact, resign in May.

26. Berger 1988, 99.

27. Luebbert 1991, 150.

28. Cited in Bobbio 1995, 33.

29. Giolitti 1923, 194.

30. Ibid., 142–43.

31. This section is based on Clark 1996.

32. See Sarti (1971) and Cotta (1992).

33. Agócs 1971, 641–42.

34. Giolitti 1923, 169. He never used this "exceptional provision" again. Throughout his memoirs he argues that he recognized that workers needed to consume in order to produce, and that it was not, in any event, the responsibility of the state to assure profits to private industry. He claims that this is why he refused to mobilize soldiers to replace striking workers. He did not want them "to receive the impression that the army, which represents the entire nation, was their enemy" (155).

35. Salomone 1945, 51.

36. Grazioli 1974, 54.

37. Here Giolitti was even ahead of the reform Socialists. See Salomone 1945.

38. Giolitti 1923, 237; Sprigge 1969, 78–79.

39. Giolitti proposed the franchise for all males over twenty-one who could read, veterans, and all illiterate males over thirty. There were only two opponents to the suffrage bill, one of whom was Gaetano Mosca.

40. See Ferrera (1993, 216–17) and Barca (1997). Giolitti describes the creation of the nationalized insurance industry (l'Istituto nazionale delle assicurazioni, or INA) as one of his greatest triumphs. See Giolitti 1923.

41. Salomone 1945, 28–29.

42. Giolitti 1923, 136.

43. Giolitti cited in Salomone 1945, 47.

44. Giolitti 1923, 227.

45. See Clark 1996.

46. The Vatican's Banco di Roma suffered from an enormous financial exposure in Tripoli and sought relief.

47. Salomone (1945, 101) makes the connection to Cavour here. See Bosworth 1979, Luebbert 1991, and Grazioli 1974 for these contrasting views.

48. Carillo 1965, 48.

49. Fermi 1961, 103.

50. See Pombeni (1985) for more on Mussolini's party tactics.
51. Salvemini 1973, 132; Row 1988.
52. Salvemini 1953, 28.
53. Mack Smith 1969, 335.
54. Salvemini described him as Mussolini's John the Baptist.
55. Clark 1996, 221. Giolitti's underestimation of Mussolini was reciprocated. Mussolini called Giolitti a "hopelessly mediocre Piedmontese." See Sprigge 1969, 91.
56. Bosworth 1998, 41.
57. Hara had once been head of operations for this Furukawa zaibatsu firm. See Nimura 1997.
58. Ramseyer and Rosenbluth 1995, 47. Also see Gordon 1991, 108–9. Hara met with Yamagata monthly during his tenure as prime minister, and always sought the elder's approval on important matters of state. See Hackett 1971, 323–26.
59. For a partisan account of how the 1918 rice riots spread across Japan, and how the government responded, see Central Committee . . . , ed., 1982, 20–21.
60. Hara quoted in Pyle 1973, 54.
61. Hara quoted in Najita 1967, 22.
62. Duus 1968, 133.
63. Hara quoted in Duus 1968, 140.
64. For details, see Ramseyer and Rosenbluth (1995) and Duus 1968.
65. Duus 1968, 139.
66. Demonstrations in support of universal suffrage were held with increasing scale, frequency, and violence during late 1919 and early 1920. The largest one occurred in February 1920, when 50,000 to 100,000 people marched through central Tokyo.
67. See Smith 1983, 191–94.
68. Pyle 1973, 55.
69. Garon (1987, 49–54) discusses the Hara/Tokonami social program and their relationship.
70. For more on this choice, see Bix 2000, chap. 4. Duus and Scheiner (1988, 673–78) reconstruct the contours of an active liberal democratic alternative to both socialism and the bureaucratic state in the early twentieth century.
71. Najita 1967, 220–21.
72. Salomone 1945, xii.
73. Sarti (1971, 3) offers this apt characterization.
74. Giolitti 1923, 247.
75. Ibid., 238.
76. Adler 1995, 33.
77. Sprigge 1969, 107.
78. Coppa 1971, 36.
79. This is the conclusion of Clark (1996) and De Grand (2001) as well.
80. Togliatti praised Giolitti in a 1950 speech as the man within the bourgeoisie who went furthest in understanding the needs of the masses. See Togliatti 1973b.
81. Pareto's evaluation is in Coppa 1971, 3–4. Mussolini's evaluation is from his memoirs, Mussolini 1998, 90.
82. See Silberman (1996) for this observation.

CHAPTER 5: THE BIRTH OF CORPORATISM

1. Johnson (1982) is the canonical work on the reinvention of the institutions of capitalism; Nakane (1970) and Dore (1973) on corporate paternalism.
2. Pareto's view of Rossi is from Lanaro 1979, 163.
3. The firm was located in a traditionally agrarian area, where Rossi could rely on cheap labor. A working class politics never developed in the Veneto. See Lanaro (1967, 67) and Lanaro (1979).
4. Lanaro 1967, 60–61.

5. Lanaro 1979, 145.

6. Avagliano (1977, 337) tells the story of Rossi's arrest in 1848 for bringing commoners to the public theater.

7. See Lanaro (1979) and Zamagni (1993, 104).

8. Romanelli 1979, 182, 295.

9. Some firms did provide social services to workers. See, for example, the case of Piaggio in Fanfani 1994.

10. Although Abegglen (1958) and Nakane (1970) treated industrial relations as an organic consequence of "Japanese culture," more recent writers have documented how much of it was the strategic consequence of creative leaders. See Hazama 1997; Dore 1973; Cole 1979; and Gordon 1998.

11. Gordon (1998) notes that the words used by capitalists to describe "traditional" practices (e.g., family-ism and warmheartedness-ism) were themselves "hastily invented" neologisms. See also Taira 1988, 607.

12. Gordon 1998, 19. See also Levine (1958) for the fine line between paternalism and despotism. Tsutsui (1997) shows how Taylorism and paternalism coexisted in Japanese practice.

13. Dore 1973, 394–95; Large 1972; Taira 1988; Pyle 1989.

14. Hazama 1994, 46; Hazama 1997, 35; and Tsutsui 1997.

15. Hazama 1997, 35.

16. Mutō quoted in Morita 1958, 144.

17. Mutō quoted in Irimajiri 1964, 136.

18. Hazama 1997, 203, n. 9.

19. Dore 1973, 394–95.

20. Irimajiri 1964; Mutō 1963, 87.

21. Gordon 1998, 21–22.

22. Dore 1973, 393, n. 5; Cole 1979, 16.

23. Irimajiri 1964; Marshall 1967, 86.

24. Hazama 1997, 157.

25. Duus 1988, 22.

26. Hazama 1997, 22, 58.

27. *Yūai Shimpō* editorial quoted by Taira 1988, 631–32.

28. Gordon 1998, 21.

29. Shōda Heigorō quoted in Gordon 1998, 21.

30. Taira (1988, 633) reports that unions and even strikes remained legal, but efforts to urge collective action were criminalized. As a result, most pre-1914 labor strikes were spontaneous and independent of the unions.

31. Large 1972, 1–2.

32. Scalapino (1983) is an excellent history of the Yūaikai. The Western influence is worth noting. Five of the six founders of the Japan Socialist Party were Christians. See Wilson 1969.

33. Harari 1973, 30–31.

34. Mutō quoted in Marshall 1967, 86.

35. See Garon 1987, 50–52; Harari 1973, 20.

36. Marshall (1967, 98) quotes an executive who claimed that this was Mitsui's "guiding principle."

37. Shibusawa quoted in Hazama 1992, 113.

38. Garon 1987, 108.

39. See Taira 1988; Totten 1967; Brown 1955; and Totten 1974.

40. Taira 1988, 646.

41. See Gordon 1985.

42. Sako 1997, xix.

43. See Samuels (1994) for more on this "technomilitary paradigm." As Roger Hackett (1971, 249) succinctly puts it: "No nation suffered less and gained more through World War I than did Japan." See also Crawcour 1988, 435.

44. Pyle 1989, 719.

45. Pyle 1973, 61–62.
46. This account is from Ogata 1923.
47. Hirota Tōsuke, the home ministry bureaucrat who authored the legislation, is quoted in Pyle 1989, 712.
48. See Garon 1997.
49. Marshall 1967, 105.
50. Tullio-Altan (1997, 106) cites fascist ideologue Enrico Corradini on this point.
51. Sarti 1971, 39–40. Adler (1995) is a particularly interesting view of these calculations.
52. Membership in the Socialist Party was 57,000 in 1914, before the war, and more than 200,000 in 1920. Trigilia 1986, 90.
53. Sarti (1971) explores this with great subtlety.
54. Sarti 1971, 2.
55. Galli della Loggia (1998, 114–15) suggests that Italy has never invented any institutions of state or economy. But corporatism was a powerfully influential invention.
56. Forsyth 1993; Seton-Watson 1967; Pombeni 1985.
57. Salvemini 1973, 419.
58. Reported by Sarti 1971, 108–9.
59. Mussolini's payback to Ansaldo is explored by Giacomo Matteoti in his memoirs, published years after he was murdered by Mussolini's thugs. See Matteoti 1969, 19–20.
60. Barca et al., 1996.
61. See Barca and Trento (1997), D'Antone (1997), and de Cecco and Giovannini (1989) for more on the origins and impact of IRI.
62. Barca et al. 1997, 6.
63. Sarti 1971, 1
64. Pietra (1985) is an excellent early history.
65. Berta 1996, xi–xii. Earle (1986, 23) reports that in September 1920 Agnelli became exasperated with a sit-in by workers at his Turin factory, and offered to sell it to a workers' cooperative. He soon backed away from that idea.
66. De Ianni 1995, 39; Pallotta 1987, 116.
67. Di Scala 1995, 240.
68. Another explanation, suggested by Pallotta (1987, 100–1) was that Agnelli's appointment was de facto recognition that the Fascists would not force Agnelli out of Fiat.
69. Pallotta 1987, 106. Actually, Agnelli's relationship to Henry Ford—and to the Fordist model of industrial production—was a complex "love-hate" relationship of "rivalry and admiration." See Pallotta 1987, 118.
70. Pallotta (1987, 121) and Castronovo (1977, 396).
71. Castronovo 1977, 399. See also Knox 2000, chaps. 2 and 3.
72. Agnelli statement to shareholders quoted in Castronovo 1977, 401–2.
73. Castronovo 1977, 438.
74. Pallotta (1987, 126) reports that Agnelli found Hitler "comical," if not a "lunatic."
75. Castronovo 1977, 446.
76. Ibid., 447–59.
77. See De Ianni 1995, 111; Ginsborg 1990, 22–23; Harper 1986, 43.
78. Duus 1988, 48.
79. The Shōwa emperor, better known in the West as Hirohito, assumed the throne in December 1926.
80. Johnson (1982) is the most important analysis of these efforts. Also see Gao (1997) and Fletcher (1998).
81. Johnson 1982, 124.
82. Kitaoka 1995, 126; Hara 1995, 14–15.
83. Kishi quoted in Hara 1995, 24. He expresses a similar sentiment in Kurzman 1960, 92.
84. See Kishi et al., 1981, and Kishi 1983.
85. See Johnson (1982) for Yoshino and the entire "control" (*tōsei*) group within the ministry.
86. Kishi et al., 1981, 15.
87. Johnson 1982, 130.

88. Noguchi 1995, 45–49.

89. For more on this trip, see Hara (1995, 38–39) and Kishi et al. (1981, 12–13). For more on "excessive competition" in Japanese thinking, see Samuels 1994. Johnson (1982, 108) speaks of how important the German industrial rationalization model was for subsequent Japanese industrial policy.

90. Kishi et al. (1981, 17) and Hara (1995, 47).

91. Kishi's group promulgated the Industrial Association Law and the Commercial Association Law to control small and medium-sized firms at the same time. See Kishi et al. 1981, 13–14.

92. See Marshall (1967, 110–11) and Samuels (1987).

93. Taking a single example, the Petroleum Industry Laws of 1934 and 1962 were virtually identical. See Samuels 1987.

94. Berger 1988, 112–14.

95. Kishi et al., 1981, 14.

96. Samuels 1987. One of these subordinates was Uemura Kōgorō, future chairman of the Federation of Economic Organizations, benefactor of Kishi's LDP. See chap. 9.

97. Kishi et al., 1981, 39.

98. Kitaoka 1995, 127; Johnson 1982, 128.

99. Manchukuo came to be governed by a cabal of five men: two "ki" (Tōjō Hide*ki* and Hoshino Nao*ki*) and three "suke": Kishi Nobu*suke*, Ayukawa Yoshi*suke*, and Matsuoka Yo*suke* (president of the South Manchurian Railway Company).

100. Kurzman 1960, 127.

101. Nish 1998, 175.

102. Young 1998, 219.

103. Kitaoka 1995, 127. Kishi claims his relations with Ishiwara were not particularly close, but he considered Ishiwara one of the "outstanding" officers of that time. See Kishi et al. 1981, 24.

104. Hara 1976, 228; Johnson (1982, 131) reviews how authorship of the Five Year Development Plan for Manchuria mattered for the Tokyo War Crimes Tribunal.

105. Jones 1949, 148; Kishi et al. 1981, 25; Hara 1995, 64. Like Kishi, Ayukawa was born in Yamaguchi Prefecture, the same region that had produced the oligarchs Ōkubo Toshimichi and Inoue Kaoru, the latter of whom helped him establish his first company, Tobata Casting, in 1910. Tobata Casting became the parent firm of Nissan Automobile. See Genther (1990) and Cusumano (1985) for useful analyses of Nissan and Japanese automobile industry policy in the 1930s. Ayukawa married into the Kuhara family, and the family company, Kuhara Mining, became the basis for his Nissan zaibatsu. See also Udagawa (1990) for details on Nissan.

106. Kishi et al. 1981, 25. For his recollections about Ayukawa, see 25–27.

107. Udagawa 1990, 5.

108. Hara 1976, 231.

109. This according to Udagawa (1990) and other secondary sources. Kishi remembers it differently. He claims that the Kwantung Army vetoed the introduction of foreign capital. See Kishi et al. 1981, 26.

110. Udagawa 1990.

111. Hara (1976, 239) dismisses the taxation explanation as a public relations ruse that Ayukawa fabricated for his shareholders.

112. Young 1998, 233.

113. Like Agnelli, he could be creative in pursing commercial advantage. Udagawa (1990, 20–24) reports that after Ayukawa failed to win Hitler's support for a large-scale swap of Manchurian agricultural products for German machinery, he tried to arrange a summit meeting between President Roosevelt and Prime Minister Konoe, proposing an anti-Soviet U.S.-Japan Pacific Alliance to replace the Axis.

114. Udagawa 1990.

115. He immodestly told the press that "the industrial world of Manchukuo is a piece of work which I created. I have an infinite affection for this creation of mine. It shall remain close to my heart always." Kishi quoted in Kurzman 1960, 143.

116. Hara 1995, 82.

117. See the account of this episode in Hara 1995, 84; Kurzman 1960, 154; and Kishi et al. 1981, 42–44.
118. Kurzman 1960, 184.
119. Indeed, they refused to cooperate in any respect. See Samuels 1994.
120. This is the central thesis of Johnson 1982. See also Noguchi 1995.
121. See Johnson (1982, 149, 309) for a partial list.
122. Hara 1995, 101. See also Johnson 1982, 171.
123. See Johnson 1982, chap. 6; Noguchi 1995.
124. Noguchi 1995, 76–84.
125. Noguchi 1995, 9–10, 39–40.
126. Noguchi 1995, 29–34.
127. Sarti 1971, 8. See also Davis 1996, 107.

CHAPTER 6: THE TOTAL LEADER

1. "Government by assassination" is from Byas 1942.
2. This section is derived from Duus 1968, Pyle 1996b, and Berger 1977. Garon (1987) offers a more positive view of Taishō democracy, but acknowledges its limits.
3. See Garon 1987, 48–49.
4. Tanaka Shōzō quoted in Pyle 1989, 716.
5. Berger 1977, 28.
6. Pyle 1996b, 178.
7. Patriotic societies first emerged in the early 1880s, when ardent followers of Saigo Takamori created an ultranationalist "Dark Ocean Society" (Genyōsha) to revive his plans to advance into Korea. In 1901 the famous "Black Dragon Society" (Kokuryūkai) was formed to advance the cause of Japanese expansion in Manchuria, Mongolia, and Siberia. Both groups targeted socialism as their sworn enemy and insinuated themselves into military and business circles.
8. The comparison to Gabriele D'Annunzio is compelling. See Hori 1990, Ogata 1964, and Wilson (1969) for analyses of Kita's plan. Maruyama (1963, 28) compares Kita's *Outline Plan* to *Mein Kampf.*
9. *Outline Plan* cited in Wilson 1969, 87.
10. Kita received enough "protection" money to support a chauffeured car and three maids for his family. See Wilson 1969, 110–11.
11. Araki quoted in Maruyama 1963, 67.
12. Byas (1942) is a dramatic account of this dramatic event. See also Wilson 1969.
13. Some Imperial Way members reported that Control faction leaders had bragged that "if the Emperor does not agree, we will make him listen at the point of a dagger." Reported by Maruyama 1963, 69. Bix (2000, 299) suggests Hirohito had his own reasons for opposing the coup.
14. Maruyama (1963, 67) offers this apt proverb.
15. Beasley 1990, 185. Garon (1997) is an excellent account.
16. Ives 1995, 18.
17. Gluck 1985, 281.
18. The most celebrated biographies are Mack Smith (1981) and DeFelice (1965). Bosworth (2002) focuses brilliantly on Mussolini's cynical amorality.
19. Mack Smith 1969, 378. Even while Mussolini was being viciously parodied by Chaplin and excoriated by Hemingway, many foreign literati supported him—for example, Wallace Stevens, T. S. Eliot, and, of course, Ezra Pound. See Diggins 1972, 245–46.
20. Bosworth (1998) addresses the links to foreign capital and to France before Mussolini split from the Socialists to support Italian entry into the war. See also Salvemini, 1973, chap. 3. See Diggins (1972) on the warm reception enjoyed by fascism in the United States.
21. Seton-Watson 1967, 519; Bellah 1980, 107.
22. Sturzo 1926, 121.
23. Salvemini 1953, 119–20.
24. Mussolini quoted in Bobbio 1995, 122.

25. Mussolini quoted in Bosworth 1998, 73.
26. See Seton-Watson (1967, 701–2) on this point.
27. This line of argument is best developed in Fogu, forthcoming.
28. Zunino 1985, 72–73.
29. Schneider and Clough 1929; Fermi 1961.
30. This design (sometimes also called the littorio) predates Mussolini's Fascism and was not used only in Italy. The frieze on Chicago's City Hall (1911) is notable for the repeated use of the rods and axe.
31. Schneider and Clough 1929, 196.
32. Ibid., 193.
33. Time always begins now for true revolutionaries. See Kertzer 1988, 183.
34. Tullio-Altan (1997, 32) labels Mussolini's use of Mazzini's ideas "consciously instrumental." See also Knox 1982, 33.
35. Fogu, forthcoming, chap. 1 (in manuscript, p. 5). For Bakunin's denunciation, see Gangulee 1987, 65.
36. Chap. 4 in Fogu (forthcoming) is a brilliant analysis.
37. See Schneider and Clough 1929, 195.
38. Becker 1994, 3. See also Tullio-Altan 1997; Salvemini 1973; Fermi 1961; Sprigge 1969; and Salomone (1945) for rich accounts of this controversial genius.
39. Fermi 1961, 217.
40. D'Annunzio quoted in Mack Smith 1969, 300–01.
41. Sprigge 1969, 98; Salomone 1945, 89. Salomone (91) also notes how the Italian glorification of militarism in Italy often invoked the Japanese example. Ledeen (2000) is a reliable biography of D'Annunzio.
42. Fermi 1961, 217.
43. Salvemini 1953, 33.
44. Tullio-Altan (1997, 138–41) is excellent on this point.
45. Mussolini quoted in Bosworth 1998, 39.
46. Fogu, forthcoming, chap. 1, lists the "terms of scorn" used to describe this "moral senility."
47. Maier (1975) is the best English language treatment of the decay of Liberal Italy.
48. Salvemini 1973, 327.
49. Adler 1995, 188.
50. See Pombeni 1985, 496.
51. Matteotti (1969) is a reprint of his diaries.
52. Pombeni 1985, 497.
53. Carillo 1965, 84. See also Maier 1975, 322.
54. Bosworth (1998, 114) makes the useful point that "The Duce had much of the 'transformist' about him." Sarti (1971, 4–6) and Di Palma (1978) also emphasize Mussolini's manipulation of and accommodation to contending factions.
55. Knox 1982, 9–10; Seton-Watson 1967, 701.
56. Sarti 1971, 34.
57. Bosworth (1998) is an excellent account. See also Kogan 1983; Fogu, forthcoming, chap. 4.
58. Cassels 1970, for example. Bosworth (1998) is a provocative review of the Italian historiography on this issue.
59. Mussolini wandered from neutralist socialist in August 1914, on the eve of World War I, to nationalist interventionist in October. He was a Mazzinian internationalist in January 1919 and a D'Annunzian nationalist nine months later. Knox (1982) forcefully argues that Mussolini's foreign policy was consistently aimed at establishing Italian hegemony in the Mediterranean, and thus he never seriously considered any of the overtures from the Allies that I recount below.
60. Sprigge 1969, 10.
61. Mussolini quoted in Ayling 1971, 105.
62. He also provided physical shelter to Hermann Goering after their failed beer hall putsch in 1923.

63. Salvemini 1953, 33.
64. Pombeni 1995, 73.
65. Pombeni 1995, 75. For his part, Lloyd George reportedly told Italian ambassador Dino Grandi in the early 1930s that "either the world decides to follow Mussolini or the world is lost." Quoted in Bosworth 1998, 68.
66. Salvemini 1953, 72.
67. Ibid., 8.
68. Ibid., 96–100, 156.
69. Ibid., 102.
70. Fermi 1961, 345.
71. Salvemini 1953, 158
72. Mussolini quoted in Salvemini 1953, 158.
73. *France Militaire* quoted in Salvemini 1953, 303.
74. Salvemini 1953, 201.
75. See Cassells (1985, 88–89) and Knox 2000, 10.
76. Years later, Clement Atlee condemned the "voluntary blindness" toward Ethiopia at Stresa, calling it "one of the most criminal blunders in the whole course of British diplomacy." Atlee quoted in Salvemini 1953, 197.
77. This account is from Salvemini 1953, 404–5. See also Knox (1982) and Ayling (1971).
78. Ayling 1971, 109.
79. Cassel 1985, 95. Mussolini was very weak relative to Germany. Within three months, he was compelled to adopt the race laws he had always disdained.
80. In March 1939 he once again increased his fortifications on the new German-Austrian frontier with Italy. See Ishida 1994.
81. Ayling 1971, 112.
82. Hitler quoted by Knox 1982, 46.
83. "Dismounting" is Knox's apt term. See Knox 1982, 42.
84. Gibson 1973, 125.
85. Knox 1982, 60.
86. Pombeni 1995, 80.
87. This is Mussolini's own observation in April 1940. Quoted in Gibson 1973, 236.
88. Germino 1971, 30.
89. Churchill quoted in Pombeni 1995, 81.
90. Churchill quoted in Kogan 1956, 175. The futile search for Churchill's correspondence with Mussolini—purportedly recovered by British agents after Mussolini's execution—has taken on the trappings of the search for the Loch Ness monster.
91. Mussolini quoted in Bosworth 1998, 112.
92. Finer 1964, 161.

CHAPTER 7: CHASING DEMOCRACY

1. Lanzarra 1998, 12–13.
2. Kōsaka 1968, 47.
3. Yoshida 1967, 4, 99, 102.
4. See Baget-Bozzo (1974, 105) on how Togliatti imagined he had captured the mantle of liberalism and democracy.
5. Doak 1997, 300. Benfell (1997) is an excellent account of the reconstruction of Japanese national identity after World War II. See Murakami (1999), Takahashi (1992), and Takahashi (2000) for scholarly Japanese analyses of postwar Italian national identity formation.
6. Salvemini 1953, 23.
7. See Cartocci 1999; Romano 1991.
8. Bollati (1983, 38) reports that Giuseppe Ferrari asked these questions in 1858.
9. Ginsborg 1990, 17. See Baget-Bozo (1974, 117) for the numbers. The geographic facts of the Resistance meant that the North could celebrate its heroism, while the South was left to ponder its capitulation.

10. On the Resistance at home and abroad, see Pombeni (1985) and Bobbio (1995).

11. Even Marxist intellectuals renounced the errors of their ways (*tenkō*), and went quietly into the authoritarian night. For the story of one such case, that of Kawakami Hajime, see Bernstein 1976.

12. Benfell 1997, chap. 3.

13. Pombeni 1979.

14. In 1949, the Vatican excommunicated those who belonged to, voted for, or participated in any activity sponsored by the Communist Party. Scoppola (1984, 32) wonders whether this was a sign of victory or defeat for the Church.

15. See Dower (1999) and Bix (2000) for the wartime role of the Shōwa emperor and the postwar preservation of his throne.

16. Benfell 1997, chap. 3.

17. See Ignazi (1995) on the strength of the neofascists.

18. McCarthy 1995, 8. According to Ginsborg (1990, 92), as late as 1960, 62 of the 64 prefects were surviving servants of the fascist state, as were all 135 police chiefs and all 139 of their deputies.

19. The fascist penal code was never abrogated and Mussolini's judges were never purged. See Barca 1997.

20. Finn 1992, 296.

21. Ginsborg 1990, 100, 152–53.

22. Steiner 1965.

23. Chubb and Vannicelli 1988, 130. See also Sarti 1971, 135–36; Hughes 1965, 171–72; and Ginsborg (1990, 91) for this view.

24. Tarrow (1994) also develops this line of argument.

25. Ginsborg (1990, 158) speaks of Bulgaria, C. Johnson (2000b) of East Germany.

26. Kogan (1983) reports that the United States financed the DC and its allied parties throughout the 1960s. The Japanese slush fund is explored in chap. 9.

27. Scalapino and Masumi 1962. Cf. Scoppola 1995, 19. For the consequences of lack of alternation in Italy, see Di Palma 1990; Tarrow 1990; Chubb and Vannicelli 1988; Ginsborg 1990; Pasquino 1992; and Golden 1999.

28. Tarrow 1990, 317.

29. Di Palma (1990) offers an excellent analysis on these points.

30. Pempel (1982) coins the apt phrase "creative conservatism." Prime Minister Alcide De Gasperi declared, "Friends, the DC is a conservative force and an innovator at the same time." Quoted by Giulio Andreotti in Orfei 1975, 122. The DC twice ran campaigns under the banner "The New DC," while the LDP periodically "abolished" factions and often claimed to have reinvented itself.

31. Cf. Weiss 1988, 142.

32. Tarrow (1990) has labeled this broadening Center "soft dominance."

33. Kogan 1983, 289–90, 334. MacDougall 1975.

34. This began to come undone in 1979 when the LDP learned how to co-opt these innovative programs. See Samuels 1982. Krauss (1982) compares leftist administrations in Bologna and Kyoto. Ferrera 1984, Dente 1985, Craveri 1995, and Fargion (1997) examine partisanship and local policy innovation in Italy during this period.

35. McCarthy 1995; Barca and Trento 1997; Scalfari and Turani 1974; Martinelli 1978; and Orefice 1993, 7. Also see Pempel (1990) for a comparative account.

36. Chubb and Vannicelli 1988, 135. See also Hellman 1993, 143. See Campbell 1984, Katō 1993, Ike 1972, and Calder (1988) on LDP factionalism.

37. Chubb and Vannicelli 1988, 136.

38. For the Italian caricature, see D'Antone 1997, 579. For the Japanese one, see Johnson 1982, 316.

39. Chubb and Vannicelli 1988, 136.

40. Cassese (1984, 40) examines the demography of Italian bureaucrats. In Japan, Tokyo University law graduates occupy senior positions in the Japanese bureaucracy in about the same proportion that Annapolis and West Point graduates occupy senior positions in the U.S. military.

41. Ginsborg 1990, 167.
42. See Samuels 1987.
43. The term *yakuza*, from "eight-nine-three," the lowest hand in a Japanese card game, reflects both an origin in gambling and an association with the lower echelons of society ("good-for-nothings"). *Bōryokudan* ("violence groups") is the official police term. See Inami 1992, 353.
44. In 1995 the bosses of the Yamaguchi-*gumi* ordered their soldiers to turn themselves in to the police when they mistakenly killed a cop. *New York Times*, 6 September 1995.
45. Finley et al. 1986, 216.
46. della Porta and Vanucci 1995, 170.
47. Rossi and Toniolo 1996.
48. Japan's economic success stimulated a spate of adulatory books. See, for example, Vogel 1979.
49. Willis (1971, 24) points out that these early liberalizations "threw the Italian economy open to the advantages and perils of European economic competition." See also Rossi and Toniolo (1996) and Barca (1997). For Japan's unequal trade, see Lincoln 1990.
50. de Cecco and Giovannini 1989, 222.
51. Hughes 1965, 171–72.
52. Cohen 1952, 89.
53. Mason (1992) is the best account.
54. Harper 1986, Barca 1997, and Barca and Trento (1997) are accounts of this important debate.
55. Gao 1997, 123–24.
56. Barca and Trento 1997, 212.
57. Barca 1997, 11; Barca and Trento 1997, 201; Rossi and Toniolo 1996, 438; Barca 1994; Martinelli 1978; D'Antone 1997.
58. Martinelli 1978, 272. See also Scoppola 1995, 19; Arighetti and Seravilli 1997; Salvatti 1981; Willis 1971.
59. Rossi and Toniolo 1996, 429. See also Mammarella 1970, 209–11.
60. 81.9%, according to the *1970 Population Census of Japan*; the Italy data are from Ginsborg 1990, 218–19.
61. On the Japanese case, see Smitka (1991) and Whittaker (1997). For Italy, see Weiss (1988) and Brusco and Paba (1997).
62. See Piore and Sabel (1984) and Cartocci (1994, 18–20) for Italy, and Friedman (1988) for Japan.
63. Ido (1998) compares postwar Italian and Japanese industrial relations.
64. Rossi and Toniolo 1996; Locke and Baccaro 1994; Weiss 1988.
65. Interview, 17 May 2000.

CHAPTER 8: WHAT KIND OF ALLY TO BE

1. See Carillo (1965) for the slightly hagiographic account of De Gasperi's life upon which this paragraph is based. Also see Gammaldi (1974) and Rossini (1984).
2. De Gasperi quoted in Carillo 1965, 13.
3. There were more Popolari than Fascists in Mussolini's first cabinet. See Formigoni 1998, chap. 4.
4. Carillo 1965, 69.
5. De Gasperi 1987.
6. June–December 1945. Palmiro Togliatti served as justice minister.
7. De Gasperi quoted in Scoppola 1974, 274.
8. De Gasperi, 1974, 110.
9. Scoppola 1974, 317.
10. Scoppola (1984, 27) speaks of this ineffability. See Pombeni (1985, 509) and Harper (1986, 59) for two interesting portraits.
11. Dower (1979, 31) speaks of "how proudly Yoshida viewed the accomplishments of the

Restoration." Yoshida celebrated the birth of Itō Hirobumi at his home, using Itō's own mortuary temple, which Yoshida had purchased and rebuilt.

12. Dower 1979, 260–65.
13. Ibid., 273. Mikuriya (1995) concurs.
14. Meiji . . . (1998, 165) is a nice account.
15. Finn 1992, part 2.
16. Yoshida 1961, 143.
17. This account is based on Yoshida 1961, chap. 13.
18. Yoshida 1961, 139 (emphasis added).
19. Yoshida quoted in Benfell 1997, 85.
20. Yoshida 1961, 285.
21. Kōsaka 1968, 51–52.
22. Interview, Nakasone Yasuhiro, 17 May 2000.
23. Dower 1979, 275.
24. Yoshida 1967, 49.
25. Pyle 1996a, 20–21.
26. Ibid.
27. See Kōsaka 1968, 49, 57–58; Dower 1979, 373.
28. Pyle 1996a, 27.
29. The comparison to Adenauer is by Ōtake 1990, 139. See also Mikuriya 1995, 42.
30. Kōsaka 1968, 49–50.
31. Mikuriya 1995, 53.
32. This famous visit is recounted in Mikuriya 1995; Dower 1979; Kōsaka 1968.
33. This, according to Miyazawa Kiichi, the future prime minister who accompanied Ikeda as an assistant in the finance ministry. See Kōsaka (1968, 56) and Dower (1979, 374–75).
34. Dower (1979, 46) reports that Yoshida and Dulles had each been minor functionaries at the Versailles Conference in 1918, where both learned of the dangers of punitive peace.
35. Yoshida 1967, 76. See also Kōsaka 1968, 56; Finn 1992, 252.
36. Yoshida 1961, 192.
37. Yoshida 1961, 191. Dower (1979, 381–83) captures this range of choice brilliantly.
38. Finn 1992, 257.
39. Yoshida 1967, 76.
40. See also the account by Secretary of State Dean Acheson 1969. Also, Mikuriya 1995, 55.
41. Tanaka (1997, 70–73) has found these documents. Ōtake (1990, 138) also speaks to the shaky legal foundation of the NPR. See Samuels (1994) for how these euphemisms persisted.
42. Mikuriya 1995, 56.
43. Tanaka (1997, 46–54) is an excellent account.
44. Acheson 1969, 426.
45. See the account of this 29 January 1951 meeting in Finn 1992, 276–77.
46. Tanaka 1997, 53; Finn 1992, 275–76; Ōtake 1990, 141.
47. Finn 1992, 279.
48. Kōsaka (1968, 57) describes the planning leading up to these negotiations.
49. Kōsaka 1968, 67. Dower (1979, 378) says that Yoshida was playing a "sophist's game."
50. Yoshida 1961, 193.
51. Yoshida 1967, 79.
52. MacArthur quoted in Acheson 1969, 428.
53. Ibid.
54. Yoshida 1961, 247. He also allows how his foreign ministry manipulated information used by the United States during the peace negotiation.
55. Acheson 1969, 433.
56. Yoshida 1967, 83–85.
57. Tanaka 1997, 42–43.
58. Mikuriya 1995, 57.
59. For the full context, see Samuels (1994, chap. 5) and Wakamiya (1994, chap. 1).
60. *Chūō Kōron* (November 1952) speculated that Kishi Nobusuke, with Hatoyama Ichirō,

Yoshida's most vocal opponent, received more than 100 million yen from the defense industry, which he distributed to one hundred politicians. The magazine predicted correctly that Kishi would become a major force in conservative politics. As we shall see in chapter 9, Kishi took the lead in establishing the "rules" for LDP dominance.

61. Yoshida (1961, 139) acknowledges that he had gone too far. See also Dower 1979, 385.
62. For details on the meetings between Ikeda and Walter Robertson, see Tanaka (1997, 122–25) and Samuels (1994, chap. 5).
63. Dower 1979, 439.
64. Tarrow 1990, 315. Also see Hellman 1988; Kogan 1956. Ignazi (1992, 30–31) quotes Togliatti's announcement of the "Italian road to Socialism." On Togliatti's relationship to the Soviet Union, see Blackmer (1968) and Urban (1986).
65. For more on this second *connubio*, see Tullio-Altan (1997, 165) and Spriano (1984, 175). Andreotti (1984) gives a personal view of the coalition from the DC right.
66. Scoppola 1974, 263.
67. Ibid., 264.
68. Ginsborg 1990, 90.
69. Baget Bozzo (1974) is an excellent account. For a nearly contemporary analysis, see Valiani 1949. See also Ginsborg (1990) and Pombeni (1997).
70. Moro quoted in Elia 1984, 181.
71. De Gasperi 1974, 108.
72. Scoppola 1974, 115.
73. De Gasperi 1974, 112–13.
74. De Gasperi quoted in Scoppola 1984, 33.
75. Baget Bozzo 1974, 125.
76. De Gasperi 1974, 111.
77. Ginsborg 1990, 153.
78. Ibid., 102.
79. Salomone 1945, 103.
80. Spain and Greece are frequently mentioned as a cohort group. See Harper (1999) and Formigoni (1996).
81. Fanfani 1958, 29.
82. Sforza had been one of Italy's earliest and most distinguished antifascists. He refused to serve in Mussolini's government in 1922, denounced fascism, and spent the war years in Parisian self-exile. See Cassels 1970.
83. Little was expected from him—which may explain the enthusiasm of both Togliatti and the Western allies for his appointment.
84. Formigoni 1996, 433.
85. De Gasperi quoted in Formigoni 1996, 56–57.
86. Formigoni 1996, 435; Taviani 1984, 194.
87. De Gasperi considered the Brenner frontier a "door" to Italy's national "house" and insisted that it be barred. See Pastorelli 1984, 75–76.
88. Seton-Watson 1991, 333; Willis 1971, 18. Ironically, Italy prevailed in Southern Tyrol (Alto Adige), where the people were effectively German, and failed in Trieste, where the people were ethnically Italian. See Kogan 1983, 3–10.
89. In De Gasperi's courageous speech on 10 August 1946 he acknowledged that the partisans did not play a decisive part in the Allied victory but nonetheless reminded the Allies that he was not representing a former Axis government. He declared that "Everything in this hall, except your personal courtesy, is against me." He was wrong, for there was not even personal courtesy. Only U.S. Ambassador Byrnes would shake De Gasperi's hand. I am grateful to Fernando Mezzetti for this account (personal correspondence).
90. See Formigoni (1996) and Kogan (1956).
91. Romano 1991, 19.
92. Kogan 1956, 132–208.
93. Formigoni 1996, 123–25.
94. Harper 1986, 119; Mammarella 1970, 147; Formigoni 1996, 123–24; Scoppola 1974, 295–99.

95. Barié 1984, 68–69.
96. Formigoni 1996, 125.
97. There is a considerable range of views about this important visit, but no definitive evidence from the archives. Some argue that De Gasperi succumbed to U.S. pressure; others are less sure. See Romano 1995b; Seton-Watson 1991; Scoppola 1974; and Pombeni 1997.
98. Orfei 1975, 48.
99. Ibid., 46–47.
100. Willis 1971, 15; Baget Bozzo 1974, 166.
101. Formigoni 1996, 142–52, and Willis 1971, 19–20.
102. Pastorelli 1987, 212–13.
103. Pastorelli 1987, 215; Kogan 1956, 206.
104. There were frequent comparisons to the temporizing and dilatory Italy of 1915 and 1938. See Varsori 1985, 104; Pastorelli 1987, 214.
105. Formigoni 1996, 220.
106. Dossetti quoted in Formigoni 1996, 160.
107. Formigoni 1996, 101.
108. Varsori 1985, 148–49; Petrilli 1990, 326.
109. Formigoni (1996, 162) quotes Moro.
110. Harper 1986, 155. Urban (1986, 180) reports that George Kennan, head of policy planning at the State Department, urged Marshall to ask the Italian government to ban the Communist Party before the April 1948 elections. His advice was rejected.
111. Kogan 1983, 39, 243.
112. Ginsborg 1990, 115.
113. The coalition of leftist parties won only 31%, lower than the combined total of votes the PCI and PSI received in 1946. See Pombeni 1997.
114. Formigoni 1996, 220.
115. The cost of the civil disturbances that resulted included nine deaths. See Scoppola 1984, 38.
116. Formigoni (1996, 253–58) is a full account of this episode.
117. Seton-Watson 1991, 340; De Gasperi 1990, 387.
118. Formigoni 1996, 314.
119. De Gasperi quoted in Formigoni 1996, 313.
120. De Gasperi quoted in Formigoni 1996, 331.
121. Churchill quoted in Willis 1971, 16.
122. Harper 1999, 4.
123. See Elia (1984) for how De Gasperi defined the democratic center of Italian politics differently than other Christian Democrats. Valiani (1949, 38) offers a similar evaluation.
124. Nenni quoted in Scoppola 1984, 40.
125. Andreotti 1984, 165.
126. For example, Silvio Berlusconi, in Milan on the fiftieth anniversary of the 1948 electoral victory that inaugurated DC dominance, proclaimed: "Today we salute the people who, on 18 April 1948, chose democracy, chose the West . . . If we celebrate 18 April 1948 today it is not to do political archeology or to pursue the ghosts of the past nor even to start an old crusade . . . We are starting this because a people that forgets the drama of its past is condemned to repeat it." (From http://www.forza-italia.it).
127. Kōsaka (1968, 234) was the first to use the term *Yoshida rōsen* ("basic line" or "doctrine"). Pyle introduced the term "Yoshida Doctrine" in English. See his explanation in Pyle 1996a, 23.
128. Kōsaka 1968, 67–68.
129. Pyle 1996a, 36. Kōsaka (1968, 7) adds that for Yoshida, "military power was second best." For close examination of these values, see Katzenstein 1996.
130. Nakasone quoted in Pyle 1987, 251.
131. Benfell 1997. Kōsaka (1968, 6) reports that in May 1946, on becoming prime minister, Yoshida told a supporter that "there is a history of lost wars but victorious diplomacy."
132. Yoshida quoted in Finn 1992, 248–49.

CHAPTER 9: PUTTING CORRUPTION IN ITS PLACE

1. Cf. Dower 1979, 275.

2. This widely used term is originally from Murobushi 1981.

3. Kishi is passed over lightly in most standard English-language analyses of the period. His political activities have also been glossed over in first-person accounts of money politics. See, for example, Uemura . . . 1979; Hanamura 1990; Kokumin Seiji Kyōkai 1991.

4. Interview, 17 May 2000.

5. Nixon quoted in Kurzman 1960, 1.

6. Kishi quoted in ibid., 1.

7. Ibid., 256.

8. See Hara 1995. Kishi, who insisted that he banned the use of opium in Manchukuo and knew nothing of its business organization elsewhere in China, acknowledged its widespread use—even among top government officials. See Kishi et al. 1981, 28–33.

9. Sakurada and Shikanai (1983, 98) and Hara (1995, 72–76, 99–100).

10. Hara 1995, 71; Kitaoka 1995, 131.

11. Future LDP leaders Hatoyama Ichirō, Kōno Ichirō, and Miki Bukichi were among the successful independent candidates, as was future political "fixer" Sasakawa Ryōichi.

12. Johnson (1982, 148–49) reminds us that Kishi was widely reviled by zaibatsu interests.

13. Wakamiya 1999, 152.

14. Mitchell (1996, 95) compares these figures to those from 1928 (10,000 cases) and 1930 (18,000 cases).

15. Meiji . . . 1998, 168.

16. Mitchell 1996, 100 2.

17. See George 1984; Castberg 1997; and Haley 1995. For a contrary view, see Ramseyer and Rasmusen (1997) and Johnson (forthcoming).

18. This account is from Mitchell (1996) and Murobushi (1981), 90–105. Sakurada and Shikanai (1983) offer a lively and intimate retrospective of the scandal.

19. Quoted in Johnson 1997, 3. One of his former colleagues, upper house member Satō Michio, disagrees. He insists that "no one ever says 'stop the investigation.' We only stopped when we had no evidence" (interview, 10 July 2000).

20. Blechinger (1999) is an excellent analysis of the way in which the LDP handled corruption cases. Kubo (1986, 25) has a full list of every Diet member arrested in each of thirteen major scandals between Shōwa Denkō and Lockheed.

21. This account is well developed by Kitaoka 1995.

22. Kishi in *Nihon Shūhō*, quoted in Kurzman 1960, 267.

23. Kishi et al. 1981, 91.

24. *Chūō Kōron* (November 1952) speculated that Kishi received more than one hundred million yen from the defense industry, which he distributed to one hundred politicians. The magazine predicted that Kishi would become a major force in conservative politics, with the strong support of the munitions industries.

25. Kurzman 1960, 270.

26. Yoshida opposed Kishi's industrial policy legislation in the 1930s, and Kishi resented Yoshida's intimacy with U.S. Ambassador Joseph Grew, whom he correctly suspected Yoshida had lobbied in a failed effort to avert the war. See Kitaoka 1995, 128.

27. This account is based on Kitaoka (1995) and Kurzman (1960).

28. Kurzman 1960, 279.

29. Kishi quoted in Kurzman 1960, 278.

30. The "show money" reportedly was no more than newspaper stuffed between real bills. See Hara 1995, 162.

31. For Kishi's reminiscences see Kishi et al. 1981, 105–18.

32. Hara 1995, 168–69.

33. *Asahi Shimbun*, 20 April 1953.

34. See Curtis 1999.

35. Kitaoka (1995, 146) and Hara (1995, 177). Former Prime Minister Nakasone insists that Miki Bukichi and Kōno Ichirō were stronger than Kishi at the time. Interview, 17 May 2000.

36. For accounts of these pressures, see Yanaga 1968; Mitchell 1996; Kokumin Kyōkai 1972; Uemura . . . 1979; Kanō and Takano 1976; and Kokumin Seiji Kyōkai 1991. See also the columns in *Yomiuri Shimbun* throughout 1955 calling for the creation of a "new conservative party" (Shin Hoshutō) by Keidanren Chairman Uemura Kōgorō, Kishi's most direct connection to the business elite. Uemura had served in the MCI under Kishi both in Manchuria and in Tokyo. Like Kishi, Uemura was purged by the Occupation, although he spent no time in jail. Although Uemura was never Japan's most powerful business leader, there was virtually no element of early postwar Japanese industrial policy in which he did not participate. Uemura had a particularly important role in organizing campaign finance for the business community, a role that anchored Kishi to "clean" money even while it freed him to explore more shady alternatives.

37. Fukui (1970, 50) offers a detailed account of these persistent cleavages.

38. Kishi explains this in Kishi et al. 1981, 124. See also Kitaoka 1995, 131.

39. Ono 1998, 91–92.

40. Tominomori 1977, 90–91; Garon 1997, 161–62.

41. Tominomori (1977, 91) and Ono (1998, 93–94).

42. Kurzman 1960, xvii. See also Kitaoka (1995, 144), who also credits Kishi with nurturing small and medium-sized firms, reforming the pension system, and developing the Income Doubling Program with which his successor and political rival, Ikeda, is widely credited.

43. Constitutional revision requires a two-thirds vote of both houses of Diet as well as a majority vote in a national referendum. The comprehensive account by Packard (1966) remains the best in English on the Security Treaty crisis of 1960. See Sakamoto (1996) and Tanaka (1997) for accounts in Japanese.

44. In 1982, former Ambassador Edwin Reischauer raised a firestorm of protest by acknowledging this arrangement. And again, in early 2000, Japanese Communist Party Chairman Fuwa Tetsuzō announced that the JCP had obtained a copy of a secret agreement between the Kishi government and the United States that allowed U.S. nuclear weapons to be brought into Japan. *Yomiuri Shimbun,* 14 April 2000.

45. Yanaga 1968, 284–85; Kishi et al. 1981, 146. In his memoirs, the Keidanren official responsible for distributing political funds says he made deliveries to the LDP secretary-general, without naming Kishi. Kishi's name is mentioned only in association with the rival Japan Chamber of Commerce and Industry. See Hanamura 1990, 96.

46. This "Group" was not formally established as part of Keidanren, but it was staffed and organized by Keidanren officials. The official history skips its relationship to Kishi Nobusuke. See Kokumin Seiji Kyōkai 1991, 31–32.

47. Masumi 1995, 218–32.

48. These funds were distributed through the so-called Hanamura List, controlled by Uemura's deputy at Keidanren. See Hanamura 1990, 19, 83.

49. Watanabe Tsuneo recounts the enormous sums of cash that were openly floating around in political circles during party presidential contests. Nomura (1977, chap. 4) tells how the anti-mainstream factions learned to use non-zaibatsu firms to circumvent the political finance laws in the 1960s.

50. Interview, Hori Wataru, former political assistant to Prime Minister Kishi Nobusuke; 28 April 2000.

51. Hanamura 1990, 16. For proportions, see Masumi (1995, 218–32) and Shinoda (2000).

52. *Asahi Shimbun,* 30 June 1960.

53. Yamaguchi 1976, 113. Uemura claims that it was *Kishi* who took the first initiatives in the autumn of 1959 to get the Keidanren to deliver more than the Economic Reconstruction Council was delivering at the time. Uemura claims that it was *Kishi* who encouraged them to create a new organization with formal nonprofit status with local branches throughout the nation. See Uemura . . . 1979, 345. Sakurada Takeshi, a former chairman of Nikkeiren, suggests that Kishi had already begun to wean the LDP from dependence on Keidanren, to move it out from "the middle of the LDP's kitchen." See Sakurada and Shikanai 1983, vol. 2.

54. Shinoda 2000; Fukui 1970, 146–47; Kokumin Seiji Kyōkai 1991, 27.

55. Kokumin Kyōkai 1972, 35.
56. Schlesinger 1997, 109.
57. Kishi et al. 1981, 126.
58. See Kitazawa 1976; Mita 1977; Shimizu 1976; Takano 1979; Yanaga 1968; Yamaguchi 1976.
59. Kishi et al. 1981, 145.
60. Yamaguchi 1976, 110–11.
61. Kojima Shinichi, president of Yahata, and Yamamoto Takayuki, vice president of Fuji, were both former vice ministers of MCI.
62. Yamaguchi 1976, 111–12.
63. Hara 1995, 238. Kishi made sure that he never came into direct contact with cash. There were always multiple filters between himself and the donor so that no matter what scandal broke out around him, he would always remain an "apparition" (*yōkai*) (Hara 1995, 238). Iwai (1990, 6) lists twenty-two corruption scandals between the Shōwa Denkō Scandal of 1948 and the Recruit Scandal of 1989. Virtually every senior politician—including six prime ministers—were caught in the prosecutors' nets, but Kishi's name never appears. One famous example of corruption, widely copied, was a gift of a painting or some other piece of relatively minor "fine art," which would subsequently be appraised by a dealer as a masterpiece and sold for an exorbitant sum to a political supporter.
64. Schaller (1995) and Kanō and Takano (1976, 36) cite an undated *New Republic* article reporting CIA funding of the LDP. Kishi was accompanied by Uemura Kōgorō, who claims to have done much of the "spade work" (*shita junbi*) for the visit. See Uemura . . . 1979, 606.
65. The most oft-cited source about the M-Fund is Takano (1980). Kanō and Takano (1976) is less fanciful, but no better documented: their sources are "M Fund brokers." Another source is Schlei (1995), written while the author was under indictment for stock fraud. See Johnson (1995a) for the background. Verification of the M-Fund awaits declassification of government documents.
66. Kanō and Takano (1976, 13–14, 38) and Takano (1980, 55).
67. Schlei 1995, 13–14.
68. Kishi et al. 1981, 118, 128. Oddly, the Foreign Correspondents' Press Club in Tokyo has no record of Kern. (5 February 2000 correspondence from a former president of the club).
69. Declassified Memorandum of Conversation, 25 July 1958, by S. S. Carpenter, first secretary of the U.S. Embassy, Tokyo. In a letter from Ambassador MacArthur to J. Graham Parsons, the deputy assistant secretary of state for Far Eastern Affairs, dated 29 July 1958, he explained: "Kishi's brother has tried to put the bite on us for financial help in fighting communism. It did not come as a surprise to us, since he suggested the same general idea last year."
70. The records pertaining to the Indonesian reparations and peace treaty were declassified in May 2000 under the category: "Items Related to the Japanese Indonesian Peace Treaty and Reparations Agreement" (*Nihon-Indoneisia Heiwa Jōyaku oyobi Baishō Kyōtei Koshō Kankei Ikken*) Code B0152–B0154.
71. Tanaka once bragged that he got his first cabinet post by giving Kishi Nobusuke a backpack stuffed with three million yen in cash. See Schlesinger 1997, 110.
72. Wakamiya (1999) is an excellent account.
73. Yoshida quoted in Arase 1995, 28.
74. The Japan-Indonesia agreement dated 2 December 1957 stipulated that reparations be paid "in the form of capital and consumer goods produced by the Japanese industries and services of the Japanese people."
75. An annex to the Indonesian treaty listed sixty-six areas in which Japanese firms could provide goods or services to satisfy the terms of the agreement. They ranged from ships and factories to large infrastructure projects such as electric power plants, harbors, and roads. Foreign ministry archives contain dozens of petitions from firms urging completion of the agreement. Many of the businessmen who signed the petitions identified themselves by their wartime Indonesian corporate identity.
76. According to the declassified foreign ministry data (vol. 20, item B'3.1.2.3, p. 59), dur-

ing a visit to Jakarta in November 1957 Kishi offered President Sukarno $50 million more than the foreign ministry had been offering, some of which was to be paid separately in cash. The agreements between Sukarno and Kishi were always reached out of earshot of foreign ministry officials.

77. This according to a political reporter who covered the LDP in the 1960s (interview, 10 March 2000). Orr (1990, 23) suggests that the Nakasone faction had special links to Oceania; the Abe faction (descended from Kishi through Fukuda) to South Korea, Thailand, and Burma; and the Tanaka faction to China and Indonesia. Data on reparation payments are in Tsūshō Sangyōshō 1979.

78. This account is from Nishihara (1976) and Yanaga (1968).

79. *Asahi Shimbun*, 29 May 2000.

80. It helped that Kinoshita personally brought Sukarno to Tokyo and arranged private meetings with Prime Minister Kishi in early 1958; it also helped that Kishi changed his transportation minister to gain official approval of the deal. Socialist representative Yanagida Hideichi attacked the deal in the House Budget Committee in February 1959 and suggested that Kishi's private villa in Atami was one result.

81. Nishihara 1976, 103; Orr 1990, 61. Sejima would remain an influential presence in LDP political strategy. A key supporter of constitutional revision, he is also referred to by many, including Prime Minister Nakasone, as a key operative (*ura no chōseikyaku*) in the administrative reform movement (Rinchō) of the 1980s. Interview, senior Rinchō official, 7 March 2000. See also Hamada 1993.

82. Nishihara 1976, 102.

83. Orr 1990, 23.

84. Diet representative quoted in Arase 1995, 109.

85. Johnson 1995b, 193. Hara (1995, 237) argues that Kishi was "in no way inferior to Tanaka in the scale and use of [political] contributions." The difference, says Hara, was that Kishi was better able to keep his transactions in the dark. Kishi had great disdain for Tanaka, whom he thought too reckless in his pursuit of political money.

86. Mitchell (1996, 118) also adds bureaucrats and other parties to the list of Tanaka's beneficiaries. Johnson (1995), Curtis (1999), and Schlesinger (1997) are reliable accounts of Tanaka's shenanigans.

87. Masumi 1995, 226.

88. Sakurada and Shikanai (1983, vol. 2, 196) discuss how Tanaka linked his money-collection schemes to his political appointments.

89. Masumi 1995, 229.

90. Tominomori 1977, 72–76; Masumi 1995, 231; Mitchell 1996, 119. Johnson, forthcoming, is a good analysis of Miki's position. He argues that Miki saw political advantage in letting the prosecutors loose on Tanaka, but that he miscalculated the costs. "Mr. Clean" was gone in short order.

91. Yasuhara 1985, 102–3.

92. Kasama 1980, 25.

93. Kokumin Seiji Kyōkai 1981, 12–22.

94. Iwai (1990, 188) notes that, on a single day, the Japan Medical Association donated one million yen to each of nine "separate" organizations affiliated with Hashimoto Ryūtarō.

95. Hanamura 1990, 20.

96. See Curtis (1999) and Sasaki (1999) for excellent accounts of this scandal. Takeshita was Tanaka's factional successor, and both Nakasone and Abe were nonmainstream successors to Kishi. (Abe was his son-in-law.) Miyazawa was very much of the old Yoshida camp.

97. Hanamura (1990, 24) opens his account of Recruit by comparing Ezoe's "dirty money" to his "clean money." Sounding a bit like Claude Rains who was "shocked, shocked that there is gambling going on in this establishment" in the film *Casablanca*, Hanamura reports that he had met Ezoe "once or twice at parties, but never imagined he would do something so atrocious."

98. The word "fixer" or political "boss" is variously translated into Japanese as *fikusaa* or *bōsu*. The Italian terms *don* and *goddofaazaa* are also used. *Kuromaku* literally means "black drapes," and is derived from traditional Japanese theater where men dressed in black—visi-

ble but unacknowledged—manipulate the props and the set. Samuels (1982) examines two such kuromaku at the local level.

99. For an overview, see Kaplan and Dubro 1986. Van Wolferen (1989, 102) sees Kodama and Sasakawa as "the two best-known rightists of recent times, privately wealthy power brokers who pulled wires for many a top politician, partly through gangster connections." Satō (1999) is a vigorous defense of Sasakawa from within Japan's academic mainstream.

100. Johnson 1995b, 8; Wakabayashi 1990, 7–8.

101. Johnson 1995b, 8; Schlesinger 1997.

102. Quote is from Schlesinger 1997, 87–88. Sukarno protection deal is from Nishihara 1976, 111.

103. Nishihara 1976, 125.

104. Kondō and Osanai 1978, 261. See Samuels (1994, chap. 7) for the full context.

105. Satō (1999) argues admiringly that Sasakawa was a true national socialist who eschewed all dependence upon the zaibatsu or the state. He dismisses claims that Sasakawa was involved in violent groups such as the Black Dragon Society. These claims, says Satō (19–20), were concocted by political enemies after the war who were "constructing alibis" for themselves through "disinformation" about Sasakawa.

106. Wakamono to Shūkyō Kenkyūkai, ed., 1992, 153.

107. Iguchi et al. 1977, 196–98. Sasakawa also says in a 1976 *Shūkan Posuto* interview that, at the time, Kodama was simply "one of his men." See also Marshall and Toyama (1994) and Wakabayashi (1990, 13).

108. Satō (1999, 23) says that Sasakawa was a genius at trading stocks and speculating, and compares him to George Soros.

109. Iguchi et al. 1977, 94 97.

110. Tajiri 1979, 131–32.

111. Iguchi et al. 1977, 225.

112. See Johnson 1995a, 3–4; Iguchi et al. 1977, 225; Schlesinger 1997, 87; Kaplan and Dubro 1983, 42.

113. Ino 1994, 90–91.

114. This estimate is from *Forbes*, 20 June 1983.

115. Iguchi et al. 1977, 250–58; Ino 1994.

116. Marshall and Toyama (1994, 31) report that Sasakawa was a board member of the National Council of Patriotic Organizations (Zenai Kaigi) "along with right-wing yakuza and with terrorists convicted of assassinating prime ministers in the 1930s." Satō (1999, 22) insists that Sasakawa was no longer a right-winger in the postwar period.

117. Ino 1994, 89. Nakasone's Institute for International Policy Studies was funded by the Sasakawa Foundation and directed by the late Professor Satō Seizaburō, author of the hagiographic Sasakawa biography.

118. *Economist*, 11 June 1994.

119. See Iguchi et al. 1977, 265–66. In 1993, Sasakawa Takashi was the wealthiest member of the Japanese Diet. *Mainichi Shimbun*, 14 June 1993.

120. These comments appeared in a 1974 *Shūkan Posuto* article quoted in Iguchi et al. 1977, 299.

121. This account is based upon Wakamono to Shūkyō Kenkyūkai, ed. (1992) and Marshall and Toyama (1994).

122. Kishi quoted in unsigned memo by a former LDP political secretary, 21 July 1993.

123. They may have had help from U.S. Ambassador MacArthur, who worked closely with Kishi on the treaty revision and who has been described as a "dear friend of Reverend and Mrs. Moon." After retiring from government service, Ambassador MacArthur became advisor to the Unification Church-related World Media Association and a member of the editorial advisory board of the Unification Church-owned *Washington Times*. See: *http://www. tparents.org/Library/Unification/Books/Tims1/Tims1-60.htm* and *http://www.tparents.org/Library /Unification/Books/Tims1/Tims1-71.htm*

For Ambassador MacArthur's view of lauded Reverend Moon, see *http://www. unification.org/globaloutreach.html.*

124. Unsigned memo by a former LDP political secretary, 3 August 1993. The Communist

Party insists this practice continued through the June 2000 lower house elections. Interview, JCP Chairman Fuwa Tetsuzō, 5 July 2000.

125. Redl 1994, 4.

126. Wakamono to Shūkyō Kenkyūkai, ed., 1992, 154. Nakasone reportedly had close connections to Kodama as well. Kaplan and Dubro 1986, 115.

127. They reportedly planned to help make him prime minister, but Abe died prematurely. Unsigned memo to Andrew Marshall and Gregg Starr, 29 July 1993.

128. List reprinted in Wakamono to Shūkyō Kenkyūkai, ed., 1992, 158. Ozawa's father, Ozawa Saeki, was a Kishi faction member in the 1950s.

129. Redl 1994.

130. Agence France Presse, 21 October 1992. Kanemaru reportedly was repaying Moon for supporting one of his disciples in a gubernatorial race in Yamanashi Prefecture.

131. Marshall and Toyama 1994, 34. Ino (1994) counts eighty retirement placements in forty-eight recipient organizations.

132. Kaplan and Dubro 1983, 28.

133. Iguchi et al. 1977, 268–69; Ino 1995, 91.

134. Iguchi et al. 1977, 270–71.

135. Ino 1994, 91; Iguchi et al. 1977, 293–301. These authors attribute a major role to Sasakawa in nurturing the Lockheed scandal.

136. Iguchi et al. 1977, 295–96.

137. Satō 1999, 17; *Wall Street Journal*, 18 August 1981.

138. Murobushi 1981. Kaplan and Dubro (1986, 116) report contacts between Kishi and yakuza, including his 1971 guarantee of bail for a Yamaguchi-gumi boss convicted of murder.

139. Tajiri 1979, 88.

140. See Yokoyama (2000) for a detailed account of the political activities of "new" religious groups.

141. Mitchell 1996, 109.

142. Ozawa (1993) is one example. Reborn as a political finance reformer after being implicated in the Recruit Scandal, he argues for funds to go directly to parties rather than to individual politicians, and argues for the transparency that was absent in the 1955 system.

143. Schaller 1995, 17.

144. Wakamiya 1999, 50, for example.

145. *Corriere della Sera*, November 22, 1999.

146. In his obituary of Fanfani for *Il Messaggero* (21 November 1999), Paolo Pombeni suggests that Fanfani was merely attracted to the technological aspects of fascism and to its promise of modernization.

147. Malgeri 1981, 224. For more on Fanfani's early years, see Galli 1975.

148. See Herf 1984.

149. Galli 1975, 12.

150. This was a central element of Catholic social ideology. See Galli and Facchi 1962, 300.

151. Ranfagni 1975, 172. Also see Galli and Facchi 1962, 305.

152. Malgeri 1981, 225 and 306. See also Galli 1975, 12. It is important to note the differences between Catholic and fascist corporatism. Fascists used corporatism to avoid class struggle in the building of national power. It was the responsibility of the state to guarantee the patriotic cooperation of economic groups. Catholics believed that class struggle could be avoided when capitalists recognize—through the Church's teaching—that they are part of a social and religious community that requires social duties. And, for their part, workers will understand class struggle as unnecessary and wrong in a society governed by Christian morality. The state has no particular role in Catholic corporatism.

153. Ranfagni is more convinced of Fanfani's adhesion to the regime than are others. See Ranfagni 1975, 59. See Bocci (1999) for a detailed review of the *Rivista Internazionale*. For Fanfani's views on social justice, see Bocci 1999, 218; on economics and the moral order, Bocci 1999, 206–9.

154. Galli 1975, 17.

155. Fanfani quoted in Galli 1975, 17.

156. Fanfani quoted in Bocci 1999, 179–80.
157. See Galli and Facchi 1962, 306; Pombeni 1979, 39; and Ranfagni 1975, 60.
158. Bellah 1980, 110.
159. Fanfani quoted in Galli 1975, 18.
160. Galli 1975, 17–18. Also see Carillo 1965, 106.
161. Some historians note that Fanfani's views were uncharacteristically obscure between 1943–1945. See, for example, Ranfagni 1975, 234–37. On the other hand, the liberal economist Luigi Einaudi remembers Fanfani without rancor or resentment as a fellow exiled professor in Switzerland. See Einaudi 1997, 109.
162. Fanfani 1948, 125.
163. Fanfani 1945, 66, 87.
164. Fanfani 1948, 124.
165. Some Italian historians do not believe that Fanfani was ever a committed fascist, e.g., Pombeni 1997, 173. See also Bocci 1999.
166. Galli 1975, 7.
167. Zangrandi (1963) is a personal account of intellectuals attracted initially to fascism who turned to communism after the war. One, Davide Lajolo, became editor of *l'Unità*, the Communist Party daily.
168. Galli 1975, 16, 50.
169. Fanfani (1958, 23) speaks here of the 1953 election campaign.
170. Mammarella 1970, 279.
171. Fanfani 1958, 94.
172. Ibid., 13.
173. For Mattei's successful confrontation with the international oil companies, see Votaw 1964. For the contemporary debates, see Senato della Repubblica 1953.
174. See Orfei 1975. Scalfari and Turani (1974) is an intimate account of the process by which state firms were transformed into instruments of DC power.
175. Martinelli 1978, 266.
176. La Malfa saw what was coming, and sought to place a wedge between the state sector and the DC. See Barca and Trento 1997, 209.
177. For its part, Confindustria "bet heavily on a losing horse, the Liberal Party." See Salvati 1981, 340.
178. On this important transformation, see Barca 1997; Baget Bozzo 1974; Scalfari and Turani 1974. Di Palma (1978, 26–27) is a particularly lucid explanation of the development of the *borghesia di stato*.
179. Barca and Trento 1997.
180. de Cecco and Giovannini 1989, 226.
181. Scalfari and Turani (1974, 60) call them Italy's "new master race."
182. See Martinelli 1978, 273. Golden (1995) suggests that this was probably the largest pool of patronage among the industrial democracies.
183. Fanfani 1958, 98.
184. Freddi 1994.
185. Barca and Trento 1997, 219, n. 8.
186. Galli 1975, 71.
187. As in Japan, the left and right wings of the Socialist Party repeatedly split. See Hellman 1988.
188. See Samuels 1987; Scalfari and Turani 1974, chap. 1.
189. Andreotti quoted in Orfei 1975, 119.
190. This account is based on Di Palma 1978; Urban 1986; Hellman 1988; Kogan 1983; and Berlinguer's biographer, Gorresio 1976.
191. Gilbert 1995, 130.
192. Years later, after the end of DC dominance, the public learned that a mid-level DC official had codified the difficult and intricate calculations for forming a new government in his "Cencelli Handbook." The relative value of each ministerial portfolio increased with the number of positions available for placement of political allies.
193. Broadcast media, three of which were state owned, were divided according to party

allegiance and in proportion to their electoral strength. The network RAI-Uno was kept under DC control, RAI-Due was the bastion of the PSI, and RAI-Tre was dominated by the PCI.

194. della Porta 1993, 108.

195. Golden (1999) provides empirical support for the view that proportional representation generates powerful incentives for the intraparty rivalries that sustain political corruption.

196. della Porta (1995, 109) rejects the term *partitocrazia*.

197. See Chubb and Vannicelli 1988.

198. Pasquino 1998, 52, calls it Italy's "voracious *lottatizione.*"

199. D'Ambrosio in a May 1993 interview in *l'Unità*, quoted in Lehner (1995, 73) and Gismondi (1996, 147).

CHAPTER 10: CHASING NORMALITY

1. See Romano (1995b) and Colajanni (1996) on Italy and Johnson (2000a) on Japan.

2. In nominal terms, Italian growth rates exceeded Japanese ones by an average of nearly 4% annually for the first decade after the end of the Cold War. *International Financial Statistics Yearbook* (Washington, D.C.: International Monetary Fund, 2000). When adjusted for inflation, Italy still grew 0.3% faster per year than Japan during this period (European Commission, 2001).

3. Hiwatari (1999) explains why the Italian reforms succeeded better than the Japanese ones.

4. See Johnson, forthcoming.

5. On the postwar Italian judiciary, see Guarnieri 1995, di Federico 1995, and Nelken 1996a.

6. Burnett and Mantovani 1998, 254. Giovanni Falcone, the anti-Mafia prosecutor murdered in May 1992, called Italy's system "absolutely irresponsible." Falcone quoted in di Federico 1998, 380.

7. di Federico 1989, 37.

8. When elected they are allowed a leave of absence, but draw both salaries and maintain their seniority within the magistracy. See di Federico 1998, 376–77.

9. On Mani Pulite, see della Porta 1993; della Porta and Vannucci 1997; Colajanni 1996; Pederezoli and Guarnieri 1997; Gismondi 1996; and Burnett and Mantovani 1998.

10. Statistics from della Porta and Vannucci 1997. Pederezoli and Guarnieri (1997) report lower numbers.

11. See Gilbert 1995, 139.

12. D'Ambrosio quoted in Lehner 1995, 65–66.

13. Nelken 1996b, 197.

14. Lehner 1995, 46; Curwen 1995, 109–10.

15. di Federico 1989, 26.

16. This criticism is found across the political spectrum. See Colajanni (1996, 127–28, 180) and di Federico (1998). Lehner (1995) compares the exercise to the Inquisition and to Stalinism. The closest American parallel was the reaction of Congress to Kenneth Starr's term as special prosecutor. By the time he had completed his investigations and laid his charges out against President Bill Clinton in 1999, Congress allowed the Special Prosecutor Law to lapse.

17. As of late 1999; *International Herald Tribune,* 1 September 1999.

18. Craxi remained a fugitive in Tunisia, where he died in 2000. An aged Andreotti, acquitted on murder charges in November 1999, moved with Nixonesque vigor toward rehabilitation.

19. Gismondi (1996, 16) used the term "decapitation." Colajanni 1996, 167, speaks of the "Republic in tatters" (*una repubblica a brandelli*).

20. Borelli quoted in Andreoli 1998, 20.

21. Silvio Berlusconi, himself a target, charged that the prosecutors had "two souls, one of justice and one of political repression." Berlusconi quoted in Colajanni 1996, 94.

22. di Federico 1989, 25.

23. Parenti quoted in Burnett and Mantovani 1998, 177.

24. Cossiga quoted in Burnett and Mantovani 1998, 11.

25. Burnett and Mantovani (1998, 239) call Mani Pulite "the first postmodern style of coup d'etat, carried out by a tiny knot of magistrates, almost certainly abetted by certain politicians and economic barons, with the complicity of the print media owned by the latter."

26. This is the view of Colajanni 1996, 72–73. Several former Communists, including Massimo D'Alema, the future prime minister, were investigated, but no evidence of cash payments was discovered.

27. *Corriere della Sera,* 30 September 1999.

28. Colajanni 1996, 57.

29. Borelli quoted in Andreoli 1998, 29.

30. *L'Espresso,* 10 May 1992.

31. See Colajanni 1996.

32. Lehner 1995, 57–58. Borelli has said that "Antonio is so stubborn, so naive. I wonder if he has the gifts of prudence, cunning, and flexibility" (Quoted in Burnett and Mantovani 1998, 226).

33. DiPietro's name appeared in the Italian print media more times in 1992–94 than the names of all other prosecutors combined. See Chiot (1996) and Moretti (1998).

34. Colajanni 1996, 139.

35. Colajanni (1996, 118) calls this a case of "ordinary trasformismo."

36. Colajanni 1996, 54.

37. By all accounts, Andreotti was the most accomplished "fixer" in postwar Italian politics. Gismondi (1996) examines Andreotti's "strategy of connivance" with the prosecutors who brought charges against him—including charges of his participation in the work of organized crime since at least 1978. For Andreotti's acquittal, see *Corriere della Sera,* 25 September 1999.

38. U.S. Government 2000.

39. National Police Agency 1989.

40. See Jamieson 2000, 105.

41. First reported by Leslie Helm in the *Los Angeles Times,* 25 January 1995.

42. See Bōzono (1998, 80) and Inami (1992, 354).

43. National Police Agency 1999.

44. Kattoulas 2002.

45. Bōzono 1998, 82.

46. Kattoulas 2002.

47. Kattoulas 2000, 93.

48. Kattoulas 2002.

49. Gambetta 1993, 348.

50. Viviano 1995. For anti-Mafia legislation that preceded the end of the Cold War, see Santino 1997.

51. della Porta and Vannucci 1997, 536.

52. Documented in chilling detail by Stille 1999, 49.

53. La Licata 2000. Gambetta (1993) is a sophisticated economic analysis of the Mafia.

54. A nationwide survey in January 2000 found 82% of Japanese voters wanted "change" in politics. *Asahi Shimbun,* 5 January 2000.

55. Morlino (1997) is a detailed analysis.

56. Curtis 1999, 137. See his chap. 4.

57. See Reed (1999) for the Japanese case and Morlino (1997) for Italy.

58. *Il Resto di Carlino,* Bologna, 17 December 1999.

59. Seiji Kōhō Center 2000. *Asahi Shimbun,* 21 March 2000, has the number (33%) prior to the election.

60. In June 1993, forty-four LDP Diet members left to form the Japan Renewal Party and ten left to form Sakigake. In April 1994 two new small parties were established. See chap. 12.

61. Curtis 1999, 27.

62. Magara (1998, 1) draws this comparison.

63. Pasquino (1993, xiii) notes that "all those who had voted for the Christian Democrats out of fear of communism are now free to vote for other parties." And this is no small part of the voting population. See Diamanti and Segatti 1994.

64. Berselli 1994, 13.

65. By then, Gianfranco Fini had given the neofascists new respectability. In March 1994 his party—now renamed—won nearly 14% of the vote and celebrated with a rally in Rome where the party faithful sang hymns to Il Duce.

66. Ozawa and D'Alema met at Liberal Party headquarters in Tokyo in June 2000, where they discussed their different paths toward "normality." Interview with meeting participant, June 2000.

67. Ozawa 1994, 95-96. Ozawa 1995, 463.

68. Ozawa 1994, 23.

69. Ozawa 1995, 462; Ozawa 1993.

70. Near the end of his life, Yoshida acknowledged: "In the matter of defense we seem to be advancing beyond the stage of depending upon the strength of other countries . . . Were Japan to persist in the policy it could not avoid in the difficult period after the Pacific War [non-rearmament], it would undoubtedly reap excessive profits but would also be criticized for not making its rightful and appropriate contribution to international cooperation." See Yoshida 1967, 106-7.

71. Ozawa 1995, 464.

72. D'Alema 1995, 168.

73. This is how Gilbert (1998a, 314) characterizes D'Alema's 1995 book. See also Cartocci 1999, 219.

74. D'Alema 1995, 17.

75. Ibid., 53-54.

76. D'Alema quoted in Gilbert 1998a, 312.

77. D'Alema 1995, 171.

78. Yoshida 1967, 110.

79. Speech by Berlusconi in Rome, 24 October 1998, and in Milan, 18 April 1998. Texts are at http://www.forza-italia.it.

80. De Mauro (1996, 95) provides a map of Italy's regional dialects. He estimates that only 14% of the Italian population uses Italian exclusively. Calvetti, 1992, compares language standardization in nineteenth-century Italy and Japan.

81. LaPalombara 1987, 86. See also Harris (1994, 39) on this same point.

82. This argument is made eloquently by Galli della Loggia 1998, 70-78. It is central to Putnam 1993. Cartocci (1999, 223) speaks of *incivismo* as the crucial "deficit in [Italy's] national identity."

83. Diamanti and Segatti 1994, 16.

84. According to *Eurobarometer* Report 51, July 1999, the average EU satisfaction with national democracy is 60%, but it is only 34% in Italy. See Cartocci (1994) and Biocca 1997.

85. See Smith and Jarkko 1998, table 3; Ceccarini 1999; Cartocci 1994.

86. *Eurobarometer* Report 51, July 1999; Ceccarini 1999, 152.

87. Diamanti and Segatti 1994, 16.

88. Japan was seventh of the twenty-three nations surveyed, while Italy was eighteenth. The United States ranked first. See Smith and Jarkko 1998, fig. 1.

89. Minami 1994, 1. Right-wing groups in Japan invoke different data and bemoan the *lack* of patriotism among Japanese youths. On regional differences within Italy, see Putnam 1993.

90. Eighty percent of Japanese and Americans are proud of their nations' economic achievements, only 40% of Italians.

91. The results reported in this paragraph are from the International Social Survey Program's National Identity Project (1995, 36, 44) and from *Tōkei Sūri Kenkyūjo* 1999, 132.

92. Compare the results in Diamanti and Segatti (1994, 22) and *Tōkei Sūri Kenkyūjo* (1999, 140).

93. *Tōkei Sūri Kenkyūjo* 1999, 711.

94. Banfield 1958.

95. The early civic culture studies were by Banfield (1958) and Almond and Verba (1963).

96. *Corriere della Sera,* 15 September 1996.

97. Bossi and the Lega are explored more fully in chap. 12.

98. Field 1991. See Lie (2001) for analysis of "multiethnic" Japan.

99. Editorial in *LiMEs: Revista Italiana di Geopolitica,* October–December 1994, 7. Galli della Loggia (1996) is the strongest argument for the uncertain existence of an Italian national identity.

100. Article 9 of the Japanese Constitution reads as follows: "Aspiring sincerely to an international peace based on justice and order, the Japanese people forever renounce war as a sovereign right of the nation and the threat or use of force as means of settling international disputes. In order to accomplish the aim of the preceding paragraph, land, sea, and air forces, as well as other war potential, will never be maintained. The right of belligerency of the state will not be recognized." Article 11 of the Italian Constitution is nearly an echo: "Italy shall repudiate war as an instrument of offence against the liberty of other peoples and as a means for settling international disputes; it shall agree, on conditions of equality with other states, to such limitations of sovereignty as may be necessary to allow for a legal system that will ensure peace and justice between nations; it shall promote and encourage international organizations having such ends in view."

101. See Dower (1979) and chap. 8 of this study for analysis of Yoshida's calculations.

102. The best accounts of these efforts and their failures are in Ward 1965; Maki 1980; and Kataoka 1991.

103. The 1970s and 1980s have been characterized as the "winter age" of constitutional debate. See Kobayashi 1997. Itoh (2001) reviews three proposals made by leading politicians after the Gulf War.

104. Odawara 1991, 11.

105. Public opinion polls initially showed strong opposition to the bill and very little support for the new interpretation of Article 9.

106. Odawara 1991, 13.

107. Asai 1991, 130–33.

108. Japan's name was markedly omitted from a Kuwaiti statement of gratitude to the allied powers.

109. *Asahi Shimbun,* 18 January 2000.

110. The new version allowed the dispatch of SDF forces to cooperate with UN peacekeeping operations, but only under severely limited constraints. New legislation was required to enable similarly restrictive Japanese participation in the U.S.-led Afghani campaign after the terrorist attacks of 11 September 2001.

111. See, for example, the editorial "To Enhance World Trust in Japan" in the *Daily Yomiuri,* 9 September 1993; Ozawa et al. 1992; and Kitaoka 1993.

112. They were Mitsuzuka Hiroshi, then chairman of the LDP's Policy Affairs Research Council, and Watanabe Michio, then foreign minister.

113. See, for example, the views expressed by Ozawa Ichirō on the 17 October 1999 "Sunday Project," a national news interview program, as well as those of Nakasone Yasuhiro in Miyazawa and Nakasone 2000, 9.

114. See Kitaoka 1999, 127.

115. See his comments on the 17 October 1999 "Sunday Project."

116. Nakasone 1997.

117. Nakasone quoted in *Mainichi Shimbun,* 15 August 1998.

118. *Yomiuri Shimbun,* 22 December 2000.

119. *Nihon Keizai Shimbun,* 2 February 2000; Odawara 2000.

120. Miyazawa 1997. Also see comments by LDP leader (and former Miyazawa protégé) Katō Kōichi on the 17 October 1999 "Sunday Project."

121. *Yomiuri Shimbun,* 3 November 1994.

122. For the personal account of the *Yomiuri* publisher, see Watanabe 1999.

123. Survey data from *Yomiuri Shimbun* (21–22 March 1998) as well as from various other sources (1994–1998) was obtained from the Japan Public Opinion Location Library (JPOLL), Roper Center for Public Opinion Research, University of Connecticut.

124. *Mainichi Shimbun,* 24 May 1997.

125. The 27 June 2000 *Asahi Shimbun* identifies the wide range of views in favor of constitutional revision within each party.

126. Interview, Nakasone Yasuhiro, 17 May 2000.

127. A 27 June 2000 *Asahi Shimbun* poll showed that of all the parties, only the JCP is monolithic.

128. Yoshida 1961, 146. See also Ozawa (1995, 467) for his appreciation of Yoshida's forecast.

129. Pasquino 2000, 105.

130. Referendum procedures had been included in the Constitution with the reluctant support of the Left and the Right as a check on government power, and were used intermittently—most dramatically in the 1970s, when Vatican and DC efforts to change divorce and abortion laws were crushed. The Italian referendum can only cancel or change existing laws—and even then, its scope is limited by the requirement that the (politicized) Constitutional Court approve its design. Referenda require a quorum of 50% plus one vote in order to carry, no matter how overwhelming the majority may be. This has enabled parties that oppose a referendum question to kill it by de-mobilizing voters and urging them to stay home. Parliament is obliged to write new laws in the spirit of a referendum decision, but legislators enjoy considerable leeway on how to implement the people's will.

131. Professor Miglio quoted in Chimenti 1999, 123.

132. Corbetta and Parisi 1995, 82.

133. Pasquino 1997, 44; D'Alimonte and Bartolini 1997, 132.

134. See Pasquino (2000), Gilbert (1998b), and Donovan (1999) for details on the ill-fated Bicamerale. Note that this was the organizational model for Japan's Constitutional Reform Committees in 2000. Fusaro (1998) is a short review of postwar constitutional reform efforts and an analysis of the Bicamerale.

135. A tentative agreement on electoral reform was included in the famous "fruit tart pact" (*patto della crostata*), reached over dessert in June at the home of an advisor to Silvio Berlusconi, leader of the largest party on the Right. Berlusconi abruptly and single-handedly scuttled parliamentary reform by withdrawing his support in June 1998.

136. *The Economist*, 24 April 1999.

137. Pasquino 2000, 118.

138. See Lewanski (1999) for broader administrative reform in Italy during the 1990s.

139. della Porta 1993, 110.

140. McCormack 1996, 33–34.

141. Blechinger 1999.

142. Rhodes 1997.

143. Johnson (1982) is the best account of Japan's economic bureaucracy. See Koh (1989) on the elite civil service and Mishima (1998) on the changing balance of power between politicians and bureaucrats. Bureaucrats had not, in fact, ever been quite as clean as their image. See Kashiwabara (1999), which draws from Hōmushō Hōmu Sōgō Kenkyūjo, ed., *Hanzai Hakusho* (Criminal White Paper), 1991 and 1996.

144. *Asahi Shimbun*, 26 February 2000. Displaced residents, including many elderly, languished in shelters for months. See Pempel 1998, 141–42; *Asahi Shimbun*, 17 January 2000.

145. Pempel 1998, 142; *Asahi Shimbun*, 29 November 1995.

146. *Asahi Shimbun*, 14 March 1995.

147. *Asahi Shimbun*, 3 September 1998.

148. *Asahi Shimbun*, 18 November 1998.

149. Blechinger dates the change from 1994. See Blechinger 1999, 43, 55.

150. *Yomiuri Shimbun*, 29 April 1998.

151. *Asahi Shimbun*, 12 October 1999.

152. *Asahi Shimbun*, 11 October 1999 and 3 March 2000.

153. *Yomiuri Shimbun*, 28 February 2000.

154. *Asahi Shimbun*, 29 January 2001.

155. *Asahi Shimbun*, 15 September 1995, 16 March 1996, and 1 August 1998. See also Pempel 1998, 142–43.

156. *Asahi Shimbun,* 17 February 1995.
157. *Asahi Shimbun,* 12 March 1997.
158. *Asahi Shimbun,* 17 April 1997.
159. *Asahi Shimbun,* 23 March 1997.
160. *Yomiuri Shimbun,* 1 and 2 October 1999; *Asahi Shimbun,* 1 and 2 October 1999.
161. Croci and Picci 1999, 20.
162. The best general accounts of concertation are Eichengreen (1996) and Iverson, Pontussen, and Soskice 2000. For the Italian case, see Regini 1997; Baccaro 2000; and Locke and Baccaro 1994. For Italy's ascension into the EMU, see Croci and Picci 1999.
163. Regini 1997. See also Locke and Baccaro 1994.
164. Barca and Trento 1997, 230. IRI was formally dissolved in July 2000.
165. Regini 1997.
166. Pasquino 1997, 43.
167. Regini and Regalia 1997, 217.
168. Ibid., 210.
169. Ibid., 225.
170. Croci and Picci 1999, 12.
171. See, for example, Makin 2001.
172. Makin 2000, 3.
173. Lincoln 2001, 65.
174. Makin (2000) estimates that the Japanese debt in 2000 was more than three times the Italian debt of the early 1990s. Asher and Dugger (2000) provide even higher estimates. See also Asher (2001, 2) who argues that in 2000 nearly 65% of Japan's tax revenues was needed to service its debt—a figure three times higher than in Italy at the same time.
175. Makin 2001, 1.
176. As much as 40% of each "new" package comprises commitments carried over from previous ones. The amount of "real water" (*mamizu*) is usually less than half the official figures.
177. Lincoln 2001, 66.
178. Most economists celebrated the forces for change. See Lincoln 2001; Katz 2001; and Makin 2001. Many sociologists worried; see Dore 2000.
179. This pithy list is from Pempel 2000.
180. Pempel (2000) stresses the irreversibility of the structural changes after the economic bubble burst.
181. Pempel 2000; Katz 2001, chap. 3; Yasukawa 1994; and Nakamura and Shibuya 1995.
182. This was just 4% in 1990. See data at http://www.mizuho-sc.com/english/ebond/equity/trends.html.
183. Lincoln (2001) is skeptical. So too are Carlile and Tilton 1998; Katz 2001; and Asher and Dugger 2000.
184. In March 2002 METI announced that Japan's five leading semiconductor manufacturers would create a research consortium with government funding, evoking 1970s industrial policy. *Asahi Shimbun,* 26 March 2002.
185. Vogel 1996; Carlile and Tilton 1998.
186. In January 2001, the LDP announced that it would use public resources to prop up equity prices on the Tokyo Stock Exchange. See *Nihon Keizai Shimbun,* 19 January 2001.
187. The real change, some would note, is on the U.S. side, where few care any longer about Japanese acquisitions of U.S. assets. In 2000, Japanese wireless giant DoCoMo bought 16% of AT&T Wireless. This elicited barely a footnote in the economic press.
188. Lincoln 2001, chap. 3.
189. Properly attributed to Chalmers Johnson in Halberstam 1991, 15–16.
190. The front page headline in the 16 May 2002 *Asahi Shimbun* blared, "Japan Alone in Last Place."
191. McKean 1981.
192. Brusco and Paba (1997, 268) report that firms with fewer than 250 employees accounted for 71.4% of Italian value-added in 1991, while in Japan the figure was a nearly identical 74.1%. Within the OECD, only Spain came close.

CHAPTER 11: CHOICES ON THE LEFT

1. On the early socialist movement in Italy, see De Grand (1989) and Di Scala 1980; on Japan, see Beckmann and Okubo (1969) and Hoston 1986. Croce (1928) is an important account by one of Italy's most influential thinkers.

2. For the party's account see Central Committee, Japan Communist Party, ed., 1982.

3. The most famous conversion was that of Kawakami Hajime. See Bernstein (1976) and his own account, Kawakami 1949. For other cases see Beasley 1990, 186.

4. See Berton (2000) and Emmerson (1972) for useful, short reviews of the Japanese case.

5. Urban 1986, 18. See also Blackmer 1968, 10–12.

6. Zangrandi (1963) is a personal account of the intellectual journeys of students and intellectuals first attracted to fascism who later became influential communists.

7. Stalin tried to undermine Togliatti's leadership. Urban 1986, Blackmer 1968, and Pombeni 1997 are excellent accounts.

8. Urban 1986, 222. He had to sacrifice colleagues in the process. See Pombeni 1997, 149.

9. Emmerson 1972, 567.

10. *Akahata* was not published again until April 1952, after the end of the Occupation.

11. Swearingen and Langer 1968, 200.

12. Beckmann and Okubo 1969. Also see Swearingen and Langer (1968) and Tagawa (1968, chap. 3).

13. Swearingen and Langer (1968, 200–202) and Koyama (1966, 23–28, 71–81, 415). The full text of Nosaka's self-criticism appeared in *Akahata* on 6 February 1950.

14. Central Committee, Japan Communist Party, ed., 1982, 181.

15. Langer 1972, 69.

16. Miyamoto was already a full member of the Central Committee in 1934. See Miyamoto (1985) for his own account.

17. Interview, Fuwa Tetsuzō, 5 July 2000. For Nosaka's dealings with the Soviets and his "betrayal," see Fuwa 1993, 63–66.

18. Berton 2000, 2.

19. Blackmer 1968, 19.

20. In 1954, Giulio Seniga, a prominent member of the central committee, bolted the party after publicly denouncing Togliatti for "temporizing" and for "capitulating" to bourgeois democratic practice. See Blackmer 1968, 19.

21. Ignazi (1992) is an excellent account.

22. He even claimed that the PCI had opposed the establishment of the Cominform. See Blackmer 1968, 50–58, 61.

23. Togliatti quoted in Blackmer 1968, 61.

24. Blackmer 1968, 239.

25. Antonio Giolitti, grandson of the Liberal premier, may have been the most prominent. See Ginsborg 1990, 207; Hughes 1965, 207–8; Urban 1986.

26. Langer, 1972, 80–82.

27. Central Committee, Japan Communist Party, ed., 1982, 225.

28. Koyama 1966, 301–6.

29. Central Committee, Japan Communist Party, ed., 1982, 205–6.

30. Koyama 1966, 319–56.

31. Koyama 1966, 403–9. See also *Akahata*, 1 and 3 January 2000. The JCP and the CCP did not normalize relations until 1998.

32. Emmerson 1972, 573.

33. Miyamoto 1985, 429.

34. Hellman 1988, 28; Kogan 1983, 134.

35. Craveri 1995, 76.

36. Berlinguer made his debut on the international scene at the Sixteenth Congress of the French Communist Party. See Gorresio 1976, 113.

37. Berlinguer 1976; Gorresio 1976.

38. Interview in *Il Messaggero*, 12 June 1975, reprinted in Berlinguer 1976, 65.

39. Romano (1995b, 146–47) argues that the Socialist Party's entry into Italian governance at the end of 1963 was possible only because the Kennedy administration assented and that the PCI admittance in the late 1970s was impossible because the Carter administration refused its assent.

40. Gorresio 1976, 137; Mammarella and Ciuffoletti 1996, 185.

41. Pasquino 1993, 169.

42. Berton 2000, 3.

43. Fuwa—born Ueda Kenjirō in 1930—worked in the iron and steel workers union for eleven years. He became a full-time staff member of the party in 1964 and within six years, at age forty, became director of the party secretariat. In 1982, Fuwa became chairman of the JCP.

44. For earlier stirrings see Blackmer 1968, 246.

45. D'Alema quoted in Gilbert 1998a, 315.

46. Occhetto 1994, 191. Elsewhere in his memoirs (81), Occhetto recalls that Berlinguer first raised with him the problem of the name "communist" in 1974, during the divorce referendum campaign. Lenin, said Berlinguer, changed the name of his party for even less of a reason than they had. But when Occhetto suggested that perhaps they should change the name from PCI to PCD (for *democratico*), Berlinguer laughed and said, "That would be like saying we were not *already* democrats!"

47. This paragraph is based on Ignazi (1992) and Pasquino 1993. See also Weinberg 1995.

48. Occhetto 1994, 183.

49. In his memoirs, Occhetto refers to Brandt as his model. See Occhetto 1994, 188.

50. See his speech in Occhetto 1988.

51. Occhetto quoted in *Italy Daily*, 12 November 1999.

52. The most vivid analysis of Occhetto's decision is Kertzer 1996. See also Weinberg 1995.

53. In so doing, he did what Gorbachev had done when he announced perestroika. Gorbachev told a group of war veterans: "You won the Second World War. If you don't want to lose it all now we must not cling to the past but devote ourselves to making great changes." Both Gorbachev and Occhetto are quoted in Kertzer 1996, 3.

54. Occhetto 1994, 59, 189.

55. Interview in *La Repubblica*, 17 November 1989, recalled in Occhetto 1994, 191. Perhaps the only person he shared his decision with was Neil Kinnock, the British Labour Party leader. See Weinberg 1995, 4.

56. Kertzer 1996, 68 (emphasis added).

57. Ibid., 69.

58. Ignazi (1992, 135) speaks of these senior leaders as "custodians of orthodoxy and the historical memory."

59. Weinberg (1995, 113) and Kertzer (1996, 18) are especially strong on this point.

60. Kertzer (1996, 7, 67) invokes Foucault and Bourdieu to make this point, but it is one that Machiavelli made in the sixteenth century.

61. *L'Espresso*, 24 February 1991.

62. Weinberg 1995, 74.

63. Pasquino (1993) and Evans (1994) are helpful snapshots of the party's platform.

64. See Occhetto (1994, chap. 5) for his own account.

65. Central Committee, Japan Communist Party, ed., 1982, 7.

66. Langer 1972, 39.

67. *Reuters World Service*, 10 October 1994.

68. This paragraph based on an interview with Chairman Fuwa, 5 July 2000.

69. Interview, Fuwa Tetsuzō, 5 July 2000.

70. Fuwa 1993, 348–51. On pages 140–43, Fuwa suggests that the PCI abetted Soviet interference in JCP affairs in 1964 and that the PCI's "independence" from Moscow was feigned.

71. *Akahata*, 16 July 1997.

72. *Akahata*, 4 October 1999.

73. *Asahi Shimbun*, 15 January 2000. Also see Fuwa (1999, 30) and *Akahata*, 1 and 3 January 2000.

74. Curtis 1999, 239.

75. *Asahi Shimbun,* 5 January 2000. In 2000 the JCP had 4,448 local assemblymen nationwide, up from 3,000 in 1977. (JCP data sheet, July 2000).

76. The JCP won 6.7 million votes, or 11.2% of the total, in the June 2000 election.

77. *Mainichi Shimbun,* 21 September 2000.

78. Berton 2000, 6. Curtis (1999, 239) comes to a similar conclusion.

79. Langer 1972, 10.

80. Interview, Fuwa Tetsuzō, 5 July 2000.

81. *Asahi Shimbun,* 25 November 2000.

82. Since the Soviet archives have been opened, there is more information available about Soviet financial support to the PCI and JCP than there is about U.S. support to the DC and the LDP. Although *l'Unità* (16 October 1991) reported that the PCI stopped receiving Soviet funding in the 1970s, President Gorbachev acknowledged that funding continued through 1990. See Burnett and Mantovani 1998, 76. Fuwa (1993) is an exhaustive review of Soviet interference in the affairs of the JCP. See chap. 9 of this book for U.S. support of the LDP.

83. Ignazi (1992, 22–23) argues that until Occhetto's svolta the communist fundamentals—socialism, the role of the party, relations between public and private ownership, and between individuals and classes—were never modified by the party's many tactical and strategic shifts.

84. Lanzarra 1998, 16.

85. *La Repubblica,* 17 December 1989.

CHAPTER 12: OPTIONS ON THE RIGHT

1. Still, when the Forza Italia came to power in 1993, the Berlusconi government blocked Slovenia's effort to join the EU, and sought to reopen talks on reparations for Italians dispossessed in Istria. See Hametz 1998.

2. *Corriere della Sera,* 17 October 1999.

3. Galli della Loggia 1998, 81.

4. Sani 1993.

5. Tarrow (1977) is impressed with the capability of Italian politicians to ameliorate regional claims through trasformismo. See also McAdam, Tarrow, and Tilly 2001, chap. 8.

6. See Cachafeiro (1999, 211) for the latter view and Diamanti (1996, 113) for the former. Bossi is not shy about taking full credit. He divides his self-indulgent autobiography into two parts, "My Life" and "My League." See Bossi 1992.

7. I borrow the metaphor of "manufacturing the North" from Cachafeiro 1999.

8. Diamanti 1996, 81. Cachafeiro (1999, 163) concurs. Forgacs and Lumley (1996) reproduce seven different maps of Italy used for seven different purposes, only one of which divides the nation into North and South.

9. Bosworth 1998, 14.

10. Quoted in Cachafeiro 1999, 231.

11. Bossi 1992, 180.

12. Cartocci 1994, 101–2. See also Clark 1996, 25.

13. "È un sistema indegno di un paese civile, uno strozzinaggio senza paragone" (It is a dishonorable system for a civil nation—usury without parallel). Bossi 1992, 131.

14. Mannheimer 1993, 98. Bossi's wife is Sicilian.

15. Farini quoted in Galli della Loggia 1998, 64.

16. Bossi quoted in Stella 1996, 47.

17. *Corriere della Sera,* 26 November 1995.

18. This is described in Cachafeiro 1999, 248–50. See also Romano 1991.

19. Cachafeiro 1999, 346.

20. See Mannheimer (1993) and Cartocci (1994) for analysis of results of the 1992 election.

21. Rocca 1999.

22. Bossi 1992.

23. Diamanti 1996, 96; Orefice 1993, 10. Cachafeiro (1999) lists the different formulations as reflected in their publications.

24. See Diamanti 1996. Stella (1996) is a thoroughly sardonic description of the journey. The account in *Corriere della Sera* by Venanzio Postiglione on 15 September 1996 also aggressively ridiculed the ceremony.

25. The full text of this declaration can be found at http://www.leganord.org/federale/gazz.htm

26. Diamanti (1996, 85) identifies five.

27. Diamanti and Segatti 1994, 18.

28. Diamanti 1996, 77.

29. Parker 1996; Mannheimer 1993; Diamanti 1996; and Cachafeiro 1999.

30. Diamanti 1996, 7.

31. *The Economist,* 22 March 2001.

32. Alessandra Stanley says that "on the stump [Berlusconi] comes off like a wired Steve Forbes with a touch of Eva Perón." *New York Times Magazine,* 15 April 2001, 40.

33. See Evans 1994, 10; and Sechi 1995, 20–21.

34. Freddi (1994) is a useful analysis. Harris (1994, 38) refers to Craxi's disgraced and corrupted party as one "for which socialism was no more than a tribal memory."

35. *Corriere della Sera,* 18 December 1993.

36. This, and the following quotations—from speeches made between 1994 and 1998—can be found at: http://www.forza-italia.it.

37. Ibid.

38. The Church even mobilized three northern cardinals to confront the Lega. See Cartocci 1994, 146.

39. http://www.forza-italia.it. The aging monk, Giuseppe Dossetti, one of the most important architects of the 1947 Constitution, reentered politics in the early 1990s. Disparaging Berlusconi, he urged a return to Catholic values of personal responsibility and faith. See *Corriere della Sera,* 4 May 1994 and 19 May 1994; *Il Sole 24 Ore,* 19 May 1994.

40. Berselli 1994, 19–20.

41. Stanley 2001, 43.

42. Bossi quoted in Evans 1994, 9.

43. Colajanni 1996, 91.

44. Bossi quoted in Evans 1994, 9.

45. "Dubious allies" is the label applied by Alessandra Stanley, *New York Times Magazine,* 15 April 2001, 42.

46. This account is based on the *Financial Times,* 23 February 2001, and *Time* magazine at http://www.time.com/time/europe/specials/ff/trip4/italypolitics.html. For a more nuanced account, see the debate in *Caffe' Europa,* 31 March 2001.

47. *Corriere della Sera,* 19 April 1998.

48. *The Economist,* 26 April 2001. *El Mundo* (Spain), *Le Monde* (France), and the *Financial Times* (Great Britain) joined *The Economist* in questioning Berlusconi's fitness for office. See *Corriere della Sera,* 1 May 2001. *New York Times,* 29 April 2001, reports on the threatened lawsuit.

49. *New York Times,* 5 May 2001.

50. See *New York Times,* 15 May 2001.

51. Tarrow (1977) is the exception.

52. Galli della Loggia (1998, chap. 3) emphasizes this fragmentation.

53. Hayasaka (1993) makes the apt comparison to Saigo. Ozawa prefers being compared to Mikhail Gorbachev. See *Newsweek,* 5 July 1993.

54. The senior Ozawa led the failed 1956 effort to change the electoral system and served as Kishi's point man on the revision of the Security Treaty.

55. Tanaka arranged Ozawa's marriage and presided over his wedding in place of his father. Ozawa was famous for attending every session of Tanaka's bribery trial. See Redl (1993) for an excellent account.

56. Ozawa reportedly went directly to Keidanren and asked whether business leaders were prepared to allow the system to dissolve. They responded by providing some twenty-five billion yen for the LDP. See Redl 1993, 39.

57. Redl 1993, 34.

58. Ushiro 1994, 47.

59. The best biography in English is in Schlesinger 1997. In Japanese, see Hirano 1996.

60. U.S. Ambassador Michael Armacost identifies Ozawa as the only nongovernment official with whom he consulted about Japan's contribution to the coalition. He also addresses the contrast between his "frequent calls on Secretary General Ozawa" and his "infrequent calls at the *kantei* [the prime minister's official residence]." See Armacost 1996, 101, 111.

61. Donald Atwood, then undersecretary of acquisitions, U.S. Department of Defense, explained that when the Japanese response to a U.S. request for a physical presence was unsatisfactory (he was appalled by Japanese offers of radios for rear area noncombatants), the United States dramatically increased its demands for financial support. Conversation, April 1995.

62. Ozawa 1994, 37.

63. *Mainichi Daily News,* 18 October 1990.

64. Hirano (1996, 36–39) is a personal account of these events.

65. MITI and Japan's major firms feared that Iraq would not pay back its debt to Japan. *Yomiuri Shimbun,* 7 August 1990.

66. Ozawa 1994, 39.

67. *Far Eastern Economic Review,* 18 July 1991.

68. *Asahi Shimbun,* 21 February 1992.

69. All surveys since 1995 show at least two-thirds of respondents supporting Japan's participation in international peacekeeping. See http://roperweb.ropercenter.uconn.edu/POLL

70. Hirano 1996, 24–30.

71. The JSP received less than half the seats it had attained in 1989; both the LDP and Komeito made large gains. Hayasaka 1993, 138–39.

72. See Hirano 1996, 59.

73. See, for example, Hayasaka 1993 and Hirano 1996.

74. In addition to Ozawa, this group, nicknamed "The G-7" by the press, comprised Kajiyama Seiroku, Okuda Keiwa, Obuchi Keizō, Hashimoto Ryūtarō, Hata Tsutomu, and Watanabe Kōzō.

75. *Japan Times,* 8 October 1992.

76. *Mainichi Shimbun,* 6 October 1992.

77. Iwami 1993, 53–55.

78. Kyodo News Service, 21 December 1992.

79. *Mainichi Shimbun,* 24 July 1993.

80. *Yomiuri Shimbun,* 25 January 1993. The *Asahi Shimbun,* 17 February 1993, found his testimony "amazing." The *Mainichi Shimbun,* 17 February 1993, called him "arrogant" and said he "sneered" at his inquisitors.

81. Firsthand accounts of the Ozawa-Yamagishi meeting are found in Hirano (1996, 69) and Uchida (1996, 119).

82. Hirano 1996, 69–71.

83. *Daily Yomiuri,* 15 June 1993.

84. Curtis 1999, 153.

85. See Hirano (1996, 79–80) and Tachibana (1993, 105–6). For a different view, see Curtis 1999, 95–96.

86. Hirano 1996, 80.

87. *Mainichi Daily News,* 15 June 1993; *The Economist,* 13 November 1993.

88. *Mainichi Shimbun,* 6 February 1999. He failed in his effort to get the LDP to agree to reinterpret the Constitution.

89. See the Liberal Party newsletter, *Liberty and Reform* 20 (August–September 2001) for Ozawa's position.

90. In a December 1992 poll by *Mainichi Shimbun,* Ishihara was the favorite for prime minister with then-Prime Minister Miyazawa tenth out of ten. See *Asahi Shimbun,* 19 February 2001, for a similar result one decade later.

91. *Chūō Kōron,* June 1999, 104.

92. *Time,* 24 January 1977, 16; *Asahi Shimbun,* 22 March 1975; Nathan 2001; *Chūō Kōron,* June 1999, 104.
93. *Chūō Kōron,* June 1999, 104; Sakurai et al. 2000, 25.
94. Ishihara 1999, 7.
95. Ibid., 16, 663–64.
96. His referenced cohort also included Goethe and Malraux; *Time,* 24 January 1977, 16. He was also alternately admired and dismissed by Mishima Yukio, Japan's other "D'Annunzio" of that period. See Nathan 2001.
97. *Mainichi Shimbun,* 1 October 1967; *Mainichi Daily News,* 12 February 1975.
98. Ishihara (1999, 66) notes that tens of thousands of votes counted for him were actually marked in his brother's name.
99. *Tokyo Shimbun,* 10 May 1970; *Time,* 15 July 1974.
100. *New York Times,* 22 May 1974.
101. Ishihara 1999, 215–25.
102. *Baltimore Sun,* 10 December 1972.
103. *Japan Times,* 7 July 1970. The Seirankai achieved instant notoriety by sealing their compact in blood.
104. *Shukan Yomiuri,* 10 October 1959. Nakasone was referred to in that article as "the Hitler of Japan." Some epithets never go out of fashion. In 2000 *Ishihara's* leadership style was compared to that of Adolf Hitler by Ministry of Finance Vice Minister Sakakibara Eisuke and in a memorandum circulated by the Japan Bankers Association. DeWit (2000, 210) and *Time,* 24 April 2000.
105. At this point, nearly half the Japanese population lived in a city or prefecture governed by a leftist chief executive. See Steiner et al. 1980.
106. *Asahi Shimbun,* 11 March 1975.
107. It did not help that Environment Agency chief Ishihara pointedly refused to meet environmental activists during his regularly scheduled tennis game. *Japan Times,* 13 November 1977.
108. *Japan Times,* 23 October 1977. Later, as transport minister in 1988, he approved construction of a new runway in Okinawa that destroyed one of the world's oldest coral reefs. See *Mainichi Shimbun,* 2 March 1988.
109. *Tokyo Business Today,* December 1989, 24.
110. Morita and Ishihara (1989) is the original. Later, Ishihara issued his own translation without Morita's participation. See Ishihara 1991.
111. Kyodo News Service, 23 June 1990.
112. *Wall Street Journal,* 28 September 1990.
113. *Asahi Evening News,* 15 June 1991.
114. *Asahi Shimbun,* 14 June 1991; Kyodo News Service, 26 January 1992.
115. Nor was his vitriol reserved for the United States. He called the Russian foreign minister a "hairy barbarian" in July 1992, and he proclaimed that Prime Minister Hosokawa's apologies for Japanese aggression "deserve death." See *Time,* 18 October 1993, and *Asahi Evening News,* 12 July 1993. In May 1994 he declared that the United States and China have deliberately overstated the number of Chinese killed in the 1937 Nanjing massacre. Earlier, in an October 1990 interview in *Playboy,* he said the massacre was a fabrication.
116. *Asiaweek,* 16 October 1998, 102.
117. *Mainichi Shimbun,* 2 July 1998.
118. Ishihara quoted in *New York Times,* 23 March 1998.
119. The resignation speech is reprinted in Ishihara 1999, 663–65.
120. Ibid.
121. *Los Angeles Times,* 15 April 1995; *Daily Yomiuri,* 23 April 1995.
122. According to one account, the idea of entering Ishihara in the 1999 governor's race first emerged as early as 1997. Sakurai et al. 2000, 18. See also Asano et al. 2000, 30–31.
123. Ishihara explained his late entry as a consequence of his own indecisiveness. See Asano et al. 2000, 34–35.
124. Sakurai et al. 2000, 19, 81; Kyodo News Service, 11 March 1999.
125. Sakurai et al. 2000, 20–24.

126. *Mainichi Shimbun,* 21 March 1999. DeWit (2000) analyzes the link between Ishihara's tax program and plans for decentralization.

127. *Japan Times,* 23 February, 25 February, and 5 March 2000; *Asahi Shimbun,* 17 February 2000; DeWit and Kaneko, 2002.

128. *Asahi Shimbun,* 24 April 2002. For earlier polls, see *Yomiuri Shimbun,* 20 July 1999, and *Asahi Shimbun,* 20 June 2001 (English edition). Even the Communist Party acknowledged that Ishihara was appealing to its own voters.

129. *Foreign Policy,* January/February 2001, 89.

130. Saito 2000, 46–47.

131. Ishihara claims that he was referring only to illegal immigrants. The last time there was a major Tokyo earthquake (1923), Japanese mobs lynched Koreans and Chinese.

132. *Mainichi Shimbun,* 27 April 1999; *Asahi Shimbun,* 14 April 2000.

133. *Mainichi Shimbun,* 27 November 1999.

134. Kyodo New Service, 15 April 2000.

135. *Mainichi Shimbun,* 21 May 2000.

136. Sakurai et al. 2000, 82 (emphasis added).

137. *Mainichi Shimbun,* 1 December 2000.

138. *Yomiuri Shimbun,* 23 April 2002, suggested that Ishihara's Tokyo administration was Japan's "shadow government" and speculated that Ishihara was prepared to move back into national politics. Like many Japanese national political figures, Ishihara has faced charges of corruption himself. In the mid-1970s, a JSP Dietman, Wada Shizuo, fingered him as a principal in a shady land deal in Oita Prefecture. See *Japan Times,* 18 March 1975. Also, Ishihara admitted receiving $3 million yen from Recruit in 1987–88 in exchange for "tickets" to his speeches. See *Mainichi Shimbun,* 6 August 1989. Innuendo surrounded a possible relationship between Ishihara and Aum Shinrikyō, through his fourth son, Nobuhiro, an artist reputed to have been a member of the cult. Ishihara resigned from the Diet in April 1995, just after Aum members indiscriminately murdered commuters on a Tokyo subway train. According to an essay and lawsuit by Nobuhiro, rumors that Ishihara paid the cult twenty million yen to make Nobuhiro leave its clutches were circulated by LDP operatives. See Ishihara 2000. In June 1992 Ishihara returned thirty million yen he had received from the head of a defunct real estate company, Ken International, whose founder was indicted for tax evasion. He had reported the donation as a series of smaller ones to keep within the legal limit. (*Mainichi Shimbun,* 3 June 1992.)

139. *Sentaku,* February 2001. See also *Themis,* March 2001.

140. Many LDP politicians posed for photographs with Ishihara during election campaigns in the summer of 2001. Even Prime Minister Koizumi declared that together they could change Japan—starting in Tokyo. *Asahi Shimbun,* 17 June 2001.

141. *Japan Digest* 12, no. 51, 22 March 2001.

142. *Asahi Evening News,* 14 April 1999.

143. *Japan Times,* 3 April 1999; *Asahi Evening News,* 30 May 1999.

144. *Asahi Evening News,* 3–4 April 1999; *Mainichi Daily News,* 5 January 2000.

145. Ozawa 1994, 46.

146. Here he is referring to the Pacific War. See Ozawa 1994, 25.

147. Ozawa 1994, 30.

148. Ibid., 31.

149. Ishihara quoted in Nathan 2001, 110.

150. Bossi's views are on-line at: http://151.4.58.42/frames/english.htm.

151. http://www.leganord.org/eng/rev_intr.htm.

152. *The Economist,* 22 March 2001.

153. Berlusconi, "Per il mio paese," 26 January 1994.

CONCLUSION: HOW LEADERS HAVE MATTERED IN ITALY AND JAPAN

1. See Kellerman 1986; Carr 1961.

2. Berlin 1954, 7.

3. Carr 1961, 55. Carr later rejected as "nonsense" the view that history is determined by "all-powerful forces guiding the unconscious will" (60).

4. Machiavelli 1995, 13.

5. Ibid., 71.

6. Ibid., 72.

7. See D. Johnson, forthcoming.

8. Greenstein 1969, 46.

9. Japanese analysts use the romanized *ridaashippu* more often than the Japanese word *shidō*, and Italian analysts prefer the English term to *direzione*.

10. Cavalli 1998, 164, 169.

11. Bellah 1980, 115. See also Gundle and Riall 1998, 153.

12. Gundle 1998, 173–74.

13. Mulgan 2000, 184. Most observers see Japanese leaders as *culturally* handicapped. See Reischauer (1988) and Van Wolferen (1989) for two prominent examples. Fukushima (2001) catalogues Japan's cultural handicaps. See Curtis (1999) for a particularly well-informed and balanced portrait of Japanese leadership.

14. See, for example, Craig 1970a, 25–26.

15. Many of the Japanese leaders examined in this book (e.g., Itō, Hara, Shibusawa, Yoshida, Kishi) were originally bureaucrats. Of the Italians, only Cavour and Giolitti had this background. Calder (1982) distinguishes between bureaucrat-politicians and pure politicians.

16. Sato, in his hagiography of Sasakawa, argues that "it is hard to be a creative leader in Japan, like Sasakawa," a situation he attributes to the "fundamental equity" of Japanese society. Sato 1999, 21. Nakane (1970), on the other hand, says that it is Japan's fundamental *hierarchy* that constrains leaders. Those atop the group are always a part of it, and have a responsibility for its survival, much as a parent must be responsible for a child.

17. *Shūkan Gendai,* 17 March 2001.

18. See the editorial in the 22 November 2000 *Nihon Keizai Shimbun.*

19. See Krauss, Steinhoff, and Rohlen (1984) and Pharr (1990).

20. See McAdam, Tarrow, and Tilly, 2001, chap. 8.

21. Mack Smith 1971, 64.

22. Di Palma (1978, 11) uses the term "manipulative absorption." I have described this process in Japan as "reciprocal consent" (Samuels 1987).

23. Di Palma 1978, 14.

24. Fogu (forthcoming, chap. 4) is particularly insightful on Mussolini in this regard, as is Kertzer (1996) for Occhetto.

25. Machiavelli 1986, 430.

26. Cotta (1992) addresses these "moments of elite consolidation" in Italy.

27. McAdam, Tarrow, and Tilly 2001, 246.

28. Johnson 1962, 21.

29. In 2002, the Joint Staff Council, the highest organ of Japanese military planning, still does not report to the prime minister or to the cabinet. Japan's senior officers can report only to the defense minister, and there is no legal way that the prime minister can even be assigned a military attaché. See Yamaguchi 2001, 43.

30. Granovetter (2001) makes the same point in a different context.

References

Abegglen, James C. 1958. *The Japanese Factory: Aspects of Its Social Organization.* Glencoe: Free Press.

Acheson, Dean. 1969. *Present at the Creation: My Years in the State Department.* New York: W. W. Norton.

Adler, Hugh Franklin. 1995. *Italian Industrialists from Liberalism to Fascism: The Political Development of the Industrial Bourgeoisie, 1906–1934.* Cambridge: Cambridge University Press.

Agócs, Sándor. 1971. "Giolitti's Reform Program: An Exercise in Equilibrium Politics." *Political Science Quarterly* 86, no. 4 (December): 637–53.

Akita, George. 1967. *Foundations of Constitutional Government in Modern Japan, 1868–1900.* Cambridge: Harvard University Press.

Albrecht-Carrié, René. 1950. *Italy from Napoleon to Mussolini.* New York: Columbia University Press.

Allinson, Gary D. 1987. "Japan's Keidanren and Its New Leadership." *Pacific Affairs* 60, no. 3 (fall): 385–407.

Almond, Gabriel A., and Sidney Verba. 1963. *The Civic Culture: Political Attitudes and Democracy in Five Nations.* Princeton: Princeton University Press.

Andreoli, Marcella. 1998. *Borelli: Direttore d'orchestra* (Borelli: Orchestra conductor). Milan: Baldini and Castoldi.

Andreotti, Giulio. 1984. "Intervento." In *De Gasperi e l'età del centrismo, 1947–1953* (De Gasperi and the age of centrism), edited by G. Rossini, 165–73. Rome: Cinque Lune.

Ansell, Christopher K., and M. Steven Fish. 1999. "The Art of Being Indispensible: Noncharismatic Personalism in Contemporary Political Parties." *Comparative Political Studies* 32, no. 3 (May): 283–312.

Apter, David E. 1963. "A Comparative Method for the Study of Politics." In *Comparative Politics: A Reader,* edited by Harry Eckstein and David E. Apter. New York: Free Press.

REFERENCES

Aquarone, Alberto. 1974. "The Rise of the Fascist State, 1926–1928." In *The Ax Within: Italian Fascism in Action,* edited by R. Sarti, 101–115. New York: New Viewpoints.

Arase, David. 1995. *Buying Power: The Political Economy of Japan's Foreign Aid.* Boulder, Colo.: Lynne Rienner.

Armacost, Michael H. 1996. *Friends or Rivals? The Insider's Account of U.S.-Japan Relations.* New York: Columbia University Press.

Arrighetti, Alessandro, and Gilberto Seravilli. 1997. "Istituzioni e dualismo dimesionale dell'industria italiana" (Institutions and dimensions of dualism in Italian industry). In *Storia del capitalismo italiano: dal dopoguerra a oggi* (The history of Italian capitalism: From the end of the war until today), edited by Fabrizio Barca, 335–88. Rome: Donizelli.

Asai Motofumi. 1991. "Pacifism in a New International Order." *Japan Quarterly* 38 (April–June): 130–33.

Asano, Shirō, et al. 2000. *Ishihara Shintaro no Tokyohatsu Nihon Kaizo Keikaku* (Shintaro Ishihara's blueprint for reforming Japan from Tokyo). Tokyo: Gakuyō Shobō.

Asher, David L. 2001. "The Bush Administration's Japan Problem." *AEI on the Issues,* March.

Asher, David L., and Robert H. Dugger. 2000. "Could Japan's Financial Mount Fuji Blow Its Top?" Working paper 00–01, MIT Japan Program. Cambridge: Massachusetts Institute of Technology.

Asukai, Masamichi. 1995. "Meiji Tennō: Kotei to Tenshi no Aida." In *Bakumatsu/Meijiki no Kokumin Kokka Keisei to Bunka Henyō* (Cultural change and the formation of the national state in the late Tokugawa Meiji period), edited by Mishikawa Nagao and Matsumiya Hideji, 45–89. Tokyo: Shinyō-sha.

Avagliano, Lucio. 1977. "Un imprenditore e una fabbrica fuori dal comune: Alessandro Rossi e il lanificio di Schio" (An Entrepreneur and a factory outside the town: Alessandro Rossi and the woolen mill of Schio). In *L'industrializzazione in Italia, 1861–1900* (Industrialization in Italy, 1861–1900), edited by G. Mori. Bologna: Il Mulino.

Ayling, S. E. 1971. *Portraits of Power: An Introduction to Twentieth-Century History.* London: George G. Harrap.

Baccaro, Lucio. 2000. "Il sistema italiano di concertazione sociale: problemi aperti e prospettive di evoluzione" (The Italian system of social concertation: Unsolved problems and prospects for evolution). Forthcoming in CESOS, *Le relazioni sindacali in Italia: Rapporto, 1998–1999* (Industrial realtions in Italy: Report, 1998–1999). Rome: Edizioni Lavoro.

Baget Bozzo, Gianni. 1974. *Il partito cristiano al potere: La DC di De Gasperi e di Dossetti, 1945–1954* (The Christian party comes to power: The DC of De Gasperi and Dossetti, 1945–1954). Florence: Vallecchi.

Baglioni, Guido. 1974. *L'ideologia della borghesia industriale nell'Italia liberale* (The ideology of the industrial middle class in liberal Italy). Turin: Einaudi.

Banfield, Edward C. 1958. *The Moral Basis of a Backward Society.* Chicago: Free Press.

Barca, Fabrizio. 1994. *Impresse in cerca di padrone* (Firms in search of leaders). Bari: Laterza.

——. 1997. "Compromeso senza riforme nel capitalismo italiano" (Compromise without reform of Italian capitalism). In *Storia del capitalismo italiano: dal dopoguerra a oggi* (The history of Italian capitalism: From the end of the war until today), edited by Fabrizio Barca, 4–115. Rome: Donizelli.

Barca, Fabrizio, and Sandro Trento. 1997. "La parabola delle partecipazioni statali: Una missione tradita" (The parabola of state participation: a mission betrayed). In *Storia del capitalismo italiano: dal dopoguerra a oggi* (The history of Italian capitalism: From the end of the war until today), edited by Fabrizio Barca, 186–236. Rome: Donizelli.

Barca, Fabrizio, Ugo Pagano, and Sandro Trento. 1996. "Postwar Property Rights Shocks: An Interpretation of the Diverging Italian and Japanese Governance Models." Unpublished paper, Bank of Italy Research Department, September.

Barié, Ottavio. 1984. "Lo scenario internazionale" (The international situation). In *De Gasperi e l'età del centrismo, 1947–1953* (De Gasperi and the age of centrism), edited by G. Rossini, 53–74. Rome: Cinque Lune.

Barzini, Luigi. 1964. *The Italians.* New York: Atheneum.

Bates, Robert H., and William T. Bianco. 1990. "Applying Rational Choice Theory: The Role of Leadership in Team Production." In *The Limits of Rationality*, edited by Karen Schweers Cook and Margaret Levi. Chicago: University of Chicago Press.

Bates, Robert H., Avner Greif, Margaret Levi, Jean-Laurent Rosenthal, and Barry R. Weingast. 1998. *Analytic Narratives.* Princeton: Princeton University Press.

Beasley, W. G. 1989. "Meiji Political Institutions." In *The Nineteenth Century,* vol. 5 of *The Cambridge History of Japan,* edited by Marius Jansen, 618–73. Cambridge: Cambridge University Press.

———. 1990. *The Rise of Modern Japan.* London: Weidenfeld and Nicholson.

Becker, Jared M. 1994. *Nationalism and Culture: Gabriele D'Annunzio and Italy after the Risorgimento.* New York: Peter Lang.

Beckmann, George M. 1957. *The Making of the Meiji Constitution: The Oligarchs and the Constitutional Development of Japan, 1868–1891.* Lawrence: University of Kansas Press.

Beckmann, George M., and Okubo Genji. 1969. *The Japanese Communist Party, 1922–1945.* Stanford: Stanford University Press.

Bellah, Robert N. 1980. "The Five Religions of Modern Italy." In *Varieties of Civil Religion,* edited by Robert N. Bellah and Phillip E. Hammond, 86–118. San Francisco: Harper and Row.

Benfell, Steven Terry. 1997. "'Rich Nation, No Army': The Politics of Reconstructing National Identity in Postwar Japan." Ph.D. diss., Department of Political Science, University of Pennsylvania.

Berger, Gordon. 1977. *Parties Out of Power in Japan, 1931–1941.* Princeton: Princeton University Press.

———. 1988. "Politics and Mobilization in Japan, 1931–1945." In *The Twentieth Century,* vol. 6 of *The Cambridge History of Japan,* edited by Peter Duus, 97–153. Cambridge: Cambridge University Press.

Berlin, Isaiah. 1954. *Historical Inevitability.* London: Oxford University Press.

Berlinguer, Enrico. 1976. *La politica internazionale dei comunisti italiani* (The international politics of the Italian Communists). Rome: Riuniti.

Bernstein, Gail Lee. 1976. *Japanese Marxist: A Portrait of Kawakami Hajime, 1879–1946.* Cambridge: Harvard University Press.

Berselli, Edmondo. 1994. "Solution on the Right: The Evolving Political Scenario." *Italian Journal* 8, nos. 1–2: 13–21.

Berta, Giuseppe. 1996. *Il governo degli interessi: Industriali, rappresentanza, e politica nell'Italia del nord-ovest, 1906–1924* (The government of interests: Industrialists, representation, and politics in northwest Italy, 1906–1924). Venice: Marsilio.

Berton, Peter. 2000. "The Japanese Communist Party and Its Transformations." Working paper 67, Japan Policy Research Institute, May.

Betts, Richard K. 2000. "Is Strategy an Illusion?" *International Security* (fall): 5–50.

Biocca, Dario. 1997. "Has the Nation Died? The Debate over Italy's Identity (and Future)." *Daedalus* 126, no. 3 (summer): 223–39.

Bix, Herbert. 2000. *Hirohito and the Making of Modern Japan*. New York: Harper-Collins.

Blackmer, Donald L. M. 1968. *Unity in Diversity: Italian Communism and the Communist World*. Cambridge: MIT Press.

Blechinger, Verena. 1999. "Changes in the Handling of Corruption Scandals in Japan since 1994." *Asia-Pacific Review* 6, no. 2: 42–64.

Blumberg, Arnold. 1990. *A Carefully Planned Accident: The Italian War of 1859*. Selinsgrove, Penn.: Susquehana University Press.

Bobbio, Norberto. 1995. *Ideological Profile of Twentieth-Century Italy*. Translated by Lydia G. Cochrane. Princeton: Princeton University Press.

Bocci, Maria. 1999. *Oltre lo stato liberale: Ipotesi su politica società nel dibattito cattolico tra fascismo e democrazia* (Beyond the liberal state: Hypotheses concerning politics and society in the Catholic debate between fascism and democracy). Rome: Bulzoni.

Bollati, Giulio. 1983. *L'italiano: Il carattere nazionale come storia e come invenzione* (The Italian: National character as history and as invention). Turin: Einaudi.

Boltho, Andrea, Alessandro Vercelli, and Hiroshi Yoshikawa, eds. 2001. *Comparing Economic Systems: Italy and Japan*. Houndsmills, U.K.: Palgrave.

Bossi, Umberto. 1992. *Vento dal Nord: La Mia Lega, La Mia Vita* (Wind from the North: My league, my life). Milan: Sperling and Kupfer.

Bosworth, R. J. B. 1979. *Italy, the Least of the Great Powers: Italian Foreign Policy before the First World War*. London: Cambridge University Press.

———. 1996. *Italy and the Wider World*. London: Routledge.

———. 1998. *The Italian Dictatorship: Problems and Perspectives in the Interpretation of Mussolini and Fascism*. London: Arnold.

———. 2002. *Mussolini*. London: Arnold.

Bourdieu, Pierre. 1991. *Language and Symbolic Power*. Translated by Gino Raymond and Matthew Adamson. Cambridge: Harvard University Press.

Bōzono, Shigeru. 1998. "Yakuza on the Defensive." *Japan Quarterly* 45, no. 1 (January–March): 79–86.

Breslauer, George W. 2002. *Gorbachev and Yeltsin as Leaders*. New York: Cambridge University Press.

Brown, Delmer. 1955. *Nationalism in Japan*. Berkeley: University of California Press.

Brown, Sidney Devere. 1962. "Ōkubo Toshimichi: His Political and Economic Policies in Early Meiji Japan." *Journal of Asian Studies* 21, no. 2 (February): 183–98.

Brownlee, John S. 1997. *Japanese Historians and the National Myths, 1600–1945: The Age of the Gods and Emperor Jimmu*. Vancouver: University of British Colombia Press.

Brusco, Sebastiano, and Sergio Paba. 1997. "Per una storia dei distretti industriali italiani dal secondo dopoguerra agli anni novanta" (Toward a history of Italian industrial districts from the Second World War to the 1990s). In *Storia del capitalismo italiano: dal dopoguerra a oggi* (The history of Italian capitalism: From the end of the war until today), edited by Fabrizio Barca, 265–333. Rome: Donizelli.

Brysk, Alison. 1995. "'Hearts and Minds': Bringing Symbolic Politics Back In." *Polity* 27, no. 4 (summer): 559–85.

Burnett, Stanton H., and Luca Mantovani. 1998. *The Italian Guillotine: Operation Clean Hands and the Overthrow of Italy's First Republic.* Lanham, Md.: Rowman and Littlefield.

Burns, James MacGregor. 1978. *Leadership.* New York: Harper and Row.

Byas, Hugh. 1942. *Government by Assassination.* New York: Alfred A. Knopf.

Byman, Daniel L., and Kenneth M. Pollack. 2001. "Let Us Now Praise Great Men: Bringing the Statesman Back In." *International Security* 25, no. 4 (spring): 107–46.

Cachafeiro, Margarita Gomez-Reino. 1999. "Redrawing the Territorial Boundaries within European States? The Rise of Lega Nord in Italian Politics." Ph.D. diss., Department of Political Science, Massachusetts Institute of Technology.

Cafagna, Luciano. 1999. *Cavour.* Bologna: Il Mulino.

Calder, Kent E. 1982. "Kanryō vs. Shomin: Contrasting Dynamics of Conservative Leadership." In *Political Leadership in Contemporary Japan,* edited by Terry Edward MacDougall, 1–28. Ann Arbor: Center for Japanese Studies, University of Michigan.

———. 1988. *Crisis and Compensation: Public Policy and Political Stability in Japan, 1949–1986.* Princeton: Princeton University Press.

Calvetti, Paolo. 1992. "Language Education and Standardization in the Formation of the Modern State: A Comparison of Italy and Japan." In *Japanese Civilization in the Modern World: Language, Literacy, and Writing,* edited by Tadao Umesao, J. Marshall Unger, and Osamu Sakiyama. Senri Ethnological Studies Volume 34, 109–121. Osaka: National Museum of Ethnology.

Cammarrano, Fulvio. 1997. "The Nationalization of Politics and the Politicization of the Nation in Liberal Italy." In *The New History of the Italian South,* edited by R. Lumley and J. Morris, 148–155. Exeter, England: Exeter University Press.

Campbell, John C. 1984. "Policy Conflict and Its Resolution within the Governmental System." In *Conflict in Japan,* edited by Ellis Krauss et al., 294–334. Honolulu: University of Hawaii Press.

Carillo, Elisa. 1965. *Alcide De Gasperi: The Long Apprenticeship.* Notre Dame, Ind.: University of Notre Dame Press.

Carlile, Lonny E., and Mark C. Tilton. 1998. "Is Japan Really Changing?" Chapter 8 in *Is Japan Really Changing Its Ways? Regulatory Reform and the Japanese Economy,* edited by Lonny E. Carlile and Mark C. Tilton. Washington, D.C.: Brookings Institution.

Carr, Edward Hallett. 1961. *What Is History?* New York: Vintage.

Cartocci, Roberto. 1994. *Fra lega e chiesa* (Between League and Church). Bologna: Il Mulino.

———. 1999. "Una scuola senza storia" (A school without history). In *La generazione invisibile* (The invisible generation), edited by Ilvo Diamanti, 219–46. Milan: Il Sole 24 Ore.

REFERENCES

Cassels, Alan. 1970. *Mussolini's Early Diplomacy.* Princeton: Princeton University Press.

——. 1985. *Fascist Italy.* 2nd ed. Arlington Heights, Ill.: Harlan Davidson.

Cassese, Sabino. 1984. "The Higher Civil Service in Italy." In *Bureaucrats and Policy Making: A Comparative Overview,* edited by Ezra N. Suleiman, 35–71. New York: Holmes and Meier.

Castberg, A. Didrick. 1997. "Prosecutorial Independence in Japan." *UCLA Pacific Basin Law Journal* vol. 16, no. 38 (fall).

Castronovo, Valerio. 1977. *Giovanni Agnelli: La Fiat dal 1899 al 1945* (Giovanni Agnelli: Fiat from 1899 to 1945). Turin: Einaudi.

——. 1995. *Storia economica d'Italia* (Economic history of Italy). Turin: Einaudi.

Cavalli, Luciano. 1998. "Considerations on Charisma and the Cult of Charismatic Leadership." *Modern Italy* 3, no. 2: 159–71.

Cavour, Camillo Benso di. 1942. *Discorsi Parlimentari* (Parliamentary speeches). Turin: Einaudi.

Ceccarini, Luigi. 1999. "Il disincanto e la radicalità" (Alienation and radicalism). In *La generazione invisibile* (The invisible generation), edited by Ilvo Diamanti, 147–71. Milan: Il Sole 24 Ore.

Central Committee, Japan Communist Party, ed. 1982. *Sixty-Year History of Japanese Communist Party, 1922–1982.* Tokyo: Japan Press Service.

Cerasi, Laura. 2002. "Anglophilia in Crisis: Italian Liberals, the 'English Model,' and Democracy in the Giolittian Era." *Modern Italy* 7, no. 1: 5–22.

Chabod, Federico. 1963. *A History of Italian Fascism.* London: Weidenfeld and Nicolson.

——. 1996. *Italian Foreign Policy: The Statecraft of the Founders.* Princeton: Princeton University Press.

Chimenti, Anna, 1999. *Storia dei referendum: Dal divorzio alla riforma elettorale* (History of the referendum: From divorce to electoral reform). Bari: Laterza.

Chiot, Loredana. 1996. "Le parole della trasizione: Nomi, tempi, e personaggi della stampa quotidiana, 1992–1994" (The words of the transition: Names, times, and personalities in the daily press). Thesis (*laurea*), Faculty of Political Science, University of Bologna.

Chubb, Judith, and Maurizio Vannicelli. 1988. "Italy: A Web of Scandals in a Flawed Democracy." In *The Politics of Scandal: Power and Process in Liberal Democracies,* edited by A. S. Markovits and M. Silverstein, 122–150. New York: Holmes and Meier.

Ciuffoletti, Zeffiro. 1980. "Le origini (1848–1891)" (The origins, 1848–1891). In *Storia del socialismo italiano* (History of Italian socialism), edited by G. Sabbatucci. Vol. 1. Rome: Il Poligono.

Clark, Martin. 1996. *Modern Italy, 1871–1995.* 2nd ed. London: Longmans.

Cohen, Jerome B. 1952. "Economic Problems of Free Japan." Working paper, Center for International Studies. Princeton: Princeton University.

Colajanni, Napoleone. 1996. *Mani Pulite? Giustizia politica in Italia* (Clean Hands? Political justice in Italy). Milan: Il Mondadori.

Cole, Robert E. 1979. *Work, Mobility, and Participation: A Comparative Study of American and Japanese Industry.* Berkeley: University of California Press.

Coppa, Frank J. 1970a. "Economic and Ethical Liberalism in Conflict: The Extraordinary Liberalism of Giovanni Giolitti." *Journal of Modern History* 42, no. 2 (June): 191–215.

——. 1970b. "The Italian Tariff and Conflict between Agriculture and Industry: The Commercial Policy of Liberal Italy, 1860–1922." *Journal of Economic History* 30, no. 4 (December): 742–69.

——. 1971. *Planning, Protection, and Politics in Liberal Italy: Economics and Politics in the Giolittian Age.* Washington, D.C.: Catholic University Press.

——. 1977. "Commercio estero e politica doganale nell'Italia liberale" (Foreign commerce and political customs in liberal Italy). In *L'industrializzazione in Italia, 1861–1900* (Industrialization in Italy, 1861–1900), edited by G. Mori. Bologna: Il Mulino.

Corbetta, Piergiorgio, and Arturo M. L. Parisi. 1995. "The Referendum on the Electoral Law for the Senate: Another Momentous April." In *Italian Politics: Ending the First Republic,* edited by C. Mershon and G. Pasquino, 75–92. Boulder, Colo.: Westview.

Cotta, Maurizio. 1992. "Elite Unification and Democratic Consolidation in Italy: A Historical Overview." In *Elites and Democratic Consolidation in Latin America and Southern Europe,* edited by J. Higley and R. Gunther. Cambridge: Cambridge University Press.

Craig, Albert M. 1970a. "Introduction: Perspectives on Personality in Japanese History." In *Personality in Japanese History,* edited by A. M. Craig and D. Shively, 1–28. Berkeley: University of California Press.

——. 1970b. "Kido Kōin and Ōkubo Toshimichi: A Psychohistorical Analysis." In *Personality in Japanese History,* edited by A. M. Craig and D. Shively, 264–308. Berkeley: University of California Press.

Craveri, Piero. 1995. *La repubblica dal 1958 al 1992* (The Republic from 1958 to 1992). Turin: UTET.

Crawcour, Sydney. 1988. "Industrialization and Technological Change, 1885–1920." In *The Twentieth Century,* vol. 6 of *The Cambridge History of Japan,* edited by Peter Duus, 385–450. Cambridge: Cambridge University Press.

——. 1989. "Economic Change in the Nineteenth Century." In *The Nineteenth Century,* vol. 5 of *The Cambridge History of Japan,* edited by Marius Jansen, 569–617. Cambridge: Cambridge University Press.

Crick, Bernard. 1986. Introduction to *The Discourses,* by Niccolò Machiavelli. London: Penguin.

Croce, Benedetto. 1928. *Storia d'Italia* (Italian history) Bari: Laterza.

——. 1982. "Il fascismo come parentesi" (Fascism as a parenthesis). Speech before the First Congress of the Parties to the Committee of National Liberation, Bari, 28 January 1944. Reprinted in *Il fascismo: antologia di scritti critici* (Fascism: An anthology of critical writings), edited by Costanzo Casucci, 347. Bologna: Il Mulino.

Croci, Osvaldo and Lucio Picci. 1999. "European Monetary Integration and Integration Theory: Insights from the Italian Case." Paper presented to the workshop on "Conceptualizing the New Europe: European Monetary Integration and Beyond," Victoria, British Columbia, October.

Curtis, Gerald. 1999. *The Logic of Japanese Politics: Leaders, Institutions, and the Limits of Change.* New York: Columbia University Press.

Curwen, Peter. 1995. "Corruption in Italy: When in Rome . . .". *Business and the Contemporary World* 3: 106–16.

Cusumano, Michael A. 1985. *The Japanese Automobile Industry: Technology and Management at Nissan and Toyota.* Cambridge: Council on East Asian Studies, Harvard University.

D'Alema, Massimo. 1995. *Un paese normale: la sinistra e il futuro dell'italia* (A normal country: The Left and the future of Italy). Milan: Mondadori.

D'Alimonte, Roberto, and Stefano Bartolini. 1997. "'Electoral Transition' and Party System Change in Italy." *West European Politics* 20, no. 1: 110–34.

D'Antone, Leandra. 1997. "'Straordinarietà' e stato ordinario" ('Extraordinariness' and the ordinary state). In *Storia del capitalismo italiano: dal dopoguerra a oggi* (The history of Italian capitalism: From the end of the war until today), edited by Fabrizio Barca, 579–625. Rome: Donizelli.

Davis, John A. 1996. "Entrepreneurs and Economic Growth: The Case of Italy." In *Enterprise and Labour: From the Eighteenth Century to the Present,* vol. 3 of *The Nature of Industrialization,* edited by P. Mathias and J. A. Davis, 106–123. London: Blackwell.

de Cecco, Marcello, and Alberto Giovannini, eds. 1989. *A European Central Bank? Perspectives on Monetary Unification after Ten Years of the EMF.* New York: Cambridge University Press.

De Felice, Renzo. 1965. *Mussolini.* Turin: Einaudi.

De Gasperi, Alcide. 1987. *Lettere dalla prigione, 1927–1928* (Letters from prison, 1927–1928). Rome: Cinque Lune.

———. 1990. *Alcide De Gasperi e la politica internazionale* (Alcide De Gasperi and international politics). Edited by Giovanni Allara and A. Gatti. Rome: Cinque Lune.

De Gasperi, Catti, and Maria Romana De Gasperi. 1964. *De Gasperi: uomo solo* (De Gasperi: A singular man). Milan: Mondadori.

De Gasperi, Maria Romana, ed. 1974. *De Gasperi Scrive: Corispondenza con capi di stato, cardinali, uomini politici, giornalistici, diplomatici* (De Gasperi writes: Correspondence with heads of state, cardinals, political men, journalists, diplomats). Brescia: Morcelliana.

Degl'Innocenti, Maurizio. 1980. "L'età del riformismo, 1900–1922" ("The age of reformism, 1900–1922). In *Storia del socialismo italiano* (History of Italian socialism), edited by G. Sabbatucci. Vol. 2. Rome: Il Poligono.

De Grand, Alexander J. 1989. *The Italian Left in the Twentieth Century: A History of the Socialist and Communist Parties.* Bloomington: Indiana University Press.

———. 2001. *The Hunchback's Tailor: Giovanni Giolitti and Liberal Italy from the Challenge of Mass Politics to the Rise of Fascism, 1882–1922.* Westport, Conn.: Praeger.

De Grazia, Sebastian. 1989. *Machiavelli in Hell.* Princeton: Princeton University Press.

De Ianni, Nicola. 1995. *Capitale e mercato azionario: La Fiat dal 1899 al 1961* (Capital and lively market: Fiat from 1899 to 1961). Naples: Scientifiche Italiane.

della Porta, Donatella. 1993. "Milan: Immoral Capital." In *Italian Politics: A Review,* edited by S. Hellman and G. Pasquino, 98–115. London: Pinter.

———. 1995. "Political Parties and Corruption: Reflections on the Italian Case." *Modern Italy* 1, no. 1: 97–114.

della Porta, Donatella, and Alberto Vannucci. 1997. "The Resources of Corruption: Some Reflections from the Italian Case." *Crime, Law, and Social Change* 27: 231–54.

———. 1995. "Politics, the Mafia, and the Market for Corrupt Exchange." In *Italian*

Politics: A Review, vol. 9, edited by Carol Mershon and Gianfranco Pasquino, 165–84. Boulder, Colo.: Westview.

Del Vecchio, Edoardo. 1979–80. *La via italiana al protezionismo* (The Italian road to protectionism), in 5 vols. Rome: Camera dei Deputati.

De Mauro, Tullio. 1996. "Linguistic Variety and Linguistic Minorities." In *Italian Cultural Studies: An Introduction,* edited by D. Forgacs and R. Lumley, 88–101. Oxford: Oxford University Press.

Dente, Bruno. 1989. "Il governo locale" (Local government). In *Scienza dell'amministrazione e politiche pubbliche* (Administrative science and public policies), edited by G. Freddi, 123–69. Rome: La Nuova Italia Scientifica.

De Rosa, Gabriele, and Francesco Malgeri. 1995. "L'impegno politico dei cattolici" (The Catholics' political commitment). In *L'età contemporanea* (The modern age), vol. 3 of *Storia dell'Italia religiosa* (History of Italian religion), edited by G. De Rosa, T. Gregory, and A. Vauchez. Bari: Laterza.

Desmond, Edward W. 1995. "Ichiro Ozawa: Reformer at Bay." *Foreign Affairs* 74 (September–October): 117–31.

DeWit, Andrew. 2000. "The Income Tax and the Tokyo Bank Tax." In "Dysfunctional Japan: At Home and in the World," a special issue, edited by Chalmers Johnson, of *Asian Perspective* 24, no. 4: 197–216.

DeWit, Andrew, and Masaru Kaneko. 2002. "Ishihara and the Politics of His Bank Tax." *JPRI Critique* vol. 9, no. 4 (May).

Diamanti, Ilvo. 1996. *Il male del nord: lega, localismo, seccessione* (What's wrong in the North: League, localism, secession). Rome: Donizelli.

Diamanti, Ilvo, and Paolo Segatti. 1994. "Orgogliosi di essere italiani" (The glories of being Italian). *LiMES* 4 (October–December): 15–36.

di Federico, Giuseppe. 1989. "The Crisis of the Justice System and the Referendum on the Judiciary." In *Italian Politics: A Review,* edited by R. Leonardi and P. Corbetta. London: Pinter.

———. 1995. "Italy: A Peculiar Case." In *The Global Expansion of Judicial Power,* edited by C. N. Tate and T. Vallinder, 233–41. New York: New York University Press.

———. 1998. "Prosecutorial Independence and the Democratic Requirement of Accountability in Italy." *British Journal of Criminology* 38, no. 3 (summer): 371–87.

Diggins, John P. 1972. *Mussolini and Fascism: The View from America.* Princeton: Princeton University Press.

Di Palma, Giuseppe. 1978. "Political Syncretism in Italy: Historical Coalition Strategies and the Present Crisis." *Policy Papers in International Affairs,* Institute of International Studies, University of California, Berkeley.

———. 1990. "Establishing Party Dominance: It Ain't Easy." In *Uncommon Democracies: The One-Party Dominant Regimes,* edited by T. J. Pempel, 162–88. Ithaca: Cornell University Press.

Di Scala, Spencer M. 1980. *Dilemmas of Italian Socialism: The Politics of Filippo Turati.* Amherst: University of Massachusetts Press.

———. 1995. *Italy: From Revolution to Republic, 1700 to the Present.* Boulder, Colo.: Westview.

Doak, Kevin M. 1997. "What Is a Nation and Who Belongs? National Narratives and the Ethnic Imagination in Twentieth-Century Japan." *American Historical Review* (April): 283–309.

Donovan, Mark. 1999. "The End of Italy's Referendum Anomaly?" Paper presented at Istituto Carlo Catteneo, Bologna, November.

Dore, Ronald. 1973. *British Factory, Japanese Factory: The Origins of National Diversity in Industrial Production.* Berkeley: University of California Press.

———. 2000. *Stock Market Capitalism: Welfare Capitalism: Japan and Germany versus the Anglo-Saxons.* London: Oxford University Press.

Dower, John. 1979. *Empire and Aftermath: Yoshida Shigeru and the Japanese Experience, 1878–1954.* Cambridge: Harvard University Press.

———. 1999. *Embracing Defeat: Japan in the Wake of World War Two.* New York: W. W. Norton.

Dunn, John. 1985. *Rethinking Modern Political Theory.* Cambridge: Cambridge University Press.

Duus, Peter. 1968. *Party Rivalry and Political Change in Taishō Japan.* Cambridge: Harvard University Press.

———. 1988. Introduction to *The Twentieth Century,* vol. 6 of *The Cambridge History of Japan,* edited by Peter Duus, 1–54. Cambridge: Cambridge University Press.

Duus, Peter, and Irwin Scheiner. 1988. "Socialism, Liberalism, and Marxism, 1901–1931." In *The Twentieth Century,* vol. 6 of *The Cambridge History of Japan,* edited by Peter Duus, 654–708. Cambridge: Cambridge University Press.

Earle, John. 1986. *The Italian Cooperative Movement: A Portrait of the Lega Nazionale delle Cooperative e Mutue.* London: Allen and Unwin.

Eichengreen, Barry. 1996. "Institutions and Economic Growth: Europe after World War II." In *Economic Growth in Europe since 1945,* edited by Nicholas Crafts and Gianni Toniolo, 38–72. Cambridge: Cambridge University Press.

Einaudi, Luigi. 1997. *Luigi Einaudi diario dell'esilio, 1943–1944* (Luigi Einaudi: Exile diary, 1943–1944). Turin: Einaudi.

Elia, Leopoldo. 1984. "Intervento." In *De Gasperi e l'età del centrismo, 1947–1953* (De Gasperi and the age of centrism), edited by G. Rossini, 181–85. Rome: Cinque Lune.

Elster, Jon, ed. 1986. Introduction to *Rational Choice,* 1–33. New York: New York University Press.

Emmerson, John K. 1972. "The Japanese Communist Party after Fifty Years." *Asian Survey* 12, no. 7 (July): 564–79.

Endo, Shigeki. 1991. *Meiji Ishin to Tennō* (The Meiji Restoration and the emperor). Tokyo: Iwanami Shoten.

Etzioni, Amitai. 1961. *A Comparative Analysis of Complex Organizations: On Power, Involvement, and their Correlates.* New York: Free Press.

Evans, Robert H. 1994. "Italy . . . Quo Vadis?" *Italian Journal* 8, nos. 1–2: 4–12.

Fanfani, Amintore. 1945. *Persona beni società in una rinnovata civiltà cristiana* (Personality, wealth, and society in a new Christian civilization). Milan: Giuffrè.

———. 1948. *Controllo sociale dell'attività economica* (Social control of economic activity). In *La nuova costituzione italiana* (The new Italian constitution). Rome: Editrice Studium.

———. 1958. *Anni difficili, ma non sterili* (Difficult years, but not barren ones). Bologna: Cappelli.

Fanfani, Tommaso. 1994. *Una leggenda verso il futuro: I centrodieci anni di storia della Piaggio* (A legend for the future: The 110-year history of Piaggio). N.p.: Piaggio Veicodi Europea.

Fargion, Valeria. 1997. *Geografia della cittadinanza sociale in Italia* (The geography of social citizenship in Italy). Bologna: Il Mulino.

Fearon, James. 1991. "Counterfactuals and Hypothesis Testing in Political Science." *World Politics* 41: 169–95.

Fermi, Laura. 1961. *Mussolini*. Chicago: University of Chicago Press.

Ferrata, Giansiro, and Niccolo Gallo, eds. 1964. *2,000 pagine di Gramsci: Nel tempo della lotta, 1914–1926* (2,000 pages of Gramsci: In the period of struggle, 1914–1926), vol. 1. Milan: Il Saggiatore.

Ferrera, Maurizio. 1984. *Il "welfare state" in Italia: Sviluppo e crisi in prospettiva comparata* (The welfare state in Italy: Development and crisis in comparative perspective). Bologna: Il Mulino.

——. 1993. *Modelli di solidarità: politica e riforma sociali nelle democrazie* (Models of solidarity: Politics and social reform in the democracies). Bologna: Il Mulino.

Field, Norma. 1991. *In the Realm of a Dying Emperor.* New York: Pantheon.

Finer, Herman. 1964. *Mussolini's Italy.* Reprint of 1935 ed. New York: Archon Books.

Finley, Moses I., Denis Mack Smith, and Christopher Duggan. 1986. *A History of Sicily.* London: Chatto and Windus.

Finn, Richard B. 1992. *Winners in Peace: MacArthur, Yoshida, and Postwar Japan.* Berkeley: University of California Press.

Fletcher, Miles. 1998. "Intellectuals and Fascism in Shōwa Japan." In *Shōwa Japan: Political, Economic, and Social History, 1926–1989,* edited by Stephen S. Large, 345–74. London: Routledge.

Fogu, Claudio. Forthcoming. *History Belongs to the Present: The Fascist Historic Imaginary.* Toronto: University of Toronto Press.

Forgacs, D., and R. Lumley, eds. 1996. *Italian Cultural Studies: An Introduction.* Oxford: Oxford University Press.

Formigoni, Guido. 1996. *La democrazia cristiana e l'alleanza occidentale, 1943–1953* (Christian democracy and the Western alliance, 1943–1953). Bologna: Il Mulino.

——. 1998. *L'Italia dei cattolici* (The Italy of the Catholics). Bologna: Il Mulino.

Forsyth, Douglas. 1993. *The Crisis of Liberal Italy: Monetary and Financial Policy, 1914–1922.* Cambridge: Cambridge University Press.

Freddi, Giorgio. 1994. "Political Change in Italy: Cultural, Political, and Institutional Factors." Paper prepared for the Japan Association for the Study of Public Administration meeting, Osaka, October.

Friedman, David B. 1988. *The Misunderstood Miracle.* Ithaca: Cornell University Press.

Fujimura, Michio. 1961. *Yamagata Aritomo* (Yamagata Aritomo). Tokyo: Toshikawa Kobunkan.

Fujitani, T. 1996. *Splendid Monarchy: Power and Pageantry in Modern Japan.* Berkeley: University of California Press.

Fujitani, Takashi. 1993. "Inventing, Forgetting, Remembering: Toward a Historical Ethnography of the Nation-State." In *Cultural Nationalism in East Asia: Representation and Identity,* edited by H. Befu, 77–106. Berkeley: Institute of East Asian Studies, University of California.

Fukui, Haruhiro. 1970. *Party in Power: The Japanese Liberal Democrats and Policy Making.* Berkeley: University of California Press.

REFERENCES

Fukushima, Glen. 2001. "Understanding 'Leadership' in Japan." *Japan Times*, 28 March.

Fukuzawa, Yukichi. 1973. *An Outline of the Theory of Civilization*. Translated by David A. Dilworth and G. Cameron Hurst. Tokyo: Sophia University Press.

Fusaro, Carlo. 1998. "The Politics of Constitutional Reform in Italy: A Framework for Analysis." *South European Society and Politics* 3, no. 2 (autumn): 45–74.

Fuwa Tetsuzō. 1993. *Interference and Betrayal: Japanese Communist Party Fights Back against Soviet Hegemonism*. Tokyo: Japan Press Service.

———. 1999. *Remaking Japan*. Tokyo: Japan Press Service.

Galli, Giorgio. 1975. *Fanfani*. Milan: Feltrinelli.

Galli, Giorgio, and Paolo Facchi. 1962. *La sinistra democristiana, storia e ideologia* (The Christian Democratic left: History and ideology). Milan: Feltrinelli.

Galli della Loggia, Ernesto. 1996. *La morte della patria: La crisi dell'idea di nazione tra resistenza, antifascismo, e repubblica* (The death of the nation: The crisis of the idea of nation across the Resistance, antifascism, and the Republic). Bari: Laterza.

———. 1998. *L'identità italiana* (The Italian identity). Bologna: Il Mulino.

Gambetta, Diego. 1993. *The Sicilian Mafia: The Business of Private Protection*. Cambridge: Harvard University Press.

Gammaldi, Anna. 1974. *Alcide De Gasperi: pensiero politico e idee ricostruttive* (Alcide De Gasperi: Political thought and reconstructive ideas). Rome: DC-Spes.

Gangulee, N., ed. 1987. *Giuseppe Mazzini: Selected Writings*. Westport, Conn.: Greenwood.

Gao, Bai. 1997. *Economic Ideology and Japanese Industrial Policy: Developmentalism from 1931 to 1965*. Cambridge: Cambridge University Press.

Garon, Sheldon. 1987. *The State and Labor in Modern Japan*. Berkeley: University of California Press.

———. 1997. *Molding Japanese Minds: The State in Everyday Life*. Princeton: Princeton University Press.

Geertz, Clifford. 1973. *The Interpretation of Cultures*. New York: Basic Books.

Genther, Phyllis. 1990. *A History of Japan's Business-Government Relationship: The Passenger Car Industry*. Ann Arbor: Center for Japanese Studies, University of Michigan.

George, B.J., Jr. 1984. "Discretionary Authority of Public Prosecutors in Japan." *Law in Japan: An Annual* 17: 42–72.

Germino, Dante L. 1971. *The Italian Fascist Party in Power: A Study in Totalitarian Rule*. New York: Howard Fertig.

Gerschenkron, Alexander. 1966. *Economic Backwardness in Historical Perspective: A Book of Essays*. Cambridge: Harvard University Press.

Gibson, Hugh, ed. 1973. *The Ciano Diaries, 1939–1943*. New York: Howard Fertig.

Gilbert, Mark. 1995. *The Italian Revolution: The End of Politics, Italian Style?* Boulder, Colo.: Westview.

———. 1998a. "In Search of Normality: The Political Strategy of Massimo D'Alema." *Journal of Modern Italian Studies* 3, no. 3: 307–17.

———. 1998b. "Transforming Italy's Institutions? The Bicameral Committee on Institutional Reform." *Modern Italy* 3, no. 1: 49–66.

Ginsborg, Paul. 1990. *A History of Contemporary Italy: Society and Politics, 1943–1988*. London: Penguin.

Giolitti, Giovanni. 1923. *Memoirs of My Life*. London: Chapman and Dodd.

Gismondi, Arturo. 1996. *La repubblica delle procure* (The republic of the prosecutors). Rome: Ideazione.

Gluck, Carol. 1985. *Japan's Modern Myths: Ideology in the Late Meiji Period*. Princeton: Princeton University Press.

——. 1998. "The Invention of Edo." In *Mirror of Modernity: Invented Traditions of Modern Japan*, edited by Stephen Vlastos, 262–84. Berkeley: University of California Press.

Golden, Miriam. 1995. "A Comparative Investigation of Political Control of the Bureaucracy: A Preliminary Review of the Italian Case." Paper presented to the annual meeting of the American Political Science Association, Chicago, September.

——. 1999. "Competitive Corruption: Factional Conflict and Political Corruption in Postwar Italian Christian Democracy." Paper presented to the MacArthur Research Network on Inequality and Economic Performance, MIT, Cambridge, October.

Gordon, Andrew. 1985. *The Evolution of Labor Relations in Japan: Heavy Industry, 1853–1955*. Cambridge: Council on East Asian Studies, Harvard University.

——. 1991. *Labor and Imperial Democracy in Prewar Japan*. Berkeley: University of California Press.

——. 1998. "The Invention of Japanese-Style Labor Management." In *Mirror of Modernity: Invented Traditions of Modern Japan*, edited by Stephen Vlastos, 19–36. Berkeley. University of California Press.

Gorresio, Vittorio. 1976. *Berlinguer.* Milan: Feltrinelli.

Gramsci, Antonio. 1957. *The Modern Prince and Other Writings*. New York. International Publishers.

Granovetter, Mark. 2002. "A Theoretical Agenda for Economic Sociology." In *The New Economic Sociology: Developments in an Emerging Field*, edited by M. Guillen et al., 35–60. New York: Russell Sage.

Granovetter, Mark, and Patrick McGuire. 1998. "The Making of an Industry: Electricity in the United States." In *The Law of Markets*, edited by M. Callon, 147–73. Oxford: Blackwell.

Grazioli, Stanislao. 1974. *Giolitti e la nascita dei partiti italiani* (Giolitti and the birth of the Italian parties). Rome: Edizioni Cremonese.

Greenfeld, Liah. 1992. *Nationalism: Five Roads to Modernity.* Cambridge: Harvard University Press.

Greenstein, Fred I. 1969. *Personality and Politics.* Chicago: Markham.

Guarnieri, Carlo. 1995. "The Political Role of the Italian Judiciary." In *Deconstructing Italy: Italy in the Nineties*, edited by S. Sechi, 90–112. International and Area Studies Research Series, no. 91. Berkeley: University of California.

Gundle, Stephen. 1998. "The Death (and Re-birth) of the Hero: Charisma and Manufactured Charisma in Modern Italy." *Modern Italy* 3, no. 2: 173–89.

Gundle, Stephen, and Lucy Riall. 1998. "Introduction." *Modern Italy* 3, no. 2: 153–57.

Hackett, Roger. 1971. *Yamagata Aritomo in the Rise of Modern Japan, 1838–1922.* Cambridge: Harvard University Press.

Haga, Yaichi. 1968. *Kokuminsei Jūron* (Ten ideas about national character). In *Meiji Bungaku Renshū* (Collection of Meiji literature), edited by Hisamatsu, Kazuichi, 235–80. Tokyo: Chikuma Shobō.

Halberstam, David. 1991. *The Next Century.* New York: Morrow.

REFERENCES

Hales, E. E. Y. 1956. *Mazzini and the Secret Societies: The Making of a Myth.* New York: P. J. Kennedy and Sons.

Haley, John O. 1995. "Judicial Independence in Japan Revisited." *Law in Japan* 25, no. 1: 1–18.

Hall, Peter. 1992. "The Movement from Keynesianism to Monetarism: Institutional Analysis and British Economic Policy in the 1970s." In *Structuring Politics: Historical Institutionalism in Comparative Analysis,* edited by K. Thelan, S. Steinmo, and F. Longstreth, 90–113. Cambridge: Cambridge University Press.

Hamada, Kengi. 1936. *Prince Ito.* Tokyo: Sanseido.

Hamada, Kōichi. 1993. *Nihon o Dame ni shita Kyūnin no Seijika* (Nine politicians who ruined Japan). Tokyo: Kōdansha.

Hametz, Maura. 1998. "Friuli-Venezia Giulia and Italian Foreign Policy: Local Identity as a Centripetal Force." *Italian Politics and Society* 49 (spring): 63–70.

Hanamura Nihachirō. 1990. *Seizaikai Paipu-yaku Hanseki* (My half-life as the pipeline between the political and business worlds). Tokyo: Tokyo Shimbun Shuppankyoku.

Hara, Akira. 1976. "Manshū ni okeru keizai tōsei seisaku no tenkai: Mantetsu kaiso to Mangyō setsuritsu o megutte" (Economic control policy in Manchuria: Concerning the establishment of south Manchurian heavy industry and the idea for the South Manchurian Railway). In *Nihon Keizai Seisaku Shiron* (Studies in the history of Japanese economic policy), edited by Ando Yoshio. Tokyo: Tokyo Daigaku Suppankai.

Hara, Shinsuke. 1995. *Kishi Nobusuke: Kensei no Seijika* (Kishi Nobusuke: Powerful politician). Tokyo: Iwanami.

Harari, Ehud. 1973. *The Politics of Labor Legislation in Japan.* Berkeley: University of California Press.

Hardacre, Helen. 1989. *Shinto and the State, 1868–1988.* Princeton: Princeton University Press.

Harootunian, H. D. 1989. "Late Tokugawa Culture and Thought." In *The Nineteenth Century,* vol. 5 of *The Cambridge History of Japan,* edited by Marius Jansen, 158–268. Cambridge: Cambridge University Press.

Harper, John Lamberton. 1986. *America and the Reconstruction of Italy, 1945–1948.* Cambridge: Cambridge University Press.

——. 1999. "Italy and the World since 1945." Unpublished manuscript.

Harris, W. V. 1994. "Italy: Purgatorio." *New York Review of Books,* 3 March.

Hayasaka, Shigezō. 1993. "Saigo ni Narikirenakatta Otoko" (The man who won't be another Saigo"). *Bungei Shunjū* (October): 128–41.

Haycraft, John. 1985. *Italian Labyrinth: Italy in the 1980s.* London: Secker and Warburg.

Hazama, Hiroshi. 1992. "Management Philosophy in the Early Years of Industrialization in Japan: In Search of a Theoretical Framework for International Comparison." *Japanese Yearbook on Business History* 9: 87–124.

——. 1997. *The History of Labour Management in Japan.* New York: St. Martin's. (Originally published in 1964 as *Nihon Rōmu Kanrishi Kenkyū* [Research on the history of Japanese labor management]. Tokyo: Daiyamondosha.)

Hearder, Harry. 1994. *Cavour.* London: Longman.

Hedström, Peter, and Richard Swedberg, eds. 1998. *Social Mechanisms: An Analytical Approach to Social Theory.* Cambridge: Cambridge University Press.

Heginbotham, Eric. Forthcoming. "Armies and Navies in Politics: The Domestic Origins of Grand Strategy in Developing States." Ph.D. diss., Department of Political Science, Massachusetts Institute of Technology.

Hellman, Stephen. 1987. "The Emergence of the Modern Italian State." In *European Politics in Transition,* edited by M. Kesselman et al., 320–43. Lexington, Mass.: D. C. Heath.

———. 1988. *Italian Communism in Transition: The Rise and Fall of the Historic Compromise in Turin, 1975–1980.* New York: Oxford University Press.

———. 1993. "Politics Almost as Usual: The Formation of the Amato Government." In *The End of Postwar Italian Politics: The Landmark 1992 Elections,* edited by Gianfranco Pasquino and Patrick McCarthy, 141–59. Boulder, Colo.: Westview.

Herf, Jeffrey. 1984. *Reactionary Modernism: Technology, Culture, and Politics in Weimar and the Third Reich.* New York: Cambridge University Press.

Hirano, Sadao. 1996. *Ozawa Ichirō to no Nijū Nen* (Twenty years with Ichiro Ozawa). Tokyo: Purejidentosha.

Hirschmeier, Joannes, and Tsunehiko Yui. 1981. *The Development of Japanese Business, 1600–1980.* 2nd ed. London: Allen and Unwin.

Hiwatari, Nobuhiro. 1999. "The Politics of Reform and the Transformation of Postwar Party Systems in Italy and Japan." Unpublished paper, Institute of Social Science, University of Tokyo.

Hobsbawm, Eric, and Terrence Ranger, eds. 1983. *The Invention of Tradition.* Cambridge: Cambridge University Press.

Holt, Edgar. 1970. *Risorgimento: The Making of Italy, 1815–1870.* London: Macmillan.

Hook, Sidney. 1943. *The Hero in History: A Study in Limitation and Possibility.* New York: John Day.

Hori, Makiyo. 1990. "Kita Ikki and Japanese Fascism." In *Social Sciences, Ideology, and Thought,* vol. 2 of *Rethinking Japan,* edited by Adriana Boscaro, Franco Gatti, and Massimo Raveri, 70–79. Sandgate, England: Japan Library.

Hoston, Germaine A. 1986. *Marxism and the Crisis of Development in Prewar Japan.* Princeton: Princeton University Press.

Huffman, James L. 1983. "The Popular Rights Debate: Political or Ideological?" In *Japan Examined: Perspectives on Modern Japanese History,* edited by Harry Wray and Hilary Conroy, 98–103. Honolulu: University of Hawaii Press.

Hughes, H. Stuart. 1965. *The United States and Italy.* Revised ed. New York: W. W. Norton.

Ido Masanobu. 1998. *Keizai Kiki no Hikō Seijigaku: Nihon to Itaria no Seido to Senryaku* (The comparative politics of economic crisis: The systems and strategies of Italy and Japan). Tokyo: Shinhyō Ron.

Ignazi, Piero. 1992. *Dal pci al pds* (From the PCI to the PDS). Bologna: Il Mulino.

———. 1995. "Movimento sociale italiano." In *Deconstructing Italy: Italy in the Nineties,* edited by S. Sechi, 292–312. International and Area Studies Research Series, no. 91. Berkeley: University of California.

Iguchi, Gō, et al. 1977. *Kuromaku Kenkyū* (Studies of political bosses). Tokyo: Shinkoku Minsha.

Ike, Nobutaka. 1972. *Japanese Politics: Patron-Client Democracy.* New York: Alfred A. Knopf.

Ilchman, Warren, and Norman Uphoff. 1969. *The Political Economy of Change.* Berkeley: University of California Press.

Immergut, Ellen M. 1998. "The Theoretical Core of the New Institutionalism." *Politics and Society* 26, no. 1 (March): 5–34.

Inami, Shinnosuke. 1992. "Going after the Yakuza," *Japan Quarterly* 39, no. 3 (July–September): 353–58.

Ino, Kenji. 1994. "'Sasakawa Teikoku' ga Yuragu: Nippon Senpaku Shinkōkai no Mae Jimukyokuchō Kiso to Naifun" ("The Sasakawa Empire" trembles: Accusations and internal discord from the former Japan Shipbuilding Promotion Association's executive director). *Ekonomisuto,* 2 August, 88–91.

Inō, Tentarō. 1966. *Nihon Gaikō Shisō-shi Ronkō Daiichi: Jōyaku Kaisei-ron no Tenkai* (The history of foreign ideas in Japan: The development of theories of treaty revision). Vol. 1. Tokyo: Komine Shōten.

———. 1976. *Jōyaku Kaisei-ron no Rekishi-teki Tenkai* (The historical development of theories about treaty revision). Tokyo: Komine Shōten.

International Social Survey Program, ed. *National Identity Project.* 1995. Ann Arbor: Inter-University Consortium for Political and Social Research, University of Michigan.

Irimajiri, Yoshinaga. 1964. *Mutō Sanji* (Mutō Sanji). Tokyo: Yoshikawa Kobunkan.

Ishida, Ken. 1994. *Chichūkai Shin Roma Teikoku e no Michi: Fuashisuto Itaria no Taigai Seisaku, 1935–1939* (The road to the new Roman Empire in the Mediterranean: The foreign policy of fascist Italy, 1935–39). Tokyo: Tokyo Daigaku Shuppankai.

Ishihara, Nobuhiro. 2000. "Watakushi o Aum ni shita Jimintō no Hiretsu" (Foul play by the LDP that put me in Aum). *Bungei Shunjū* (April): 122–32.

Ishihara, Shintarō. 1991. *The Japan that Can Say "No": Why Japan Will Be First among Equals.* New York: Simon and Schuster.

———. 1999. *Kokka Naru Genei: Waga Seiji e no Hankaisō* (Illusions of the state). Tokyo: Bungei Shunjū.

Itō, Hirobumi. 1906. *Commentaries on the Constitution of the Empire of Japan.* Tokyo: Chūō University Press.

Itoh, Mayumi. 2001. "Japanese Constitutional Revision: A Neo-liberal Proposal for Article 9 in Comparative Perspective." *Asian Survey* 41, no. 2 (March–April): 310–27.

Iverson, Torben, Jonas Pontussen, and David Soskice, eds. 2000. *Unions, Employers, and Central Banks: Macroeconomic Coordination and Institutional Change in Social Market Economies.* New York: Cambridge University Press.

Ives, Christopher. 1995. "Ethical Pitfalls in Imperial Zen and Nishida Philosophy." In *Rude Awakenings: Zen, the Kyoto School, and the Question of Nationalism,* edited by James W. Heisig and John C. Maraldo, 16–39. Honolulu: University of Hawaii Press.

Iwai, Tomoaki. 1990. *Seiji Shikin no Kenkyū* (Research on political funds). Tokyo: Nihon Keizai Shimbunsha.

Iwami, Takao. 1993. "Shin Jimintō Sengokushi" (The new history of LDP civil war). *Chūō Kōron* 108, no. 3 (February): 52–61.

Iwata, Masakazu. 1964. *Ōkubo Toshimichi: The Bismarck of Japan.* Berkeley: University of California Press.

Izzo, Luigi, 1978. "Commercio estero e sviluppo economico dell'Italia tra liberismo e protezionism, 1869–1890" (Foreign commerce and economic development in Italy between liberalism and protectionism, 1869–1890). In *Storia del commercio italiano* (History of Italian commerce), edited by Aldo Spranzi. Milan: Etas libri.

Jamieson, Alison. 2000. *The Antimafia: Italy's Fight against Organized Crime.* New York: St. Martin's.

Jansen, Marius. 1989. "The Meiji Restoration." In *The Nineteenth Century,* vol. 5 of *The Cambridge History of Japan,* edited by Marius Jansen, 308–66. Cambridge: Cambridge University Press.

Johnson, Chalmers. 1962. *Peasant Nationalism and Communist Power.* Stanford: Stanford University Press.

——. 1982. *MITI and the Japanese Miracle: The Growth of Industrial Policy, 1925–1975.* Stanford: Stanford University Press.

——. 1995a. "The 1955 System and the American Connection: A Bibliographic Introduction." Working paper no. 11, Japan Policy Research Institute, July.

——. 1995b. "Tanaka Kakuei, Structural Corruption, and the Advent of Machine Politics in Japan." In *Japan: Who Governs? The Rise of the Developmental State,* edited by Chalmers Johnson, 183–211. New York: W. W. Norton.

——. 2000a. *Blowback: The Costs and Consequences of American Empire.* New York: Metropolitan Books.

——. 2000b. "Nihon Bashingu no 'Don' to Iwarete" (Being called the "Don" of Japan bashing). Special edition of *Bungei Shunjū,* "Dō Suru? Dō Naru? Watakushitachi no 21 Seiki" (What to do? What will be? Our twenty-first century), June: 122–37.

Johnson, David T. 1997. "Why the Wicked Sleep: The Prosecution of Political Corruption in Postwar Japan." Working paper no. 34, Japan Policy Research Institute, June.

——. Forthcoming. "A Tale of Two Systems: Prosecuting Corruption in Japan and Italy." In *The State of Civil Society in Japan,* edited by Susan Pharr and Frank Schwartz. New York: Cambridge University Press.

Johnson, James. 1997. "Symbol *and* Strategy in Comparative Political Analysis." *APSA-CP: Newsletter of the APSA Organized Section in Comparative Politics* 8, no. 2 (summer): 6–9.

——. 2000. "Why Respect Culture?" *American Journal of Political Science* 44, no. 3 (July): 405–18.

Jones, F. C. 1949. *Manchuria since 1931.* New York: Oxford University Press.

Kanō Akihiro and Takano Hajime. 1976. *Uchimaku: Ayatsutte Kita Kenryoku no Rimenshi* (Inside story: The hidden background of how power came to be manipulated). Tokyo: Gakuyō Shobō.

Kaplan, David E., and Alec Dubro. 1986. *Yakuza: The Exclusive Account of Japan's Criminal Underworld.* Reading, Mass.: Addison-Wesley.

Kasama, Tetsuhito. 1980. *Dokō Toshio no Keiei Tetsugaku: Shigen wa Yūgen, Zunō wa Mugen* (The management philosophy of Dokō Toshio: Finite resources, unlimited imagination). Tokyo: Yamate Shobō.

Kashiwabara Yutaka. 1999. "Japanese Bureaucrats in the 1990s: Their Relationship with the Politicians." Master's thesis, Department of Political Science, Massachusetts Institute of Technology, June.

Kataoka Tetsuya. 1991. *The Price of a Constitution: The Origin of Japan's Postwar Politics.* New York: Crane Russak.

Katō, Junko. 1993. "Party Dominance and Organizational Change in Comparative Perspective." Working paper, University of Tokyo.

Katō Shūichi. 1998. "Taishō Democracy as the Pre-stage for Japanese Militarism."

In *Shōwa Japan: Political, Economic, and Social History, 1926–1989,* edited by Stephen S. Large, 31–46. London: Routledge. (Originally published in *Japan in Crisis: Essays on Taishō Democracy.* 1974. Edited by Bernard S. Silberman and H. D. Harootunian. Princeton: Princeton University Press.)

Kattoulas, Velisarios. 2000. "Taking Care of Business." *Far Eastern Economic Review,* 30 November, 92–95.

———. 2002. "The Yakuza Recession." *Far Eastern Economic Review,* 17 January.

Katz, Richard. 2001. *Japan, the System that Soured: The Rise and Fall of the Japanese Economic Miracle.* 2nd ed. Armonk, N.Y.: M. E. Sharpe.

Katzenstein, Peter J. 1996. *Cultural Norms and National Security: Police and Military in Postwar Japan.* Ithaca: Cornell University Press.

Katznelson, Ira. 1997. "Structure and Configuration in Comparative Politics." In *Comparative Politics: Rationality, Culture, and Structure,* edited by Mark Irving Lichbach and Alan S. Zuckerman, 81–112. Cambridge: Cambridge University Press.

Kawada, Minoru. 1998. *Hara Kei to Yamagata Aritomo: Kokka Kōsō o meguru Gaiko to Naisei* (Hara Kei and Yamagata Aritomo: Diplomacy and domestic politics in state-building). Tokyo: Chūō Kōronsha.

Kawakami, Hajime. 1949. *Jijoden* (Autobiography). Tokyo: Sekai Hyōronsha.

Kellerman, Barbara. 1986. *Political Leadership: A Sourcebook.* Pittsburgh, Penn.: University of Pittsburgh Press.

Kemp, Tom. 1985. *Industrialization in Nineteenth-Century Europe.* 2nd ed. London: Longman.

Kertzer, David I. 1980. *Comrades and Christians: Religion and Political Struggle in Communist Italy.* Cambridge: Cambridge University Press.

———. 1988. *Ritual, Politics, and Power.* New Haven: Yale University Press.

———. 1996. *Politics and Symbols: The Italian Communist Party and the Fall of Communism.* New Haven: Yale University Press.

Khong, Yuen Foong. 1992. *Analogies at War: Korea, Munich, Dien Bien Phu, and the Vietnam Decisions of 1965.* Princeton: Princeton University Press.

Kikuchi, Taketoshi. 1992. *Issan seitōjin Hara Takashi* (Hara Takashi: Indefatigable party politician). Morioka: Iwate Nippōsha.

Kimeldorf, Howard. 1988. *Reds or Rackets? The Making of Radical and Conservative Unions on the Waterfront.* Berkeley: University of California Press.

Kingdon, John W. 1995. *Agendas, Alternatives, and Public Policies.* 2nd ed. Boston: Little, Brown.

Kishi Nobusuke, Yatsugi Kazuo, and Itō Takashi, eds. 1981. *Kishi Nobusuke no Kaisō* (The remembrances of Kishi Nobusuke). Tokyo: Bungei Shunjū.

———. 1983. *Waga no Seishun* (My springtime). Tokyo: Kōsaidō.

Kitaoka, Shinichi. 1993. "The Constitution: Ready for Revision?" *Japan Echo* 20, no. 2 (summer): 6–7.

———. 1995. "Kishi Nobusuke: Yashin to Zassetsu" (Kishi Nobusuke: Ambition and failure). In *Sengo Nihon no Saishōtachi* (The prime ministers of postwar Japan), edited by Watanabe Akio, 121–48. Tokyo: Chūō Kōronsha.

———. 1999. "Kenpō Kyōjō no Jubaku kara Nukedasu Toki" (Time to break the spell of Article 9). *This Is Yomiuri* (March): 126–35.

Kitazawa, Yoko. 1976. "Nihon no Ōshoku Kōzō to Ajia: Indonesia Baishō o meguru Kuroi Riken" (Japanese structural corruption and Asia: Black concessions in Indonesian compensation). *Ushio* 203 (May): 154–62.

Kitschelt, Herbert. 1992. "Political Regime Change: Structure and Process-Driven Explanations?" *American Political Science Review* 86, no. 4 (December): 1028–1034.

Knox, MacGregor. 1982. *Mussolini Unleashed, 1939–1941: Politics and Strategy in Fascist Italy's Last War.* Cambridge: Cambridge University Press.

———. 2000. *Hitler's Italian Allies: Royal Armed Forces, Fascist Regime, and the War of 1940–1943.* London: Cambridge University Press.

Kobayashi, Masaaki. 1985. "Japan's Early Industrialization and the Transfer of Government Enterprises: Government and Business." *Japanese Yearbook on Business History* 2: 54–80.

Kobayashi, Setsu. 1997. "Kaishaku Kaiken ga Maneita Kudōka" (Amending the Constitution through changing interpretation invited hollowing). *This Is Yomiuri,* May.

Kogan, Norman. 1956. *Italy and the Allies.* Westport, Conn.: Greenwood.

———. 1983. *A Political History of Italy: The Postwar Years.* New York: Praeger.

Koh, Byung Chul. 1989. *Japan's Administrative Elite.* Berkeley: University of California Press.

Kokumin Kyōkai, ed. 1972. *Kokumin Kyōkai 10 Nen no Ayumi* (The course of ten years of the Kokumin Kyōkai). Tokyo: Kokumin Kyōkai.

Kokumin Seiji Kyōkai, ed. 1981. *Kokumin Seiji Kyōkai 20 Nenshi* (The twenty-year history of the Kokumin Seiji Kyōkai). Tokyo: Kokumin Seiji Kyōkai.

———. 1991. *Sōritsu 30 Nen no Ayumi* (The course of thirty years since the founding). Tokyo: Kokumin Seiji Kyokai.

Kondō, Kanichi, and Osanai, Hiroshi, eds. 1978. *Sengo Sangyōshi e no Shōgen* (Testimony related to postwar industrial history). Vol. 3. Tokyo: Mainichi Shimbunsha.

Kōsaka, Masataka. 1968. *Saishō Yoshida Shigeru* (Prime Minister Yoshida Shigeru). Tokyo: Chūō Sōsho.

Koyama, Kōken. 1966. *Sengo Nihon Kyōsantō Shi* (The postwar history of the Japan Communist Party). Tokyo: Hōga Shoten.

Krasner, Stephen. 1984. "Approaches to the State: Alternative Conceptions and Historical Dynamics." *Comparative Politics* 16, no. 2 (January): 223–46.

Krauss, Ellis S. 1982. "Kyoto and Bologna: Communist Power and Alternative Models of Local Development." Paper presented at the Conference on Local Institutions in National Development: Strategies and Consequences of Local-National Linkages in the Industrial Democracies, Bellagio, Italy, 15–19 March.

Krauss, Ellis S., Patricia G. Steinhoff, and Thomas P. Rohlen, eds. 1984. *Conflict in Japan.* Honolulu: University of Hawaii Press

Kubicek, Brett. Forthcoming. "Locating Political Creativity." Ph.D. diss., Department of Political Science, Massachusetts Institute of Technology.

Kubo, Hiroshi. 1986. *Nihon no Kensatsu* (Japan's prosecutors). Tokyo: Kōdansha.

Kuran, Timur. 1995. *Private Truths, Public Lies: The Social Consequences of Preference Falsification.* Cambridge: Harvard University Press.

Kurzman, Dan. 1960. *Kishi and Japan: The Search for the Sun.* New York: Ivan Obolensky.

Laitin, David. 1986. *Hegemony and Culture.* Chicago: University of Chicago Press.

———. 1998. *Identity in Formation: The Russian-Speaking Population in the Near Abroad.* Ithaca: Cornell University Press.

Laitin, David, and Carolyn M. Warner. 1992. "Structure and Irony in Social Revolutions." *Political Theory* 20, no. 1 (February): 147–51.

La Licata, Francesco. 2000. "Niente appalti alle imprese che pagano il pizzo" (No public works contracts to firms that pay Mafia overhead). *La Stampa*, 27 August, 7.

Lanaro, Silvio. 1967. "Nazionalismo e ideologia del blocco corporativo-protezionista in Italia" (Nationalism and the ideology of the corporative-protectionist bloc in Italy). *Ideologie: quaderni di storia contemporanea* 2: 36–93.

———. 1979. *Nazione e lavoro: Saggio sulla cultura borghese in italia, 1870–1925* (Nation and work: Essay on bourgeois culture in Italy, 1870–1925). Venice: Marsilio.

Langer, Paul F. 1972. *Communism in Japan: A Case of Political Naturalization*. Stanford: Hoover Institute Press.

Lanzara, Giovan Francesco. 1998. "Self-Destructive Processes in Institution Building and Some Modest Countervailing Mechanisms." *European Journal of Political Research* 33: 1–39.

———. 1999. "Institutional *Bricolage:* Notes on the Evolutionary Dynamics of the Italian Code of Parliamentary Procedure." Paper presented at the joint session of the European Consortium for Political Research, Mannheim, 26–31 March.

LaPalombara, Joseph. 1987. *Democracy, Italian Style*. New Haven: Yale University Press.

Large, Stephen S. 1972. *The Yūaikai, 1912–19: The Rise of Labor in Japan*. Tokyo: Sophia University Press.

Lebow, Richard Ned. 2000. "What's So Different about Counterfactuals?" *World Politics* 53 (July): 550–85.

Lebra, Joyce C. 1973. *Ōkuma Shigenobu: Statesman of Meiji Japan*. Canberra: Australia National University Press.

Ledeen, Michael Arthur. 2000. *D'Annunzio: The First Duce*. New Brunswick, N.J.: Transaction Publishers.

Lehner, Giancarlo. 1995. *Borelli: 'Autobiografia' di un inquisitore* (Borelli: An 'autobiography' of an inquisitor). Turin: Quaderni.

Levi, Margaret. 1997. "A Model, a Method, and a Map: Rational Choice in Comparative and Historical Analysis." In *Comparative Politics: Rationality, Culture, and Structure*, edited by Mark Irving Lichbach and Alan S. Zuckerman, 19–41. Cambridge: Cambridge University Press.

Lévi-Strauss, Claude. 1966. *The Savage Mind*. London: Weidenfeld and Nicolson.

Levine, Solomon B. 1958. *Industrial Relations in Postwar Japan*. Urbana: University of Illinois Press.

Lewanski, Rodolfo. 1999. "Italian Administrtation in Transition." *South European Society and Politics* 4, no. 1 (summer): 97–131.

Lie, John. 2001. *Multiethnic Japan*. Cambridge: Harvard University Press.

Lincoln, Edward J. 1990. *Japan's Unequal Trade*. Washington, D.C.: Brookings Institution.

———. 2001. *Arthritic Japan: The Slow Pace of Economic Reform*. Washington, D.C.: Brookings Institution.

Locke, Richard M., and Lucio Baccaro. 1994. "Pedagogy and Politics in the Italian Union Movement: A Tale of Administrative Failure." Unpublished manuscript, Massachusetts Institute of Technology, June.

Lockwood, William W. 1955. *The Economic Development of Japan: Growth and Structural Change, 1868–1938*. London: Oxford University Press.

Losito, Marta, and Sandro Segre. 1992. "Ambiguous Influences: Italian Sociology and the Fascist Regime." In *Sociology Responds to Fascism,* edited by Stephen P. Turner and Dirk Kasler, 42–87. London: Routledge.

Lovett, Clara M. 1982. *The Democratic Movement in Italy, 1830–1876.* Cambridge: Harvard University Press.

Luebbert, Gregory M. 1991. *Liberalism, Fascism, or Social Democracy: Social Classes and the Political Origins of Regimes in Interwar Europe.* New York: Oxford University Press.

Lustick, Ian S. 1996. "History, Historiography, and Political Science: Multiple Historical Records and the Problem of Selection Bias." *American Political Science Review* 90, no. 3 (September): 605–18.

MacDougall, Terry Edward. 1975. "Localism and Political Opposition in Japan." Ph.D. diss., Department of Political Science, Yale University.

Machiavelli, Niccolò. 1986. *The Discourses.* London: Penguin.

———. 1995. *The Prince.* London: Penguin.

Mack Smith, Denis. 1959 and 1969 (rev. ed.). *Italy: A Modern History.* Ann Arbor: University of Michigan Press.

———. 1971. *Victor Emmanuel, Cavour, and the Risorgimento.* London: Oxford University Press.

———. 1981. *Mussolini.* London: Weidenfeld and Nicolson.

———. 1985. *Cavour.* London: Methuen.

Magara, Hideko. 1998. *Tuisei Ikkō no Seiji Guku. Ituria to Nihon no Seiji Keizai Henyō* (The politics of system change: Transformation of the Italian and Japanese political economies). Tokyo. Waseda University Press.

Mahoney, James. 2000. "Path Dependence in Historical Sociology." *Theory and Society* 29: 507–48.

Maier, Charles S. 1975. *Recasting Bourgeois Europe: Stabilization in France, Germany, and Italy in the Decade after World War I.* Princeton: Princeton University Press.

Maki, John M., trans. 1980. *Japan's Commission on the Constitution: The Final Report.* Seattle: University of Washington Press.

Makin, John. 2000. "Japan: It's the Economy, Stupid!" *AEI Economic Outlook,* April.

———. 2001. "Japan's Lost Decade: Lessons for America." *AEI Economic Outlook,* February.

Malgeri, Francesco, ed. 1981. *Storia del movimento cattolico in Italia* (History of the Catholic movement in Italy). Vol. 4. Rome: Poligono.

Mammarella, Giuseppe. 1970. *L'Italia dopo il fascismo, 1943–1968* (Italy after fascism, 1943–1968). Bologna: Il Mulino.

Mammarella, Giuseppe, and Zeffiro Ciuffoletti. 1996. *Il declino: Le origine storiche della crisi italiana* (The decline: The historical origins of the Italian crisis). Milan: Mondadori.

Manacorda, Gastone, ed. 1966. *Il socialismo nella storia d'Italia* (Socialism in the history of Italy). Bari: Laterza.

Mannheimer, Renato. 1993. "The Electorate of the Lega Nord." In *The End of Postwar Italian Politics: The Landmark 1992 Elections,* edited by Gianfranco Pasquino and Patrick McCarthy, 85–107. Boulder, Colo.: Westview.

Marshall, Andrew, and Michiko Toyama. 1994. "In the Name of the Godfather." *Tokyo Journal* (October): 29–35.

Marshall, Byron K. 1967. *Capitalism and Nationalism in Prewar Japan: The Ideology of the Business Elite, 1868–1941.* Stanford: Stanford University Press.

Martinelli, Alberto. 1978. "Borghesia industriale e potere politico" (Industrial middle class and political power). In *La politica nell'Italia che cambia* (The changing politics of Italy), edited by A. Martinelli and G. Pasquino. Milan: Feltrinelli.

Maruyama, Masao. 1963. *Thought and Behaviour in Modern Japanese Politics*. London: Oxford University Press.

Marx, Karl. 1972. *The Eighteenth Brumaire of Louis Napoleon*. New York: International Publishers.

Mason, Mark. 1992. *American Multinationals and Japan: The Political Economy of Capital Controls, 1899–1980*. Cambridge: Harvard University Press.

Masumi, Junnosuke. 1995. *Contemporary Politics in Japan*. Berkeley: University of California Press.

Matteotti, Giacomo. 1969. *The Fascisti Exposed: A Year of Fascist Domination*. (First published, 1924.) New York: Howard Fertig.

McAdam, Doug, Sidney Tarrow, and Charles Tilly. 2001. *Dynamics of Contention*. Cambridge: Cambridge University Press.

McCarthy, Patrick. 1995. *The Crisis of the Italian State: From the Origins of the Cold War to the Fall of Berlusconi*. New York: St. Martin's.

McCormack, Gavan. 1996. *The Emptiness of Japanese Affluence*. St. Leonard's, New South Wales, Australia: Allen and Unwin.

McKean, Margaret A. 1981. *Environmental Protest and Citizen Politics in Japan*. Berkeley: University of California Press.

Mehl, Margaret. 1998. *History and the State in Nineteenth-Century Japan*. New York: St. Martin's.

Meiji Daigaku Shakai Kagaku Kenkyūjo, ed. 1998. *Seiji Shikin to Hōseido* (Political finance and the legal system). Tokyo: Meiji Daigaku Seiji Shikin Kenkyūkai.

Mikuriya, Takashi. 1995. "Tanaka Kakuei: Kaihatsu Seiji no Tōtatsuten" (Tanaka Kakuei: The goals of developmental politics). In *Sengo Nihon no Saishōtachi* (The prime ministers of postwar Japan), edited by Watanabe Akio, 209–38. Tokyo: Chūō Kōronsha.

Minami, Hiroshi. 1994. *Nihonjinron: Meiji kara Konnichi Made* (The theory of Japaneseness: From Meiji to the present day). Tokyo: Iwanami Shoten.

Mishima, Ko. 1998. "The Changing Relationship between Japan's LDP and the Bureaucracy: Hashimoto's Administrative Reform Effort and Its Politics." *Asian Survey* 37, no. 10 (October): 968–86.

Mita, Hideaki. 1977. "Kishi Nobusuke: Musessō na Kinken Seiji no Genkei" (Kishi Nobusuke: The model of unprincipled political finance). *Gendai no Me* 18, no. 4 (April): 204–11.

Mitani, Taichirō. 1988. "The Establishment of Party Cabinets." In *The Twentieth Century*, vol. 6 of *The Cambridge History of Japan*, edited by Peter Duus, 55–96. Cambridge: Cambridge University Press.

———. 1995. *Nihon Seitō Seiji no Keisei: Hara Takashi no Seiji Shidō no Tenkai* (The state of Japanese party politics: The evolution of Hara Takashi's party politics). Tokyo: Tokyo Daigaku Shuppankai.

Mitchell, Richard H. 1996. *Political Bribery in Japan*. Honolulu: University of Hawaii Press.

Mitsubishi Jūkōgyō Kabushiki Gaisha Shashi Hensan Iinkai, ed. 1990. *Umi ni, Oka ni, Soshite Uchū e: Mitsubishi Jūkōgyō Shashi* (To the sea, to the land, and then to space: The company history of Mitsubishi Heavy Industries). Tokyo: Mitsubishi Jūkōgyō.

Miyamoto, Kenji. 1985. *Selected Works*. Tokyo: Japan Press Service.

Miyamoto Masao. 1995. "Group Think Meets Individualism: The Saga of Dr. Miyamoto Masao and the Japanese Bureaucracy." *JPRI Critique* (Japan Policy Research Institute) 2, no. 10 (November): 1–2.

Miyazawa, Kiichi. 1997. "Rethinking the Constitution—A Document Tested by Time." *Japan Quarterly* 44, no. 3 (July–September): 11–14.

Miyazawa, Kiichi, and Nakasone, Yasuhiro. 2000. *Kenpō Daironsō* (The great constitutional debate). Tokyo: Asahi Shimbunsha.

Moore, Barrington, Jr. 1966. *Social Origins of Dictatorship and Democracy: Lord and Peasant in the Making of the Modern World*. Boston: Beacon.

Moretti, Ottaviano. 1998. "La popularità di DiPietro rilevata attratverso l'analisi del contenuto de 'la stampa' dal 1992–1997" (The popularity of DiPietro as revealed through analysis of the press from 1992–1997). Thesis (*laurea*), Faculty of Political Science, University of Bologna.

Mori, Toshihiko. 1969. *Ōkubo Toshimichi* (Ōkubo Toshimichi). Tokyo: Chūō Kōronsha.

Morita, Akio, and Ishihara Shintarō. 1989. *"No" to Ieru Nippon* (The Japan that can say "no"). Tokyo: Kobunsha.

Morita, Yoshio. 1958. *Nihon Keieisha Dantai Hattenshi* (History of the development of Japanese managers' associations). Tokyo: Nikkan Rōdō Tsushinsha.

Morlino, Leonardo. 1997. "Is There an Impact? And Where Is It? Electoral Reform and the Party System in Italy." *South European Society and Politics* 2, no. 3 (winter): 103–30.

Morris-Suzuki, Tessa. 1989. *A History of Japanese Economic Thought*. London: Routledge.

——. 1998. *Re-inventing Japan: Time, Space, Nation*. Armonk, N.Y.: M. E. Sharpe.

Mulgan, Aurelia George. 2000. "Japan's Political Leadership Deficit." *Australian Journal of Political Science* 35, no. 2: 183–202.

Murakami Shinichirō. 1999. *Itaria Kingendaishi no Shomondai* (Several issues in research on modern Italian history). In *Seiyō Kingendai Kenkyū Nyūmon* (An introduction to research on modern Western history), edited by Mochida Yukio et al., 251–71. Nagoya: Nagoya Daigaku Shuppankai.

Murobushi, Tetsurō. 1981. *Oshoku no Kōzō* (The structure of corruption). Tokyo: Iwanami Shoten.

Mussolini, Benito. 1998. *My Rise and Fall*. New York: Da Capo Press.

Mutō, Sanji. 1963. *Mutō Sanji Zenshū* (The collected works of Mutō Sanji). Vol. 1. Tokyo: Shinjusha.

Najita, Tetsuo. 1967. *Hara Kei in the Politics of Compromise, 1905–1915*. Cambridge: Harvard University Press.

Nakamura, Yoshiaki, and Minoru Shibuya. 1995. "The Hollowing-out Phenomenon in Japanese Industry." *Studies in International Trade and Industry 19*. Tokyo: Research Institute of International Trade and Industry.

Nakane, Chie. 1970. *Japanese Society*. Berkeley: University of California Press.

Nakasone, Yasuhiro. 1997. "Rethinking the Constitution—Make It a Japanese Document." *Japan Quarterly* 44, no. 3 (July–September): 4–9.

Nathan, John. 2001. "Tokyo Story." *New Yorker,* 9 April.

National Police Agency. 1989. *Heisei Gannen Keisatsu Hakusho* (1989 police white paper). Tokyo: National Police Agency.

Nelken, David. 1996a. "The Judges and Political Corruption in Italy." *Journal of Law and Society* 23, no. 1: 95–112.

——. 1996b. "Stopping the Judges." In *Italian Politics: The Stalled Transition*, edited by M. Caciagli and D. I. Kertzer. Boulder, Colo.: Westview.

Nimura, Kazuo. 1997. *The Ashio Riot of 1907: A Social History of Mining in Japan.* Durham, N.C.: Duke University Press.

Nisbett, Richard, and Lee Ross. 1980. *Human Inference: Strategies and Shortcomings of Social Judgment.* Englewood Cliffs, N.J.: Prentice-Hall.

Nish, Ian. 1990. "Some Thoughts on the Origins of the Meiji Constitution." In *Social Sciences, Ideology, and Thought*, vol. 2 of *Rethinking Japan*, edited by Adriana Boscaro, Franco Gatti, and Massimo Raveri, 42–47. Sandgate, England: Japan Library.

——. 1998. "Conflicting Japanese Loyalties in Manchuria." In *Shōwa Japan: Political, Economic, and Social History, 1926–1989*, edited by Stephen S. Large, 172–85. London: Routledge.

Nishihara, Masashi. 1976. *The Japanese and Sukarno's Indonesia: Tokyo-Jakarta Relations, 1951–1966.* Honolulu: University of Hawaii Press.

Nitobe, Inazo. 1912. *The Japanese Nation: Its Land, Its People, Its Life.* New York: George Putnam's Sons.

——. 1936. *Bushido: The Soul of Japan.* Tokyo: Kenkyusha.

Noguchi, Yukio. 1995. *1940 Nen Taisei: Saraba "Senji Keizai"* (The 1940 system: In that case, "wartime economy"). Tokyo: Toyo Keizai Shimposha.

Nomura, Jirō. 1977. *Nihon no Kensatsu* (Japan's prosecutors). Tokyo: Nihon Hyōronsha.

North, Douglass C. 1990. "A Transaction Cost Theory of Politics." *Journal of Theoretical Politics* 2, no. 4 (October): 355–67.

Notehelfer, Fred. 1990. "Meiji in the Rearview Mirror: Top-down vs. Bottom-up History." *Monumenta Nipponica* 42, no. 2: 207–28.

Novack, Bogdan C. 1970. *Trieste 1941–1954: The Ethnic, Political, and Ideological Struggle.* Chicago: University of Chicago Press.

Occhetto, Achille. 1988. "The Themes and Stages for the 'Reconstruction' of the Party." *The Italian Communists* 2 (April–June): 32–52.

——. 1994. *Il sentimento e la ragione* (Sentiment and reason). Milan: Rizzoli.

Odawara, Atsushi. 1991. "The Kaifu Bungle." *Japan Quarterly* 38, no. 1 (January–March): 6–14.

——. 2000. "The Dawn of Constitutional Debate." *Japan Quarterly* 47, no. 1 (January–March): 17–22.

Ogata, Kiyoshi. 1923. *The Co-operative Movement in Japan.* London: P.S. King and Son.

Ogata, Sadako N. 1964. *Defiance in Manchuria: The Making of Japanese Foreign Policy, 1931–1932.* Berkeley: University of California Press.

Oguma, Eiji. 1995. *Tanitsu Minzoku Shinwa no Kigen* (The origins of the myth of the homogeneous people). Tokyo: Shinyōsha.

Oka, Yoshitake. 1958. *Aritomo Yamagata* (Aritomo Yamagata). Tokyo: Iwanami.

Okamoto, Shumpei. 1970. *The Japanese Oligarchy and the Russo-Japanese War.* New York: Columbia University Press.

Ono, Koji. 1998. *Nihon Seiji no Tenkanten* (Reversals in Japanese politics). Tokyo: Aoki Shoten.

Ordeshook, Peter C. 1990. "The Emerging Discipline of Political Economy." In *Perspectives on Positive Political Economy,* edited by James E. Alt and Kenneth A. Shepsle, 9–30. Cambridge: Cambridge University Press.

Orefice, Gastone Ortona. 1993. "The End of the First Republic in Italy." *Italian Journal* 7, no. 6 (December): 7–11.

Orfei, Ruggero. 1975. *Andreotti.* Milan: Feltrinelli.

Orr, Robert M., Jr. 1990. *The Emergence of Japan's Foreign Aid Power.* New York: Columbia University Press.

Ōtake, Hideo. 1990. "Defense Controversies and One-Party Dominance: The Opposition in Japan and West Germany." Chapter 4 in *Uncommon Democracies: The One-Party Dominant Regimes,* edited by T.J. Pempel. Ithaca: Cornell University Press.

Ozawa, Ichirō. 1994. *Blueprint for a New Japan: The Rethinking of a Nation.* New York: Kodansha.(Originally published in 1994 as *Nihon Kaizō Keikaku.* Tokyo: Kōdansha.)

———. 1995. "Futsū no Kuni ni Nare" (Become a normal country). In *Sengo Nihon Gaikō Ronshi* (A collection on postwar Japanese diplomacy), edited by Kitaoka Shinichi, 461–81. Tokyo: Chūō Kōronsha.

Ozawa, Ichirō, et al., 1992. "Tabū wa Mohayanai" (No more taboo). *Chūō Kōron* 105 (May): 33.

Packard, George R. 1966. *Protest in Tokyo: The Security Treaty Crisis of 1960.* Princeton: Princeton University Press.

Pallotta, Gino. 1987. *Gli Agnelli: Una dinastica italiana* (The Agnellis: An Italian dynasty). In *Storia e cronache d'Italia* (The history and chronicles of Italy), vol. 5. Rome: Newton Compton.

Parker, Simon. 1996. "Political Identities." In *Italian Cultural Studies: An Introduction,* edited by D. Forgacs and R. Lumley, 107–28. Oxford: Oxford University Press.

Pasquino, Gianfranco. 1992. *La nuova politica* (The new politics). Bari: Laterza.

———. 1993. "Programmatic Renewal, and Much More: From the PCI to the PDS." *West European Politics* 16, no. 1 (January): 156–73.

———. 1997. "No Longer a Party State? Institutions, Power, and the Problems of Italian Reform." *West European Politics* 20, no. 2 (January): 34–53.

———. 1998. "Reforming the Italian Constitution." *Journal of Modern Italian Studies* 3, no. 1: 42–54.

———. 2000. "A Postmortem of the *Bicamerale.*" In *Italian Politics: The Return of Politics,* edited by David Hine and Salvatore Vassallo, 101–20. New York: Berghahn.

Pastorelli, Pietro. 1984. "L'Adesione dell'italia al patto atlantico" (The addition of Italy to the Atlantic Pact). In *De Gasperi e l'età del centrismo, 1947–1953* (De Gasperi and the age of centrism), edited by G. Rossini, 75–93. Rome: Cinque Lune.

———. 1987. *La politica estera italiana del dopoguerra* (Postwar Italian foreign policy). Bologna: Il Mulino.

Pederezoli, Patrizia, and Carlo Guarnieri. 1997. "The Judicialization of Politics, Italian Style." *Journal of Modern Italian Studies* 2, no. 3: 321–36.

Pempel, T. J. 1982. *Policy and Politics in Japan: Creative Conservatism*. Philadelphia: Temple University Press.

——, ed. 1990. *Uncommon Democracies: The One-Party Dominant Regimes*. Ithaca: Cornell University Press.

——. 1998. *Regime Shift: Comparative Dynamics of the Japanese Political Economy*. Ithaca: Cornell University Press.

——. 2000. "Tokyo's Little Italy." *International Economy* (May–June): 34–37.

Perrow, Charles. 1985. *Normal Accidents: Living with High-Risk Technologies*. New York: Basic Books.

Pescosolido, Guido. 1995. *Arretratezza e sviluppo* (Backwardness and development). In *Storia d'Italia* (History of Italy), edited by G. Sabbatucci and V. Vidotto. Vol. 2. Bari: Laterza.

Petrilli, Giuseppe. 1990. "La politica estera ed europea di De Gasperi" (De Gasperi's Europe and foreign policy). In *Alcide De Gasperi e la politica internazionale* (Alcide De Gasperi and international politics), edited by Giovanni Allara and A. Gatti. Rome: Cinque Lune.

Pharr, Susan J. 1990. *Losing Face: Status Politics in Japan*. Berkeley: University of California Press.

Pierson, Paul. 2000. "Increasing Returns, Path Dependence, and the Study of Politics." *American Political Science Review* 94, no. 2 (June): 251–68.

Pietra, Italo. 1985. *I tre Agnelli: Giovanni, Edoardo, Gianni* (The three Agnellis: Giovanni, Edoardo, and Gianni). Milan: Garzanti.

Piore, Michael J., and Charles F. Sabel. 1984. *The Second Industrial Divide: Possibilities for Prosperity*. New York: Basic Books.

Plutarch. 1979. *The Lives of the Noble Grecians and Romans*. Translated by John Dryden. New York: Modern Library.

Pombeni, Paolo. 1979. *Il gruppo dossettiano e la fondazione della democrazia italiana, 1938–1948* (Dossetti's faction and the foundation of Italian democracy). Bologna: Il Mulino.

——. 1985. *Partiti e sistemi politici nella storia contemporanea* (Parties and political systems in modern history). Bologna: Il Mulino.

——. 1994. *Partiti e sistemi politici nella storia contemporanea, 1830–1968* (Parties and political systems in modern history, 1830–1968). Bologna: Il Mulino.

——. 1995. "Churchill and Italy, 1922–1940." In *Winston Churchill: Studies in Statesmanship*, edited by R. A. C. Parker, 65–82. London: Brassey's.

——. 1997. "I partiti e la politica dal 1948 al 1963" (Parties and politics from 1948 to 1963). In *La Repubblica* (The Republic), vol. 5 of *Storia d'Italia* (The history of Italy), edited by G. Sabbatucci and V. Vidotto, 127–251. Bari: Laterza.

Procacci, Giuliano. 1968. *The History of the Italian People*. London: Penguin.

Prodi, Romano. 1965 and 1966. "Il protezionismo nella politica e nell'industria italiana dall'unificazione al 1887" (Protectionism in Italian politics and industry from unification to 1887). Parts 1 and 2. *Nuova Rivista Storica* 49 (September–December, 1965): 597–626; 50 (January–April, 1966): 42–86.

Putnam, Robert D. 1993. *Making Democracy Work: Civic Traditions in Modern Italy*. Princeton: Princeton University Press.

Pye, Lucian. 1991. "Political Culture Revisited." *Political Psychology* 12, no. 3 (September): 487–508.

Pyle, Kenneth B. 1969. *The New Generation in Meiji Japan: Problems of Cultural Identity, 1885–1895*. Stanford: Stanford University Press.

——. 1973. "The Technology of Japanese Nationalism." *Journal of Asian Studies* 33, no. 1 (November): 51–65.

——. 1987. "In Pursuit of a Grand Design: Nakasone Betwixt the Past and the Future." *Journal of Japanese Studies* 13, no. 2: 243–70.

——. 1989. "Meiji Conservatism." In *The Nineteenth Century*, vol. 5 of *The Cambridge History of Japan*, edited by Marius Jansen, 674–720. Cambridge: Cambridge University Press.

——. 1996a. *The Japanese Question: Power and Purpose in a New Era*. Washington, D.C.: AEI Press.

——. 1996b. *The Making of Modern Japan*. 2nd ed. Lexington, Mass.: D. C. Heath.

Ranfagni, Paolo. 1975. *I clerico fascisti: Le riviste dell'università cattolica negli anni del regime* (The fascist clerics: The journals of the Catholic University during the years of the regime). Florence: Cooperativa Editrice Universitaria.

Ramseyer, J. Mark, and Eric B. Rasmusen. 1997. "Judicial Independence in a Civil Law Regime: The Evidence from Japan." *Journal of Law, Economics, and Organization* 13, no. 2 (October): 259–86.

Ramseyer, J. Mark, and Frances McCall Rosenbluth. 1995. *The Politics of Oligarchy: Institutional Choice in Imperial Japan*. Cambridge: Cambridge University Press.

Redl, Christopher. 1993. "Curse of the Kingmakers." *Tokyo Journal* (May): 34–41.

——. 1994. "Japan's Divine Seduction: How the Unification Church Infiltrated the Japanese Government." Unpublished manuscript.

Reed, Steven R. 1993. *Making Common Sense of Japan*. Pittsburgh, Penn.: University of Pittsburgh Press.

——. 1999. "Political Reform in Japan: Combining Scientific and Historical Analysis." *Social Science Japan Journal* 2, no. 2: 177–93.

Regini, Marino. 1997. "Still Engaging in Corporatism? Recent Italian Experience in Comparative Perspective." *European Journal of Industrial Relations* 3, no. 3: 259–78.

Regini, Marino, and Ida Regalia. 1997. "Employers, Unions, and the State: The Emergence of Concertation in Italy?" *West European Politics* 20, no. 1 (January): 210–29.

Reischauer, Edwin O. 1988. *The Japanese Today: Change and Continuity*. Cambridge: Harvard University Press.

Rhodes, Martin. 1997. "Financing Party Politics in Italy: A Case of Systemic Corruption." *West European Politics* 20, no. 1: 54–80.

Riker, William. 1986. *The Art of Political Manipulation*. New Haven: Yale University Press.

Rocca, Francis X. 1999. "Out of Their League." *American Spectator*, March, 34–39.

Romanelli, Raffaele. 1979. *L'Italia liberale, 1861–1900* (Liberal Italy, 1861–1900). Bologna: Il Mulino.

Romano, Sergio. 1991. "La cultura della politica esterna italiana" (The culture of Italian foreign policy). In *La politica esterna italiana, 1860–1985* (Italy's foreign policy), edited by R. J. B. Bosworth and Sergio Romano, 17–34. Bologna: Il Mulino.

——. 1995a. "The Foreign Policy that Was Not There." In *Deconstructing Italy: Italy in the Nineties,* edited by S. Sechi, 140–52. International and Area Studies Research Series, no. 91. Berkeley: University of California.

——. 1995b. *Lo scambio ineguale. Italia e Stati Uniti da Wilson a Clinton* (Unequal exchange: Italy and the United States from Wilson to Clinton). Bari: Laterza.

Rossi, Nicola and Gianni Toniolo. 1996. "Italy." In *Economic Growth in Europe since 1945,* edited by Nicholas Crafts and Gianni Toniolo, 427–54. Cambridge: Cambridge University Press.

Rossini, Giuseppe, ed. 1984. *De Gasperi e l'età del centralismo, 1947–1953* (De Gasperi and the age of centrism). Rome: Cinque Lune.

Row, Thomas. 1988. "Economic Nationalism in Italy: The Ansaldo Company, 1861–1921." Ph.D. diss., Johns Hopkins University. (Published in 1997 as *Il nazionalismo economico nell'italia liberale: L'Ansaldo, 1903–1921* (Economic nationalism in liberal Italy: Ansaldo, 1903–1921. Bologna: Il Mulino.)

Rustow, Dankwart A. 1970. "The Study of Leadership." In *Philosophers and Kings: Studies in Leadership,* edited by Dankwart A. Rustow, 1–32. New York: George Braziller.

Saito, Takao. 2000. "Bōsai Supekutakuru no Ichinichi" (The one-day disaster prevention spectacle"). *Sekai* 681 (October): 38–48.

Sakamoto, Kazuya. 1996. "Kishi Shusho to Anpō Kaitei no Ketsudan" (Prime Minister Kishi and the decision to revise the Mutual Security Treaty). *Journal of the Osaka University Law Faculty* vol. 45, no. 1 (June).

Sakamoto, Tarō, ed. 1989. *Nihonshi Shojiten* (Dictionary of Japanese history). 8th ed. Tokyo: Yamakawa Shuppansha.

Sako, Mari. 1997. "Foreword: Part I—Professor Hiroshi Hazama on the Firm as Family." In *The History of Labor Management in Japan,* edited by Hazama Hiroshi, xv–xxi. New York: St. Martin's.

Sakurada, Takeshi, and Shikanai, Nobutaka. 1983. *Ima Akasu Sengo Hishi* (Secret postwar history now revealed). Tokyo: Sankei Shuppan.

Sakurai, Akio, and the Tokyo Shimbun "Watching Ishihara" Team. 2000. *Ishihara Shintarō no Tokyo Daikaikaku* (Ishihara Shintarō's overhaul of Tokyo). Tokyo: Seishun Shuppansha.

Salomone, A. William. 1945. *Italian Democracy in the Making.* Philadelphia: University of Pennsylvania Press.

Salvati, Michele. 1981. "May 1968 and the Hot Autumn of 1969: The Responses of Two Ruling Classes." In *Organizing Interests in Western Europe: Pluralism, Corporatism, and the Transformation of Politics,* edited by Suzanne Berger, 329–63. Cambridge: Cambridge University Press.

Salvemini, Gaetano. 1953. *Prelude to World War II.* London: Victor Gollancz.

——. 1973. *The Origins of Fascism in Italy.* New York: Harper and Row.

Samuels, Richard J. 1982. "Local Politics in Japan: The Changing of the Guard." *Asian Survey* (July): 630–37.

——. 1987. *The Business of the Japanese State: Energy Policy in Comparative and Historical Perspective.* Ithaca: Cornell University Press.

——. 1994. *Rich Nation, Strong Army: National Security and the Technological Transformation of Japan.* Ithaca: Cornell University Press.

Sani, Giacomo. 1993. "The Anatomy of Change." In *The End of Postwar Italian Politics: The Landmark 1992 Elections,* edited by Gianfranco Pasquino and Patrick McCarthy, 108–20. Boulder, Colo.: Westview.

Santino, Umberto. 1997. "Law Enforcement in Italy and Europe against the Mafia and Organized Crime." In *Crime and Law Enforcement in the Global Village,* edited by W. F. McDonald, 151–66. Cincinnati, Ohio: Anderson.

Sarti, Roland. 1971. *Fascism and the Industrial Leadership in Italy, 1919–1940: A Study in the Expansion of Private Power under Fascism.* Berkeley: University of California Press.

Sasaki, Suguru. 1995. "Meiji Tennō Imeji Keisei to Minshu" (The formation of the Meiji emperor's image and the people). In *Bakumatsu/Meijiki no Kokumin Kokka Keisei to Bunka Henyō* (Cultural change and the formation of the national state in the late Tokugawa Meiji period), edited by Mishikawa Nagao and Matsumiya Hideji, 117–42. Tokyo: Shinyosha.

Sasaki, Takeshi, ed. 1999. *Seiji Kaikaku 1800 Hi no Shinjitsu* (The reality of 1,800 days of political reform). Tokyo: Kodansha.

Satō Seizaburō, ed. 1999. *Za Raito uingu no Otoko: Senzen no Sasakawa Ryōichi Goroku* (The right-wing man: The prewar analects of Sasakawa Ryōichi). Tokyo: Chūō Kōronsha.

Scalapino, Robert A. 1983. *The Early Japanese Labor Movement: Labor and Politics in a Developing Society.* Berkeley: Center for Japanese Studies, Institute of East Asian Studies, University of California.

Scalapino, Robert A., and Junnosuke Masumi. 1962. *Parties and Politics in Contemporary Japan.* Berkeley: University of California Press.

Scalfari, Eugenio, and Giuseppe Turani. 1974. *Razza padrona: Storia della borghesia di stato* (The master race: The history of the state bourgeoisie). Milan: Feltrinelli.

Schaller, Michael. 1995. "America's Favorite War Criminal: Kishi Nobusuke and the Transformation of U.S.-Japan Relations." Japan Policy Research Institute working paper no. 11, July: 17–20.

Schlei, Norbert A. 1995. "Japan's 'M-Fund' Memorandum, January 7, 1991." Japan Policy Research Institute working paper no. 11, July: 10–16.

Schlesinger, Jacob M. 1997. *Shadow Shoguns: The Rise and Fall of Japan's Postwar Political Machine.* New York: Simon and Schuster.

Schneider, Herbert W., and Shepard B. Clough. 1929. *Making Fascists.* Chicago: University of Chicago Press.

Schumpeter, Joseph A. 1950. *Capitalism, Socialism, and Democracy.* New York: Harper and Row.

Scoppola, Pietro. 1974. *La proposita politica di De Gasperi* (De Gasperi's political plan). Bologna: Il Mulino.

———. 1984. "Per una storia del centrismo" (Toward a history of centrism). In *De Gasperi e l'età del centrismo, 1947–1953* (De Gasperi and the age of centrism), edited by G. Rossini, 23–51. Rome: Cinque Lune.

———. 1995. "The Christian Democrats and the Political Crisis." *Modern Italy* 1, no. 1 (autumn): 18–29.

Sechi, Salvatore, ed. 1995. Introduction to *Deconstructing Italy: Italy in the Nineties,* 1–38. International and Area Research Studies Series, no. 91. Berkeley: University of California.

Seidelman, Raymond. 1979. "Neighborhood Communism in Florence: Goals and Dilemmas of the Italian Road to Communism." Ph.D. diss., Department of Government, Cornell University.

Seiji Kōhō Center, ed. 2000. *Seiji Handobukku* (Politics handbook). Vol. 37 (September). Tokyo: Seiji Kōhō Center.

Senato della Repubblica. 1953. "Relazione di maggioranza della V commissione permanente (finanze e tesoro)" (Majority report of the Fifth Permanent Commission for Finance and Treasury), no. 2489–A. Rome: Senato della Repubblica.

Sengoku Tamotsu. 1998. *Nihon no Kōkōsei* (Japan's high school students). Tokyo: NHK Books.

Seton-Watson, Christopher. 1967. *Italy from Liberalism to Fascism, 1870–1925.* London: Methuen.

——. 1991. "La politica estera della repubblica italiana" (The foreign policy of republican Italy). In *La politica estera italiana, 1860–1985* (Italy's foreign policy, 1860–1985), edited by R.J.B. Bosworth and S. Romano. Bologna: Il Mulino.

Sewell, William H., Jr. 1992. "A Theory of Structure: Duality, Agency, and Transformation." *American Journal of Sociology* 98, no. 1 (July): 1–29.

Shibusawa, Eichi. 1994. *The Autobiography of Shibusawa Eichi.* Tokyo: University of Tokyo Press.

Shimizu, Kazuyuki. 1976. "Seizaikai no Kage no Jitsuryokusha Kishi Nobusuke no Shōtai" (The true character of Kishi Nobusuke, power holder in the shadows of the political and business worlds). *Hōseki* 4, no. 1 (January): 86–98.

Shimomura, Fujio. 1962. *Meiji Shōnen Jōyaku Kaisei-shi no Kenkyu* (Research on the history of treaty revision in the early years of the Meiji period). Tokyo: Yoshikawa Kobunkan.

Shinoda, Tomohito. 2000. *Leading Japan: The Role of the Prime Minister.* Westport, Conn.: Praeger.

Silberman, Bernard S. 1993. *Cages of Reason: The Rise of the Rational State in France, Japan, the United States, and Great Britain.* Chicago: University of Chicago Press.

——. 1996. "The Continuing Dilemma: Bureaucracy and Political Parties." *Social Science Japan* vol. 7 (August).

Skocpol, Theda. 1979. *States and Social Revolutions: A Comparative Analysis of France, Russia, and China.* Cambridge: Cambridge University Press.

Smith, Henry D., Jr. 1983. "The Nonliberal Roots of Taishō Democracy." In *Japan Examined: Perspectives on Modern Japanese History,* edited by Harry Wray and Hilary Conroy, 191–98. Honolulu: University of Hawaii Press.

Smith, Thomas C. 1955. *Political Change and Industrial Development in Japan: Government Enterprise, 1868–1880.* Stanford: Stanford University Press.

Smith, Tom W., and Lars Jarkko. 1998. "National Pride: A Cross-national Analysis." GSS Cross-national Report, no. 19 (May). Chicago: National Opinion Research Center, University of Chicago.

Smitka, Michael J. 1991. *Competitive Ties: Subcontracting in the Japanese Automotive Industry.* New York: Columbia University Press.

Sommer, Dorris. 1991. *Foundational Fictions: The National Romances of Latin America.* Berkeley: University of California Press.

Spriano, Paolo. 1984. "Intervento." In *De Gasperi e l'età del centrismo, 1947–1953* (De Gasperi and the age of centrism), edited by G. Rossini, 175–79. Rome: Cinque Lune.

Sprigge, Cecil J. S. 1969. *The Development of Modern Italy.* New York: Howard Fertig.

Stanley, Alessandra. 2001. "Berlusconi, the Rerun." *New York Times Magazine,* 15 April, 40–43.

Steiner, Kurt. 1965. *Local Government in Japan.* Stanford: Stanford University Press.

Steiner, Kurt, Ellis Krauss, and Scott A. Flanagan, eds. 1980. *Political Opposition and Local Politics in Japan.* Princeton: Princeton University Press.

Stella, Gian Antonio. 1996. *Dio Po: Gli uomini che fecero la Padania* (God Po: The men who made Padania). Milan: Baldini and Castoldi.

Stille, Alexander. 1999. "Palermo: The Photography of Death." *New York Review of Books,* 15 July, 49–54.

Sturzo, Luigi. 1926. *Italy and Fascismo.* New York: Harcourt Brace.

Swearingen, Rodger A., and Paul Langer. 1968. *Red Flag in Japan: International Communism in Action, 1919–1951.* New York: Greenwood Press.

Swidler, Ann. 1986. "Culture in Action: Symbols and Strategies." *American Sociological Review* 51, no. 2 (April): 273–86.

Swidler, Leonard, and Edward James Grace, eds. 1988. *Catholic-Communist Collaboration in Italy.* Lanham, Md.: University Press of America.

Tachibana, Takashi. 1993. "Ososugita Shuen" (The end that came too late). *Bungei Shunjū* (August): 94–111.

Tagawa Kazuo. 1968. *Nihon Kyōsantō Shi* (The history of the Japan Communist Party). Tokyo: Gendai Shichōsha.

Taira, Koji. 1988. "Economic Development, Labor Markets, and Industrial Relations in Japan, 1905–1955." In *The Twentieth Century,* vol. 6 of *The Cambridge History of Japan,* edited by Peter Duus, 606–53. Cambridge: Cambridge University Press.

———. 1997. "Troubled National Identity: The Ryukyuans/Okinawans." In *Japan's Minorities: The Illusion of Homogeneity,* edited by Michael Weiner, 140–77. London: Routledge.

Tajiri, Ikuzo. 1979. *Shōwa no Yōkai: Kishi Nobusuke* (The monster of Shōwa: Kishi Nobusuke). Tokyo: Gakuyōshobō.

Takahashi, Susumu. 1992. "Itaria ni okeru Sengo Taisei no Keisei to Reisen" (The postwar political situation in Italy and the Cold War). In *1940 Nendai Yooroppa no Seiji to Reisen* (The Cold War and politics in 1940s Europe), edited by S. Ishii, 205–42. Tokyo: Minerva.

———. 2000. "De Gasperi to Sengo Itaria Seiji Taisei no Keisei" (De Gasperi and the postwar Italian political structure). *Ryūkoku Hogaku* vol. 32 (March).

Takano, Hajime. 1980. *M-Shikin: Shirarezaru Chika Kinyū no Seikai* (M-Fund: The unknown world of underground finance). Tokyo: Nihon Keizai Shimbunsha.

Takano, Takeshi. 1979. "Kishi Nobusukeshi no Kuhaku no Rirekisho" (The blank spaces in Mr. Kishi Nobusuke's résumé). *Asahi Jaanaru,* no. 1058 (25 May): 10–32.

Tamura, Sadao. 1977. *Shokusan Kōgyō* (Production promotion). Tokyo: Kyoikusha.

Tanaka, Akihiko. 1997. *Anzen Hoshō: Sengo 50 Nen no Mosaku* (National security: Fifty years of postwar groping). Tokyo: Yomiuri Shimbunsha.

Tanaka, Akira. 1979. *Kindai Tennō-sei e no Michi* (The road to the modern emperor system). Tokyo: Yoshikawa Kobunkan.

Tarrow, Sidney. 1977. *Between Center and Periphery: Grassroots Politicians in Italy and France.* New Haven: Yale University Press.

———. 1990. "Maintaining Hegemony in Italy: 'The Softer They Rise, the Slower

They Fall!'" In *Uncommon Democracies: The One-Party Dominant Regimes,* edited by T.J. Pempel, 306–32. Ithaca: Cornell University Press.

———. 1994. "The Odd Couple: Political-Institutional Change in Italy and Japan after the Cold War." Paper presented to the Seminar on Institutional Change in Europe, Nuffield College, Oxford, 21 January.

Taviani, Paolo Emilio. 1984. "Intervento." In *De Gasperi e l'età del centrismo, 1947–1953* (De Gasperi and the age of centrism), edited by G. Rossini, 193–200. Rome: Cinque Lune.

Titus, David Anson. 1974. *Palace and Politics in Prewar Japan.* New York: Columbia University Press.

Tocqueville, Alexis de. 1949. *The Recollections of Alexis de Tocqueville.* Edited by J.P. Mayer. New York: Columbia University Press.

Togliatti, Palmiro. 1973a. *Gramsci.* Rome: Riuniti.

———. 1973b. *Discorso su Giolitti* (Discourse on Giolitti). Rome: Riuniti.

Tōkei Sūri Kenyūjo, ed. 1999. *Ishoku no Kokusaika Hikō ni okeru Rensateki Chōsa Bunseki Hōhō no Jitsuyōka ni kansuru Kenkyū* (Application of cultural link analysis for comparative social research). Tokyo: Tōkei Sūri Kenkyūjo.

Tominomori, Eiji. 1977. *Sengo Hōshu Tōshi* (Postwar conservative parties). Tokyo: Nihon Hyōronsha.

Toniolo, Gianni. 1990. *An Economic History of Liberal Italy, 1850–1918.* London: Routledge.

Totten, George O. 1967. "Collective Bargaining and Works Councils as Innovations in Industrial Relations during the 1920s." In *Aspects of Social Change in Modern Japan,* edited by R.P. Dore, 203–43. Princeton: Princeton University Press.

———. 1974. "Japanese Industrial Relations at the Crossroads: The Great Noda Strike of 1927–1928." In *Japan in Crisis: Essays on Taishō Democracy,* edited by B.S. Silberman and H. Harootunian, 398–436. Princeton: Princeton University Press.

Trigilia, Carlo. 1986. *Grandi partiti e piccole impresse* (Big parties and small firms). Bologna: Il Mulino.

Trimberger, Ellen Kay. 1972. "A Theory of Elite Revolution." *Studies in Comparative International Development* 10: 191–203.

Tsebelis, George. 1990. *Nested Games: Rational Choice in Comparative Politics.* Berkeley: University of California Press.

Tsūshō Sangyōshō, ed. 1979. *Keizai Kyōryoku no Genjō to Mondaiten* (Problems and the current status of economic cooperation). Tokyo: Tsūshō Sangyōshō.

Tsutsui, William M. 1997. "Rethinking the Paternalist Paradigm in Japanese Industrial Management." *Business and Economic History* 26, no. 2 (winter): 561–72.

Tullio-Altan, Carlo. 1997. *La coscienza civile degli italiani: valore e disvalore nella storia nazionale* (Civil consciousness of the Italians: Positive and negative values in national history). Udine: Paolo Gaspari.

Twain, Mark. 1911. *The Innocents Abroad.* New York: Harper and Brothers.

Uchida, Kenzō. 1996. "'Ozawa Ichirō' to wa Nan Datta no Ka" (What was 'Ichirō Ozawa'?). *Bungei Shunjū* (December): 118–26.

Udagawa, Masaru. 1990. "The Move into Manchuria of the Nissan Combine." *Japanese Yearbook on Business History* 7: 3–30.

Uemura Kōgorō Denki Henshūshitsu, ed. 1979. *Ningen: Uemura Kōgorō Sengo Keizai Hatten no Kiseki* (Personage: Uemura Kōgorō, the path of postwar economic development). Tokyo: Sankei Shuppan.

Urban, Joan Barth. 1986. *Moscow and the Italian Communist Party: From Togliatti to Berlinguer.* Ithaca: Cornell University Press.

U.S. Government. 2000. *International Crime Threat Assessment Report.* Washington, D.C.: Government Printing Office.

Ushiro, Fusao. 1994. *Seiken Kōtai no aru Minshushugi* (Democracy with an alternating power system). Tokyo: Madosha.

Valiani, Leo. 1949. *L'Avvento di De Gasperi: Tre anni di politica italiana* (The advent of De Gasperi: Three years of Italian politics). Turin: Francesco da Silva.

Van Wolferen, Karel. 1989. *The Enigma of Japanese Power.* New York: Alfred A. Knopf.

Varsori, Antonio. 1985. "La scelta occidentale dell'Italia, 1948–1949" (Italy's Western choice, 1948–1949). *Italia contemporanea* 1: 95–159.

Viviano, Frank. 1995. "The New Mafia Order." *Mother Jones,* May–June, 44–50.

Vlastos, Stephen. 1986. *Peasant Protests and Uprisings in Tokugawa Japan.* Berkeley: University of California Press.

———. 1989. "Opposition Movements in Early Meiji, 1868–1885." In *The Nineteenth century,* vol. 5 of *The Cambridge History of Japan,* edited by Marius Jansen, 367–431. Cambridge: Cambridge University Press.

———, ed. 1998. *Mirror of Modernity: Invented Traditions of Modern Japan.* Berkeley: University of California Press.

Vogel, Ezra F. 1979. *Japan as Number One: Lessons for America.* Cambridge: Harvard University Press.

Vogel, Stephen E. 1996. *Freer Markets, More Rules: Regulatory Reform in Advanced Industrial Countries.* Ithaca: Cornell University Press.

Votaw, Dow. 1964. *The Six-Legged Dog: Mattei and ENI, a Study in Power.* Berkeley: University of California Press.

Wakabayashi, Bob Tadashi. 1990. "Sasakawa Ryoichi: A Brief Sketch." *Active Voice* 2, no. 6 (27 February): 6–12.

Wakamiya, Yoshibumi. 1994. *Wasurerarenai Kokkai Ronsen: Saigunbi kara Kōgai Mondai Made* (Unforgettable Diet debates: From rearmament to environmental problems). Tokyo: Chūō Kōronsha.

———. 1999. *The Postwar Conservative View of Asia.* Tokyo: LTCB International Library Foundation.

Wakamono to Shūkyō Kenkyūkai, ed. 1992. *Tōitsu Kyōhai no Uchimaku* (The inside story of the Unification Church). Tokyo: Eeru Shuppankai.

Waltz, Kenneth N. 1954. *Man, the State, and War: A Theoretical Analysis.* New York: Columbia University Press.

Ward, Robert E. 1965. "The Commission on the Constitution and Prospects for Constitutional Changes in Japan." *Journal of Japanese Studies* 24, no. 3 (May): 401–29.

Watanabe, Tsuneo. 1999. "Waga jissenteki janarizumu-ron" (My theory of activist journalism). *Chūō Kōron* 114 (August): 156–82.

Weber, Max. 1949. *The Methodology of the Social Sciences.* Translated and edited by Edward A. Shils and Henry A. Finch. New York: Free Press.

———. 1958. *From Max Weber: Essays in Sociology.* Edited by H. H. Gerth and C. Wright Mills. Oxford: Oxford University Press.

Webster, R. A. 1975. *Industrial Imperialism in Italy, 1908–1915.* Berkeley: University of California Press.

Weinberg, Leonard. 1995. *The Transformation of Italian Communism.* New Brunswick, N.J.: Transaction.

Weiner, Michael. 1997. "The Invention of Identity: 'Self' and 'Other' in Prewar Japan." In *Japan's Minorities: The Illusion of Homogeneity,* edited by Michael Weiner, 1–16. London: Routledge.

Weiss, Linda. 1988. *Creating Capitalism: The State and Small Business since 1945.* London: Blackwell.

White, James W. 1995. *Ikki: Social Conflict and Political Protest in Early Modern Japan.* Ithaca: Cornell University Press.

Whittaker, D. H. 1997. *Small Firms in the Japanese Economy.* Cambridge: Cambridge University Press.

Willis, F. Roy. 1971. *Italy Chooses Europe.* New York: Oxford University Press.

Wilson, George Maklin. 1967–68. "A New Look at the Problem of 'Japanese Fascism'." *Comparative Studies in Society and History* 10: 401–12.

——. 1969. *Radical Nationalist in Japan: Kita Ikki, 1883–1937.* Cambridge: Harvard University Press.

Yamaguchi, Asao. 1976. "Kishi, Ikeda, Satō Shushō no Kinmyaku Uramenshi" (The inside history of the financial connections of Prime Ministers Kishi, Ikeda, and Satō). *Hōseki* 4, no. 4 (April): 106–15.

Yamaguchi, Noboru. 2001. "Japan: Completing Military Professionalization." In *Military Professionalism in Asia,* edited by Muthiah Alagappa, 35–46. Honolulu: East-West Center Press.

Yanaga, Chitoshi. 1968. *Big Business in Japanese Politics.* New Haven: Yale University Press.

Yasuhara, Kazuo. 1985. *Keidanren Kaichō no Sengoshi, Kenryokusha no Jinbutsu Shōwashi* (The postwar history of Keidanren chairmen, the Shōwa history of the personalities of power). Tokyo: Bijinesusha.

Yasukawa, Tatsuo. 1994. "Kūdōka to Kōreika e no Shohōsen" (A prescription for hollowing out and an aging society). *This Is Yomiuri* 5, no. 9 (November): 260–82.

Yokoyama Michiyoshi. 2000. "Mō Hitosu no Senkyōse: Shigatsukai vs. Sōkagakkai" (Another election campaign: The Shigatsukai versus the Sokagakkai). *Chūō Kōron* (July): 76–83.

Yoshida, Shigeru. 1961. *The Yoshida Memoirs: The Story of Japan in Crisis.* London: Heinemann.

——. 1967. *Japan's Decisive Century, 1867–1967.* New York: Praeger.

Young, Louise. 1998. *Japan's Total Empire: Manchuria and the Culture of Wartime Imperialism.* Berkeley: University of California Press.

Zamagni, Vera. 1993. *The Economic History of Italy, 1860–1990.* Oxford: Oxford University Press.

Zangheri, Renato. 1997. "Dalle prime lotte nella Valle Padana ai fasci siciliani" (From the first struggles in the Po Valley to the Sicilian fasci). In *Storia del socialismo italiano* (History of Italian socialism), edited by G. Sabbatucci. Vol. 2. Turin: Einaudi.

Zangrandi, Ruggero. 1963. *Il lungo viaggio attraverso il fascismo* (The long journey from fascism). Milan: Feltrinelli.

Zunino, P. G. 1985. *L'ideologia del fascismo: Miti, credenze, e valori nella stabilizzazione del regime* (The ideology of fascism: Myths, credibility, and values in the stabilization of the regime). Bologna: Il Mulino.

Index